D1221583

Laurens County

South Carolina

Deed Abstracts

Books E-F

1793-1800
(1767-1800)

Vol. #2

Compiled By:

Larry Vehorn

Copyright © 2006 by:

Larry Vehorn

Please Direct All Correspondence and Book Orders to:

Southern Historical Press, Inc.
PO Box 1267
375 West Broad Street
Greenville, S.C. 29602

ISBN # 0-89308-815-3

Printed in the United States of America

INTRODUCTION

This volume of abstracts includes all deeds found in Deed Books E and F, for Laurens County, South Carolina. The deeds were recorded between 1793 and 1800. The earliest recorded deed, during this period, was executed in 1767. A South Carolina Archives microfilm copy was the basis for the abstracts. Those deeds in Book F not completely readable on film were checked at the Clerk's office in Laurens. The original Book E has been missing since before the move from the old Courthouse. Therefore, deeds in Book E not completely readable on film were checked against the WPA abstracts. In 1940, the Works Progress Administration (WPA) abstracted the early deed books; copies are retained by the South Carolina Archives. The WPA abstracts were checked for any deeds missing from the film, or the original Book F; no additional deeds were found.

Each deed originated in Laurens County, unless stated otherwise. Courts and local officials are in Laurens County, unless explicitly stated. All places are in South Carolina, unless another state or country is named. Adjacent landowners and natural features are included; metes and bounds are not included.

In the index, the modern spelling is used for rivers, creeks, branches, shoals, etc. Personal names in the index retain literal spellings from the deeds. When searching for a surname, each spelling variant must be checked. Besides personal names and names of corporations, the major index entries are: Cemeteries, Creeks and Branches, Places, Rivers, Roads and Streets, Slaves.

In many deeds, a clerk was inconsistent in spelling a name. Some clerks wrote certain letters nearly the same, for example, L and S, I and J. Lower case letters were often alike within the same deed, for example, a, o, and e. The similarities account for many of the variations in spelling of personal names.

The individual named in a dower release is the wife of the grantor, unless another relationship is stated in the abstract.

This book of abstracts is a guide to the original books. Whenever possible, the deed books should be consulted, either on film, or at the Clerk's office in Laurens.

Larry Vehorn
22 September 2005

Page [1]-[2] 1793, Alexander **McNary** (Laurens Co.) yeoman to William **Warrant** (same), for £20 Sterling sold a certain tract of land containing 100 acres in sd. Co. on N.W. side of Duncans creek on a branch called beards fork. Bounded when Surveyed, N.E. on lands laid out, S.W. by John **McNairy** [sic], all other sides vacant. Being the whole tract granted to sd. Alexander **McNairy** [sic] by William **Bull** Esq. Lieut. Governor, 17 Mar 1775, recorded in book WWW, page 407. Witness John **Harris**, Gilbert **Mcnary**. Signed Alexander **Mcnary**. Witness oath by Gilbert **Mcnary** 30 Mar 1793 to Roger **Brown** J.P., Laurens Co., 96 Dist. Rec. 1 Aug 1793.

Page [2]-5 Lease & Release, 27 & 28 Feb 1789, Patrick **Cuningham** (Ninety six Dist.) Planter & Ann **Cuningham** his wife, to James **Green** yeoman (same), for £40 Sterling, sold all that tract of land containing 100 acres on waters of Durbins creek. Surveyed for John **Audibert** 20 June 1773. Granted unto sd. Patrick **Cuningham** by Wm. **Moultrie** Gov. 4 Apr 1785. Witness David **Green**, Joel **Burgess**, Richard **Duty**. Signed P. **Cuningham**, Ann **Cuningham**. Witness oath by David **Green** 27 June 1789 to George **Anderson** J.P. Laurens Co. Rec. 1 Aug 1793.

Page 5-7 28 Mar 1791, John **Gammel** & his wife Sarah (Laurens Co.) to John **Adair** (same), £20 Sterling sold a certain parcel of land containing 175 acres more or less, being part of 221 acres as shown in the original plat dated 2 June 1788, granted by Thomas **Pinckney** Gov. at Charleston. Being on Allisons creek, waters of Duncans creek, waters of Enoree river, in sd. Co. Border: Ishem **East**, old bounty land, **Ravenell**, sd. John **Gamble** [sic]. Witness James **Gamble**, Ayres **Gorely**. Signed John **Gamble**, Sarah (x) **Gamble** [sic]. Witness oath by James **Gamble** 17 July 1793 to Charles **Saxon** J.P. Rec. 3 Aug 1793.

Page 7-8 26 Jan 1793, Drury **Smith** (Laurens Co.) to Laurens **Barker** [Laurence in one ref.] (same), for £30 sold a certain tract of land containing 140 acres more or less, on S side of Warrior creek, waters of Enoree river. Originally granted to sd. Drury **Smith** 5 June 1786 by William **Moultrie**, then Gov., and recorded in Secretary's office in book NNNN, page 59. Witness John (x) **Winn**, James (x) **Barker**. Signed Drury (x) **Smith**, Sarah (x) **Smith**. Witness oath by James (x) **Barker** 7 Feb 1793 to John **Hunter** [No title.], Laurens Co. Rec. 3 Aug 1793.

Page 9-10 8 Feb 1793, Laurens **Barker** [Laurence in one ref.] (Laurens Co.) to Moses **Sanders** (same), for £44 Sterling convey a certain tract of land containing 140 acres more or less, on S side of Warrior creek, waters of Enoree river. Originally granted to Drury **Smith** 5 June 1786 by William **Moultrie**, then Gov. Recorded in Secretary's office in book NNNN, page 59. Witness Charles **Henderson**, William **Mountgomery**. Signed Laurence (x) **Barker**, Mary (W) **Barker**. Witness oath by Charles **Henderson**, 17 July 1793 to Joseph **Downs** J.P. Laurens Co. Rec. 3 Aug 1793.

Page 11-13 (Newberry Co.) Lease & Release, 25 Nov 1792, Thomas **Chapell** (Newberry Co.) and Delilah his wife to Richard **Griffen** (Laurens Co.), for £150 sterling, sold all that tract of land containing 150 acres in Laurens Co. on N side of Saluda River at mouth of Cain Creek. Bounding S.E. on **Savage**, S & S.W. by sd. River & Creek, N & N.W. by **Griggby**. Originally granted to Robert **Long** and by sd. **Long** conveyed to James **Chappell** [sic] by Lease and Release 1 & 2 Apr 1756, and devolving to sd. Thomas **Chapell** by Heirship. Witness William **Day**, Wm. (x) **Jones**, James **Chapell**. Signed Thomas **Chapell**, Delily (x) **Chapell** [sic]. Witness oath by Wm. **Day** 9 July 1793 to R. **Brown** Judge, Newberry Co. Rec. 5 Aug 1793.

Page 14-16 Lease & Release, 11 & 12 Mar 1793, Richard **Griffen** (Laurens Co.) to William **Day** (Newberry Co.), for £150 Sterling sell all that tract of land containing 300 acres, being in Laurens and Newberry Counties, on waters of Mudlick, whereon sd. William **Day** now lives, on the Main Road leading from Fishdam ford on Broad River to the Island Ford on Salluda. Bounded at time of original Survey: N by William **Neily** and Anthony **Griffen**, other sides Vacant. Originally granted to John **Ray**, and by sd. **Ray** conveyed to Richard **Griffen** by Lease and Release 3 & 4 Feb 1772. Witness Bernardi **Sweeny** [Barnard M. **Sweeny** in one ref.], Martin **Lawless**, Amry **Day**. Signed Richard **Griffen**. Witness oath by Amry **Day** 9 July 1793 to J. R. **Brown** Judge, Newberry Co. Rec. 5 Aug 1793.

Page 16-18 12 May 1791, John **Lindsey** (Laurens Co.) and Mary his wife to Thomas **Holden** (same), for £350 Sterling sold part of a tract of 150 acres in sd. Co. on S side of Enoree River, being part of 300 acres granted to James **Steen** 3 Mar 1767. Border: widow **Lindsey** on Enoree River, a waggon road. Also all that part between the waggon road & the river, 162 acres, adjoining the tract above mentioned. Granted unto sd. John **Lindsey** 5 June 1786. Also part of two tracts containing in the whole 155 acres, adjoining the tracts above mentioned & conveyed to sd. John **Lindsey** by Bartlet **Brown** 7 Jan 1779. The sd. 155 acres more or less, as 15 being part of a tract granted to William **Cannon** containing 150 acres and conveyed by Henry **Hamilton** to sd. John **Lindsey**. And also one other tract of 40 acres more or less, being part of 600 acres conveyed by Benjamin **Brown**, lawful Heir to Bartlet **Brown**, 14 Oct 1785, unto sd. John **Lindsey**. The three last mentioned tracts being bounded by sd. John **Lindsey** Survey as far as the Waggon road, by sd. Road to James **Oliphant**, by **Oliphant** to **Hannah's** path, Enoree River, dividing corner between sd. John **Lindsey** and Abraham **Gray**. Being in the whole 500 acres more or less. Witness Edwerd (x) **Lindsey**, John **Newberry**, John **Pearson**. Signed John **Lindsey**, Mary (x) **Lindsey**. Witness oath by John **Pearson** 8 June 1793 to Daniel **Wright** J.P., Laurens Co. Rec. 6 Aug 1793.

Page 19-22 Lease & Release, 27 Oct 1775, Hans **Hendrick** (Ninety six Dist.) planter to John **West** (same) planter, for £20 Current Money of the Province, sell 20 acres of land, being part of 150 acres, in Berkly Co. in S.W. side of Reedy River, granted unto sd. **Hendrick** by Lord Charles Griville **Montague**, Gov., 7 Feb 1773. Bounded on two sides by land laid out unto Robert **Long**, one side laid out unto Theodocias **Turk** [Theodocia in one ref.], one other part sd. Reedy River, one side Vacant land. Witness William **Parker**, Richard **Lang**. Signed Hans **Hendrick**. Survey certified 16 Oct 1775, by Pat. **Cuningham**, D.S. Oath by Patrick **Cuningham** 15 May 1793, that he made the plat and did write the Leases. Also that by the hand writing, Richard **Lang** & Wm. **Parker**, did sign their names as witnesses. Oath by John **Shirly**, 16 May 1793, that he is well acquainted with sd. Richard **Lang's** writing. Oath by Wm. **Anderson**, 16 May 1793, that he is well acquainted with the hand writing of Hans **Hendrick**, Richard **Lang** & William **Parker**. Given before George **Anderson** J.P. Laurens Co. Rec. 6 July 1793 [sic]. [Includes plat.]

Page 22-25 Lease & Release, 16 & 17 July 1793, John **Hunter** Esq. Attorney for Fredrick **Frasure** (Charleston) to Angus **Campbell** Esq. (Laurens Co.), for £10 Sterling sold all that tract of land containing 250 acres in Craven Co. on Warriors creek, bounding S.W. on William **Berry**, Vacant and land laid out to Robert **McCreery** & James **Allison**, N.E. on William **Sims**. Being granted to William **Williamson** Esq. by **George III** on 2 Apr 1773, and conveyed by Wm. **Williamson** to Fredrick **Freasure** [sic] and now by virtue of Power of Attorney dated 13 [30 in one ref.] Mar 1792. Witness Richard **Pollard**, James **Creswell**. Signed John **Hunter**, Attorney for Fredrick **Freasure**. Witness oath by Richd. **Pollard** 17 July 1793 to Joseph **Downs** J.P. Rec. 6 Aug 1793.

Page 25-26 18 Jan 1793, David **Gibson** (Laurens Co.) to John **Coker** (same), for £15 sold a certain tract of land containing 100 acres more or less, being in the fork of Beaverdam creek of Enoree River. Being part of a tract granted to sd. John **Coker** [sic], joining lands granted to Edwerd **Arnald** & lands granted to Henry **Bramlet**. Also joins a tract where Reubin **Bramlet** now has possession. Also joins David **Gipson's** [sic] land where he now lives. Witness Henry **Jones**, Aaron (x) **Jones**. Signed David (x) **Gibson**. Witness oath by Henry **Jones** 16 July 1793 to Danl. **Wright** J.P. Laurens Co. Rec. 6 Aug 1793.

Page 26-27 20 Apr 1793, Soloman **Niblet** (Laurens Co.) to John **Coker** (same), for £50 sold 100 acres of land more or less, being part of a tract of 406 acres granted to sd. **Niblet**. Being on waters of Warrior Creek, where sd. Soloman **Niblet** now lives. Border: Aaron **Niblet's** spring, Samuel **Dunlap**, sd. Spring branch. Including the house & plantation that Soloman **Niblet** has now in possession. Witness William **Hellum**, Aaron (A) **Niblet**. Signed Soloman (x) **Niblet**. Witness oath by William **Helloms** [sic] 16 July 1793 to Danl. **Wright** J.P. Laurens Co. Rec. 6 Aug 1793.

Page 27-28 23 Jan 1793, John **Young** (Laurens Co.) to John **Coker** (same), for £44 sold all that tract of land containing 80 acres more or less, being on N side of a branch of Beaverdam Cr. Being part of a tract granted to Edwerd **Arnald**. Border: sd. Branch, John **Coker**, spring on sd. **Coker's** side of branch with a square rod of land with it. Including the houses & plantation that John **Coker** has now in his possession. Witness William **Helloms**, Henry **Jones**. Signed John (J) **Young**. Witness oath by William **Helloms** 16 July 1793 to Danl. **Wright** J.P. Laurens Co. Rec. 7 Aug 1793.

Page 28-29 23 Jan 1793, David **Gibson** (Laurens Co.) to Henry **Jones** (same), for £15 sell all that tract of land containing 100 acres more or less, in the fork of Beaverdam creek of Enoree River. Being part of a tract granted to John **Coker**. Border: North fork of sd. creek, Peter **Hammons**, South fork of sd. creek, John **Coker**. Including the house with plantation that Henry **Jones** has now in possession. Witness John **Coker**, William **Helloms**. Signed David (+) **Gibson**. Witness oath by William **Helloms** 28 Feb 1793 to Danl. **Wright** J.P. Laurens Co. Rec. 7 Aug 1793.

Page 30-31 21 Feb 1793, James **Floyd** (Laurens Co.) to John F. **Wolff** Merchant (same), for £20 Sterling sold one tract of land on branches of Warrior creek, bounded S.W. by Thomas **Buckel**, S.E. unknown, N.E. by Thomas **Warring**, N.W. by Drury **Smith**. Granted by Charles **Pinckney** 7 July 1788, containing 295 acres. Witness Ishem (J) **Hestelow**, Oliver **Mathews**. Signed James **Floyd**. Witness oath by Ishem (J) **Hestelow** 28 May 1793 to Joseph **Downs** J.P. Laurens Co. Rec. 10 Aug 1793.

Page 32-33 23 Oct 1792, Whereas Isaac **Delyon** (Charleston) lately in the Court of Common Pleas at Cambridge obtained a Judgment against John **Moffet** & Charles **Saxon** Esq. (Ninety six Dist.) for £2,000 with Interest. A writ by John **Rutledge** Chief Justice at Cambridge, 9 May 1790, directed the Sheriff to levy the above sum. By virtue of the writ, Samuel **Saxon**, Sheriff of Ninety six Dist., did seize one tract of land containing 140 acres more or less, in sd. Dist. in Pendleton Co. on waters of BrassTown creek, waters of Togoloe river. Bounded N.E. by land laid out to James **Millwee**, all other sides by vacant land at time of Original Survey. Granted to sd. Charles **Saxon** 5 Jan 1789, by Thomas **Pinckney** Esq. Gov. and recorded in Secretary's office in Grant book YYYY, page 268. Samuel **Saxon** did on 6 Aug 1792 dispose of the tract at public auction to John Francis **Wolff** for £3 14sh. Witness Joshua **Downs**, LitB. **Willson**. Signed S. **Saxon**, Sheriff 96 Dist. Witness oath by Joshua **Downs** 14 Aug 1793 to Lewis **Saxon** J.P. Laurens Co. Rec. 14 Aug 1793.

Page 33-35 16 July 1792, William **Donohoe** (Laurens Co.) to Thomas **Wadsworth** & William **Turpin** otherwise called **Wadsworth** & **Turpin** (S.C.) Merchants, for £35 Sterling sold all that tract of land on which I now live, together with every improvement, containing 462 acres more or less, on waters of Beaverdam of Little river in sd. Co. Bounded by Thomas **Boyce**, Duncan **Obryant**, John **Donohoe**, John **Younghusband**. Surveyed by John **Hunter** & granted to me by Charles **Pinckney** Esq. Gov. 2 Jan 1792. Together with the present crop as it is now Situate. Witness James **Young**, John **Eastland**. Signed William **Donohow** [sic]. Witness oath by James **Young** 27 July 1792 to John **Hunter** [No title.]. Rec. 15 Aug 1793.

Page 35-36 10 Aug 1793, Whereas Robert **Culbertson** (Laurens Co.) by note 10 Aug 1793, became indebted to James **Parks** (same) for £17 Sterling with Interest from the date. For the better securing payment, sold unto sd. James

Parks, three head of horses: one brown horse, two years old last spring, neither Docked nor branded, the others are both bays, two years old, Stallion Colts; six head of cattle, marked with a Crop in left ear & slit in right ear; one old Waggon with the hind Geers; one rifle gun. Together with my household furniture. Provided that if sd. Robert **Culbertson** shall on 1 Aug 1794, pay the full sum with Interest, then this Deed shall be void. Witness Lewis **Saxon**, Lydall **Allen**. Signed Robert **Culbertson**. Witness oath by Lydall **Allen** 10 Aug 1793 to Jonathan **Downs** J.P. Laurens Co. Rec. 15 Aug 1793.

Page 37-38 (Fairfield Co.) [No date.], Thomas **McClurkin** (same) & Jane his wife, in consideration of 10sh Sterling paid by William **Glidewell** (Laurens Co.) planter, sold all that tract of land containing 100 acres in ninety six Dist. on Beards fork of Duncans creek. Bounding N.W. by land laid out to Alexander **Fairbarn**, S.W. vacant, S.E. on land laid out to John **Cuningham**, N.E. vacant. Granted to Thomas **Cuningham** 2 Apr 1773 by William **Bull** Esq. Lieut. Gov. with a memorial entered in Secretary's office in Grant book OOO, page 280. Transferred from sd. **Cuningham** unto sd. Thomas **McClurkin** 27 Jan 1780. Jean **McClurkin** made over all my right of Dower of the above mentioned land & premises. Witness Francis (+) **Lufey**, Robert (x) **Glidewell**, Abraham **Myers**. Signed Thomas **McClurkin**, Jenny **McClurkin**. Witness oath by Francis (x) **Lufey** 6 Aug 1793 to Roger **Brown** J.P. Laurens Co. Rec. 11 Aug 1793.

Page 38-39 9 Dec 1791, Silvanus **Walker** [sic] (Laurens Co.) to Benjamin **Milam** (same), for £30 sold one certain Tract of land in sd. co. containing 200 acres more or less, & is part of a grant of 245 acres, granted unto sd. **Walker**. Bound: Hardy **Curnant**, Thomas **Dandy**, Cornelus **Cargill** old line, Thomas **Jones**, John **Cargill** old line, Ambrous **Hall**. Witness Thomas **Jones**, Ambrous **Hall**, John **Milam**. Signed Syvs. **Walker**, Sarah **Walker**. Oath by John **Milam** and Thomas **Jones** that they saw Sylvs. **Walker** and Sarah his wife sign the deed. Given 18 July 1792, before Angus **Campbell** J.P. Laurens Co. Rec. 27 Aug 1793.

Page 40 22 Aug 1703 [sic], Jesse **Owley** and Keziah his wife to Thomas **Milam**, for £20 Sterling sold one certain Tract of land in Laurens Co. on N side of Norths creek, containing 50 acres more or less, being part of 300 acres granted unto John **Cargill** and conveyed by him to Thomas **Dendy** and him to Robert **Hall**. Bound: sd. Creek, Elisebeth **Tinsly**. Witness Benjn. (+) **Milam**, John **Milam**. Signed Jese (O) **Owley** [sic], Keziah (+) **Owley**. Witness oath by Benjn. (+) **Milam** 27 Aug 1793 to Charles **Saxon** J.P. Laurens Co. Rec. 27 Aug 1793.

Page 41-42 23 June 1793, Edwerd **Gideon** and Elizebeth my wife (Laurens Co.) planter in consideration of £30 paid by Adam **Gorden** planter (same), sold a certain tract of land of 117 acres more or less. Bounded N.W. Andrew **Endsley**, S.E. Adam **Gorden** & vacant. Witness William **Hall**, John **Robinson**. Signed Edward **Giddeon** [sic], Elizabeth (x) **Giddeon** [sic].

Witness oath by William **Hall** 23 June 1793 to Roger **Brown** J.P. Laurens Co. Rec. 16 Sept 1793.

Page 42-43 13 Mar 1793, Thomas **McClurkin** (Fairfield Co., Camden Dist.) in consideration of £50 Sterling paid by Adam **Gorden** (Laurens Co.), sold a certain tract of land containing 100 acres more or less. Bounded E by lands surveyed by Roland **McCurley**, S by Robert **Taylor** and **Cradock**. Originally granted to Jannet **McWilliams** and situate in Laurens Co., Ninety six Dist. on long branch of Duncans creek. Witness William **Hall**, Lydia (x) **Brown**. Signed Thomas **McClurkin**. Witness oath by Wm. **Hall** [No signature.] 30 Mar 1793 to Roger **Brown** J.P. Laurens Co. Rec. 16 Sept 1793.

Page 43-44 4 Oct 1793, John **Willson** (Laurens Co.) planter to James **Gilbert** (same) planter, for £15 Sterling sell a Tract of Land supposed to be about 20 acres more or less, in Laurens Co. on Durbins Creek, being part of a tract granted by **George III** to Richard **Fowler** 28 Nov 1771, for 200 acres on Durbins Creek, being then Berkley Co. Transferred by sd. **Fowler** to Joshua **Fowley** his heir of Dower, then from Joshu **Fowler** [sic] to John **Willson**. Border: Muddy Branch, Durbins Creek. Witness John **Coker**, William **Jones**. Signed John (J) **Willson**. Witness oath by Wm. **Jones** [No day.] Oct 1793 to Hudson **Berry** J.P. Laurens Co. Rec. 14 Oct 1793.

Page 44-45 1 Aug 1793, George **Willson** (Laurens Co.) planter to William **Jones** (Caswell Co., N.C.) planter, for £150 Sterling sold 200 acres in Laurens Co. on both sides Dirbins, granted by **George III** unto John **York**, being then in Berkly Co. Transferred from John **York** to Amanuel **York** and Thomas **York**, his heirs of Dowry. From sd. Amanuel **York** & Thomas **York** to George **Willson**. Witness Richard **Jones**, James **Wilson**. Signed George (O) **Willson**. Witness oath by Richard **Jones** 12 Oct 1793 to Hudson **Berry** J.P. Laurens Co. Rec. 14 Oct 1793. [Includes plat.]

Page 46-47 1 Oct 1793, Joshua **Fowler** (Pendleton Co.) planter to John **Willson** (Laurens Co.), for £30 sold a tract of Land in Laurens Co. on Durbins Creek, containing about 60 acres more or less, being part of a tract granted to Joseph **Burchfield** by Benjamin **Guerard** Gov., for 204 acres on Dirbins creek, in 1785, and recorded in book AAAA, page 256. From sd. **Burchfield** by Lease & release to Joshua **Fowler**. Border: Richard **Fowler** old line, George **Willson**. Witness Richard **Jones**, Wm. **Jones**. Signed Joshua **Fowler**. Witness oath by Richard **Jones** 12 October 1793 to Hudson **Berry** J.P. Laurens Co. Rec. 14 Oct 1793.

Page 47-49 Lease & Release, 17 & 18 Aug 1787, Joseph **Burchfield** (Laurens Co.) to Joshua **Fowler** (same), for £9 Sterling sold all that tract of land containing 100 acres, whereon sd. Joshua **Fowler** now liveth, being part of 204 acres granted to Joseph **Burchfield** by Benjamin **Guerard** Esq. Gov., in 1785, and recorded in book AAAA, page 256. Witness Daniel **Wright**, Josear **Fowler** [Jesar **Fowler** in one ref.]. Signed Joseph (J) **Burchfield**. Witness oath by Daniel **Wright** 14 Oct 1793 to Hudson **Berry** J.P. Laurens Co. Rec. 14 Oct 1793.

Page 49-50 30 Sept 1793, Joshua **Fowler** (Pendleton Co.) planter to John **Willson** (Laurens Co.), for £100 sold a tract of land supposed to contain 125 acres more or less, in Laurens Co. on Dirbins creek, a branch of Enoree river, being part of a grant 28 Nov 1771, by **George III** unto Richard **Fowler**, 200 acres, being then Berkly Co, entered in Auditor's Office in book 4, No.11, page 127, 21 Feb 1772. From sd. Richard **Fowler** to his son Joshua **Fowler** & his heirs of Dowery. Witness Richard **Jones**, William **Jones**. Signed Joshua **Fowler**. Witness oath by Richard **Jones** 12 Oct 1793 to Hudson **Berry** J.P. Laurens Co. Rec. 14 Oct 1793.

Page 50-51 7 Sept 1793, Daniel **Wright** Esq. (Laurens Co.) hath given to Jonathan **Davis** planter, a tract of land containing 426 acres, being part of a grant 5 Dec 1791, recorded in grant book D, No.5, page 235, by Charles **Pinckney** Gov. unto Daniel **Wright**, 640 acres in sd. Co. on branches of Dirbins creek, a branch of Enoree River. Border: Thomas **Nix**, **Bowen** old corner. Witness Jonathan **Wallace**, Edward **Howard**. Signed Daniel **Wright**. Witness oath by Jonathan **Wallace** 7 Sept 1793 to Hudson **Berry** J.P. Laurens Co. Rec. 14 Oct 1793.

Page 52-54 Lease & Release, 21 Feb 1783, James **Dougherty** and Agness his wife (Ninety six Dist.) to James **Young** (same), for £200 Current money sold all that tract of land containing 150 acres in Craven Co. on waters of Bush River and Duncans creek. Bounding N.E. on land laid out on Bounty of John **Brown**, W on Thomas **Donalson** & Michael **Dickson** [**Dixon** in one ref.], S.E. on James **Anderson** and Endsworth **Middleton**. Certified 24 Mar 1772 by William **Bull** Esq. Lieut. Gov. Witness John **Riely**, Patrick (x) **Riely**, William **Moore**. Signed James **Dougherty**, Agness **Dougherty**. Witness oath by John **Riely** 4 June 1791 to George **Ruff** Judge Newberry Co. Rec. 14 Oct 1793.

Page 54-55 6 Mar 1793, David **Gibson** (Laurens Co.) to John **Young** (same), for £60 sold a certain tract of land on waters of Enoree River on Beaverdam creek, Ninety six Dist. & sd. Co., including the plantation whereon sd. David **Gibson** now lives, containing 100 acres more or less. Border: old Survey line, **Hammons**, Beaverdam Creek, mouth of Bare branch, Rubin **Bramlet**. Being part of 481 acres granted to John **Coker**. Witness William **Helloms**, Henry **Jones**. Signed David (x) **Gibson**. Witness oath by Henry **Jones** 13 Aug 1793 to Danl. **Wright** J.P. Laurens Co. Rec. 14 Oct 1793.

Page 55-57 1 Apr 1783, Thomas **Wadsworth** & William **Turpin** Merchants to John **Stephens** (Laurens Co.), for £7 Sterling sold all their Right to 180 acres [185 in one ref.] of land, in Laurens Co. on waters of Cain Creek, waters of Saluda, being part of a tract granted to William **Donohow** by Charles **Pinckney** Esq. 2 Jan 1792. By sd. **Donohow** conveyed to **Wadsworth** & **Turpin** for more secure payment of a Debt due from sd. **Donohow**. Border: Thos. **Boyse**, John **Younghusband**, Duncan **Obryant**. Witness James **Young**,

James **Boyce**. Signed Thos. **Wadsworth**, Wm. **Turpin**. Witness oath by James **Young** 8 Aug 1793 to John **Hunter** [No title.]. Plat certified 10 Jan 1793 by Patrick **Cuningham** D.S. Rec. 14 Oct 1793. [Includes plat.]

Page 57 (Charleston) 1 Feb 1793, Memwan **Walker** (Orangburgh Dist.) in consideration of £50 Sterling paid by Patrick **Cunningham** (Laurens Co., Ninety six Dist.), sold one Negro Boy about 16 years old, named Absalum. Witness John **Cunningham**, Samuel **Brown**. Signed Memwan **Walker**. Witness oath by Samuel **Brown** 22 Feb 1793 to Stephen **Ravenel** J.P. Charleston Dist. Rec. 14 Oct 1793.

Page 57-59 16 Dec 1792, Jacob **Back** and Brigatha his wife (Berkly Co.) planters to John **Prather** (Laurens Co.) planter, for £30 Sterling sold a Certain tract of land containing 150 acres in Craven Co. on waters of Enoree between Broad and Saluda Rivers. Bounding S.E. John **Mchan**, S.W. and S.E. Robert **Smart**, S.W. Bazel **Prather** on land laid out to Joseph **Greer** and all other sides vacant. Granted unto sd. Jacob **Back**, recorded in Book MM, 13, page 78, in Mar 1775. Witness James **Adair**, Hanner (x) **Jones**, Jo. **Mikler**. Signed Jacob **Back**, Brigatha (x) **Back**. Witness oath by James **Adair** [No signature.] 2 Feb 1792 [sic] to Roger **Brown** J.P. Rec. 14 Oct 1793.

Page 59 13 May 1793, Amalichiah **Powell** (S.C.) sold a Negro man Gim, about 22 years of age, unto David **Madden** (same), for £12 Sterling, £10 paid in hand, balance to be paid in Charleston. Witness John **Baugh** Jur., Mabra **Maddin**. Signed Malichiah **Powell** [sic]. Witness oath by John **Baugh** Jur. 17 July 1793 to Joseph **Downs** J.P. Laurens Co. Rec. 14 Oct 1793.

Page 59-60 18 Mar 1792, John **Cockran** (Laurens Co.) in consideration of £30 Sterling paid by Richard **Pugh** (same), sold all the Goods, Household Stuff and implements of household & all other Goods & Chattels to me belonging. Together with my Crop of Corn, wheat, Oats, Rye, Barley &c. I have put sd. Richard **Pugh** in possession of one Sorrel Mare, branded C. Witness John (x) **McClanahan**, William **McClanahan**. Signed John **Cockran**. Witness oath by John (x) **McClanahan** 10 Sept 1793 to Joseph **Downs** J.P. Laurens Co. Rec. 14 Oct 1793.

Page 60-62 31 Oct 1793, Samuel **Eakin** and Jean his wife to Joseph **Blackerby**, for £85 Sterling sold all that tract of land on which sd. Samuel & Jean now live, containing 250 acres more or less, being a tract originally granted to Thomas **Clark** by Charles G. **Montague** 6 Apr 1768, & by sd. **Clark** conveyed to Hambleton **Murdock**, & by him conveyed to Samuel **Eakin** by Lease & Release 18 & 19 Apr 1783. Situate on waters of Little river in Laurens Co., waters of Saluda. Witness James **Boyce**, Benjamin **Blackerby**. Signed Samuel **Eakin**, Jean (x) **Eakin**. Witness oath by Benjamin **Blackerby** [No date.] to Thomas **Wadsworth** J.L.C. Rec. 2 Nov 1793.

Page 62-64 18 Apr 1793, Whereas Ann **Craddock** (S.C.) by her obligation dated this date, in the penal sum of £49 19sh Sterling with a consideration written for payment of £24 14sh 6p with Interest to be paid annually unto Thomas **Wadsworth** & William **Turpin**, otherwise called **Wadsworth** & **Turpin** (same) Merchants, on or before 1 Jan 1794. Ann **Craddock** for the better securing payment sold two fellows, one called Reubin about 19 years old, the other called David about 17 years old, yellow complexion. Provided that if sd. Ann **Craddock** shall pay the sum, then this deed shall be void. Witness Abiram **Lawrence** [**Laurence** in one ref.], James **Young**. Signed Ann **Craddock**. Witness oath by James **Young** 1 Oct 1793 to John **Hunter** [No title.] Rec. 2 Nov 1793.

Page 64-65 18 July 1793, Whereas John **Woods** planter (Laurens Co.) became indebted to J. F. **Wolff** Merchant for £8 9sh 6p Sterling to be paid on or before 1 Nov 1793. For the better securing payment, Mortgage unto J. F. **Wolff**, one white cow with black Ears, one white spotted Cow with a calf, one Chesnut Sorrel Mare named fly with a colt, and the growing crop now belonging to sd. John **Woods**. Provided that if sd. John **Woods** shall pay the sum, then this Instrument shall be void. Witness James **McCaa**, Gershom **Kelley**, James **Floyd**. Signed John **Woods**. Witness oath by James **McCaa** 29 Oct 1793 to Joseph **Downs** J.P. Laurens Co. Rec. 2 Nov 1793.

Page 65 14 Apr 1792, Shadrach **Martin** planter in consideration of £80 Sterling paid by Thomas **Wadsworth** & William **Turpin**, otherwise called **Wadsworth** & **Turpin** Merchants, (all of S.C.), sold one Negro fellow Isaac about 50 years old; one Bay Mare, three white feet, star in her forehead, branded SS on the near shoulder & Buttock; one Bay horse, two hind feet white, six years old, neither Docked nor branded; two cows & calves, one white with black ears, the other prided with red & white; five yearlings without either mark or brand; seven sheep; one bed & furniture; six chairs; twelve pounds of pewter; three bowls; one set of cups & saucers; one barshear plow; one shovel plough; one large pott; one Dutch oven; two axes; two broad hoes; one Iron Wedge. Witness William **Young**, James **Young**. Signed Shadrach **Martin**. Witness oath by James **Young** 10 Nov 1793 to Lewis **Saxon** J.P. Rec. 10 Nov 1793.

Page 66-67 22 Aug 1793, William **Cason** and Ann his wife to Thomas **Wadsworth** & William **Turpin**, otherwise called **Wadsworth** & **Turpin** Merchants (S.C.), for 5sh Sterling sold that tract of land on both sides of Little river in Laurens Co. Ann **Cason** doth renounce her right of Dower to sd. tract containing 200 acres, originally granted to John **Pursell** by William **Bull** Esq. 21 June 1765, and since purchased by William **Cason** & by him sold to Joseph **Blackerby**, which is recorded in Clerks office Book C, page 286, and since conveyed by sd. **Blackerby** to **Wadsworth** & **Turpin**. Including every part & privilege that was received in their Titles to Joseph **Blackerby**, either to themselves or either of them, except only what the Law shall Determine, was conveyed by sd. William **Cason** to Hugh **ONeal**, respecting his Will by an Instrument signed by sd. William **Cason** & recorded in the Clerks office. Witness James **Young**, Samuel **Wier**. Signed William **Cason**, Ann **Cason**.

Witness oath by James **Young** 4 Nov 1793 to John **Hunter** [No title.] Ninety six Dist. Rec. 10 Nov 1793.

Page 67-69 31 Oct 1793, Joseph **Blackerby** & Jadah his wife to Thomas **Wadsworth** & William **Turpin**, otherwise called **Wadsworth** & **Turpin** (S.C.) Merchants, for £85 Sterling sold all that tract of land containing 100 acres in Laurens Co. on a Simmonses Creek, a branch of Little river of Saluda. Granted to Hugh **Young** by Wm. **Bull** Esq. 10 Jan 1771. Bounded on all sides by vacant land at time of original Survey. Recorded in Secretary's office in book GGG, page 54. Sd. **Young** conveyed to Luke **Waldrop** by Lease & release 21 & 22 Aug 1772, & Willed by sd. **Waldrop** Sen. to his son Jachonias **Waldrop**, & by sd. **Waldrop** conveyed to Ambrose **Hudgins** by Lease & Release 27 & 28 Jan 1780, & by sd. Ambrose **Hudgins** & Joanna his wife conveyed to Joseph **Blackerby** by Lease & Release 21 June 1784. The whole tract more or less. Witness James **Young**, Benjamin **Blackerby**. Signed Joseph **Blackerby**, Judah (x) **Blackerby** [sic]. Witness oath by James **Young** 4 Nov 1793 to John **Hunter** [No title.]. Rec. 10 Nov 1793.

Page 69-71   7 Aug 1793, Joseph **Young** & Mary his wife to Thomas **Wadsworth** & William **Turpin**, otherwise called **Wadsworth** & **Turpin** (S.C.) Merchants, for £8 15sh Sterling sold all that tract of land containing 17-1/2 acres, being the N & E part of a tract of 100 acres, whereon sd. Joseph & Mary **Young** now reside, in Laurens Co. on waters of Simmonses creek. Bounded: N & E on **Wadsworth** & **Turpin**, W & S.W. on Joseph **Young** land part of this original Survey, S.E. on Joseph **Blackerby**. Witness James **Young**, John **Crawford**. Signed Joseph **Young**, Mary (x) **Young**. Dower relinquished by Mary (x) **Young** 7 Aug 1793. Witness James **Young**, John **Crawford**. Witness oath by James **Young** 4 Nov 1793 to John **Hunter** [No title.]. Rec. 10 Nov 1793.

Page 71-73 28 May 1793, Joseph **Blackerby** & Judah to Thomas **Wadsworth** & William **Turpin**, otherwise called **Wadsworth** & **Turpin** (S.C.) Merchants, for £77 Sterling sold all that tract of land containing 200 acres more or less, on both sides of Little River, waters of Saluda in Laurens Co. Originally granted to John **Purcell** by William **Bull** Esq. 21 June 1765. And by Terrel **Reily** administrator to sd. **Purcell**, conveyed to William **Cason** by Lease & Release 5 & 6 Mar 1787, and by sd. **Cason** conveyed to Joseph **Blackerby** by Lease & Release 5 & 6 Aug 1790. With such incumbrance that shall be by Law determined in consequence of an Instrument given by William **Cason** to Hugh **ONeal**, which is Recorded in the Clerk's office of Laurens Co. Witness James **Young**, James **Boyce**. Signed Joseph **Blackerby**, Judah (x) **Blackerby**. Dower relinquished by Judah (x) **Blackerby** 8 May 1793 [sic]. Witness James **Young**, James **Boyce**. Witness oath by James **Young** 4 Nov 1793 to John **Hunter** [No title.]. Rec. 10 Nov 1793.

Page 73-76 24 Oct 1793, Whereas William **Arnold** Sen. and Mary his wife by his obligation 1 Apr 1793, stands bound unto Thomas **Wadsworth** & William **Turpin**, otherwise called **Wadsworth** & **Turpin** (S.C.) Merchants, for the penal sum of £204 1sh Sterling, conditioned for the payment of £102 6p Sterling with Interest. For the better securing the payment, William **Arnold** Sen. & Mary his wife sold all that tract of land on which they now live, containing 200 acres more or less, being part of a tract originally granted to John **Ritchey** by William **Moultrie** Esq. 6 Feb 1786. The 200 acres being part of 300 acres that John **Richey** conveyed to sd. William **Arnold** by Lease and release 15 Aug 1790, recorded in Clerk's office in Laurens Co. in book D, page 289. Provided that if the sum shall be paid, then this Indenture shall be void. Witness James **Young**, William **Cason**, William (x) **Arnold** Jun. Signed William **Arnold** Sen., Mary (x) **Arnold**. Witness oath by James **Young** 4 Nov 1793 to John **Hunter** [No title.]. Rec. 10 Nov 1793.

Page 76-79 5 June 1793, Machones **Goode** (Edgefield Co., Ninety six Dist.) planter, to Patrick **Cuningham** (Laurens Co.) planter, for £400 Sterling sell the following tracts of land containing in the whole 900 acres more or less, each tract adjoining each other & being in Laurens Co. One tract of 200 acres more or less, originally granted unto sd. Machones **Goode** by William **Bull** Esq. Lieut. Gov. 12 Apr 1771. One tract containing 200 acres more or less, originally granted unto William **Martin** dec. by Lord Charles Griville **Montague** Capt. Genl. Gov. 29 Apr 1768, sold away by Berrs **Martin**, being the oldest son & Heir of sd. William **Martin** dec., unto sd. Machones **Goode** by Lease & release 1 & 2 June 1793. One tract containing 100 acres more or less, originally granted unto William **McClaughlin** by Lord Charles **Montague** Gov. 13 Oct 1767, sold away by sd. **McLaughlin** [sic] unto sd. Machones **Goode** by Lease & release 2 & 3 Sept 1771. One tract containing 150 acres more or less, originally granted unto Samuel **Caldwell** dec. by Gov. **Montague** 1 Feb 1768, sold away by John **Caldwell**, being the oldest brother & Heir unto sd. Samuel **Caldwell** dec., unto sd. Machones **Goode** by Lease & release 14 & 15 July 1773. One tract containing 250 acres more or less, bordering Christopher **Rowland's** spring branch to N as has been agreed upon between sd. Machones **Goode** & John **Ozborn**. Originally granted unto Moses **Yarborough** by Gov. William **Bull**, 15 July 1768, sold away by sd. **Yarborough** unto sd. Machones **Goode** by Lease & release 9 & 10 Mar 1769. One tract containing 41 acres more or less, being part of 176 acres, in sd. Co. between waters of Little river & Beaverdam creek, originally granted unto sd. John **Osborn** 14 Apr 1785, sold away unto sd. Machones **Goode** by Lease and release 2 & 3 June 1793. Bounding E, S & W on sd. Machones **Goode's** land, to N on part of original Survey, but now belonging unto John **Walker**. Witness James **Burnsides** Jun., John **Bowman**, John **Dunklin**. Signed Machones (MG) **Goode**. Witness oath by James **Burnsides** Jun. 15 Nov 1793 to Angus **Campbell** J.P. Laurens Co. Rec. 30 Nov 1793.

Page 79-81   21 Feb 1793, John **Hunter** Esq. (Laurens Co.) to Ezekiel **Mathews** (same), for £14 8sh Sterling sold all that tract of land containing 46 acres more or less. Border: **Mathews**, **Dunlap**, Reaburns creek. Also another tract containing 60 acres more or less, both which are part of 950 acres more or less, in sd. Co. on N fork of Reaburns creek. Border: Ezekiel **Mathews**, Waggon Road. Granted to William **Williamson** 20 July 1772, & by him conveyed to Fredrick **Frasure** by Lease & release 23 & 24 Nov 1779, and now by sd. John **Hunter** by a Power of Attorney from sd. Fredrick **Freasure** [sic], dated 30 Mar 1792. Witness J. F. **Wolff**, James **McCaa**, Jonathan **Downs**. Signed John **Hunter** Atty. for Frederick **Freasure**. Plat of 60 acre tract certified 1 Feb 1793, by John **Hunter** D.S. Plat of 46 acre tract certified 10 Nov 1793, by John **Hunter** D.S. Witness oath by John F. **Wolff** 14 Aug 1793 to Joseph **Downs** J.P. Laurens Co. Rec. 30 Nov 1793. [Includes two plats.]

Page 81-82 1 Oct 1791, John **McCullock** Trader (S.C.) in consideration of £150 Sterling paid by Edwerd **Hooker** [Edward in one ref.] (Spartan Co.) farmer, sold all that tract of land containing 700 acres in Laurens Co. on S side of Enoree River, although by mistake the Surveyor called it Tyger River in original plat as granted to William **Miller** by Wm. **Bull** Esq. Lieut. Gov. 10 Feb 1775. Bounded S.E. David **Childers**, S.W. an old Survey, N.W. land surveyed, N.E. Enoree River. Conveyed by William **Miller** 10 Mar 1775 to Martemer **Harris** & Charles **Harris** (Charleston), and again conveyed by sd. **Harris** & Co. 11 Nov 1788 to me, John **McCullock**. Witness Thomas **Todd**, Thomas **McCullock**, Mark (xx) **Powell**. Signed John **McCullock**. Witness oath by Mark (xx) **Powell** 3 Dec 1793 to Roger **Brown** J.P. Laurens Co. Rec. 3 Dec 1793.

Page 82-83 5 Sept 1789, Whereas John **McCullock** am bound by an obligation this date in the Penal sum of £163 16sh 8p conditioned for payment of £81 13sh 4p unto Mauris **Murphey** (S.C.). For the better securing the payment, sold unto sd. Mauris **Murphey**, a tract of land containing 700 acres more or less, on Enoree River. Bounding S.E. David **Childers**, S.W. on an old Survey, N.E. on sd. River. Provided that if the debt is paid, this Deed shall be void. Witness John **Mell**, Sparks **Findley**. Signed John **McCullock**. Witness oath by Sparks **Findley** [No signature.] 5 Sept 1789 to Wm. M. **Mell** J.P. Charleston Dist. Rec. 3 Dec 1793.

Page 83-85 8 Apr 1790, James **Carter**, formerly of Ninety six, but now of Rawden, Hants Co., Novascotia, yeoman, am seized in fee of a certain tract of land which I have agreed to sell unto James **Nickels** of Rawden, Hants Co., Novaschosha, yeoman, say 225 acres upon Cain Creek in Laurens Co., whereof 125 acres was by me purchased of my father Richard **Carter** and the other 100 acres was to me granted by S.C. I appoint my trusty friends Patrick **Cunninham** of Salluda River in Laurens Co. Esq. and Anthony **Golden** of Little River in Laurence Co. Husbandman, my Attorneys to sell the 225 acres unto James **Nickels**. Witness William **Densmore**, Thomas **Pearson**. Signed James **Carter**. Acknowledged by James **Carter** 8 Apr 1790 before Thomas **Pearson** J.P. Hants Co. Nova Scotia. Certification of Thomas **Pearson** Esq. 15 Apr 1790, by John **Parr** Esq. Lieut. Gov. Nova Scotia. Rec. 3 Dec 1793.

Page 85-87 Lease & Release, 28 & 29 Oct 1793, James **Carter** by his Attorneys Patrick **Cuningham** Esq. & Anthony **Golden** (Laurens Co.) to James **Nickels** (same), for £100 Sterling sold all that tract of land containing

125 acres more or less, in sd. Co. on Cain creek, being the upper part or N part of 200 acres originally granted to Richard **Carter** 25 June 1769, and conveyed by Richard **Carter** & Margaret his wife to sd. James **Carter** by Lease & release 5 & 6 June 1777. Bounded: Robert **Carter** & Benjamin **Carter**. Includes the plantation whereon sd. Richard **Carter** formerly lived. Power of Attorney dated 8 Apr 1790. Witness Lewis **Saxon**, William **Dunlap**. Signed Patrick **Cuningham** Attorney for James **Carter**, Anthony **Golden** Atty. for James **Carter**. Witness oath by Wm. **Dunlap** 29 Oct 1793 to John **Hunter** [No title.] Laurens Co. Rec. 3 Dec 1793.

Page 87-89 31 Dec 1791, Elizabeth **Gray** & Jacob **Gray** the father of sd. Elizabeth (Newberry Co.) to William **McCard** [**McCord** in one ref.] (Laurens Co.), for £60 sold all that tract of land containing 200 acres more or less, on waters of Cain Creek a branch of Salada river. Bounding S.E. John **Carter**, N.W. James **McGill**, S.W. Patrick **Cuningham**. Granted 23 Aug 1774, & sold away by William **Gray** unto sd. Elizabeth **Gray** by Lease & release 4 May 1791. Witness Benjn. **Carter** Jun., Wm. **Carter**, John **Carter**. Signed Elizabeth (x) **Gray**, Jacob **Gray**. Witness oath by John **Carter** Sen. 25 June 1792 to George **Anderson** J.P. Laurens Co. Rec. 30 Dec 1793.

Page 89-92 (Newberry Co.) Lease & Release, 4 & 5 May 1791, William **Gray** (Pendleton Co.) & Catharine his wife to Elizebeth **Gray** (Newbery Co.), for £100 Sterling sell a certain tract of land containing 200 acres in Craven Co. on waters of Salluda. Bounding S.E. John **Carter**, N.W. James **McGill**, all other sides owners unknown. Granted 23 Aug 1774. Witness John **Pollock**, Daniel Johnson **Gray** [Johnston in one ref.], Elisebeth **Pollock** [Elizabeth in one ref.]. Signed William (W) **Gray**, Catharine (C) **Gray**. Witness oath by John **Pollock** 20 May 1791 to Andw. **Pickens** J.P. Pendleton Co. Rec. 30 Dec 1793.

Page 92 (Charleston) 26 Apr 1791, I inform you that my Brother Langston & myself have agreed and sold all my father's land & that I bought of you to Silvanus **Walker**. As you know that I have paid you for the land, be so good as to make the right to sd. **Walker** or my Brother as it may best suit them, and this shall be a Clear Discharge to you & your Heirs &c and from me & my Heirs forever. Witness Wm. **Sims**, Aaron (a) **Starns**, Capt. Samuel **Wharton**. Signed William **Drew**. Witness oath by Aaron (a) **Starns** 10 Aug 1793 to George **Anderson** J.P. Laurens Co. Rec. 31 Dec 1793.

Page 92-94 18 July 1793, Randolf **Cook** and Stephen **Potter** (Laurens Co.) planters in consideration of £40 Sterling paid by John **Brown** Jun. (same) planter, sold a certain tract of land containing 50 acres more or less, being part of a tract originally granted to David **Smith** by William **Moultrie** 3 Apr 1786, in sd. Co. on Reedy fork, a branch of Little River. By sd. **Smith** conveyed to sd. Stephen **Potter**, and by him given to sd. Randolph **Cook** as a Marriage Dowery with sd **Potter's** daughter Mary. Land lies in the fork of Reedy fork. Bounded on Lower side by sd. John **Brown**, S by John **Rodgers**. Plat certified 6 June 1793 by Jonathan **Downs** D.Sur. Witness David **Dunlap**, Boland (m)

Bishop. Signed Stephen **Potter**, Randolph (x) **Cook**. Witness oath by David **Dunlap** [No signature.] 18 July 1793 to Roger **Brown** J.P. Laurens Co. Rec. 31 Jan 1794.

Page 94 8 July 1793, Jonathan **Williams** (Laurens Co.) in consideration of the Love, good will & affection I bear toward my Loving father Benjamin **Williams** (same) farmer, give all my lands which I now live on in sd. Co. with the Houses & all things thereunto belonging, of which I have delivered him an Inventory bearing even date. Witness Oliver **Matthews**, Benjamin **Williams**. Signed Jonathan **Williams**. Witness oath by Oliver **Matthews** 16 July 1793 to Joseph **Downs** J.P. Laurens Co. Rec. 1 Feb 1794.

[Page 95 skipped.]

Page 96-97 8 Feb 1791, Thomas **Richerson** (Ninety six Dist., Laurens Co.) to Thomas **Norris** (same), for £30 Current money sold 100 acres of land, of the S end of a tract containing 200 acres, in sd. Dist. on waters of Reedy River. Bounding N.E. James **Ryan**, S.E. & S.W. John **Baugh**. Original grant to William **Elser** by William **Bull** Esq. Lieut. Gov. 23 June 1774, and from thence conveyed unto Patrick **Cuningham** esq., and further to John **Kersterson**, & further to Thomas **McClurkin**, and further to Thomas **Richerson**. Witness Thomas **Cuningham**, John **Cuningham**, David **Dunlap**. Signed Thomas **Richerson**, Keothern (x) **Richerson**. Witnesses to receipt of payment: Richard **Pugh**, Jeremiah (x) **Leatham**. Witness oath by David **Dunlap** 26 Mar 1791 to Joseph **Downs** J.P. Laurens Co. Rec. 5 Feb 1794.

Page 97-100 Lease & Release, 9 & 10 Sept 1793, John **Hunter** Esq. (Laurens Co.) to William **Dorough** (same), for £27 6sh Sterling, sell all that tract of land containing 182 acres of land in sd. Co. on waters of Reedy River. Bounded by Arther **Taylor**, James **Dorough**, Samuel **Cooper**, **Townsend**, part of Survey. Being part of 500 acres in sd. Co. granted to Pierce **Butler** on 5 May 1772, & by him conveyed to Harculas Daniel **Beze** 9 July 1792, and now conveyed by sd. John **Hunter** by virtue of a Power of Attorney dated 1 June 1793. Witness William **Norris**, John **Dorough**. Signed John **Hunter** Attorney for Harculas Danl. **Beze**. Plat certified 3 Sept 1793 by John **Hunter** D.S. Witness oath by John **Dorough** 14 Feb 1794 to Joseph **Downs** J.P. Laurens Co. Rec. 17 Feb 1794. [Includes plat.]

Page 101-102 8 Apr 1793, Whereas **Saxon** & **Willson** & Co. stands Indebted to Robert **Ross** (Laurens Co.) for £145 5sh sterling, to be paid on or before 1 Mar 1795, with Interest. Samuel **Saxon** (same) for the better securing the payment, Mortgage the following slaves: 1 Negro man Peter, one Ditto Bob, one negro woman Aggy & her child, a Girl Milley. Provided that if **Saxon** & **Willson** & Co. pay the sum, then this Instrument to be void. Witness Joshua **Downs**, Nethaniel **McCay**. Signed S. **Saxon**. Witness oath by Joshua **Downs** 26 Aug 1793 to William **Hunter** J.P. Laurens Co. Rec. 22 Feb 1794.

Page 102-103 22 June 1792, James **McCurley** (Pendleton Co.) Blacksmith to Samuel **Saxon** and James **Saxon** (Laurens Co.), for £200 Sterling sold one tract of land containing 100 acres on Warrior Creek. Bounded on W by land conveyed by William **Bourland** to Elisha **Atteway**, E by lands laid out unto William **Berry**, S by Thomas **Dean** &c. Granted unto William **Bourland** 1 Dec 1769, and by sd. **Bourland** conveyed to sd. James **McCurley** by Lease & release 24 Sept 1779. Also one other tract of 136 acres on Warriors creek in sd. Co., bounding N.E. on land laid out for Wm. **Berry**, N.W. & S.W. on Vacant land, S.E. on above mentioned tract. Granted unto sd. James **McCurley** by Wm. **Moultrie** Esq. Gov. 3 July 1786. Witness Joshua **Downs**, James (J) **Rains**, Thomas **Dean**. Signed James **McCurley**, Jane (RU) **McCurley**. Witness oath by Thomas **Dean** 18 Feb 1794 to Joseph **Downs** J.P. Laurens Co. Rec. 22 Feb 1794.

Page 104-105 [No date.], William **Craig** (Laurens Co.) in consideration of £45 Sterling paid by George **Leviston** (same), sell a certain tract of land containing 100 acres on Allisons Branch of Duncans creek. Granted to James **Hanna** 12 Jan 1769 & recorded in Secretary's office in book J, No.9, page 308 & made over by Lease & release to James **Craig** & recorded in Clerk's office of sd. Co. in book D, page 282. William **Craig** says he is the true owner of the premises as an absolute Estate of Inheritance in fee Simple. Witness David **Graham**, John **Hanna**. Signed William **Craig**, Susanna **Craig**. Oath by John **Hanna** 10 Feb 1794, that he did see William **Craig** & Susanna his wife sign the deed. Given before William **Hunter** J.P. Laurens Co. Rec. 22 Feb 1794.

Page 105-107 15 Nov 1793, Whereas John **Edwards** (Laurens Co.) by his two obligations of 13 Nov Inst. acknowledged himself bound for payment of £100 Sterling to William Henry **Crouch** (Charleston). Under one of sd. Bonds a condition is written that it shall be void on payment of £50 with Interest on or before 13 May next & under the other a like condition for payment on or before 13 Mar 1795. For the better securing the payment, sold a tract of land on Indian Creek in sd. Co. granted 8 May 1758 to Abraham **Crouch**, formerly of Charleston, dec., for 100 acres, then bounding upon all sides on vacant land. Provided that if John **Edwards** shall pay the sum, then these presents shall be void. Witness John **Dunlap**, John **Cox**. Signed John **Edwards**. Witness oath by John **Cox** [No signature.] 22 Nov 1793 to Stephen **Ravenell** J.P. Charleston Dist. Rec. 17 Feb 1794.

Page 107-109 20 Dec 1792, Thomas **Norris** to Thomas **Wadsworth** & William **Turpin**, otherwise called **Wadsworth** & **Turpin** (S.C.) Merchants, for £100 Sterling sold three several Tracts of land in Ninety six Dist., 300 acres on waters of Little River of Saluda, bounding N.W. on land laid out to Thomas **Edghill**, N.E. on land laid out to Samuel **Ford** and vacant land and land laid out to William **Simpson**, S.E. on Elizabeth **Caldwell**, all other sides vacant. Surveyed 28 July 1774 by John **Caldwell** Dep. Sur., granted 1 Mar 1775 to Thomas **Edghill** by Wm. **Bull** esq., then Lieut. Gov., recorded in book WWW, page 211. Also 100 acres on a branch of Little River of Saluda, bounding on all sides by vacant land. Surveyed for John **Simmons** 26 May

[No year.] by John **Fairchild**, and granted 15 Feb 1769 to Thos. **Edghill** by order of Council 3 Oct 1765, by Charles Griville **Montague**, then Gov., recorded in Secretary's office in book DDD, page 99. Also a tract of 100 acres on waters of Little River of Saluda. Surveyed by John **Caldwell** and granted by Charles Griville **Montague** to Thomas **Edghill** Jun. Bounding on lands laid out to Thomas **Edghill** S.E. and on land laid out Moses **Grigory**, John **Chesnut** and vacant land. Witness A. **Hammond**. Signed Thos. **Norris**. Witness oath by Abner **Hammond** to William **Hunter** J.P. Laurens Co. and certification that witness signed his name as Magistrate of Cambden Co., Ga., and release has form that Laws of Georgia require. Rec. 17 Feb 1794.

Page 109-112 21 Oct 1793, Whereas William **Arnold** Jun. stands bound unto Thomas **Wadsworth** and William **Turpin**, otherwise called **Wadsworth & Turpin** Merchants (S.C) for £112 1sh 2d Sterling conditioned for the payment of £46 7p Sterling. For the better securing the payment with Interest, William **Arnold** Jun. and Ann his wife sold all that tract of land on which they now live, containing 100 acres more or less, being part of a tract originally granted to John **Ritchey** by William **Moultrie** 6 Feb 1786, and by John **Richey** [sic] sold to William **Arnold** Sen. Sd. tract being on Reaburns Creek in Laurens Co. Bound: sd. creek, plantation which Wm. **Arnold** Sen. bought of John **Richey**, Roger **Murphey** Sen., Patrick **Cuningham**. Provided that if sd. Wm. **Arnold** Jun. shall pay the sum, then this Indenture shall be void. Witness James **Young**, William **Carson**, William **Arnold** Sen. Signed William (x) **Arnold**, Ann (x) **Arnold**. Witness oath by James **Young** 4 Nov 1793 to John **Hunter** [No title.]. Rec. 17 Feb 1794.

Page 113-114 17 Feb 1794, John **Milam** & Nancy his wife (Laurens Co.) to Crystopher **Roland** [sic] (same), for £30 sold one certain tract of Land in sd. Co. on S side of little River, containing 30 acres more or less. Bound: Tandy **Walker**, sd. River, John **Walker**, Mcness **Good**, Mansfield **Walker**. Being granted to Thomas **Dandy**, conveyed from him to Wm. **Dandy** & from him to John **Milam** & **Milam** to Cristopher **Roland** [Christopher in one ref.]. Witness Ezekl. **Roland**, Mansfield **Walker**. Signed John **Milam**, Nancy (x) **Milam**. Witness oath by Ezekiel Stephen **Roland** 17 Feb 1794 to Angus **Campbell** J.P. Rec. 17 Feb 1794.

Page 114-116 28 Aug 1793, Charles **Kelley** & Mary his wife (Union Co.) to John **Cambell** (Laurens Co.), for £40 Sterling sold a tract of land containing as is supposed about 50 acres more or less, being on S side of Enoree River in Laurens Co. Being part of a Survey of 100 acres. Originally granted to sd. Charles **Kelley** 26 Oct 1785, and recorded in Secretary's office in grant book RRRR, page 86. Witness Wm. (x) **Cooper**, Charles (x) **Cambell**, James **Burk**. Signed Charles (C) **Kelly** [sic], Mary [I] **Kelly**. Witness oath by William (x) **Cooper** 24 Jan 1794 to Roger **Brown** J.P. Laurens Co. Rec. 17 Feb 1794.

Page 116-117 17 Aug 1792, John **Smith** & Susannah his wife (Laurens Co.) to William **Ball** Sen. (same), for £30 Sterling sold one certain tract of land lying between cain creek & Saluda River in sd. Co., containing 25 acres more or less, being part of a tract Granted to Alexander **Hamilton** by Letter Patent in 1768 by **Montague** Lieut. Gov. Border: near **Coals** Spring, old path, near John **Smiths** spring. Witness Hugh **Crumbless**, John **Smith**. Signed John (J) **Smith**, Susanah (x) **Smith**. Witness oath by John **Smith** 4 Sept 1792, that he saw John **Smith** Jun. & Susanah his wife, sign the deed. Given before Angus **Campbell** J.P. Laurens Co. Rec. 17 Feb 1794.

Page 118 3 Aug 1793, We, the sons-in-law & daughters of George **Peterson**, late of Laurens Co., give our Interest & Claim in a certain tract of land in sd. Co., the late property of our Father George **Peterson** and the place of his abode at the time of his death, unto our Brother Jon. **Peterson**. Nevertheless, we desire that our dear Mother may enjoy the third of the Tract until her Decease unless our Mother Margret **Peterson** & our Brother John **Peterson** should jointly agree to sell the land, then the money arising from the sale, after just debts paid, go unto our mother & all the Movable property of our late father toward maintaining her. Witness William (R) **Smith**, Benjamine **Peterson**, Robert **Hogan**. Signed Wm. **Day**, Mary (x) **Day**, Marget (x) **Holt**, Thoms. (x) **Chapman**, Nancy **Chapman**, Richard (x) **Hogan**, Francis (x) **Hogan**. Witness oath by William (R) **Smith** 24 Oct 1793 to Angus **Campbell** J.P. Laurens Co. Rec. 17 Feb 1794.

Page 118-119 18 Jan 1791, James **White** (Laurens Co.) to Hugh **Monford** (same), for £6 Sterling sold a certain tract of land containing 16 acres more or less, part of 200 acres, granted to James **Willson** by Wm. **Bull** Esq. 1 Sept 1768, lying on S side of Enoree River, in Ninety six Dist. Witness James **Monford**, William **Gray**. Signed James **White**. Witness oath by James **Monford** 25 May 1793 to William **Hunter** J.P. Laurens Co. Rec. 17 Feb 1794.

Page 119-121 30 Dec 1791, John **Gray** (Laurens Co.) to Hugh **Monford** (same), for £6 Sterling sold a certain tract of land containing 16 acres more or less, part of 325 acres, granted to sd. John **Gray** by William **Moultrie** Esq. 1 May 1786, lying between Duncans creek & Enoree River in Ninety six Dist. Witness James **Monford**, John **Gray** Jun., Wm. **Gray**. Signed John **Gray**, Dally (x) **Gray**. Witness oath by James **Monford** 25 May 1793 to William **Hunter** J.P. Laurens Co. Rec. 17 Feb 1794.

Page 121-122 2 Nov 1793, Jacob **Bowen** (Laurens Co.) to Jonathan **Davis** (same), for £60 sold all that tract of 250 acres of land, being granted to John **Bowen** dec., and willed in the last Will & Testament of sd. dec. to Jacob & Isaac **Bowen**, & Isaac **Bowen's** part conveyed to Jacob **Bowen**. Being in sd. Co. on S side of Enoree River on a N branch of Dirbins creek. Bounding N by lands laid out for David **Anderson**. Witness James **Russell**, James **Killgore**. Signed Jacob **Bowen**. Witness oath by James **Russell** 27 Nov 1793 to Hudson **Berry** J.P. Laurens Co. Rec. 17 Feb 1794.

Page 122 5 Oct 1793, John **Penington** in consideration of £40 Sterling paid by James **McClintock**, sold a Negro Boy Jack. Witness John **McClintock**

Jun., Jacob **Penington**. Signed John **Penington**. Witness oath by John **McClintock** 17 Feb 1794 to Angus **Campbell** J.P. Laurens Co. Rec. 17 Feb 1794.

Page 123   14 Feb 1794, Francis **Harden**, Poor Girl (Laurens Co.) by the consent of her father Henry **Harden**, hath bound herself to Elisha **Holcomb** Blacksmith (same), from present date until 8 July 1797, or until the day of Marriage. During which time she is to obey sd. Master & mistress in all commands and orderly & Honestly behave herself towards the rest of the family. Sd. Elisha **Holcomb** is to find Sufficient Diet, Clothing, Lodging, washing & all other things needful for an apprentice. In presence of & by approbation & consent of Hudson **Berry** J.P. Signed Frances (x) **Harden**, Henry **Harden**, Elisha **Holcomb**. Rec. 17 Feb 1794.

Page 123-124   14 Feb 1794, Mark **Harden**, poor Boy (Laurens Co.) by consent of his father Henry **Harden** hath bound himself to Elisha **Holcomb** Black Smith (same), to Dwell from the present date until 14 Aug 1804, at which time he will be 21 years of age or until the day of Marriage. During which time he is to obey sd. Master in all commands & honestly & orderly behave himself towards his Master and honestly & orderly toward the rest of the family. Sd. Elisha **Holcomb** is to give sd. Mark **Harden** one year Schooling, and Teach & Instruct him in the art & mistery of Blacksmith Trade, on condition he serves out his time, sd. Elisha **Holcomb** to give him a reasonable set of Black Smith's Tools, find him Sufficient Clothing, Diet, Lodging, Washing & all other things Needful for an apprentice. In presence & consent of Hudson **Berry** J.P. Signed Mark (x) **Harden**, Henry **Harden**, Elisha **Holcomb**. Rec. 17 Feb 1794.

Page 124-125   20 Aug 1793, John **Goodwin** (Franklin Co., Ga.) to Benjamin **Mcgee** (Laurens Co.), for £60 Sterling sold a Tract of land in Laurens Co., Ninety Six Dist., on Beaverdam, a branch of Reedy River, bounding on land laid out to sd. **Goodwin** & lands of William **Arthor**. Originally granted to sd. **Goodwin** 15 Oct 1784, for 184 acres more or less. Witness John (x) **Mcgee**, Ansel (x) **Mcgee**. Signed John **Goodwin**. Witness oath by John (x) **Mcgee** 15 Feb 1794 to George **Anderson** J.P. Rec. 17 Feb 1794.

Page 125-126   6 Dec 1793, Langston **Drew** (Laurens Co.) & Nancy his wife to John **Stanfield** (same), for £150 sold one certain tract of land in sd. Co. containing 150 acres more or less. Bound: Andrew **Rodgers**, Jeremiah **Glenn**, Beaverdam creek, **Good**, James **Clardy**, mouth of a branch. Witness Silvanus **Walker**, Joshua (x) **Roberts**. Signed Langston **Drew**, Nancy (x) **Drew**. Witness oath by Silvanus **Walker** 17 Feb 1794 to Joseph **Downs** J.P. Laurens Co. Rec. 17 Feb 1794.

Page 126-128   24 Aug 1793, Archibald **Mchurg** (Laurens Co.) to Benjamin **Camp** (same) planter, for £12 Sterling sold a certain tract of land containing 100 acres more or less,, in sd. Co. on Mountain creek, a branch of Reaburns creek. Granted to sd. **Mchurg** by Charles **Pinckney**, then Gov. 2 Aug 1790.

Border: Jonathan **Downs**, unknown, Benjamin **Camp**, Calvin **Coker** claim, Road to **Wolff's** Store. Witness Jonathan **Downs**, J. F. **Wolff**. Signed Archabald (A) **Mchurg** [sic]. Witness oath by J. F. **Wolff** 28 Jan 1794 to Joseph **Downs** J.P. Laurens Co. Rec. 17 Feb 1794. [Includes plat.]

Page 128-129 31 Dec 1791, James **Green** (Laurens Co.) to Thomas **Goodwin** (same), for £20 sold all that tract of land of 70 acres more or less, being part of land originally granted to sd **Green** by Charles **Pinckney** Esq. Gov. Border: Bowens branch. Witness Moses **Holcomb**, Jesse **Wallace**. Signed James (x) **Green**. Witness oath by Jesse **Wallace** 31 Dec 1792 to Hudson **Berry** J.P. Laurens Co. Rec. 17 Feb 1794. [Includes plat.]

Page 129-130 1794, Mansfield **Walker** & Jinney his wife (Laurens Co.) to James **Bailey** (same), for £20 sold one certain tract of land in sd. Co. on N side of Little River containing 18 acres more or less, being part granted to William **Dendy** & part to John **McKinsey**. Conveyed from Wm. **Dendy** to sd. **Walker**, the other conveyed from sd. John **McKinzie** [sic] to Tobias **Miars** & from him to Wm. **Dendy** & from sd. **Dendy** to sd. Mansfield **Walker**. Border: sd. **Bailey**, Samuel **Powel**, McNees **Good**, branch on the River, mouth of **Powels** spring branch. Witness Silvanus **Walker** Jun., William **Bailey**. Signed Mansfield **Walker**, Jinny (x) **Walker**. Witness oath by William **Bailey** 17 Feb 1794 to Charles **Saxon** J.P. Rec. 17 Feb 1794.

Page 131 16 May 1793, Benjamin **Camp** (Laurens Co.) having bought a Tract of 500 acres of land from John **Hunter** Esq. (same), sd. John **Hunter** binds himself for £80 Sterling in Horses, & Calves at the Rate of Good Cows & Calves at £3 Sterling, or any other kind of Good Trade that sd. **Camp** & sd. **Hunter** can agree about, without interest. Provided that an older Right for sd. tract should appear and take sd. land within the Term of five years from date. Bordering sd. **Camp** and Widow **Morgan**, Wm. **Gary**, unknown. Witness John **Woods**, Milley **Downs**. Signed John **Hunter**, Benjamin (xx) **Camp**. Witness oath by John **Woods** 16 May 1793 to Joseph **Downs** J.P. Laurens Co. Rec. 17 Feb 1794.

Page 132-133 13 Oct 1793, William **Arnold** Sen. (Reaburns Creek, Laurens Co.) Yeoman in consideration of £100 Sterling paid by William **Arnold** Jun. (Laurens Co.) Yeoman, sold a certain piece of land of 100 acres on reaburns creek in sd. Co. Bounded: sd. creek, plantation which I bought of John **Richey**, Roger **Murphey** Sen., Patrick **Cuningham**. Witness Samuel **Arnold**, Reubin **Arnold**. Signed Wm. **Arnold**, Mary (x) **Arnold**. Oath by Samuel (x) **Arnold** 15 Oct 1793, that he saw William **Arnold** Sen. & Mary his wife sign the deed. Given before George **Anderson** J.P. Laurens Co. Rec. 17 Feb 1794.

Page 133-134 18 Dec 1778, John **Williams** (Craven Co.) & his wife to Abraham **Holingsworth** (same), for £300 Current money sold all that tract of land containing 150 acres, in sd. Co. on waters of Saludy. Bound: N.E. on Zachariah **Tenison**, S.E. on William **Burges**, all other sides on vacant land. Granted 8 July 1774. Witness J. **Burnsides** Jun., E. A. **Williams**, Ja.

Thurston. Signed John **Williams**, Mary (x) **Williams**. Witness oath by James **Burnside** Jun. [sic] 11 June 1792 to Angus **Campbell** J.P. Laurens Co. Rec. 17 Feb 1794.

Page 135-136   14 Dec 1793, Richard **Hancock** (Laurens Co.) to Elisha **Mitchell** (same), for £60 Sterling sold a certain tract of land containing 250 acres more or less, in sd. Co. on a branch of Cain creek, originally granted to James **White** by Lord Charles G. **Montague** for 450 acres. Bounded on all sides by vacant land at time of original survey, Memorial is in Auditors office in book J, No.9, page 108. Conveyed by sd. **White** or his heirs to sd. **Hancock**. Witness Mansil **Crisp**, Clayborn **Sims**, William (X) **Crisp**. Signed Richard **Hancock**. Witness oath by Mansil **Crisp** 17 Feb 1794 to Joseph **Downs** J.P. Laurens Co. Rec. 17 Feb 1794.

Page 136-137   28 Dec 1792, William **Anderson** (Laurens Co.) to David **Anderson** (same), for £75 sold one certain Tract of land containing 200 acres more or less, in sd. Co. on Long lick Creek of Reedy River. Border: Reaburns creek, George **Wright's** old Mill, lands granted to **Foster**, lands sold by sd. William **Anderson** to Wm. **Hughes**, Stephen **Wood**, William **Mitchell**. Granted to sd. William **Anderson** by William **Bull** Esq. in 1774. Witness James **Middleton**, George **Anderson**, Molley (M) **Anderson**. Signed William **Anderson**, Molley (x) **Anderson**. Oath by James **Middleton** 27 Dec 1792 that he saw William **Anderson** and Molley his wife sign the deed. Given before George **Anderson** J.P. Laurens Co. Rec. 17 Feb 1794.

Page 137-138   18 Nov 1793, William **Morgan**, a Poor Boy (Laurens Co.) and with consent of Elizabeth **Jackson** (his mother) (same), has placed himself to be apprentice with Thomas **Kivell** (same) to dwell from the present date until 9 Jan 1801, at which time sd. William **Morgan** is 21 years of age, or until the day of Marriage. During which time he shall serve his said Master Thomas **Kivil** [sic], and behave himself towards his master and the rest of the family. Thomas **Kivel** shall Teach & Instruct the Art of making Common Course shoes and give him one year's schooling. When sd. **Morgan** is 21 years old,, sd. **Kivel** shall give one Horse to value of £10, one common Saddle & Bridle, with a reasonable Suit of Clothes. During the time, sd. **Kivel** shall allow sufficient meat, apparel, washing, Lodging & other things necessary. Witness Hudson **Berry** J.P. Signed Elizabeth (x) **Jackson**, William (x) **Morgan**, Thomas **Kivell**. Rec. 17 Feb 1794.

Page 138-139   4 Mar 1792, Joseph **Griffen** (Laurens Co.) planter to James **Griffen** (same) Gent., for £50 sold a certain Tract of land in sd. Co. on head of Carsons creek, in W corner of an original survey containing 350 acres, granted to Wm. **Griffen** Sen. by William **Bull** Esq. Lieut. Gov. for time being. Being a Long Square piece bounding N on unknown, W on William **Truman**, S & E on original Survey. Containing 130 acres. Witness William **Griffen**, Ben **Butler**. Signed Joseph **Griffen**, James **Griffen**. Witness oath by William **Griffen** 11 Feb 1794 to Pro. **Williams** J.P. Rec. 17 Feb 1794.

Page 140-141 4 Jan 1788, Joseph **Turner** (Abeville Co.) to Stephen **Potter** (Laurens Co.) Planter, for £50 sold all that tract of land containing by Estimation 200 acres, in Abeville Co. on N branches of Eighteen mile creek, waters of Savannah River. Granted unto sd. **Turner** (a Soldier in the Bounty) by Benjamin **Guerard** Esq. Gov. 21 Jan 1785, and recorded in the Secretary's office in Grant book BBBB page 104. Witness John (J) **Arnold**, Samuel **Burton**. Signed Joseph (J) **Turner**. Witness oath by John (J) **Arnol** [sic] and Saml. **Burton** 7 Jan 1788, that they saw Joseph **Turner**, late of Abeville Co., now of sd. Co., sign the deed. Given before Jonathan **Downs** J.P., Joseph **Downs** J.P. Laurens Co. Rec. 17 Feb 1794.

Page 141-142 10 Sept 1793, John **Watts** (Laurens Co.) planter in consideration of £20 Sterling paid by Michael **Finney** (same) planter, sold this Sorrel horse 14 hands high six years old Trots & Canters. Likewise one Bay horse 4 years old about 14 hands high Trots & Canters, branded on near shoulder D, and a horse Dittos. Witness William **Finney**, Jeremiah **Ward**. Signed John **Watts**. Witness oath by Jeremiah **Ward** 16 Oct 1793 to Angus **Campbell** J.P. Laurens Co. Rec. 17 Feb 1794.

Page 142-144 19 Aug 1793, Thomas **Adkins** and Ruth **Adkins** wife (Laurens Co.) in consideration of £9 Sterling paid by Aaron **Harlin**, sold a certain tract of land containing 100 acres more or less, bounded: E & S.E. by Robert **Taylor**, N.E. by Joshua **Palmer** where a line runs from William **Sparks** line to sd. **Taylor**, N.W. by sd. **Harlin**. Land is part of a tract containing 146 acres originally granted to sd. Thomas **Adkins** by Charles **Pinckney** Gov. 5 Mar 1792, recorded in Secretary's office in Grant book D, No.5, page 428. To be measured off the original 146 acres, and Joshua **Palmer** to have the remaining 46 acres, divided by sd. line to be run with consent of Joshua **Palmer** & Aaron **Harlin**. Witness Roger **Brown**, Joshua **Palmer**. Signed Thomas (T) **Adkins**, Ruth (x) **Adkins**. Witness oath by Joshua **Palmer** 1 Feb 1794 to Roger **Brown** J.P. Laurens Co. Rec. 17 Feb 1794.

Page 144-145 7 Nov 1793, John **Newill** (Pendleton Co.) planter to John **Howard** (Greenville Co.) planter, for £50 Sterling sold a tract of 150 acres in Laurens Co. on waters of Dirbins creek. Granted 30 Sept 1774, entered in Secretary's office in book TTT, page 247. Granted by George III to Mayo **Newill**, 150 acres on waters of Dirbins creek, being then Berkley Co. Then from sd. **Newill** to John **Newill** his heir of Dowery. Witness James **Gilbert**, John (x) **Gilbert**. Signed John **Newill**. Witness oath by James (x) **Gilbert** 13 Feb 1794 to Hudson **Berry** J.P. Laurens Co. Rec. 17 Feb 1794.

Page 145-147 17 Nov 1793, John **Johnson** (96 Dist.) Gent. in consideration of the Love & affection he hath unto Dugal **Johnson** (same), give all that tract of land that I live upon containing 350 acres, on Mudlick creek in the fork between broad & Saluda Rivers. Bounded at present by land laid out to Daniel **Mcgin** & part laid out to James **Williams** & part on land laid out to W. **Thompson**. Granted by William **Bull** Esq. Lieut. Gov. Witness John **ONeal**, James **Willson**, Charles **Willson**. Signed John (x) **Johnson**. Witness oath by

Charles **Willson** 15 Jan 1794 to James **Mayson** J. Abeville Co. Rec. 17 Feb 1794.

Page 147-148   23 Oct 1793, John **Willson** (Laurens Co.) planter to James **Gilbert** (same) planter, for £18 sold a tract of land in sd. Co. on Durbins creek, supposed to be about 60 acres more or less, being part of the following tract. Border: old tract, first branch, N course of Muddy branch, **Parris'** road. Granted 30 Sept 1774, recorded in book JJJ, page 247. Granted by **George III** to Mayo **Nevill** 150 acres on waters of Durbins Creek, being then Berkly Co. Then from sd. **Nevill** to John **Howard**, then from him to John **Willson**. Witness William **Gilbert**, Jonathan (x) **Davis**. Signed John (J) **Willson**. Witness oath by William **Gilbert** 23 Oct 1793 to Hudson **Berry** J.P. Laurens Co. Rec. 17 Feb 1794.

Page 148-149   6 Mar 1793, John **Young** (Laurens Co.) to David **Gibson** (same), for £50 sold a certain tract of land on S side of Warrior creek, waters of Enoree River in sd. Co. Including the plantation whereon William **Cockerham** now lives, containing 50 acres more or less. Being part of 200 acres now in possession of Charles **Henderson**. Witness Henry **Jones**, William **Hellums**. Signed John (I) **Young**. Witness oath by Henry **Jones** 13 Aug 1793 to Danl. **Wright** J.P. Laurens Co. Rec. 17 Feb 1794.

Page 149-150   13 Dec 1792, Robert **Swain** and Elizabeth (Abiville Co.) Heirs at Law of estate of John **Ward** dec., in consideration of £60 paid by Aaron **Harlin** (Laurens Co.) sold a certain tract of land containing 300 acres, granted to sd. John **Ward** dec. 24 Aug 1771, on Dunkins Creek in Laurens Co. Certified by Francis **Bremar** Esq. Surv Genl. Witness John **Brown**, William **Brown**. Signed Robert **Swain**, Elizabeth (x) **Swain**. Witness oath by William **Brown** 13 Feb 1794 to Roger **Brown** J.P. Laurens Co. Rec. 17 Feb 1794.

Page 150-151   28 Jan 1794, John **Prude** in consideration of Two Cows and Calves and one Earling Calf, one black Mare, Saddle & Bridle, one Bed & Bed cloaths & wearing apparel, and parcel of pork, being as Mary **Prude** believes her Legal share of sd. John **Prude's** Real & Personal Estate, to the Intent that she may become a Sole Trader as though she was never under Covert and that they may both be considered different Traders in Law. John **Prowd** [sic] & his wife Mary **Prowd** [sic] agree that she does Renounce all Claims to any Dowery. Witness Silas (e) **Garret**, Enoch **Garret**. Signed John **Prowd**, Mary (x) **Prowd**. Witness oath by Silas **Garret** [No signature.] 28 Jan 1794 to Roger **Brown** J.P. Laurens Co. Rec. 17 Feb 1794.

Page 152-153   17 Sept 1793, Thomas **Griggory** planter (Greenville Co.) became indebted to John F. **Wolff** Merchant (Laurens Co.) for £7 10sh 2-1/2p Sterling to be paid on or before 17 Sept ensuing with Interest from date. For the better securing the payment, Thomas **Griggory** does Mortgage all my Crop of Corn & Tobacco now on my Plantation, one Shovel plow, one Bearshear plow, two weading Hoes, two Pole axes, two feather beds & furniture, two bed steeds, one Iron pott, one Dutch oven, two Pewter Basons, eight pewter plates, one pewter dish, four Earthen plates, two Trunks, one Loom, two flat Irons, knives and forks, three Chairs, one Cow, one Calf, one Heifer, nine Hoggs, one Iron Wedge, one Wooden Waggon. Provided that if the sum shall be paid then this Instrument of writing shall be void. Witness James **McCaa**, James **Floyd**. Signed Thomas **Griggory**. Witness oath by James **McCaa** 29 Oct 1793 to Joseph **Downs** J.P. Laurens Co. Rec. 17 Feb 1794.

Page 153-154 21 Jan 1794, Samuel **Allison** and Charity his wife (Laurens Co.) to John **Garret** (same), for £65 sold all that tract of land containing 100 acres more or less, on Warrior creek, waters of Enoree River, being part of 200 acres granted unto William **Vaughn** by William **Bull** Esq. Gov. 26 July 1764, and Recorded in Secretary's office in book RRR, page 519. Sold by sd. William **Vaughan** unto Samuel **Allison** 13 Oct 1791 and recorded in Clerk's Office in sd. Co. in book D, page 312. Bound: N.E. by Stephen **Mullins**, N.W. by James **Garret**, S.W. by sd. **Garret**, N.W. by Mr. **Bell**. Witness Stephen **Garret**, Stephen **Mullings** [sic]. Signed Samuel (A) **Allison**, Charity (x) **Allison**. Witness oath by Stephen **Mullings** 18 Feb 1794 to Roger **Brown** J.P. Laurens Co. Rec. 18 Feb 1794.

Page 154-156 Jan 1794, James **Garret** (Laurens Co.) with Dorcas his wife to John **Garret** (same), for £25 sold a certain tract of land containing 50 acres more or less, on Warrior creek, waters of Enoree River, being part of 313 acres granted to sd. James **Garret** by Charles **Pinckney** Esq. Gov. 9 Feb 1792 & Recorded in Secretary's office in book D, No.5, page 451. Witness Stephen **Mullings**, Stephen **Garret**. Signed James **Garret**, Dorcas (x) **Garret**. Witness oath by Stephen **Mullings** 18 Feb 1794 to Roger **Brown** J.P. Laurens Co. Rec. 18 Feb 1794.

Page 156-158 18 Aug 1793, James **Thompson** and Hugh **Thompson** (Laurens Co.) to James **Myers** (same), for £26 Sterling sold all that tract of land containing 100 acres more or less. Being part of 250 acres granted unto James **Rosamond** by his Excellency. Being in sd. Co. on Saludy River. Witness Daniel **South**, James (S) **Saxon**. Signed James **Thompson**, Hugh (W) **Thompson**. Witness oath by James (S) **Saxon** 18 Feb 1794 to Joseph **Downs** J.P. Laurens Co. Rec. 18 Feb 1794. [Includes plat.]

Page 158-159 12 Sept 1793, William **Bean** (Laurens Co.) and Ann his wife to Robert **Burns** (Union Co.), for £70 Sterling sold a tract of 100 acres of land on S fork of Duncans creek in Laurens Co. Bounded E by Josiah **Prather**, W by Reubin **Roland**. Being part of 250 acres formerly granted to William **Bean** Sen., the father of sd. William **Bean** and devolved on him as heir at Law. Witness Reubin **Roland**, John **Martindale**, Henry (W) **Owins**. Signed William **Bean**, Ann (A) **Bean**. Witness oath by John **Martindale** 21 Feb 1794 to Roger **Brown** J.P. Laurens Co. [No record date.]

Page 160-161 24 Feb 1794, Whereas David **Simpson** (Laurens Co.) by my obligation dated 16 Nov 1791, became indebted to Alexander **Hamilton** (same), for £50, one of which was due 1 Dec 1792, the other 1 Dec 1793, with Interest from date, for £25 each. For the better securing the debt, sold 100 acres of land whereon sd. David **Simpson** now lives, one Bay Mare & Sorrel colt, one Sorrel horse with one blind Eye, six head of Cattle, Eighteen head of Hoggs, one man's Saddle & woman's Saddle, with all my house hold furniture of every kind. Provided that if David **Simpson** shall pay the sum on 25 Dec next, then this Deed shall be void. Witness Lydall **Allen**, James **Floyd**. Signed David **Simpson**. Oath by Joshua **Downs** 24 Feb 1794, that he subscribed his name with the witnesses. Given before Jonathan **Downs** J.P. Laurens Co. Rec. 24 Feb 1794.

Page 161-162   16 Oct 1793, Harculas Daniel **Bezi** by his Attorney John **Hunter** (Laurens Co.) in consideration of £11 5sh Sterling sold unto John **Mathis** (same), all that tract of land containing 100 acres in sd. Co., bounding on Robert **McNees**, Robert **Bolt**, John **King**, Waggon Road & part of sd. Survey. Being part of 500 acres originally granted to Pierce **Butler** Esq., and by him conveyed to Harculas Daniel **Bezi**, 9 July 1792. Power of Attorney dated 1 June 1793. Tract lies on branches of Reaburns creek, waters of Reedy River. Witness Lewis **Saxon**, Benjn. (x) **Williams**. Signed John **Hunter** Atty. for Harculas D. **Bezi**. Survey certified 10 Oct 1794 by John **Hunter** D. Surv. Witness oath by Lewis **Saxon** 18 Feb 1794 to Joseph **Downs** J.P. Laurens Co. Rec. 24 Feb 1794.

Page 163-164   2 Jan 1794, Whereas Thomas **Elliott** Sen. (Laurens Co.) by his obligation 1 Jan 1794, for £60 Sterling with condition for payment of £30 Sterling, to be paid unto Lewis **Saxon** (same). For the better securing the payment, sell one Negro woman Pegg, between 30 & 40 years old. Provided that if Thomas **Elliott** shall pay the sum on 1 Jan 1796, then this Deed shall be void. Witness John **Abercrombie**, Lydall **Allen**, Wm. **Abercrombie**. Signed Thomas **Elliott**. Witness oath by Lydall **Allen** 22 Jan 1794 to Charles **Saxon** J.P. Laurens Co. Rec. 24 Feb 1794.

Page 164-165   6 Jan 1794, Whereas John **Manly** Jun. (Laurens Co.) by his obligation 15 Oct 1793 for £40 with condition for payment of £20 Sterling to be paid unto Harculas Daniel **Bize** (Charleston) in three Equal annual payments, the first to commence 1 Jan 1795 &c, to which bond Lewis **Saxon** (same) is bound as Security. For the better securing the payment, sold unto Lewis **Saxon** all that tract of 100 acres of land in sd. Co. on waters of Reaburns creek, bounding on Berry **Harvey**, John **Cammoch**, Harculas Daniel **Bezi** [sic]. Having such shape as a plat to a deed from John **Hunter** Esq. (Attorney for sd. Harculas D. **Bize** to sd. John **Manly** Jun.). Also one white mare, 11 years old; one Grey mare, 2 years old; one yearling filly; one Sorrel mare, 5 years old; ten head of Cattle; five head of Sheep, with their Increase; also all my household furniture of every kind. Provided that if the sum is paid, then this Deed shall be void. Witness Lydall **Allen**, Polley (x) **Garner**. Signed John (J) **Manley** [sic]. Witness oath by Lydall **Allen** 22 Jan 1794 to Charles **Saxon** J.P. Laurens Co. Rec. 24 Feb 1794.

Page 166-167 2 Mar 1793, John **Hudson** to David **Madden**, for £40 Sterlg. Sell all that Messuage on Reedy River, whereon sd. John **Hutson** [sic] now lives. Provided that if the sum shall be paid with Interest on 1 June 1794, then these presents shall cease. Witness Samuel **Saxon**, James **Saxon**, Litt.B. **Willson**. Signed John (x) **Hudson**. Witness oath by Little Berry **Willson** 22 Feb 1794 to Joseph **Downs** J.P. Laurens Co. Rec. 24 Feb 1794.

Page 167-170 Lease & Release, 3 & 4 Feb 1794, Daniel **OHara** and Peter **Bounetheau** (Charleston) Admrs. of Estate of William **Downs** late (same) Gentleman dec. to John **Lynch** (Laurens Co., Ninety six Dist.) Planter, for £25 Current money sell all that Tract of land containing 500 acres, more or less, being in Ninety six Dist. on waters of Enoree River, on Coxes Creek. Bounding S.W. on Angus **Campbell**, S.E. on land laid out, S.W. on John **Cox** [**Casey** in one ref.] & Aaron **Lynch**, E on land laid out. Originally granted to James **Smith** (Charleston) 15 Sept 1775. Witness Waltr. **Hall**, Henry **OHara**. Signed Daniel **OHara**, Peter **Bounetheau**. Witness oath by Henry **OHara** [No signature.] 4 Feb 1794 to John **Mitchell** Esq. J.Q. Rec. 1 Mar 1794.

Page 170-171 28 Dec 1793, Oliver **Mathis** (Laurens Co.) to Boling **Bishop** (same), for £36 10sh Sterling sold one grey horse, two brown bay mares, Jackling of sd. Waggon and other appurtenances belong to sd. Waggon, two Cows and Calves, and all my house hold stuff, with hoggs, and 146 acres of land more or less, bounding on Benjn. **Elliott**, John **Cammoch**, John **Cockran**. Being part of a Survey belonging to Harculas Danl. **Bezi**. Provided that if Oliver **Mathis** shall pay unto Harculas Danl. **Bezi** the sum of money in the space of three years so that sd. Boling **Bishop** does not come to Damage, from this date 1 Jan 1794, then these presents shall be void. Witness Joseph **Mathis**, Penine (x) **Mathis**. Signed Oliver **Mathis**. Witness oath by Joseph **Mathis** 19 Feb 1794 to Roger **Brown** J.P. Laurens Co. Rec. 1 Mar 1794.

Page 171-172 30 May 1792, Thomas **Dendy** Sen. and Mary his wife (Laurens Co.) to Cornelius **Dendy** (same), for 20sh sterling sold one certain Tract of land in sd. Co. containing by Estimation 180 acres more or less. Bound: N side of Norths creek, old line. Being part of land granted unto Benjamin **Powell** 23 June 1771 & conveyed by him unto Thomas **Dendy** Sen. by Lease & release 20 Dec 1773. Witness Daniel **Dendy**, William **Dendy**, William **Dendy** [sic]. Signed Thomas **Dendy**, Mary (x) **Dendy**. Witness oath by William **Dendy** 19 Feb 1794 to Charles **Saxon** J.P. Laurens Co. Rec. 1 Mar 1794.

Page 172-175 Lease & Release, 14 & 15 Nov 1793, Elizebeth **Greene** (Cambridge), heir to Henry **Green** [sic], in consideration of £30 Sterling paid by Charles **Braudy** (Laurens Co.) planter, sold all that Tract of 150 acres of land. Granted 1 Sept 1768, by William **Bull** Esq., at that time Gov., to Henry **Greene** 150 acres on waters of Reedy River. Recorded in Secretary's office in book DDD, page 449. Witness Jane (x) **Dixon**, Thomas **Dixon**, Thomas **Richardson**. Signed Elizabeth (x) **Greene** [sic.]. Witness oath by Thomas **Richardson** 20 Nov 1793 to Jas. **Mayson** J. Newberry Co. Rec. 1 Mar 1794.

Page 175-178 Lease & Release, 5 & 6 Sept 1793, John **Hunter** Esq. (Laurens Co.) to Hugh **Henderson** (same), for £17 14sh sterling sold all that tract of land containing 177 acres more or less, on waters of Reedy River, being part of 1,300 acres originally granted to Thomas **Shubrick** & by him conveyed to Wm. **Williamson**, and by him to John **Rutledge** Jun., & now by John **Hunter** by virtue of a Power of Attorney from sd. John **Rutledge** dated 31 Jan 1791 & recorded in clerk's office of sd. Co. on 14 Mar in same year in book C, page 332. Border: Wm. **Allison**, William **Wadkins**, part of Survey. Witness John **Brodey**, John **Henderson**. Signed John **Hunter** Atty. for John **Rutledge** Jun. Plat certified 3 Sept 1793 by John **Hunter** D.Surv. Witness oath by John **Brodey** 18 Feb 1794 to Joseph **Downs** J.P. Laurens Co. Rec. 3 Mar 1794. [Includes plat.]

Page 178-179 16 Oct 1793, Harculas Daniel **Bize** by his Attorney John **Hunter** (Laurens Co.) to Benjamin **Williams** (same), for £8 7sh 6p sold a certain tract of land containing 67 acres more or less, in sd. Co. on waters of Reaburns creek, bounding on fork of branch, sd. Benjamin **Williams**, Lewis **Saxon**, John **Cockran** & part of the Survey. Being part of 500 acres originally granted to Pierce **Butler**, and by him conveyed to Harculas Daniel **Bize** 9 July 1792. Witness Jonathan **Williams**, Benjamin **Williams** Jun. Signed John **Hunter** Atty. for Harculas Danl. **Bize**. Recd. a bond from Benjamin **Williams** & Jonathan **Williams** payable to Harculas Danl. **Bize**, 17 Oct 1793. Witness oath by Benjamin **Williams** 2 Mar 1794 to Joseph **Downs** J.P. Laurens Co. Rec. 3 Mar 1794. [Includes plat.]

Page 180-181 9 Aug 1793, Whereas John **Simpson** (Laurens Co.) did on 16 Dec 1789, in County Court of Laurens obtain a judgment against Richard **Carrol** for £6 9sh. By virtue of a writ dated 17 Dec 1789, issued by Lewis **Saxon** Clerk of sd. Court directed the Sheriff of sd. Co. to cause to be made the sum from the goods of sd. **Carrol**. William **Hunter**, former Sheriff, did seize one tract of land containing 230 acres more or less, in sd. Co. on Carrols branch of Little River. Bounding at time of original Survey on Thomas **Cargill**, Robert **Cooper**, Hugh **Young**, Richard **Carrol**, Sarah **Cargill** & Thos. **Dendey**. Granted unto Ratclift **Jowell** 4 Apr 1785 by William **Moultrie** Esq. Gov. Sold on 25 Feb 1790 at public auction to Robert **Ross** (same), for £10 Sterling. Witness Gilbert **Menary**, Nathaniel **McCay**. Signed William **Hunter** Sheriff. Witness oath by Nathaniel **McCay** 10 Apr 1794 to Lewis **Saxon** [No title.] Rec. 10 Apr 1794.

Page 181-183 26 Oct 1793, Whereas Richard **Hix** (Laurens Co.) by my obligation of this date became indebted to Robert **Ross** Hatter (same), for £40 Sterling with Interest from 1 Jan 1794, to be paid: £10 on 1 Jan 1795, £10 on 1 Jan 1796, £10 on 1 Jan 1797, and £10 on 1 Jan 1799. Said sum to be paid in Tobacco delivered in Charleston at the highest price Tobacco then bears in half cash & half goods. For the better securing the sum, sold one tract of land containing 230 acres more or less, in sd. Co. on Carrols branch, of Little River. Bounding at time of original Survey on Thomas **Cargill**, Robt. **Cooper**, Hugh **Young**, Richard **Carrol**, Sarah **Cargill** & Thomas **Dendy**. Granted unto

Ratclift **Jowell** 4 Apr 1785 by Wm. **Moultrie** Esq. Gov. Provided that if the sum is paid, then this Instrument of Writing shall be void. Witness Joshua **Downs**, Joel **Walker**. Signed Richard (V) **Hix**. Witness oath by Joshua **Downs** 10 Apr 1794 to Lewis **Saxon** [No title.]. Rec. 10 Apr 1794.

Page 183-184   28 Oct 1788, Richard **Jowell** am bound unto Richard **Carrol** for £60 Sterling. Condition that if Richard **Jowell** makes a firm Title to a tract of 230 acres of land, known by name of Samuel **Boyd's** old place, bounding on land where sd. **Carrol** now lives, on or before 10 Oct next ensuing. Witness James **McNees**, Francis **Lester**. Signed Richard **Jowell**. Witness oath by James **McNees** 17 Feb 1794 to Joseph **Downs** J.P. Laurens Co. Rec. 10 Apr 1794.

Page 184-186   27 July 1793, Whereas James **Layson** planter & Morgan **Layson** planter (Laurens Co.) by their obligation dated 27 July 1793, stand bound unto Robert **McCrery** planter & George **Gordon** & Company Merchants (S.C.), for £21 13sh Sterling, conditioned for payment with Interest. For the better securing the payment, sold all that tract of land of 150 acres, originally granted to James **Layson** & bounded N.E. on lands granted to William **Layson**, other sides by lands Granted to Mark **Littleton**, vacant land & land granted to Robert **Mann**. Provided that if the sum is paid, then this Indenture shall be void. Witness Robert **Hanna**, David **Templeton**. Signed James **Layson**, Morgan **Layson**. Witness oath by Robert **Hanna** 8 Mar 1794 to Roger **Brown** J.P. Laurens Co. Rec. 10 Apr 1794.

Page 186-188   15 Oct 1793, John **Hunter** Esq. to William **Simmons** (Laurens Co., Ninety six Dist.), for £25 13sh Sterling sold all the tract of land contained in 171 acres more or less, on S side of Long Shoals of Reedy River, adjoining John **Pringle**, David **Green** & River. Being part of 3,000 acres originally granted to Thomas **Shubrick**, and by him conveyed to William **Williamson**, & by him conveyed to John **Rutledge** Jun. & now by John **Hunter** by power of Attorney from sd. John **Rutledge** 31 Jan 1791. Witness John **Pringle**, David **Madden**. Signed John **Hunter** Atty. of John **Rutledge** Jun. Plat certified 10 Oct 1793 by John **Hunter** D.S. Received a bond from William **Simmons** & John **Pringle** 15 Oct 1793. Witness oath by John **Pringle** 14 Apr 1794 to Joseph **Downs** J.P. Laurens Co. Rec. 14 Apr 1794. [Includes plat.]

Page 188-190   15 Oct 1793, John **Hunter** Esq. to John **Pringle** (Laurens Co., Ninety six Dist.), for £42 3sh Sterling sold all that tract of land containing 281 acres more or less, on long shoal branch of Reedy River & on Joseph **Mayhon** [**Mahon** in one ref.], sd. Survey, lands laid off for John **Robinson**, William **Simmons** at time of Surveying. Being part of 3,000 acres originally granted to Thomas **Shubrick** & by him conveyed to William **Williamson** & conveyed by him to John **Rutledge** Jun. & now conveyed by sd. John **Hunter** by Power of Attorney from sd. John **Rutledge** 31 Jan 1791 & Recorded in Clerk's office in book C, page 332 on 14 Mar in same year. Witness Joseph **Mayhon**, David **Green**. Signed John **Hunter** Atty. for John **Rutledge** Jun. Certification of plat of 251 acres [sic] 10 Oct 1793 by John **Hunter** D.S. Witness oath by Joseph

Mayhon 14 Apr 1794 to Joseph **Downs** J.P. Laurens Co. Rec. 14 Apr 1794. [Includes plat.]

Page 190-192 15 Oct 1793, John **Rutledge** Esq. Jun. (Charleston) by his Attorney John **Hunter** Esq. (Laurens Co.) to Joseph **Mayhon** (Laurens Co.), for £20 Sterling sold all that tract of land containing 162 acres more or less, being part of 3,000 acres originally granted to Thomas **Shubrick** 15 May 1772, and by him conveyed to **Williamson** & by him to sd. John **Rutledge**. Power of Attorney dated 31 Jan 1791 and recorded in Clerk's office 14 Mar in same year in book C, page 332. Sd. land lying in Laurens Co. on Reedy River, bounding on William **Simmons**, John **Pringle**, part of sd. Survey & Joseph **Mayhon**. Witness John **Pringle**, William **Simmons**. Signed John **Hunter** Atty. for John **Rutledge** Jun. Plat certified 10 Oct 1794 by John **Hunter** D.S. Witness oath by John **Pringle** 14 Apr 1794 to Joseph **Downs** J.P. Laurens Co. Rec. 14 Apr 1794. [Includes plat.]

Page 192-194 15 Oct 1793, Harculas Daniel **Bize** by his Attorney John **Hunter** Esq. (Laurens Co.) to Berry **Harvey** (same), for £32 10sh Sterling sold all that tract of land containing 200 acres more or less, in sd. Co. on waters of Reaburns creek, joining lands of James **Cuningham**, part of sd. Survey, John **Manly**, John **Cammoch** & Samuel **Elliott**. Being part of 500 acres originally granted to Pierce **Butler**, and by him conveyed to Harculas Daniel **Bize** 9 July 1792. Power of Attorney dated 1 June 1793. Witness Joseph **Mathis**, Robert **McNees**. Signed John **Hunter** Atty. for Harculas Danl. **Bize**. Plat certified 10 Oct 1793 by John **Hunter** D.S. Witness oath by Robert **McNees** 2 Mar 1794 to Joseph **Downs** J.P. Laurens Co. Rec. 15 Apr 1794. [Includes plat.]

Page 194-195 [Two pages numbered 194.] 7 Oct 1792, John **Hunter** esq. (Laurens Co.) to John **Folconer** [**Falconer** in one ref.] (same), for £28 10sh Sterling sold one certain tract of land, joining John **Chandler**, Wm. **Edin**, William **Carter**, Soloman **Southerland**, Thomas **Dendy**, William **Bryson** & Robert **Conine**, containing 190 acres in sd. Co. on waters of Norths & Simmons creek, being part of 2,000 acres originally granted to William **Bull** Jun. & conveyed by him to William **Williamson** Esq. and by him to Fredrick **Freasure** Esq. and now by John **Hunter** Esq. by Power of Attorney from sd. **Freasure**. Witness Benjamin **Jones**, John **Cargill**. Signed Fredrick **Freasure** by his Atty. John **Hunter**. Plat certified 11 Oct 1792 by John **Hunter** D.S. Witness oath by Ben. **Jones** 7 Nov 1793 to William **Hunter** J.P. Laurens Co. Rec. 15 Apr 1794. [Includes plat.]

Page 195-196 6 Nov 1793, John **Falconer** (Laurens Co.) to James **Henderson** Sen. (same), for £20 sold all that tract of land containing 190 acres more or less, in sd. Co. on waters of Norths and Simmons creek, adjoining John **Chandler**, William **Edin**, William **Carter**, Joshua **Southerland**, Daniel **Dendy**, William **Bryson** and Robert **Conine**, being part of 2,000 acres originally granted to William **Bull** Jun. & conveyed by him to **Williamson** & by him to Fredrick **Freasure** Esq. and by Power vested into John **Hunter** Esq.

conveyed to sd. **Falconer**. Provided if John **Falconer** shall pay Joseph **Winthrop** Esq. (Charleston) £28 10sh and Interest that may become due on a bond given by sd. **Falconer** for which sd. James **Henderson** stands Security, then the conveyance shall be void. Signed John **Cargill**, Benj. **Jones**. Signed John (x) **Falconer**. Witness oath by Ben. **Jones** 7 Nov 1793 to William **Hunter** J.P. Laurens Co. Rec. 15 Apr 1794.

Page 196-197   14 Sept 1793, John **Norris** planter (Laurens Co.) in consideration of £10 15sh 2p Sterling paid by David **Mcgladery** planter, all my present this year's crop of Tobacco & corn standing on the plantation of sd. David **Mcgladery**, likewise one grey mare, also one feather bed & furniture to the bed, one pott, one pewter Dish, half Doz. Pewter Plates, one Cotton wheel, one pair Cotton cards, half Doz. Earthen plates, knives & forks, one old man's Saddle, two side of Shoe Leather, in Jann, half Doz. Tin cups, one pott, one weading hoe, one water pail, one Churn, one Tub, one Piggin, one Cann, one homespun woman's gown. Provided that if the sum is paid on 14 Oct 1794, then this Bill of Sale shall be void. Witness J. F. **Wolff**, James **McCaa**, Nathaniel **Sullivant**. Signed John (x) **Norris**. Witness oath by J. F. **Wolff** 28 Jan 1794 to Joseph **Downs** J.P. Laurens Co. Rec. 15 Apr 1794.

Page 197-200   Lease & Release, 10 & 11 Feb 1788, Henry **Geddes** Merchant (Charleston) to James **McLaughlin** (Laurens Co.), for £30 current money sell a certain tract of land containing 200 acres in Ninety six Dist. on a branch of Duncans creek called in the original Isaacs branch, originally granted to Zepheniah **Kinsley** by Wm. **Bull** Lieut. Gov. 3 Apr 1775. Sold by William **Hist** at Public Vendue in Charleston, as Attorney for sd. **Kinsly** [sic] by Lease & release 6 & 7 Mar 1786, to sd. Henry **Geddes**. Witness Adam C. **Jones**, Jonathan **Downs**, John **Hunter**. Signed Henry **Geddes**. Witness oath by John **Hunter** 12 June 1788 to John **Rodgers** J.P. Rec. 16 Apr 1794.

Page 200-201   26 Apr 1794, William **Olifant** (Laurens Co.) in consideration of £15 10sh paid by James **Underwood** (same), sold a certain Waggon & the hind Giers. Sd. Waggon is branded with a heart in four places upon the hind gate & now in possession of sd. **Underwood**. Witness Robert **Anderson**. Signed William **Oliphent** [sic]. Witness oath by Robert **Anderson** 29 Apr 1794 to William **Hunter** J.P. Laurens Co. Rec. 29 Apr 1794.

Page 201-203   Lease & Release, 20 & 21 Jan 1794, Daniel **Wood** (Ninety six Dist.) to James **Criswell** & Co. (same), for £30 Sterling sold a certain tract of land containing 91 acres in Laurens Co. Bounded S.W. on Frederick **Ward**, N.E. on John **Sills** Jun., S.W. on James **Mayson**. Granted to Robert **Gilliam** esq. by William **Moultrie** Esq. Gov. 21 May 1786. Witness Richard **Watts**, Elihu **Criswell**, John **Sills** Jun. Signed Daniel **Wood**. Witness oath by Richard **Watts** 25 Apr 1794 to James **Mayson** J.P. Rec. 29 Apr 1794.

Page 204-205   4 Nov 1793, William **Yarbrough** & Frances **Savage** mother to sd. **Yarbrough** (Edgfield Co.) to Joseph **Cox** (Laurens Co.), for 10sh Sterling sold a certain Tract of land, being part of a Tract originally granted unto

Moses **Yarbrough**, for 500 acres. Being in Laurens Co. on the Westernmost side of Little River. Border: Vincen **Glass**, Joseph **Cox**, John **Cox**, Mark **Moore**, Wm. **Martin**, John **Wigenton**, John **Manley**, John **Boyd**, . Containing & now laid out for 321 acres in the original Deed. [Plat shows 379 acres.] Witness Gilson **Yarbrough**, John **Cornelison**. Signed William **Yarbrough**, Frances (x) **Savage**. Witness oath by John **Cornelison** 18 Jan 1794 to Jonathan **Downs** J.P. Laurens Co. Rec. 2 May 1794. [Includes plat.]

Page 206-209   Lease & Release, 9 & 10 Sept 1793, John **Hunter** Esq. (Laurens Co.) to Arther **Taylor** [Arthor in one ref.] (same), for £51 14sh Sterling sold all that Tract of land containing 232 acres, in sd. Co. on waters of Reedy River. Bounding on David **Dunlap**, Samuel **Cooper**, Richard **Pugh** & William **Dorough**. Being part of 500 acres originally granted to Pierce **Butler** 5 May 1772, and by him conveyed to Harculas Daniel **Bize** 9 July 1792, and now conveyed by sd. John **Hunter** by Power of Attorney dated 1 June 1793. Witness William **Norris**, John **Dorough**. Signed John **Hunter** Atty. for Harculas Danl. **Bize**. Plat certified 9 Sept 1793 by John **Hunter** D.Surv. Witness oath by John **Dorough** 14 Feb 1794 to Joseph **Downs** J.P. Laurens Co. Rec. 5 May 1794. [Includes plat.]

Page 209-210   5 May 1794, Whereas William **Martin** & Shadrach **Martin** (Laurens Co.) stand indebted to **Saxon** & **Willson** (same) Merchants, for £13 3sh 1p 1f Sterling, to be paid by 25 Dec next. For the better securing the payment, sold one tract of land containing 180 acres more or less, being part of 300 acres granted unto sd. Shadrach **Martin** & whereon sd. Shadrach & Wm. **Martin** now live. Lying on W side of a branch of Little River, which sd. branch runs threw the 300 acres. Provided that if the sum is paid, then this agreement shall be void. Witness Joshua **Downs**, Lydall **Allen**. Signed Wm. **Martin**, Shadrach **Martin**. Witness oath by J. **Downs** 7 May 1794 to Joseph **Downs** J.P. Laurens Co. Rec. 7 May 1794.

Page 211-212   7 May 1794, Whereas Samuel **Saxon** is bound as Security for Little Berry **Harvey** (Laurens Co.) for £31 18sh 4p, payable to Harculas Daniel **Bize**, one third to be paid 1 Jan 1795, one other third 1 Jan 1796 & the other third 1 Jan 1797. For the better securing payment, sold unto sd. Samuel **Saxon** one Tract of 200 acres in sd. Co. on waters of reaburns creek, being part of a Tract granted to sd. **Bize** & whereon sd. Little Berry **Harvey** now lives. Also one Sorrel horse, one Black Mare, five head of Cattle, two feather beds & furniture, two Iron potts, one Dutch oven, one frying pan and all my plantation & working Tools. Nevertheless, if the sum is paid, then this Instrument of Writing shall be void. Witness Stainback **Willson**, Joshua **Downs**. Signed Little Berry **Harvey**. Witness oath by J. **Downs** 7 May 1794 to Joseph **Downs** J.P. Laurens Co. Rec. 7 May 1794.

Page 212-213   10 Nov 1793, James **Flin**, now of Laurens Co., in consideration of £150 Sterling paid by John **Wright**, sold a Negro woman Sela, about 30 years of age, County born; also one Negro girl Tabby, about 13 years of age; also one other Negro Girl Milley, about 9 years of age; and one other Negro

Girl child Dicey, about 6 years of age, all three children of sd. Ceala [sic].
Witness Silvanus **Walker**, Wm. (x) **Ramsey**. Signed James (x) **Flin**. Witness
oath by Silv. **Walker** 8 May 1794 to Charles **Saxon** J.P. Rec. 8 May 1794.

Page 213-214 20 Apr 1792, James **Flin**, now of Laurens Co., in consideration
of £120 Sterling paid by John **Doyel**, sold a Negro woman Cela, about 35 or
36 years of age, county born, also one Negro girl Tabbey, about 10 or 11 years
of age, also one other Negro Girl child named Milley, about 7 years of age,
and one other negro Girl child Dicey, about 2 years old, all three the children
of Ceala [sic]. Witness Robert **Adair**, James **Adair**. Signed James (x) **Flin**.
Witness oath by Robert **Adair** 11 May 1792 to Roger **Brown** J.P. Oath by
John **Huston** that sd. John **Doyel** was going to North Carolina and Endorsed
the Bill of Sale to this Deponent & left it with him to keep sd. **Huston** free
from Damages on account of his being Security for sd. **Doyel** to Benjn. **Bird**
for one Hogshead of Tobacco, which this Deponent has been obliged to pay
since. When sd. **Doyel** came back & commenced a Suit against sd. **Flin** for sd.
Negroes, that this Deponent was advised to Cross sd. Endorsement, which he
did. Given 15 Oct 1793 before John **Hunter**. Received of John **Wright** by
hand of Silvanus **Walker** Esq. £7 which is full Satisfaction to me for the Bill
of Sale, which I sign over all my right to sd. John **Wright**, this 24 Oct 1793.
Witness John **Hunter**. Oath by Silvs. **Walker** 8 May 1794, that he saw John
Huston sign the receipt. Given before Charles **Saxon** J.P. Rec. 8 May 1794.

Page 215-216 15 July 1793, Joseph **Whitmore** (Laurens Co.) in consideration
of the natural Love & affection I bear to Alis **Whitmore** widow and Sarah,
Lyddia, Margaret, Ann & Mary **Whitmore** (Daughters of sd. Alis **Whitmore**)
(same), my grand Daughters, give all that tract of land containing 150 acres on
S side of Enoree River on a small spring branch thereof. Bounded on all sides
by vacant land when Surveyed. Granted to Joseph **Whitmore** 11 Aug 1774 by
Wm. **Bull** esq., recorded in Secretary's office in book RRR, page 662 Also
another tract of 150 acres on drafts of Duncans creek upon School house
branch. Bounded N.E. by above tract, all other sides vacant when Surveyed.
Granted to sd. Joseph **Whitmore** 21 Apr 1774, and recorded in Secretary's
office in Book 32, page 30, by Wm. **Bull** esq. Witness John **Garret**, George
Whitmore. Signed Joseph (x) **Whitmore**. Witness oath by John **Garret** [No
signature.] 7 May 1794 to Roger **Brown** J.P. Laurens Co. Rec. 12 May 1794.

Page 216-217 16 Oct 1793, Elisha **Attaway** (Laurens Co.) & Lettuce his wife
to John **Moore**, late of sd. Co., for £100 Sterling sold all that tract of land
containing by Estimation 150 acres, being part of land originally granted to
Joseph **Attaway** by Letter patent 22 Mar 1768. Witness James **Attaway**, John
(B) **Brown**, James (x) **Dunlap**. Signed Elisha (x) **Attaway** [Alisha in one ref.],
Lettuce (m) **Attaway**. Witness oath by John (B) **Brown** 12 May 1794 to
Charles **Saxon** J.P. Laurens Co. Rec. 12 May 1794.

Page 217-218   5 Aug 1793, Thomas **Wadsworth** & William **Turpin**,
otherwise **Wadsworth** & **Turpin** Merchants (S.C.) to John **Robinson**
[**Robertson** in one ref.] (Laurens Co.), for £25 Sterling sold all that tract of

land on Bush River, waters of Saluda, in sd. Co., containing 116 acres more or less. Bound: Benjamin **Jones**, Jacob **Niel**, Wm. **Williamson** & Wm. **Millwee**, at time of original Survey. Run by Wm. **Hunter** 19 Oct 1786, granted by William **Moultrie** esq. 5 Feb 1787. Witness James **Young**, James **Boyce**. Signed Willm. **Turpin**, Thomas **Wadsworth**. Witness oath by James **Boyce** 5 Aug 1793 to John **Hunter** [No title.] Rec. 12 May 1794.

Page 219-222   Lease & Release, 12 & 13 Feb 1794, Britain **Jones** (Statesborough) & Mary **Jones** his wife to John **Roberson** (Laurens Co.), for £70 Sterling sold a certain tract of land containing 250 acres more or less, originally granted unto William **Wheeler** by Charles G. **Montague** Gov. 21 May 1772. Transferred by sd. **Wheler** [sic] to sd. Britain **Jones** 14 & 15 Jan 1773. Situate in Laurens Co. on N side of Saluda River on a small branch of Cain Creek. Bounded S.E. on Wm. **Burges** now Peter **Smith**, N.E. Wm. **Purse** now John **Watts**, N.W. by Jonathan **Pucket**, S.W. by Patrick **Cuningham** Esq. Witness Joshua **Draughon**, Elizabeth **Jones**, Benjamin **Mitchell**. Signed Britain **Jones**, Mary **Jones**. Copy of original grant drawn 9 Jan 1794 by Robert **Mayson** D.S. (Edgfield Co.). Oath by Benjamin **Mitchell** 13 Feb 1794, that he saw Britain **Jones** & Elizabeth **Jones** his wife [sic] sign the deed. Given before John **McDonell** J.P. (Claremont Co.) Rec. 12 May 1794. [Includes plat.]

Page 222-223   10 Oct 1793, Thomas **Wadsworth** & Wm. **Turpin** (S.C.) Merchants to Elijah **Elverson** (Laurens Co.) planter, for 5sh Sterling sold Their Right only to 190 acres of land more or less, being part of land granted to Wm. **Donohoe** by Charles **Pinckney** Esq. 2 Jan 1792, and by sd. **Donahoe** conveyed to **Wadsworth** & **Turpin** for payment of a Debt. Sd. land situated in sd. Co. on waters of Cain creek, waters of Saluda, bounded S.W. by lands held by heirs of John **Stephens**, W & S on Robert **Shaw**, S.E. by lands granted to James **Burgess**, E by John **Donohoe**, N by Duncan **Obryant**. They only Warrant land from Claim of the heirs & assigns, but not from claim of any other person. Witness James **Young**, James **Boyce**. Signed Thomas **Wadsworth** for himself & partner William **Turpin**. Witness oath by James **Young** 4 Nov 1793 to John **Hunter** [No title.] Rec. 12 May 1794.

Page 223-224   6 July 1793, Jonathan **Downs** & John **Hunter** Esqs. Judges of Laurens Co. Court to John Frances **Wolff** (Laurens Co.) Merchant, for £13 10sh sold one Lot of land containing 22 feet 6 inches in front & 244 feet in length, being part of 4 acres sold by Samuel **Saxon**, one of the Judges of sd. Court, 15 Mar 1792. Sd. Lot known in plat of sd. 4 acres and plan of public Lots laid out as No.2. Bounded on front by now Public land of sd. Co. (part of 4 acres), S on John **Simpson** Merchant, W & N on a Street. Witness Lewis **Saxon**, Joshua **Downs**, John A. **Elmore**. Signed Jonthn. **Downs**, John **Hunter**. Witness oath by Joshua **Downs** 28 Jan 1794 to Joseph **Downs** J.P. Laurens Co. Rec. 12 May 1794.

Page 224-226   28 Aug 1793, John **Hunter** Esq. (Laurens Co.) to John F. **Wolff** Merchant (same), for £40 Sterling sold all that tract of land containing

300 acres more or less, in sd. Co. on waters of Reaburns creek, being part of 950 acres originally granted to William **Williamson** by Charles G. **Montague** Esq. then Gov., and by sd. **Williamson** conveyed by Lease & release to Fredrick **Freasure** 23 & 24 Nov 1779, and conveyed by sd. John **Hunter** by Power of Attorney dated 13 Mar 1792. Witness Jonathan **Downs**, William **Dunlap**. Signed John **Hunter** Atty. for Fredrick **Freasure**. Witness oath by Wm. **Dunlap** 13 May 1794 to Joseph **Downs** J.P. Laurens Co. Rec. 13 May 1794.

Page 226   17 Mar 1794, Mary **Goodman** (Laurens Co.) sold all my right of a certain piece of land containing, as supposed, 40 acres. Border: **Vaughan**, **Calweld** [sic], **Caldwell**, branch, Nicholas **Vaughan**. Sold unto Clabourn **Goodman** in consideration of £9 Sterling. Witness George **Anderson**, Stephen **Wood**, John **Hazlet**. Signed Mary **Goodman**. Witness oath by Stephen **Wood** 5 Apr 1794 to George **Anderson** J.P. Laurens Co. Rec. 13 May 1794.

Page 227   5 Mar 1794, Robert **McFadden** [sic], Mary **McFaden** his wife, Jean **Bryant** [sic] wife of Dunkin **OBryant** (Laurens Co.) to John **Hendrick** (same), for £45 Sterling sold one certain tract of land containing 100 acres in sd. Co. on waters of Beaver dam, being land sd. Robert **McFaden** bought of Dunkin **OBryant**, recorded in Laurens Co. in book C, page 315-317. Bound: Zachariah **Bailey**, John **Davis**, Thomas **Wadsworth**. Witness William **Bryant** [**OBryant** in witness oath.], Daniel **Duprie**, John **Crisp**. Signed Robert **McFaden**, Mary (x) **McFaden**, Jean (x) **OBryant**. Witness oath by Daniel **Duprie** 13 May 1794 to William **Hunter** J.P. Laurens Co. Rec. 13 May 1794.

Page 228-229   15 Oct 1793, Harculas Daniel **Bize** by his Attorney John **Hunter** (Laurens Co.) to John **Manley** (same), for £20 Sterling sold all that tract of land containing 100 acres more or less, in sd. Co. on waters of Reaburns creek, bounding on Berry **Harvey**, John **Cammoch** & part of sd. Survey. Being part of 500 acres originally granted to Pierce **Butler**, and by him conveyed to Harculas Daniel **Bize** 9 July 1792, and now conveyed by sd. John **Hunter** by Power of Attorney dated 1 June 1793. Witness Lewis **Saxon**, Little Berry **Harvey**. Signed John **Hunter** Atty. for Harculas Danl. **Bize**. Witness oath by Little B. **Harvey** 2 Apr 1794 to Joseph **Downs** J.P. Laurens Co. Plat certified 3 Sept 1794 [sic] by John **Hunter** D.Surv. Rec. 13 May 1794. [Includes plat.]

Page 230-232   20 Feb 1794, Abner **Babb** (Laurens Co.) planter & Mary [Martha in one ref.] his wife to Joseph **Babb** (same), for 10sh sold all that tract of land containing 293-1/2 acres more or less, in sd. Co. on Beaverdam creek, waters of Little River. Bounding S.W. on John **Filpot**, S.E. on **Fuller** & Jeremiah **Glen**, N.E. on **Rodgers**, N.W. on sd. Abner **Babb**. Being part of two different tracts, one of 200 acres, originally granted to Joseph **Babb** dec. 24 Nov 1767. The other containing 150 acres, originally granted to William **Wright** 14 June 1771, and by him conveyed to Joseph **Babb** dec., 31 May & 1 June 1772. And by sd. Abner **Babb**, oldest son & Heir to sd. Joseph **Babb** dec.

to sd. Joseph **Babb**. Witness John **Stanfield**, James **Culberson**, James (x) **Babb**. Signed Abner **Babb**. Witness oath by John **Stanfield** 12 May 1794 to William **Hunter** J.P. Laurens Co. Plat certified 19 Oct 1793 by John **Hunter** D.Surv. Rec. 13 May 1794. [Includes plat.]

Page 232-233 20 Jan 1794, John **Williams** (Edgfield Co.) to James **Thurston** (Laurens Co.), for £5 sold one certain tract of land in Laurens Co. on a branch of Mudlick, containing by Estimation 100 acres more or less, being part of 200 acres. Border: James **McGill**, Nathaniel **Nichols**. Witness Duke **Williams**, James Atwd. **Williams**. Signed John **Williams**, Ann Meriah (x) **Williams**. Witness oath by James At. **Williams** 12 May 1794 to Angus **Campbell** J.P. Laurens Co. Rec. 13 May 1794.

Page 233-235 5 June 1792, Charles **McKnight** (Spartanburgh Co., Ninety six Dist.) to Simeon **Thedford** (Laurens Co.), for £50 Sterling sold all that tract of land in S.C. on S side of Enoree River on a branch called the South fork of Dunkins creek, originally granted by Gov. **Montague** to Robert **Fleming**, and by power of Attorney dated 13 June 1785, conveyed to Obediah **Roberts**, and by sd. **Roberts** to Charles **McKnight** 10 Nov 1785. A Memorial of original Patent entered in Auditor's office 5 Sept 1768 in book J, No.9, page 70. Containing 100 acres more or less. Witness Thomas **McKnight**, George **Reese**, Thomas **Reese**. Signed Charles **McKnight**. Witness oath by Thomas **McKnight** 6 May 1794 to James **Hooper** J.P. Spartanburgh Co. Rec. 13 May 1794.

Page 235-236 5 June 1792, Charles **McKnight** (Spartanburgh Co., Ninety six Dist.) to Simeon **Thedford** (Laurens Co.), for £50 Sterling sold all that tract of land in S.C. on S side of Enoree River on a branch called the South fork of Dunkins creek, originally granted by Gov. **Montague** in the 13th year of King **George III**, to Ralph **Fleming**, and by power of Attorney dated 13 June 1785, conveyed to Obediah **Roberts**, and by sd. **Roberts** to Charles **McKnight** 10 Nov 1785. A Memorial of original Patent entered in Auditor's office 5 Sept 1768 in book J, No.9, page 70. Containing 100 acres more or less. Witness Thomas **McKnight**, George **Reese**, Thomas **Reese**. Signed Charles **McKnight**. Witness oath by Thomas **McKnight** 6 May 1794 to James **Hooper** J.P. Spartanburgh Co. Rec. 13 May 1794.

Page 236-240 Lease & Release, 26 & 27 Aug 1792, Robert **Finney** (Laurens Co.) to Richard **Griffen** (same), for £150 current money, sold a certain tract of land containing 150 acres, in sd. Co. on N side of Saluda River & bounding S on sd. River, S.E. on Cain Creek, all other sides by Vacant land at time of original Survey. Granted by Robert **Johnson** Esq. Gov. unto John **Dingle** on or about 15 Jan 1736, and by him sold unto Thomas **Anderson** Sen., and by him sold unto Michael **Finney** in 1764. Evidenced & probated before James **Mayson** Esq. J.P. (Colleton Co.). Witness John **Grigsby**, Stephen **Watson**, Robert **Clark**. Signed Robert **Finney**. Pursuant to a Warrant from the late Robert **Johnson** Esq. Gov. 25 Oct 1733 & a receipt from John **St. John** Esq. late Surv. Genl. 15 Jan 1736 & a Deput. from George **Hunter** Esq. Surv. Genl.

Survey certified 14 Oct 1749 by John **Fairchild** Dep. Surv. Oath by Stephen **Watson** that he saw Robert **Finney** & Elizabeth his wife sign the deed. Given before Angus **Campbell** J.P. Laurens Co. Oath by Robert **Finney** that he is possessed of a tract as heir at Law & oldest son of Michael **Finney** Sen. dec. (Laurens Co., then Craven), on Saluda River. To his knowledge the Title to Michael **Finney** was executed before James **Mayson** Esq. at his house and sd. **Mayson** with Gideon **Beck** and James **Anderson** Sen. were the other Subscribing Evidences to sd. Deed. At time of the British Evacuating Ninety six on or about 12 Oct 1781, Deponents house, furniture & all papers were burnt by a party under William **Cuningham**, a britsh officer, in which Conflagration was burnt the plat & Grant to John **Dingle** with all Title Deeds & other papers. Given 25 Aug 1792 before Jas. **Mayson** J. Newberry Co. Oath by James **Mayson** J. (Colleton Co. now Abiville Co.) 1 Sept 1792, that at my office in sd. Co. & at my plantation called Glasgow, I did write & probate a set of Leases & releases from Thomas **Anderson** Sen. to Michael **Finney** (Laurens Co.) for the Tract above described by oath of Robert **Finney** Son & Heir to Michael **Finney** dec. Rec. 13 May 1794. [Includes plat.]

Page 241-243 Lease & Release, 5 & 6 Mar 1790, Lewis **Banton** (Laurens Co.) to William **Goodman** (same), for £20 Sterling sold a Tract of land containing 55 acres, in sd. Co. on Long lick branch of Reedy River, bounding on William **Goodman**, David **Caldwell**, Lewis **Banton** & Aaron **Starnes**. Being part of 300 acres that was granted unto sd. Lewis **Banton** by Lord Charles Griville **Montague** Gov. 22 Nov 1771. Witness John **Carter**, Clabourn **Goodman**, Mary (x) **Banton**. Signed Lewis **Banton**, Jedidah (J) **Banton**. Witness oath by Clabourn **Goodman** 12 May 1794 to Jonathan **Downs** J.P. Laurens Co. Rec. 13 May 1794.

Page 243-244 2 Jan 1794, William **Griffen** & Nancy his wife (Laurens Co.) Sadler to James **Griffen** (same) Gent., for £60 Sterling sold a certain tract of land, being part in Newberry Co. & part in Laurens Co. on W side of Carsons creek, containing 85 acres more or less. Being part of 350 acres granted to William **Griffen** Sen. by Wm. **Bull** Esq. then Lieut. Gov. 5 June 1771. Bounding on Ambrose **Hudgins**, Joseph **Galegey**, James **Lafan** and part on original Survey. Witness Ambrose **Hudgins** Sen., Wm. **Grimes**, Jane **Clark**. Signed William **Griffen**, Agnes (x) **Griffen**, James **Griffen**. Witness oath by Ambrose **Hudgins** Sen. 21 Feb 1794 to William **Hunter** J.P. Memorial sent to Secretary's office 1 July 1794. Rec. 3 July 1794.

Page 244-245 4 Jan 1794, Nathaniel **Vance** (Laurens Co.) planter in consideration of £30 Sterling paid by John **Simpson** Merchant (same) Storekeeper, sold one Waggon with Utensils; one Mare branded with H on near buttock & Shoulder, 13 years old; Bay horse with a Star in his face, not branded nor Docked; 2 yearling colts, one black with a Star in her face & one Sorrel with a Star in his face; Ten head of Cattle; Six head of Sheep; 2 feather Beds and furniture; 1 Sorrel horse, 12 years old, a Star in his face, branded T on a buttock, and A on the near shoulder; likewise all my plantation tools and all my house hold furniture. One Sorrel horse delivered in behalf of the whole of the above. Witness John **Willson**, Andw. **Smith** Jun. Signed Nathaniel **Vance**. Witness oath by Andrew **Smyth** Jun. [sic] 24 Mar 1794 and sworn 1 July 1794 to R. **Brown** J.N.C. Rec. 4 July 1794.

Page 245-247 29 May 1794, Whereas William **McTeer** (Laurens Co.) by his bond 4 Jan 1794, for £70 5sh Sterling. For the better securing the payment, binds himself for sum of £140 10sh Sterling to John **Simpson** (same). Sold a Negro man Caroline [sic]; four horse creatures, one Bay horse branded with three crooks, one Bay mare branded MC wrong end upwards on shoulder, one Sorrel mare branded, one Bay mare not branded, 2 years old with a Star in her face; three Milk cows marked in each Ear, one Swallow fork & under keel; five head of young Cattle of same mark; three feather beds & furniture; & two potts & two ovens & likewise all my plantation utensils. Provided that if the sum is paid, then these presents shall be void. Witness Andw. **Smith** Jun., John **Willson**, Nathaniel **Vance**. Signed William **McTear** [sic]. Witness oath by John **Willson** 1 July 1794 to R. **Brown** J.N.C. Rec. 4 July 1794.

Page 247-248 29 May 1794, Whereas William **McTeer** (Laurens Co.) by his bond 1 Feb 1794, for £80 Sterling with condition for payment of £40 by two Installments, 1 June 1794 & 1795 with Interest, unto John **Simpson**. For the better securing payment sold a certain tract of land containing 100 acres more or less, being in sd. Co. on a branch of Carsons creek, waters of Little River, whereon sd. **McTeer** now lives, originally granted to Charles **Harvey**, bounded by Wm. **Freeman**, John **Simpson**, Alexd. **Simpson** and William **Griffen**. Provided that if the sum is paid, then this Deed shall be void. Witness Andw. **Smyth** Jun., John **Wilson**, Nathl. **Vance**. Signed William **McTeer**. Witness oath by John **Wilson** 1 July 1794 to R. **Brown** J.N.C. Rec. 4 July 1794.

Page 248-249 24 June 1794, Barnard **ONeal** (Laurens Co.) planter in consideration of £5 Sterling paid by John **Simpson** Merchant (same), sold one mare with a Blaze face, hind foot white, branded O on near shoulder, about 9 Years old & a bright Sorrel. Witness John **Willson**, James (x) **Griffen**. Signed Barnard **ONeall** [sic]. Above Bill of Sale is void if sum paid before the Middle of Nov next after above date. Witness oath by John **Wilson** [sic] 1 July 1794 to R. **Brown** J.N.C. Rec. 4 July 1794

Page 249-250 28 Feb 1794, BordWin **Waters** & Jean [Jane in one ref.] his wife (Spartan Co.) to Benjamin **Byrd** (Laurens Co.), for £10 Sterling sold one certain tract of land granted unto sd. Bordwin **Waters** 1 Apr 1793, containing 125 acres, Surveyed for him 22 Sept 1792. Situate in Ninety six Dist. on a branch of Warrior creek in Laurens Co. Bounded S.E. & N.E. by John **Linch** & Vacant land, N.W. by Angus **Campbell** Esq. & Esq. **Fakes**, S.W. Joseph **Caldwell**, John **Collins**. Witness John **Lynch**, Thomas (T) **Adkins**. Signed BordWin **Waters**, Jean (n) **Waters**. Witness oath by John **Lynch** 18 July 1794 to Jonthn. **Downs** J.P. Laurens Co. Rec. 17 July 1794.

Page 251-252   24 Oct 1793, John **Watson** (Laurens Co.) to Thomas **Moore** (same), for 10sh Sterling sold 10 acres of land more or less, being the S part of 311 acres granted to sd. John **Watson** 2 July 1792, on branches Derbins Creek, waters of Enoree River. Joining James Walker **Moore**. Witness Stephen **Griffith**, Benjamin **Griffith**. Signed John (O) **Watson**. Witness oath by Stephen **Griffith** 25 Oct 1793 to Hudson **Berry** J.P. Laurens Co. Rec. 17 July 1794.

Page 252-253   18 Nov 1793, William **Fowler** Sen. (Laurens Co.) planter to John **Brockman** (same) planter, for £50 Sterling sold 120 acres of land more or less, on S side of Dirbins creek, being part of 300 acres on S side of Enoree River, granted 2 May 1785 unto William **Fowler** Sen. by William **Moultrie** Esq. Gov. at Charleston and recorded in Secretary's office in Grant book HHHH, page 77, examined by Peter **Freneau** Dep. Surv. Bound: Dirbins creek, Joseph **Lyon**, branch above **Lyons** Spring, above Wm. **Fowler's** old spring. Witness Joseph **Lyon**, James **Allison**. Signed William (F) **Fowler**. Witness oath by Joseph **Lyon** 24 May 1794 to Daniel **Wright** J.P. Laurens Co. Rec. 17 July 1794.

Page 254-255   25 May 1794, John **Rodgers** (Laurens Co.) Surveyor to Boling **Bishop** (same), for £60 Sterling sold one certain tract of land on branches of Reedy fork of Little River, containing 200 acres more or less, being part of 400 acres originally granted to Garner **Williams** & conveyed by him to John **Rodgers**. Original grant recorded in Grant book AAAA, page 359. Border: Robt. **McNees**, John **Brown**. Witness Wm. T. **Rodgers**, John **Cargill** Jun. Signed John **Rodgers**. Witness oath by William **Rodgers** 18 July 1794 to Roger **Brown** J.P. Laurens Co. Rec. 18 July 1794. [Includes plat.]

Page 255-257   19 Aug 1793, Thomas **Adkins** & Ruth his wife (Laurens Co.) in consideration of £6 Sterling paid by Joshua **Palmer** Minister of the Gospel (same), sold a certain tract of land containing 46 acres, part of 146 acres originally granted to sd. Thomas **Adkins** by Charles **Pinckney** 5 Mar 1792, recorded in Secretary's office in book D, No.5, page 428. Sd. 46 acres is to be measured off along Joshua **Palmer's** line and to include the house where sd. Thomas **Adkins** now lives, with all land under fence. Border: Joshua **Palmer**, Wm. **Sparks**, land run by Robert **Taylor**, Aaron **Harlin**. Witness Roger **Brown**, Aaron **Harlin**. Signed Thomas (T) **Adkins**, Ruth (x) **Adkins**. Witness oath by Aaron **Harlin** [No signature.] 28 Feb 1794 to Roger **Brown** J.P. Laurens Co. Rec. 18 July 1794.

Page 257-258   16 Jan 1794, John **Endsley** (Laurens Co.) planter in consideration of £15 Sterling paid by Moses **Madden** (same) planter, sold one bay horse with a Star in his forehead, about 14 years old; one young black [blank] marked with a Crop & Slit in each ear; one other black Cow with a Swallow fork in the right ear & a crop in the other; one new man's Saddle; one woman's Saddle; one Dutch oven; half a Dozen pewter plates; one feather bed & furniture; half a Dozen Delph plates &c. Provided that if £7 10sh Sterling with Interest is paid on 1 Sept next ensuing, then this bill of Sale to be void.

Witness Saml. C. **Stedman**, David **Craddock**. Signed John **Endsley**. Witness oath by Saml. C. **Stedman** 18 July 1794 to Joseph **Downs** J.P. Laurens Co. Rec. 18 July 1794.

Page 258-259 14 Dec 1793, John **Coker** to Bradock **Harris**, for £5 Sterling sold a Tract of land in Laurens Co. on Beaverdam creek, waters of Enoree River. Border: branch of Beaverdam. Witness William **Helloms**, Aaron (x) **Niblet**. Signed John **Coker**. Witness oath by Aaron (A) **Niblet** 14 Dec 1793 to Jonthn. **Downs** J.P. Laurens Co. Rec. 18 July 1794.

Page 259-260 28 Jan 1794, James **Tate** (Union Co.) to David **Ridgway** (Laurens Co.), for £50 Sterling sold all that tract of land containing 96 acres more or less, in Laurens Co. on Reedy River, bounding S.W. by sd. **Ridgaway** [sic], N.W. by Wm. **Turner**, N.E. Reedy River. Being a tract originally Surveyed by David **Ridgway** & Granted to James **Tate** by William **Moultrie** 4 Feb 1793, recorded in Grant book [blank] No.5, page 517. Witness Thomas **Lamar**, Harris **Mullings**, James **Lamar**. Signed James (T) **Tate**. Witness oath by Harris **Mullins** [sic] 28 Mar 1794 to Joseph **Downs** J.P. Laurens Co. Rec. 18 July 1794.

Page 260-261 18 July 1794, John **Milam** & Nancy his wife (Laurens Co.) to Mansfield **Walker** (same), for £50 sold one certain Tract of land containing 180 acres more or less, in sd. Co., being part granted to Thomas **Dendy** Sen. & part granted to John **McKinzie**, and conveyed by John **McKinsey** to Tobias **Myers** & from him to William **Dendy** & from him to John **Milam**. The rest conveyed from Thomas **Dendy** to Wm. **Dendy** and from him to John **Milam**. Situate on both sides Little River. Bounded on sd. River, Christopher **Rowland** [**Roland** in one ref.], Patrick **Cuningham**, sd. **Walker**, William **Hall**, James **Young**. Witness Edmond **Grinage**, James (x) **Ramsey**. Signed John **Milam**, Nancy (x) **Milam**. Witness oath by Edmond **Grinage** 18 July 1794 to Joseph **Downs** J.P. Laurens Co. Rec. 18 July 1794.

Page 261-262 14 Apr 1794, William **Stone** (Laurens Co.) to William **Cannon** (same), for £10 sold a certain tract of land containing 134 acres, being part of a Tract granted to William **Stone** by Charles **Pinkney** 6 Apr 1789. Situate on Twenty Six Mile creek. Witness Roger **Brown**, Edwerd **Cox**. Signed William **Stone**. Witness oath by Edwerd **Cocks** [sic] [No signature.] 14 Apr 1794 to Roger **Brown** J.P. Laurens Co. Rec. 18 July 1794.

Page 262-263 22 Apr 1794, William **Cannon** (Laurens Co.) to Edwerd **Cox** (same), for 10sh sold a certain tract of land containing 72 acres, being part of a Tract granted to William **Stone** by Charles **Pinckney** by Patent 6 Apr 1789. Situate on Twenty Six Mile creek. Witness Roger **Brown**, William (x) **Cooper**. Signed William (M) **Cannon**. Witness oath by William **Cooper** [No signature.] 22 Apr 1794 to Roger **Brown** J.P. Laurens Co. Rec. 18 July 1794.

Page 263-265 30 May 1794, John **Hunter** and his wife Margaret, William **Thompson** & his wife Agnes, and Daniel **Thompson** & his wife Isabella, planters (Laurens Co.) to John **Bryson**, for £18 Sterling sold all their Right to one tract of land containing 100 acres more or less, granted to Martha **Hunter** dec. on the bounty, grant dated 6 Feb 1773, by Charles G. **Montague** Esq. Bounded S.E. on Jane **Hunter** & Christopher **Neiley**, all other sides vacant land at time of original Survey. Situate in sd. Co. on waters of Beaverdam creek, a branch of Little River of Saluda. Witness Samuel **Fleming** Sen., Samuel **Fleming**, James **Fleming**. Signed John **Hunter**, Margaret (x) **Hunter**, William **Thompson**, Agnes (x) **Thompson**, Daniel **Thompson**, Isabella (O) **Thompson**. Witness oath by Samuel **Fleming** Sen. 17 July 1794 to Thos. **Wadsworth** J.L.C. Rec. 18 July 1794.

Page 265-266 28 Jan 1793, Reubin **Flanagin** and Ann his wife (Laurens Co.) to George **Whitmore** (same), for £1 5sh Sterling sold 39 acres more or less, of a certain Tract of land in the fork between broad & Saluda Rivers in sd. Co. on a branch of Duncans creek. Being part of 87 acres, N.W. & S.E. by sd. George **Whitmore**, N.E. by other part of Tract. Originally granted unto Reubin **Flanagan** [sic] 6 Aug 1792, recorded in Secretary's office in book F, No.5, page 86. Witness Nicholas (x) **Welsh**, James **Duncan**, John (J) **Duncan** Jun. Signed Reubin **Flanagan** Jun., Ann **Flanagan**. Witness oath by James **Duncan** 23 June 1794 to James **Dillard** J.P. Laurens Co. Rec. 18 July 1794.

Page 267 16 May 1793, Malachiah **Powell** (S.C.) sold a Bay stud horse about 13 years of age, branded on mounting shoulder HH, about 14-1/2 hands high, unto John **Baugh** (same), for £4. Saddle & Bridle is concluded also in Bill of Sale. Witness George **Madden**, Mabra **Madden**. Signed Malachiah **Powell**. Witness oath by Mabra **Madden** 17 July 1794 to George **Anderson** J.P. Laurens Co. Rec. 18 July 1794.

Page 267-269 28 Feb 1792, Isaac **Bean** (Chester Co.) to Soloman **Duty** (Laurens Co.), for £50 Sterling sold all that Tract of land containing 150 acres in Berkley Co., when Surveyed, but now Laurens, being in the fork between broad & Saluda Rivers on a Draft of Enoree River called the South fork of Duncans creek. Bounded S.E. by William **Bean** at time of Surveying but now Reubin **Rowland**, N by David **Baty**, other sides by vacant land at time of Surveying. Original grant to William **Bean** 11 Aug 1774, recorded in Secretary's Office in book RRR, page 545. Isaac **Bean** now stands seized of a good Indefeasible Estate of Inheritance in sd. Tract. Witness George **Whitmore**, Nicholas (x) **Welch**, Odell (O) **Garret**. Signed Isaac **Bean**. Witness oath by George **Whitmore** 28 June 1794 to James **Dillard** J.P. Laurens Co. Rec. 18 July 1794.

Page 269-270 14 [No month.] 1793, Arthur **Taylor** & Margaret **Taylor** his wife (Laurens Co.) to James **Sullivant** (same), for £40 sold all that Tract of land containing by Estimation 100 acres, being in sd. Co. on a Ryans creek, a branch of Little River. Bounded when Surveyed on all sides by Vacant land. Granted to Margret **Spence**, and Registered in Auditor's office in book J, No.9, page 192, 29 Dec 1788, then conveyed by Adam **Taylor**, husband to sd. Margaret **Spence** [sic], but then Margret **Taylor**, to sd. Arthur, son & Heir to

Adam **Taylor** dec. Witness Ezel. **Roland**, Frederick **Sullivant**. Signed Arthur **Taylor**, Margret (x) **Taylor** [sic]. Oath by Ezel. **Roland** 14 Oct 1793 that he saw the deed signed and Margaret **Taylor** give up her Right of Dower. Given before Charles **Saxon** J.P. Laurens Co. Rec. 26 July 1794.

Page 270-271 23 July 1794, Frederick **Sullivant** (Laurens Co.) Shoemaker to John **Godfrey** late of same place Carpenter, for £100 Sterling sold all that Tract of land containing by Estimation 83 acres more or less, in sd. Co. on a South branch of Ryans creek, bounded when Surveyed: N by James **McDowall**, Thomas **Jones** & **Taylor**, E on William **Martin**, S unknown, W by Nancy **Barkee**. Laid out to John **Martin** first, then conveyed by him to sd. **Sullivant**. Witness Ezel. **Roland**, David **Burris**. Signed Fredrick (x) **Sullivant**. Witness oath by Ezel. **Roland** 25 July 1794 to Charles **Saxon** J.P. Rec. 26 July 1794.

Page 272-274 15 Oct 1793, John **Rutledge** Esq. Jun. (Charleston) by his Attorney John **Hunter** Esq. (Laurens Co.) to David **Green** (Laurens Co.), for £58 6sh 8p Sterling sold all that tract of land containing 281 acres more or less, in Laurens Co. on Reedy River. Bound: Arthur **Durham**, William **Simmons**, Widow Kesiah **Swain**, John **Robinson**, sd. River. Being part of 3,000 acres originally granted to Thomas **Shubrick** by **George III** 15 May 1772, & by him conveyed to William **Williamson**, and by him to John **Rutledge** Jun., and now by sd. John **Hunter** by Power of Attorney dated 31 Jan 1791, recorded in Clerks office in Laurens in book C, page 332, 14 Mar in same year. Witness John **Pringle**, Wm. **Simmons**. Signed John **Hunter** Atty. for John **Rutledge** Jun. Witness oath by Wm. **Simmons** 18 July 1794 to Danl. **Wright** J.P. Laurens Co. Plat certified 10 Oct 1793 by John **Hunter** D.Surv. Rec. 26 July 1794. [Includes plat.]

Page 274-276 10 Sept 1793, John **Hunter** Esq. (Laurens Co.) to James **Green** (same), for £48 1sh Sterling sold all that tract of land containing 93 acres more or less, in sd. Co. on Reedy River, bounding on David **Dunlap**, John **Rodgers**, **Beard** & reedy river. Being part of 500 acres originally granted 5 May 1772 to Pierce **Butler** & by him conveyed to Harculas Daniel **Bize** 9 July 1792 & now conveyed by John **Hunter** by Power of Attorney dated 1 June 1793. Witness David **Green**, Samuel **Green**. Signed John **Hunter** Atty. for Harculas Danl. **Bize**. Witness oath by Samuel **Green** 23 Aug 1794 to Danl. **Wright** J.P. Laurens Co. Plat certified 10 Sept 1793 by John **Hunter** D.Surv. Rec. 26 Aug 1794. [Includes plat.]

Page 276-277 1 Mar 1788, Elisha **Attaway** (Laurens Co.) to John **Attaway**, for £10 Sterling sold all that tract of 200 acres, being part of land originally granted to Joseph **Attaway** by his Majesty's Letter Patent in 1768. Witness Harley **Attaway**, John **Power**, Jesse (x) **Attaway**. Signed Elisha (x) **Attaway**. Witness oath by John **Power** 28 Aug 1794 to Roger **Brown** J.P. Laurens Co. Rec. 28 Aug 1794.

Page 277-278 28 Sept 1793, Archabald **McHurgh** (Laurens Co.) to Salatheil **Shockley** (same), for £50 sold all that tract of land containing 150 acres on Mchurgs creek, a branch of Reaburns creek, which Salathiel **Shockley** has now in possession. Being a tract granted to Nehemiah **Franks**. Joining Charles **Garey**, Stephen **Potter** & Vacant land. Witness James **Floyd**, Drew **Coker**, Thomas **Coker**. Signed Archibel (A) **Mchurg** [sic], Rebeccah (x) **Mchurg**. Witness oath by Drwry **Coker** [sic] 29 Aug 1794 to Jonthn. **Downs** J.P. Laurens Co. Rec. 29 Aug 1794.

Page 278-281 19 Sept 1794, Samuel **Scott** (Laurens Co.) to David **McCaa** (same), for £10 Sterlg. sold all that tract of land originally granted to Samuel **Scott** 21 Jan 1785, containing 150 acres, on waters of Reyburns creek & bounded W on Miss **Millhouse**, S by James **Williams**, all other sides vacant at time of original Survey. Judgment now extent by a Power of Attorney in possession of Hezekiah **Alexander** (Mecklinburgh Co., N.C.) to sell sd. premises to best advantage whenever such a step shall in the opinion of David **McCaa** become necessary for affecting purposes of the Trust. After the judgment shall be paid, then in Trust to convey the whole or so much as shall remain to such persons as Samuel **Scott** by Deed or by his last Will & Testament shall appoint. In Default of appointment, to use of the children of Samuel **Scott** now born or to be born on the body of any future wife and their heirs. Witness LitB. **Willson**, William **Harris**. Signed Samuel **Scott**. Witness oath by William **Harris** 20 Sept 1794 to Charles **Saxon** J.P. Laurens Co. Rec. 20 Sept 1794.

Page 281-282 17 Sept 1794, Robert **Barnet** (Cumberland, Western Territory) to Robert **Bolt** Jun. (Laurens Co.), for £50 Sterling sold all that Tract of Land originally Granted to James **Boyd** and by him in his last Will and Testament conveyed to sd. Robert **Barnet**, containing 300 acres in Laurens Co. (then Craven) on N side of Saluda on small branches of Rayburns creek. Bounded N.W. by John **Maharg**, N.E. vacant, all other sides by Larger Surveys. Witness B. H. **Saxon** [Benjamin **Saxon** in witness oath.], Andw. **Rodgers** Jun. Signed Robert **Barnet**. Witness oath by Andw. **Rodgers** Jun. 18 Sept 1794 to Joseph **Downs** J.P. Laurens Co. Rec. 20 Sept 1794.

Page 282-284 18 Aug 1794, John **Martin** Planter (Laurens Co.) to John **Godfrey** (same) House Carpenter, for £100 sold all that tract of land containing by estimation 157-1/2 acres [152-1/2 in one ref.] more or less, in sd. Co. Being part of 640 acres Granted by William **Moultrie** Gov. Border: Isaac **Rodgers**, Ezel. T. **Roland**, John **Martin**, Fredrick **Sullivant**, road to **Swancies** ferry. Witness Ezel. **Roland**, Fredrick (FS) **Sullivant**. Signed John **Martin**. Plat certified 23 Sept 1794 by Ezel. **Roland**. Quit claim by Thomas **Wadsworth** for **Wadsworth** & **Turpin**. Witness oath by Ezel. **Roland** 30 Sept 1794 to Charles **Saxon** J.P. Rec. 30 Sept 1794. [Includes plat.]

Page 284-285 1 Aug 1793, Thomas **Wadsworth** & William **Turpin** (S.C.) Merchants to Doctor George **Ross** (Laurens Co.), for £14 Sterling sold all their Right to a Tract of 100 acres of land Surveyed for sd. George **Ross** 11 May

1785, and Granted 5 Feb 1787 by William **Moultrie** Esq., & by Augustus **Merrick** conveyed to **Wadsworth** & **Turpin** in Mar 1787. Situate on a small branch of Duncans creek in sd. Co. Bounded S.W. on sd. Ross, S.W. on Elleanor **Craig**, all other sides on Vacant land at time of original Survey. Witness James **Young**, James **Boyce**. Signed Thos. **Wadsworth**, Willm. **Turpin**. Witness oath by James **Boyce** 5 Aug 1793 to John **Hunter** Ninety six Dist. Rec. 13 Oct 1794.

Page 285 26 Apr 1794, Isaac **Wilburn** (Laurens Co.) sold unto John **Pinson** (same), for £10 Sterling, one Sorrel Horse with White on his nose, about 5 years old; also one Bay Mare Branded G on near shoulder; also one Hatters Kettle of a large Size. Until the sum is paid off. Witness George **Anderson**, William **Sims**, Roger **Murphey**. Signed Isaac **Wilborn** [sic]. Witness oath by Wm. **Sims** 13 Oct 1794 to George **Anderson** J.P. Laurens Co. Rec.13 Oct 1794.

Page 286-287 20 Dec 1792, John T. **McElroy**, late of Laurens Co., to Sterling **Tucker** (same), for £160 Sterling sold all that Tract of land containing 200 acres more or less, in sd. Co. Bounded by Enoree river & Beaverdam creek, John **Dening**, Abraham **Gray**, James **Oliphent**, Ellis **Cheek**, mouth of creek. Being part of 600 acres originally granted to James **Kilgore** by Benjamin **Guerard** Gov. 31 Jan 1785, recorded in Secretary's office in Grant Book CCCC, and by sd. **Kilgore** conveyed by Lease & release 1 Dec 1786. Witness John **Denning** [sic], James **Attaway**, Priscilla (x) **McElory** [sic]. Signed John Thos. (x) **McElroy**, John **McElroy**. Witness oath by John **Denning** 19 Feb 1793 to Daniel **Wright** J.P. Laurens Co. Rec. 13 Oct 1794.

Page 287-288 3 Apr 1794, John **Lynch** Jun. (Laurens Co.) planter in consideration of £9 Sterling paid by Henry **Langston** (same), sold a certain tract of land containing 40 acres more or less, in sd. Co. on S side of Enoree River on waters of Coxes creek, being part of 500 acres, originally granted unto James **Smith** 15 Sept 1775, recorded in Book X, No.4, page 147. Bound: Christian **McCulla**, Margret **McCulla**, spring branch near fall of Rocks, Angus **Campbell**. Witness Joseph **Lynch**, Jesse **Lynch**. Signed John **Lynch**. Witness oath by Joseph **Lynch** 21 July 1794 to Roger **Brown** J.P. Laurens Co. Rec. 13 Oct 1794.

Page 289-290 13 Jan 1794, James **Box** planter to John **Orsborn** [**Osborn** in one ref.], for £50 sold all that tract of land containing by Estimation 130 acres (on head waters of the long lick) more or less, in Laurens Co. Bounded on Samuel **Wharton**, meeting house branch, line from **Ditney** hill, Claburn **Sims**. Being part of a Tract laid for sd. **Box**. Granted by Commander in Chief over sd. State to sd. **Box**. Witness Thomas **Hughes**, James **Sullivant**, Isaac **Wilborn**. Signed James **Box**. Witness oath by James **Sullivant** 13 Oct 1794 to Charles **Saxon** J.P. Rec. 13 Oct 1794.

Page 290-292 Lease & Release, 20 Apr 1792, Baily **Duvall** planter (Laurens Co.) to James **Simpson** planter (same), for £40 Sterling sold all that Tract of land containing the full measure of 200 acres laid of the N.E. & N.W. Square of 640 acres originally granted to sd. Bailey **Duvall** [sic] in 1785. Witness John **Simpson**, David **Speers**. Signed Bailey **Duvall**. Witness oath by John **Simpson** 15 Oct 1794 to William **Hunter** J.P. Laurens Co. Rec. 1 Nov 1794.

Page 292-295 [Page 293 skipped.] 29 Oct 1794, John **Woods** planter (Laurens Co.) to Jesse **Garret** (same), for £75 Sterling sold one parcel of land in sd. Co. in the N fork of Reaburns creek containing 150 acres more or less, being part of 950 acres granted to Wm. **Williamson** 20 July 1772, and by him conveyed to Fredrick **Freasure** by Lease & release 23 & 24 Nov 1779, and by John **Hunter** Esq. by Power of Attorney dated 30 Mar 1792, to John **Woods** by Lease & release 17 & 18 July 1794. Witness James **McCaa**, J. F. **Wolff**. Signed John **Woods**, Susannah (S) **Woods**. Witness oath by John F. **Wolff** 6 Nov 1794 to Daniel **Wright** J.P. Laurens Co. Rec. 6 Nov 1794.

Page 295-297 Lease & Release, 17 & 18 July 1794, John **Hunter** Esq. (Laurens Co.) planter in consideration of £22 sold unto John **Woods** (same), all that Tract of land containing 150 acres more or less, in sd. Co. on N fork of Reaburns creek, being part of 950 acres granted 17 July 1772 to William **Williamson**, and by him conveyed to Fredrick **Freasure** by Lease & release 23 & 24 Nov 1779, and now by John **Hunter** by Power of Attorney from sd. **Freasure** dated 30 Mar 1792. Border: **Garner**, **Dunlap**, Reaburns creek. Witness Jonathan **Downs**, Joseph **Downs**. Signed John **Hunter** Atty. for Fredrick **Freasure**. Witness oath by Joseph **Downs** 6 Nov 1794 to Danl. **Wright** J.P. Laurens Co. Plat certified 10 Nov 1792 by John **Hunter** D.Sur. Rec. 6 Nov 1794. [Includes plat.]

Page 298-299 2 May 1794, George **Bush** (Laurens Co.) to Jesse **Brooks** (same), for £100 Sterling sold a Tract of land containing 200 acres more or less, being part of two Surveys, one granted to John **Grey** by Charles **Montague** 15 May 1792, recorded in book LLL, page 92, entered in Auditor's office in book J, No.11, page 284. The other granted to sd. George **Bush** by William **Moultrie** 5 June 1786, recorded in book LLLL, page 41. Situate in sd. Co. in forks of Duncans creek. Witness Soloman **Duty**, William **Bush**, Stephen (S) **Williams**. Signed George **Bush**. Witness oath by Williams **Bush** 31 May 1794 to Roger **Brown** J.P. Laurens Co. Rec. 6 Nov 1794.

Page 299-300 2 Oct 1794, Robert **Sims** (Laurens Co.) Miller, in consideration of the Love & affection I bear toward my Loving friend Drury **Boyce** (same), Give all my goods, one Negro wench Atha; four Head of Cattle; two feather beds & furniture; Silver Watch, with all I now possess in my Dwelling house in sd. Co. Witness Fleman (x) **Hatcher**, Nancey (x) **Hatcher**. Signed Robt. **Sims**. Witness oath by Fleman (x) **Hatcher** 24 Oct 1794 to Jonathan **Downs** J.P. Laurens Co. Rec. 6 Nov 1794.

Page 300-301 25 Aug 1794, William **Helloms** & Mary his wife (Laurens Co.) to John **Robinson** [Roberson in one ref.] (same), for £110 sold all that Tract of land containing 350 acres more or less, on a branch of Beaverdam creek of

Enoree River. Including the house with plantation where sd. William **Hellums** now lives. One hundred acres of above land granted to sd. William **Hellums**, including house where sd. **Hellums** resides. Also 50 acres of above land conveyed from John **Coker** to sd. **Hellums**, being part of 489 acres granted to John **Coker**. Also 200 acres of sd. land granted to Soloman **Niblet**, then conveyed to sd. **Hellums**. Border: **Harris'** spring branch, Peter **Hammons**, mill branch. Witness Elisha **Halcomb**, John **Meadar**, Wm. Robt. **Stone**. Signed William **Hellums**, Mary (x) **Hellums**. Witness oath by Elisha **Halcomb** 13 Nov 1794 to Hudson **Berry** J.P. Laurens Co. Rec. 14 Nov 1794.

Page 302-303   8 Apr 1789, James **Adair** and James **Templeton** (S.C.) to Elisha **Attaway** (Laurens Co.), for £5 Sterling sold land in sd. Co. on [blank] of Enoree on Rockey creek now Warrior creek, and when first run joining a Survey of Walter **Carruth's**, being part of a Tract originally granted to David **Templeton** by the King's Office by patent 16 May 1754, and afterwards in 1761, the Right of Sale was Vested in Archabald **Templeton** by last Will & Testament of sd. David **Templeton**, and by sd. Archabald **Templeton** conveyed to sd. James **Templeton** 25 Nov same year. Containing by computation 400 acres, included in lines of Joseph **Attaway's** old original lines containing by computation 220 acres more or less now granted to sd. Elisha **Attaway**. Witness Joseph **Adair**, John **Brown**, Rebecah **Adair**. Signed James **Adair**, Ja. **Templeton**. James **Adair** showed his Power of Attorney from James **Templeton** to recover & make sale of sd. land, dated 30 Apr 1783. Witness oath by James **Brown** Sen. 19 Sept 1794 to Roger **Brown** J.P. Laurens Co. Rec. 15 Nov 1794.

Page 303-304   (State of Georgia) 11 Feb 1788, Joseph **Attaway** (Burke Co.) to Elisha **Attaway** (Ninety six Dist., S.C.), for £30 Specia sold all that tract of land containing 550 acres in Laurens Co., formerly known by Craven Co., on Warriors creek of Enoree River, on all sides by Vacant land at time of Survey by Patent, 22 Mar 1768 as by sd. grant in Record in Registers of Grants office in Book DDD, page 163. Witness W. **Baduly** J.P., James **Attaway**, Jesse (x) **Attaway**. Signed Joseph **Attaway**. Witness oath by James **Attaway** [No signature.] 9 Dec 1788 to Joseph **Downs** J.P. Laurens Co. Rec. 15 Nov 1794.

Page 305-306   7 Apr 1791, Thomas **Deen** Taylor, late of Laurens Co., to Elisha **Attaway** (same), for £25 sold all that Tract of land containing 130 acres, on Buckhead branch of Enoree River. Granted to Thomas **Deen** by Charles **Pinckney** Esq. Gov. 1 Mar 1790, recorded in Secretary's Office in Grant book B, No.5, page 135. Witness Harley **Attaway**, Joseph **Deen**, John (J) **Attaway**. Signed Thos. **Dean** [sic]. Witness oath by John (J) **Attaway** 19 July 1791 to Joseph **Downs** J.P. Laurens Co. Rec. 15 Nov 1794.

Page 306-307   30 Oct 1794, John **Dunklin** (Ninety six Dist.) to Joseph **Dunklin** (Washington Dist.), for £100 Sterling sold a certain Tract of land on W side of Reaburns creek, containing 137 acres more or less, being granted by William **Moultrie** Esq. Gov. to John **Richey**, and recorded in Secretary's Office in Grant book, 6 Feb 1786. Bounding N.W. on John Ewin **Calhound**,

S.W. on John **Gocher**. Witness Nathaniel **Sullivant**, Hulet **Sullivant**, Charles **Sullivant**. Signed John **Dunklin**. Witness oath by Hewlet **Sullivant** [sic] 24 Nov 1794 to Joseph **Downs** J.P. Laurens Co. Rec. 24 Nov 1794.

Page 307-308   30 Oct 1794, John **Dunklin** (Laurens Co.) to Joseph **Dunklin** (Greenville Co.), for £4 Sterling sold a certain Tract on W side of Reaburns creek, containing 36 acres more or less. Bounded N.E. on land originally granted to John **Richey**, S.E. on Patrick **Cuningham**. Being part of land originally granted to John **Gocher** by Wm. **Moultrie** Esq. Gov. Witness Nathaniel **Sullivant**, Hewlet **Sullivant**, Charles **Sullivant**. Signed John **Dunklin**. Witness oath by Hewlet **Sullivant** 24 Nov 1794 to Joseph **Downs** J.P. Laurens Co. Rec. 24 Nov 1794.

Page 308-309   4 July 1794, David **Smith** and Ann my Wife in consideration of £30 Sterling paid by Hanna **Musgrove**, sold to her during the Term of my wife's life the following negroes, Tom, a fellow; Phillis a wench; Lott a Girl; Joe & Tom, two boys. Also two Beds and one Pott & two Tables & bedding. Witness Edwerd **Hooker**, Anty. **Foster** Jun. Signed David **Smith**, Ann **Smith**. Witness oath by Edwerd **Hooker** 13 Dec 1794 to Roger **Brown** J.P. Laurens Co. Rec. 14 Dec 1794.

Page 309   4 July 1794, David **Smith** & Ann my wife in consideration of £10 Sterling paid by Landen **Waters**, sold a Negroe Girl Kize, with her future Issue, during the Term of my wife's natural life. Witness Edwerd **Hooker**, Anty. **Foster** Jun. Signed David **Smith**, Ann **Smith**. Witness oath by Edward **Hooker** [sic] 13 Dec 1794 to Roger **Brown** J.P. Laurens Co. Rec. 14 Dec 1794.

Page 310-312   Lease & Release, 3 & 4 Dec 1770, Hugh **Brown** (Berkly Co.) to Jonathan **Downs** (same), for £100 Current money, sold all that Tract of land containing 100 acres in sd. Co. on Horse Creek, on S side of Reedy River. Bounding N by sd. River, S.W. by land claimed by Moses **Tomlin**, other side by Vacant land. Witness Pa. **Cuningham**, John **Brown**. Signed Hugh **Brown**. Witness oath by Patrick **Cuningham** 14 Jan 1771 to Robt. **Cuningham** J.P. Craven Co. Rec. 29 Dec 1794.

Page 312-315   9 Sept 1789, Elisha **Ford** & Sarah his wife (Newberry Co.) to Thomas **Horner** (same), for £60 Sterling sold 200 acres of land, being granted 21 May 1772 by Ld. Charles Greville **Montague** Capt. Genl. Gov. unto Samuel **Worthington**. Situate in Berkly Co. (but now in Laurens Co.) on waters of Indian creek. Bounding N.E. on Reubin **Pactson**, S.E. & S.W. on Thomas **Green**, all other sides Vacant. Samuel **Worthington** did appoint by his last Will & Testament Samuel **Pearson**, Mercer **Babb** as sole Exors., who conveyed sd. Tract unto Elisha **Ford** 13 July 1786. Witness James **Ballenger**, Samuel (S) **Edwards**. Signed Elisha **Ford**, Sarah **Ford**. Witness oath by James **Ballenger** 24 Apr 1790 to John **Hunter** J.P. Rec. 12 Jan 1795.

Page 315-316   17 Nov 1788, Martin **Williams** (Laurens Co.) planter to Holloway **Power** (same) planter, for £8 Stlg. Sold all that Tract of 100 acres, being granted 1 Jan 1787, by William **Moultrie** then Gov. unto Grieff **Williams**, being on Enoree River, recorded in Secretary's office in book OOOO, page 501. Witness Benjamin **Rainey**, Alxd. **Harper**. Signed Martin **Williams**. Witness oath by Benjamin **Rainey** [sic] 17 Nov 1788 to Danl. **Wright** J.P. Laurens Co. Rec. 12 Jan 1795.

Page 317-319   18 July 1789, Holloway **Power** (Laurens Co.) & Elizabeth his wife to Thomas **Holden** (same), for £80 Sterling sold a Tract of land on S side of Enoree River in sd. Co., containing 100 acres, which was Granted to Grieff **Williams** 1 Jan 1787, and by him conveyed unto Martin **Williams** 25 Oct 1788, and by him conveyed unto sd. Holloway **Power** 17 Nov 1788. Also a Tract containing 40 acres more or less, adjoining the premises above. Border: above Tract, River, mouth of a Large Branch. Being part of Tract whereon sd. Holloway **Power** now Dwells. Sd. Holloway **Power** until Execution of these presents stands seized of a good & Indefeasible Estate of Inheritance in sd. Tract of 140 acres. Witness Enoch **Pearson**, Soloman **Bond**, Holloway **Power** Jun. Signed Holloway **Power**, Elizabeth (O) **Power**. Witness oath by Enoch **Pearson** 17 Oct 1789 to Danl. **Wright** J.P. Laurens Co. Rec. 13 Jan 1795.

Page 319-320   16 Oct 1794, William **Hix** (S.C.) planter to John **Martin** (same) planter, for £500 Sterling sold all that Tract of land containing 640 acres more or less, being in Laurens Co. on Burrises creek and some other Branches. Bounded on N by Duncan **OBryant** & Haistings **Doyal**, E by lands not known, all other sides not known. Granted by Wm. **Moultrie** Esq. Gov. in 1705 [sic], recorded in Secretary's office in Grant Book KKKK, page 260. Witness Martin (8) **Martin**, James **Sullivant**. Signed William (x) **Hix**. Witness oath by James **Sullivant** 3 Jan 1795 to Charles **Saxon** J.P. Laurens Co. Rec. 13 Jan 1795.

Page 320-322   25 Oct 1788, Grief **Williams** (Georgia) to Martin **Williams** (Laurens Co.), for £32 Sterling sold all that Tract of 100 acres, being granted 1 Jan 1787 by William **Moultrie** Esq. Gov. unto sd. Grieff **Williams** [sic], on Enoree River, recorded in Secretary's Office in book OOOO, page 501. Witness John **Denning**, Luis **Murphey** [Lewis in witness oath.]. Signed Grief (x) **Williams**. Witness oath by John **Denning** 1 Nov 1788 to Thomas **Jenkins** J.P. Greenville Co. Rec. 13 Jan 1795.

Page 322-323   18 Aug 1794, John **Martin** (Laurens Co.) planter to Frederick **Sullivant** (same) Shoemaker, for £100 sold all that tract of land containing by Estimation 233 acres more or less, in sd. Co., being part of 640 acres. Witness Ezekiel **Roland**, John **Godfrey**. Signed John **Martin**. Quit claim by Thomas **Wadsworth** 19 Aug 1794, for **Wadsworth** and **Turpin**. Witness oath by Ezekiel Stephen **Roland** 30 Sept 1794 to Charles **Saxon** J.P. Plat certified 18 Aug 1794 by John **Rodgers** D.S. Rec. 14 Jan 1795. [Includes plat.]

Page 324-325 19 Aug 1794, John **Martin** (Laurens Co.) planter to Nancy **Barley**, widow of William **Barley** dec., for £20 Sterling sold all that Tract of land containing by Estimation 51 acres more or less, being part of 640 acres Granted by William **Moultrie** Esq. Gov. Border: John **Martin** and unknown. Witness Ezel. **Roland**, Fredrick (F) **Sullivant**. Signed John **Martin**. Quit claim 19 Aug 1794 by Thos. **Wadsworth** for **Wadsworth** & **Turpin**. Witness oath by Ezel. **Roland** 20 Sept 1794 to Charles **Saxon** J.P. Plat surveyed 18 Aug 1794 by John **Rodgers** D.S. Rec. 14 Jan 1795. [Includes plat.]

Page 325-327 Lease & Release, 13 Dec 1791, Leanna **Arnald** [**Arnall** in one ref.] (Laurens Co.) widow woman, Exor. of Joshua **Arnall**, to Benjamin **Jones** (same) Blacksmith, for £30 Sterling sold a certain Tract of land containing 161 acres in sd. Co. on Mchurgs creek, waters of Reaburns creek. Granted 4 Jun 1787 to John **Williams** by Thomas **Pinckney** esq. Gov. & recorded in Secretary's office in Grant Book TTTT, page 264. Conveyed by sd. John **Williams** to sd. Leanna **Arnall**. Witness Stephen **Potter**, William **Franks**. Signed Leanna (x) **Arnall**. Witness oath by Stephen **Potter** 23 Jan 1795 to Joseph **Downs** J.P. Laurens Co. Rec. 23 Jan 1795.

Page 328-330 Lease & Release, 7 & 8 Oct 1793, John **Hunter** esq. (Laurens Co.) to Ambrose **Hudgins** Jun. (same), for £35 Sterling sold all that Tract of land containing 148 acres more or less, being part of 500 acres originally Granted to Pierce **Butler**, and by him conveyed to Harculas Daniel **Bize** 9 July 1792 & now conveyed by John **Hunter** by Power of Attorney from sd. Harculas Danl. **Bize** 1 June 1793. Situate in sd. Co. on waters of Reaburns creek. Border: John **Rodgers**, Saml. **Elliott**, part of sd. Survey, vacant. Witness Margret **Hunter**, Alexander **Mcnary**. Signed John **Hunter** Atty. for Harculas Danl. **Bize**. Witness oath by Alexander **Menary** 14 Oct 1794 to Joseph **Downs** J.P. Laurens Co. Plat certified 5 Oct 1793 by John **Hunter** D.Surv. Rec. 30 Jan 1795. [Includes plat.]

Page 331-332 8 Jan 1795, Stephen **Potter** (Laurens Co.) & Jemima his wife to Peter **Skeen** (same), for £50 Sterling sold one certain Tract of land joining Salathiel **Shockley**, Charles **Gary**, Benjamin **Jones** & Jonathan **Skeen**, containing 110 acres more or less, in sd. Co. on waters of Lick Creek, being part of 350 acres originally Granted to Joshua **Arnall** 5 June 1786, by Wm. **Moultrie** Gov., and from sd. **Arnall** conveyed to Stephen **Potter**. Witness Benjamin **Jones**, Robert **Franks**. Signed Stephen **Potter**, Jemima (x) **Potter**. Witness oath by Benjamin **Jones** 2 Feb 1795 to Joseph **Downs** J.P. Laurens Co. Rec. 9 Feb 1795. [Includes plat.]

Page 332-333 12 Nov 1792, Samuel **Ewing** and Elizabeth his wife (Laurens Co.) to Adam **Bell** (same) farmer, sold 100 acres more or less, in consideration of £10 Sterling. Being part of a Large tract granted unto sd. **Ewing** for 454 acres, by Thomas **Pinckney** then Gov. Border: Adam **Bell**, John **Walker**. Lying in sd. Co. on both sides of Hendricks branch. Witness James **Lindsey**, John **Walker**, John **Coleghan**. Signed Samuel **Ewing**, Elizabeth (x) **Ewing**.

Book E

Witness oath by James **Lindsey** 26 Jan 1793 to William **Hunter** J.P. Rec. 9 Feb 1795.

Page 333-335 25 Feb 1794, John **Walker** farmer (Laurens Co.) to Adam **Bell** (same), for £9 Sterling sold all that Tract of land containing 59 acres, being part of 454 acres Granted by Thomas **Pinckney** then Gov. unto Samuel **Ewing**, and from him conveyed to sd. John **Walker**, 100 acres as by a plat certified by Robert **Hannah** Dep. Surv. Witness James **Lindsey**, Menassah **Willson**. Signed John **Walker**, Mary (x) **Walker**. Witness oath by James **Lindsey** 3 Jan 1795 to William **Hunter** J.P. Rec. 9 Feb 1795.

Page 335-338 9 Apr 1794, Whereas James **Sullivant** (Laurens Co.) planter by his obligation 9 Apr 1794, stands bound unto Thomas **Wadsworth** & Wm. **Turpin**, otherwise called **Wadsworth** & **Turpin** (S.C.) Merchants, for £960 8sh 6p Sterling, conditioned for payment of 404sh 5p [£490 4sh 5p in one ref.] Sterling with Interest. For the better securing payment, sold all that Tract of land containing by Estimation 200 acres more or less, in sd. Co. on head waters of Beaverdam creek. Being the plantation on which I now live. Also a tract containing by estimation 100 acres more or less, in sd. Co. on Ryans Cr. Being a Tract on which Ezekiel S. **Roland** now lives. Provided that if the sum is paid, then this Indenture shall be void. Witness Ezekl. **Roland**, James **Young**. Signed James (J) **Sullivant**. Witness oath by Ezel. **Roland** [No date.] to William **Hunter** J.P. Rec. 17 Feb 1795.

Page 338-341 20 Aug 1794, Whereas John **Godfrey** by his obligation 19 Aug 1794 stands bound unto Thomas **Wadsworth** & William **Turpin**, otherwise **Wadsworth** & **Turpin** (S.C.) Merchants, for £80 Sterling, conditioned for payment of £40 Sterling with Interest. For the better securing payment sold two tracts of land, one the sd. John **Godfrey** bought of Fredrick **Sullivant** containing 83 acres, which sd. **Sullivant** bought of John **Martin**. Other tract containing 157-1/2 acres. Both tracts part of land in Laurens Co. on Red Lick branch of Willsons creek. Survey by John **Rodgers** for John **Martin** 2 May 1785 & Granted to him by Wm. **Moultrie** 6 Mar 1786, both which tracts contain 240-1/2 acres. Provided that if the sum is paid, then this Indenture shall be void. Witness James **Boyce**, Ezel. S. **Roland**. Signed John **Godfrey**. Witness oath by Ezel. S. **Roland** [No date.] to Wm. **Hunter** J.P. Rec. 17 Feb 1795.

Page 341-345 [Page 343-344 skipped.] 4 July 1794, Larkin **Sullivant** to Thomas **Wadsworth** & William **Turpin**, otherwise **Wadsworth** & **Turpin** Merchants (S.C), for £30 Sterling sold a certain Tract of land containing 67 acres more or less, on Beaverdam branch of Little River, being part of 248 acres granted by Wm. **Moultrie** Gov. and recorded in Secretary's office in grant book FFFF, page 166. Bounding E on Alexd. **Hambleton**, S on Patrick **Cuningham**, W on James **Sullivant**, N on sd. Beaverdam branch. Conveyed by Jesse **Meeks** to sd. **Sullivant** 13 Mar 1791. Witness James **Young**, James **Boyce**. Signed Larkin **Sullivant**. Witness oath by James **Young** 17 Feb 1795 to Jonthn. **Downs** J.P. Rec. 17 Feb 1795. [Includes plat.]

48

Page 345-346 1794, John **Rodgers**, son of Andrew **Rodgers** (Duncans creek) & his wife to Thomas **Wadsworth** & Wm. **Turpin**, otherwise **Wadsworth** & **Turpin** (S.C.) Merchants, for £22 10sh Sterling sold all that tract of land containing 313 acres more or less, being in Laurens Co. on Beards fork of Duncans creek of Enoree river. Bounding N.E. on unknown, E & N.E. on lands Surveyed for Alexd. **McNary**, S.W. & N.W. by Andrew **Rodgers**, N.W. by Alexd. **McNary**, S.E. by Adam **Gordon** and unknown. Granted to John **Rodgers** by Charles **Pinckney** Esq. Gov. at Columbia 4 July 1791. Witness James **Young**, James **Boyce**. Signed John **Rodgers**, Sisley (x) **Rodgers**. [No witness oath.] Rec. 18 Feb 1795.

Page 346-347 5 Nov 1793, Alexander **Mcnary** to Thomas **Wadsworth** & Wm. **Turpin**, otherwise **Wadsworth** & **Turpin** (S.C.) Merchants, for £15 Sterling sold 225 acres of land on waters of Duncans creek in Laurens Co., being part of a tract granted to sd. Alexd. **Mcnary** by Charles **Pinckney** Esq. 6 Dec 1790. Witness James **Young**, James **Boyce**. Signed Alexd. **Mcnary**. Witness oath by James **Young** 18 Feb 1795 to Jonathan **Downs** J.P. Rec. 18 Feb 1795.

Page 348-349 16 Nov 1793, Wm. **Osborn** & Salley his wife to Thomas **Wadsworth** & Wm. **Turpin**, otherwise **Wadsworth** & **Turpin** (S.C.) Merchants, for £5 Sterling sold 6 and 8 Perches of land, being part of a tract originally granted to John **Rainey** by Charles **Pinckney** Esq. 1 June 1789, containing 199 acres, which was by sd. **Rainey** conveyed to Wm. **Osborn** by Lease & release 27 Feb 1792. Border: branch, Joseph **Blackerby**. Tract includes a spring. Witness James **Young**, Benjamin **Blackerby**. Signed William **Ozborn** [sic], Salley (x) **Osborn**. Dower relinquished by Salley (x) **Osborn** 30 Oct 1793. Witness oath by James **Young** 18 Feb 1795 to Jonthn. **Downs** J.P. Rec. 18 Feb 1795.

Page 349-351 3 Nov 1794, John **Hurskerson** planter to Thomas **Wadsworth** & William **Turpin**, otherwise **Wadsworth** & **Turpin** (S.C.) Merchants, for £30 Sterling sold two separate tracts of land, one containing 330 acres in Laurens Co. on Beaverdam & branches of Walnut creek of Reedy River, bound N.W. by Joshua **Saxon** & David **Braden**, S.E. by Mathew **Gaits**, N.E. & S.E. by Thomas **Foster**, N.E. vacant. Granted to John **Hurskurson** 15 Feb 1794 by William **Moultrie** Esq. The other tract containing 155 acres, in sd. Co. on branches of Walnett creek [sic] of Reedy River, bounded S.W. by Patrick **Cuningham** & David **Braden**. N.E. by Joshua **Saxon**, N.W. by John **Mcgee**. Witness James **Young**, James **Boyce**. Signed John **Hurskerson**. Witness oath by James **Young** 18 Feb 1795 to Jonathan **Downs** J.P. Rec. 18 Feb 1795.

Page 351-352 20 Nov 1794, Elias **Holingsworth** to Thomas **Wadsworth** and Wm. **Turpin**, otherwise **Wadsworth** & **Turpin** (S.C.) Merchants, for £12 10sh Sterling sold a certain tract of land containing 50 acres more or less, in Pendleton Co. on a branch of Twenty three mile creek. Border: sd. Creek,

William **Turpin**, land granted to **Martin**, Hugh **Rodgers**, unknown, land granted to Thomas **Wadsworth**. Originally granted to Samuel **Gillison**, son & Minor to James **Gillison** by William **Moultrie** 18 Oct 1784. Recorded in Grant book JJJJ, page 685 & by James **Gillison** the father conveyed to Elias **Holingsworth** 25 May 1793. Witness James **Young**, James **Boyce**. Signed Elias **Holingsworth**. Witness oath by James **Young** 18 Feb 1795 to Jonathan **Downs** J.P. Rec. 18 Feb 1795.

Page 353-359   Lease & Release, 6 & 7 July 1792, Honorable Pierce **Butler** Esq. (S.C.) to Harculas Daniel **Bize** Esq., for 5sh sold all those several Tracts & Lots of land herein described, 500 acres in Craven Co. between Broad & Saluda Rivers, on Beaverdam Branch of Reedy River. Bound S & S.W. by land laid out to Elias **Brock** & James **Pew**, N.W. by Jonathan **Downs**, all other sides by Vacant land; 500 acres between sd. two Rivers, bounded N.E. by sd. Pierce **Butler**, S.W. & S.E. by lands laid out by Richard **Winn**, N.W. by Benjamin **Williamson**, N.E. & N.W. by Benjamin **Elliott** & Samuel **Elliott**, N.W. by Kitt **Shoats**; 500 acres between sd. Rivers, bounded N.W. by Benjamin **Elliott** & Samuel **Elliott**, S.W. & N.W. by Paddy **Cuningham**, S by **Grant**, E, S & W by James **Lindley** [**Lindsey** in one ref.], S.E. by sd. Pierce **Butler**; 500 acres between sd. Rivers, bounded N.E. & N.W. by sd. Pierce **Butler**, W by James **Lindley** & **Grant**, S.E. & S by Surveyed lands; 500 acres on branches of Browns creek, bounded S.W. & E by Daniel **Huger**, N & E by Phillip **Waters**, N by William **Grant** [**Gant** in one ref.], N.W. by William **Pelmon**, other sides by Vacant land; 300 acres on Dutchmans Creek of Tyger River, bounded S.E. by Isaac **Peters** [**Paten** in one ref.]; 300 acres on Fergusons Creek, a branch of Tyger River, bounded S.W. by Daniel **Brewton**; 500 acres on branches of Little River of Saluda, bounding N.E. on Thomas **Woodward**, N.W. on John **Rodgers**, Vacant & then vacant, S.E. on Robert **Tweedy**; 500 acres on branches of Buffow, bounded S.E. & S.W. by Jonathan **Parker**, W by Hillery **Gee**, all other sides Vacant; 500 acres on Dry Branch of Enoree, bounded N & W by Alexander **Freasure**, W by Robert **Goodwin**, all other sides Vacant; 200 acres on a branch of Elisha Creek, bound N.W., S.W., S.E. & N.E. by William **Dodd**, N.E. on **Whitiker**; 200 acres on a branch of Fergusons Creek, bounded S.E. by Daniel **Huger**, S.W. by James **Brewton**, N.W. & S.W. on James **Wafford**; 500 acres in forks of Broad & Saluda Rivers, bounded S.W. by Benjamin **Elliott** & Pierce **Butler**, N.W. & N.E. by John **Helmes** and Roger **Brown**, N.W. by Benjamin **Williamson**; 500 acres on N side of Reedy River, bounding N.E. & N.W. on Hugh **Beard**, N.E. by James **Read**, S.E. & N.E. by Richard **Pew**, S.W. & S.E. by Elias **Brock**, N.W. by Paddy **Cuningham**; 200 acres on a branch of Fair Forest, bounded on all sides when Granted by Vacant land; 500 acres in the fork between Great Saluda & Broad Rivers on Buffelow & a branch of Camping creek, waters of Saluda, bounding N.W. on Michael **Wrigah**, all other sides by vacant land when granted; 500 acres in fork of Broad & Saluda Rivers, bound N.E. & N.W. by James **Boyd**, N.W. & S.W. by land laid out to Richard **Winn**, S.W. by Kitt **Shoats**, N.W. & S.W. by Paddy **Cuningham**, S & W by James **Lindley** [**Lindsay** in one ref.], S by **Grant**; 500 acres on a branch of Little River, bounded S.E. by John **Caldwell**, S.W. by unknown, W & S by John **Hunter**,

S.W. by Dick **Neily**, N.W. by **Lowery**, N.E. & N.W. by **Williamson**, N.E. by George **Ankrum** [**Ankerhom** in one ref.], all other sides by vacant land; 200 acres on Widow Stuarts branch, Wateree River, said in Grant to be Surveyed 6 July 1785, but in fact Surveyed in 1775; 200 acres Surveyed for sd. Pierce **Butler** 27 June 1775, on Beaver Dam Creek on N.E. side of Wateree River; also all that part of a Town Lot in Charleston containing on the Western most line next to a Lot heretofore conveyed to William **Miller**, border on Parapet line, Estate of John **Edwards** Esq., John **Morris**, Josiah **Smith**, the whole being high ground. Also all that Low Water Lot exclusive of land left for a Street, on Ashly River. Also 1,167 acres more or less in Parish of Saint Andrew, bounding N.E. on William **Wood** & Major **Fuller** dec., N.W. on Benjamin **Fuller** Esq. [dec. in one ref.] & Isaac **DeCosta** & Ashly River, S.W. & S.E. on hands heretofore of Edmond **Petrie**, but now Christopher **Willimon**. Witness Thomas **Marshall**, Edward **Rutledge**. Signed Pierce **Butler**. Witness oath by Edward **Rutledge** [No signature.] (Charleston) Attorney at Law 21 Mar 1793 to D. **Mazyck** J.P.Qu. Release of Major **Butler** from covenant hearing respecting the Lands mentioned except those Mary Ville and the Lot in Charlest. Given 10 July 1792 by Herculas Danl. **Bize**. Rec. 18 Feb 1795.

Page 360-362 1 Apr 1790, Patrick **Cuningham** & Ann **Cuningham** his wife (Laurens Co.) Planter to John **Dacus** (same), for £35 Sterling sold all that Tract of land containing 100 acres more or less, in sd. Co. on waters of Little River, granted by William **Moultrie** Esq. Gov. 4 Apr 1785. Witness S. **Saxon**, Charles **Allen**, Charles **Simmons**. Signed Patrick **Cuningham**, Ann **Cuningham**. Witness oath by Charles **Allen** 12 May 1794 to Charles **Saxon** J.P. Laurens Co. Rec. 18 Feb 1795.

Page 362-363 14 Mar 1791, Thomas **Williams**, Grand Son of James **Williams** dec., being his Lawful Heir of a Tract of land containing 300 acres, sold unto William **Moore** my Title of sd. Land for £25. Witness Jesse **Moore**, James **McClawnahan** [**McClannahan** in one ref.]. Signed Thomas (x) **Williams**. Witness oath by Jesse **Moore** 17 Mar 1791 to Joseph **Downs** J.P. Laurens Co. Rec. 18 Feb 1795.

Page 363-364 13 Aug 1793, John **Nutt** (Washington Co., Ga.) to Robert **McCrery** Esq. (Laurens Co.), for valuable consideration give a certain Tract of land containing 150 acres more or less, in Laurens Co. on Warriors Creek, a branch of Enoree. Witness John **Nutt**, James **Martin**, Margaret **Greer**. Signed John **Nutt**. Witness oath by Margaret **Greer** 14 Aug 1793 to H. **Breazeal** J.P. Washinton Co., Ga. Rec. 18 Feb 1795.

Page 364-366 15 Jan 1795, Robert **McCrery** & Mary his wife (Co. aforesaid) to William **Ward** [**Word** in one ref.] (same), for £42 Current money sold a certain tract of land containing 105 acres on Warriors creek in sd. Co. Border: E side of Lynches Branch. Originally granted to John **Nutt** and by him conveyed to sd. Robert **McCrery** 13 Aug 1793. Witness Thomas **Word**, Robert **Word**. Signed Robert **McCrery**, Mary (m) **McCrery**. Witness oath by

Thomas **Word** 15 Jan 1795 to Roger **Brown** J.P. Laurens Co. Rec. 18 Feb 1795. [Includes plat.]

Page 366-367 18 Oct 1793, Nathan **Jones** (S.C.) in consideration of £20 Current money paid by Soloman **Langston**, sold all that Tract of land containing 84 acres, being part of 200 acres granted to William **Cooper** Sen., on S side Enoree River in Laurens Co. Bounded W by land granted to John **Blackstock**, E by land granted to Jonathan **Johnston**, N by William **Cooper's** 200 acres. Witness Jesse **Holder**, Soloman **Holder**. Signed Nathan **Jones**. Witness oath by Jesse **Holder** 24 Dec 1793 to Roger **Brown** J.P. Laurens Co. Rec. 18 Feb 1795.

Page 367-369 Lease & Release, 9 Dec 1790, Agnes **Couch** (Laurens Co.) to Nathan **Jones** (same), for £10 sold all that tract of land containing 84 acres, originally granted to Agnes **Couch** in a grant of 200 acres, on which sd. **Jones** now lives, on S side of Enoree River, on both sides of Warrior Creek trading Road. Bounded W by land formerly granted to John **Blackstock**. Witness Thomas **Springfield**, Jesse (x) **Benton**. Signed Agnes **Couch**. Witness oath by Jesse (x) **Benton** 16 Aug 1793 to Roger **Brown** J.P. Laurens Co. Rec. 18 Feb 1795.

Page 369-370 28 Jan 1795, Soloman **Langston** (Laurens Co.) planter in consideration of £100 paid by Jesse **Holder** planter (same), sold a certain tract of land containing 100 acres more or less, originally granted to Margaret **McCuller** and recorded in Secretary's office Book EEE, page 1. Being on Coxes Branch of Enoree River. Bounded S.W. on lands laid out to Christian **McCulle** [sic], all other sides at time of original Survey on Vacant land. Witness Henry **Langston**, Samuel **Stiles**. Signed Soloman **Langston**. Witness oath by Henry **Langston** 20 Jan 1795 [sic] to Roger **Brown** J.P. Laurens Co. Rec. 18 Feb 1795.

Page 370-371 12 Feb 1795, Patrick **OBryant** (Laurens Co.) Planter in consideration of £60 Sterling paid by Joseph **Adair** (same), sold one Negro Wench Poll, aged about 40 years old; one Negro Boy Jacob; one Grey Horse; one Black Mare; one bay colt mare; three cows, one Black, one Spotted, one red & three calves, all Heifers; four Heifers, one red, one Brindled, two grown; nine head of Sheep; three Sows & sixteen Piggs; five fat Hoggs; about 100 Bushells of Corn; one feather bed & furniture; two Chests; one Table; four chairs; two Dishes; six plates; one half Dozen Earthen plates; one Cup board; two potts; one oven; one Skillet; one Loom & Jackling; Cards & two wheels; one big plow; one Shovel plough; two Bed steads; one Hackel; one side Saddle; one ax; one Matlock & tops & bades. Witness John **Adair**, James **Adair**. Signed Patrick (O) **OBryant**. Witness oath by John **Adair** 14 Feb 1795 to Roger **Brown** J.P. Laurens Co. Rec. 18 Apr 1795 [sic].

Page 371-372 16 Oct 1794, Elijah **Elberson** (S.C.) to William **Hall** (Laurens Co.), for 5sh sold all that Tract of land containing 190 acres more or less, being part of a tract granted to William **Donohoe** by Charles **Pinckney** Esq. 2

Jan 1792, and by sd. **Donohoe** conveyed to **Wadsworth & Turpin** for more sure payment of a Debt. Situate in sd. Co. on waters of Cain Creek, waters of Saluda River. Bounded S.W. by Heirs of John **Stephens**, W & S by Robert **Shaw**, S.E. by land granted to James **Burgess**, E by John **Donohoe**, N by Duncan **OBryant**. Witness Benjn. **Carter** Jun., Wm. **Coleman**. Signed Elijah (O) **Elberson**. Witness oath by Wm. **Coleman** 17 Jan 1795 to Zachariah **Bailey** J.P. Rec. 18 Feb 1795.

Page 372-374 6 Nov 1794, Thomas **Dendy** Lawful Heir to Daniel **Dendy** dec. (Laurens Co.) planter to William **Mitchell** planter, for £70 Sterling sold all that Tract of land containing 300 acres more or less, in sd. Co. on Norths Creek, waters of Little River, being part of 2,000 acres granted to William **Bull** Jun. 21 Feb 1772, and by him conveyed 17 and 18 June 1772 to William **Williamson**, and by him to Fredrick **Freasure** by Lease & Release 23 and 24 Nov 1779, and by John **Hunter** Esq. Attorney for sd. **Freasure** to Daniel **Dendy**. Bounding on Thomas **Dendy**, William **Bryson** Jun., Wm. **Leek**, part of original 2,000 acres. Witness Jeremiah **Glen**, William **Leak** [sic], Cornelius **Dendy**. Signed Thomas **Dendy**. Witness oath by Cornelius **Dendey** [sic] 17 Feb 1795 to George **Anderson** J.P. Laurens Co. Rec. 18 Feb 1795.

Page 374-376   15 Aug 1789, Whereas Robert **Reatherford** (S.C.) at Sept Sessions in 1789 in Laurens Co. Court on an Action of Debt against Robert Henry **Hughes** late of sd. Co. did Emplify Robert **Reatherford** and John A. **Elmore** for Recovery of £49 5sh 10p, as also £2 9sh 11p Cost in Suit. By virtue of sd. Judgment, tested by Lewis **Saxon** Clerk, 28 Mar 1789, by a writ, David **Anderson**, Sheriff of sd. Co., did take into Execution a tract of land containing by Estimation 909 acres more or less, on a small branch of Enoree River, on S side of sd. River. Bounded by Elenor **Craig**, Robert **Hannah**, Wm. **Craig**, Elizabeth **Briggs**, Wm. **McCluer**, James **Burk**, John **Newman**, **Pearson**, Mathew **McCrery**, James **Adair**, Doctor **Ross**. Surveyed and Granted unto Robert Henry **Hughes**. Sold at Public Auction 8 June 1789 unto William **Darby** for £5 5sh Sterling. Witness Joshua **Downs**, Robert **Culbertson**. Signed David **Anderson** Sheriff. Witness oath by Robert **Culbertson** [No signature.] 18 Feb 1795 to Lewis **Saxon** J.P. Laurens Co. Rec. 18 Feb 1795.

Page 376-379   14 June 1794, William **Darby** (Union Co.) Merchant to William **Shaw** (Abeville Co.) Attorney at Law, for £250 Sterling sold all that Tract of land supposed to contain 909 acres more or less, on a small branch of Enoree River in Laurens Co., originally granted to Robert Henry **Hughes**, and at Public Sale by an Execution at Instance of Robert **Reatherford** Esq. against sd. **Hughes**, on 8 June 1789, by David **Anderson** Esq. Sheriff of sd. Co. sold to sd. **Darby**. Border: Elenor **Craig**, Robt. **Hand**, Wm. **Craig**, Elizabeth **Brigg**, Wm. **McCluer**, James **Burk**, John **Newman**, **Pearson**, Mathew **McCrerie**, James **Adair**, Doctor George **Ross**. Witness Wm. **Lancaster** clerk of Spartanburgh Co., John **Wright** Revenue Collector. Signed Wm. **Darby**. Witness oath by W. **Lancaster** 14 June 1784 to James **Jourdan** J.S.C. Pursuant to a Warrant from John **Thomas** Esq. Commissioner of Locations 10

Jan 1787, North of Saluda River, I have laid out unto Robert Henry **Hughes** 909 acres. Surveyed 25 Jan 1787 by Robert **Hanna** D.Sur. Recorded 5 Feb 1787 in Book C page 159 by John **Thomas** Comnr. of Locations. Certified by Andrew **Thomson**. Rec. 18 Feb 1795. [Includes plat.]

Page 379-380   5 Nov 1792, Robert **Culbertson** (Laurens Co.) to Daniel **Martin** (same), for £100 Sterling sold all that Tract of Land in sd. Co. on waters of Little River of Saluda. Bounded at time of original Survey: N on Richard **Robertson**, S.W. on Nehemiah **Franks**, S on Vacant, E on Charles **Allen**. Containing 100 acres more or less, granted to James **Beard** 7 May 1774 by William **Bull** Esq. Gov., conveyed by sd. **Beard** by Lease & release to Richard **Robertson**, and by him to Robert **Ross**, and by him to Hugh **McVay** by Lease & release, and by him to Robert **Culbertson**. Witness Joshua **Downs**, Robert **Ross**, Saml. **Stedman**. Signed Robert **Culbertson**. Witness oath by Robt. **Ross** 15 Feb 1795 to Charles **Saxon** J.P. Laurens Co. Rec. 18 Feb 1795.

Page 380-381   20 Jan 1795, Charles **Merril** [sic] (Ninety six Dist.) for £8 Sterling paid by Benjamin **Willson** (same), sold my Smiths Tools, one Anville, one Vice, one Bellows & Hammers, for £5 Sterling. One Bed and furniture at £1 10sh. One big Pott & one Dutch oven at £1. One Yearling Heifer at 10sh. Witness John **Robinson**, James (x) **Robinson**. Signed Charles **Merrill**. Witness oath by John **Robinson** 14 Feb 1795 to William **Hunter** J.P. Laurens Co. Rec. 18 Feb 1795.

Page 381-383   5 Nov 1794, John **Hanna** (Laurens Co.) planter for £10 paid by Alexander **Morison** Merchant (same), sold a certain Tract of Land containing 251 acres more or less, being on a small branch on S side of Enoree River in sd. Co. Border: Robert **Hanna**. Being part of 592 acres granted to sd. John **Hanna** 2 Jan 1792, and recorded in grant book D, No.5, page 296. Border: Vacant, William **Craig**, John **Hanna**, Robert **Hanna**, Thos. **Logan**, Robt. **Templeton**, Wm. **Johnston**, Robt. H. **Hughes**. Witness Edwerd **Giddeon**, Ann **Gordan**, Robert **Hanna**. Signed John **Hanna**. Witness oath by Ann **Gordan** 15 Nov 1794 to Roger **Brown** J.P. Laurens Co. Rec. 18 Feb 1795. [Includes plat.]

Page 383-385   Lease & Release, 27 & 28 May 1794, Andrew **Smyth** Jun. (Laurens Co.) to John **Simpson** Merchant (same), for £25 Sterling sold a certain Tract of land containing 94 acres more or less, in sd. Co. on Cross road from Charleston to the Golding Grove and from fish Dam ford on Broad River to Cambridge. Bounded N.W. by **Simpson**, S.W. by Widow **Lenord**, S.E. & S.W. by James **Bryson**, S.E. by John **Simpson**, late John **Hunter's** land. Witness Jacob **Crosthwait**, John **Willson**, James **Waldrop**. Signed Andrew **Smyth** Jun. Witness oath by John **Willson** 26 Nov 1794 to Prv. **Williams**. [No title.] Laurens Co. Rec. 18 Feb 1795.

Page 385-386   22 Jan 1795, William **Thompson** (Laurens Co.) to Nicholas **Garret** (same), for £45 sold all that tract of land containing 150 acres more or less, in sd. Co. on Beaver Dam Creek, waters of Enoree River. Granted to Wm. **Thompson** dec. by **Bull** then Gov. 18 May 1773. Witness Nuton **Higgins** [sic], Joseph **Camp**. Signed William **Thompson**. Witness oath by Newton (x) **Higgins** 17 Feb 1795 to Joseph **Downs** J.P. Laurens Co. Rec. 18 Feb 1795.

Page 386-387 1794, John **Gray** (Laurens Co.) for £5 10sh paid by James **Kelly** dec., sold unto William **Kelley** & James **Kelley**, sons of sd. James **Kelley** [sic] dec. (same) on Duncans creek, a certain tract of land containing 25 acres more or less, on waters of Duncans creek in sd. Co., part of 325 acres granted to me 1 May 1786. Bounded S.W. on Estate of sd. James **Kelley** dec., N.W. by George **Young**, N.W. by Joseph **Jeans** and Eliz. **Miller**, S.W. by other part of sd. 325 acres. Witness Joseph **Jeanes** [sic], George **Young**. Signed John **Gray**, Salley (x) **Gray**. Oath by George **Young** 17 Feb 1795, that he saw John **Gray** & Alse **Gray** sign the deed. Given before Joseph **Downs** J.P. Laurens Co. Rec. 18 Feb 1795.

Page 387-388 6 Feb 1795, Moses **Halcomb** (Laurens Co.) Blacksmith to Jonathan **Wallace** (same) planter, for £40 Sterling sold a tract of 173 acres of land on both sides of North fork of Dirbins creek, waters of Enoree River, being granted 6 Feb 1786 & recorded in Grant book HHHH, page 84, by William **Moultrie**, then Gov. unto William **Young**. Then by lawful Titles from Thomas **Brandon**, exor. of sd. William **Young**, to Moses **Halcomb**. Including the plantation whereon sd. Jonathan **Wallace** now lives. Witness Thomas **Jones**, Elisha **Halcomb**. Signed Moses **Halcomb**. Witness oath by Thomas **Jones** 17 Feb 1795 to Hudson **Berry** J.P. Laurens Co. Rec. 18 Feb 1795.

Page 389-390 17 Feb 1795, Jonathan **Wallace** (Laurens Co.) planter to Thomas **Jones** (same), for £50 Sterling sold a Tract of 107 acres, being part of 173 acres granted 6 Feb 1786, recorded in Grant book HHHH, page 84, by William **Moultrie** then Gov. unto William **Young**. Then by titles from Thomas **Brandon** Exor. of sd. William **Young**, to Moses **Halcomb**, then from him to Jonathan **Wallace**. Lying on both sides of North fork of Dirbins creek, waters of Enoree River, including the plantation whereon sd. Thomas **Jones** now lives. Witness William **Brown**, Moses **Wright**. Signed Jonathan **Wallace**. Witness oath by William **Brown** 17 Feb 1795 to Hudson **Berry** J.P. Laurens Co. Rec. 18 Feb 1795.

Page 390-391 28 June 1794, John **Willson** (Laurens Co.) planter to Richard **Jones** (Greenville Co.) planter, for £75 Sterling sold a tract of land containing 110 acres, being part of two certain Grants, one by **George III** to Mayo **Nevel**, 150 acres on waters of Dirbins Creek, being then Berkly Co., 30 Sept 1774, recorded in book TTT, page 247. Then from sd. **Nevel** to John **Howard**, then from him to John **Willson**. The other granted to Joseph **Burchfield** by Benjamin **Guerard** Esq. Gov. for 204 acres on Dirbins Creek, waters of Enoree River in sd. Co., in 1785, recorded in book AAAA, page 256. Then from sd. **Burchfield** to Joshua **Fowler**, then from him to John **Willson**. Situate part in Laurens & part in Greenville Co. Witness William **Jones**, James **Russell**. Signed John (J) **Willson**. Witness oath by William **Jones** Sen. 14 Feb 1795 to Hudson **Berry** J.P. Laurens Co. Rec. 18 Feb 1795.

Page 391-393   23 July 1790, John **Ritchey**, Margret his wife, William **Caldwell** & Elizabeth his wife (Ninety Dist. [sic]) planters to Lewis **Banton** (same), for £81 Sterling sold all that Tract of land containing 328 acres in Laurens Co. on waters of Reaborns creek on Reedy River. Being part of 637 acres originally granted unto sd. John **Ritchey** by William **Moultrie** Esq. Gov. 15 Oct 1784. Witness John **Rodgers**, John **Carter**, Sarah (x) **Banton**. Signed John **Ritchey**, Margret (M) **Ritchey**, William **Caldwell**. Witness oath by John **Carter** 23 July 1790 to William **Caldwell** J.P. Newberry Co. Rec. 18 Feb 1795.

Page 393-394   9 Jan 1794, William **Anderson** and Mary his wife (Laurens Co.) planter to Lewis **Banton** (same) planter, for £92 10sh Sterling sold one certain Tract of land on branches of long lick creek, waters of Reedy River, containing 208 acres more or less, being part of 500 acres granted to sd. William **Anderson** 1 Oct 1784 & recorded in book DDDD, page 143. Border: David **Caldwell**, Stephen **Wood**, John **Middleton**, Lewis **Banton**, road. Witness George **Anderson**, John **Rodgers**, Stephen **Wood**. Signed William **Anderson**, Molly (x) **Anderson**. Witness oath by Stee. **Wood** 9 Jan 1794 to George **Anderson** J.P. Laurens Co. Rec. 18 Feb 1795. [Includes plat.]

Page 394-395   29 Feb 1794, Ann **Scurlock** & John **Scurlock** (Laurens Co.) planter to Lewis **Banton** (same), for £10 Sterling sold one certain Tract of Land on Hendricks Branch, waters of Reedy River, containing 97 acres more or less, being part of 197 acres granted to James **Goodman**, and conveyed by him to sd. Ann **Scurlock** by Lease & release. Witness William **Hughes**, Lazarus **Wood**, Margret (x) **Hendrick**. Signed Ann (x) **Scurlock**, John (J) **Scurlock**. Witness oath by William **Hughes** 29 Mar 1794 to George **Anderson** J.P. Laurens Co. Rec. 18 Feb 1795.

Page 395-396   11 Oct 1794, William **McCall** (Laurens Co.) Weaver in consideration of Love and good Will I have towards my Loving Daughter Ellinor **McClain** Widow (same), give all my goods & Chattels in my possession with all Debts, Book accounts or otherwise. Witness John **Cook**, Angus **Campbell**. Signed William (D) **McCall**. Witness oath by John **Cook** [No signature.] 18 Feb 1795 to Angus **Campbell** J.P. Laurens Co. Rec. 18 Feb 1795.

Page 396-397   16 Aug 1794, William **Crisp** (S.C.) & Elizabeth his wife to Charles **Parks** (same), for £70 sold one certain Tract of land in sd. Co. on both sides of Rockey branch of Burrises creek. Border: sd. **Crisp**, sd. **Parks**, branch, **Lemare**, **Burris**. Containing 100 acres more or less, being part of 155 acres granted by Charles **Pinckney** Gov. to sd. William **Crisp**. Recorded in Secretary's office in book E, No.5, page 62. Witness Thomas **Babb**, Elisha

Mitchell. Signed William (W) **Crisp**, Elizabeth (x) **Crisp**. Witness oath by Thomas **Babb** 18 Feb 1795 to Zachariah **Bailey** J.P. Rec. 18 Feb 1795.

Page 397-398 Jan 1795, Stephen **Mullings** (Laurens Co.) to William **Renolds** (same), for £20 Sterling sold a certain Tract of land containing 50 acres in sd. Co. on waters of Beaver Dam Creek, waters of Little River, originally granted to sd. Stephen **Mullins** [sic] by Charles **Pinckney** Gov. in 1792. Bound: creek, **Chesnut**, Zachariah [blank], Saml. **Hall**, Mcernees **Good**. Witness Whitfield **Willson**, John **McLaughlin**. Signed Stephen **Mullings**. Witness oath by John **McLaughlin** 18 Feb 1795 to George **Anderson** J.P. Laurens Co. Rec. 18 Feb 1795.

Page 398-399 26 Nov 1792, William **Moore** (Laurens Co.) to Wiseman **Box** (same), for £41 Sterling sold a certain Tract of land containing 300 acres more or less, in sd. Co. on both sides of Reaburns creek, including the Plantation where William **Moore**, Edward **Box** & Henry **Box** is now living. Joining lands of Charles **Braidey** and **Millhouse**. Witness John **Wadkins**, John **Moore**, Henry **Box**. Signed William **Moore**. Witness oath by Henry **Box** 18 Feb 1794 [sic] to Joseph **Downs** J.P. Laurens Co. Rec. 18 Feb 1795.

Page 399-400 22 Aug 1794, Wiseman **Box** (Laurens Co.) to Hugh **Henderson** (same), for £26 10sh sold a Tract of land containing 40 acres more or less, being part of 300 acres laid out for James **Williams** under the hand of James **Glenn**, on waters of Reaburns creek in sd. Co. Recorded in Secretary's office in Book RR, page 84. Tract lies on N side of Reaburn's creek in N.E. corner of sd. Tract and down Burrises creek unto the mouth. Border: Reaburn's creek, William **Bradey**, **Broadway**, Burrises creek. Witness James **Robinson**, Jonathan (<) **Box**. Signed Wiseman (x) **Box**. N.B. Hugh **Henderson** grant sd. Wiseman **Box** the privilege of lifting & carrying water from the Spring. Witness oath by Jonathan (8) **Box** [sic] 18 Feb 1795 to Zachariah **Bailey** J.P. Rec. 18 Feb 1795.

Page 400-402 10 Mar 1792, John **Ritchey** (Laurens Co.) to Charter **Nichols** (same), for £20 Sterling sold all that Tract of land containing 30 acres more or less, in sd. Co. on Cain Creek. Bounded W on sd. creek, S.E. John **Cuningham**, N.E. George **Carter**. Being part of a tract granted to Samuel **Harris** by the Gov. 1 Jan 1787, and conveyed by sd. **Harris** to sd. John **Ritchey** by Lease & release 14 & 15 Feb 1790. Witness James **Nickels**, David **Whiteford**, William **Nickels**. Signed John **Ritchey**. Witness oath by James **Nickels** 18 Feb 1795 to William **Hunter** J.P. Laurens Co. Plat on 10 Mar 1792, by William **Caldwell** D.S. Rec. 18 Feb 1795. [Includes plat.]

Page 402-403 10 Jan 1795, Samuel **Ewing** (Laurens Co.) to Thomas **East** (same), for £50 Sterling sold all that Tract of land containing 233 acres which was granted to him by Wm. **Moultrie** 6 Mar 1786, recorded in Grant Book JJJJ, page 54. Being in sd. Co. on waters of Hedler creek, and when laid out all sides on Vacant land. Witness James **Lindsey**, James **Ramage**, John

Cologhan. Signed Samuel **Ewing**. Witness oath by James **Ramage** 31 Jan 1795 to William **Hunter** J.P. Laurens Co. Rec. 18 Feb 1795.

Page 404-405 10 Jan 1795, Thomas **East** (Laurens Co.) to John **Calaghan** (same), for £15 Sterling sold all that Tract of land containing 50 acres more or less, being part of 233 acres granted to Samuel **Ewing** by Wm. **Moultrie** Gov., recorded in Grant book JJJJ, page 54. Being in sd. Co. on Hedleys creek, and when laid out all sides on Vacant land. Sd. 50 acres on S side of Hedleys creek, whereon sd. John **Calaghan** now lives. Witness James **Lindsey**, John **Walker**, Nathan **Davis**. Signed Thomas **East**. Witness oath by John **Walker** 31 Jan 1795 to William **Hunter** J.P. Laurens Co. Rec. 18 Feb 1795.

Page 405-406 30 Sept 1794, John **Hansel** and Sarah his wife, late wife of John **Wattson** and John **Adair** dec., and Benjamin **Adair** Jun., her son and Heir of dec. John **Adair** (Laurens Co.) to Benjamin **Adair** Sen. (same), for £106 Sterling sold all that Tract of land containing 100 acres, one of 60, one of 13, in the fork between Broad & Saluda Rivers on Duncans creek. The 100 acres bounded by Joseph **Adair** Sen., John **Brotherton**, John **McCrery**, and land Surveyed by Andrew **Paul**. The 60 acres bounding E on James **Adair**, W on other part of **Brotherton's** land, all other on Vacant. The 13 acres a part of 200 acres on S side of Duncans creek laid out to James **Adair** Sen. Witness James **Howerton**, James **Adair** Jun., John **Robinson**. Signed John (H) **Hansel**, Sarah **Hansel**, Benjamin **Adair** Jun. Witness oath by John **Robinson** 24 Dec 1794 to James **Dillard** J.P. Rec. 18 Feb 1795.

Page 406-407 12 Feb 1791, William **Read** (S.C.) appoint George **Vaughan** (same) my Attorney to Contract and sell all that Tract of land containing 250 acres more or less, on Reaburns Creek in Ninety Six Dist., either by public or private Sale. Witness Silvanus **Walker** Sen., John **Cuningham**. Signed William (8) **Read**. Witness oath by Silvanus **Walker** 18 Feb 1795 to John **Davis** J.P. Laurens Co. Rec. 18 Feb 1795.

Page 408-409 2 May 1791, James **Goodman** (Newberry Co.) to Ann **Scurlock** (Laurens Co.), for £20 Sterling sold all that Tract of Land containing 193 acres more or less, in Laurens Co. on waters of Reedy River, bounded N.E. on Thomas **Carter**, N.W. on George **Anderson**, S.W. on Lewis **Banton** & George **Anderson**, S.E. on old Survey. Granted to sd. James **Goodman** 7 June 1790 by Charles **Pinckney** Esq. Gov. Witness Wm. **Caldwell**, John **Ritchey**, Lewis **Banton**. Signed James **Goodman**. Witness oath by Lewis **Banton** 18 Feb 1795 to George **Anderson** J.P. Laurens Co. Rec. 18 Feb 1795.

Page 409-412 1 Sept 1794, Whereas Wade **Hampton** survivor of Richard and Wade **Hampton**, late in Court of Common Pleas at Cambridge obtained a Judgment for £16 7sh 2p against Richard **Carroll** (Laurens Co.) Planter. Also £11 14sh 4p 1f for Damage by Detention of sd. Debt and Costs. Witness John **Rutledge** Esq., one of the Justices of sd. Court 24 Apr 1794. By virtue of a writ, Samuel **Saxon** Esq. Sheriff of sd. Dist. did seize a Tract of Land of 150 acres more or less, on Little River, waters of Saluda River in sd. Co. Bounding on lands granted to James **Boyd** now belonging to Abraham **Boyd**, Bartholomew **Cradock**, James **Martin**. Samuel **Saxon** did on 1 Sept 1794 at Cambridge, sell the tract unto Charles **Goodwin** Esq. Attorney at Law for £24 10sh. Witness Benjamin H. **Saxon**, Richard **Gantt**. Signed S. **Saxon** S. 96 Dist. Witness oath by Richard **Gantt** 18 Feb 1795 to Thomas **Wadsworth** J.L.C. Rec. 18 Feb 1795.

Page 412-413   24 Dec 1794, Benjamin **McGee** (Laurens Co.) to Thomas **Williamson** (same), for £30 Sterling sold all that Tract of Land containing 100 acres more or less, in sd. Co. on Beaverdam Creek, waters of Reedy River. Being part of a Tract that John **Goodwin** sold to sd. **Mcgee**. Witness Cornelius **Cook**, Thomas **Williamson**, Dieson (x) **Waldrop**. Signed Benjamin **McGee**. Witness oath by Cornelius **Cook** 13 Feb 1795 to Joseph **Downs** J.P. Laurens Co. Rec. 18 Feb 1795.

Page 413-414   10 Nov 1794, John **Page** (Laurens Co.) sold to Benjamin **Drummond** (same), for £15 Stg., a Bay Horse 12 Years old, 14 hands high, a blaze in his face partly to the nose, branded O on the buttock; one bay mare 9 years old, 13 hands high, branded CL on the shoulder; six head of Cattle, two cows & calves, a Red cow & brown sided; one two [sic] heifers a Red one & a pyded one, their marks is a Crop & two Slits in left Ear, the other a hole & underbit, the calves are the same mark; 17 head of Hoggs, one Sow marked with a Swallow fork in Right Ear, and left a crop & Slit, all the rest the same mark; Two feather beds & furniture; two potts and eight plates; two Basons; the present Crop of corn & Tobacco. Witness William **Rowland**, Elizabeth (x) **Drummond**. Signed John **Page**. Witness oath by William **Rowland** 4 Dec 1794 to Joseph **Downs** J.P. Laurens Co. Rec. 18 Feb 1795.

Page 414-415   3 Sept 1794, Silvanus **Walker** Sen. (Laurens Co.) to James **Clardy** (same), for £5 sold one certain Tract of land in sd. Co. on waters of Little River, containing by estimation 50 acres more or less. Being part of 400 acres granted to Canelius **Cargill** [sic] dec. and conveyed by his son Cornelius **Cargill** to sd. Silvanus **Walker**. Bounded: John **Cargill** dec. old line, Indigo Branch, Reedy Branch, sd. Canelius **Cargill's** old line. Witness Tandy **Walker**, Silvanus **Walker** Jun. Signed Slvs. **Walker**. Witness oath by Silvanus **Walker** Jun. 17 Feb 1795 to Jno. **Davis** J.P. Laurens Co. Rec. 18 Feb 1795.

Page 415-416   15 July 1793, John **Caldwell** & Jane his wife, son of William (Ninety six Dist.), Eldest Brother & heir of Samuel **Caldwell**, late of Virginia, dec., to Macherness **Good** Sen. (same), for £250 Current money sold all that Tract of Land containing 150 acres, being in fork between Broad & Saluda Rivers in sd. Dist. on Beaverdam Branch of Little River of Saluda. Bounding at time of original Survey S.E. on Joseph **Babb**, part Vacant land, N.E. on land laid out to William **Bayley** & part Vacant, all other sides by Vacant land. Originally granted to Samuel **Caldwell** dec. by Lord Charles Greville **Montague** Gov. And did Descend unto sd. John **Caldwell** by virtue of his being Eldest Brother to sd. Samuel **Caldwell** dec. Grant recorded in

Secretary's office in Book BBB, page 461. Reserving to his Majesty one Tenth part of Mines of Gold and Silver only. Witness Richard **Golding**, John **Saturwhite**, Frances **Taylor**. Signed Jno. **Caldwell**, Jane **Caldwell**. Witness oath by Frances **Taylor** 26 May 1775 to Jas. **Mayson** J.P. Rec. 18 Feb 1795.

Page 417-418 3 Sept 1771, William **McLaughlin** (Virginia) to Mack **Goode** (S.C.), for £90 Current money sold all that Tract of Land containing 100 acres on Beaver Dam Branch in Berkly Co. Bounded on all sides by Vacant land at time of original Survey. Granted to sd. **McLaughlin** by Lord Charles Greville **Montague** Gov. 30 Oct 1767. Witness Jane **Caldwell**, Martha **Caldwell**, Wm. Thomas **Caldwell**. Signed William **McLaughlin**. Witness oath by Wm. Thomas **Caldwell** 4 Aug 1771 to Jno. **Caldwell** J.P. Craven Co. Rec. 18 Feb 1795.

Page 418-420 3 Nov 1774, Peter **Meal** (Ninety six Dist.) and Mary his wife planter to Patrick **Cuningham** Esq. (same), for £100 Current money sold all that Tract of land containing 200 acres in Craven Co. on waters of Reedy River. Bounding W on Lewis **Banton**, N on Enos **Stimson**, E on George **Wright**, S on not known. Granted unto sd. **Meal** by William **Bull** Esq. Lieut. Gov. 23 June 1774. Witness Christopher **Humble**, Henry **Strum**. Signed Peter **Mehl** [sic], Mary (O) **Meal**. Witness oath by Christopher **Humble** 16 Apr 1774 to Robt. **Cuningham** J.P. Ninety Six Dist. Rec. 18 Feb 1795.

Page 420-421 13 May 1794, John **Chesnut** (Camden) to Patrick **Cuningham** (Laurens Co.), for £40 Sterling sold 150 acres of land on Beaver Dam creek of Saluda. Bounded when Surveyed on N.W. by **McCollough** & Vacant land, N.E. by M. **Goode**, S.E. by Samuel **Caldwell** & Vacant land. Originally granted to William **Downs** 9 Sept 1774, and by him sold unto sd. John **Chesnut**. Witness E. **Ramsay**, James **Saxon**. Signed John **Chesnut**. Witness oath by James **Saxon** 18 Feb 1795 to Daniel **Wright** J.P. Laurens Co. Rec. 18 Feb 1795.

Page 422-423 3 Sept 1774, Jacob **Withrow** (Ninety Six Dist.) & Margaret his wife to Patrick **Cuningham** Esq. (same) planter, for £60 Current Money sold all that Tract of land containing 100 acres in Colleton Co. on S.W. side of Saluda River. Bounding S.W. on not known, N.E. by Saluda River, other sides on Vacant. Granted by William **Bull** Esq. Lieut. Gov. unto Margaret **Hen** on the Bounty by Grant 25 May 1774. Sd. Margaret **Hen** now married unto sd. Jacob **Withrow**. Witness David **Cuningham**, Jeremiah (C) **Cummans**. Signed Jacob **Withrow**, Margaret (x) **Withrow**. Witness oath by Jeremiah (C) **Cummans** 17 Apr 1775 to Robt. **Cuningham** J.P. Ninety Six Dist. Rec. 18 Feb 1795.

Page 423-425 2 June 1793, Reeves **Martin** (Edgfield Co.), Eldest Son and Heir of William **Martin** dec., planter to Machonus **Goode** (same) planter, for £50 Current money sold all that Tract of land containing 200 acres more or less, in Laurens Co. on Beaver Dam, waters of Little River. Originally granted by Lord Charles Griville **Montague** Gov. unto sd. William **Martin** dec. 29

Apr 1768. Witness Dennett **Hill**, John **Pulliam** Jun., Garland **Goode**. Signed Reeves **Martin**. Witness oath by John **Pulliam** Jun. [No date.] to John **Moore** J.P. Rec. 18 Feb 1795.

Page 425-427 18 May 1792, Margaret **Cuningham** (Laurens Co.) Widow Woman to Patrick **Cuningham** (same) planter, for £100 Sterling sold all that Tract of land containing 300 acres more or less, on S side of Reaburns Creek, waters of Reedy & Saluda Rivers, being part of 500 acres formerly in Berkly Co. but now in Laurens Co. Originally granted unto Richard **Shurley** by Lord Charles Griville **Montague** Capt. Genl. 15 Feb 1769, and bounded on all sides by Vacant land when laid out. Sold by Robert **Shurley** and Mary **Shurley** his mother unto Andrew **Cuningham**, now dec., by Lease & release 9 & 10 Jan 1775, the sd. Robert **Shurley** being the eldest son and Heir of Richard **Shurley**, which land was confiscated by the Assembly of the State by an Act passed at Jacksonburough in 1780, on account of sd. Andrew **Cuningham** being a British Subject, and sd. Tract was Granted by the Legislature unto sd. Margaret **Cuningham**, relict of sd. Andrew **Cuningham**, and his children by sd. Andrew **Cuningham**, by an Act passed in Charleston Mar 1785. Bounding N.E. on Reaburns creek & Sarah **Hodges**, S.W. on Richard **Pinson**, W on Jacob **Bowman**, N.W. on lands formerly John **Ritchies**. Witness Isaac **Gray**, Charles **Simmons**, Wm. **Cuningham**. Signed Margaret (x) **Cuningham**. Witness oath by Charles **Simmons** 18 Feb 1795 to Daniel **Wright** J.P. Laurens Co. Rec. 18 Feb 1795.

Page 428-430 3 June 1793, John **Osborn** (Edgefield Co.) planter to Machones **Goode** (same), for £15 Sterling sold all that Tract of Land containing 47 acres more or less, being part of 176 acres in Laurens Co. betwixt waters of Little River & Beaverdam Creek. Originally granted unto sd. John **Osborn** by William **Moultrie** Esq. Gov. 4 Apr 1785. Sd. 47 acres bounding on three sides by sd. Machonus **Goode's** [sic] land & N on original Survey, granted to John **Osborn** but now belonging to John **Walker**. Witness P. **Cuningham**, John **Walker**, Kiturah **Walker**. Signed John **Osborn**. Witness oath by Patrick **Cuningham** 18 Feb 1784 [sic] to Daniel **Wright** J.P. Laurens Co. Plat certified 1 June 1793 by P. **Cuningham** D.S. Rec. 18 Feb 1795. [Includes plat.]

Page 430-431 16 July 1794, Andrew **Rodgers** Jun. (Laurens Co.) to Patrick **Cuningham** (same), for £2 14sh Sterling sold a certain Tract of land in sd. Co. containing 12-1/2 acres, being part of 701 acres originally granted to Andrew **Rodgers** Jun. Border: land originally granted to William **Bailey**, Saml. **Caldwell**, Moses **Yarborough**. Witness Isaac **Gray**, Fielder **Wells**. Signed A. **Rodgers** Jun. Witness oath by Fielder **Wells** 12 Feb 1795 to George **Anderson** J.P. Laurens Co. Plat certified 16 July 1794 by P. **Cuningham** D.S. Rec. 18 Feb 1795. [Includes plat.]

Page 432-434 26 Apr 1790, James **Pucket** & Martha his wife (Laurens Co.) planter to Patrick **Cuningham** (same) planter, for £30 Sterling sold all that Tract of Land containing 71 acres in sd. Co. on N.E. side of Saluda River, being part of 244 acres originally granted unto sd. James **Puckett** [sic] by Charles **Pinckney** Esq. Gov. 10 June 1789. Border: P. **Cuningham**, James **Pucket, Griffen**, Saluda River, Rob. **Swansy's** road. Witness Memn. **Walker**, Nancy (8) **Walker**, Wm. **Cuningham**. Signed James **Pucket**, Martha **Pucket**. Witness oath by Memwan **Walker** 18 Feb 1795 to Daniel **Wright** J.P. Laurens Co. Plat certified 23 Apr 1790 by P. **Cuningham** D.S. Rec. 18 Feb 1795. [Includes plat.]

Page 434-436   Lease & Release, 24 & 25 Aug 1794, Moses **Lawson** (Meclinburgh Co., N.C.) to James **Downen** (Laurens Co.) planter, for £275 Current money paid unto William **Galaspy** dec. and £10 Sterling paid unto sd. Moses **Lawson**, sd. **Galaspy's** heirs, sold all that Tract of land containing 250 acres in Laurens Co. on S fork of Reaburns creek, originally granted unto Peter **Dinner** by Charles Griville **Montague** 13 May 1769 [15 May in release.]. Recorded in Secretary's office in Book DDD, page 148, and from thence conveyed by Lease & release unto William **Galaspy** dec., and by Heirship unto Moses **Lawson**. Bounded on three sides by Vacant land at time of Surveying. Witness Elisha **Hunt**, William **Kellett**. Signed Moses **Lawson**, Catrine (x) **Gelaspy**. Or other ways Catrin **Harris**. Oath by Elisha **Hunt** on 19 Feb 1795 that he saw Moses **Lawson** & Catren **Galaspy** [sic] other wise called Catrin **Harris**, sign the Deed. Given before Joseph **Downs** J.P. Laurens Co. Rec. 19 Feb 1795.

Page 436-438   5 Jan 1788, Joseph **Turner** planter (Abeville Co.) to Stephen **Potter** (Laurens Co.), for 5sh sold all that Tract of land containing by Estimation 200 acres in Abeville Co. on N branches of Eighteen Mile creek, waters of Savanah River. Granted unto sd. Joseph **Turner** (a Soldier) on the Bounty by Benjamin **Guerard** Esq. Gov. 21 Jan 1785. Recorded in Secretary's office in Grant book BBBB, page 104. Witness John (J) **Arnol**, Samuel **Burton**. Signed Joseph (xx) **Turner**. Witness oath by John (J) **Arnall** [sic] 24 July 1793 to Charles **Saxon** J.P. Laurens Co. Rec. 19 Feb 1795.

Page 438-441   Lease & Release, 18 & 19 May 1774, John **Willard** (St. Mark Parish, Ninety six Dist.) & Martha his wife to Joseph **Atkins** (same), for £375 Current money sold a certain Tract of land containing 179 acres, being part of 250 acres granted to sd. John **Willard** 30 Feb 1768 [3 Feb in release.], for a Mill seat. Situate in Berkley Co. on both sides of Reedy Creek. Bounding S.W. on lands when Surveyed of John **Brown**, N.W. on lands laid out to John **Cargill**, S.E. on lands laid out to Hanse **Hendrick** [Hans in one ref.], all other sides on Vacant land. Sd. 179 acres on S side of Reedy Creek. The Dividing line extending to the Center of sd. Creek. Witness John **Cobbs**, William **Burges**, Patrick **Cuningham**. Signed John **Willard**, Martha **Willard**. Witness oath by John **Cobbs** 19 May 1774 to Patrick **Cuningham** J.P. Ninety Six Dist. Rec. 2 Mar 1795.

Page 441-442   9 Nov 1790, Richard **Jowell** (Laurens Co.) to Thomas **Babb**, for £100 Current money sold one certain Tract on Beaver Dam Creek, waters of Little River, waters of Saluda, containing 196 acres more or less, being part of 510 acres granted by William **Moultrie** Esq. Gov. to Richard **Jowell** and recorded in book DDDD, page 92. Bounding N by William **Drew**, W on Joel **Burgess**, S on Wm. **Hail**, Richard **Roland**, S.E. on James **Holingsworth**. Witness John **Rodgers**, Joshua **Downs**, Charles **Simmons**. Signed Richard **Jowell**. Witness oath by John **Rodgers** 18 Feb 1792 to George **Anderson** J.P. Laurens Co. Rec. 2 Mar 1795. [Includes plat.]

Page 442-443   28 July 1792, James **Clardy** (Laurens Co.) to Joshua **Sutherland** [**Sutherlin** in one ref.] (same), for £30 sold a certain Tract of land on N side of Little River containing by Estimation 100 acres more or less, being part of 200 acres granted to Cornelius **Cargill** dec. Bounded on Richard **Carrell**, Thomas **Jones**, Nathan **Cranshaw**, Samuel **Boyd**. Witness Peter (x) **Flinn**, Jemimah **Moore**. Signed James (x) **Clardy**, Sarah (x) **Clardy**. Oath by Jemima **Moore** 18 July 1794 that she saw James **Clardy** & his wife sign the Deed. Given before Wm. **Hunter** J.P. Laurens Co. Rec. 2 Mar 1795.

Page [444]   17 June 1794, John **McCarty** (Laurens Co.) for £10 Sterling paid by Alexander **Simpson** Sen. (same), sold one Red Cow & Calf, one Red Bullock, one pyed cow & Calf, one pyed Heifer, all marked with one crop of right Ear, one Sorrel Mare, 2 years old with a blaze face, one Black yearling filly, one Black Mare, 8 years old, supposed natural Trotter, one Bay horse about 10 years old. Witness David **Speers**, Mary **Simpson**. Signed John (x) **Macarty** [sic]. Witness oath by David **Speers** 1 Apr 1795 to Wm. **Hunter** J.P. Laurens Co. Rec. 2 Apr 1795.

Page [444]-446   Lease & Release, 1 & 2 Feb 1790, Joseph **Scott** (S.C.) Planter to Sarah **Evens** [**Evans** in one ref.] (same), for £20 Sterling sold all that Tract of land containing 150 acres more or less, in Laurens Co. on Cain creek, waters of Great Saluda River, bounding at time of original Survey S.E. on John **Evans** and Mary **Edwards**, all other sides Vacant land. Granted to sd. Joseph **Scott** 8 Feb 1773 by Lord Charles Griville **Montague** Gov. Witness A. **Robinson**, Mercer **Babb**. Signed Joseph **Scott**. Witness oath by Mercer **Babb** 8 May 1794 to Elisha **Ford** J.P. Newberry Co. Rec. 2 Apr 1795.

Page 446-448   6 Apr 1795, James **McDowall** (Laurens Co.) to Soloman **Goodwin** (same), for £30 sold a certain Tract of land on the head of Duncans creek, waters of Enoree River in sd. Co., including the plantation where sd. **Goodwin** now lives, containing 100 acres. Witness Thomas **Goodwin**, Theophiless **Goodwin**. Signed James (x) **McDowel** [sic]. Witness oath by Thomas **Goodwin** [No signature.] 6 Apr 1795 to John **Davis** J.P. Laurens Co. Rec. 6 Apr 1795.

Page 448   20 Feb 1795, Lewis **Saxon** and John **Boyd** are bound unto J. G. **Guignard** Treasurer at Columbia for £1,000. Condition that Lewis **Saxon** shall perform the Duties of Tax Collector, Enquirer & assessor of Laurens Co. to which he has been appointed, then the obligation to be void. Witness Jonathan **Downs** J.L.C., Thomas **Wadsworth** J.L.C. Signed Lewis **Saxon**,

John **Boyd**. Lewis **Saxon** took oath as assessor & Collector of Public Tax on 20 Feb 1795. Rec. 6 Apr 1795.

Page 448-449 5 Jan 1795, Archibald **McDanald** (Laurens Co.) & Editha his wife to Thomas **Childers** (same), for £35 Sterling sold a certain Tract of land on waters of Reaburns creek in sd. Co. Granted to William **McDanald** by Lord Charles **Montague** by Patent Dec 1772. Tract contains 100 acres. Witness Isaac **Norman**, Samuel **Green**. Signed Archd. **McDaniel** [sic], Editha (x) **McDaniel**. Witness oath by Samuel **Green** 16 Mar 1795 to Jonathan **Downs** J.P. Laurens Co. Rec. 6 Apr 1795.

Page 449-450 12 May 1795, Jonathan **Downs** & John **Hunter** Esq. Judges of Laurens Co. Court to Thomas **Wadsworth** and William **Turpin**, otherwise called **Wadsworth** & **Turpin** (S.C.) Merchants, for £10 10sh sold one Lot of Land containing 72-ft 6-in in front and 244-ft in Length, being part of 4 acres sold by Samuel **Saxon** to the Judges of the Court 15 Mar 1792. Lot is known in the plan as No.3. Bounded on front by the now public Lands of the County, N on a Lot held by Lewis **Saxon**, other sides by a passage or Street. **Wadsworth** & **Turpin** to have free Egress & Regress to and from the spring of Waters made use of by people living near the Court House. Witness Lewis **Saxon**, Wm. **Dunlap**. Signed Jonthn. **Downs**, John **Hunter**. Witness oath by William **Dunlap** 12 May 1795 to Joseph **Downs** J.P. Laurens Co. Rec. 12 May 1795.

Page 450-452 Lease & Release, 6 & 27 Nov 1784 [sic], Jonathan **Downs** Esq. (Berkley Co.) to James **Pool** (same), for £40 Stlg. sold all that Tract of Land containing 100 acres in sd. Dist. on Horse Creek on S side of Reedy River. Bounding N by sd. River, S.W. by land claimed by Moses **Tomlin**, other sides by Vacant land. Witness William **Burton**, Robt. **Parker**. Signed Jonathan **Downs**, Sarah **Downs**. Oath by Wm. **Burton** 23 May 1785 that he saw Jonathan **Downs** & Sarah his wife sign the Deed. Given before Joseph **Downs** J.P. Laurens Co. Rec. 18 Feb 1795 [sic].

Page 452-454 Lease & Release, 7 & 8 Sept 1773, John **Cary** and Mary **Cary** his wife (Mechlinburgh Co., N.C.) Weaver to Matthew **Gasten** weaver (Rowan Co., N.C.), for £75 current money sold all that Tract of land containing 150 acres in Berkley Co., waters of Duncans Creek, bounded all sides on vacant land. Granted 12 Sep 1768 by William **Bull** Esq. Lieut. Gov. unto John **Cary**. Witness James **McCluer**. Signed John (x) **Cary**, Mary (x) **Cary**. Witness oath by Joseph **Gasten** 27 Jan 1795 to Andw. **Hamphill** J.P. Chester Co. Rec. 18 Feb 1795.

Page 454-455 23 Nov 1794, Matthew **Gasten** (Greene Co., Ga.) planter for £50 Sterling paid by Joshua **Palmer** (Laurens Co.) Clergyman, sold a certain Tract of Land containing 150 acres more or less, in Laurens Co. on waters of Duncans Creek, originally granted to John **Cary** by William **Bull** Esq. 12 Sept 1768. Recorded in Secretary's office in Book EEE, page 36. And by sd. **Cary** conveyed to sd. **Gasten**. Witness Saml. **Reed**, George **Reid** Jun. Signed

Matthew **Gasten**. Witness oath by George **Reid** 23 Nov 1794 to Geo. **Reid** J.P. Greene Co., Ga. Rec. 19 Feb 1795.

Page 455 8 May 1795, William **Black** (Laurens Co.) planter for £25 Sterling paid by John **Simpson** Mercht. (same), sold one Ridgland Horse, bright bay with a Star in the face; one 4 year old Dark Bay Horse, branded WT with two white hind feet and a Star in his face; one red Cow & Bull calf; one yellow Cow & Heifer calf; one yearling red & white; four Sheep with smooth crop and Swallow fork; nine head of hogs with one hole in right ear and swallow fork in left; one large pot; one Dutch oven; all the present Crop and plantation Tools, Corn, potatoes, Tobacco &c. Witness Wm. **Ross**, Saml. **Word**. Signed William (x) **Black**. Witness oath by Wm. **Ross** 11 May 1795 to Zachariah **Bailey** J.P. Rec. 12 May 1795.

Page 456 7 Jan 1795, John **McCarly** (Laurens Co.) planter for [blank] paid by John **Simpson** Mercht. (same), sold twenty head of hogs, two ploughs and all plantation Utensils, two Beds and furniture, three pots, six pewter plates, one set knives and forks, with all my household furniture, one man's Saddle, one woman's Saddle, plough giers & Gridles, 100 Bushels of Corn and also a quantity of Fodder. Witness David **Speers**, William **Rees**. Signed Jno. (x) **McCarly**. Witness oath by William **Reese** [sic] 23 Mar 1795 to Charles **Griffen** J.P. Rec. 12 May 1795.

Page 456-457 11 May 1795, William **Warren** (Laurens Co.) Yeoman for £25 paid by Andw. **Rodgers** Jun. (same), sold a certain Tract of land containing 100 acres in sd. Co. on N.W. side of Duncan's Creek on Beard's fork. Bounded when surveyed N.E. on lands laid out, S.W. by John **McNary**, all other sides by Vacant land. Being granted to Alexd. **McNary** 17 Mar 1775, recorded in Book WWW, page 407. Conveyed by sd. **McNary** to Wm. **Warren**. Witness John **Rodgers**, Andrew **Rodgers** Jun., John **Studdard**. Signed William (x) **Warren**. Witness oath by John **Rodgers** 11 May 1795 to William **Hunter** J.P. Laurens Co. Rec. 13 May 1795.

Page 457-458 17 Dec 1794, Caleb **Davis** (Laurens Co.) planter to William **Rodgers** (same), for £32 10sh Sterling sold one certain Tract of land on branches of Duncans Creek, containing 126 acres more or less, having such bounds as a plat dated 5 May 1795. Bounding N.E. on Andw. **Rodgers**, William **Rodgers**, S.E. on James **Cummings**, W on Moses **Cerkland**, Alexr. **McNary**. Recorded in Grant book F, No.5, page 84. Witness Andw. **Rodgers**, Abner **Rodgers**. Signed Caleb (x) **Davis**. Witness oath by Andw. **Rodgers** Sen. 11 May 1795 to Wm. **Hunter** J.P. Laurens Co. Rec. 14 May 1795.

Page 458 1 Apr 1795, Richard **Fowler** (Laurens Co.) planter to James **Gilbert** (same) planter, for £60 Sterling sold a tract supposed to be about 100 acres more or less, being part of 200 acres on Durbins Creek, waters of Enoree River, then Berkley Co., granted 1 Oct 1771, by **George III** to Richard **Fowler** Sen., recorded in Book L, No.11, page 127. Sd. tract being the South part, on S side of Durbins Creek, willed from Richard **Fowler** dec. to Richd.

Fowler Jun. Tract lies on both sides of the new Line between Laurens and Greenville Co. Border Edward **Wilson**, Durbins Creek. Witness James **Kilgore**, William **Gilbert** Jun. Signed Richard **Fowler**. Witness oath by William **Gilbert** Jun. 9 May 1795 to Hudson **Berry** J.P. Laurens Co. Rec. 14 May 1795.

Page 459 1 Apr 1795, William **Bowen** (Laurens Co.) to Richard **Fowler** (same), for £30 sold all that tract of Land containing 112 acres in sd. Co. on S side of Durbins Creek, waters of Enoree River, being part of 3,000 acres granted to Alexr. **Frazer** in 1772, and conveyed to William **Bowen**. Border: Wm. & James **Gilbert**, Rd. **Fowler** dec., **Fowler**, William **Bowen**. Witness William **Gilbert** Jun., James **Kilgore**. Signed William **Bowen**. Witness oath by William **Gilbert** Jun. 9 May 1795 to Hudson **Berry** J.P. Laurens Co. Rec. 15 May 1795. [Includes plat.]

Page 459-460 1 Apr 1795, Richd. **Fowler** (Laurens Co.) to James **Gilbert** (same), for £50 Sterling sold a certain Tract of Land containing 170 acres more or less, on both sides of new line between Laurens & Greenville Co. in Ninety Six Dist. & Pendleton Dist. on S side of Durbin's Creek, waters of Enoree River. Bounding on William **Gilbert**. Sd. tract partly in a grant to Alexd. **Frazer** 12 May 1772, supposed to include 3,000 acres, and from sd. **Frazer** to James **Frazer** and from him to William **Bowen**, and from him to Richd. **Fowler**, 112 acres being part of above 170 acres. Witness James **Kilgore**, William **Gilbert** Jun. Signed Richard **Fowler**. Witness oath by William **Gilbert** Jun. 9 May 1795 to Hudson **Berry** J.P. Laurens Co. Rec. 15 May 1795.

Page 460-461 24 Feb 1794, Andr. **Rodgers** Jun. (Laurens Co.) to James **Boyce**, Elizabeth **Boyce**, Sarah **Boyce**, John **Boyce** & Jesse **Boyce**, for £5 Sterling sold a certain Tract of Land containing by Grant 104 acres in sd. Co. on a branch of Cane Creek, waters of Saluda. Bound S by land laid out to Cornelius **Cargill** & George **Carter**, N.E. by Thomas **Boyce**, N.E. and E by Dunkin **OBryant**, W by **White**. Originally granted to sd. Andrew **Rodgers** Jun. by Charles **Pinckney** Gov. 17 Aug 1786. Witness John (J) **Gotherd**, Stephen **Wood**. Signed A. **Rodgers** Jun. Oath by Thomas **Wadsworth** 10 Apr 1795, that he saw Andrew **Rodgers** sign the receipt. Given before Zechariah **Bailey** J.P. Witness oath by John (J) **Gothard** [sic] 2 May 1795 to Zech. **Bailey** J.P. Rec. 15 May 1795.

Page 461-462 25 Oct 1793, Andrew **McCreary** (Laurens Co.) to George **Young** (same), for £60 Sterling sold all that Tract of Land containing 100 acres more or less, in Ninety six Dist. on S side of Broad River on a branch thereof. Granted to Michael **Snider** by William **Bull** Esq. 28 Jan 1771. Witness James Noteman **McCreary**, Andrew **McCreary** Jun. Signed Andrew **McCreary**, Sarah (O) **McCreary**. Oath by James Noteman **McCreary** 24 Apr 1795 that he saw Andw. **McCreary** with Sarah his wife sign the Deed. Given before Geo. **Whitmore** J.P. Laurens Co. Rec. 11 May 1795 [sic].

Page 462-463 4 Dec 1794, Andw. **McCreary** (Laurens Co.) to James Noteman **McCreary** (same), for £60 Sterling sold a certain Tract of Land containing 100 acres more or less. Granted to sd. Andw. **McCreary** 1 Oct 1765, lying on S side of Enoree River on Duncans Creek in ninety six Dist. Witness John (x) **McCreary** Jun., Robet **McCreary**. Signed Andrew **McCreary**. Witness oath by John (x) **McCreary** Jun. 24 Apr 1795 to Geo. **Whitmore** J.P. Laurens Co. Rec. 15 May 1795.

Page 463-465 Lease & Release, 22 & 23 Sept 1775, William **Watson** (Ninety Six Dist.) planter with Ann [sic] his wife to William **Cason** (same) planter, for £250 Current money sold a certain Tract of Land containing 200 acres more or less, in Craven Co. on Banks Creek, a branch of Saluda River. Bounding N.W. on Richd. **Griffin**, S.W. on James **Cook**, N.W., S.W. and S.E. by vacant land & Alexr. **Deall**. Part of 300 acres originally granted unto sd. **Watson** 7 June 1774 by Wm. **Bull** Esq. Lieut. Gov. Recorded in Secretary's office in Book QQQ, page 467. Witness John **Thomas**, John (x) **McGregor**, Ann (x) **Thomas**. Signed William **Watson**, Sarah (x) **Watson**. Wm. **Watson** & his wife Sarah signed the Lease & Release. Given 2 Oct 1777 before James **Pollard** J.P. Ninety six Dist. [No witness oath.] Rec. 15 May 1795. [Includes plat.]

Page 465-466 7 Feb 1795, William **Nichols** (S.C.) sold unto Joshua **Hammond** all my Stock and household furniture: one black mare about 9 years old and about 12 hands high; three cows & calves and one yearling; five head of Sheep; one feather Bed and furniture; two Bedsteads; two Spinning wheels; one Clack reel; one dish; six plates; three Basons; three pots; dutch oven; one Iron Tea kettle; two falling axes; one broad ax; one hatchet; one howel; one drawing knife; two screw Augers; one hand saw; one Iron Square; one Chizzel; one Cart; one Table and five Chairs; one Chest; one Trunk; two water Pails; one Tub; small Lot of Crockery ware; one Sett of Shoe makers Tools and a set of Tanners tools; one set of Saddlers tools; one Skillet; one Grindstone, concluding with all my property, in consideration of £15 Sterling. Witness Frances (x) **Casterson**, Sally (G) **Harris**. Signed William **Nichols**. Witness oath by Frances (x) **Casterson** 17 Feb 1795 to Charles **Saxon** J.P. Laurens Co. Rec. 22 July 1795.

Page 466-468 7 Aug 1771, George **Carter** (Berkly Co.) planter and Naomi **Carter** his wife to William **Turk** (same) planter, for £60 Current money sold 150 acres on a fork of Cane Creek in Berkley Co. Bounded on all sides on Vacant Land at time it was laid out. Granted by **George III** 22 Feb 1771 and Tested by Wm. **Bull** esq. Lieut. Gov., unto George **Carter**. Witness Pat. **Cuningham**, Hugh **Brown**, Robert **Carter**. Signed George **Carter**, Naomi (N) **Carter**. Witness oath by Hugh **Brown** 24 Aug 1771 to Robert **Cuningham** J.P. Craven Co. Rec. 13 July 1795. [Includes plat.]

Page 1 18 Aug 1795, John **Templeton** (Laurens Co.) planter for £83 paid by Alexander **Morrison** (same), sold a certain brown bay mare and colt, near 10 years old, 14 hands, star and snip, branded on near jaw & near buttock with a heart, and on near shoulder with an R; a bright bay horse about 14 hands, natural trotter, no visible marks; a young grey filly, 2 years old, trots naturally, no visible marks, about 13-1/2 hands high; two pied cows and calves; three heifers, two of them pied and one brown; two pied yearling; twenty head of hogs marked crop and a hole in left ear and an under keel in right; eight head of Sheep marked same as hogs; two beds and Bedsteads with a pair of Sheets, two blankets, a Coverlet, Bolster and two pillows, which constitutes the furniture of each; Chest of drawers made of Walnut; one side cupboard made of pine. Provided if the sum is paid to sd. **Morrison** on 1 Jan nest ensuing, then this bill of Sale to be void. Witness Joseph **Hanna**, John **Nugent**. Signed John **Templeton**. Witness oath by John **Nugent** 19 Aug 1795 to Joseph **Downs** J.P. Laurens Co. Rec. 19 Aug 1795.

Page 1-2 17 Jan 1792, David **Burns** and Massey **Burns** his wife (Laurens Co.) to Bryant **Leak** and George **Leak** (same), for £100 sold all that Tract of land containing 100 acres more or less, in the fork of Broad and Saluda Rivers, on a fork of Enoree called Duncans Creek, which was Granted to Patrick **Cuningham** 21 Apr 1775 by William **Bull** esq. Lieut. Gov., then conveyed to James and Samuel **Saxon**, and then sd. **Saxon** conveyed to sd. **Burns**. Witness Robert **Oliphant**, James (J) **Underwood**. Signed David (D) **Burns**, Massey (x) **Burns**. Witness oath by James (J) **Underwood** 4 Aug 1792 to John **Hunter** [No title.] Laurens Co. Rec. 29 May 1795.

Page 2-6 Lease & Release, 21 & 22 Oct 1774, William **Sanders** (Charleston) and Ann his wife to Capt. Thomas **Woodward** (Craven Co.) planter, for £5 sold a certain Tract of Land containing 375 acres, in Craven Co. on Bush river Creek, bounded N.E. on **Mulvey** & William **Nealy**, Kitt **Smith**, James **Anderson**, Ansley **Anderson**, N.W. James **Barton** and Benjamin **Barton**, S.E. on William **Gibbs** & James **Fenlow**, S.W. on William **Nealy** and William **Bull** Jun. Originally granted 31 Aug 1774, by **George III**. Witness Issachar **Willcock**, Mary **Porcher**. Signed William **Sanders**, Ann **Sanders**. Witness oath by Issachar **Wilcocks** [sic] [No signature.] 22 Oct 1774 to Richard **Lembton** J.P. Berkley Co. Grant reserves to **George III** all white pine Trees and 1/10 of Mines of Gold and Silver. On 25 Mar in every year, pay 3sh Sterg. or 4sh proclamation money, for every hundred acres, to commence after two years. Also to clear and cultivate 3 acres each year for every hundred. Signed William **Bull** by Thos. **Winstanley** Prob.C. Memorial entered in Aud. Genl. Office in Book M, No.13, page 350, 23 Feb 1775. Rec. 30 July 1795. [Includes plat.]

Page 6-7 Lease & Release, 10 Dec 1793, John **Simpson** Mercht. (Laurens Co.) to Alexr. **Simpson** Sen. planter (same), for £70 9sh 4d Sterling sold a certain Tract of Land containing 302 acres, being part of 350 acres granted on or about 18 May 1771 by William **Bull** Esq. unto Charles **Harvey** Carpenter now of Laurens Co., in sd. Co. on a small branch of Little River. Bounded

N.E. on John **Miligan**, N.W. by William **McTeer** & lands laid off to Thos. **Davison**. Transferred by sd. **Harvey** by Lease and Release 22 June 1772 unto Jacob **Jones** & by him unto Henery [sic] and Rowland **Rugeley** 22 Feb 1773, and by James **Mayson** Atty. for Henry **Rugely** [sic], surviving partner of Henry & Rowland **Rugely** [sic], unto John **Simpson** Mercht. 13 July 1793. Witness Andrew **Smyth** Jun., David **Speers**, John **Wilson**. Signed John **Simpson**. Witness oath by David **Speers** 30 Jan 1794 to William **Hunter** J.P. Laurens Co. Rec. 25 Aug 1795.

Page 8-9 1 Aug 1795, Hannah **Jones** widow of John **Jones** dec. and William **Jones** her Son and Mary his wife (Laurens Co.) to John **Craig** (same), for £17 10sh Sterling sold all that Tract of Land containing 50 acres more or less, in sd. Co. on Duncans Creek, being part of 200 acres granted to James **Adair** Sen. 11 Aug 1774, recorded in Secretary's Office in Book RRR, page 597, and by sd. James **Adair** & Eleanor his wife 25 Feb 1784, conveyed unto sd. John **Jones** 150 acres of aforesd. 200 acres. Bordering on John **McCreary's** Spring Branch, W on John **Adair**, N on Vacant Land, N.E. on James **Montgomery**, S.E. on John **McCreary**. Sd. 50 acres lying on N side of tract aforesd. on Montgomery's Branch. Witness John **Robertson**, Alexr. **Fillson**, John **Owens**. Signed Hannah (x) **Jones**, William **Jones**, Mary (x) **Jones**. Witness oath by Alexander **Fillson** 3 Aug 1795 to Roger **Brown** J.P. Laurens Co. Rec. 0 Aug 1795 [sic].

Page 9-10 1 Aug 1795, Hannah **Jones** widow of John **Jones** dec. and William **Jones** her son and Mary his wife (Laurens Co.) to Alexr. **Fillson** (same), for £17 10sh sterling sold all that Tract of Land containing 100 acres more or less, in sd. Co. on Duncans creek, being part of a Tract granted to James **Adair** Sen. 11 Aug 1774, recorded in Secretary's' Office, in Book RRR, page 597, and sd. James **Adair** & Eleanor did on 25 Feb 1784 convey to John **Jones** 150 acres of aforesd. 200 acres. Bounding on John **McCreary's** spring branch, W on John **Adair**, N on vacant Land, N.E. on James **Montgomery**, S.E. on John **McCreary**. Witness John **Robinson**, John **Craig**, John **Owens**. Signed Hannah (x) **Jones**, William **Jones**, Mary (x) **Jones**. Witness oath by John **Craig** 3 Aug 1795 to Roger **Brown** J.P. Laurens Co. Rec. 13 Aug 1795.

Page 10-12 Lease & Release, 24 & 25 Feb 1784, James **Adair** Sen. cooper and Eleanor his wife (Ninety six Dist.) to John **Jones** blacksmith (same), for £200 Sterling sold a Tract of land containing 150 acres more or less, being part of 200 acres in Craven Co., on Duncans Creek, between Broad and Saluda Rivers. Bounding on John **McCreary's** spring branch, W & S on John **Adair**, N.E. James **Montgomery**, S.E. on John **McCreary**. Survey certified 3 June 1773, and granted 11 Aug 1774, a Memorial entered in Auditor's Office in Book M, No.13, page 230, 7 Jan 1775. Witness James **Adair** Saddler, James **Adair** Jun., James **Miller**. Signed James (J) **Adair**, Eleanor (x) **Adair**. Witness oath by James **Adair** sadler 3 Aug 1795 to Roger **Brown** J.P. Laurens Co. Rec. 14 Aug 1795.

Page 12-13 9 Apr 1794, Whereas James **Sullivant** by his Bond in 1794 for £960 8sh 10p Sterling unto Thomas **Wadsworth** & William **Turpin** (S.C.), payable on or before 10 Nov 1799. For the better securing the debt and 7% per annum, sold 12 [sic] Negro Slaves, Jane, Ned, Lewis, Lid, Peter, Andrew, Lucy, Bartley, Tom, Primus, Isaac, all Country Born; one Stud horse; 6 head of other Horse beasts; 4 feather Beds & furniture; 16 head of Cattle; 14 head of Sheep; 80 head of Swine; all my working tools; all my household and kitchen furniture; Corn, Wheat & Tobacco from time to time that is made on any of my land. Provided that if the sum is paid, then these presents shall be void. Witness Eze. S. **Roland**, James **Young**. Signed James (J) **Sullivan** [sic]. Witness oath by James **Young** 5 Aug 1795 to John **Hunter** [No title.] Rec. 25 Aug 1795.

Page 13 1 Aug 1795, Whereas John **Martin** (Laurens Co.) by his note 1 Aug 1795 for £7 13/3 to be paid to James **Sullivan** (same), on or before 1 Oct next. For the better securing the payment, sold all my crop of Corn where I now live and all my hogs and a certain colt called Piram. Provided that if the sum is paid, then this note shall be void. Witness Eze. S. **Roland**, Aaron **Casey**. Signed John **Martin**. Witness oath by Ezekiel S. **Roland** 8 Oct 1795 to Jno. **Cochran** [No title.] Laurens Co. Rec. 9 Oct 1795.

Page 13-14 27 Jan 1795, Nicholas **Davis** (Laurens Co.) to Valentine **Nix** (Newberry Co.), for £75 sold a tract supposed to contain 129 acres, being granted 5 June 1786 by William **Moultrie** Esq. Gov. unto Chas. **Finley**, 400 acres on Durbin Creek, waters of Enoree River, recorded in Secretary's office in Book SSSS, page 105. Conveyed by Benj. **Raney** to William **Jackson**, late of sd. Co., then sold by Exctn. at instance of William **Shaw** 10 Apr 1788, and then struck off to Benj. **Raney**, then conveyed from him to William **Manly**, and from him to Nicholas **Davis**. Sd. tract being on S side of North fork of Durbins Creek. Bounding sd. Creek, Wm.. **Young**, John **Williams**, Joseph **Barton**. Conveyance made by David **Anderson** Sheriff of sd. Co. 12 Mar 1789. Witness Wm. **Birdsong**, Thos. (x) **Nix**. Signed Nicholas (x) **Davis**. Witness oath by Thos. (x) **Nix** 6 Jun 1795 to Danl. **Wright** J.P. Laurens Co. Rec. 12 Aug 1795.

Page 14-15 1 Mar 1795, Nathan **Austin** (Pendleton Co.) to John **Henderson** (Laurens Co.), for £50 Sterling sold a Tract of Land containing 100 acres more or less, originally granted to Duke **Pinson** by William **Bull** Esq. and conveyed to David **Morgan**, and conveyed by him to Nathan **Austin**. Lying on waters of Reedy River in Laurens Co.. Grant recorded in Book OOO, page 398. Bounding Reedy River, S.W. on John **Reed**, S.E. Joshua **Saxon**, John **Moore**. Witness Wm. **Henderson**, Saml. **Burton**. Signed Nathan **Austin**. Witness oath by Wm. (W) **Henderson** 18 July 1795 to Wm. **Hunter** J.P. Laurens Co. Rec. 22 July 1795.

Page 15 18 Apr 1792, Langston **Drew**, son and Heir of William **Drew** dec. (Laurens Co.) and Nancy his wife to Jeremiah **Glenn** (same), for £50 sold one certain Tract of Land in sd. Co. on N side of Beaverdam Creek, a branch of

Little River, containing 102 acres, part of two Grants, one granted unto Wm. **Drew** dec. and the other granted unto David **Craddock**, and by him conveyed unto Wm. **Drew** dec., which by the testimony of Danl. **Osbourn** and Saml. **Powel**, and bounded on sd. **Glenn**, Beaverdam creek, Andw. **Rodgers**. Witness Silvs. **Walker** Sen., John **Rodgers**, Tyree **Glenn**. Signed Langston **Drew**, Nancy (x) **Drew**. Witness oath by Silvs. **Walker** 17 July 1792 to Chas. **Saxon** J.P. Laurens Co. Rec. 28 May 1795.

Page 16   18 Mar 1795, Thos. **Roberts** (Laurens Co.) to Revd. Robert **McClintock** (same), for £15 Ster. sold a certain Tract of Land on S side of North fork of Bush River, in sd. Co., containing 66 acres more or less. Witness Jas. **Young**, James **Boyce**. Signed Thomas **Roberts**. Witness oath by James **Young** 7 Aug 1795 to Thomas **Wadsworth** J.L.C. Rec. 25 Aug 1795.

Page 16-17   6 Feb 1795, John **Smith** (Fairfield Co.) to Robert **Hutcheson** planter (Laurens Co.), for £30 Sterling sold all that Tract of Land containing 100 acres, granted to sd. **Smith** in 1773, recorded in Secretary's office in Book NNN, page 436. Lying on a branch of Duncans Creek in Laurens Co. Bounded N.E. by land laid out to William **Raily**. Witness Robt. **McClintock**, H. **Milling**. Signed John **Smith**. Witness oath by Rev. Robert **McClintock** 21 Aug 1795 to John **Hunter** [No title.]. Rec. 25 Aug 1795.

Page 17-18   19 June 1794, Elizabeth Jane **Ravenel** widow of Daniel **Ravenel** dec. and qualified Exrx to his last Will and Testament, to Samuel **Henderson** (Laurens Co.), for £32 Sterling sold all that Tract of Land containing 400 acres more or less, and numbered No.17. Bounding: S & E on part of original Survey, now divided into Tracts & Numbered 11, 12 & 13, W on Samuel **Henderson**, N by William **East**. Survey by John **Diamond** Surv. Nov 1791. Part of 3,000 acres more or less, granted to Danl. **Ravenel** Esq. 30 Oct 1772, situate on waters of Bush River in Ninety Six Dist.. Sd. Danl. **Ravenel** died possessed of same and by his last Will & Testament did order that the Tract should be sold for certain purposes therein by his Widow; all other Exors. mentioned in sd. Will are now dead. Witness Peter **Porcher** Jun., Willm. **Turpin**. Signed Elizabeth Jane **Ravenel**. Witness oath by William **Turpin** 19 June 1794 to Danl. **Stevens** Q.U. Rec. 14 Sept 1795. [Includes plat.]

Page 18-19   9 Mar 1791, Jonathan **Hollingsworth** (Laurens Co.) blacksmith to David **Hollingsworth** (same), for £30 Sterling sold all that Tract of Land containing 100 acres more or less, in sd. Co. on waters Mudlick Creek, being part of a tract granted to John **Thornton**, containing 350 acres, by William **Bull** esq. 14 July 1774, and conveyed by sd. **Thornton** to Wm. **ONeal** by lease and release, and by Exor. of sd. **ONeal** dec. to sd. Joh. **Hollingsworth**. Bounding N.W. & N.E. on part of original Survey, S.E. on John **Cook**, S.W. on Liberty Springs. Witness Robt. **Hollingsworth**, Isaac **Hollingsworth**, Abram **Hollingsworth**. Signed Jonathan **Hollingsworth**. Witness oath by Robert **Hollingsworth** 9 Mar 1791 to William **Caldwell** J.P. Laurens Co. Plat certified 30 Aug 1789 by William **Caldwell** D.S. Rec. 17 July 1795. [Includes plat.]

Page 19-20 24 Sept 1794, Jonathan **Hollingsworth** (Laurens Co.) Blacksmith to David **Hollingsworth** (same), for £30 Sterling sold one Tract of land in sd. Co. on waters of Mudlick, containing 100 acres, being part of land granted to John **Thornton** by William **Bull** esq., and by Sundry conveyances became the property of sd. Jonathan **Hollingsworth**. Bounding Liberty Spring, David **Hollingsworth**, John **Hollingsworth**, Jno. **Williams**. Reserving to myself that part of sd. Tract that lies on N side of **Good's** Road, as it now runs to be the line, containing by estimation 12 acres more or less. Witness Simpson **Warrin**, Joseph **Hollingsworth**. Signed Jon. **Hollingsworth**. Witness oath by Simpson **Warrin** 9 Oct 1794 to Angus **Campbell** J.P. Laurens Co. Rec. 17 July 1795. [Includes plat.]

Page 20-21 17 July 1795, Jamima **Hollingsworth** & Hannah **Hollingsworth** spinsters (Laurens Co.) to George **Hollingsworth** planter (same), for £50 Sterling sold 200 acres in sd. Co., waters of Mudlick, bounding S.E. on Joseph **Atkins**, all other sides on vacant land. Granted 23 Dec 1771 by Lord Chas. Greville **Montague** Gov. unto William **ONeal**. Recorded in Secretary's office in Book KKK, page 259. Witness David **Hollingsworth**, Simpson **Warrin**, Joseph **Hollingsworth**. Signed Jamima **Hollingsworth**, Hannah (x) **Hollingsworth**. Witness oath by David **Hollingsworth** [No signature.] 17 July 1795 to Angus **Campbell** J.P. Laurens Co. Rec. 17 July 1795.

Page 21 1795, John **Jones** (Pendleton Co.) to John **Pyles** (Laurens Co.), for value recd. sold a certain Tract of land Surveyed for Lewis **Saxon**, on Beaverdam, on a branch of Reedy River, in Laurens Co., containing 50 acres more or less. Bounding Reuben **Pyles**, Patrick **Ryley**, Eliz. **McDowell**, John **Taylor**, Beaver Dam Creek. Witness Reuben **Pyles**, Anthony **Ginings**. Signed John (J) **Jones**. Payment receive 14 Mar 1795. Witness oath by Anthony **Jennings** [sic] [No date.] to Reuben **Pyles** J.P. Rec. 28 May 1795.

Page 21-22 4 Oct 1792, Jacob **Gibson** (Laurens Co.) to William **Moore** (same), for £40 sold one certain Tract of Land on W side of Reaburns Creek, containing 100 acres more or less, bonding N.E. on John Ewing **Calhoun**, S.W. on William **McPherson**. Witness John **Moore**, Jno. **Henderson**, Hugh **Henderson**. Signed Jacob **Gibson**. Witness oath by John **Henderson** 10 Mar 1794 to Geo. **Anderson** J.P. Laurens Co. Rec. 28 May 1795.

Page 22 (Pendleton Co.) 6 Aug 1792, John **Gocher** (Pendleton Co.) to Jacob **Gibson** (Laurens Co.), for £30 sold one certain Tract of land on N side of Reedy River, containing 200 acres more or less, being granted by Wm. **Moultrie** esq. Gov. to John **Gocher**. Bounding N.E. on Robt. **Box** dec. and joining land with John Ewing **Calhoun**. Being land formerly titled from sd. **Gocher** to sd. **Gibson** and agreeable to the old lines. Witness Wm. **Wright**, John **Dunklin**, Wm. (M) **McPherson**. Signed John (x) **Gotcher** [sic]. Witness oath by Jno. **Dunklin** 10 Mar 1794 to Geo. **Anderson** J.P. Laurens Co. Rec. 31 May 1795.

Page 22-23   20 Mar 1793, David **Gibson** (Laurens Co.) to Peter **Hammond** (same), for £5 sold a certain Tract of land containing 50 acres more or less, in sd. Co. on Beaverdam creek, waters of Enoree River. Border: sd. **Hammond**, near fence, near North fork of sd. Beaver dam creek, near road. Witness Henry **Jones**, John (J) **Young**. Signed David (x) **Gibson**. Witness oath by John (J) **Young** 17 July 1793 to Danl. **Wright** J.P. Laurens Co. Rec. 19 Aug 1795.

Page 23   2 Jan 1792, William **Hamby** and Jamima **Hamby** (Greenville Co., Washington Dist.) to Peter **Hammond** (Laurens Co.), for £80 Sterlg. sold all that certain tract of land in Laurens Co. on Beaverdam creek, waters of Enoree River, containing 100 acres more or less, originally granted unto Saml. **Hamby** by William **Bull** esq. 18 May 1773. Also a Tract on sd. Beaverdam creek, and joining above mentioned Survey containing 100 acres more or less, signed by Chas. G. **Montague** 7 Feb 1773. Witness Fedderick **Craft**, Walter **Austin**. Signed William (x) **Hamby**, Jamima (x) **Hamby**. Witness oath by Frederick **Croft** [sic] 13 Jan 1792 to James **Harrison** J.P. Greenville Co. Rec. 19 Aug 1795.

Page 23-24   30 May 1795, Danl. **Williams** Sen. (Ninety Six Dist.) for £168 Sterling paid by Saml. **Williams**, sell four Negroes, Phill, a man of 45 years age; Franky, a woman of about 50 years; Ruth, a woman of about 20 years; Granville, a boy of about 3 years; also one bay mare; one sorrel gelding; one bay colt. Witness William **Neely**, William **Golding**. Signed Daniel **Williams** Sen. Acknowledged before R. **Brown** J.N.C. Witness oath by William **Neely** 2 June 1795 to Thomas **Wadsworth** J.L.C. Rec. 21 July 1795.

Page 24   30 May 1795, Daniel **Williams** Sen. (Ninety Six Dist.) for £434 Sterling paid by Elizabeth **Williams** & Ursla **Williams**, sell 15 Negro Slaves, Jack, a man of about 52 years; Jacob, a man about 21 years old; Rose, a woman about 52 years old; Salt, a woman of about 14 years; Aaron, a boy of about 7 years; John, a boy of about [blank] years; James, a boy of about 6 years; Winney, a girl of about 5 years; Virgin, a female child of about 3 months; Easter, a woman of about 17 years; Ben, a boy of about 1 year; Sukky, a woman of 15 years; Aggy, a woman of about 45 years; Philo, a boy of about 6 years; Joham, a boy of about 1 year. Witness Wm. **Neely**, William **Golding**. Signed Danl. **Williams** Sn. Acknowledged before R. **Brown** J.N.C. Witness oath by William **Neely** 2 June 1795 to Thomas **Wadsworth** J.L.C. Rec. 21 July 1795.

Page 24   30 May 1795, Daniel **Williams** Sen. (Ninety Six Dist.) for £289 10sh Sterling paid by Danl. **Williams** Jun., sell six negro slaves, Peter, a man about 55 years of age; Isabella, a woman about 21 years old; Edom, a boy about 8 years of age; Solomon, a boy about 3 years old; Collin, a man child about 3 months of age; William about 40 years of age; also one bay Gelding, one brown bay mare; two roan Geldings; one Book case. Witness William **Neely**, William **Golding**. Signed Danl. **Williams** Sn. Acknowledged before R. **Brown** J.N.C. Witness oath by William **Neely** 2 June 1795 to Thomas **Wadsworth** J.L.C. Rec. 21 July 1795.

Page 24-25 13 Mar 1794, James **Puckett** (Laurens Co.) for £30 paid by John **Templeton** (same), sold a certain Tract of Land containing 100 acres in sd. Co. on a branch of Enoree, originally granted to John **McUlure** [sic], bounded W by Edd. **Musgrove**, S by John **Hanna**, N by Alexr. **George**, E by sd. **Hanna**. I am possessed of the same as an absolute Estate of inheritance. Witness Joseph **Hanna**, Alexr. **George**. Signed James **Puckett**. Witness oath by Joseph **Hanna** 15 Nov 1794 to Roger **Brown** [No title.]. Rec. 22 Oct 1795.

Page 25 6 Mar 1794, Robert **Rutherford** (Newberry Co.) Esq. to William **Shaw** (Abbeville Co.) Attorney at Law, for £50 sold all that Tract of land containing 164 acres more or less, on Harolds creek, a branch of Enoree River, in Laurens Co. Bounding N.W. on lands laid out to John **Coulter**, S.E. on lands laid out to Wm. **Layson**, all other sides on unknown or vacant lands at time of original Survey. Granted to Matthew **McCreary**, and by him conveyed to Robert Henry **Hughs**, formerly of sd. Co., and afterwards sold by virtue of a writ out of the Laurens Co. Court, by David **Anderson** esq. (Shff. of sd. Co.) to Robt. **Rutherford**. Witness Joseph **Goodman**, J. **Dunlap**, Fred. **Nance** [sic] J.P. Signed Robt. **Rutherford**. Witness oath by John **Dunlap** [No signature.] 29 July 1795 to Frederick **Nanance** Esq. Clerk of Newberry Co. Court. Rec. 22 Sept 1795.

Page 26-27 Lease & Release, 17 July 1795, Abner **Babb** and Martha his wife (Laurens Co.) planter to Robert **Pasley** (same), for £145 Sterling sold all that Tract of land containing 200 acres more or less, in sd. Co. on Beaverdam, water of Little River, bounding Andrew **Rogers**, creek, Joseph **Babb**. Being part of two Tracts, one of 250 acres originally granted to Joseph **Babb** dec. 24 Nov 1767, the other containing 150 acres originally granted to Wm. **Wright** 14 June 1771, and by him conveyed to Joseph **Babb** dec. by lease & release 31 May and 1 June 1772, and by sd. Abner **Babb**, oldest son and heir of sd. Joseph, to sd. Robt. **Pasley**. Witness A. **Rodgers** Jun., Wm. A. **Rodgers**. Signed Abner **Babb**, Martha (x) **Babb**. Witness oath by Andw. **Rodgers** Jun. 17 July 1795 to John **Davis** J.P. Laurens Co. Rec. 22 July 1795.

Page 27-28 24 June 1795, William **McPherson** (Laurens Co.) planter by his bond dated 24 June 1795, stands bound unto Thomas **Wadsworth** and William **Turpin**, otherwise **Wadsworth** & **Turpin** (S.C.) Merchants, for £22 6sh 8-1/2p Sterling, conditioned for payment of £11 3sh 4p 1f Sterling. For the better securing payment sell all that tract of land containing 100 acres more or less, in sd. Co. on waters of Reedy River, being the lower part of a Tract granted to John **Gocher** containing 200 acres, including the plantation whereon Jacob **Gibson** lived, joining John **Box** & John **Lewis**. Provided that if the sum is paid, then this Indenture shall be void. Witness Jas. **Young**, James **Boyce**. Signed William (m) **McPherson**. Witness oath by James **Young** 5 Aug 1795 to John **Hunter** [No title.]. Rec. 22 Sept 1795.

Page 28 9 Jan 1795, William **Arnold** Jun. (Laurens Co.) planter for £80 Sterling paid by Thomas **Wadsworth** & William **Turpin**, otherwise

Wadsworth & Turpin, sold one negro woman, Hannah & her child, Tom, 2 years old; one black mare, 5 years old next spring; one sorrel Colt; three cows; three yearlings; eleven head of Hogs, marked with a crop and slit in right ear and slit in left ear; two feather beds & furniture; two pots; one dutch oven; two black walnut Tables; one doz. Pewter plates; two dishes; one bason; & all my household furniture; one weavers loom; five axes; one mattock; one Bar-share plough; one Shovel plough; & all the corn I have and the barley I have now growing. Provided that if the sum is paid on 1 Dec next, then this Bill of Sale shall be void. Witness James **Young**, James **Boyce**. Signed William (x) **Arnold** Jun. Witness oath by James **Young** 5 Aug 1795 to Jno. **Hunter** [No title.]. Rec. 22 Sept 1795.

Page 29   13 Nov 1794, John **Powell** & James **Powell** (Laurens Co.) planters for £24 Sterling paid by Thomas **Wadsworth** & William **Turpin**, otherwise **Wadsworth** & **Turpin** (S.C.) Merchants, sold one sorrel mare 7 years old, branded on near buttock C, with a Star in her forehead, about 14 hands high with her horse colt; three cows, one yearling marked with crop and slit in left ear and swallow fork under keel in right ear; ten head of Hogs with the same mark of Cattle; four feather beds & furniture; two pots; one dutch oven; six pewter plates; three basons; one large dish. Witness James **Young**, James **Boyce**. Signed John **Powell**, James **Powell**. Witness oath by James **Young** 14 Aug 1795 to John **Hunter** [No title.]. Rec. 22 Sept 1795.

Page 29   4 July 1794, Larkin **Sullivant** (Laurens Co.) for £16 14sh Sterling paid by Thomas **Wadsworth** & William **Turpin**, otherwise **Wadsworth** & **Turpin** (S.C.) Merchants, sold one Sorrel mare about 10 years old, no brands perceivable; two cows and calves, one cow red & other dun; two Sows & four pigs & nine shoats; six head of sheep; one feather bed & all my household furniture & plantation Tools; and all the crop that I have growing on my plantation where I now live. Witness James **Young**, James **Boyce**. Signed Larkin **Sullivant**. Witness oath by   James **Young** 14 Aug 1795 to John **Hunter** [No title.]. Rec. 22 Sept 1795.

Page 29-30   11 Oct 1794, William **Norris** and Anna his wife (Laurens Co.) planter to Rodger **Murphy** Sen. (same) planter, for £7 10sh sold all that tract of 100 acres more or less, in sd. Co., being part of Land granted to James **Box** by Wm. **Moultrie** esq. Lieut. Gov. 4 Feb 1793. Bounded: Ditany hill, John **Osbourn**, Long lick creek. Being the west end of the 382 Acres granted to James **Box**. Witness Wm. (x) **Camon**, Isaac (B) **Bailey**, Wm. **Sims**. Signed William (x) **Norris**, Anna (a) **Norris**. Witness oath by William (x) **Camon** 31 Dec 1794 to Thomas **Wadsworth** J.L.C. Rec. 10 Aug 1795.

Page 30-31   30 Jan 1795, Thomas **Holden** (Laurens Co.) & Margaret his wife to John **Cain** (Union Co.), for £100 Sterling sold a tract of 150 acres more or less, in sd. Co. on S side of Enoree river, being part of 300 acres which was granted to James **Steen** 3 Mar 1767. Bounding: widow **Lindsay**, Enoree River, waggon road. Also all that part between the waggon road & river of a tract of 162 acres, adjoining the tract above, granted unto sd. John **Lindsay** 5 June

1786. Also part of two tracts containing in the whole 155 acres more or less, adjoining the Tracts above and conveyed to John **Lindsey** [sic] by Bartlett **Brown** 7 Jan 1779. Also 15 acres, being part of a Tract granted to William **Cannon**, containing 150 acres, and conveyed by Henry **Hamilton** to sd. John **Lindsay**. Also one Tract of 40 acres more or less, being part of 600 acres and conveyed by Benjamin **Brown**, lawful heir to Bartlett **Brown**, 14 Oct 1785, unto sd. John **Lindsey**. The three last tracts being bounded by sd. John **Lindsey's** survey as far as the Waggon road, James **Oliphant**, **Hanna's** path, Enoree River. The river bank being the dividing line between John **Lindsey** & Abraham **Gray**. Being computed in the whole to be 500 acres more or less. Witness Stacey **Cooper**, John **Holden**, John **Pearson**. Signed Thos. **Holden**, Margaret **Holden**. Witness oath by Stacey **Cooper** 12 Sept 1795 to Hudson **Berry** J.P. Laurens Co. Rec. 18 Oct 1795.

Page 31-32 12 Sept 1795, Thomas **Gitzendanner** (Union Co.) to John **Cain** (same), for £130 Sterling sold a Tract of land containing 200 acres more or less, being part of two surveys, the one granted to John **Gray** 15 May 1772. The other granted to Geo. **Bush** 5 May 1786. Sd. Tract of 200 acres was conveyed by George **Bush** unto Jesse **Brooks** 2 May 1794. Situate in Laurens Co. in fork of Duncans Creek. Border: head of a branch. Above 200 acres conveyed to Thos. **Gitzendanner** by Jesse **Brooks** 20 July 1795. Witness Stacey **Cooper**, Sarah (x) **Berry**. Signed Thomas **Gitzendanner**. Witness oath by Stacey **Cooper** 12 Sept 1795 to Hudson **Berry** J.P. Laurens Co. Rec. 18 Oct 1795.

Page 32-33 12 Sept 1795, John **Cain** (Union Co.) for £160 Sterling paid by Thos. **Gitzendanner**, sold part of a Tract of 150 acres on S side of Enoree River in Laurens Co., being part of 300 acres granted to James **Steen** 3 Mar 1767. Bounds of 150 acres on widow **Lindsey**, Enoree river, Waggon road. For 100 acres more or less, also all that part between the Waggon road & river of a Tract of 162 acres, adjoining the Tract above mentioned, which was granted unto John **Lindsey** 5 Jun 1786. Also part of two Tracts containing in the whole 150 acres, adjoining the above & conveyed to John **Lindsey** by Bartlett **Brown** 7 Jan 1779, sd. Tract being 155 acres more or less. Also 15 acres, being part of 150 acres granted to Wm. **Cannon** & conveyed by Henry **Hamilton** to sd. John **Lindsey**. Also 40 acres more or less, being part of 600 acres, and conveyed unto sd. John **Lindsey** by Benjamin **Brown**, lawful heir to Bartlett **Brown** 14 Oct 1785. The three last mentioned Tracts being bounded by sd. John **Lindsey's** survey, Waggon road, James **Oliphant**, **Hanna's** path, Enoree river, Abraham **Gray**, being computed in the whole to be 500 acres more or less & was conveyed by John **Lindsey** to Thos. **Holden**, who conveyed same unto sd. John **Cain** 30 Jan 1795. Witness Stacey **Cooper**, Sarah (x) **Berry**. Signed John **Cain**. Witness oath by Stacey **Cooper** 12 Sept 1795 to Hudson **Berry** J.P. Laurens Co. Rec. 18 Oct 1795.

Page 33 20 July 1795, Jesse **Brooks** (Laurens Co.) to Thomas **Gitzendanner** (Union Co.), for £130 Sterling sold a Tract of Land containing 200 acres more or less, being part of two Surveys, the one granted to John **Gray** by Chas.

Montague 15 May 1772, recorded in Book LLL, page 32, entered in Auditors Office in Book 1, No.11, page 284. The other granted to Geo. **Bush** by William **Moultrie** 5 June 1786, recorded in Book SSSS, page 41. Situate in Laurens Co. in fork of Duncan's Creek. Border: head of a branch. Witness William **Bush**, Levina **Brooks**. Signed Jesse **Brooks**, Ann (x) **Brooks**. Oath by George **Bush** 10 Sept 1795 that he saw Jesse **Brooks** with Ann his wife, sign the within Deed. Given before George **Whitmore** J.P. Laurens Co. Rec. 18 Oct 1795.

Page 33 21 Oct 1795, William **Burris** (Laurens Co.) appoint David **Burris** my Attorney to recover & Receive all sums owing unto me. Witness Wm. P. **Culbertson**, Wm. **Donohow**. Signed William (W) **Burris**. Witness oath by Wm. P. **Culbertson** 21 Oct 1795 to Jno. **Cochran** D.C. Laurens Co. Rec. 22 Oct 1795.

Page 34 27 Dec 1794, Stephen **Roach** & Rebeckah his wife & William **Corsly** & Grace his wife (Pendleton Co.) to Moses **Sanders** (same), for £120 Sterling sold a Tract of land containing 250 acres more or less, in Laurens Co., originally granted to Thomas **Carter** on Beaverdam branch, bounding S.E. on land laid out to Henry **ONeal**, N.W. on lands laid out to Henry Stone **Parish**, all other sides on Vacant land. Granted 21 Dec 1772, made over by Thos. **Carter** to John **ONeal** by Lease & Release 2 Dec 1773, recorded in Secretary's Office in Book NNN, page 338. Witness Stephen (x) **Harris**, Moses **Sanders** Jun., Wm. **Land**. Signed Stephen (x) **Roach**, Rebeckah (x) **Roach**, Wm. **Crosby** [sic], Grace (m) **Crosby** [sic]. Witness oath by Moses **Sanders** Jun. 17 Sept 1795 to Thomas **Wadsworth** J. L.C. Rec. 25 Sept 1795.

Page 34-35 9 May 1795, James Atwood **Williams** & Mary his wife (Laurens Co.) to Anthony **Golding** (same), for £200 Sterling sold all that Tract of Land containing 214 acres in sd. Co. on Mudlick creek, bounding: mouth of Shoal House Branch, Jacob **Gray**, mudlick creek. Being part of two Tracts laid out to Jacob **Gray** & one to Nathan **Moats**, and conveyed to John **Williams** L.D. dec. 28 Mar 1795. Bounded by Sarah **Neely**, Estate of James **Williams**, Archd. **Sawyer**, Danl. **McGuinn**, Jas. Atd. **Williams**. Witness J. R. **Brown**, Wm. **Fulton**, Danl. (x) **McGinn** [sic]. Signed James Atd. **Williams**, Mary **Williams**. Witness oath by Daniel (x) **McGinn** 23 May [1795] to Thomas **Wadsworth** J.L.C. Rec. 22 Aug 1795.

Page 35-36 28 Mar 1795, William **Caldwell** (Newberry Co.), Joseph **Williams** (Edgefield Co.) exors. of Estate of John **Williams** L.D. (Edgefield Co.) dec. to James Atwood **Williams** (Laurens Co.), for £190 sold all that certain Tract of land containing 214 acres in Laurens Co. on Mudlick Creek, bounding: mouth of School house branch, Jacob **Gray**, Mudlick creek. Being part of two Tracts laid out to Jacob **Gray** & one laid out to Matthew **Mottes**, & sd. 214 acres bounded James Atwood **Williams**, Danl. **McGinn**, Archd. **Sawyer**, Sarah **Neely**. Witness Danl. **Williams** Jun., Abel **Pearson**, Elizabeth Ann **Caldwell**. Signed William **Caldwell**, Joseph **Williams**. Witness oath by

Danl. **Williams** Jun. [No date.] to Thomas **Wadsworth** J.L.C. Rec. 22 Oct 1795. [Includes plat.]

Page 36-37 2 Dec 1773, Thomas **Carter** (Craven Co.) planter with Mary his wife to John **ONeal**, brother to Wm. (same), for £400 current money sold all that certain Tract of land containing 250 acres in Berkley Co. on Beaverdam branch, bounding S.E. on land laid out to Henry **ONeal**, N.W. on land laid out to Henry Stone **Parish**, all other sides by vacant land. Granted 24 Dec 1772. Witness Anthony **Griffin**, Mary **ONeal**. Signed Thomas **Carter**, Mary (x) **Carter**. Witness oath by Mary **ONeal** 1 Jan 1794 to Elisha **Ford** J.P. Newberry Co. Rec. 15 Oct 1795.

Page 37 20 July 1791, Moses **Sullivant** (Greenville Co.) to Jeremiah **Glenn** (Virginia), for £150 Virginia money sold a certain Tract of land containing 150 acres more or less, in Laurens Co. on waters of Beaverdam Creek, bounding S & W on Joseph **Babb**, N on David **Cradock**, E on Wm. **Drew**. Originally granted by James **Glenn** Esq. Gov. to Christopher **Plens** 3 June 1755. Witness Tyree **Glenn**, Hewlet **Sullivant**, Chas. **Sullivant**. Signed Moses (M) **Sullivant**, Milly (x) **Sullivant**. Witness oath by Tyree **Glenn** 18 Jan 1792 to Thos. **Wadsworth** J.L.C. Rec. 15 Oct 1795.

Page 37-38 6 Mar 1795, Gassaway **Rodgers** (Laurens Co.) & Margaret his wife to Wm. **Patridge**, Joel **Whitten**, Joseph **Whitmore**, Thomas **Duncan**, Danl. **Young**, Henry **Hill**, Joseph **Jones**, John **Robertson** & John **Whitten**, Trustees appointed by Methodist Episcopal Church, for 10sh sell a Lot of 3 acres of Land, being part of 180 acres in sd. Co. on a small branch of Enoree River, granted to sd. Gassaway **Rogers** [sic]. Witness Geo. **Whitmore** J.P., Jacob Ducket **Masters**, Henry **Davis**. Signed Gassaway **Rogers**, Margaret **Rogers**. [No witness oath.] Rec. 24 July 1795.

Page 38 8 July 1794, George **Whitmore** & Martha his wife (Laurens Co.) to William **Partridge** (same), for £5 Sterling sold 62 acres more or less, of a certain Tract of land in the fork between Broad & Saluda Rivers, upon two small Drafts of Duncans Creek, waters of Enoree River. Border: Henry **Davis**, land surveyed for Andw. **McCreary**, sd. **Whitmore**. Being half of 124 acres survey. Granted unto sd. **Whitmore** 6 Aug 1792 by Charles **Pinckney** Esq. Gov. & recorded in Secretary's Office in Grant Book F, No.5, page 113. Witness Henry **Davis**, Odell (O) **Garret**. Signed George **Whitmore**, Martha (x) **Whitmore**. Witness oath by Henry **Davis** 20 July 1794 to James **Dillard** J.P. Laurens Co. Rec. 24 July 1795.

Page 38-39 18 July 1795, John Prather **Odell** (Laurens Co.) and his wife Mary **Odell** to Wm. **Liles** (same), for £40 Sterling sold a Tract of land containing & laid out for 81 acres, being part of 120 acres on branches of Duncans creek, in sd. Co. Originally granted to sd. John Prather **Odell** 3 Mar 1788, recorded in Grant Book 8888, page 416. Bound: E on James **Duncan**, N.E. by other part of sd. Tract, all other sides by vacant land. Witness Wm. **Prather**, Alexr. **Abram**, Arthur **McCrokin**. Signed John Prather **Odell** (x), Mary Prather (x)

Odell [sic]. Witness oath by Arthur **McCrokin** 18 July 1795 to Willm. **Turpin** J.Q. Rec. 24 July 1795.

Page 39 29 Dec 1794, James **Odell** Admr. & Eleanor **Odell** Admx. of the Estate of John **Odell**, late of Newberry Co. dec., in compliance with the will of sd. decd. give to Joel & Sarah **Whitten** (she being the daughter of sd. John **Odell** dec. and one of his heirs at Law), a Tract of 66 acres of Land in Laurens Co., adjoining land laid out to sd. Joel **Whitten**, being part of 500 acres granted to sd. John **Odell** 1 Aug 1785. Witness Henry **Davis**, Rignal **Odell**, Abel **Pearson**. Signed James **Odell**, Eleanor (x) **Odell**. Witness oath by Henry **Davis** 29 Dec 1794 to Levi **Casey** J. Newberry Co. Rec. 22 July 1795.

Page 39-40 4 Apr 1795, Joseph **Mahon** (Laurens Co.) for the natural love & affection I bear unto my Son Bailey **Mahon** (same), give all my Goods, chattels, leases, lands and debts & all other substance. Witness Saml. **Shaw**, Nelly (x) **Mahon**. Signed Joseph **Mahon**. Memorandum of Particulars: one Negro Girl Gin, 162 acres of land, all my Horses and Mares branded 3, two feather beds with furniture, other household property, 30 head of Cattle branded 3. Witness oath by Saml. **Shaw** 24 July 1795 to Reuben **Pyles** J.P. Laurens Co. Rec. 24 July 1795.

Page 40 1795, William **Hanna** Sen. (Laurens Co.) for £25 paid by William **Cuningham** (same), sold a certain Tract of Land in sd. Co. on branches of Duncans Creek, containing 107 acres, part of 320 acres granted to sd. William **Hanna** 6 Jan 1794, recorded in Secretary's Office in Grant book K, No.5, page 79. Border: Heirs of A. **Millan**, Wm. **Cuningham**, James **Blakeley**, Widow **Ritchie**, Adam **Gorden**, Wm. **Hanna**. Witness John **Templeton**, John **Rodgers**. Signed Wm. **Hanna** Sr. Witness oath by John **Templeton** and John **Rogers** [sic] 18 July 1795 to James **Dillard** J.P. Rec. 25 July 1795. [Includes plat.]

Page 40-41 24 Feb 1795, Wm. **Thomason** Sen. (S.C.) for £5 sterling sold to John **Thomason** (Laurens Co.), one red cow with a white face marked with a crop & an under Bit in left ear & crop & two Slits in right ear; a black cow marked with a Slit & under bit in left ear & right ear a crop; three calves. Witness Anderson **Arnold**, Micajah **Sims**. Signed William (x) **Thomason**. Witness oath by Anderson **Arnold** 16 Mar 1795 to Jonthn. **Downs** J.P. Laurens Co. Rec. 25 July 1795.

Page 41 15 Aug 1789, Middleton **Prater** (Laurens Co.) am bound to George **Morgan** (same) for £5. Condition that Middleton **Prater** & Geo. **Morgan** hath Jointly purchased a certain Tract of land of John **Adkins** and sd. **Morgan** hath taken **Adkins'** right for same and made **Prayter** [sic] a good right to his part of same & not knowing whether **Adkins'** right may stand good, therefore if **Adkins'** right should prove deficient, above bound **Prayter** shall not sue **Morgan** for more than his part of such damages, then the obligation to be void. Witness Lewis **Graves**, Zacharias **Sims**. Signed Middleton (x) **Prayter**.

Witness oath by Lewis **Graves** 14 June 1795 to Geo. **Anderson** J.P. Laurens Co. Rec. 28 July 1795.

Page 41   28 Sept 1792, Jacob **Gibson** (Laurens Co.) to William **McPherson** (same), for £40 sterling sold a certain Tract of land containing 100 acres more or less, in sd. Co. on waters of Reedy River, being the lower part of a Tract granted to John **Gocher**, containing 200 acres, including the plantation whereon Jacob **Gibson** lived. Joining John **Box** & John **Lewis**. Witness Isaac (IB) **Bailey**, Notley **Gore**, Wm. **Wright**. Signed Jacob **Gibson**, Mary (x) **Gibson**. Witness oath by Notley **Gore** 18th day above mentioned [sic] to Zech. **Bailey** J.P. Rec. 28 July 1795.

Page 41-42   8 Jan 1795, Wm. **Norris** & Anna **Norris** his wife (Laurens Co.) to Joel **Hughes** (same), for £50 Sterling sold all that Tract of land containing by Estimation 100 acres more or less, bounded: Roger **Murphy** Sen., watery Branch, James **Wells**, **Burris**, Wm. **Crisp**, Walls branch, Wm. **Osbourn**, Ready road, Danl. **Osbourn**. Lying in sd. Co., being part of land laid out to James **Box** 30 Jan 1793 & granted by William **Moultrie**, Gov. & recorded in Grant book E, No.5, page 528, to sd. Jas. **Box**. Witness Thos. **Hughs** [sic], John (O) **Osbourn**, Danl. (x) **Osbourn**. Signed William (x) **Norris**, Anna (A) **Norris**. Witness oath by Thos. **Hughes** 17 July 1795 to Zech. **Bailey** J.P. Laurens Co. Rec. 28 July 1795.

Page 42   16 July 1794, Andw. **Anderson** (Laurens Co.) to Thomas **Roberts** planter, for £30 Sterling sold a certain Tract of Land containing 66 acres more or less, joining land of James **Young**, Robert **McClintock**, Andrew **Anderson**, Thos. **Roberts**. Witness Lit. B. **Wilson**, James **Brown**, Wm. **Hunter**. Signed Andrew **Anderson**. Witness oath by Wm. **Hunter** 11 May 1795 to Joseph **Downs** J.P. Laurens Co. Plat certified 11 Dec 1794 by Wm. **Hunter** D.S. Rec. 28 July 1795. [Includes plat.]

Page 43   13 Oct 1794, John **Hunter** (Laurens Co.) & Geo. **Anderson** (same) Exors. of Estate of James **Anderson** dec. to Thomas **Roberts**, for £20 Sterling sold one certain Tract of land in sd. Co. on waters of Bush river, containing 79 acres, being part of 250 acres originally granted to sd. Jas. **Anderson** dec. Border: Thos. **Roberts**, vacant, Ainsworth **Middleton**, Jas. **Young**, Bush River, Rev. Robt. **McClintock**. Witness Jno. **Simpson**, Saml. **Saxon**. Signed John **Hunter** Exor., Geo. **Anderson**. Witness oath by John **Simpson** 11 May 1795 to Wm. **Hunter** J.P. Laurens Co. Plat certified 8 Oct 1794 by John **Hunter** D.S. Rec. 28 July 1795. [Includes plat.]

Page 43-44   11 Mar 1795, Saml. **Saxon** & James **Saxon** (Laurens Co. to Thomas **Roberts** (same), for £80 Sterling sold one certain Tract of land in sd. Co. on waters of N fork of Bush river, containing 140 acres more or less. Bounding N.E. on **Anderson**, S.E. & N.E. on Ainsworth **Middleton**, N.W. on Wm. **Saxon**, N.W. on Geo. **Leak**, N.E. on **McClintock**. Originally granted to James **Doherty**, conveyed from him to James **Young**, and from him to Saml. **Saxon**. Witness Moses **McCreary**, Benjamin **Wilson**. Signed Saml. **Saxon**,

James **Saxon**. Witness oath by Moses **McCreary** 11 May 1795 to Wm. **Hunter** J.P. Laurens Co. Plat certified 11 Mar 1795 by Robt. **Young** D.S. Rec. 28 July 1795. [Includes plat.]

Page 44   14 Sept 1795, Clabourn **Simms** (Laurens Co.) to John **Walker** (same), for £65 9sh sterling sold a certain Tract of land containing 164 acres more or less, in sd. Co. on waters of Cane Creek, being part of 800 acres, originally granted to James **Harley** by Chs. Greville **Montague**, 20 July 1772. Border: **Carter**, branch, **Mitchell**, **White**, **Crisp**, Eli **Bailey**, **Gibson**. Witness Horatio **Walker**, A. **Rodgers** Jun. Signed Clabourn **Sims** [sic]. Witness oath by Hor. **Walker** 13 Oct 1795 to Jno. **Davis** J.P. Laurens Co. Rec. 13 Oct 1795.

Page 44-45   18 Sept 1795, John **Walker** (Laurens Co.) & Keturah his wife to Horatio **Walker** (same), for £40 sold one certain Tract of land on S side of Little River, in sd. Co., containing by estimation 83 acres more or less, bounded: Silvanus **Walker** Jun., Pat. **Cuningham**, Tandy **Walker**, Christopher **Roland**. Being part of a Tract granted originally to John **Osbourn** Sen. & conveyed by him to sd. John **Walker**. Witness Francis **Ross**, John **Simmons**. Signed John **Walker**, Keturah **Walker**. Witness oath by John **Simmons** 13 Oct 1795 to John **Davis** J.P. Laurens Co. Rec. 13 Oct 1795.

Page 45-46   Lease & Release, 17 July 1795, Joseph **Babb** & Mary his wife (Laurens Co.) planter to Robert **Pasley** (same), for £91 Sterling sold all that Tract of Land containing 130 acres more or less, in sd. Co. on Beaverdam creek, waters of Little River, bounding: **Glenn**, **Rodgers**, Abner **Babb**, Creek, old Spring on S side of Creek. Being part of 250 acres originally granted to Joseph **Babb** dec. 24 Nov 1767 & conveyed by Abner **Babb** to Joseph **Babb**. Witness Andw. **Rodgers** Jun., Wm. A. **Rodgers**. Signed Joseph **Babb**, Mary (x) **Babb**. Witness oath by A. **Rodgers** Jun. 17 July 1795 to John **Davis** J.P. Laurens Co. Rec. 14 Oct 1795.

Page 46-47   Lease & Release, 25 Dec 1794, David **Greene** (Laurens Co.) to Nebo **Gaunt** (same), for £50 Sterling sold a certain tract of land containing 55 acres more or less, in sd. Co. on N.E. side of Reedy River, bounded S.E. on David **McGladdry**, S.W. and N.W. on Reedy River, N.W. on Saml. **Green**. Being part of a Tract originally granted 20 July 1785, to Patrick **Cuningham** by Benjamin **Gerard** Gov., & from sd. **Cuningham** conveyed to sd. David **Greene**. The other part granted to sd. David **Greene** 3 Mar 1788 by Thomas **Pinckney** Gov. Witness William **Norris**, Nathaniel **Greene**, Jonathan **Cox**. Signed David **Greene**, Leannah **Greene**. Witness oath by Jonath. **Cox** 20 July 1795 to Joseph **Downs** J.P. Laurens Co. Rec. 22 July 1795. [Includes plat.]

Page 47-48   15 July 1795, John **Davis** and Susannah **Davis** his wife (Greenville Co.) to Zachary **Baily** [Zachariah **Bailey** in one ref.] (Laurens Co.), for £100 sold all that Tract of Land containing 96 acres, being part of 100 acres granted to Pat. **Cuningham** by Patent 4 Apr 1785, recorded in Secretary's Grant Book DDDD, page 53. Situate in Laurens Co. on waters of Philpots branch, waters of Little River, originally surveyed for John **Audibert**

& conveyed from sd. **Cuningham** to sd. John **Davis**. **Davis** having heretofore sold and laid off 4 acres of E side of sd. Tract to John **Philpot**, the balance is 96 acres. Witness Jas. **Kilgore**, Wm. **Mitchusson**, William **OBryant**. Signed John **Davis**, Susannah (x) **Davis**. Witness oath by Wm. **Mitchusson** 17 July 1795 to Chas. **Saxon** J.P. Laurens Co. Rec. 23 July 1795.

Page 48 8 Dec 1793, Lazarus **Hitt** planter (Laurens Co.) to John **Smith** Jun. (same), for £55 Sterling sold part of a certain Tract of Land in sd. Co. on waters of Saluda River & on N side of Bank's Branch, containing 100 acres more or less. Granted to Wm. **Esler** in 1773, by Wm. **Bull** Gov. Witness Wm. (x) **Smith**, James (O) **Smith**, Henry **Hitt**. Signed Lazarus **Hitt**. Witness oath by Willm. **Smith** [No signature.] 19 Mar 1795 to Angus **Campbell** J.P. Laurens Co. Rec. 22 Aug 1795.

Page 48-49 18 July 1795, Solomon **Langston** (Laurens Co.) planter for £30 sterling paid by Henry **Langston** (same) planter, sold a certain tract of land containing 50 acres more or less, in sd. Co. on N side of Cox's Creek, a branch of Enoree, being part of 200 acres originally granted to Christian **McCullee**, by Wm. **Bull** esq. & recorded in Secretary's Office in Book EEE, page 89. Sd. tract is N.W. part of original tract. Witness Gabl. **Bumpass**, Jesse **Holder**. Signed Solomon **Langston**. Witness oath by Jesse **Holder** 20 July 1795 to Roger **Brown** J.P. Laurens Co. Rec. 23 Oct 1795.

Page 49 31 Aug 1795, George **Berry** for £75 Sterling paid by James **McClintock**, sold a Negro fellow named Man. Witness John **McClintock** Jun., Starling **Tucker**. Signed George **Berry**. Witness oath by John **McClintock** Jun. 12 Oct 1795 to John **Hunter** [No title.]. Rec. 12 Oct 1795.

Page 49-50 Lease & Release, 1 & 2 Dec 1778, John **Adair** & Sarah his wife (Ninety Six Dist.) farmer to James **Adair** (same) Saddler, for £50 sold all that Tract of Land containing 100 acres in Craven Co. on waters of Duncan's creek. Bounding N on sd. James **Adair**, S.E. on Joseph **Adair** and vacant land, all other sides vacant land. Survey certified 18 Aug 1772 and granted 11 Aug 1774, a memorial entered in Auditor General's Office in Book M, No.13, Page 230, 7 Jan 1775. Witness Wm. **Adair**, Wm. **Ross**, John **Finney**. Signed John **Adair**, Sarah **Adair**. Witness oath by William **Adair** 23 Dec 1778 to George **Ross** J.P. Ninety Six Dist. Rec. 12 Oct 1795.

Page 50-51 12 Mar 1795, Laurens Co. in behalf of a poor Apprentice Mulatto Boy Henry, the Issue of Jenny **Langston** and John **Adams** (same), bound the sd. Henry to sd. John **Adams** to dwell from this date until he comes to the age of 21 years, which will be on 1 Apr 1815. During which time he shall serve his Master and behave himself towards his Master and the rest of the family. John **Adams** shall teach in the best way he can the Art of Farming and give the boy learning sufficient to read the Holy Write & find sufficient meat, drink, washing & lodging and apparel. Witness Hudson **Berry** J.P. Signed John **Adams**. Indenture executed 18 July 1795. Rec. 15 Aug 1795.

Book F

Page 51   18 July 1795, Sarah **Wright** hereby revokes the power of Att. to Jacob **Bowman** (Laurens Co.). Witness Stevn. **Wood**. Signed Sarah **Wright**. Rec. 22 July 1795.

Page 51   1 June 1795, Morgan **Layson** (S.C.) planter for £10 paid by George **Gordon** & Alexr. **Morison** (Laurens Co.), sold a certain Tract of Land containing 115 acres in sd. Co. on waters of Enoree river, bounded N.E. by Eliphaz **Reyley**, N.W. by Jas. **Mahon**, S.W. by William **Lacey**, S.E. & N.E. by Robt. **McCrady**. Originally granted to James Mahon **Layson** 7 May 1792, recorded in Grant Book D, No.5, page 589. Witness James **Adair**, Douglass **Puckett**. Witness oath by Douglass **Puckett** 23 Oct 1795 to Roger **Brown** J.P. Laurens Co. Rec. 14 Nov 1795.

Page 51-52   1 Apr 1795, John **Martin** (Laurens Co.) planter to James **Sullivan** planter (same), for £50 sold all that Tract of Land containing 21-1/2 acres in sd. Co. on Ryan's Creek of Little river, bounding S.E. by Jno. **Martin**, N.W. by James **Wilson**, N.E. by Margaret **Spence**. Witness Ezekl. **Roland**, Andw. **Rodgers**. Signed John **Martin**. Witness oath by Ezekl. **Roland** 13 Nov 1795 to Jno. **Cochran** D.C. Laurens Co. Rec. 13 Nov 1795.

Page 52-53   16 Dec 1784, Andrew **Anderson** (Ninety Six Dist.) planter to Robert **Anderson** (same), for £2 3sh 6p Sterling sold part of a certain Tract of land containing one acre on a branch of Santee, otherwise called Saluda River, called Bush creek. Bounded S.E. & N.E. on sd. Andw. **Anderson**, N.W. on sd. Robert **Anderson**. Being part of land of sd. Andrew **Anderson's** containing 100 acres, being granted to sd. Andw. **Anderson** by William **Bull** esq. Lieut. Gov. 12 July 1771. Witness Ambrose **Hudgens** Sen., Kitt **Smith**, Jas. **Milwee**. Signed Andw. **Anderson**. Witness oath by Kitt **Smith** 18 July 1795 to Wm. **Hunter** J.P. Laurens Co. Rec. 22 Aug 1795.

Page 53   28 Mar 1795, Whereas Danl. **Williams** Sen. (Laurens Co.) planter is indebted to Saml. **Henderson** and Jas. **Waldrop** (same), for £400 Sterling to be paid partly upon a Bond with condition of payment. For the better securing payment on or before 1 Jan 1797, sold one negro fellow Harry and one named Moses & one negro wench Jude & her two children George & Levi, one negro girl Sarah. Provided that if the sum is paid, then this Grant to be void. Witness William **Caldwell**, Jn. **Simpson**. Signed Daniel **Williams**. Witness oath by Jno. **Simpson** 18 July 1795 to William **Hunter** J.P. Laurens Co. Rec. 23 July 1795.

Page 53-54   9 May 1795, Thomas **Wilks** and Mary his wife & Francis **Lester** (Laurens Co.) to James **Clardy** (same), for £82 Sterling sold one certain tract of land in sd. Co. on a branch of North's Creek containing 150 acres more or less, being part of Land granted to Geo. **Anderson**, bounded on Maria **Goodman**, James **Cook**, Thomas **Woodward**, Stephen **Harris**. Witness Jno. **Cargill** V. [sic], John **Chandler**. Signed Thos. **Wilks**, Mary (x) **Wilks**, Frans. **Lester**. Witness oath by John **Cargill** V. 15 Sept 1795 to Thomas **Wadsworth** J.L.C. Rec. 12 Oct 1795.

Page 54 15 July 1795, Michael **McGee** & Anna his wife (Abbeville Co.) to Wm. **Powell** (Laurens Co.), for £28 Sterling sold all that Tract of land containing 100 acres more or less, in Laurens Co. on N side of Saluda River. Bound: Joseph **South**, Wm. **Powell**, Saluda river. Witness Thos. **Sims**, Matthew (x) **Bolton**, Ann (x) **Delph**. Signed Michael (x) **McGee**, Anna (x) **McGee**. Witness oath by Thos. **Sims** 17 July 1795 to Danl. **Wright** J.P. Rec. 22 July 1795.

Page 55 20 July 1795, Joshua **Roberts** & Sarah **Roberts** wife to sd. Joshua (Laurens Co.) sold unto Sally **Drew** (same), a certain negro woman Jane, for £5 Sterling. Witness Thomas **Owens**, Mary (M) **Owens**. Signed Joshua (x) **Roberts**, Sarah (x) **Roberts**. Witness oath by Thomas **Owens** 28 July 1795 to Jno. **Davis** J.P. Laurens Co. Rec. 7 Aug 1795.

Page 55 28 July 1795, Joshua **Roberts** and Sarah **Roberts** wife to Joshua (Laurens Co.) sold unto Daniel **Osbourn** a certain negro James, for £5 sterling. Witness Thomas **Owens**, Mary (M) **Owens**. Signed Joshua (x) **Roberts**, Sarah (x) **Roberts**. Witness oath by Thomas **Owens** 28 July 1795 to Jno. **Davis** J.P. Laurens Co. Rec. 7 Aug 1795.

Page 55-56 7 Oct 1789, Richard **Owens** (Laurens Co.) to David **McCaa** (same), for £20 Sterling sold all that Tract of 163 acres more or less in sd. Co. Being part of 260 acres originally granted unto Richard **Owings** [sic] by William **Moultrie** Gov. 1 May 1786, a memorial entered in Secretary's office in Grant book JJJJ, page 413. Border: Reaburn's Creek, Robert **Cooper**, Wm. **Millwee**, Old Survey. Witness Jonathan **Downs**, William **Owings**. Signed Richard **Owings**, Sarah (x) **Owings**. Oath by Jnthn. **Downs** 19 Dec 1794 that he saw Richard **Owings** & Sarah his wife sign the deed. Given before Joseph **Downs** J.P. Rec. 14 Nov 1795. [Includes plat.]

Page 56 20 Dec 1794, David **McCaa** (Laurens Co.) to Charles **Wilson** (same), for £31 sterling sold all that Tract of 163 acres of Land more or less, in sd. Co., being part of 260 acres originally granted unto Richard **Owens** by Wm. **Moultrie** Gov. 1 May 1786, a memorial entered in Secretary's Office in Grant Book JJJJ, page 413. Witness James **Wilson**, John (x) **McCurly**, William (x) **Comar**. Signed David **McCaa**, Polly (x) **McCaa**. Oath by James **Wilson** 24 Feb 1795 that he saw David **McCaa** & Polly his wife sign the deed. Given before Angus **Campbell** J.P. Laurens Co. Rec. 14 Nov 1795. [Includes plat.]

Page 57 2 Nov 1795, John **Templeton** (Laurens Co.) for £20 Sterling paid by Walter **Stewart** (same), sold a certain Tract of Land containing 185 acres in sd. Co. on waters of Enoree River, originally granted to John **Templeton**, bounding on Robert **Templeton**, John **Campbell**, Jas. **Adair**, vacant Land, William **Clinton**, John D. **Kern**. Witness James **Couch**, Jas. **Hanna** Jun. Signed John **Templeton**. Witness oath by James **Couch** 16 Nov 1795 to Roger **Brown** J.P. Laurens Co. Rec. 17 Nov 1795.

Page 57-58   14 June 1795, Whereas on 4 Mar 1795, a writ by Laurens Co. Court was lodged on the Office of William **Dunlap** esq., then Sheriff, against David **Smith**, late of your Co. for £5 9sh 9p, which Geo. **Gordon**, lately in our Co. Court recovered against him for debt, also 3sh for Cost expended. Sd. sums of money to be recovered on 17 July next. Witness Lewis **Saxon** Clerk. William **Dunlap** as Sheriff by virtue of sd. Writ, did on 15 Apr in year last, seize a certain Tract of land containing 75 acres on Enoree river on S side, being granted to Ann **Musgrove**, now Ann **Smith**, 20 Dec 1791, bounded N.E. by W. **Berry**, S.E. by Douglas **Pucket**, N.W. Enoree River. On 6 June in year last, sold at public Auction to George **Gordon** & Alexr. **Morison** (Laurens Co.) Merchants for £3 Sterling. Witness John **Wallis**, Jon. **Coker**. Signed William **Dunlap** Sheriff. Witness oath by Jon. **Coker** 18 June 1795 to John **Hunter** [No title.]. Rec. 29 Dec 1795.

Page 58-59   16 June 1795, Whereas on 4 Mar 1795, a writ by the Laurens Co. Court was entered against David **Smith**, late of your Co., for £5 9sh 9p which Geo. **Gordon** lately in our Court recovered against him for Debt, also 3sh for Cost. The several sums of money before the Court on 7 July next. Witness Lewis **Saxon** Clerk. William **Dunlap** as Sheriff did on 15 Apr seize a certain Tract of Land containing 65 acres on Enoree river on S side, being originally granted Ann **Musgrove**, now Ann **Smith**, 20 Dec 1791. Bounded on S by Enoree river, N on Edward **Musgrove**, N.W. on Douglas **Pucket**, S.E. [blank.]. On 6 June in year last, sold at public Auction to George **Gordon** & Alexr. **Morison** (Laurens Co.) Merchants for £3 Sterling. Witness Jno. **Cocker** [**Coker** in one ref.], Jno. **Wallis**. Signed William **Dunlap** Shff. Witness oath by John **Wallis** 18 June 1795 to John **Hunter** [No title.]. Rec. 29 Dec 1795.

Page 59-60   Lease & Release, 23 & 24 Aug 1795, Joseph **Parsons** (Laurens Co.) planter to Solomon **Langston** Sen. (same), for £100 sold a tract of land containing 250 acres more or less, on Coxes creek, runs into Enoree on S side in sd. Co. Joining Jesse **Holder** on upper side, James **Miller** on lower side, all on sd. Coxes creek, corner held at time of Surveying by Angus **Campbell**, **Kates** old plantation. Part of 640 acres granted to Joshua **Kates** by Wm. **Moultrie** 6 Feb 1786, recorded in Secretary's Office in Book JJJJ, page 489. Witness Silas **McBee**, William **Owings**. Signed Joseph (J) **Parsons**. Witness oath by Silas **McBee** 26 Aug 1795 to Roger **Brown** J.P. Laurens Co. Rec. 16 Nov 1795.

Page 60   27 Oct 1795, Solomon **Langston** (Laurens Co.) planter for £50 Sterling paid by Samuel **Stiles** (same), sold all that tract of land containing 250 acres more or less, on Cox's creek, a branch on S side of Enoree in sd. Co. Joining Jesse **Holder** on upper side, James **Miller** on lower side, Cox's Creek, Angus **Campbell** (at time of Survey), **Kate's** old plantation. Witness Solomon **Langston** Jun., Jesse **Holder**, Solomon **Holder**. Signed Solomon **Langston**. Witness oath by Jesse **Holder** 27 Oct 1795 to Roger **Brown** J.P. Laurens Co. Rec. 16 Nov 1795.

Page 60-61 Lease & Release, 14 & 15 Apr 1795, John **Russel** (Abbeville Co.) weaver to Geo. **Swindle** (Laurens Co.) planter, for £150 Sterling sold all that tract of land containing by estimation 300 acres on N side of Saluda River, granted unto sd. John **Russel** 8 Mar 1768 by Lord Chas. Greville **Montague**. Witness James **Hathorn**, Wm. **Russel**, Jos. **Wardlaw**. Signed John **Russel**. Witness oath by James **Hathorn** 11 Nov 1795 to Hugh **Wardlaw** J.P. Abbeville Co. Laid out pursuant to order by John **Troup** Esq. D.S.Genl. 22 June 1767, 300 acres on N side of Saluda River in Granville Co., bounded all sides by vacant land. J. **Bremar** Surv.Gen. [Plat labeled Bounty.] Plat certified 18 Dec 1767 by Jared **Nelson** D.S. 2 Dec 1795. [Includes plat.]

Page 62 5 Apr 1780, Richd. **North** planter (Ninety Six Dist.) to Hamilton **Murdoch** (same) planter, for £5,000 Current money sold all that tract of land containing 250 acres, being part of 300 acres including the plantation whereon Robt. **Wood**, late lived, in sd. Dist. in the fork between Broad & Saluda Rivers on waters of Long Lick & Reaburns creek, bounding S on Ebenezer **Starnes**, land laid out to John **Cuningham**, Jas. **Williams**, N.E. on unknown, N.W. on Saml. **Milhous**, vacant, W on rem. part of original Survey. Sd. 300 acres granted to sd. Richd. **North** 10 Feb 1775, by Wm. **Bull** esq. Lt.Gov. Witness Jno. **Caldwell**, Jno. **Thompson**, A. **Rodgers**. Signed Richard (No) **North**. Witness oath by Andw. **Rodgers** 4 Jan 1796 to John **Hunter** [No title.] Rec. 5 Jan 1796.

Page 62-63 15 June 1784, Hamilton **Murdoch** planter (Ninety Six Dist.) to Jas. **Sims** (same) planter, for £5,000 old currt. sold all that tract of land containing 250 acres, being part of 300 acres, including the plantation whereon Robt. **Wood**, late lived, in sd. Dist. in the fork between Broad & Saluda Rivers, on waters of Long lick & Reaburns Creeks. Bounding S on Ebenr. **Starnes**, land laid out to Jno. **Cuningham**, James **Williams**, N.E. on unknown, N.W. on Saml. **Milhouse**, vacant, W on rem. part of original survey. Granted to sd. Richd. **North** 10 Feb 1775 by Wm. **Bull** esq. Lt. Gov. Witness Henry (H) **Butler**, George **Goggans**, John **Fletchall**. Witness oath by Henry (H) **Butler** 26 Nov 1795 to Thos. **Wadsworth** J.L.C. Rec. 14 Dec 1795.

Page 63-64 7 Jan 1791, Wm. **McDonald** & Jamima his wife (S.C.) to Drury **Dupree** planter (same), for £55 sterling sold a certain tract of Land containing 150 acres more or less, on waters of Beaverdam, a branch of Little River. Bounded at time of original Survey, N.E. on Henry **ONeil**, Thos. **Carter**, vacant, S.E. on John **ONeil**, vacant. Granted to Henry **ONeil** by Wm. **Bull** esq. 8 July 1774, & by sd. **ONeil** conveyed to Wm. **McDonald**. Witness Joseph **Blackerby**, Thos. **McDonald**. Signed William **McDonald**, Jamima (C) **McDonald**. Signed 1 Sept 1794 in presence of Jas. **Young**, Ths. **McDonald**. Witness oath by Thos. **McDonald** 15 Sept 1795 to Thos. **Wadsworth** J.L.C. Rec. 2 Dec 1795.

Page 64 27 Nov 1792, John **Billups** & Chloe his wife (Laurens Co.) to Landon **Waters** (same) planter, for £50 Sterling sold by estimation 100 acres of Land, being part of 150 acres granted to John **Owen**, surveyed by John **Rodgers** 24 Aug 1773, on S side of Enoree river, bounded N on sd. River, E on Edward **Musgrove**, S by Strange lands. Witness W. **Farrow**, Bordwine **Waters**. Signed John **Billups**, Chloe (x) **Billups**. [No witness oath.] Rec. 24 Dec 1795.

Page 64-65 9 Dec 1795, Gasper **Trotti** (Orangeburgh Dist.) planter to Reuben **Martin** (S.C.) planter, for $500 [sic] sold all that tract of land containing 500 acres, in Craven Co. (now Laurens) on Warriors creek, bounding by Original survey, N.E. on Pat. **Cuningham**, S.E. on **Gordon**, Abner **Bishop**, & unknown, N.W. on Bounty land, N.E. unknown. Granted to Thos. **Farr** 26 July 1774, & by Nath. **Farr**, one of the sons & heirs of sd. Thos. **Farr**, sold to sd. Gasper **Trotti** by Lease & Release 1 & 2 Jan 1784, recorded in Orangeburgh Dist. Public register in Office Book No.2, Page 13 & 14. Witness William (T) **Ball**, John **McDowell**. Signed Gaspar **Trotti** [sic]. Witness oath by John **McDowell** 21 Dec 1795 to Danl. **Wright** J.P. Laurens Co. Rec. 23 Dec 1795.

Page 65 Dec 1795, Thomas William **Fakes** (Laurens Co.) for £30 paid by Sanford **Berry**, sold a certain tract of land containing 168 acres, in sd. Co. on Lynch's creek, a branch of Enoree River & is part of a Survey of 535 acres originally granted to Thos. **Farr** 8 July 1774. Witness Wm. **Day**, Angus **Campbell** Jun. Signed Thos. Wm. **Fakes**. Witness oath by Angus **Campbell** Jun. 29 Dec 1795 to Angus **Campbell** J.P. Laurens Co. Rec. 4 Jan 1796.

Page 65-66 15 Sept 1795, John **Blackwell** (Laurens Co.) to Solomon **Goodwin** (same), for £40 Sterling sold a certain tract of Land containing 300 acres, being part of 475 acres granted to sd. John **Blackwell** by Wm. **Moultrie** Esq. Gov. 3 Mar 1794. Situate in Greenville Co. on Beaver Dam, a branch of Mountain Creek of Saluda River. Bounding N by Athy. **Meeks**, N.W. vacant, E by Joel **Chandler**, S by Isaac **Jones**. Witness Gabriel **Bumpass**, Chas. **Smith**. Signed John (B) **Blackwell**. Witness oath by Chas. **Smith** 12 Dec 1795 to Reuben **Pyles** J.P. Laurens Co. Rec. 28 Dec 1795.

Page 66 29 Aug 1795, Saml. **Henderson** (Laurens Co.) planter to John **Crawford** (same) Blacksmith, for £20 Sterling sold all that Tract of Land containing 198-3/4 acres more or less, being part of 400 acres more or less, formerly granted to Danl. **Ravenel** esq. & by his wife as Exrs. to his last Will and Testament, conveyed by Lease & Release to sd. Saml. **Henderson**. Border: Wm. **Young**, Edmond **Drake**, Saml. **Henderson**, part of Larger Survey, Wm. **East**, Old Waggon Road, Great Waggon Road, New Road. Witness Jno. **Davis**, Jas. **Young**. Signed Saml. **Henderson**. Witness oath by James **Young** 29 Aug 1795 to Thos. **Wadsworth** J.L.C. Rec. 28 Dec 1795. [Includes plat.]

Page 66-67 8 Sept 1795, Thos. **Wadsworth** & Wm. **Turpin** (S.C.) Merchants to Edmond **Drake** planter, for £30 Current money sold all that tract of land containing 120 acres more or less, in Laurens Co. Bounded E by Saml. **Eakin**,

S by John **Rainey**, W by **Hancock**, N by Wm. **Young**. Granted to Saml. **Henderson** by William **Moultrie** 3 Oct 1785. Witness James **Young**, Jas. **Boyce**. Signed Thomas **Wadsworth**, Willm. **Turpin**. Witness oath by James **Young** 1 Oct 1795 to John **Hunter** [No title.]. Rec. 28 Dec 1795.

Page 67 25 Mar 1795, John **Martin** (Laurens Co.) planter to William **Wilson** planter (same), for £100 Sterling sold one certain tract of land containing 260 acres in sd. Co. on head waters of Burris' creek, being laid out by Jno. **Rodgers** esq. D.S., being part of a Tract granted to John **Martin**. Witness Ezel. **Roland**, Alexr. **Grant**. Signed John **Martin**. Witness oath by Ezel. **Roland** 28 Oct 1795 to James **Saxon** J.P. Laurens Co. Rec. 28 Oct 1795.

Page 67-68 17 Mar 1795, John **Martin** (Laurens Co.) to Robert **Todd** (same), for £50 Sterling sell a tract of 220 acres in sd. Co. on waters of Dirty Creek. Witness William **Sooter**, Benjam. (x) **Sooter** [sic]. Signed John **Martin**, Elizabeth (x) **Martin**. Witness oath by Benjamin (x) **Sooter** 8 Jan 1796 to John **Cochran** D.C. Laurens Co. Surveyed 14 Mar 1795 by John **Rodgers** D.S. Rec. 8 Jan 1796. [Includes plat.]

Page 68 8 May 1795, Robert **Bolt** Jun. (Laurens Co.) to Charles **Henderson** (same), for £10 Sterling sell part of that Tract of Land originally granted to James **Boyd** & by him in his last Will & Testament conveyed to Robert **Barnett** & by him conveyed to Robt. **Bolt** Jun. 17 Sept 1794. Containing 65 acres in sd. Co. on N side of Saluda, on a small branch of Reaburns Creek. Witness Ezekl (x) **Matthews**, Saml. **Downs**. Signed Robert (x) **Bolt** Jun. Witness oath by Ezekiel (x) **Matthews** 8 May 1795 to Jonthn. **Downs** J.P. Laurens Co. Rec. 8 May 1795. [Includes plat.]

Page 68-69 26 Dec 1795, John **Adams** (Laurens Co.) planter in consideration of the love, good will & affection I bear to my loving son Abraham **Adams** (same), give a certain tract of Land containing 150 acres more or less, on N prong of Reaburns creek in sd. Co. Witness Richard **Childress**, Jesse **Childress**. Signed John **Adams**. Witness oath by Richd. **Childress** 2 Jan 1796 to Joseph **Downs** J.P. Laurens Co. Rec. 2 Jan 1796.

Page 69 22 Dec 1795, John **Adams** (Laurens Co.) appoint my trusty friend Jesse **Childress** (Laurens) Gentleman my lawful Attorney to recover from Zechariah **Bailey** & Andw. **Rodgers** (Laurens), £45 Sterling. Witness Abraham **Adams**, Richd. **Childress**. Signed John **Adams**. Witness oath by Abraham **Adams** 2 Jan 1796 to Joseph **Downs** J.P. Laurens Co. Rec. 2 Jan 1796.

Page 69-70 Lease & Release, 3 & 4 July 1795, Joseph **Mahon** to Bailey **Mahon** (Ninety Six Dist.), for £50 Sterling sold all that tract of land containing 162 acres more or less, adjoining John **Pringle**, Wm. **Simmons**, long Shoal of Reedy River, Joseph **Mahon**, same survey. Being part of 300 acres originally granted to Thomas **Shurbrick** & by him conveyed to Wm. **Williamson**, & conveyed by him to John **Rutledge** Jun. & conveyed to John

Hunter by power of Attorney 31 Jan 1791 & recorded in Clerk's Office Book C, page 332, 14 Mar of same year & next conveyed by sd. **Hunter** to Joseph **Mahon**. Witness John **Pringle**, Benjamin **Box**. Signed Joseph **Mahon**. Witness oath by John **Pringle** 10 Dec 1795 to Joseph **Downs** J.P. Laurens Co. Rec. 10 Dec 1795.

Page 70   10 Feb 1795, Benjamin **Jones** (Laurens Co.) to Charles **Henderson** (same), for £60 sold all that tract of land containing 150 acres more or less, in sd. Co. on McHurg's creek, waters of Reaburns creek. Bounded S on Jas. **Boyd** dec., S.W. not known, S.E. on Joshua **Arnold**. Granted to John **Williams** 4 June 1787 by Thos. **Pinckney** esq. Gov., recorded in Secretary's Office in Book TTTT, page 264. Witness John (x) **Henderson**, Thos. (x) **Henderson**. Signed Benjamin **Jones**, Cloe (x) **Jones**. Witness oath by John (x) **Henderson** 29 Dec 1795 to Joseph **Downs** J.P. Rec. 29 Dec 1795.

Page 71   25 Aug 1795, Arthur **Taylor** (Laurens Co.) to Richard **Pugh** (same), for £20 Sterling sold a Tract of Land containing 105 acres more or less, on waters of Reedy River in sd. Co., originally granted to Pierce **Butler** esq. & by him conveyed to Hercules Danl. **Bize**, and by his attorney John **Hunter** esq. conveyed to sd. Arthur **Taylor**. Bounding: Arthur **Taylor**, unknown, William **Dorrah**, Rd. **Pugh**. Witness Benjamin **Box**, Wm. **McClanahan**. Signed Arthur **Taylor**, Margaret (x) **Taylor**. Witness oath by Wm. **McClanahan** 26 Dec 1795 to John **Cochran** [No title.] Laurens Co. Rec. 26 Dec 1795. [Includes plat.]

Page 71-72 11 Sept 1793, John **Hunter** esq. (Laurens Co.) to Richd. **Pugh** (same), for £15 Sterling sold all that tract of Land containing 100 acres more or less, in sd. Co. on waters of Shirrels Branch, waters of Reaburns Creek. Bounded on land laid out to sold to [sic] John **Manly** & Oliver **Matthews**, being part of 500 acres originally granted to Pierce **Butler** & conveyed by him 9 July 1792 to Hercules Danl. **Bize** & now conveyed by John **Hunter** by power of Atty. dated 1 June 1793. Border: Ben. **Williams**, John **Manly**, Parts of Land. Witness David **Greene**, Jno. **Cochran**. Signed John **Hunter** Atty. for Hercules Danl. **Bize**. Witness oath by John **Cochran** 21 Jan 1796 to Reuben **Pyles** J.P. Laurens Co. Plat certified 3 Sept 1793 by John **Hunter** D.S. Rec. 21 Jan 1796. [Includes plat.]

Page 72   10 Sept 1793, John **Hunter** esq. (Laurens Co.) to Richard **Pugh** (same), for £7 7sh Sterling sold all that Tract of Land containing 42 acres more or less, being part of 500 acres originally granted to Pierce **Butler** 5 May 1772, & by him conveyed to Hercules Danl. **Bize** 9 July 1792, & now conveyed by John **Hunter** by Power of Attorney dated 1 June 1793. Situate in sd. Co. on waters of Reedy River. Bounding on Richd. **Pugh**, James **Dorah**, part of sd. Survey. Witness David **Green** [**Greene** in witness oath.], Jno. **Cochran**. Signed John **Hunter** Atty. for Hercs. Danl. **Bize**. Witness oath by John **Cochran** 21 Jan 1796 to Reuben **Pyles** J.P. Laurens Co. Rec. 21 Jan 1796. [Includes plat.]

Page 72-73 19 Jan 1773, John **Williams** (Craven Co.) planter to Capt. James **Lindley** esq. (same) planter, for £300 sold all that tract of land containing 150 acres on Hallums Branch in sd. Co., bounded on all sides by vacant land at time of original Grant. Granted 7 May 1767 by Lord Chas. Greville **Montague** then Gov. unto John **Williams**. Witness Geo. **Wright** Jun., John **Madden**, Benjn. **Wood**. Signed John **Williams**. Witness oath by John **Madden** 17 Dec 1784 to Jonthn. **Downs** J.P. 96 Dist. Rec. 23 Jan 1796.

Page 73-74 28 Aug 1778, James **Lindley** (Ninety Six Dist.) planter to John **McClanahan** (same) planter, for £800 Current money sold all that tract of land containing 150 acres in sd. Dist. on Hallams branch, a branch of Reaburns Creek. Bounded on all sides by vact. Land when surveyed for John **Williams**. Granted by Patent 7 May 1767 by Lord Chas. Greville **Montague** then Gov. unto John **Williams**. Witness Thos. **McClurkin**, Robt. (R) Jno. **Wood**, John **AbCrombie** [sic]. Signed Jas. **Lindley**, Mary **Lindley**. Witness oath by John **Abercrombie** 14 Jan 1784 to Robert **Hanna** J.P. 96 Dist. Rec. 23 Jan 1796.

Page 74 15 Jan 1779, James **Mayson** (Saluda River, Colleton Co.) in £2,400 Current money to be paid to Chas. **Simmons**, to which payment I bind myself. Condition that James **Mayson** does make a good Title to a certain Tract of land containing 200 acres more or less, on both sides of Little River, known by **Anderson's** Old Field Tract, adjoining to land since laid out to David **Anderson** esq. & by vacant land on all other sides at time of original survey. Granted by Thos. **Boone** esq. Gov. If condition met on or before 20 June next, then the obligation to be void. Witness John **Rodgers**, John **Ritchey**. Signed Jas. **Mayson**. [No witness oath.] Rec. 20 Aug 1795.

Page 74 9 Apr 1794, Recd. of Lewis **Banton** £500 former currency of S.C., in full discharge of all accts. Due & Demands of the estate of Capt. Wm. **Ritchey** dec. Witness Nimrod **Williams**, Clabourn **Goodman**. Signed Wm. (x) **Goodman**, Mary **Goodman**. Witness oath by Clabourn **Goodman** 5 Apr 1794 [sic] to Geo. **Anderson** J.P. Laurens Co. Rec. 22 Nov 1795.

Page 74-75 26 Jan 1796, Newton **Higgins** & his wife Sarah (Laurens Co.) to John **Paterson** (same), for £33 Sterling sold one certain Tract of Land containing 200 acres. Bounded W by William **Bramlett** & old line, N.W. by James **Higgins** & old lines, all other sides by Vacant lands. Witness Starling **Tucker**, John **Moore**. Signed Newton (x) **Higgins**, Sarah (x) **Higgins**. Witness oath by Starling **Tucker** [No signature.] to James **Saxon** J.P. Laurens Co. Rec. 1 Feb 1796.

Page 75 (Orangeburgh Dist.) 22 Aug 1785, Oath by Aaron (x) **Niblett** that he bit a piece off John **Bowen's** ear in a fight, about 5 or 6 years ago. Given before John **Heminton** J.P. Orangeburgh Dist. Acknowledged by Aaron (x) **Niblett** 21 July 1795 to Wm. **Hunter** J.P. Rec. 10 Aug 1795.

Page 75 28 Mar 1795, Robert **Allison**, late of Spartanburgh Co., to Zechariah **Turner** (Laurens Co.), for £40 Sterling sold a certain tract of land containing

100 acres more or less, on a small branch of Beaverdam creek, waters of Enoree river, below the line. Bounded S by Robt. **Allison** Sen., N by old lines, all other sides by vacant land at time of being granted. Granted unto Thomas **Allison** by Wm. **Bull** esq. then Gov., 2 Feb 1773. Witness William **Parker**, Mary (x) **Parker**. Signed Robert (A) **Allison**. Witness oath by William **Parker** 27 July 1795 to Danl. **Wright** J.P. Laurens Co. Rec. 6 Feb 1796.

Page 75-76   28 Nov 1795, William **Vaughan** & Daniel **Spillars** (Hancock Co., Ga.) to Reuben **Kelly** (Laurens Co.), for £40 sold all that tract of land containing 100 acres more or less, in Laurens Co. on N.E. side of Warrior, on Vaughan's Branch, water of Enoree River. Bounded S by Wm. **Vaughan** Sen., N.W. by unknown, S.W. by Jno. **Cox**, all other sides by vacant land at time of being granted. Granted unto John **Vaughan** by William **Bull**, then Gov., 8 July 1774. Recorded in Book M, No.13, page 190. Witness Willm. **Turner**, Zachr. **Turner**. Signed William (x) **Vaughan**, Danl. (x) **Spillars**. Witness oath by Zachr. **Turner** 21 Jan 1796 to Danl. **Wright** J.P. Laurens Co. Rec. 6 Feb 1796.

Page 76-77   29 Dec 1795, Oath by John **Pringle** that some time about 2 years ago, he wished to purchase a Cow of Joseph **Mahon**, which was not his but belonged to his Son Bailey **Mahon**, which sd. Cow was lately executed as property of Joseph **Mahon** at the Inst. of Joseph **Waldrop**. Given before Jonthn. **Downs** J.P. Laurens Co. Oath on 29 Dec 1795, by Bailey **Mahon** (being of full age) that a certain Sorrel Mare now present, was given to him by his Grandmother, Eleanor **Mahon**, some time before her death in 1788, & has been ever since in his possession. That 14 head of Black Cattle, which sprang from & is the increases of two Cows, given to him by his sd. Grandmother before her dec., which is his just right & property, and is now under Execution on the property of Joseph **Mahon** at instance of Joseph **Waldrop**. Given before Jonthn. **Downs** J.P. Laurens Co. Oath on 29 Dec 1795, by Nelly **Mahon** that the above Mare has been claimed & in possession of her Brother Bailey **Mahon** since 1788, & that before the death of her Grandmother, he heard her say her Brother Bailey **Mahon** should have sd. Mare. Given before Jonthn. **Downs** J.P. Oath on 19 Dec 1795, by Isaac **Mitchell** of lawful age that he has lived at the House of Joseph **Mahon** for some considerable time, during which time he always knew the Sorrel Mare was called Bailey's Mare, & Deponant borrowed sd. Mare of Bailey **Mahon** to ride several times and believes her to be his property. Given before Jonthn. **Downs**. J.P. Laurens Co. Oath on 29 Dec 1795, by Nelly **Mahon** that some time about 1 May 1788, she was present & did hear her Grandmother a few days before her Death, give unto Drury **Silvey** her Grandson, one horse, he being then a Boy, which sd. Horse was given in a swap for a Mare & the Mare was given in a swap for a Dun horse now present, in custody of sd. Drury, which Horse was lately executed as the property of Joseph **Mahon**. Given before Jonthn. **Downs** J.P. Laurens Co. Oath on 29 Dec 1795, by Nelly **Mahon** (being of full age) that her Grandmother Eleanor **Mahon** did some time before her death give her a certain Sorrel Mare, which is the Mother of a Sorrel Horse now present, 4 or 5 years old, is her just right & property, and was folded her property. Her

Grandmother did give unto her one red coloured Cow, just before she deceased, and that a certain Brindled Cow and young Calf, one black & white Cow & yearling same colour & one red and white Heifer yearling, are likewise her property, as they are all the increase & offspring of the first given Cow, and is now under execution as property of Joseph **Mahon** at inst. of Jos. **Waldrop**. Given before Jonthn. **Downs** J.P. Laurens Co. Oath [No date.] by Benjamin **Box** (being of full age) that the sorrel Horse now present, he has known ever since he was a colt and was called Nelly's Horse & believes sd. Horse to be Nelly **Mahon's** property, as she has offered to trade him to this Depont. Given before Jonthn. **Downs** J.P. Laurens Co. Rec. 18 Feb. 1796.

Page 77   10 Feb 1796, Christian **Atkins** for £3 10sh Sterling sold unto Joseph **Atkins**, one roan Stallion Colt, 2 years old next Spring, Trots natural. Witness Robt. **Atkins**, Bartlet **Atkins**. Signed Christian (x) **Atkins**. Witness oath by Robt **Atkins** 22 Feb 1796 to Jonthn. **Downs** J.P. Laurens Co. Rec. 22 Feb 1796.

Page 77   10 Feb 1796, Christian **Atkins** sold unto Bartlet **Atkins**, for £5 Sterling one Sorrel Mare, 3 years old, blazed face, trots natural. Witness Robt. **Atkins**, Joseph **Atkins**. Signed Christian (x) **Atkins**. Witness oath by Robt. **Atkins** 22 Feb 1796 to Jonthn. **Downs** J.P. Laurens Co. Rec. 22 Feb 1796.

Page 77   (Abbeville Co.) 9 May 1792, Meshic **Overby** [sic] (Laurens Co.) to Robert **Swanzy** (Abbeville Co.), for 30sh sterling sold all that Tract of land containing one whole acre more or less, being part of a Tract named **Goudy's** quarter, on great Saluda river. Border: sd. river, below **Swanzy's** Mill dam, above ferry road. Witness James **Brown**, John **Mitchel**. Signed Meshech (x) **Overby**. Witness oath by Jas. **Brown** 7 Feb 1796 to Joseph **Downs** J.P. Laurens Co. Rec. 17 Feb 1796.

Page 78 6 Oct 1795, Little Berry **Harvey** and Nancy his wife (Laurens Co.) to Jno. **Cargill** (same), for £38 Sterling sold all that tract of Land containing 200 acres more or less, in sd. Co. on waters of Reaburn's Creek, joining lands of James **Cuningham**, part of sd. **Harvey**, John **Manly**, John **Cammoch** & Samuel **Elliot**. Being part of 400 acres originally granted to Pierce **Butler**, and by him conveyed to Hercules Daniel **Bize**, & by John **Hunter** esq. Atty. for sd. **Bize**, conveyed to sd. **Harvey** 9 July 1793. Witness John **Martin**, John **Dendy**. Signed Littleberry **Harvey** [sic], Nancy **Harvey**. Witness oath by John **Dendy** and John **Martin** 6 Oct 1795 to Thomas **Wadsworth** J.L.C. Rec. 17 Feb 1796.

Page 78 12 Oct 1795, Little Berry **Harvey** & Nancy his wife, formerly Nancy **Cargill**, Daughter of Daniel **Cargill** dec., (Laurens Co.), appoint our Brother & friend John **Cargill** our Attorney to settle our part of sd. Father's, Danl. **Cargill** dec. Estate, in Common Wealth of Virginia. Witness Samuel **Saxon**, Whitf. **Wilson**. Signed Littleberry **Harvey** [sic], Nancy **Harvey**. Witness oath by Whitfield **Wilson** 12 Oct 1795 to Wm. **Hunter** J.P. Laurens Co. Rec. 17 Feb 1796.

Page 78-79   3 Mar 1794, Lewis **Devall** (Laurens Co.) to William **Putman** (S.C.), for £20 Sterling sold a certain tract of land containing 100 acres more or less, being in sd. Co., part of a tract laid out for sd. Lewis **Devall** containing 903 acres & recorded in Book F, No.5, page 552, lying on E side of branch of Warriors Creek, where Solomon **Niblet** now lives. Border: sd. branch, John **Higgins**. Witness David (x) **Duke**, Wm. (x) **Norton**. Signed Lewis **Devall**. Witness oath by William (x) **Norton** 8 Aug 1794 to Danl. **Wright** J.P. Laurens Co. Rec. 17 Feb 1796.

Page 79   7 Aug 1795, Hugh **Crumbliss** (Greenville Co.) to Joseph **Banner** (Laurens Co.), for 10sh Sterling sold the third part of a certain Tract of land on waters of Cane Creek. Surveyed for him in the year 90, by John **Hunter** esq. Surveyor. Signed 31 Aug in year above. Witness Alexr. **Deale**, Warwick (x) **Bristoro**. Signed Hugh **Crumbliss**. Witness oath by Alexr. **Deale** 24 Feb 1796 to Angus **Campbell** J.P. Laurens Co. Rec. 25 Feb 1796.

Page 79   1 Jan 1795, Alexr. **Grant** (Laurens Co.) sold unto William **Moore** (same), seven head of Hogs, two feather Beds & furniture, one large pot, one Dutch oven, two pewter basons, five pewter plates, twelve table spoons, seven tin cups, one pare of cotton Cards, one flax wheel, one poll ax, two Sheep, with all my Household & kitchen furniture. Being for 10 English Guineas. Witness Ezekl. **Roland**, James **Wilson**. Signed Alexr. **Grant**. Witness oath by James **Wilson** 13 June 1795 to Chas. **Saxon** J.P. Laurens Co. Rec. 17 Feb 1796.

Page 79-80   16 Feb 1792, James **Pucket** [sic] (Laurens Co.) to Robert **Swanzy** (Abbeville Co.) for £10 Sterling sold all that Tract of Land containing half of an acre more or less, joining & below **Goudy's** Quarter, on great Saluda River. Together with the Liberty of a Road from thence into the old land through sd. James **Puckett's** Land. Witness Richard **Puckett**, James **Brown**. Signed James **Puckett**. Witness oath by James **Brown** 17 Feb 1796 to Joseph **Downs** J.P. Laurens Co. Rec. 17 Feb 1796.

Page 80-81   10 Nov 1795, Whereas William **Arnold** Sen. planter (Laurens Co.) by his obligation dated 5 Nov 1795, stands bound unto Thomas **Wadsworth** & William **Turpin**, otherwise **Wadsworth** & **Turpin** (S.C.) Merchants, for £72 11sh 1-1/2p Sterling, conditioned for payment of £36 5sh 6-3/4p Sterling with interest. For the better securing of payment sold all that tract of land containing 78 acres more or less, in sd. Co. on Beaverdam branch of Reedy River, bounded N.E. on Widow **Madden**, S.W. on Widow **Bowman**. Granted to Jacob **Wright** by William **Moultrie** esq. 6 Mar 1786, & descended to Elizabeth his wife & George **Wright** his Son, & by them conveyed to William **Arnold** Sen. 6 Nov 1795. Provided that if the sum is paid then this Indenture to be void. Witness James **Young**, James **Boyce**. Signed William **Arnold** Sen. Witness oath by James **Young** 13 Feb 1796 to William **Hunter** J.P. Rec. 17 Feb 1796.

Page 81   30 Jan 1796, Hugh **ONeall** & Elizabeth **ONeall** (Laurens Co.), for £173 6sh 8p Sterling paid by Thomas **Wadsworth** and William **Turpin**, otherwise **Wadsworth** & **Turpin** Merchants (S.C.), sold all that tract of land containing 150 acres more or less, which was granted to my Father Hugh **ONeall** by William **Bull** esq. 26 July 1774, and by my father willed to me. Situate on both sides of Little River, waters of Saluda, and at time of original Survey bounded on W side of sd. river by vacant land & by land laid out to Thomas **Carter**, Henry **ONeall** & Hugh **ONeall** on outermost sides, and on inner side by land laid out to John **Purcell**, on E side on land laid out to Hugh **ONeal**, John **Chesnut**, vacant land and land laid out to John **Purcell**. Also one other Tract which is also on both sides of Little River, adjoining the S.E. of above Tract, which was also granted to my father Hugh **ONeall** and by him willed to me. Together with the Mill, mill dam, dwelling house, out houses and every thing else thereon. Witness James **Boyce**, Thos. **McDonnald** [**McDonald** in one ref.]. Signed Hugh **ONeall**, Elizabeth (x) **ONeall**. Witness oath by James **Boyce** 30 Jan 1795 to Wm. **Hunter** J.P. Laurens Co. Dower renounced by Elizabeth **ONeall** wife of Hugh **ONeall**, 30 Jan 1796 to John **Hunter** J.L.C. Rec. 17 Feb 1796.

Page 81-82   29 Jan 1796, Gallanus **Winn** & Rebekah my wife (Laurens Co.) for £68 paid by Thomas **Wadsworth** & Wm. **Turpin** Merchants (S.C.), sold 100 acres of land, being all that remains of a Tract that was originally granted to John **Young** for 200 acres by William **Bull** 15 Feb 1770, the other half being sold to **Wadsworth** & **Turpin** by Lease & Release 11 & 12 Feb 1793. Situate on a branch of Little River, waters of Saluda, bounded at time of original Survey by vacant land on all sides. Witness Jonathan **Parker**, Tandy **Walker**. Signed Gallanus **Winn**, Rebekah (x) **Winn**. Dower renounced by Rebekah **Winn** 30 Jan 1795 to John **Hunter** J.L.C. Witness oath by Jonathan **Parker** [No date.] to John **Hunter**. Rec. 17 Feb 1796.

Page 82   19 Sept 1795, William **OBryant** & Elizabeth his wife (Greenville Co.) to Thomas **Wadsworth** & William **Turpin**, otherwise **Wadsworth** & **Turpin** (S.C.) Merchants, for £127 12sh Sterling sold all that Tract of Land containing 319 acres more or less, in Laurens Co. on waters of Cane Creek of Saluda and Beaverdam of Little River. Originally granted to Chesley **Davis** by Lieut. Gov. **Bull** 2 Sept 1773, and by him sold to Duncan **OBryant**, and by him conveyed to me. Witness John **Dacus**, Joseph **Babb**, Joseph **Groves**. Signed William **OBryant**, Elizabeth (x) **OBryant**. Witness oath by Joseph **Groves** 31 Oct 1795 to Jno. **Davis** J.P. Rec. 17 Feb 1796.

Page 82-83   19 Feb 1796, Hutchin **Burton** & Patty his wife (Laurens Co.) for £75 paid by Thomas **Wadsworth** & William **Turpin**, otherwise called **Wadsworth** & **Turpin** (S.C.), sold all that Tract of land containing 100 acres more or less, in sd. Co. on Ryan's Creek, a branch of Little River, bounded at time of original survey, under side by Adam **Taylor** & James **Blakely**, all other sides being Vacant. Granted by William **Moultrie** esq. to John **Manly** 2 Oct 1786, & by sd. **Manly** conveyed to Wm. **Wilson** 30 Aug 1787, & by him conveyed to Jesse **Meeks** 28 Feb 1789, & by him conveyed to James

McDowell 14 Mar 1791, & by him conveyed to Hudgen **Burton** [sic] 29 July 1793. Witness James **Young**, Wm. **Dunlap**, Lewis **Saxon**, Aaron **Casey**. Signed Hutchin (x) **Burton**, Patty (x) **Burton**. Witness oath by Lewis **Saxon** 19 Feb 1796 to John **Hunter**. Dower renounced by Patty **Burton** 19 Feb 1796 to John **Hunter** J.L.C. Rec. 19 Feb 1796.

Page 83　22 Apr 1794, Clement **Deale** planter (Pendleton Co.) to Peter **Hitt** (Laurens Co.) planter, for £100 Sterling sold one certain tract of land on waters of Saluda River, N side, sd. Co., containing 150 acres, granted to Philip **Good** in 1767. Witness Thomas **Hitt**, Alexr. **Deale**. Signed Clement **Deale**. Witness oath by Thos. **Hitt** and Alexr. **Deale** 3 Aug 1794 to Angus **Campbell** J.P. Laurens Co. Rec. 17 Feb 1796.

Page 83　12 Oct 1795, Little Berry **Harvey** & Nancy his wife for £100 Sterling sold unto John **Cargill** one part of our father Dl. **Cargill's** dec. Estate. Witness S. **Saxon**, Robt. **Hanna** Jr. [**Hannah** in one ref.]. Signed Littleberry **Harvey** [sic], Nancy **Harvey**. Witness oath by Saml. **Saxon** 12 Oct 1795 to William **Hunter** J.P. Laurens Co. Rec. 17 Feb 1796.

Page 83-84　1 Feb 1796, Ambrose **Hugens** Sen. [sic] & Joanna his wife (Laurens Co.) to Hugh **ONeall** Junr. (same), for £70 Sterling sold all that Tract of Land containing 150 acres more or less, as it is now laid off and on which sd. Ambrose now lives. Joining lands of Wm. **Freeman**, Wm. **McEnture**, a large Survey. Being part of 350 acres granted to Wm. **Griffin** by Wm. **Bull** esq. Lieut. Gov. 5 June 1770. Situate in sd. Co. on waters of Little River. Witness James **Young**, James **Boyce**. Signed Ambrose **Hudgens**, Joanna (x) **Hudgens**. Witness oath by James **Young** 13 Feb 1796 to Wm. **Hunter** J.P. Rec. 17 Feb 1796.

Page 84　2 Nov 1795, Joseph **Thompson** & Mary his wife (Laurens Co.) for £70 sterling paid by John **Garret** (same), sold a certain tract of Land containing 150 acres in sd. Co. on Enoree river, bounded E by land granted to John **Garret**. Border: land laid out to James **Mahon**, sd. river. Witness Eliphaz **Riley**, William **Dollon**, Robert **King**. Signed Joseph **Thompson**, Mary (M) **Thompson**. Witness oath by Eliphaz **Riley** 21 Nov 1795 to James **Dillard** J. Rec. 17 Feb 1796.

Page 84　1 Jan 1796, Charles **Pucket** (Laurens Co.) planter for £20 paid by George **Gordon** & Co. Merchants (same), sold one Sorrel Mare, branded on mounting shoulder 2, about 9 years old; one Sorrel Colt, near one year old; one feather bed with furniture & bed stead. Provided that if sd. **Pucket** pays the sum by 1 Nov ensuing, then this Bill of Sale to be void. Witness William **Byrd**. Signed Charles (x) **Puckett** [sic]. Witness oath by William **Byrd** 18 Feb 1796 to Danl. **Wright** J.P. Laurens Co. Rec. 18 Feb 1796.

Page 85　2 Aug 1793, John **Hunter** esq. (Laurens Co.) to William **Dandy** (same), for £25 2sh 6p Sterling sold all that tract of Land containing 201 acres more or less, in sd. Co. on waters of North's Creek. Being part of 2,000 acres originally granted to Wm. **Bull** Junr. by Chas. Gr. **Montague**, 21 Feb 1772 & conveyed by Lease & release by sd. **Bull** to Wm. **Williamson** 26 & 27 June 1772, and by sd. **Williamson** unto Frederick **Freasure** 23 & 24 Nov 1779 & now by John **Hunter**, by power of Attorney from sd. **Freasure** dated 30 Mar 1792. Border: Thomas **Dandy**, Wm. **Leek**, land surveyed for Wm. **Dandy**, Wm. **Carter**, John **Falconer**. Witness James **Brown**, Joel **Dendy**. Signed John **Hunter** Atty. for Frederick **Freasure**. Received from Wm. **Dendy** [sic] and Joel **Dendy** a Bond for £25 2sh 6p Sterling payable to Joseph **Winthrop**, this 2 Aug 1793. Witness oath by Joel **Dendy** 12 May 1794 to William **Hunter** J.P. Laurens Co. Plat certified 2 Aug 1793 by John **Hunter** D.S. Rec. 17 Feb 1796. [Includes plat.]

Page 85-86 5 Apr 1796, Saml. **Scott** (Laurens Co.) to John **Sims** (same), for £100 Sterling sold all that tract of Land containing 50 acres more or less, being part of 150 acres on which sd. Saml. **Scott** now lives in sd. Co. on waters of Reaburns Creek. Border: Dittany hill, old line. Witness S. **Saxon**, Jno. **Rowland**. Signed Saml. **Scott**. Witness oath by Saml. **Saxon** 5 Apr 1796 to John **Cochran** D.C. Laurens Co. Rec. 5 Apr 1796.

Page 86 4 Apr 1796, David **McCaa** (Laurens Co.) to Saml. **Scott** (same), for £100 sold all that Tract of Land whereon sd. Saml. now lives containing 150 acres, on waters of Reaburns Creek, bounded W by Miss **Millhouse**, S by James **Williams**, all other sides by vacant when laid out. Witness John **Sims**, John (J) **Manly**. Signed David **McCaa**. Witness oath by John **Sims** 5 Apr 1796 to John **Cochran** D.C. Laurens Co. Rec. 5 Apr 1795 [sic].

Page 86-87 23 Jan 1796, John **Weathers** (Laurens Co.) to John **Pinson** (same), for £25 sterling sold a certain tract of Land in sd. Co. containing 75 acres, being part of 300 acres originally granted unto Richd. **Carter**, and sold by him unto Robert **Carter**. Bounding to S.W. & N on Patrick **Cuningham**, E on sd. John **Pinson**, part on Robert **Carter's** [Richd. **Carter** in plat.] land & part on land not known. Being upon waters of Cane Creek. Witness Ste. C. **Wood**, Richd. **Duty**, Robt. **Carter**, John **Pinson**. Signed John **Weathers**. Witness oath by Stephen C. **Wood** 18 Feb 1796 to Geo. **Anderson** J.P. Laurens Co. Plat certified 12 Jan 1796 by P. **Cuningham** D.S. Rec. 18 Feb 1796. [Includes plat.]

Page 87 10 Sept 1791, John Prather **Odell** (Laurens Co.) to Joseph **Hudleston** (same), for £36 5sh sterling sold all that tract of Land containing 120 acres in Ninety Six Dist. on a small branch of Duncans Creek in sd. Co., bounded S.E. by Geo. **Whitmore** & John **Watson**, N.W. by David **Beaty**, N.W. and S.W. by Wm. **Bean**, S.W. by vacant land. Granted to sd. John Prather **Odell**. Witness Thomas **McCreary**, David (D) **Beaty**, John **Robinson**. Signed John Prather (x) **Odell**. Dower relinquished by Mary (x) **Odell**, wife of John Prather **Odell**, 15 Feb 1796 before John **Hunter** J.L.C. [No witness oath.] Rec. 17 Feb 1796.

Page 87-88 6 Apr 1795, Benjamin **Carter** & his wife Mary **Carter** (Laurens Co.) to William **Greene** (same), for £100 current money sold a certain Tract of

Land containing 70 acres more or less, in sd. Co. on waters of Saluda, granted by William **Moultrie** unto sd. Ben. **Carter** 5 Dec 1785. Witness Samuel (x) **Simmon**, Thos. **Morrow**, Sarah **Green**. Signed Benjamin **Carter**, Mary (x) **Carter**. Witness oath by Thomas **Morrow** 26 Dec 1795 to Zechr. **Bailey** J.P. Laurens Co. Rec. 17 Feb 1795 [sic].

Page 88   25 Nov 1795, James **McNess** (York Co.) to Elisha **Mitchel** (Laurens Co.), for £25 Sterling sold a certain tract of Land containing 240 acres, being part of 380 acres in Ninety six Dist. on a branch of Tweddys creek, waters of Little River. Bounded S by Shadrach **Martin**, W by William **Tweddy**, N.E. by Nathaniel **McCoy**, E by Robert **Cooper**. Being first granted by Charles **Pinkney** to sd. James **McNess** & recorded in Book F, No.5, page 344. Witness Abner **Pyles**, Wm. T. **Rodgers**. Signed Jas. **McNees** [sic]. Witness oath by Wm. T. **Rodgers** 18 Feb 1796 to James **Saxon** J.P. Laurens Co. Rec. 18 Feb 1796.

Page 88   16 Sept 1795, Mansfield **Walker** (Laurens Co.) & Jenny his wife to James **Young** (same), for £35 sold one certain tract of land in sd. Co. on N side of Little River of Saluda, containing 125 acres more or less. Border: Little River, James **Young**, Thos. **Dendy** Sen., Wm. **Hall** Sen., spring branch. Originally granted to Thos. **Dendy** and conveyed by him to John **Milam**, and by him conveyed to sd. Mansfield **Walker**. Witness Horatio **Walker**, John **Walker**. Signed Mansfield **Walker**, Jenny (I) **Walker**. Witness oath by John **Walker** 18 Feb 1796 to John **Davis** J.P. Laurens Co. Rec. 18 Feb 1796.

Page 89   11 Nov 1795, Alexander **Roseborough** (Fairfield Co.) to Mattw. **McCreary** (Laurens Co.), for £15 sterling sold a tract of Land containing 50 acres, being part of 100 acres granted by Wm. **Bull** esq. 19 Sept 1794, being in sd. Co. on waters of Enoree River. Bounded by land granted to Hugh **Monford**, Thomas **McCreary**, Joseph **Martindale**. Witness James **Monford**, John **Tomson**. Signed Alexander **Roseborough**, Jane **Roseborough**. Witness oath by James **Monford** 17 Dec 1795 to Geo. **Whitmore** J.P. Laurens Co. Rec. 17 Feb 1796.

Page 89   (Cambridge Dist., Laurens Co.) 3 Sept 1795, Edward **Gidden** (Laurens Co.) & Elizabeth his wife to Robert **Glidewell**, for £2 Sterling sold part of a certain tract of Land in sd. Co. on waters of Beard's fork, a branch of Duncan's creek, containing 100 acres more or less, granted by William **Moultrie** esq. to Edward **Gidden**, 5 Jun 1786. Border: Wm. **Williamson**, Francis **Luffry**, Robt. **Glidewell**, vacant. Plat certified 6 May 1785. Witness William (x) **Glidewell**, James **Leak**. Signed Edward **Giddens** [sic], Elizabeth (e) **Giddens** [sic]. Witness oath by William (x) **Glidewell** 20 Nov 1795 to Roger **Brown** J.P. Laurens Co. Rec. 17 Feb 1796.

Page 89-90   18 Feb 1796, Hugh **Crumbless** (Laurens Co.) to John **Sample** & Peter **Smith** (same), for £16 Sterling sold a certain parcel of Land in sd. Co. on waters of Cane creek, containing 82 acres more or less, being part of 249 acres granted to sd. **Crumbless** in 1791. Border: Jonathan **Puckett**, branch, Joseph

Hollingsworth, Wm. **Wheeler**, **Parsons**. Witness John **Cole**, Jno. **Estes**. Signed Hugh **Crumbless**. Witness oath by John **Cole** 18 Feb 1796 to John **Cochran** D.C. Laurens Co. Rec. 18 Feb 1796.

Page 90   16 Feb 1796, William **Salmon** (Laurens Co.) for £75 paid by Mary **Criswell** (same), sold all that parcel of Land containing 88 acres, in sd. Co. on Saluda River. Border: sd. Mary **Criswell**, William **Anderson**, sd. River. Witness Robert **Criswell**, Dickie **Garlington**. Signed William (WS) **Salmon**. Witness oath by Robert **Criswell** 19 Feb 1796 to John **Cochran** D.C. Laurens Co. Rec. 19 Feb 1796.

Page 90-91   13 Jan 1796, Merick **Fowler** (Spartanburgh Co.) planter to Jesse **Fowler** (Laurens Co.), for £20 Sterling sold 50 acres, being part of 200 acres granted 2 May 1785, by Wm. **Moultrie** esq. Gov. unto John **Fowler**. Situate in Ninety six Dist. on waters of Enoree River & recorded in Grant Book DDDD, page 230. Which sd. John **Fowler** made over 50 acres as a Legacy unto his Son Merick **Fowler**. Border: Jesse **Fowler**, Joel **Fowler**, branch. Witness Reuben (R) **Stone**, Nancy **Wright**. Signed America (A) **Fowler** [sic]. Witness oath by Reuben (R) **Stone** 13 Jan 1796 to Danl. **Wright** J.P. Laurens Co. Rec. 19 Feb 1796.

Page 91   21 Jan 1796, John Prather **Odell** (Laurens Co.) for £65 paid by Saml. **Bishop** (same), sold a Tract of Land containing 100 acres, bounding on S fork of Duncan's Creek. Bound on all sides by vacant land. Original grant to James **McCord** 2 Apr 1773 by William **Bull** esq. & recorded in Secretary's office in Book OOO, page 391. Witness George **Bush**, Saml. **Bishop**, Simon **Thetford**. Signed John Prather (x) **Odell**. Witness oath by Saml. **Bishop** Sen. 23 Jan 1796 to George **Whitmore** J.P. Laurens Co. Dower relinquished by Mary (x) **Odell** 15 Feb 1796 before John **Hunter** J.L.C. Rec. 19 Feb 1796.

Page 91   25 Nov 1795, James **Sullivant** planter to Benjamin **Atkins** (Laurens Co.) (late) planter, for £100 Sterling sold all that tract of Land containing by estimation 125 acres more or less, in sd. Co. on Ryan's Creek, a branch of Little River, 100 acres of which was originally granted to Margaret **Spence**, afterward sold by Arthur **Taylor**, son & heir to sd. **Spence**, to sd. James **Sullivant**. The other 25 acres originally granted to John **Martin**, and conveyed by him to sd. **Sullivant**, adjoining the first mentioned on the West. The whole bounded E by John **Godfrey** & Hutchins **Burton**, S by sd. **Godfrey**, W by Frederick **Sullivan** & John **Wilson**, N by H. **Burton** & **Kennedy**. Witness Ezekl. **Roland**, Larkin **Sullivan**. Signed James (J) **Sullivant**. Witness oath by Ezekl. **Roland** 11 Mar 1796 to John **Cochran** D.C. Laurens Co. Rec. 11 Mar 1796.

Page 91-92   9 Jan 1795, Alexander **Roseborough** (Fairfield Co.) to Hugh **Monford** (Laurens Co.), for £15 Sterling sold a tract of Land containing 50 acres more or less, being part of 100 acres granted by Wm. **Bull** esq. 9 Sept 1774. Being in Laurens Co. on waters of Enoree River. Witness James **Monford**, John **Tomson**. Signed Alexr. **Roseborough**, Jane **Roseborough**.

Oath by James **Monford** 17 Dec 1795, that he saw Alexr. **Roseborough** & Jane his wife sign the deed. Given before Geo. **Whitmore** J.P. Laurens Co. Rec. 17 Feb 1796.

Page 92 29 Feb 1796, William **Harris** for £30 paid by way of Mortgage, a certain negro girl Reena to Thomas **Murphey**, for term of 2 years from date, at which time sd. **Harris** may reclaim sd. Negro Girl by payment of the sum. If he should fail to pay the sum, sd. Thomas keeps possession one year longer. At expiration of sd. term, if **Harris** shall fail to pay, the Negro is to be the property of sd. **Murphey**. Witness Saml. **Saxon**, Henry **Langston**. Signed William **Harris**. Witness oath by Henry **Langston** 11 Apr 1796 to John **Cochran** D.C. Laurens Co. Rec. 11 Apr 1796.

Page 92 11 Nov 1793, Recd. of Anna **Starns** Extx. Of Ebenezer **Starns** dec., £15 Sterling. I acknowledge myself fully paid for all Legacies to me arising from the Estates of either my father or mother, namely Ebenezer & Anna **Starns**. I assign over all rights I have against the estate to Anna **Starns**. And also all claims that I or my heirs shall have to the Lands of John **Starns**, should he die without Issue. Witness Wm. **Mitchel**, Geo. **Wright**, Saml. **Anderson**. Signed Ebenezer **Starns**. Witness oath by William **Mitchel** 17 Feb 1796 to Danl. **Wright** J.P. Laurens Co. Rec. 18 Feb 1796.

Page 92 6 Feb 1796, John **Gray** Sen. (Laurens Co.) for £10 Sterling paid by William **Gray** (same), sold 113 acres of Land, upon S side of Duncans creek. Bounded by lands laid out to John **McCreary**, now belonging to Chas. **Jones**, lands laid out to David **Beaty**, lands laid out to Thos. **McCreary**, sd. creek. Being part of 150 acres granted to Reuben **Flannagan**, 11 Aug 1774, by William **Bull** esq. Lieut. Gov. & recorded in Secretary's Office in Book RRR, page 585. Witness Charles **Jones**, John **Watson**. Signed John **Gray**. Witness oath by Charles **Jones** 6 Feb 1796 to Geo. **Whitmore** J.P. Laurens Co. Rec. 17 Feb 1796.

Page 93 27 Feb 1794, James **Griffin** and Martha his wife (Laurens Co.) to Ambrose **Hugins** [**Hudgens** in one ref.] (same), for £75 Sterling sold all that tract of land containing 150 acres more or less, as it is now laid off. Joining Wm. **Freeman**, Wm. **McEntire**, Large Survey, part of original Tract. Being part of 350 acres granted to Wm. **Griffin** by Wm. **Bull** esq. Lieut. Gov. 5 June 1770. Situate in sd. Co. on waters of Little River. Witness Saml. **Freeman**, Wm. H. **Howard**, Susannah (x) **Freeman**. Signed James **Griffin**, Martha **Griffin**. Witness oath by Samuel **Freeman** 13 Mar 1794 to William **Hunter** J.P. Rec. 17 Feb 1796.

Page 93 30 Jan 1789, John **Williams** (Laurens Co.) planter to James **Russel** (same) planter, for £80 Sterling sold 144 acres more or less, being part of 640 acres in sd. Co. on Durbins creek, waters of Enoree River, granted 15 Oct 1784, by Benjamin **Guerard** esq. Gov. unto Alexr. **Harper**. Recorded in Secretary's office in Book AAAA, page 174. Conveyed unto John **Williams** by sd. Alexr. **Parker** [sic]. Border: old line, S side of sd. Creek, **Harper**, Wm.

Gilbert. Witness Elisha **Halcom**, Caleb **Hughes**. Signed John (W) **Williams**. Witness oath by Caleb **Hughes** 6 Jan 1796 to Hudson **Berry** J.P. Laurens Co. Rec. 7 Feb 1796.

Page 93-94   19 Oct 1793, Jonathan **Wallace** (Laurens Co.) to John **Meders** (same), for £20 Sterling sold 16 acres of Land, being the South part of 173 acres granted 6 Feb 1786, on both sides of Durbins creek, waters of Enoree river, unto Wm. **Young** and made to Thomas **Brandon**, and from him to Moses **Halcom**, and from him to Jonathan **Wallace**. Border: sd. John **Meders**. Witness James **Russell**, Richard **Jones**. Signed Jonathan **Wallace**. Witness oath by James **Russell** 19 Oct 1793 to Hudson **Berry** J.P. Laurens Co. Rec. 17 Feb 1796.

Page 94   13 Jan 1789, John **Williams**, Rachel his wife (Laurens Co.) to John **Meador** (same), for £50 Sterling sold a certain Tract of Land on both sides of Durbins creek, waters of Enoree River in sd. Co., being different tracts, part of one Tract in part granted to John **Humphreys** 15 July 1768 & part surveyed for Chas. **Finley** & made to sd. John **Williams**. Border: branch, creek. Laid off for 160 acres more or less, bordering E by Benjamin **Rainey**. Witness Hudson **Berry**, Joseph (I) **Halcom**. Signed John (M) **Williams**, Rachel (x) **Williams**. Witness oath by Hudson **Berry** 29 Dec 1789 to Danl. **Wright** J.P. Laurens Co. Rec. 18 Feb 1796.

Page 94-95   15 Jan 1791, John **Bowen** & Sarah his wife (Laurens Co.) for £100 Sterling paid by Wm. **Bowen** (same) Merchant, sold the Right to their part of the Estate of Isham **Cleaton** dec. Witness John **Wright**, John (J) **Wilson**. Signed John **Bowen**, Sarah **Bowen**. Witness oath by Jno. (J) **Wilson** 14 July 1791 to Danl. **Wright** J.P. Laurens Co. Rec. 18 Apr 1796.

Page 95   12 Jan 1796, John **Meador** (Laurens Co.) planter for the love & affection I bear towards my loving Nieces, Mary **Hughes**, Jinny Meador **Hughes**, Charity Anderson **Hughes** & Elizabeth **Hughes**, the daughters of Caleb **Hughes** Sen. (same), give the property sd. John **Meador** purchased at public Sale, being the property of Caleb **Hughes** Sen., eleven head of Cattle with their increase, two old mares and Colts with their increase, two feather beds & furniture, two pots, one dutch oven, two pewter Basons, six plates & two dishes, one chest & two saddles. I lend unto Caleb **Hughes** Sen. & Mary **Hughes** his wife till their decease & after their decease to be equally divided among the above named. Witness Joseph **Lyon**, Micajah **Hughes**. Signed John **Meador**. Witness oath by Joseph **Lyon** 12 Jan 1796 to Hudson **Berry** J.P. Laurens Co. Rec. 22 Feb 1796.

Page 95   28 Nov 1795, Joseph **Halcomb** (Laurens Co.) to Sarah **Halcomb** (same) Widow woman, for £10 Sterling sold a tract of 25 acres more or less, in sd. Co. on Durbins Creek, being part of 340 acres granted 6 Feb 1786, recorded in Grant Book FFFF, page 484, signed by William **Moultrie** Gov. unto Joseph **Halcomb**. Border: **Berry**, Creek, **Roberts**. Witness William (W) **Wood**, Sarah (x) **Wood**. Signed Joseph (h) **Halcomb**. Witness oath by

William (x) **Wood** 16 Dec 1795 to Hudson **Berry** J.P. Laurens Co. Rec. 22 Feb 1796.

Page 95-96   28 Aug 1792, Hastings **Dial** (Laurens Co.) to John **Madden** (same), for £1 Sterling sold one certain Tract of land on Burris' Creek, waters of Reaburns Creek, containing 59 acres more or less, being part of 640 acres granted by Wm. **Moultrie** Gov. to John **Sims** & conveyed to Hasting **Dial** [sic], recorded in Secretary's office in Book JJJJ, page 385. Border: John **Sims**, John **Madden**. Witness David **Madden**, John **Rodgers**. Signed Hastings **Diel** [sic]. Witness oath by David **Madden** 17 Feb 1796 to Charles **Saxon** J.P. Laurens Co. Rec. 22 Feb 1796. [Includes plat.]

Page 96-97   15 Mar 1796, Patrick **Cuningham** & Ann **Cuningham** his wife (Laurens Co.) to James **Kinman** (same), for £100 Sterling sell all that tract of land containing 300 acres, being part of a large tract originally granted unto sd. Patrick **Cuningham**, in sd. Co. on N side of Saluda River, adjoining the old Indian Boundary. Border: Patrick **Cuningham**, Saluda River. Witness Memn. **Walker**, John **Cuningham**, Thomas **Meares**. Signed Pat. **Cuningham**, Ann **Cuningham**. Witness oath by John **Cuningham** 15 Mar 1796 to Geo. **Anderson** J.P. Laurens Co. Dower relinquished by Ann **Cuningham** in 1796 before John **Hunter** J.L.C. Plat certified 1 Apr 1795 by P. **Cuningham** D.S. Rec. 21 Mar 1796. [Includes plat.]

Page 97   21 Nov 1795, Thomas **Eliott** Sen. & Lucy **Eliott** his wife (Laurens Co.) to Lewis **Saxon** (same), for £66 Sterling sold a Tract of 110 acres more or less, in sd. Co. on Reaburns Creek. Bounding on sd. Lewis **Saxon**, **Mazick**, John **McCain**, James **Findley**, Reaburns Creek. Granted to sd. Thomas **Elliott** [sic] by Chas. **Pinkney** esq. Gov. 6 Nov 1789. Witness Wm. **Simmons**, Isom (x) **Elliott**, John (o) **Simmons**. Signed Thomas **Elliott**, Lucey **Elliott** [sic]. Witness oath by Wm. **Simmons** 21 Mar 1796 to Joseph **Downs** J.P. Laurens Co. Rec. 2 Apr 1796.

Page 97-98   12 Feb 1796, John **Fields** (Laurens Co.) for £10 Sterling paid by Anna **Starns** (same), sold a certain tract of Land containing 25 acres, being part of 196 acres granted to sd. John **Fields** in 1786, bounding on Anna **Starns**, Roger **Murphey**. Witness John **Starns**, Jacob (J) **Paulk**, John **Creecy**. Signed John **Fields**. Witness oath by John **Creecy** 18 Feb 1796 to Reuben **Pyles** J.P. Laurens Co. Plat certified 13 Jun 1794 by P. **Cuningham** D.S. Rec. 19 Feb 1796. [Includes plat.]

Page 98   1 Jan 1796, Alexander **Hamilton** (Ninety six Dist.) planter to Charles **Simmons** (same), for £80 Sterling sold all that Tract of land containing 100 acres in Laurens Co. on a Branch of Little River of Saluda, granted to Wm. **Martin** in 1778, by Charles Greville **Montague** Gov. & made over to Alexr. **Hamilton** by Lease & Release 30 May 1786. Witness David **Madden**, Thomas **Wood**. Signed Alexander **Hamilton**, Agnes (x) **Hamilton**. Witness oath by David **Madden** 17 Feb 1796 to Charles **Saxon** J.P. Laurens Co. Laid out in Craven Co. at direction of John **Troup** Esq. Dep. Surv. Gen. 22 July

1767. Plat certified 23 Nov 1767 by Ralf **Humphreys** Dep. Sur. Copy taken 30 Sep 1785 by F. **Bremar** Surv.Gen. Rec. 14 Mar 1796. [Includes plat.]

Page 98-99 18 July 1795, Jesse **Holder** (Laurens Co.) planter for £20 Sterling paid by Henry **Langston** (same) planter, sold a certain tract of Land containing 30 acres more or less. Bounding: small branch, mouth of a creek. Being part of 100 acres originally granted unto Margt. **McCulle** by William **Bull** esq. and recorded in Secretary's office in Book EEE, page 1. Witness Gabl. **Bumpass**, Solomon **Holder**. Signed Jesse **Holder**. Witness oath by Gabl. **Bumpass** 18 Feb 1796 to Roger **Brown** J.P. Laurens Co. Rec. 29 Feb 1796.

Page 99 9 Mar 1796, Solomon **Langston** (Laurens Co.) for £100 Sterling paid by Henry **Langston** (same), sold a certain Negro Boy Adam, aged 16 years next April. Witness Bennet **Langston**, Solomon **Langston**. Signed Solomon **Langston**. Oath by Bennet **Langston** 10 Apr 1796, that he saw his father Solomon **Langston** sign the Bill of Sale to his Brother Henry **Langston**. Given before Roger **Brown** J.P. Rec. 12 Apr 1796.

Page 99 1 Sept 1795, Ezekiel S. **Roland** (Laurens Co.) by his bond dated this date for £40 sterling, payable by 1 Nov 1797, to John F. **Wolff** Merchant (same), sold one Negro Girl Lucey, six head of Cattle, thirteen head of hogs, two new feather Beds & furniture & his working tools, with all his crop of Corn, fodder &c. & all his household & Kitchen furniture. Provided that if the sum is paid, then these presents shall be void. Witness Edward **Morgan**, Isom (I) **Hiteloe**. Signed Ezekl. S. **Roland**. James **Sullivan** Sen. does quit claim right & title claimed in the within Mortgage. Signed James (J) **Sullivan**. Witness oath by Edward **Morgan** 16 Feb 1796 to Joseph **Downs** J.P. Laurens Co. Rec. 29 Feb 1796.

Page 100 3 Sept 1795, Edward **Gidden** (Laurens Co.) to James **Leake**, for £50 sterling sold part of a certain Tract of land in sd. Co. on waters of Beard's fork, a branch of Duncans Creek, containing 300 acres more or less, granted by Wm. **Moultrie** esq. to Edward **Gidden**, 5 June 1786. Bounding N.E. on Joseph **Glenn**, N.W. on vacant, S.W. on vacant, S.W. [sic] on John **Cuningham**. Witness William (x) **Glidewell**, Robert (x) **Glidewell**. Signed Edward **Giddens** [sic], Elizabeth (x) **Giddens**. Witness oath by Robert (x) **Glidewell** 20 Nov 1795 to Roger **Brown** J.P. Laurens Co. Rec. 11 Mar 1796.

Page 100-101 1 Aug 1772, John **McCullee** (Craven Co.) planter to Robert **Ellison** (same), for £100 current money sold 100 acres, being granted 12 Sept 1768, by Wm. **Bull** esq. Lieut. Gov. unto John **McCullee**. Situate in sd. Co. on a small branch, S side Enoree, bounding all sides by vact. Land. Witness John **Ellison**, Saml. **Clegg** [John **Clegg** in one ref.]. Signed John (JM) **McCullee**. Witness oath by John **Ellison** 22 June 1785 to John **McCaw** J.P. Camden Dist. Rec. 11 Apr 1796.

Page 101 Lease & Release, 10 & 11 Mar 1789, John **Simpson** (Laurens Co.) Merchant to John **Compton** (same) planter, for £10 Sterling sold that tract containing 100 acres [83 acres in plat.] in sd. Co. on a branch of Duncans Creek, bounding on sd. **Compton**, Benjamin **Byrd**, sd. John **Simpson**. [Plat has bounding: Lewis **Devall**, Benj. **Byrd**.] Witness Nathan **Barksdale**, James **Park**. Signed John **Simpson**. Witness oath by James **Park** 18 Mar 1789 to John **Rodgers** J.P. Rec. 24 Mar 1796. [Includes plat.]

Page 101-102 28 Feb 1795, John **Huskerson** (Laurens Co.) to Henry **Hasel** (same), for £65 Sterling sold two certain tracts of land, containing 485 acres more or less. One tract of 330 acres surveyed for me 5 Feb 1794, being in sd. Co. on Beaverdam & branches of Walnut creek of Reedy River. Bounded S.W. by Joshua **Saxon**, David **Braden**, S.E by Matthew **Gailie**, N.E. & S.E. Thomas **Foster**, N.E. vacant. The tract of 155 acres surveyed for me at above date in sd. Co. on sd. waters, bound S.W. by Pat. **Cuningham** & David **Braden**, N.E. by Joshua **Saxon**, N.W. by John **McGee**. Above lands granted to me by William **Moultrie** esq. & recorded in Book K, and No.5 & the 330 acres on page 182 and the other on page 183 & both examined by Peter **Bremar** pro Secretary. Witness Wm. **Washington**, Wm. (x) **Rasdale**, George (x) **Gorard** [**Gothard** in one ref.], ~~Hannah (x) Gothard~~. Signed John **Huskerson**, Mary (x) **Huskerson**. Witness oath by Wm. (x) **Ragsdale** [sic] 19 Mar 1795 to William **Hunter** J.P. Thomas **Wadsworth** & Wm. **Turpin** agree to relinquish all our right to the within land, 18 May 1795. Witness James **Young**. Rec. 10 May 1796.

Page 102-103 Lease & Release, 17 & 18 July 1793, John **Hunter** esq. (Laurens Co.) to Benjamin **Camp** (same), for £80 sterling sold all that tract of Land containing 407 acres more or less, on S.W. side of Mountain Creek, being part of 500 acres granted to John **Hunter** by William **Moultrie** esq., on Reaburns Creek & Mountain Creek in sd. Co. Bound: David **Morgan**, William **Gary**, Bengn. **Camp**, unknown. Witness S. **Saxon**, John **Cammack**. Signed John **Hunter**. Witness oath by Saml. **Saxon** 9 May 1796 to John **Cochran** D.C. Laurens Co. Plat certified 15 July 1793 by John **Hunter** D.S. Rec. 9 May 1795 [sic]. [Includes plat.]

Page 103 12 Apr 1796, Thomas **Davison** (Newberry Co.) to William **Galligly** (same), a certain white Mare branded a7; one Sorrel Mare; ten head of horned Cattle, some marked half crop under side of both Ears, and some not marked at all; seventeen head of Sheep, the above mark; plantation tools; Household furniture & this ensuing crop, in consideration of £240 sterling. If the sum is paid in one year & nine months after date, the obligation to be void. Witness John **Galligly**, James **Galligly**. Signed Thos. **Davison**. Witness oath by John **Galligly** [No signature.] 18 Apr 1796 to William **Neill** J.P. Laurens Co. Rec. 18 Apr 1796.

Page 104 26 Dec 1795, Samuel **Reed** (Abbeville Co.) to William **Arnold** & Tea **Arnold** (Laurens Co.), for £120 sterling sold all that tract of land containing 300 acres more or less, in Laurens Co. on Horse creek. Border:

ancient Boundary. Being a Tract originally granted to James **Reed** 13 May 1768, recorded in Secretary's office in Grant Book DDD, page 53. Witness Benjn. **Arnold**, Starling **Camp**, John (x) **Camp**. Signed Samuel **Reed**. Witness oath by B. **Arnold** 14 Mar 1796 to Reuben **Pyles** J.P. Laurens Co. Rec. 15 Mar 1796.

Page 104-105   10 Sept 1793, John **Hunter** Esq. (Laurens Co.) to William **Norris** (same), for £33 sterling sold all that tract of land containing 60 acres more or less, in sd. Co. on waters of Reedy River. Bounding on David **Dunlap**, Richd. **Pugh**, William **Norris**, **Beard**, A. **Taylor**. Being part of 500 acres originally granted to Pierce **Butler** 5 May 1772, & by him conveyed to Hercules Danl. **Bize** 9 July 1792, & now conveyed by John **Hunter** by power of Attorney dated 1 June 1793. Witness David **Dunlap**, David **Greene**. Signed John **Hunter** Atty. for Hercules Danl. **Bize**. Witness oath by David **Greene** 12 Apr 1796 to John **Cochran** D.C. Laurens Co. Plat certified 10 Sept 1793 by John **Hunter** D.S. Rec. 12 Apr 1796. [Includes plat.]

Page 105   25 Sept 1795, William **Dendy** & Clary his wife (Laurens Co.) planter to William **Mitchel** planter, for £14 sterling sold one tract of Land containing 126 acres more or less, in sd. Co. on a branch of Norths creek, waters of Little River, being part of two tracts, 86 acres being part of 201 acres conveyed to sd. Wm. **Dendy** by John **Hunter** esq., being part of 2,000 acres granted to William **Bull** Jun. 21 Feb 1772, & by him conveyed 26 & 27 June 1772 to William **Williamson** & by him to Fredrick **Freasure**, by Lease & Release 23 & 24 Nov 1779 & by him to Wm. **Dendy** by John **Hunter** esq. 2 Aug 1793 by power of Attorney from sd. **Freasure**. Together with a tract of 40 acres more or less, being part of 128 acres granted to sd. William **Dendy** by William **Moultrie** esq. Gov. 3 June 1793, adjoining and makes a tract of 126 acres. Border: Wm. **Mitchell** [sic], Wm. **Leek**, Lewis **Young**, **Williamson's** old line, Willm. **Carter**, Wm. **Owens**. Witness Elliott **Clardy**, Wm. **Dendy** Jun., William **Carter**. Signed William **Dendy** Sen., Clary (C) **Dendy**. Witness oath by William **Dendy** Jun. 12 Mar 1796 to Zechr. **Bailey** J.P. Laurens Co. Rec. 11 Apr 1796.

Page 105-106   22 July 1791, David **Allison** & Dorcas his wife (Laurens Co.) to George **Hollingsworth**, for £80 Sterling sold all that tract of Land containing 100 acres, or half of 200 acres granted to William **Allison**, my father, & did Will & bequeath the sd. 100 acres, or half of land, to me. Lying on S side of the 200 acres, where sd. David **Allison's** plantation now is, in Craven Co. on waters of Reaburns creek. Bounding N.E. on land laid out to sd. Wm. **Allison**, N.W. on land laid out to Robert **Box**. Witness John (x) **Hutson**, Charles **England**. Signed David (A) **Allison**, Dorcas (x) **Allison**. Witness oath by John (J) **Hutson** 2 May 1795 to Jonthn. **Downs** J.P. Laurens Co. Rec. 7 Apr 1796.

Page 106   12 Mar 1790, John **Swering** (Laurens Co.) & Anna his wife freeholder to William **Hobbs** (same), for £30 Sterling sold one certain Tract of Land on Muddy Branch, waters of Dirty Creek & Reaburns Creek, being 100 acres, part of 247 acres conveyed unto sd. John **Swering** by Lease & release in 1788 by Hasting **Dial**. Being part of 570 acres granted to sd. Hasting **Dial** by Wm. **Moultrie** esq. 3 Oct 1785. Border: John **Swering**, Thos. **Allison**. Witness Joel **Hart**, Robert **Todd**. Signed John **Swering**, Anna (x) **Swering**. Witness oath by Robt. **Todd** 11 Apr 1796 to John **Cochran** D.C. Laurens Co. Rec. 11 Apr 1796. [Includes plat.]

Page 106-107 21 Sept 1795, Wilson **OBryant** & Jane **OBryant** his mother (Spartanburgh Co.) & Wm. **OBryant** & Elizabeth **OBryant** his wife (Greenville Co.) to Stephen **Jones** (Laurens Co.), for £30 current money sold all that tract of Land containing 100 acres more or less, being part of a tract originally granted to Chesley **Davis** by Lieut. Gov. **Bull** 2 Sept 1773. Situate in Laurens Co. on waters of Cane Creek, bounded by John **Hendrick**, **Wadsworth** & **Turpin**, Estate of Thomas **Boyce**, Widow **Stephans**. Witness John **Dacus**, Susanna (x) **Dacus**, Josep **Groves** [sic]. Signed Wilson **OBryant**, Jane (x) **OBryant**, William **OBryant**, Eliza. (x) **OBryant**. **Wadsworth** & **Turpin** renounced title 31 Oct 1795. Witness oath by Joseph **Groves** 31 Oct 1795 to Jno. **Davis** J.P. Rec. 2 May 1796.

Page 107 19 Nov 1795, George **Walton** to Josiah **Leak**, for £65 Virginia Currency sold one tract of land on Rocky creek, waters of Enoree River, Laurens Co., which sd. **Walton** bought of Caleb **Hughes**, consisting of several parcels adjoining. Containing 200 acres more or less, bounded by John **Williams**, John **Meadows**, Capt. **Russel**. Witness Robt. **Thomson**, Cynthia H. **Thomson**, Philip **Johnson**. Signed George **Walton**. Witness oath by Robert **Thomson** [No signature.] 2 Oct 1795 to Jas. A. **Whyte** J.P. Union Co. Rec. 6 May 1796.

Page 107-108 13 Feb 1796, William **Harris** (Laurens Co.) to John **Cuningham** esq. Merchant (Charleston), for £61 Sterling sold one tract of Land containing 200 acres, in sd. Co. on waters of Little River, bounding by Wm. **Rodgers**, Thos. **Blakely**. Being whereon sd. Wm. **Harris** formerly lived. And also five negroes, one fellow Absalom, one other Sam, one named Peter, one wench Melila, one other wench Kinday; also five head of Horses, one Gray, two Bays, one Sorrel Mare, one black Mare, one black Horse Colt. Also seven Cows & five Calves; also three Feather Beds. Provided that if the sum shall be paid as by a Judgment obtained against sd. Wm. **Harris** in the Laurens County Court, before 1 Dec next ensuing, with interest, then these presents shall cease. Witness Willm. (F) **Underwood**, Nelly (x) **Underwood**. Signed William **Harris**. Witness oath by Wm. **Underwood** (x) 13 Feb 1796 to John **Hunter** J.L.C. Rec. 7 May 1796.

Page 108 21 Sept 1795, Wilson **OBryant** & Jane **OBryant** his mother (Spartanburgh Co.), with William **OBryant** & Elizabeth his wife (Greenville Co.), for £50 current money sold all that tract of Land containing 100 acres more or less, in Laurens Co. Bounding on widow **Stevens**, Wm. **Hall**, John **Donahow**, Zechr. **Bailey**, John **Hendrick**. Being part of a tract originally granted unto Chesley **Davis** by Lieut. Gov. **Bull** 7 Sept 1773. Witness John

Dacus, Susanna (x) **Dacus**. Signed Wilson **OBryant**, Jane (x) **OBryant**, William **OBryant**, Elizabeth (x) **OBryant**. Witness oath by John **Dacus** 28 Dec 1795 to Thomas **Wadsworth** J.L.C. **Wadsworth** & **Turpin** renounced title, 31 Oct 1795. Rec. 9 May 1796.

Page 108 22 Feb 1794, Lewis **Duvall** and Thomas **Nobles** (Laurens Co.) for £14 Sterling paid by Danl. **Wright** esq. (same), sold one negro boy Absalom, about 3 years old. Witness John **Brockman**, Joseph **Lyon**, Francis **Ross**. Signed Lewis **Duvall**, Thomas (T) **Nobles**. N.B. If Daniel **Wright** shall conceive that the above Negro could be obtained from me according to Law, it shall be at my pleasure to give up sd. negro without entering into a course of Law. Lewis **Duvall** & Thos. **Nobles** shall pay me all damages that I may sustain by sd. Negro. Witness oath by John **Brockman** 15 Oct 1794 to Hudson **Berry** J.P. Laurens Co. Rec. 9 May 1796.

Page 109 12 Feb 1796, Joseph **Adair** Jun. (Laurens Co.) for £100 Sterling paid by William **Holland** (same), sold all that Tract of land containing 120 acres more or less, in sd. Co. on a small branch of Duncan's Creek, bounding N by Jno. **McCreary** now John Archer **Elmore**, S.W. by John **Adair** now Benjamin **Adair**, S by Joseph **Adair**. Granted 2 Oct 1786. Also all that tract of Land containing 100 acres more or less, purchased from Samuel **Euring** 16 Dec 1778, being part of 150 acres granted to sd. Saml. **Euring** 30 Sept 1774, adjoining the above tract. Excepting out of the last described Tract 20 acres, being the S.W. part of sd. Tract, extending on both sides of Duncans Creek, heretofore by me laid out, sold unto John Archer **Elmore**. Witness Benjamin H. **Saxon**, John A. **Elmore**, Basil **Holland**. Signed Joseph **Adair** Jun. Dower renounced by Sarah, wife of Joseph **Adair** Jun., also Eleanor **Adair**, widow of James **Adair** dec., 12 Feb 1796 to John **Hunter** J.L.C. Witness oath by John A. **Elmore** 3 May 1796 to James **Dillard** J.P. Laurens Co. Rec. 9 May 1796. [Includes plat.]

Page 109-110 4 Jan 1796, By virtue of a writ issued from the Court of Common Pleas at suit of Charles **Sims** against Ann **Musgrove** Exrx. of Edward **Musgrove** dec., William **Tennent** (Sheriff of Ninety Six Dist.) seized a certain tract of Land and did on the date above publicly sell the tract to George **Gordon** for £27 1sh 4p Sterling. Tract lies in Laurens Co. on Enoree River, and known as **Musgrove's** Mill Tract, containing 150 acres more or less. Witness Wm. **Dunlap**, Andw. **Torrence**. Signed Wm. **Tennent** S. 96 Dt. Witness oath by Wm. **Dunlap** 13 Apr 1796 to John **Hunter** [No title.]. Rec. 9 May 1796.

Page 110-111 Lease & Release, 26 & 27 Feb 1794, James **Wright** (Charleston) Baker to Nathan **Davis** (Ninety Six Dist.), for £10 sterling sold all that half of 200 acres granted to William **Walton** 4 May 1775. Situate on waters of Indian Creek, a branch of Enoree River, bounded N.E. on Clement **Davis**, all other sides vact. N.B. the 100 acres conveyed is the S.W. half of sd. 200 acres. Witness John **Diamond**, Simon **Thelford**. Signed James **Wright**.

Witness oath by Simon **Thelford** esq. [No signature.] 26 Jan 1796 to James **Dillard** J.P. Laurens Co. Rec. 9 May 1796.

Page 111 10 Jan 1795, Thomas **East** (Laurens Co.) Blacksmith to Nathan **Davis** (same), for £10 sold all that tract of land containing 50 acres, being part of 200 acres granted to Clement **Davis** by the Gov., 150 acres conveyed to sd. Thomas **East** by Lease & Release & sd. 50 acres being the place and part of the land where sd. Nathan **Davis** now lives. Being in sd. Co. on waters of Headless Creek. Witness James **Lindsey**, John **Callaghan**, John **Walker**. Signed Thomas **East**. Witness oath by John **Walker** 31 Jan 1795 to Wm. **Hunter** J.P. Laurens Co. Rec. 9 May 1796.

Page 111 14 Mar 1796, Nathan **Davis** (Laurens Co.) for £70 sterling paid by Benjamin **Wilson** (same), sell a tract of land containing 150 acres, being part of two tract, one being granted to William **Walton** for 200 acres by Willm **Bull**, then Gov. 15 May 1775, recorded in Book XXX, page 262, conveyed by Wm. **Walton** unto James **Wright** & by him conveyed 100 acres of same unto Nathan **Davis** by Lease & Release 26 & 27 Feb 1794, being in sd. Co. on waters of Duncans Creek & waters of Indian Creek, for £10 sterling. Adjoining land formerly laid out to Clement **Davis** & adjoining Jno. **Walker** and others. Aforesd. 50 acres being formerly granted to Clement by the Gov. for 200 acres & sd. **Davis** did convey the same unto Thomas **East**, Blacksmith, by Lease & Release, & sd. **East** did convey the 50 acres unto sd. Nathan **Davis** 10 Jan 1795, for £10 Sterling. Witness Samuel **Ewing**, James **Lindsey**. Signed Nathan **Davis** (ND), Jean (J) **Davis** (JD). Oath by Saml. **Ewing** 9 Apr 1796, that he saw Nathan **Davis** and Jane [sic] his wife sign the deed. Given before William **Hunter** J.P. Laurens Co. Rec. 9 May 1796.

Page 111-112 10 Jan 1795, Thomas **East** (Laurens Co.) to Saml. **Ewing** (same), for £20 Sterling sold all that tract of Land containing 50 acres, being part of 200 acres granted to Clement **Davis** by the Gov., being in sd. Co. on Headless Creek, a small branch of Enoree, & sd. **Davis** did convey 150 acres, being the part where Saml. **Ewing** now lives. Witness James **Lindsey**, John **Callaghan**, Jas. **Rammage**. Signed Thomas **East**. Witness oath by John **Callaghan** 31 Jan 1795 to Wm. **Hunter** J.P. Laurens Co. Rec. 9 May 1796.

Page 112 26 Sept 1794, John **Powell** (Laurens Co.) am bound unto Joshua **Noble** (same) for £60 sterling for value received. Condition that if John **Powell** shall on or before 15 Dec next make good titles unto a certain tract of Land on waters of Cane Creek, containing 100 acres more or less, laid out to Clabourn **Sims**, bounded on An. **Burnside**, then the obligation to be void. Witness Clabourn **Sims**, Wm. **Sims**. Signed John **Powell**. Witness oath by Wm. **Sims** 8 June 1796 to Zechr. **Bailey** J.P. Laurens Co. Rec. 9 June 1796.

Page 112-113 28 May 1796, John **Martin** (Laurens Co.) planter to Hutchins **Burton** (same), for £60 Sterling sold all that tract of Land containing 100 acres more or less, in sd. Co. on a branch of Beaverdam, bounding W on Frederick **Sullivan**, S on Moses **Madden** & Isaac **Rodgers**, E on John

Godfrey. [Plat includes border on Stephen **Plant**.] Being part of 640 acres granted to John **Martin** by the Gov. Witness John **Cochran**, Ezekl. **Roland**. Signed John **Martin**. Witness oath by Ezek. S. **Roland** 9 June 1796 to Charles **Saxon** J.P. Laurens Co. Certification of replat 30 Apr 1796 by John **Rodgers** Dep. Sr. Rec. 9 June 1796. [Includes plat.]

Page 113 9 Aug 1794, Benjamin **Williams** (Laurens Co.) to Charles **Lowry** Jun. (same), for £60 Sterling sold one certain Tract of Land, on a branch of Dirty Creek, waters of Reaburns Creek, containing 100 acres more or less. Witness Thos. **Burton**, Wm. **Burton**. Signed Benjamin (x) **Williams**, Lucretia (x) **Williams**. Oath by Thos. **Burton** 25 June 1796, that he saw Benjamin **Williams** & Lucretia his wife sign the deed. Given before John **Cochran** D.C. Laurens Co. Rec. 25 June 1796. [Includes plat.]

Page 113-114 5 Jan 1796, James **Vaughan** & Susanna **Vaughan** his Wife (Laurens Co.) for £80 Sterling paid by Wm. **Dunlap** (same), sold all that tract of Land containing 153 acres more or less, in sd. Co. on Simmons Creek, waters of Little River. Being part of 300 acres granted to Edward **Osbourn** 26 July 1774, and which sd. 153 acres was conveyed to John **Young** by sd. **Osbourn** 5 Apr 1777, and by sd. **Young** to Thomas **Elliott** 20 Feb 1779, & by him to Willm. **Irby**, and by him to Ambrose **Hudgins**, & by him to James **Vaughan**. Border: John **Hunter**, Alexr. **Adair**, John **Chandler**, James **Henderson**, Simmons' Creek. Witness William (x) **Eddins**, John **Hunter** Jun. Signed James **Vaughan**, Susanna (-) **Vaughan**. Dower relinquished by Susannah **Vaughan** [sic] 5 Jan 1796 before John **Hunter** J.L.C. Witness oath by John **Hunter** Jun. 2 July 1796 to John **Hunter** [No title.]. Certification of plat 4 Jan 1796 by John **Hunter** D.S. Rec. 2 July 1796. [Includes plat.]

Page 114 5 Mar 1796, Manassah **Mann** (Laurens Co.) planter for £10 Sterling paid by John Daniel **Kern** (Charleston) Merchant, sold all that tract of land containing 66 acres, on waters of Duncan's Creek. Border: John **Rammage**. Being part of 350 acres granted to Robert **Mann** 1 Sept 1768. Witness John **Luke**, F. C. **Bertzou**, John **Jerra**. Signed Manassa **Mann** [sic]. Witness oath by John **Luke** [No signature.] 3 Apr 1796 to Roger **Brown** J.P. Laurens Co. Rec. 2 July 1796.

Page 114-115 24 Feb 1796, Daniel **Osborn** (Laurens Co.) planter for £100 sterling paid by Richard **Shakelford** (same) planter, sold all that tract of Land containing 150 acres more or less, being part of 200 acres in sd. Co. on a branch of Beaverdam creek, waters of Little River, originally granted to Samuel **Whaton** [sic] 5 Mar 1771. Witness James **Boyce**, Tyree **Glenn**. Signed Daniel **Osborn**. Dower relinquished by Maudlin **Wharton** wife of Saml. **Wharton** & Elizabeth **Osborn** wife of Danl. **Osborn** 18 Feb 1796 before Thomas **Wadsworth** J.L.C. Witness oath by James **Boyce** 3 Mar 1796 to Thomas **Wadsworth** J.L.C. Rec. 8 July 1796.

Page 115 2 June 1796, John **Baugh** Jun. (Laurens Co.) to Thomas **Hood** (same), for £30 sterling sold all that tract of Land containing 84 acres more or less, in sd. Co. on waters of Reedy River, in the fork between sd. River and Reedy Fork. Being part of 150 acres granted to Wm. **Baugh** dec., and by him Willed to sd. John **Baugh**. Border: Reedy Fork, Reedy River, Pat. **Cuningham**. Witness John **Cochran**, Wm. **Baugh**. Signed John **Baugh** Jun. Dower relinquished by Dorcas (x) **Baugh**, wife of John **Baugh**, 18 July 1796 before Jonthn. **Downs** J.L.C. Witness oath by John **Cochran** [No signature.] 19 July 1796 to James **Saxon** J.P. Certification of plat 2 June 1796 by John **Cochran** [No title.]. Rec. 19 July 1796. [Includes plat.]

Page 116 25 Nov 1793, Stephen **Potter** (Laurens Co.) freeholder to Jonathan **Skeen** (same), for £40 Sterling sold one certain tract of Land in Ninety six Dist. on McHerg's Creek, a branch of Reaburns Creek. Originally granted to Nehemiah **Franks** by Wm. **Moultrie** by Patent 5 June 1786, the tract of 340 acres more or less, & conveyed to sd. Stephen **Potter**. Sold a part of sd. tract, containing 100 acres to sd. **Skeen**. Witness Benjamin **Jones**, John **Potter**. Signed Stephen **Potter**. Witness oath by Benjamin **Jones** 6 Dec 1793 to Joseph **Downs** J.P. Laurens Co. Rec. 15 Aug 1796.

Page 116-117 11 July 1796, William **Hunter** esq. (Laurens Co.) to Joseph **Galligly** & Thomas **Roberts** (same), for £86 Sterling paid by Moses **McCreary** & Samuel **Dillard** Admrs. to Estate of Matthew **McCreary** dec. in the purchase of a Negro fellow, sold to sd. Wm. **Hunter** and for which sd. **Galligly** & **Roberts** stand security. To save them from loss, sell one tract of 150 acres of Land, whereon sd. William **Hunter** now lives, in sd. Co. on waters of Indian Creek, bounded by Elia. **Teague**, land formerly Susanna **Dean** & Large Survey. Being originally granted to William T. **Caldwell** & by him conveyed to Josiah **East** & by him to sd. Wm. **Hunter**. Also one Negro fellow Sam & one Negro Woman Amey with all her future increase. Provided that if the sum is paid, then these presents shall be void. Witness Jno. **Cargill** Va., Peter (x) **Kelly**, George (x) **Davis**. Signed William **Hunter**. Witness oath by John **Cargill** Va. 13 July 1796 to John **Hunter** [No title.]. Rec. 15 July 1796.

Page 117 6 Feb 1796, Nancy **Campbell** single woman (Laurens Co.) in behalf of her daughter Jenny **Campbell**, bound her daughter Jenny unto William **Jones** (same) planter, with the consent of Hudson **Berry** , Justice (same), as an apprentice to dwell from this date until she come to the age of 18 years old, which will be on the last of Jan 1810, or until the death of sd. Wm. **Jones'** wife Mary, during which time she shall serve her Master. Wm. **Jones** will give her a reasonable time of Schooling, sufficient to read the Holy Writ; also find & allow sufficient Meat, drink, apparel, washing, lodging & all other things needful. Witness Hudson **Berry** J.P. Signed Nancy (x) **Campbell**, William **Jones**. Acknowledged by Hudson **Berry** J.P. Laurens Co. Rec. 18 July 1796.

Page 117 25 Sept 1794, Whereas 640 acres were granted 15 Oct 1784, recorded in Grant Book AAAA, 174, by Benjamin **Guerard** esq. Gov. unto Alexr. **Harper**, Lying in sd. Co. on branches of Durbins Creek, waters of Enoree River. Conveyed from Alexr. **Harper** unto Nicholas **Davis**, then from him unto Saml. **Goodwin**. Sold by Saml. **Goodwin** for £60 to Richard **Jones** (Laurens Co.) & the sd. **Jones** to William **Jones** (same) planter, for £60 sterling, sold 100 acres of Land more or less, being part of the above at the East end. Border: James **Gibson**. Witness William **Jones**, Solomon **Jones**. Signed Richard **Jones**. Witness oath by William **Jones** 16 July 1796 to Hudson **Berry** J.P. Laurens Co. Rec. 18 July 1796.

Page 118   30 Mar 1796, James **White** (Laurens Co.) for £50 Sterling paid by John **Brown** (same), sold all that tract of Land containing 100 acres more or less, on waters of Duncans Creek in sd. Co. Bounded S.E. by land laid out to John Danl. **Kern**, N.W. by John **Hunter**, S.W. & N.W. by sd. John **Brown**, other sides by vacant land at time of Surveying. Grant recorded in Secretary's Office in Book C, No.5, page 44. Witness Francis **Tillotson**, William **Brown**. Signed James (W) **White**. Witness oath by Francis **Tillotson** 16 July 1796 to Roger **Brown** J.P. Rec. 18 July 1796.

Page 118   19 Feb 1796, John **Rutledge**, by his Attorney John **Hunter** (Laurens Co.) to Joseph **Culbertson** & John **Culbertson** (same), for £35 14sh sold all that tract of Land containing 153 acres, in sd. Co. on branches of Reedy River. Bounding on Patrick **Cuningham**, spring. Being part of 1,300 acres originally granted to Thomas **Shubrick**, & by him conveyed to William **Williamson**, & by him to John **Rutledge** esq. Sd. 153 acres known as **Brewers** old place. Witness Lewis **Saxon**, James **Parks**. Signed John **Hunter** Atty. for John **Rutledge** Jun. Witness oath by Lewis **Saxon** 7 July 1796 to Joseph **Downs** J.P. Laurens Co. Plat certified 14 Nov 1792 by John **Hunter** D.S. Rec. 7 July 1796. [Includes plat.]

Page 118-119   13 Jan 1795, John **Walker** Cooper (Laurens Co.) in consideration of the love and affection for his son Jethro **Walker**, conveyed 100 acres of Land, part of a Survey granted to sd. John **Walker**, and part being granted to Saml. **Ewing**, so as to reserve a Mill Seat to which sd. John **Walker** reserves 30 acres with it, during his natural life, after that descend to sd. Jethro **Walker**, adjoining Adam **Bell**, sd. John **Walker**. Witness James **Lindsey**, Thos. **East**, John **Callaghan**. Signed John **Walker**. Witness oath by John **Callaghan** 31 Jan 1795 to William **Hunter** J.P. Laurens Co. Rec. 18 July 1796.

Page 119   22 Dec 1795, David **Gibson** (Laurens Co.) to Enoch **Jones**, for £30 Sterling sold a certain tract of Land in sd. Co. on Beaverdam Branch. Border: Henry **Bramlet**, branch, Bear branch. Containing in the whole 100 acres more or less. Witness Reuben **Bramlet**, James **Jones**. Signed David (x) **Gibson**. Witness oath by James **Jones** 19 Feb 1796 to Hudson **Berry** J.P. Laurens Co. Rec. 19 July 1796.

Page 119-120   1 Jan 1796, John **Young** (Laurens Co.) to Mordecai **Moore** (same), for £36 sold a certain Tract of Land containing 100 acres more or less, in sd. Co., being part of land laid out to John **Coker**, containing 489 acres on W side of Beaverdam Creek. Recorded in Grant Book D, No.5, page 160.

Border: creek, Henry **Bramblet**, conditional line. Witness Jacob (x) **Maner**, Joseph (x) **Hammond**. Signed John (J) **Young**. Witness oath by Jacob (J) **Maner** 19 Feb 1796 to Hudson **Berry** J.P. Laurens Co. Rec. 18 July 1796.

Page 120   7 May 1796, William **Bowen** (Laurens Co.) to John **House** (same), for £30 sold all that tract of Land containing 175 acres, including the plantation whereon sd. **House** now lives, being part of a Tract granted to Alexander **Frasure** by Patent 20 July 1772. Border: S bank of Enoree River at mouth of Big Branch. Witness Thos. (x) **Westmoreland**, Jacob **Bowen**. Signed Wm. **Bowen**, Mary **Bowen**. Oath by Thos. (x) **Westmoreland** that he saw William **Bowen** & Mary **Bowen** his wife sign the deed. Given before Hudson **Berry** J.P. Laurens Co. Rec. 18 July 1796.

Page 120   10 Feb 1775, Richard **North** (Columbia Co., Ga.) for £6 Sterling paid by Roger **Murphey** (Laurens Co.), sold all that Tract of Land containing 50 acres, being part of 300 acres laid off for sd. **North** & granted by William **Bull** esq. Gov., & bounded on vacant Land one square & on James **Williams** on another square, and John **Cuningham** on another. Witness Joshua **Noble**, John **Motes**. Signed Richard (N) **North**. Witness oath by Joshua **Noble** 20 Aug 1796 to Thomas **Wadsworth** J.L.C. Rec. 23 Aug 1796.

Page 121   12 May 1796, Jacob **Bowman** and Sarah **Bowman** his mother (Laurens Co.) for £100 sterling paid by Jacob **Niswanger** (same), sold all that tract of Land containing 100 acres, in sd. Co. on Reedy River, granted to John **Bryan** by Ld. Chas. Greville **Montague** Gov. 28 Aug 1767, conveyed by Lease & Release to Jacob **Bowman** Sen. Witness Lewis **Graves**, Geo. **Anderson**, Ste. C. **Wood**. Signed Jacob **Bowman**, Sarah (S) **Bowman**. [No witness oath.] Rec. 19 July 1796.

Page 121   14 May 1796, William **Montgomery** (Laurens Co.) to Saml. **Potts** (same), for £50 sterling sold all that tract of Land containing 100 acres more or less, in sd. Co. on N side of Reedy River. Border: hollow Branch, River. Being part of 200 acres granted to Roger **Brooks** by Thomas **Pinkney** esq. in 1787, recorded in Book FFFF, page 30. Witness Hezekiah **Dyer**, Thomas **Kelly**, Nicholas **Smith**. Signed William **Montgomery**, Eley (x) **Montgomery**. Witness oath by Hezekiah **Dyar** [sic] 15 July 1796 to Reuben **Pyles** J.P. Laurens Co. Rec. 19 July 1796.

Page 122-123   Lease & Release, 8 & 9 Mar 1784, James **Brownlee** & Sarah his wife, formerly widow of Hugh **Trimble** dec., (Long Cane Settlement, Ninety six Dist.) to James **Dorrah** (Duncan's Creek Settlement, Ninety six Dist.), for £16 16sh sterling sold all that tract of land containing 250 acres, being in Berkley Co. on Beaverdam, a small branch of Reedy River & bound part to S.E. & S.W. on land laid out to Robert **Dennis** & on all other sides on vacant land. Being granted to Hugh **Trimble** 13 May 1768 by patent by William **Bull** esq. Lieut. Gov. Witness Richd. **Pugh**, Geo. **Brownlee**. Signed James **Brownlee**, Sarah (S) **Brownlee**. Witness oath by Richard **Pugh** [No signature.] 14 Aug 1796 to John **Cochran** D.C. Laurens Co. Rec. 14 Aug 1796.

Page 123 [No date.], John **Wallis** & Mary his wife is seized of a good right to the estate of inheritance of 100 acres of Land, and convey the same unto James **Jones**. Witness David **Welch**, Roley **Bowen**. Signed John **Wallis**, Mary (x) **Wallis**. Oath by Rolley (R) **Bowen** [sic] 9 July 1796, that he saw the deed signed, for 100 acres, on South fork of Durbins Creek, just above the Waggon ford, adjoining land laid out to Robert **McCreary** & land laid out to Ralph **Humphreys**. Given before Danl. **Wright** J.P. Laurens Co. Rec. 19 July 1796.

Page 123 10 Sept 1795, John **Baugh** & Rosanna **Baugh** (Laurens Co.) to George **Cuningham** (same), for £80 sterling sold a tract of 100 acres of Land on waters of Reedy River, bounded on all sides by vacant land. Being laid out for John **Baugh**. Witness Philip **Malkey**, John **Cuningham**. Signed John **Baugh**, Rosanna (x) **Baugh**. Witness oath by John **Cuningham** 19 July [No year.] to Joseph **Downs** J.P. Laurens Co. Rec. 19 Aug 1796.

Page 124 5 Apr 1795, Thomas **Cuningham** (Laurens Co.) to Samuel **Cuningham** (same), for £30 sterling sell a Tract of 139 acres of Land more or less, on waters of Reaburns Creek, bounded on lands laid out for Thos. **Cuningham**, John **Hollingsworth**, John **Cuningham**, Jonathan **Cox**. Being part of 600 acres laid out for David **Webb**. Witness David **Dunlap**, Geo. (x) **Cuningham**. Signed Thos. **Cuningham**. Witness oath by David **Dunlap** 19 July 1796 to Joseph **Downs** J.P. Laurens Co. Rec. 19 July 1796.

Page 124 12 Apr 1796, John **Rodgers** (Laurens Co.) for £30 sterling paid by Saml. **Cuningham**, sold one Negro Girl Happ. Witness McNess **Rodgers**, John **Waldrop**. Signed John **Rodgers**. Witness oath by McNees **Rodgers** [sic] 19 July 1796 to Joseph **Downs** J.P. Laurens Co. Rec. 19 July 1796.

Page 124 18 Feb 1785, I sell my right & title of a certain land Warrant of 200 acres that I obtained from John **Thomas** unto Andrew **Cuningham**, which I oblige myself to make titles as soon as the plat comes to my hand to sd. **Cuningham**, him paying for the titles, for which I bind myself in the sum of £100 current money. Witness Zach. **Carwiles**. Signed James (x) **Hamilton**. I endorse the Bond to Hugh **Young**, this 15 Dec 1792. Witness Thos. **Wood**, Richard **Giddens**. Signed James **Cuningham**. Witness oath by Zach. **Carwiles** 19 July 1796 to Geo. **Anderson** J.P. Laurens Co. Rec. 19 July 1796.

Page 124-125 23 Oct 1790, Tilly **Merrick** (Pendleton Co.) to Henry **Davis** (Laurens Co.) planter, for £10 Sterling sell all that tract containing 196 acres of Land more or less. Situate in Ninety Six Dist. on a small Branch of Enoree River, below the Indian Boundary line, certified for Augustus **Merrick** 13 Jan 1787 & granted by Willm. **Moultrie** esq. 5 Feb 178[blank]. Witness Thos. **Wadsworth**, John **Raney**. Signed Tilly **Merrick**. Witness oath by Thos. **Wadsworth** 2 Aug 1791 to John **Hunter** J.L.C. Rec. 19 July 1796.

Book F

Page 125   6 Dec 1795, Samuel **Weathers** & Martha his wife (Wilks Co., Ga.) to Wm. **Whitehead** (Laurens Co.), for £100 Sterling sold all that tract of land in sd. Co. on waters of Cane Creek, being the land whereon sd. Saml. **Weathers** formerly lived. Border: E side Cane Creek, Salt Spring, John **Carter**, widow **Armstrong**, Allen **Brown**, Margt. **Durham**, John **Griffin**, Charter **Nochol**. Containing by estimation 200 acres more or less. Witness Benj. **Carter**, Robt. (x) **Shaw**. Signed Samuel **Wethers** [sic], Martha (x) **Weathers**. Witness oath by Robert (x) **Shaw** 20 Feb 1796 to Geo. **Anderson** J.P. Laurens Co. Rec. 19 July 1796.

Page 125-126   21 Apr 1796, William **Whitehead** & Frances his wife (Laurens Co.) to Mary **Strain** (same), for £25 sterling sell 100 acres of land on waters of Cane Creek, being part of 300 acres originally granted to Saml. **Weathers** by Lord Chas. **Montagu** 24 Dec 1772. Bounded by Mary **Durham**, widow **Armstrong**, Allen **Brown**, Margt. **Durham**. Witness Thos. Wm. **Fakes**, Jno. **Abernathy**, Jno. Caldwell **Burns**. Signed Wm. **Whitehead**, Frances (x) **Whitehead**. Witness oath by Thos. Wm. **Fakes** 23 Apr 1796 to Angus **Campbell** J.P. Laurens Co. Rec. 19 July 1796.

Page 126   30 Dec 1795, William **Fountain** & Sarah his wife (Laurens Co.) to Jesse **Adams** (same), for £40 sterling sold one certain tract of land containing 137 acres more or less, on a Branch of Reaburns Creek in sd. Co., being part of a tract formerly belonging to John **Williams** & conveyed from him to Stephen **Potter**, & conveyed from him to Sarah **Fountain** & given to William **Fountain** by Marriage. Border: Chas. **Henderson**, Robt. **Bolt**, John **Lowry**, Isom **Histeloe**. Witness Isom (x) **Histeloe**, Charles (x) **Miles**. Signed William (x) **Fountain**, Sarah (V) **Fountain**. Witness oath by Isom (x) **Histeloe** 27 June 1796 to Joseph **Downs** J.P. Laurens Co. Rec. 19 July 1796.

Page 126-127   13 Apr 1796, Benjamin **Adair** (Laurens Co.) for £25 sterling paid by Alexr. **Filson** (same), sold all that tract of land containing 75 acres more or less, all that lies on N side of Duncan's Creek, being part of 100 acres surveyed for Anthony **Funderburgh** & granted to Benjn. **Kilgore**. Situate on Duncan's Creek in sd. Co. Bounded N on John **Craig** & James **Adair**, N.E. on John A. **Elmore**, E on Wm. **Holland**. Witness John **Jones**, Alexr. **Morison**. Signed Benjamin **Adair**. Dower relinquished by Nancy (^) **Adair** wife of Benjn. 13 Apr 1796 before John **Hunter** J.L.C. Witness oath by John **Jones** 29 Aug 1796 to James **Dillard** J.P. Laurens Co. Rec. 30 Aug 1796.

Page 127   20 Oct 1788, John **Williams** (Laurens Co.) to Wm. **Allison** (Abbeville Co.), for 20sh current money sold a certain tract of Land containing 200 acres, being part of a survey containing 640 acres, on South fork of Durbins creek & on S.E. end or corner of sd. 640 acres, according to the old lines made by James **Wafford** in 1774, the place whereon sd. **Allison** formerly lived & where sd. **Williams** now lives, that was vacant land in 1774. Witness Martin **Williams**, Andw. **Cuningham**, Robt. (A) **Allison**. Signed John (M) **Williams**. Witness oath by Robt. (x) **Allison** 16 Mar 1795 to Bayley **Anderson** J.P. Pendleton Co. Rec. 19 July 1796.

Page 127   22 Jan 1789, William **Allison** (Abbeville Co.) weaver to Francis **Allison** planter (same), for 20sh current money, sold a certain tract of land containing 200 acres, being part of a Survey containing 640 acres. Situate on South fork of Durbin's creek & on S.E. end or corner of sd. 640 acres, the place whereon Wm. **Allison** formerly lived & where John **Williams** now lives, that was vacant land in 1774. Witness Moses (x) **Allison**, Robert (R) **Allison**, Thomas **Forster**. Signed William **Allison**. Witness oath by Moses (x) **Allison** 19 July 1796 to Joseph **Downs** J.P. Laurens Co. Rec. 19 July 1796.

Page 128   15 Feb 1794, Joshua **Sutherland** & Nelly his wife (Laurens Co.) to Joel **Dendy** (same), for £30 sell one certain tract of Land in sd. Co. on N side of Little River, containing by estimation 100 acres more or less, being part of 200 acres granted unto Cornelius **Cargill** dec. and conveyed by Cornelius **Cargill**, son & heir to sd. Cornelius dec. to James **Clardy**, & by him to sd. Joshua **Sutherland**. Border: Richd. **Carrol**, Thos. **Jones**, part of sd. tract sold to Thos. **Jones**, Nathan **Crenshaw**, Saml. **Boyd** old line. Witness William **Dendy** Jun., Langston **Drew**, Michael (x) **Gifford**. Signed Joshua (x) **Sutherland**, Nelly (x) **Sutherland**. Witness oath by William **Dendy** 12 May 1794 to Charles **Saxon** J.P. Laurens Co. Rec. 19 July 1796.

Page 128-129   24 Aug 1795, Solomon **Duty** & Susannah his wife (Laurence Co.) to John **Pearson** blacksmith (Union Co., Pinckney Dist.), for £90 current money sell all that tract of land containing 150 acres more or less, in Berkley Co. (but now Laurens) between Broad & Saluda River, on a Draught of Enoree River called the South fork of Duncan's Creek. Bounded S.E. by Wm. **Bean**, N by David **Beaty**, other sides on vacant land at time of Original Survey. Granted to Wm. **Bean** 11 Aug 1774 by Wm. **Bull** esq., then Lieut. Gov. A memorial is entered in the Audt. Gen. Office in Book M, No.13, page 235. Witness John **Watson**, John **Brooks**, Wm. (x) **Gray**. Signed Solomon **Duty**, Susannah (x) **Duty**. Witness oath by John **Watson** 15 July 1796 to George **Whitmore** J.P. Laurens Co. Rec. 19 July 1796.

Page 129   8 Aug 1796, Matthew **Brown** (Laurens Co.) Miller for £25 Sterling paid by Robert **Gilliland** (same) Hatter, sold all that tract of Land containing 113 acres more or less, in sd. Co. along N.E. side of the Branch where sd. **Gilliland** now lives. Witness Joseph **Leeke**, William **Brown**. Signed Matthew **Brown**, Jane (x) **Brown**. Witness oath by Joseph **Leeke** 8 Aug 1796 to Roger **Brown** J.P. Laurens Co. Rec. 8 Aug 1796.

Page 129   2 Aug 1796, Nathaniel **Ashley** (Laurens Co.) for $57 [sic] paid by Robert **Gilliland** (same), sell all that tract of Land containing 57 acres more or less, on waters of Duncan's Creek on N.E. side of sd. Creek, in sd. Co., part of a tract originally granted to Roger **Brown** by William **Moultrie** by patent 3 Apr 1796. Witness Matthew **Brown**, John **Brown**. Signed Nathaniel **Asley** [sic]. Witness oath by John **Brown** 2 Aug 1796 to Roger **Brown** J.P. Laurens Co. Rec. 8 Aug 1796.

Page 129   4 Mar 1796, Joseph **Lynch** (Laurens Co.) planter for £14 paid by Thomas **Adkins** (same), sell all that tract of Land containing 80 acres more or less, being part of land originally granted unto James **Smith** containing 500 acres 31 July 1775, on waters of Coxes creek, being waters of Enoree in Laurens Co. Border: John **Lynch**, Aaron **Lynch**, Jesse **Holder**, Thos. **Adkins**. Witness Edward **Cox**, Solomon **Langston**. Signed Joseph **Lynch**. Witness oath by Solomon **Langston** 15 July 1796 to Roger **Brown** J.P. Laurens Co. Rec. 19 July 1796.

Page 130   4 Mar 1796, Thomas **Adkins** (Laurens Co.) planter for £10 paid by James **Griffin** (same), sold all that tract of land containing 50 acres more or less, being part of 500 acres, dated 31 July [sic] & granted to James **Smith** & lying on Coxes Creek, being waters of Enoree in Laurens Co. Border: sd. **Griffin**, Spring Branch, Jesse **Holder**, Samuel **Stiles**, Joseph **Lynch**, Aaron **Lynch**. Witness Edward **Cox**, Solomon **Langston**. Signed Thomas (T) **Adkins**. Witness oath by Solomon **Langston** 15 July 1796 to Roger **Brown** J.P. Laurens Co. Rec. 19 July 1796.

Page 130   25 Mar 1793, Ezekiel **Akins** & Benjamin **Kivell** (S.C.) Exors. of estate of Lewis **Akins** dec. to William **Bowen** (same), for £40 sold a certain tract of Land in Laurens Co. on S fork of Durbin's Creek. Tract lies on N side of sd. Creek, the Creek to be the dividing line, being part of 200 acres granted to David **Welch** by Wm. **Bull**, then Gov. in 1773 & recorded in Book M, No.12, page 173. Supposed to contain 100 acres more or less. Witness Edwd. **Michusson**, Burrel **Thompson**. Signed Ezekiel **Akins**, Benj. **Kivell**. Witness oath by Edwd. **Mitchusson** [sic] 25 Mar 1793 to Danl. **Wright** J.P. Laurens Co. Rec. 20 July 1796.

Page 130-131   6 Nov 1795, Elizabeth **Wright** & George **Wright** her Son (Laurens Co.) to William **Arnold** Sen., for £40 current money sold a certain tract of Land containing 78 acres more or less, in sd. Co. on Beaverdam, a branch of Reedy River. Granted to Jacob **Wright** by William **Moultrie** esq. 12 Nov 1784, & descended to his Widow Elizabeth & Son George. Witness Jno. **Bowman**, Jacob **Wright**, Thos. (x) **Wright**. Signed Elizabeth (x) **Wright**, George **Wright**. Witness oath by Jno. **Bowman** 18 Mar 1796 to Geo. **Anderson** J.P. Laurens Co. Rec. 20 July 1796.

Page 131   Lease & Release, 24 & 25 Sept 1779, William **Bourland** (Ninety six Dist.) to Elisha **Attway**, for £200 sold a tract of land containing 200 acres on Warriors creek, bounded on W on land laid out for Joseph **Attway**, on E on land lately conveyed to James **McCarley** by sd. Wm. **Bourland** & on all other sides by vacant Land. Being part of 300 acres granted to Wm. **Bourland** 1 Dec 1769. A memorial is entered in Auditor's Office in Book K, No.10, page 35, 25 Jan 1770. Witness John **Deen**, Willm. (C) **Crow**. Signed William **Bourland**, Mary (M) **Bourland**. Oath by John **Deen** 25 Sept 1779, that he saw Wm. **Bourland** & Mary his wife sign the deed. Given before George **Ross** J.P. Ninety Six Dist. Rec. 20 July 1796.

Page 132 21 Aug 1794, Fredrick **Freasure** (Charleston) by his Attorney John **Hunter** to Henry **Byram**, for £20 sterling sell all that tract of land containing 100 acres more or less, in Laurens Co. on waters of Reaburns Creek on a branch called Moll Kelley's, bounding at time or original Survey on Robert **Milhouse** & James **Williams**. Granted to Wm. **Williamson** & by him conveyed to Fredrick **Freasure** by Lease & Release 23 & 24 Nov 1779, & by sd. **Freasure** by his Attorney John **Hunter** by Power of Attorney dated 31 Mar 1792. Witness Jos. **Galligly**, Mansd. **Walker**. Signed Fredrick **Freasure** by his Atty. John **Hunter**. Received from Henry **Byram** & David **McCaa** a Bond for £20 payable to Joseph **Winthrop** (Charleston), 21 Aug 1794. Signed John **Hunter**. Witness oath by Mansfield **Walker** 18 July 1796 to Jonthn. **Downs** J.P. Laurens Co. Rec. 21 July 1796.

Page 132 18 Apr 1796, William **Butler** (Laurens Co.) planter for £22 sterling paid by John **Simpson** Mercht. (same), sold two feather beds, clothes & furniture belonging to sd. Beds, six pewter plates, two Basons, one dish of pewter & also all my Share of the crop of corn fodder, rye & barley & all that I make as my part on sd. Jno. **Simpson's** plantation this year, of grain of any kind, & likewise one knife. One knife delivered in behalf of the whole crop & property. Witness Francis **Higgins**, James **Stewart**. Signed William **Butler**. Witness oath by Francis **Higgins** 1 June 1796 to Charles **Griffin** J.P. Newberry Co. Rec. 20 July 1796.

Page 132-133 13 Jan 1795, Thomas **East** (Laurens Co.) to James **Ramage** (same) for £20 sterling sold all that tract of Land containing 115 acres more or less, being part of 233 acres granted by Wm. **Moultrie**, then Gov., & recorded in Grant book JJJJ. Border: John **Walker**, Clement **Davis** old line, branch. Witness James **Lindsey**, John **Walker**, Nathan **Davis**. Signed Thomas **East**. Witness oath by John **Walker** 31 Jan 1795 to William **Hunter** J.P. Laurens Co. Rec. 20 July 1796.

Page 133 10 July 1795, Danl. **Deupree** (Laurens Co.) to Joseph **Babb** (same), for £75 Sterling sold one certain tract of land in sd. Co. on waters of Cane Creek containing 100 acres more or less, being part of 350 acres granted to Cornelius **Cargill** dec. Border: head of Bee Branch, **White**, John **Carter**, Tumbling Branch, Paul **Findley**, **Dudgin**. Witness Wm. **Coleman**, William **Hall**. Signed Daniel **Deupree**, Sarah **Deupree**. Witness oath by Wm. **Coleman** 20 June 1796 to Zechr. **Bailey** J.P. Laurens Co. Rec. 20 July 1796.

Page 133 29 Dec 1795, John B. **Bennet** (Newberry Co.) is bound in a Mortgage of a Negro Boy Quillo, 11 years old, unto Lud **Dulen** (Laurens Co.) for £51 1sh 11p sterling [Spanish Mill Dollars at 4 & 8 pence in another ref.] with interest for £20. Condition that if the sum is paid, then the obligation shall be void. Witness John **Bourland**. Witness to receipt, John **Ballau**. Witness oath by John **Bolland** [sic] 16 Aug 1796 to Geo. **Whitmore** J.P. Laurens Co. Rec. 18 Aug 1796.

Page 133 20 July 1796, County in behalf of an Orphan Girl Pamelia **Tomlin**, the Issue of Rachel **Tomlin** (sd. Co.), placed & bound sd. Pamelia **Tomlin** to Thomas **Allison** & Catherine his wife, to dwell from this date until she shall come to the age of 18 years, which will be 17 years & 4 months. She shall be put unto the command of her Master & Mistress, obedient in all things and orderly toward the rest of the Family. Sd. Thomas & Catherine **Allison** shall instruct sd. Girl in the best ways the art of Family Business, to give her sufficient learning to read the hold Writ & find her sufficient meat, drink, washing, lodging & apparel. Certified by James **Saxon** J.L.C. Signed Thos. (T) **Allison**, Catherine (O) **Allison**. Rec. 18 Aug 1796.

Page 134 19 Mar 1793, William **Taylor** Wheel wright (Laurens Co.) to the dissenting Presbyterian Congregation of Rocky Spring (same), for 10sh sterling sold a tract of Land containing 1-1/2 acres more or less, being laid out of a Tract originally granted to sd. **Taylor** on a Branch of Duncan's Creek. Witness Robert **Hutcheson**, John (O) **Taylor**. Signed William **Taylor**. Witness oath by Robert **Hutcheson** 28 July 1796 to John **Cochran** D.C. Laurens Co. Rec. 18 Aug 1796.

Page 134 27 July 1796, Robert **Hood** & Jean **Hood** his wife (Laurens Co.) to Danl. **Osbourn** (same), for £15 sold a certain tract of Land containing by Estimation 150 acres more or less, in sd. Co. on waters of Little River, adjoining Richard **Shackleford**, Wm. **Lowe**, Mr. **Geddis**, Pat. **Cuningham**, sd. **Osbourn**. Being part of 400 acres originally granted to Robert **Hood** by Wm. **Bull** Lieut. Gov. 19 Aug 1774. Recorded in Autr. Office in Book M, No.13, page 267, 1 Feb 1775 & since granted to Ratliff **Joel** by Wm. **Moultrie** esq. Gov. 4 Apr 1785, for 250 acres. This conveyance being part of sd. Tract. Witness Charles **Simmons**, Thomas **Hood**. Signed Robert (x) **Hood**, Jean (x) **Hood**. Witness oath by Charles **Simmons** 16 Aug 1796 to John **Cochran** D.C. Laurens Co. Rec. 18 Aug 1796.

Page 134-135 Lease & Release, 9 & 10 Sept 1793, John **Hunter** esq. (Laurens Co.) to David **Ross** Hatter (same), for £6 6sh sterling sell all that tract of Land containing 138 acres in sd. Co. and waters of Reedy River, bounding on David **Ross**, David **Greene**, John **Rodgers**, Reedy River. Being part of 500 acres originally granted 5 May 1772 to Pierce **Butler** & by him conveyed to Hercules Danl. **Bize** 9 July 1792, & now conveyed by John **Hunter** by Power of Attorney from sd. **Bize** dated 1 June 1793. Witness Saml. **Cooper**, Francis **Ross**. Signed John **Hunter** Atty. for Hercules Danl. **Bize**. Witness oath by Francis **Ross** 12 Mar 1794 to Joseph **Downs** J.P. Laurens Co. Plat certified 10 Sept 1793 [No signature.]. Rec. 25 Aug 1796. [Includes plat.]

Page 135-136 23 Dec 1795, William **Fountain** planter & Sarah his wife to Cornelius **Hooker**, for £20 sterling sold one certain tract of Land in sd. Co. on branches of Reaburns Creek containing 50 acres more or less, being part of Land granted to John **Williams** & conveyed from him to Stephen **Potter** & from him to Sarah **Durham**, and from sd. **Durham** given to Wm. **Fountain** in marriage. Bounded on James **Smith's** big Survey, Burgess **Goolsby**, Isham

Histeloe. Witness James **McCaa**, John **Cochran**. Signed Sarah **Fountain** (x), William **Fountain** (x). Witness oath by John **Cochran** 14 Sept 1796 to Chas. **Saxon** J.P. Laurens Co. Rec. 14 Sept 1796.

Page 136 28 Mar 1796, John **Sims** (Laurens Co.) to Samuel **Scott** (same), for the yearly rent of 20sh for the Term of 20 years, all that parcel of Land on which sd. Saml. **Scott** now lives. Witness Wm. **Dunlap**, John **Cochran**. Signed John **Sims**. Witness oath by John **Cochran** 14 Sept 1796 to Chas. **Saxon** J.P. Laurens Co. Rec. 14 Sept 1796.

Page 136-137 24 Aug 1796, Joseph **Halcomb** (Laurens Co.) Planter to Obediah **Halcomb** (same) planter, for £15 Sterling sold a tract of land Supposed to contain 50 acres more or less, in sd. Co. on waters of Durbins Creek, being the S.E. part of 340 acres in Ninety six Dist. granted 6 Feb 1796, recorded in Grant Book FFFF, page 484, signed by Wm. **Moultrie** Gov. Border: old tract, **Locock**, near a spring. Witness Joshua **Halcomb**, Beacy (x) **Halcomb**. Signed Joseph (x) **Halcomb**. Witness oath by Joshua **Halcomb** 24 Aug 1796 to Hudson **Berry** J.P. Laurens Co. Rec. 19 Oct 1796.

Page 137 ~~10 Nov 1790, Abner **Babb** (Laurens Co.) to John **Blackwell** (same), for £200 Sterling sell one certain Plantation of Land containing by estimation 200 acres more or less, in sd. Co. on Raiborns Creek, a branch of Saluda. Bounded on all sides by vacant land when Surveyed. Granted to Oliver **Matthews** and by him conveyed to Joseph **Babb** and including the plantation whereon sd. John **Blackwell** now lives. Witness Richard **Jowell**, Thos. **Babb**. Signed Abner **Babb**, Martha (x) **Babb**. Rec. 19 Oct 1796.~~

Page 138 13 Jan 1795, John **Walker** cooper (Laurens Co.) in consideration of pure good will, love & affection for his Daughter Martha **Roberts**, wife of Evans **Roberts**, and her kin and heirs of her Body lawfully begotten, give a Tract of Land containing 50 acres, granted to sd. John **Walker**, being part of 125 acres and being the place where sd. Evans **Roberts** now lives, adjoining sd. John **Walker**, James **McClure**. Evans **Roberts** and Martha his wife shall possess the tract during their Natural lives and then to the next heir at law. Witness James **Lindsey**, Thomas **East**, John **Callaghan**. Signed John **Walker**. Witness oath by Thomas **East** 31 Jan 1795 to Wm. **Hunter** J.P. Laurens Co. Rec. 19 Oct 1796.

Page 138-139 11 Nov 1795, James **Tweedy** (Laurens Co.) to William **Montgomery** (S.C.), for £30 Stlg., sold all that tract of Land containing by estimation 100 acres more or less, in sd. Co. on N side of Reedy River. Border: Hallow branch, Reedy River. Being part of a Bounty of Land formerly belonging to Roger **Brooks**, for 200 acres granted by Thomas **Pinckney** Esq. in 1787. Recorded in Secretary's grant Book FFFF, page 30. Witness Thomas **Kelley**, Hezekiah **Dyer**, John **Dorroh**. Signed James **Tweedy**, Rachel **Tweedy**. Witness oath by Thomas **Kelley** 19 Mar 1796 to Reuben **Pyles** J.P. Laurens Co. Rec. 20 Oct 1796.

Page 139   13 Aug 1796, John **Martin** & Elizabeth **Martin** his wife and William **Martin** & Sarah **Martin** his wife (Laurens Co.) to Horatio **Walker** (same), for £50 sell all that tract of land containing 150 acres more or less, in sd. Co. on red lick branch, waters of Beaver Dam. Part of 640 acres, originally granted to sd. Wm. **Martin** 3 Apr 1786. Bounded S by Wm. **Martin**, W by John **Todd**, N on Wm. **Martin**, E on Nancey **Barbie** [**Barbey** on plat.] & Fredrick **Sullavant**. Witness Ezel. S. **Roland**, John **Rodgers** D.S. Signed John **Martin**, Elizabeth (x) **Martin**, William **Martin**, Salley (x) **Martin** [sic]. Witness oath by Ezekl. S. **Roland** 10 Oct 1796 to John **Cochran** D.C. Laurens Co. Plat surveyed 30 Aug 1796 by John **Rodgers** D.S. Rec. 20 Oct 1796. [Includes plat.]

Page 139   4 Apr 1796, Pleasant **Sullivant** (Greenville Co.) sell unto Stephen **Mullings** (Laurens Co.), one Negro Boy Hall, about 7 or 8 years old, in consideration of 160 Silver Dollars. Witness Owen **Sullivant**, Hewlet **Sullivant**. Signed Pleasant **Sullivant**. Witness oath by Hewlet **Sullavant** [sic] 3 Oct 1796 to Thomas **Camp** J.P. Greenville Co. Rec. 20 Oct 1796.

Page 140   10 Oct 1796, Patrick **Cuningham** and Ann **Cuningham** my wife (Laurens Co.) for $25 paid by John **Pinson** (same), sold all that tract of Land containing 32 acres more or less, on E side of Road leading from Laurens Court house to Swanceys ferry, being part of 300 acres originally granted to Richard **Carter** on waters of cain Creek & goldmans Creek. Out of sd. 300 acres, Richard **Carter** sold away unto his son John **Carter** 100 acres, and John **Carter** as the oldest son & heir at law, sold the sd. 100 acres unto sd. Patrick **Cuningham**. The sd. 32 acres is part of the 100 acres. Border: John **Pinson**, Patrick **Cuningham**. Witness Memuca **Walker**, Howard **Pinson**, John **Cuningham**. Signed P. **Cuningham**, Anne **Cuningham** [sic]. Witness oath by Howard **Pinson** 10 Oct 1796 to Geo. **Anderson** J.P. Laurens Co. Plat certified 1 June 1796 [No signature.]. Rec. 21 Oct 1796. [Includes plat.]

Page 140-141   11 Mar 1796, John **Simpson** (Laurens Co.) to Samuel **Simpson** (same), for £10 sold a certain tract of land on waters of Beaver Dam Creek, waters of Enoree River in sd. Co., including the plantation where sd. Samuel **Simpson** now lives, containing 151 acres. Border: **Lightcap**. Witness John **Wallis**, Thos. **Barnes**. Signed John (x) **Simpson**. Witness oath by John **Wallis** 28 May 1796 to Daniel **Wright** J.P. Laurens Co. Rec. 21 Oct 1796.

Page 141   11 Mar 1796, John **Young** (Laurens Co.) to Samuel **Simpson** (same), for £5 sold a certain tract of land on waters of Beaver Dam Creek, on E side of sd. Creek, waters of Enoree River in sd. Co., including the sd. Samuel **Simpsons** field, containing 50 acres more or less. Border: **Lightcap's** old line, Creek, bare Branch. Being part of the tract whereon John **Young** now lives. Originally granted to John **Coaker**, containing 489 acres, 7 Nov 1791. Witness John **Wallis**, John (x) **Simpson**. Signed John (J) **Young**. Witness oath by John **Wallis** 28 May 1796 to Daniel **Wright** J.P. Laurens Co. [No record date.]

Page 141-142 20 June 1796, Alexander **Morrison** (Laurens Co.) Merchant for $50 paid by George **Gordon** Merchant (same), sold two Tracts of Land, both on S side of Enoree River, one tract containing 75 acres more or less, granted to Ann **Musgrove**, now Ann **Smith**, 20 Dec 1791. Bounded N.E. by Wm. **Berry**, S.E. by Duglass **Puckett**, N.W. by River Enoree. The other Tract granted to Ann **Musgrove**, now Ann **Smith**, 9 Feb 1792, bounded N on Edwd. **Musgrove** dec., E on Duglass **Puckett**. Containing 65 acres more or less. Two tracts were sold by William **Dunlap** Sheriff of sd. Co. for Debt due to George **Gordon**, 6 June 1795, with titles to George **Gordon** & Alexr. **Morrison**, the first dated 14 June & the next dated 16 June in the year last mentioned. Recorded in sd. Co. in Book F, page 57 & 58. Certified for 29 Dec in year last mentioned. Witness John **Lynch**, William **Johnston**. Signed Alexr. **Morison** [sic]. Witness oath by William **Johnston** 4 July 1796 to Roger **Brown** J.P. Laurens Co. Rec. 22 Oct 1796.

Page 142 3 Sept 1796, William **Bowen** (Laurens Co.) for £20 paid by Joseph **Lyon** (same), sold a parcel of land containing 111 acres, being part of 3,000 acres granted 20 July 1772 unto Alexr. **Fraser** & conveyed to James **Fraser**, then from him conveyed to sd. Wm. **Bowen**. Situate in sd. Co. on S side of Durbins Creek, waters of Enoree River. Border: Waggon road, Levy **Young**, Joseph & Elisha **Holcomb**. Witness Thos. **Parks**, Wm. **Arnold**. Signed William **Bowen**. Witness oath by William **Arnold** 17 Sept 1796 to Hudson **Berry** J.P. Laurens Co. Rec. 23 Oct 1796.

Page 142-143 3 Sept 1796, William **Bowen** (Laurens Co.) for £30 paid by Elisha **Holcomb** (same), sold a parcel of Land containing 145 acres, being part of 3,000 acres granted 20 July 1772, unto Alexr. **Fraser** & conveyed unto James **Fraser**, then from him conveyed to sd. William **Bowen**. Situate in sd. Co. on S fork of Durbins Creek, waters of Enoree River. Border: Elisha **Holcomb**, Hudson **Berry**, John **Meader**, Levy **Young**, branch, Joseph **Lyon**, Joseph **Holcomb**. Witness Thos. **Parks**, Wm. **Arnold**. Signed William **Bowen**. Witness oath by William **Arnold** 17 Sept 1796 to Hudson **Berry** J.P. Laurens Co. Rec. 23 Oct 1796.

Page 143 22 Sept 1796, William **Bowen** (Laurens Co.) for £15 paid by Joseph **Holcomb** (same), sold a parcel of land containing 83 acres, being part of 3,000 acres granted 20 July 1772, unto Alexr. **Fraser** & conveyed unto James **Fraser** & from him conveyed to sd. William **Bowen**. Situate in sd. Co. on S fork of Durbins creek, waters of Enoree River. Border: Elisha **Holcomb**, Joseph **Lyon**, sd. Joseph **Holcomb**. Witness Jesse **Wallace**, Obediah **Holcomb**. Signed William **Bowen**. Witness oath by Obediah **Holcomb** 6 Oct 1796 to Hudson **Berry** J.P. Laurens Co. Rec. 23 Oct 1796.

Page 143-144 25 July 1796, James **McDowell** Sen. & Mary his Wife (Laurens Co.) to Henry **Atkinson** (same), for £60 Sterling sold one certain tract of land in sd. Co. on S side of Little River, containing by estimation 100 acres more or less, being part of land granted to David **Craddock** dec., conveyed by John **Craddock** son & heir unto Richd. **Hix**, and by him unto sd. James **McDowell**.

Border: Little River, **Boyd's** old line, Silv. **Walker**, branch, John **Davis**, Joseph **Cox**, Vincent **Glas**. Witness Silv. **Walker** Jun., George **Watts**, Lewis J. W. (x) **Dupree**. Signed James (x) **McDowell**, Mary (O) **McDowell**. Witness oath by George **Watts**, Silvs. **Walker**, Lewis J. W. **Dupree** 25 July 1796 to John **Davis** J.P. Laurens Co. Dower relinquished by Mary (S) **McDowell** 11 Oct 1796 before John **Hunter** J.L.C. Rec. 23 Oct 1796.

Page 144-145   21 Aug 1796, Margaret **Cuningham** (Laurens Co.) for £30 Sterling paid by Clement **Wells** (same), sold all that Tract of Land containing 50 acres in sd. Co. on waters of Cain Creek, being part of 250 acres originally granted unto John **Owens** and part of 97 acres originally granted unto Patrick **Cuningham** and now the property of sd. Margaret **Cuningham**. Border: **Crossen**, M. **Cuningham**. Witness John **Wells**, John **Morris**, John **Cuningham**. Signed Margaret (m) **Cuningham**. Witness oath by John **Wells** 8 Oct 1796 to Angus **Campbell** J.P. Laurence Co. Plat certified 20 Aug 1796 by John **Cuningham**. Rec. 23 Oct 1796. [Includes plat.]

Page 145-146   28 July 1796, Samuel **Henderson** (Laurence Co.) for £7 8sh Stlg., paid by William **East** (same), sold all that certain tract of Land whereon sd. **East** now lives containing 100 acres, bounding on sd. Samuel **Henderson**, William **East** Sen., John **Croford**. Being part of a tract granted to Daniel **Revenall** for 3,000 acres & conveyed by heirs or Exors. of sd. **Revenal** [sic] to sd. **Henderson**. Situate in sd. Co. on waters of Simmons Creek, waters of Little River. Witness Joseph **East**, Samuel **Mathis**. Signed Samuel **Henderson**. Dower relinquished by Mary Ann (M) **Henderson**, wife of Samuel **Henderson**, 28 July 1796 before John **Hunter** J.L.C. Receipt witnessed by John **Sinclear**, Joel **East**. Plat certified 28 July 1796 by John **Hunter** D.S. Rec. 23 Oct 1796. [Includes plat.]

Page 146   8 Aug 1796, David **Gibson** planter (Laurens Co.) to Stephen **Garrett** (same) planter, for $150 sold a certain tract of land containing 50 acres more or less, in sd. Co. on S side of Warriers Creek, waters of Enoree River, being part of 200 acres granted unto John **Cox**, including the plantation where David **Gibson** now lives. Witness William **Turner**, Moses **Sanders** Jun. Signed David (x) **Gibson**. Witness oath by Moses **Sanders** 11 Oct 1796 to Reuben **Pyles** J.P. Laurens Co. Rec. 23 Oct 1796.

Page 147   31 Aug 1796, James **McClintock** (Laurens Co.) to John **McClintock** (same), for £50 Sterling sell all that tract of Land containing 224 acres more or less, in sd. Co. on Bratchers Branch, a branch of Warriors Creek. Bounded N.E. on land laid out for James **Crook**, S.W. on lands claimed by John **McClintock**, all other sides by Vacant land at time of Surveying. Being granted to sd. James **McClintock** by William **Moultrie** esq. Gov. 3 Apr 1786, & recorded in Book HHHH, page 419. Witness John **Simpson**, Alexr. **Mills**. Signed James **McClintock**. Witness oath by Alexander **Mills** 10 Oct 1796 to John **Cochran** D.C. Laurens Co. Rec. 23 Oct 1796.

Page 147-148   9 Sept 1796, Watson **Allison** (Laurens Co.) to John **Childers** (same), for £50 Sterling sold all that Tract of Land supposed to contain 103 acres more or less, being part of a Tract granted by Letter Patent to William **Hellems**, in sd. Co. on both sides of Raburns Creek. Border: Richard **Owings**, Creek, Hasting **Dial**, Isaac **Hugar**. Witness Richard **Owings**, Thomas **Childers**. Signed Watson (A) **Allison** Witness oath by Richard **Owings** 22 Sept 1796 to Hudson **Berry** J.P. Laurens Co. Rec. 23 Oct 1796.

Page 148   12 Feb 1796, Bartholemew **Cradock** planter (Laurens Co.) to Robert **Taylor** planter (same), for £5 Sterling sell part of a Tract of Land granted unto sd. **Craddock** [sic] 6 Jan 1794, on waters of Duncans Creek, bounded by Robert **Taylor**, Alexr. **McNairy**. Containing 47 acres more or less. Witness Cornelius **Craddock**. Signed Bartholemew **Craddock**, Elizabeth (x) **Craddock**. [No witness oath.] Rec. 24 Oct 1796.

Page 149   18 Oct 1796, Robert Goodloe **Harper** (Laurens Co.) for £20 Sterling paid by Abiram **Laurence** (same), sold all that part of Land containing 2 acres more or less, on waters of Little River, in sd. Co., being part of 600 acres granted to John **Rodgers**, and by him sold to Samuel **Saxon** Esq., & by him conveyed to sd. Robert Goodloe **Harper**. Bounded E by the big Road leading from the Mountain Shoals on the Enoree River through sd. Co. to Swansays ferry on Saluda, all other sides by Robert Goodloe **Harper**. Witness B. H. **Saxon**, James **Saxon** Esq. Signed Robert Goodloe **Harper**. Witness oath by B. H. **Saxon** 18 Oct 1796 to James **Saxon** J.P. Laurens Co. Rec. 24 Oct 1796. [Includes plat.]

Page 149   29 Oct 1796, Solomon **Langston** Sen. (Laurens Co.) for £20 Sterling paid by Bennet **Langston** (same), sold all that Tract of Land containing 125 acres more or less, being part of 200 acres originally granted to William **Cooper** Jun. 4 Dec 1786 & recorded in secretary's Grant book BBBB, page 406, in sd. Co. on the dividing ridge between Enoree & Duncans Creek. Border: William **Cooper** Sen., Anthony **Miller**, John **Blackstock**. Witness Mathew **Brown**, Ephraim **Christopher**. Signed Solomon **Langston**. Witness oath by Mathew **Brown** 29 Oct 1796 to Roger **Brown** J.P. Laurens Co. Rec. 11 Nov 1796.

Page 150   31 Oct 1796, Thomas **Hughes** planter (Laurens Co.) to Lewis **Saxon** (same) planter, for £30 sold all that tract of Land containing 326 acres more or less, in sd. Co. on Buckhead, a branch of Enoree. Bounding when surveyed S on Joseph **Parson**, all other sides on Vacant land. Originally granted to sd. **Hughes** by William **Moultrie** Esq. Gov. Witness Chas. **Smith**, John **Hughes**. Signed Thomas **Hughes**. Witness oath by Chas. **Smith** 8 Nov 1796 to Charles **Saxon** J.P. Laurens Co. Rec. 8 Nov 1796.

Page 150-151   10 Nov 1796, Jesse **Adams** (Laurens Co.) to Charles **Henderson**, for £30 Sterling sold one certain Tract of Land containing 137 acres more or less, on a branch of Raiburns Creek in sd. Co., being part of a Tract formerly belonging to John **Williams** & conveyed to Stephen **Potter** &

conveyed from him to Sarah **Fountain** & given to William **Fountain** by Marriage. Border: sd. Charles **Henderson**, **Bolt**, Isham **Histelow**. Witness Jesse **Garrett**, James (V) **Vines**. Signed Jesse **Adams**. Witness oath by Jesse **Garrett** 11 Nov 1796 to Chas. **Smith** J.P. Laurens Co. Rec. 11 Nov 1796.

Page 151-152 19 Mar 1796, John **Bowman** (Laurens Co.) to Reuben **Arnold** (same), for £23 6sh 8p Sterling sold all that Tract of Land containing 50 acres on N.E. side of Reedy River in sd. Co., being part of 150 acres granted to Richard **Balard** 2 Mar 1773, by William **Bull** Esq. Witness John **Kinton**, John **Shurley**, Wm. **Moore**. Signed John **Bowman**. Witness oath by John **Shurley** 18 Aug 1796 to George **Anderson** J.P. Laurens Co. Rec. 17 Nov 1796.

Page 152 2 Feb 1795, John **Hellums** (Laurens Co.) to Watson **Allison** (same), for £50 sold all that tract of Land supposed to contain 103 acres more or less, being part of a tract originally granted by letter patent to William **Hellums**, in sd. Co. on both sides of Raiborns Creek. Border: Richard **Owens**, sd. Creek, Hasting **Dial**, Isaac **Hugar**. Witness Richard **Owings**, John **Woody**. Signed John **Hellums**. Witness oath by Richard **Owings** 22 Sept 1796 to Hudson **Berry** J.P. Laurens Co. Rec. 18 Nov 1796.

Page 152-153 2 Feb 1795, Hasting **Dial** (Laurens Co.) to Watson **Allison** (same), for £20 sold all that tract of Land supposed to contain 100 acres more or less, being part of a Tract granted to Hasting **Dial** by Thomas **Pinckney** 2 June 1788, in sd. Co. on a branch of Raiborns Creek. Recorded in grant Book XXXX, page 73. Bounded by land laid out for William **Hellums**, old survey, old line supposed to be run by a warrant of Jane **McClurkin**. Witness Henry **Stover**, Richard **Owings**, John **Woody**. Signed Hasting **Dial**. Witness oath by Richard **Owings** 22 Sept 1796 to Hudson **Berry** J.P. Laurens Co. Rec. 18 Nov 1796.

Page 153 18 July 1796, William **Hunter**, Samuel **Saxon** & John **Simpson** are bound unto the Treasurer of this State for £1,500. Condition is such that the above bound William **Hunter** is appointed Sheriff of Laurens Co. If he shall well and faithfully discharge the Trust reposed in him, then the obligation shall be void. Witness Lewis **Saxon** C.C. Signed William **Hunter**, Samuel **Saxon**, John **Simpson**. [No record date.]

Page 153 12 Oct 1796, Charles **Smith**, Joseph **Downs**, William **Dunlap** and John **Simpson** are bound unto John G. **Guignard** Treasurer of the State for £1,000 Sterling. The above bound Charles **Smith** Esq., is by the Judges of Laurens Co. appointed Clerk of sd. County Court. Condition that if Charles **Smith** shall faithfully discharge the duty of Clerk of the Court, then the obligation to be void. Witness Jonthn. **Downs** J.L.C., John **Hunter** J.L.C. Signed Chas. **Smith**, Joseph **Downs**, William **Dunlap**, John **Simpson**. [No record date.]

Page 154 17 Mar 1794, James **Thompson** & Hugh **Thompson** (Laurens Co.) to Samuel **Neighbours** (same), for £20 4sh 4p Sterling sell all that tract of

Land containing by Computation 50 acres, in sd. Co. on Saluda River. Border: James **Mares**. Being part of land that James **Rosemand** sold unto sd. James **Thompson** & Hugh **Thompson** & made over by Lease & release. Witness Wm. **Ware**, Thos. **Meares**, James (x) **Waldrop**. Signed Hugh (N) **Thompson**, James **Thompson**. Witness oath by Thomas **Meares** 7 Nov 1795 to Reuben **Pyles** J.P. Laurens Co. Witness oath by James (x) **Waldrop** 19 Dec 1795 to Reuben **Pyles** J.P. Laurens Co. Rec. 26 Nov 1796.

Page 154-155 27 May 1796, Elijah **Tucker** (Halifax Co., Va.) sell to Sarah **Wright** (Laurens Co.), one Negro man Sam, about 25 years old, about 6 feet high, a Blacksmith to trade, in consideration of £70 Sterling. Witness William **Obannon**, James (J) **Clements**, Ste. C. **Wood**, Signed Elijah (x) **Tucker**. Witness oath by James (J) **Clements** 4 Aug 1796 to George **Anderson** J.P. Laurens Co. 4 Aug 1796, I assign the within Bill of Sale to Andrew **Rodgers** for value recd. and not return to me. Witness Lewis **Banton**, Geo. **Anderson**. Signed Sarah **Wright**. Rec. 3 Dec 1796.

Page 155 5 Dec 1796, John **Simmons** (Laurens Co.) sold unto John **Hunter** (same), two Negroes, one a Girl about 9 years, named Jane, the other a Boy named Will, about 6 years old. In consideration of £84 10sh Sterling. Witness Reuben **Pyles**, Chas. **Smith**. Signed John **Simmons**. Witness oath by Chas. **Smith** 5 Dec 1796 to Reuben **Pyles** J.P. L.C. Rec. 5 Dec 1796.

Page 155-156 18 Mar 1796, James **Giddeon** (Laurens Co.) planter for £50 paid by Richard **Giddeon** (same) planter, sold all that part of a Tract of Land containing 100 acres, being part of 200 acres granted to Stephen **Hutson**, and conveyed by him to James **Giddeon**. Lying on Dunkins Creek and all sides on Vacant Land. Witness Alexr. **Mills**, John **Power**. Signed James **Giddins** [sic]. Oath by John **Power** 16 Dec 1796, that he saw James **Giddens** Sen. [sic] sign the deed. Given before Chas. **Smith** J.P. Laurens Co. Rec. 16 Dec 1796.

Page 156 9 Aug 1792, Bailey **Devall** (Laurens Co.) to John **Power**, for £20 Sterling sold all that Tract of Land of 110 acres, being part of Land originally granted to sd. Bailey **Devall** by William **Moultrie**. Border: Richd. **Winn**, Stephen **Hutson** Bounty. Witness William **Power**, Judith (x) **Belue**, Elizabeth (x) **Power**. Signed Bailey **Devall**. Witness oath by William **Power** 16 Dec 1796 to Chas. **Smith** [No title.] Laurens Co. Rec. 16 Dec 1796. [Includes plat.]

Page 156-157 [Marked "error" in margin.] 23 Aug 1795, Joseph **Parsons** (Laurens Co.) planter to Solomon **Langston** Sen. (same), for 20sh Sterling sold a tract of land containing 250 acres more or less, on Coxes Creek, which runs into the Enoree on the S side & in sd. Co. Bounded by Jesse **Holder** on upper side & James **Millar** on lower side, corner of a tract held at time of Surveying by Anguish **Campbell**, **Kates** old plantation. Part of 640 acres granted to Joshua **Cates** by Wm. **Moultrie** 6 Feb 1786 & recorded in secretary's Office in Book JJJJ, page 489. [No witnesses, signature or witness oath.] Rec. 19 Dec 1796.

Page 157-158 (Beaufort Dist., Prince Wm. Parish) 20 Dec 1796, William **Smith** (one of the Exors. of James **Smith** dec.) (Beaufort Dist., Prince Wm. Parish), for 12,000 Weight of Tobo. paid by Elizabeth **Goodwin** Admx. of Mark **Goodwin** dec. (Laurens Co.), sold unto Elizabeth **Goodwin**, Widow & relict of Mark **Goodwin** dec. & Admx. of same, all that tract of Land containing 1,000 acres more or less, being at time of original Survey in Craven Co., at this time in Laurens Co., on waters of Duncans Creek & Little River, waters of Enoree & Saluda Rivers. Border: Charles **Allen**, vacant land, Stephen **Hudson**. Witness Martha **Goodbe**, David **Liles**. Signed William **Smith** Exr. of J. **Smith**. Witness oath by David **Liles** 28 Dec 1796 to Chas. **Smith** J.P. Laurens Co. Rec. 6 Jan 1797.

Page 158-159   21 June 1796, John **Carter** (Laurens Co.) planter for £17 Sterling paid by John **Pinson** (same) planter, sold all that tract of Land containing 50 acres more or less, on E side of Road leading from Laurens Courthouse to Swancys Ferry, being part of 300 acres originally granted unto Richard **Carter** on waters of Cain Creek & Golemans Creek & out of sd. 300 acres, sd. **Carter** sold away unto his son Joseph **Carter** 125 acres & he sold unto sd. John **Carter** by Lease & release 22 & 23 Apr 1784 & sd. 50 acres is part of the 125 acres. Border: Jno. **Pinson**, Patrick **Cuningham**. Witness Ste. C. **Wood**, Henery **Thompson**, Sarah **Wood**. Signed John **Carter**. Witness oath by Sarah **Wood** 24 Dec 1796 to George **Anderson** J.P. Laurens Co. Dower relinquished by Zebiah (x) **Carter**, wife of John **Carter**, 22 Sept 1796 before Thomas **Wadsworth** J.L.C. Plat certified 1 June 1796 by P. **Cuningham** D.S. Rec. 10 Jan 1797. [Includes plat.]

Page 159   12 Apr 1796, William **Hall** (Charleston Dist.) for £55 paid by Abraham **Box** (Laurens Co.), sold all that tract of Land containing by original Survey 100 acres more or less, in Laurens Co. on Ready River & bounding S by sd. River, all other sides by vacant land at time of original Survey. Originally granted to James **Abercromby** and by him sold to Acquilla **Hall**, and now by William **Hall**, oldest son & heir to sd. Acquilla **Hall** dec. to sd. Abraham **Box**. Witness Lewis **Saxon**, Thomas **Lindley**. Signed William **Hall**. Witness oath by Lewis **Saxon** 9 Jan 1797 to Reuben **Pyles** J.P. Laurens Co. Rec. 16 Jan 1797.

Page 160-161   29 Oct 1796, John **Rodgers** Esq. (Laurens Co.) to John Francis **Wolff** esq., for £50 Sterling sold all that parcel of Land containing 100 acres more or less, in sd. Co. on waters of Raibarns Creek. Bounded S by Isaac **Abercrombie** [**Crumby** on plat.], N on sd. **Rodgers**, W on Raiborns Creek. Being part of 333 acres originally granted to sd. **Rodgers** 2 Mar 1795. Witness Charles **Smith**, James **McCaa**. Signed John **Rodgers**. Witness oath by James **McCaa** 18 Jan 1797 to Chas. **Smith** J.P. Laurens Co. Plat surveyed 6 Sept 1796 by John **Rodgers** D.Sur. Rec. 18 Jan 1797. [Includes plat.]

Page 161   27 Sept 1796, William **Dunlap** & Benjamin **Dunlap** (Laurens Co.) to Ellie **Cheek** [Ellis in one ref.] (same), for £40 Sterling sold all that tract of land containing by estimation 100 acres more or less, in sd. Co. Border: mouth of widow **Dunlaps** spring branch, James **Waldrop**, Enoree River, mouth of Beaverdam Creek. Being part of 600 acres granted to James **Kilgore** by Benjamin **Garrard**, 21 Jan 1785. Witness Sterling **Tucker**, Elisha (x) **Attaway**. Signed William (x) **Dunlap**, Benjamin (x) **Dunlap**. Witness oath by Sterling **Tucker** 25 Oct 1796 to James **Saxon** J.P. Laurens Co. Rec. 18 Jan 1797.

Page 161-162 2 Nov 1788, John **McElroy** late of Laurens Co. to William & Benjamin **Dunlap** (Laurens Co.), for £25 Sterling sold all that tract of Land containing by Estimation 100 acres more or less, being in sd. Co. on beever dam Creek on Enoree River. Border: mouth of Widow **Dunlap's** spring branch on S side of sd. Creek, James **Waldrop**. Being part of 600 acres granted to James **Killgore** [sic] by Benj. **Garrard** 21 Jan 1785, and by sd. **Kilgore** transferred to sd. John **McElroy** by Lease & release 1 Dec 1785. Witness Jesse (x) **Higgens**, James (x) **Cheek**. Signed John **McElroy**. Witness oath by James (x) **Cheek** 25 Oct 1796 to James **Saxon** J.P. Laurens Co. Rec. 18 Jan 1797.

Page 162-163   21 Mar 1796, Reuben **Rowland** (Laurens Co.) for £130 Sterling paid by Robert **Burns** formerly of Union Co., sold 150 acres of Land upon both sides of S fork of Duncans Creek. Being part of 250 acres granted to William **Bean** Sen. 12 Aug 1768, by William **Bull** Esq. Gov. at that time and Recorded in Secretary's Office in Book DDD, page 41. Including the plantation and Improvement. Also another tract containing 49 acres, being part of 120 acres originally granted to John Prather **Odell** by Thomas **Pinckney** Esq. Gov. 3 Mar 1788 and Recorded in Secretary's Office in Book WWWW, page 355. Sd. John Prather **Odell** did convey 49 acres of sd. Tract to Joseph **Huddleston**, and he conveyed to Reuben **Rowland**. Being laid out at S side of above Tract. Including all Improvements upon waters of Duncans Creek in sd. Co. Also another Tract containing 74 acres. Bounded W by John **Pearson** & Elisha **Rodes**, S by land laid out to Mathias **Gore**, E by land laid out to Josiah **Prather**. Witness Joseph **Huddleston**, George **Bush**. Signed Reuben **Rowland**, Anna (x) **Rowland**. Oath by George **Bush** 3 Dec 1796, that he saw Reuben **Rowland** & his wife Ann **Rowland** [sic] sign the deed. Given before Roger **Brown** J.P. Laurens Co. Rec. 30 Jan 1797.

Page 163-165 (Newbury Co.) Lease & Release, 14 & 15 Apr 1788, James **Cook** & Deborah his wife (same) to John **Williams** Jun. (Laurens Co.), for £200 Sterling sell Two Certain Tracts of Land containing 250 acres in Laurens Co. on Little River. One Tract containing 150 acres originally granted to Elizebeth **Keltenon** [Elizabeth **Kelterson** in release.] by bounty Grant 11 Oct 1755 by James **Glenn** then Gov. The other Tract of 100 acres adjoining the above mentioned & was originally granted to Richard **Turner** 4 July 1769 by Charles G. **Montague** then Gov. & conveyed by sd. **Turner** unto William **Turner** by Lease & Release 21 & 22 Mar 1774. Where Especially Bequeathed by the last will & Testament of sd. William **Turner** unto his Daughter Deborah, the wife of sd. James **Cook**. Witness Henry (x) **Irby**, William **Irby**.

Signed James **Cook**, Deborah (x) **Cook**. Witness oath by William **Irby** 16 Feb 1797 to Robert **Gillam** J.P. Newberry Co. Rec. 19 Feb 1797.

Page 165 13 Dec 1796, James **Green** (Laurens Co.) for £60 Sterling paid by James **Holcomb** (same), sell that parcel of Land where sd. **Holcomb** now lives, being part of Two Tracts. One granted 26 Feb 1785 to Patrick **Cuningham** by William **Moultrie** then Gov., 100 acres. Recorded in Grant Book DDDD page 54. The other Tract granted to sd. James **Green** 5 May 1791, by Charles **Pinckney**, then Gov. Recorded in Grant Book C, No.5, page 397, 120 acres in sd. Co. on waters of South Durbins Creek. Supposed to include 150 acres [sic] more or less. Witness Obediah **Halcomb**, Caleb **Halcomb**. Signed James (x) **Green**. Witness oath by Obediah **Halcomb** 13 Dec 1796 to Hudson **Berry** J.P. Laurens Co. Rec. 18 Feb 1797.

Page 166-167 13 Feb 1797, Ebenezar **Starns** & Mary his wife (Laurens Co.) to Aaron **Starns** (same), for £50 Sterling sold one Certain Tract of Land in sd. Co. on waters of Ready River on W side of Long lick Creek, containing 114 acres more or less. Border: Roger **Murphey**, Ann **Starns**, Aaron **Starns**. Being part of a Tract that was originally granted unto Ebenezar **Starnes** Sen. [sic]. Witness Rachel (x **Tumblin**, Roger **Murphey**, Ste. C. **Wood**. Signed Ebenezar **Starns**, Mary (x) **Starns**. Witness oath by Ste. C. **Wood** 20 Feb 1797 to Reuben **Pyles** J.P. L. Co. Rec. 20 Feb 1797.

Page 167 13 Nov 1796, William **Davis** (Laurens Co.) Planter for £12 Sterling paid by Joseph **Adare** Sen. [**Adair** in one ref.] (same), sold one Brindle Cow with a Crop on right Ear, half Crop on left ear; Calf; one red Cow with a white back, two Swallow Forks; one yellow Cow unmarked with a small white spot in her forehead; Steer yearling with a Crop & under bit in right Ear; one Red & white Cow with two Crops; Calf; one yearling heifer with a Crop & under bit in right Ear; one black & white yearling heifer with a Crop & under bit in right Ear; three Featherbeds & furniture & household furniture. Witness Robt. **Adair**, Elisha **Adair**. Signed William (x) **Davis**. Witness oath by Robert **Adair** 18 Feb 1797 to James **Dillard** J.P. Laurens Co. Rec. 18 Feb 1797.

Page 167 1 June 17[blank], Rec. 18 Feb 1797. [Remainder of deed not completed.]

Page 167 8 Mar 1797, Whereas I did appoint Silvanus **Walker** Sen. Esq. my Lawful Attorney, I do from this day revoke sd. power of attorney. Witness Lydall **Allen**. Signed James **Irwin**. Witness oath by Lydall **Allen** 9 Mar 1797 to Chas. **Smith** J.P. Laurens Co. Rec. 9 Mar 1797.

Page 168 21 Jan 1797, Boland **Bishop** (Laurens Co.) for £30 Sterling paid by Aron **Harlin** (same), sold all that tract of Land containing 77 acres more or less, on S side of Dunkins Creek in sd. Co., originally granted to me by a patent 3 Apr 1786 and Recorded in Secretary's Office in Grant Book KKKK, page 146. Witness Mathew **Brown**, Thomas **Parker**. Signed Boling (x)

Bishop [sic]. Witness oath by Mathew **Brown** 21 Jan 1797 to Roger **Brown** J.P. Laurens Co. Rec. 21 Feb 1797.

Page 168-169 31 Oct 1796, Thomas **Hughes** planter (Laurens Co.) to George **Hearn** (same), for £30 Sterling sold all that tract of land containing 314 acres more or less, in sd. Co. on Beaverdam branch of Ready River. When surveyed on lands of John **Reid**, Nathan **Austin**, David **Alexander**, Jacob **Wright**, Widow **Madden** & unknown. Originally granted to sd. Thomas **Hughes**. Witness Chas. **Smith**, John **Hughes**. Signed Thomas **Hughes**. Witness oath by John **Hughes** 17 Feb 1797 to Joseph **Downs** J.P. Laurens Co. Rec. 21 Feb 1797.

Page 169 24 Dec 1792, Hasting **Dial** [sic] (Laurens Co.) to David **Helloms** (same), for £10 Sterg., sell one Certain Tract of Land on branches of Durty Creek, waters of Raiborns Creek, containing 91 acres more or less, being part of a larger tract granted [blank]. Border: Saml. **Williams**, Jno. **Owens**, Hastings **Dial**, Maj. **Butler**, **Laydecake**. Witness Samuel **Williams**, Isaac **Dial**, Rebecca (D) **Dial**. Signed Hastings **Dial**, Rebecca (D) **Dial**. Witness oath by Samuel **Williams** 3 Feb 1795 to Joseph **Downs** J.P. Laurens Co. [No record date.] [Includes plat.]

Page 170 27 Jan 1797, Charles **North** (Edgefield Co.) for £20 Sterling paid by Benjamin **Drummond** (Laurens Co.), sold all that tract of Land in Laurens Co. on waters of Mudlick, containing 100 acres, being the lower end of 200 acres granted to William **Marsh** in 1769. Border: sd. **Drummond**, Benjamin **Drummond**. Witness Nethl. **Drummond**, Benjn. **Drummond**. Signed Charles (x) **North**. Witness oath by Benjamin **Drummond** 17 Feb 1797 to Zech. **Bailey** J.P. Laurens Co. Rec. 21 Feb 1797.

Page 170-171 9 Nov 1795, David **Ragsdal** & Alse **Ragsdal** his wife (Laurens Co.) Planter to John **Watson** (same) Planter, for £26 Sterling sold a certain tract of land containing 100 acres in sd. Co. on waters of Ready River. Border: Jacob **Wright**, not known, vacant. Original being land warranted to Elizabeth **Hen** Bounty from King **George III** 6 May 1774 & then granted to her 25 May & Witnesseth by William **Bull** Esq. & examined by Thos. **Skolloure**, and recorded in B[ook] FFF, 362. Witness Wm. **Washington**, George (x) **Gothard**. Signed David (x) **Ragsdal**, Alsey (-) **Ragsdal** [sic]. Witness oath by George (x) **Gothard** 23 Apr 1796 to George **Anderson** J.P. Laurens Co. Rec. 21 Feb 1797.

Page 171 3 Feb 1797, Benjn. **Couch** (Laurens Co.) to Charles **Henderson** (same), for $60 sold one certain tract of land in sd. Co. on branches of Raiborns Creek, containing 50 acres more or less, being part of a tract granted to John **Williams** & conveyed from him to Stephen **Potter** & from him to Sarah **Durham** & given to William **Fountain** in Marriage. Border: James **Smith's** big survey, Burgess **Goldsbey**, Isham **Histelow**. Witness Wm. **King**, Rebeckah **Downs**. Signed Benjamin (C) **Couch**. Witness oath by Wm. **King** 3 Feb 1797 to Joseph **Downs** J.P. Laurens Co. Rec. 21 Feb 1797.

Page 172   9 Sept 1796, John **West** (Laurens Co.) for £60 paid by David **McCleure** (same), sold all that Tract of Land of 50 acres, on waters of Dunkins Creek in sd. Co. Being part of 100 acres granted to Robert **Flamon**. Witness Richard **Bell**, John **Finney**. Signed John (x) **West**, Mary (x) **West**. Witness oath by Richard **Bell** 16 Feb 1797 to George **Whitmore** J.P. Laurens Co. Rec. 21 Feb 1797.

Page 172-173   9 May 1795, John **Cargill** and Rachel his Wife (Laurens Co.) to Thomas **Wilks** and Frances **Lester** (same), for £60 sell one tract of Land in sd. Co. on both sides of Norths Creek, containing 135 acres more or less, 100 acres granted to Margaret **Wiseman** & by her granted to George **Norwood** dec. & conveyed by Nethl. **Norwood**, son & heir to sd. George, to Thos. **Gifford** & conveyed by him to sd. John **Cargill** & Raichel [sic] his wife. The 35 acres part of a large grant unto sd. George **Norwood** dec. Border: James **Burnside**, sd. Creek, sd. **Wilks** & **Lester**, **Harde** [**Hardie** in one ref.], William **Hall**, **Owens**, Tyre **Glenn**. Witness John **Chandler**, James **Clardy**. Signed John **Cargill**, Rachel (x) **Cargill**. Witness oath by James **Clardy** 15 Sept 1795 to Thomas **Wadsworth** J.L.C. Rec. 21 Feb 1797.

Page 173   18 Jan 1796, Patrick **Gibson** (Abeville Co.) for £30 Sterling paid by William **Crisp** (Laurens Co.), sell all that Tract of Land containing 100 acres, being part of a Tract originally granted to James **Harley** containing 850 acres in sd. Co. on waters of Cain Creek, a branch of Saludy. Border: S by James **White** old line now held by Elisha **Mitchell**, E by Abel **Bowlan**, Eli **Bailey**, John **Walker**. Part conveyed by sd. **Harley** to Patrick **Gibson**. Witness John **Walker**, William **Walker**. Signed Patrick (O) **Gibson**. Witness oath by William **Walker** 18 Feb 1797 to Zech. **Bailey** J.P. Laurens Co. Rec. 21 Feb 1797.

Page 173-174   23 Dec 1796, Jacob **Williams** & Mary his Wife (Laurens Co.) planter to John **Cornelison** (same), for £30 Sterling sold a certain Tract of Land on waters of Raburns Creek in sd. Co., granted to sd. Jacob **Williams** by James **Abercrombie** by deed 3 Jan 1785. The tract containing 100 acres more or less. Border: land laid out for Samuel **Williams** Sen., William **Owings**, William **Boyd**. A stated line agreed upon between sd. **Williams** & sd. **Cornelison** running with a certain cross fence. Witness Saml. **Cuningham**, Jonathan **Cox**. Signed Jacob **Williams**, Mary (x) **Williams**. Witness oath by Jonathan **Cox** 18 Feb 1797 to Reuben **Pyles** J.P. Laurence Co. Rec. 21 Feb 1797.

Page 174-175   1 Feb 1797, William **Dendey** Sen. [sic] & Clary his Wife (Laurens Co.) to William **Leek** Sen. (same), for 20sh sell one certain Tract of Land whereon sd. **Dendy** now lives, in sd. Co., containing 177 acres, being part originally granted to Thomas **North** & the other part granted to sd. **Dendy**. Border: William **Leed** [**Leek** in one ref.], **Yancy**, creek, Samuel **Powel** [**Powell** in one ref.], Thomas **Dendy**. Witness William **Dendy** son of Wm., William **Dendy** s. of Tho., Samuel (x) **Leek**. Signed William **Dendy**,

Clary (C) **Dendy**. Witness oath by William **Dendy** s. of Wm. 20 Feb 1797 to John **Davis** J.P. [No record date.]

Page 175 8 Feb 1797, John & Moses & Clement **Wells** (Laurens Co.) for £30 Sterling paid by Margret **Cuningham** (same), sell all that tract of Land containing 50 acres in sd. Co. on waters of Cane Creek, being part of 100 acres originally granted from Peter **Caseity** to John **Wells** and being part of Land where sd. **Wells** now lives. Witness Robt. Andw. **Cuningham**, John **McGowen**, Caleb (x) **Maulden**. Signed John **Wells**, Moses **Wells**, Clemment **Wells** [sic]. [No witness oath.] [No record date.]

Page 175-176 20 Nov 1787, John **Bell** (Chester Co.) to Henry **Davis** (Laurens Co.), for £50 Sterling sell all that tract of land containing 100 acres, at time of surveying in Barkley now in Laurens Co., on Whitmores branch of Duncans Creek in fork between Broad & Saluda Rivers. Original grant to John **Bell** 17 June 1774, and recorded in Secretary's Office in Book QQQ, page 397. Witness George **Whitmore**, Robert **Whitton**, John **Boys**. Signed John **Bell**. Witness oath by Robert **Whitton** 15 Feb 1797 to George **Whitmore** J.P. Laurens Co. [No record date.]

Page 176-177 29 Jan 1789, Mordecai **Moore** (Laurens Co.) planter to Ezekiel **Griffith** (same) planter, for £30 Sterling sold 268 acres of Land, being part of 325 acres granted 6 Feb 1786 by William **Moultrie** Esq. Gov. unto Mordecai **Moore**. Situate on N fork of Durbins Creek on S.W. side of Enoree River in sd. Co. Recorded in Surveyor General's office 19 Aug 1784, likewise recorded in Secretary's Office in Book KKKK, page 80. But with 50 acres only excluded at N end of 350 acres joining Thomas **McGriger**. Witness Thomas (D) **McGreger**, Alxr. **Harper**. Signed Mordecai **Moore**, Silvey (x) **Moore**. Oath by Thomas **McGrigger** [No signature.] 16 Apr 1789, that he saw Mordecai **Moore** and Silvey **Moore** his wife, sign the deed. Given before Daniel **Wright** J.P. Laurens Co. Rec. 21 Feb 1797.

Page 177-178 9 Mar 1797, James **Lowry** & James Hamilton **Lowry** (Laurens Co.) to James **Irwin** (Pennsylvania), for £75 Sterling sold all that tract of land containing 150 acres on Raiburns Creek in Laurens Co. Bounded S on land formerly sd. **Irwin**, E on land laid out to Majr. **Butlar**, N & W on land laid out to Robert **Cooper**, S.W. on Alexr. **Mazyck**. Condition that if James **Lowry** & James Hamilton **Lowry** shall pay the sum, 20 on or before 1 Jan 1798, 25 on or before 1 Jan 1799, the remaining 25 on or before 1 Jan 1800, agreeable to three Notes bearing equal date, then these presents shall be void. Witness B. H. **Saxon**, John **Hughes**. Signed James **Lowry**, James Hamilton **Lowry**. Witness oath by John **Hughes** 9 Mar 1797 to Chas. **Smith** J.P. Laurens Co. [No record date.]

Page 178-179 7 Jan 1775, Henry **Stoneparish** (Camden Dist.) to William **Pitts** (Ninety six Dist.), for £500 current money sell all that tract of Land containing 350 acres in Ninety six Dist. on Beverdam branch, a small Creek of Little River. Granted to sd. Henry **Stoneparish** 1 Feb 1768 by Lord Charles

Greville **Montague**, then Gov. Witness John **Caldwell**, Jenet **Burns**, Sarah (x) **Burns**. Signed Henry (H) **Stoneparish**. Witness oath by John **Caldwell** 17 Feb 1777 to John **Satterwhite** J.P. Ninety six Dist. Rec. 21 Feb 1797.

Page 180 11 Feb 1796, James **Young** (Laurens Co., Cambridge Dist.), for £100 Current money paid by Robert **Young**, sold one certain tract of Land on N fork of Bush River containing 222 acres more or less, being a Tract granted to William **Young** & conveyed from him to James **Young**. Granted by William **Moultrie** 26 Jan 1766, recorded in Book K, No.10, p.55, 20 Oct 1770. Border: Matthew **Hunter**, William **Garey**, William **Barksdale**, Bush River, Thomas **Roberts**. Witness William **Osborn**, Alexr. **McNair** [**Mair** in one ref.], Answorth **Middleton**. Signed James **Young**, Anne **Young**. Witness oath by Answorth **Middleton** 20 Feb 1797 to Reuben **Pyles** J.P. L.C. Rec. 21 Feb 1797. [Includes plat.]

Page 180-181 10 Nov 1796, Dower relinquished by Ann **Young**, Widow of James **Young** dec., unto Joseph **Young**, for a tract of 150 acres on Little River, granted to James **Young** dec. & by him in his lifetime conveyed to sd. Joseph **Young**. Given before Jno. **Hunter** J.L.C. Oath by William **Young** 17 Feb 1797, that he saw James **Young** dec. assign a Lease & deliver the deed to Joseph **Young** and saw his Wife Ann **Young** assign with her husband. Given before Wm. **Neill** J.P. Laurens Co. [No record date.]

Page 181 13 Nov 1795, Benjamin **Wofford** (Spartenburg Co.) to John **Wright** (Abevill Co.), for £100 Sterling sold a tract of Land containing 176 acres more or less, on S side of Enoree River in Laurens Co. Border: sd. River, Joseph **Lyons**, swamp in Hollaway **Powers** field. Signed Daniel **Wright**, William **Wofford**. Signed Benjamin **Wofford**. Witness oath by Daniel **Wright** 18 Feb 1797 to Jno. **Davis** J.P. Laurens Co. Rec. 21 Feb 1797.

Page 181-182 29 Sept 1796, Joel **Rucks** (Laurens Co.) for £40 paid by Peter **Smith** (same), sold all that tract of Land in sd. Co. containing 100 acres more or less, on Cane Creek, a branch of Saluda. Border: John **Robertson**. Witness Elisha **Weatherford**, John **Smith**. Signed Joel **Rucks**. Witness oath by Elisha **Weatherford** 11 Jan 1797 to Angus **Campbell** J.P. Laurens Co. [No record date.]

Page 182 12 Dec 1796, Peter **Smith** & James **Smith** (Laurens Co.) for £50 paid by John **Robertson** (same), sell all that tract of Land in sd. Co. containing 178 acres more or less, on Cane Creek, a branch of Saluda. Border: John **Robertson**. Witness Elisha **Weatherford**, Joseph **Pollard**, Michael **Finney**. Signed Peter **Smith**, James (x) **Smith**. Witness oath by Elisha **Weatherford** 11 Jan 1797 to Angus **Campbell** J.P. Laurens Co. Rec. 21 Feb 1797.

Page 182-183 28 Dec 1796, Cornelius **Hooker** (Laurens Co.) to Benjamin **Couch** (same), for £20 Sterling sold one certain tract of Land in sd. Co. on branches of Raiborns Creek containing 50 acres more or less, being part of a tract granted to John **Williams** & conveyed form him to Stephen **Potter**, and from him to Sarah **Durham** & from her given to William **Fountain** in marriage. Border: James **Smith's** big Survey, Burgess **Goldsby**, Isham **Histelow**. Witness James (C) **Couch**, Anderson **Arnold**. Signed Cornelius (x) **Hooker**. Witness oath by James (C) **Couch** 18 Feb 1797 to Jas. **Dillard** J.P. Laurens Co. Rec. 21 Feb 1797.

Page 183   30 July 1796, William **Thompson** (Greenville Co.) to John **Robertson** (Laurens Co.), for £10 sold all that tract of land containing 100 acres more or less, on a branch of warrier Creek where Aaron **Niblet** formerly lived, being part of a tract granted to Solomon **Niblet**. Border: head of branch near Georgia road, Samuel **Dunlap**, spring, William **Hellums**. Including the house with the plantation where Aron **Niblet** [sic] formerly lived. Witness J. F. **Wolff**, Martin **Killet**, Robt. (x) **Jones**. Signed William **Thompson**. Witness oath by Robert (x) **Jones** 25 Aug 1796 to Daniel **Wright** J.P. Laurens Co. Rec. 21 Feb 1797.

Page 184   12 Jan 1797, William **McClure** (Laurens Co.) Cotton Manufactr. for £35 Sterling paid by John **Simpson** Mert. (same), sold one spinning Cotton Machine draws 84 threads, one Narrow Loom, three feather Beds, Furniture & bed steads, sheets, blankets, coverings, 1 Trunk with close & house hold furniture, one warping machine, one chesnut Mare about 6 years old, small star in her face & one white foot, one Saddle & bridle. Witness Jno. **Gallegly**, James **McCary**. Signed William **McClure**. Witness oath by John **Gallegly** 18 Feb 1797 to Charles **Griffin** J.P. Laurens Co. Rec. 21 Feb 1797.

Page 184   15 Dec 1796, Joseph **Adair** Sen. & Thomas **Hughey** (Laurens Co.) planters for $152 paid by Bryant **Leek** (same), sold one Negro Boy Jacob. Witness Robert **Adair**, William **Saxon**. Signed Joseph **Adair**, Thomas **Hughey**. Witness oath by William **Saxon** 4 Jan 1797 to Roger **Brown** [Rodger in one ref.] J.P. Laurens Co. [No record date.]

Page 184-185   27 Aug 1796, James **Jones** (Laurens Co.) planter in consideration of the love, good will & affection I have towards my Son Jesse **Jones** (same), give a Negro man George, about 22 Years of age, also a Negro Girl Clark, about 9 years old, like wise a Negro Boy Toney about 2 years old. Witness Joseph **Jones**, Martha (x) **Whitmore**. Signed James (x) **Jones**. Witness oath by Joseph **Jones** 27 Aug 1796 to George **Whitmore** J.P. Laurens Co. Rec. 21 Feb 1797.

Page 185-186   29 Aug 1796, James **Rosamond** & Mary his wife (Abeville Co.) to John **Moore** (Laurens Co.), for £30 Sterling sell all that tract of Land containing 125 acres more or less, in Laurens Co. on both sides of Ready River. Border: John **Henderson**, Vacant land, **Box**, River, Henry **Box**. Witness Jas. **Watts**, Robert **Moore**, William **Powell**. Signed James **Rosamond**, Mary (x) **Rosamond**. Witness oath by William **Powell** 24 Jan 1797 to George **Anderson** J.P. Rec. 21 Feb 1797.

Page 186   20 Dec 1796, Charles **Allen** Esq. appointed Judge of Laurens Co. Court. Commission to continue during good Behavior. Certified by Stephen **Ravenel** Secretary. Signed Charles **Pinckney** Esq. Gov. (Columbia). [No record date.]

Page 186   20 Dec 1796, William **Mitchell** Esq. appointed Judge of Laurens Co. Court. Commission to continue during good Behavior. Certified by Stephen **Ravenel** Secretary. Signed Charles **Pinckney** Esq. Gov. (Columbia). [No record date.]

Page 186   9 Apr 1796, Plat certified represents shape of a tract of 6-1/4 acres of Land in Laurens Co. on Little River, being part of 150 acres granted to Hugh **ONeal**. I have laid off at the Instance of the Exors. of the Last Will & Testament of sd. Hugh **ONell** [sic]. Includes the Mill & Dwelling House where sd. Hugh **ONell** formerly lived. Border: Waggon Road, Little River, Thos. **Wadsworth**. Signed John **Hunter** D.S. 9 Apr 1796, Exors. of the Estate of Hugh **ONeall** [sic] dec. in complying with Hugh **ONeall**, agreeable to the Last Will and Testament of sd. dec., valued the three tracts of Land left to his three Sons, Hugh, Charles & Thomas **ONeall**. The upper tract on Little River left to Hugh **ONeall** we value to £150. The Lower Division on Little River left to Charles **ONeall** was valued to £65. The other tract of 270 acres on waters of Ready River was valued at £80. Agreeable to sd. Will, we have admeasured the Lower tract of Little River, 6-1/4 acres which contains the Mill, Dam and Dwelling house. Signed Mercer **Babb**, Elisha **Ford**, Hugh **ONeall**. Rec. 15 Mar 1797. [Includes plat.]

Page 187   18 Mar 1797, William **Moore** (Abeville Co.) for £51 11sh current money paid by Aaron **Clore** (Laurens Co.), sold all that tract of Land containing 158 acres in Laurens Co. on both sides of Walnut Creek, waters of Ready River. Whereon sd. Aaron **Clore** now lives, being part of 300 acres granted unto sd. William **Moore** by William **Bull** 16 June 1768. A memorial entered in Audt. Office in Book I, No.9, page 94, 7 Sept 1768. Sd. tract lies on N.W. side of the 300 acres. Witness James **Powell**, John **Moore** Robert **Moore**. Signed William (U) **Moore**. Witness oath by James **Powell** 3 Apr 1797 to Charles **Saxon** J.P. Rec. 4 Apr 1797.

Page 188-189   16 Feb 1795, Whereas Ralph **Izard** the Younger and Joshua **Ward**, two of the acting Exors. of the last will and Testament of Thomas **Farr**, late of St. Andrew Parish Esq. dec. on 13 Mar 1793 did file their Bill of Complaint in the Court of Equity at Charleston against William Brandford **Farr**, one of the Exors. of sd. Thomas **Farr**, on his own account as Heir and Legatee of his Father, the sd. Thomas **Farr**, and on behalf of the other children, to direct sale of all real and personal Estate of sd. Thomas **Farr**, for discharging his debts. Decretal order made at Mar Term 1793, that the whole of the Estate should be sold by the master of sd. Court. William Hazell **Gibbs** Master of the Court of equity at Charleston Esq. did at public auction on 16 Feb sell the tract of Land to John **McDowall** (same), for £70. Sold all that Tract of Land in Ninety Six Dist. on Maple Swamp Creek, a branch of Tyger

River. Bound N by the Indian line, E by **Heyward**, all other sides by vacant Land at time of original Grant. Containing together 700 acres, originally granted to sd. Thomas **Farr**. Witness Oliver **Cromwell**, Cs. **Stewart**. Signed William Hazell **Gibbes** Master in Equity. Witness oath by O. **Cromwell** 18 Mar 1797 to John **Johnson** J.P. Charlestown Dist. on a Credit of 1, 2, 3, 4, & 5 years [sic]. [No record date.]

Page 189-190 16 Feb 1794, Whereas Ralph **Izard** the Younger and Joshua **Ward**, two of the acting Exors. of the last will and Testament of Thomas **Farr**, late of St. Andrew Parish Esq. dec. on 13 Mar 1793 did file their Bill of Complaint in the Court of Equity at Charleston against William Brandford **Farr**, one of the Exors. of sd. Thomas **Farr**, on his own account as Heir and Legatee of his Father, the sd. Thomas **Farr**, and on behalf of the other children, to direct sale of all real and personal Estate of sd. Thomas **Farr**, for discharging his debts. Decretal order made at Mar Term 1793, that the whole of the Estate should be sold by the master of sd. Court. William Hazell **Gibbs** Master of the Court of equity at Charleston Esq. did at public auction on 16 Feb sell the tract of Land to John **McDowall** (same), for £12 10sh. Sold all that Tract of Land in Craven Co. containing 500 [acres] granted 17 May 1774 to Peter **Porcher**, on Cabbin Crauch, a branch of Ready River, then bounded by Thomas **McDonel**, Thomas **Matthews**, James **Ryan** and others. Witness Chas. **Stewart**, Oliver **Cromwell**. Signed William Hazell **Gibbes** Master in Equity. Witness oath by O. **Cromwell** 18 Mar 1797 to John **Johnson** J.P. Charlestown Dist. [No record date.]

Page 190 2 Feb 1797, John **Boyd** (Laurens Co.) for 10sh Sterling paid by Bridget **McLallen** [**McLellen** in one ref.] (same), sold all that Tract of Land on W side of Little River. Being part of Land originally granted unto James **Ryan** for 100 acres. Bounded S & W by Silvanus **Walker**, N by Henry **Atkinson**, E by main run of Little River. Except that part that lyeth on N side of the main run of a branch upon which John **Davis'** Spring stands. Containing & now laid out for 89 acres more or less. Witness Silvs. **Walker** Sen., Henry **Atkinson**, John **Davis**. Signed John **Boyd** Atty. for Ephm. **McLain**. Witness oath by Henry **Atkinson** 15 Mar 1797 to John **Davis** J.P. Laurens Co. Rec. 4 Apr 1797.

Page 191-192 1 June 1789, Lewis **Saxon** Clerk of Laurens Co. & Sally his Wife to James **Tweedy** planter (Laurens Co.), for £20 Sterling sold all that Tract of Land containing 200 acres in Ninety Six Dist. on Ready River, bounding N.E. & S.E. on Hugh **Beard**, N.E. on William **Norris**, all other sides on vacant Land at time of original survey. Being first granted to Roger **Brooks**, and since conveyed by lease & release to sd. Lewis **Saxon**. Witness Lydall **Allen**, Samuel **Nelson**. Signed Lewis **Saxon**, Sally **Saxon**. Witness oath by Lydall **Allen** 8 Apr 1797 to Joseph **Downs** J.P. Laurens Co. Rec. 17 Feb 1797.

Page 192 26 Nov 1796, Robert **Pasley** (Laurens Co.) for £75 Sterling paid by James **McCaa** (same), sold one outlandish Negro woman about 30 years old,

Charlotte, with her female Child about 17 months old, Jeane. Witness Charles **Allen**, Joseph **Cox**. Signed Robert **Pasley**. Witness oath by Chas. **Allen** 13 Apr 1797 to Chas. **Smith** J.P. Laurens Co. Rec. 13 Apr 1797.

Page 192-193 16 Jan 1797, Robert **Todd** & Jane **Todd** his Wife (Laurens Co.) to Daniel **Osborn** (same), for £50 Sterling sell all that tract of Land containing 150 acres more or less, being the S.W. part of 250 acres granted to Ratliff **Joel** 4 Apr 1786 by William **Moultrie** then Gov. & situate in sd. Co. on waters of Little River. Dividing line is between Richard **Joel** & Robert **Todd**, to be S end of a tract run for Young McNees **Good**. Border: Daniel **Osborn**, Ratliff **Jowell** [sic], old McNees **Good**, Richard **Jowell** [sic] son & heir to sd. Ratliff **Jowel** [sic], conveyed to Robert **Todd**. Witness Ezekiel S. **Roland**, Benjamin **Burton**. Signed Robert **Todd**, Jane (n) **Todd**. Witness oath by Ezekiel S. **Roland** 16 Feb 1797 to Chas. **Smith** J.P. Laurens Co. Rec. 16 Feb 1797.

Page 193 16 Jan 1797, Robert **Todd** (Laurens Co.) is bound unto Daniel **Osbourn** for £100 Sterling. Condition that if Robert **Todd** does indemnify sure rights to sd. Daniel **Osburn** [sic] for a piece of land sold sd. **Osburn**, which sd. **Todd** bought of Richard **Jowel** from claim of sd. Richard **Joel's** [sic] Mother, widow of Ratliff **Jowel** dec. so that the widow does not Distress possess or gain any part of sd. Land, then the obligation to be void. Witness Ezekiel S. **Roland**, Benjamin **Burton**. Signed Robert **Todd**. Witness oath by Ezekiel S. **Roland** 13 Feb 1797 to Chas. **Smith** J.P. Laurens Co. [No record date.]

Page 194 3 Nov 1796, Moses **Madden** & Caty **Madden** his Wife (Laurens Co.) to Thomas **Burton** late of same place, for £100 sold all that tract of Land containing 64 acres more or less, in sd. place on a branch of Rians Creek of Little River. Witness Ezel. S. **Roland**, James **Sullivant**. Signed Moses **Madden**. Witness oath by Ezel. S. **Roland** 14 Dec 1796 to Chas. **Smith** J.P. Laurens Co. Rec. 28 Apr 1797.

Page 194-195 25 Feb 1797, David **Madden** & Moses **Madden** are bound unto Thomas **Burton** for £100 Sterling. Condition that if David **Madden** and Moses **Madden** shall make good rights to a certain tract of Land containing 8 acres, adjoining sd. **Burton**, being granted to Jesse **Meeks** and at present occupied by sd. **Burton**, within 12 months of date, then the obligation shall be void. Witness Ezel. S. **Roland**, Benjn. **Burton**. Signed David **Madden**, Moses **Madden**. Witness oath by Ezel. S. **Roland** 25 Apr 1797 to Chas. **Smith** J.P. Laurens Co. Rec. 28 Apr 1797.

Page 195 31 Oct in 21st year of Independence, John **Lynch** Jun. (Laurens Co.) for £30 Sterling paid by Benjamin **Byrd** (same), sold all that tract of Land granted unto me 4 June 1787, containing 200 acres more or less, in sd. Co. on Lynches Creek, bounded N.W. by William **Hutcheson**, S.W. by Thos. **Murphey**, other sides belonging to sd. **Byrd**. Witness Solomon **Langston**, Henry **Langston**. Signed John **Lynch**. Witness oath by Henry **Langston** 25 Apr 1797 to Roger **Brown** J.P. Laurens Co. Rec. 29 Apr 1797.

Page 195-196 28 Apr 1797, Whereas Fredrick **Sullivant** (Laurens Co.) by his bond dated 28 Apr 1797 for £50 Stg., unto Ezekiel S. **Roland** & Benjamin **Burton** (same), on or before 28 Apr 1798. For the better securing payment of £25, sold one certain tract of Land containing [blank] acres more or less, being part of 640 [acres] originally granted to John **Martin** and is the tract where sd. Fredrick **Sullivant** now lives. Also one Mare 3 years old, part of Yellow bay with a blaze in her face, Two Cows, two heifers, some Calves, two feather beds & furniture, fifteen head of hogs & all my household & kitchen furniture. Provided that if the sum is paid, then the sale to be void. Witness John **Ritchey**, Chas. **Smith**. Signed Fredrick (F.S.) **Sullivant**. Witness oath by John **Ritchey** 28 Apr 1797 to Charles **Saxon** J.P. Laurens Co. [No record date.]

Page 196-197 12 July 1790, Hugh **Wardlaw** (Abbeville Co.) Esq. to James **King** (Laurens Co.), for 5sh sold all that tract of Land containing by Estimation 100 acres, on N side of Saluda River in Laurens Co. on Indian Hut Creek. When surveyed bounding S.E. & N.E. by Obediah **Edwards**, S.E. by Edward **Connoway**, S.W. by vacant land, other sides by Saluda River. Surveyed for Obediah **Edwards** 15 Nov 1769 & certified for Hugh **Wardlaw** by order of Council 4 Dec 1770, and granted by Wm. **Bull** Esq. Lieut. Gov. on or about 22 Feb 1771 to sd. Hugh **Wardlaw**. Witness William **Beneson**, Thomas **Ware**, James (J) **King** Jun. Signed Hugh **Wardlaw**. Witness oath by James **King** [No signature.] 14 Jan 1794 to Adm. Cr. **Jones** J.P. Abbeville Co. Rec. 8 May 1797.

Page 197-198 6 Apr 1797, Robert **Hood** (Laurens Co.) Planter for $12 paid by Richard **Shackelford** (same) planter, sold all that Tract of Land containing 15 acres more or less, being part of 400 acres in sd. Co. on a branch of Beaverdam Creek, waters of Little River, granted to sd. Robert **Hood** 23 June 1773. Land laid out for Samuel **Wharton** 5 Mar 1771. Border: land laid out for McNees **Goode, Eaten**. Witness Thomas **Hood**, Daniel **Osborn**. Signed Robert (x) **Hood**. Witness oath by Daniel **Osborn** 8 May 1797 to Wm. **Mitchell** J.P. Rec. 8 May 1797.

Page 198-199 12 May 1796, Jacob **Bowman** & Sarah **Bowman** his Mother (Laurens Co.) to Jacob **Niswanger** (same), for £200 Sterling sell three tracts of Land containing 277 acres in sd. Co. on S side of Ready River. First tract border: Ready River. Original grant for 77 acres. Second tract border: Ready River. Original grant for 100 acres. Third tract border: Ready River. Original grant for 100 acres. Witness George **Anderson**, Ste. C. **Wood**, Lewis **Graves**. Signed Jacob **Bowman**, Sarah (S) **Bowman**. Witness oath by Lewis **Graves** 8 May 1797 to Zech. **Bailey** J.P. Laurens Co. Rec. 8 May 1797.

Page 199 12 May 1796, Jacob **Bowman** & Sarah **Bowman** (Laurens Co.) for £100 Sterling paid by Jacob **Niswanger** (same), sold all that tract of Land containing 100 acres in sd. Co. on Ready River. Granted to John **Bryan** by Charles Greville **Montague** Gov. 28 Aug 1767. Conveyed by lease & release to Jacob **Bowman** Sen. Witness Lewis **Graves**, George **Anderson**, Ste. C.

Wood. Signed Jacob **Bowman**, Sarah (S) **Bowman**. Full possession given by Jacob **Bowman** and Sarah **Bowman** his mother unto Jacob **Niswanger**. Witness oath by Lewis **Graves** 8 May 1797 to Zech. **Bailey** J.P. Laurens Co. Rec. 8 May 1797.

Page 199-200 12 May 1796, Jacob **Bowman** & Sarah **Bowman** (Laurens Co.) for £100 Sterling paid by Jacob **Niswanger** (same), sold all that tract of Land containing 200 acres in sd. Co. on Ready River. Granted unto John **Kesterson** by William **Bull** Esq. Lieut. Gov. 25 June 1771. Conveyed by Lease & release to Jacob **Bowman** Sen. Witness Lewis **Graves**, George **Anderson**, Ste. C. **Wood**. Signed Jacob **Bowman**, Sarah (S) **Bowman**. Full possession given by Jacob **Bowman** and Sarah **Bowman** his Mother unto Jacob **Niswanger**. Witness oath by Lewis **Graves** 8 May 1797 to Zech. **Bailey** J.P. Laurens Co. [No record date.]

Page 200 22 July 1795, Gasper **Trotti** (Orange Co.) [sic] Planter to John **Garret** (Laurence Co.) Planter, for £35 sold all that parcel of Land containing 150 acres more or less, in Laurens Co. on Warrier Creek, waters of Enoree River, which is half of 300 acres granted to Thomas **Farr** 8 July 1774, and by his heirs conveyed to sd. Gasper **Trotti** by Lease & release 1 & 2 Jan 1784. Bounding at time of grant, N on John **Waun**, W on John **Cox**? & Jonthn. **Downs**, S by other half of tract yet unsold & property of Gasper **Trotti**, E on William **Waun** now land of Anne **Garret**. Witness Reuben **Martin**, John (x) **Ashley**. Signed Gasper **Trotti**. Witness oath by Reuben **Martin** 21 Dec 1791 [sic] to Daniel **Wright** J.P. Laurens Co. Rec. 8 May 1797.

Page 201 16 Feb 1797, Nathan **Fowler** (Warren Co., Ga.) to James **King** (Laurens Co.), for one guinea sold a certain Tract of Land on waters of Saluda in Laurens Co., being granted to Nathan **Fowler** 3 Nov 1767, containing 100 acres more or less. Witness Adam **Jones**, James (J) **King** Jun. Signed Nathan **Fowler**. Witness oath by James (x) **King** 2 Mar 1797 to Reuben **Pyles** J.P. Rec. 8 May 1797.

Page 201 1 Jan 1796, Elizabeth Jane **Ravenel** Exrx. of Daniel **Ravenel** dec. for £30 paid by John **Gray** Gentleman, sell all that tract of Land on waters of Bush River in Ninety Six Dist., containing 260 acres more or less, part of 3,000 acres originally granted to sd. Daniel **Ravenel** and by him in his last Will & Testament directed to be sold by his Exrs. or Exor. and is known in the general plan of same by number 6. Witness George **Porcher**, Isaac **Porcher**, Peter **Porcher** Jun. Signed Elizabeth Jane **Ravenel**. Witness oath by Peter **Porcher** Jun. 19 Dec 1796 to R. **Brown** J. Newberry Co. [No record date.]

Page 201-202 30 Apr 1796, Jorden **Jones** (Meclenburg Co., N.C.) for $260 paid by John **McClintic** (Laurens Co.), sell a likely sensible well grown Country born Negro Boy named [blank]. With affirmation of Wyche **Goodwin** Esq. (Georgia). Witness George **Berry**. Signed Jorden (8) **Jones**, Wyche **Goodwin**. Witness oath by George **Berry** 3 Aug 1796 to James **Saxon** J.P. Laurens Co. Rec. 8 May [No year.].

Page 202-203 Lease & Release, 17 & 18 Nov 1794, Elizabeth Jane **Ravenel** Exrx. of her late Husband Daniel **Ravenel** to John **Monro**, for £52 14sh current money sold a certain Tract of Land on waters of Bush River containing 240 acres more or less, part of 3,000 acres originally granted to sd. Daniel **Ravenel** and by him in his last Will & Testament directed to be sold by his Exrx. & Exors. and known in the General plan by Number 7. Also all that other Tract containing 35 acres more or less, being also part of sd. 3,000 acres and known in the General plan by number 8. Also all that other tract containing 147 acres more or less, being also part of sd. 3,000 acres & known in the General plan by Number 10. Witness D. **Ravenel**, Rene **Ravenel**, Peter **Porcher** Jun. Signed Elizabeth Jane **Ravenel**. Witness oath by Peter **Porcher** Jun. 15 Dec 1796 to J. R. **Brown** J. Newberry Co. Rec. 8 May 1797.

Page 203 (Halifax Co., Va.) 7 Apr 1797, I empower Jesse **Wood** as my Lawful Attorney in So. Carolina to receive from Lewis **Banton** that part of My Wife's Estate due to her from Lewis **Banton** Admr. of the Estate of Peter **Wood** dec. Witness Andw. **Rodgers** Jun., Elisha (x) **Tucker**. Signed Moses **Hubbard**, Sarah (x) **Hubbard**. Oath by A. **Rodgers** Jun. 8 May 1797, that he saw Moses **Hubbard** & his Wife Sarah sign the power of Attorney. Given before Joseph **Downs** J.P. Laurens Co. Rec. 8 May 1797.

Page 203-204 26 Apr 1797, Jesse **Wood**, Lawful Representative of Peter **Wood** dec., have settled all Accounts Relating to the Estate of sd. Peter **Wood** dec. and Release Lewis **Banton** Admr. from any other Claims. Witness Jas. **Arnold**, Tho. **Davenport**, Ste. C. **Wood**. Signed Jesse **Wood**. Witness oath by Ste. C. **Wood** 8 May 1797 to Zech. **Bailey** J.P. Laurens Co. [No record date.]

Page 204 1 Aug 1796, William **Freeman** (Laurens Co.) for £40 Sterling paid by John **Simpson** Mercht. (same), sell all that tract of Land containing 79 acres more or less, being part of a Tract originally granted to sd. William **Freeman** containing 150 acres & sold to John **McCarter**. The 79 acres being laid off the S.E. and N.E. ends of the original Survey. Bounding Saml. **Freeman**, S.W. on John **Gray**, S.E. on James **Little**, N.E. on original Survey, N.W. on large Survey. Being on waters of Little River on Carsons Creek & sd. Co. Witness Jas. **Stewart**, Robert **Freeman**, Samuel **Freeman**. Signed William (x) **Freeman**. Dower relinquished by Mary (x) **Freeman**, wife of William **Freeman**, 25 Aug 1796 before Jno. **Hunter** J.L.C. [No witness oath.] Plat certified 1 Oct 1794 by John **Hunter** D.S. Rec. 8 May 1797. [Includes plat.]

Page 205 2 Mar 1797, James **Young** and his Wife Elizabeth (Laurens Co.) for £38 Sterling paid by John **Neighbours** (same), sold all that tract of Land which sd. **Young** lives on, containing 127-3/4 acres more or less. Being on waters of Little River on Tods Creek, being part of a Tract originally granted to James **Young** Sen., it being Willed to James **Young** Jun. by James **Young** Sen. dec., containing originally 150 acres. Border: Wm. **Smith**, Wm. **Taylor**. Witness Robt. (R) **Spence**, David **Speers**, John **Boyd**. Signed James **Young**,

Elizabeth (x) **Young**, Robt. **Young** Exor. Witness oath by David **Speers** 8 May 1797 to Charles **Saxon** J.P. Laurens Co. Rec. 8 May 1797. [Includes plat.]

Page 205-206 1 Feb 1797, Joseph **Adair** (Laurens Co.) for £35 Sterling paid by Thomas **McCrery** (same), sold a certain tract of Land containing 100 acres more or less. Witness Elisha **Adair**, James **Adair**. Signed Joseph **Adair**. Witness oath by Elisha **Adair** 9 May 1797 to Jonthn. **Downs** J.P. Laurens Co. Rec. 9 May 1797.

Page 206 26 Nov 1796, John **Adair** and his wife Jean (Laurens Co.) to Francis **Braddock** (same), for £12 Sterling sell a certain parcel of Land containing 75 acres more or less, being part of 221 acres granted to John **Gamble** by Thomas **Pinckney** Esq. Gov. at Charleston, 2 Jun 1788 & conveyed by sd. **Gamble** to John **Adair**. Being on Allisons Creek, waters of Duncans Creek, waters of Enoree River. Situate in sd. Co. Border: Robert **Scott**. Witness Joseph (x) **Chumbley**, James **Adair**. Signed John **Adair**, Jean (x) **Adair**. Witness oath by Joseph (x) **Chumley** [sic] 9 May 1797 to Jonthn. **Downs** J.P. Laurens Co. [No record date.]

Page 207 25 Feb 1797, Samuel **Saxon** (Laurens Co.) for £100 Sterling paid by Little Berry & Whitfield **Wilson** (same), sold all that Lot of Land containing one acre or thereabouts, being at or near Laurens Courthouse. Bounded W by Road leading from Swansays ferry on the Saluda to the Mountain Shoals on Enoree River, S by Road leading from Greenville by Laurens Court House to Charleston, both other sides by sd. Samuel **Saxon**. Witness B. H. **Saxon**, Stainback **Wilson**. Signed Samuel **Saxon**. Dower relinquished by Mary **Saxon**, wife of Samuel **Saxon**, 25 Feb 1797 before Chas. **Allen** J.L.C. Witness oath by B. H. **Saxon** 25 Feb 1797 to Chas. **Allen** J.P. Laurens Co. [No record date.] [Includes plat.]

Page 207 1 Dec 1787, Mark **Goodwin** (Laurens Co.) Planter am bound unto Joshua **Arnall** (same) for £100 Sterling. Condition that if Mark **Goodwin** makes unto Joshua **Arnall**, sufficient Title to a certain Tract of 250 acres, being part of a Tract where sd. **Goodwin** now lives, on or before 1790, then this obligation to be void. Witness Charles **Smith**, John **Williams**. Signed Mark **Goodwin**. Witness oath by John **Williams** 24 May 1797 to Chas. **Smith** J.P. Laurens Co. Rec. 24 May 1797.

Page 208-209 Lease & Release, 27 & 28 Dec 1795, James **Burnside** Sen. (Laurens Co.) to Abraham **Hollingsworth** (same), for £35 Sterling sold all that tract of Land containing 47 acres on Mudlick Creek, adjoining James A. **Williams**, Widow **Armstrong** [Rhebecca **Armstrong** in one ref.], James **Burnside**, Widow **Hollingsworth**. Being a tract originally granted to sd. James **Burnside** Sen. by Charles Griville **Montague** 8 Feb 1773. Witness Isaac **Hollingsworth**, John **Nickles**. Signed James (J) **Burnside**. Witness oath by Isaac **Hollingsworth** and John **Nickles** 30 Dec 1795 to Angus **Campbell** J.P. Laurens Co. [No record date.]

Page 209-210 7 Jun 1796, James **Burnside** Jun. (Laurens Co.) for £3 Sterling paid by Abraham **Hollingsworth** (same), sold that Corner of the land on which sd. James **Burnside** now lives that lies on N side of Mudlick Creek, computed at 5 acres more or less. Original Survey granted to Nethaniel **Abney** by Charles Graville **Montague** 4 Aug 1767, and by sd. **Abney** conveyed by Lease & release to James **Burnside** Sen. & by him given as a Marriage Gift to his Son James **Burnside** `Jun. 8 Feb 1777. Witness George **Hollingsworth**, John **Nickles**. Signed J. **Burnside** Jun. Witness oath by John **Nickels** 20 Dec 1796 to Angus **Campbell** J.P. Rec. 2 Jun 1797.

Page 210-211 31 Jan 1772, Ralph **Humphres** (Craven Co.) to James **Lindley** (same), for £350 sell all that Tract of Land containing 250 acres in sd. Co. on a Branch S side of Reed River. Bounding on all sides by vacant land at time of Survey. Witness Adam Crain **Jones**, Daniel **Allen**, Jas. **Morrison**. Signed Ralph **Humphreys** [sic]. Witness oath by Adam Cr. **Jones** 17 Nov 1773 to Patrick **Cuningham** J.P. Rec. 17 July 1797.

Page 211-212 2 Sept 1768, Josiah **Faugett** (Craven Co.) to Ralph **Humphreys** (same), for £200 sold all that Tract of land containing 250 acres in sd. Co. on a Branch S side of Ready River. Bounding on all sides by vacant land at time of Survey. Witness George **Hollingsworth**, James **Hollingsworth**, Isaac **Hollingsworth**. Signed Josiah **Feugitt** [sic]. Affirmation by George **Hollingsworth**, he being one of the people called Quaker, 5 Mar 1772 to Jas. **Lindley** J.P. Craven Co. Rec. 17 July 1797.

Page 212-213 10 Jan 1775, Robert **Shirley** (Craven Co.) planter and Jane his Wife & Mary **Shirely** [sic] his Mother to Andrew **Cuningham** planter, for £450 Current money sell 350 acres of Land, being the place that sd. Robert **Shirley** & Mary **Shirley** now live on and being part of 500 acres originally granted unto Richard **Shirley** dec., which was sd. Robert **Shirley's** Father and sd. Mary **Shirley's** husband. Situate in Craven or Barkley Co. on Raborns Creek, waters of Reedy River & Saluda River, bounded on all sides by vacant Land at time it was laid out. Granted unto sd. Richard **Shirley** by Lord Charles Graville **Montague** Gov. 15 Feb 1769. Witness David **Cuningham**, Godfrey **Isbell**, Joseph (J) **Pinson**. Signed Robert **Shirley**, Jane (x) **Shirley**, Mary (W) **Shirley**. Witness oath by David **Cuningham** 5 Sept 1788 to William **Moore** J.P. Aberville Co. [No record date.]

Page 213-214 14 Mar 1796, Andrew **Rodgers** Jun. (Laurens Co.) for $30 paid by Patrick **Cuningham** (same), sold all that Tract of Land in sd. Co. on Beaverdam Creek, waters of Little River, containing 60 or 61 acres more or less, being part of 701 acres originally granted to sd. Andw. **Rodgers**. Bounded: **Chesnut**, Saml. **Caldwell**, David **Craddock**, Robert **Pasley**, Patrick **Cuningham**. Witness John **Cuningham**, Memn. **Walker**, Thomas **Meares**. Signed Andw. **Rodgers** Jun. Witness oath by Memn. **Walker** 18 July 1797 to Zech. **Bailey** J.P. Laurens Co. Dower relinquished by Letty **Rodgers** wife of

Andw. **Rodgers** 22 Apr 1797 before Thomas **Wadsworth** J.L.C. Plat certified 14 Mar 1796 by Patrick **Cuningham** D.S. Rec. 17 July 1797. [Includes plat.]

Page 214-215 8 July 1791, John **Carter** (Laurens Co.) Tavern Keeper to Patrick **Cuningham** (same) Planter, for £30 Sterling sold Two tracts of Land, one Tract containing 100 acres more or less, and one Tract containing 3 acres. Bounding upon Each other, in sd. Co., being part of 300 acres originally granted unto Richard **Carter** on waters of Cane Creek and Golmans Creek, by Lord Charles Granville **Montague** Gov. 11 Feb 1773. Sd. 100 acres was sold away by sd. Richard **Carter** unto George **Carter**, his Son, by lease & release 5 & 6 Aug 1777, and now the above named John **Carter**, being the Oldest Son & heir of sd. George **Carter**, who is dec., hath sold unto sd. **Cuningham**. Sd. 100 acres bounding E on John **Weathers** & John **Pinson**, N & W on sd. Patrick **Cuningham**, S on land formerly held by Joseph **Carter** but now by sd. John **Carter**. Sd. 3 acres, being part of 125 acres that sd. Richard **Carter** originally sold unto Joseph **Carter**, being part of sd. original grant of 300 acres. Witness Reuben **Pyles**, John (S) **Donnaho**, John **Pinson**. Signed John **Carter**. Witness oath by Reuben **Pyles** 18 July 1797 to Zech. **Bailey** J.P. Laurens Co. Plat certified 8 July 1791 by Patrick **Cuningham** D.S. Rec. 17 July 1797. [Includes plat.]

Page 215-216 21 June 1796, John **Carter** (Laurens Co.) planter for £13 Sterling paid by Patrick **Cuningham** (same) planter, sold all that tract of Land containing 72 acres more or less, on W side of the Road leading from Laurens Courthouse to Swanceys ferry, being part of 300 acres originally granted unto Richard **Carter**, on waters of Cain Creek & Goodmans Creek. [Plat description includes, "on waters of Saluda River."] Out of sd. 300 acres, sd. Richard **Carter** sold away unto his Son Joseph **Carter** 125 acres, and he sold away unto sd. John **Carter** by lease & release 22 & 23 Apr 1784. Border: Patrick **Cuningham**, John **Pinson**. Witness Ste. C. **Wood**, Flanders **Thompson**, Sarah **Wood**. Signed John **Carter**. Witness oath by Ste. C. **Wood** 18 July 1797 to Zech. **Bailey** J.P. Laurens Co. Dower relinquished by Zebiah (x) **Carter**, wife of John **Carter**, 22 Sept 1796 before Thomas **Wadsworth** J.L.C. Plat certified 1 June 1796 by P. **Cuningham**. Rec. 17 July 1797. [Includes plat.]

Page 216-217 13 June 1797, Silvanus **Walker** Jun. (Laurens Co.) to John **Cuningham** (Charles Ton), for £5 Current money sell a Certain Tract of Land in sd. Co. on both sides of Little River, containing by a resurvey 713 acres, being the Land sd. **Walker** now lives on. Witness John **Cuningham**, George **Watts**. Signed Silvanus **Walker**. Witness oath by John **Cuningham** [No date.] to Zech. **Bailey** J.P. Laurens Co. Rec. 17 July 1797.

Page 217 14 June 1797, Whereas Silvanus **Walker** (Laurens Co.) by my bond of this date to John **Cuningham** (Charleston) stands bound for $5,000 with Condition for payment of whatsoever sums shall be recovered against sd. **Cuningham** by the U.S. in consequence of sd. John being Security in a bond to the U.S. for $4,000 conditioned for faithful performance of duties of

Collector of Revenues. For the better securing the sum, sell three Negroes, Toby, Harry & Jane, with the Issue of the female. Also all my stock of Different kinds consisting of one bay Mare about 4 feet 7 inches high, 7 or 8 years old; Two sorrel mares, one is one year, the other four years old & about 4 feet 8 inches high; one black mare about 4 feet 10 inches high & about 7 or 8 years old; Ten head of Sheep; about forty head of hogs, marked with a Swallow fork in left ear, a Crop & a nick in the right; twelve head of Cattle, some marked as above, some not the same, others at marked, also all my household furniture. Provided that if sd. **Walker** shall pay the sum which may be recovered against sd. **Cuningham** on which an action is now brought in the Court of U.S., then this deed shall be void. Witness John **Cuningham**, George **Watts**. Signed Silv. **Walker**. Witness oath by John **Cuningham** 18 July 1797 to Zech. **Bailey** J.P. Laurens Co. Rec. 18 July 1797.

Page 218 14 June 1797, Whereas John **Cuningham** (Charleston) by his bond dated 24 Sept 1794, stands bound with Silvanus **Walker** (Laurens Co.) to the U.S.A. for $4,000, conditioned for faithful performance of the duty of inspector of duties for survey No.3. Whereas an action has been instituted in the Circuit of the U.S. on sd. bond against sd. John **Cuningham** for recovery of certain monies said to be received by sd. Silvanus and not paid over. In consideration of the above and also 5sh and for the better securing the payment, sell unto sd. **Cuningham** all that Tract of Land in sd. Co. on both sides of Little River, containing by resurvey 713 acres, being the plantation which sd. Silvanus now lives on. Provided that if sd. **Walker** shall pay all sums which may be recovered of sd. John **Cuningham** by the U.S., then these presents to be void. Witness John **Cuningham**, George **Watts**. Signed Silvanus **Walker**. Dower relinquished by Sarah **Walker**, wife of Silvanus **Walker**, 17 July 1797 before Wm. **Mitchell** J.L.C. [No witness oath.] Rec. 18 July 1797.

Page 219 14 June 1797, Silvanus **Walker** (Laurens Co.) is bound unto John **Cuningham** (Charleston) for $5,000. Whereas Silvanus **Walker** and John **Cuningham** are bound unto the U.S.A. for $4,000. Condition that sd. Silvanus **Walker** shall faithfully discharge his duty as Inspector of the Revenue of the U.S.A. for Survey No.3 District. Whereas an action is pending in the Circuit Court of the U.S. for Survey No.3 for purpose of recovering certain moneys said to be received by sd. **Walker** and not Accounted for and forthcoming to the U.S. Condition that if the suit is carried to Judgment, that sd. **Walker** will pay whatever sums which may be recovered. Witness John **Cuningham**, George **Watts**. Signed Silv. **Walker**. Witness oath by John **Cuningham** 18 July 1797 to Zech. **Bailey** J.P. Laurens Co. Rec. 18 July 1797.

Page 219-220 Lease & Release, 8 & 9 July 1792, Samuel **Scott** (Laurens Co.) to John **Ritchey** (same), for £50 Sterling sold all that tract of Land containing 150 acres more or less, being a Tract granted unto sd. **Scott**. Being in sd. Co. on waters of Ready River, bound S.W. by Ms. **Milhoun**, S.E. by James **Williams**, N.E. by vacant Land. Witness Thos. **Wadsworth**, Thomas **Meaid**.

Signed Samuel **Scott**. Witness oath by Thomas **Wadsworth** 25 May 1797 to Zech. **Bailey** J.P. Rec. 18 July 1797.

Page 220-221 10 May 1791, Zekiel **Griffith** [sic] (Laurens Co.) to William **Stone** (same), for £20 sold part of a Tract of Land on Beaverdam Creek, waters of Enoree River. Border: N & S side of Creek, mouth of Spring branch. To contain 50 acres more or less. Granted to sd. Zekiel **Griffith** 24 Jan 1770 by William **Bull** then Gov. and recorded in Secretary's Office in Book EEE, page 681. Witness Nathan **Bramlett**, John **Bramlett**. Signed Ezekiel (E) **Griffith**. Witness oath by John **Bramlett** 10 May 1791 to Daniel **Wright** J.P. Laurens Co. Rec. 18 July 1797.

Page 221 [This deed is crossed out.] 1 Dec 1791, William Hasell **Gibbes** (Charleston) for £109 paid by James **Underwood** (Laurens Co.) Planter, sold all that Body of Land in Laurens, formerly Craven Co., on branches of Duncans Creek containing about 1,090 Acres more or less, bounding S.E. on Edmund **Reily**, unknown, Patrick **Bryant**, Michael **Dixon**, S.W. on James **Barton**, William **Sanders**, N.W. on Benjamin **Barton**, on or near William **Ball** Jun., N.E. on William **Taylor**, Andrew **Rodgers**. [No witness.] Signed W. Hasell **Bigges**. [No witness oath.] [No record date.]

Page 222 22 Aug 1796, Thomas **Ewing** (Laurens Co.) planter for $100 paid by Alexander **Leeke** (same), sold all that Tract of Land granted to me, being in sd. Co. containing 100 acres more or less, bounded S.E. on land laid out to me, N.W. on James **Adair**, W on Joseph **Adair**, N on Hannah **Glenn** and land lately laid out to sd. Alexander **Leeke**. Witness David **Grayham**, Alexr. **Filson**, Robt. **Hanna**. Signed Thomas **Ewing**. Witness oath by David **Grayham** 14 July 1797 to Roger **Brown** J.P. Laurens Co. Rec. 18 July 1797.

Page 222-223 30 Jan 1797, William **Bell** (Laurens Co.) Mortgage unto James **Rammage** (same), one Sorrell horse about 13-1/2 hands high, about 6 years old with a large Star in his forehead, also two cows & yearlings, one brindle Cow marked -, also one pided Cow and a feather Bed & furniture, a loom & her tackling and all my house hold furniture. For the payment of the sum to which sd. **Rammage** stands Bail and Surety & on non performance of an obligation. Witness Mos. **Lindsey**, Joseph **Rammage**. Signed William **Bell**. Witness oath by Joseph **Rammage** 15 June 1797 to James **Dillard** J.P. Laurens Co. Rec. 18 July 1797.

Page 223 10 Sept 1796, John **Cole** (Laurens Co.) to Jonathan **Johnston** (same), for £40 Sterling sold part of a Certain tract of Land in sd. Co. on Cane Creek, waters of Saluda and on E side of sd. Creek principally, being 75 acres more or less, being the remainder of the tract originally granted to sd. **Cole**. Border: Peter **Smith's** Spring branch on Cane Creek. Excepting what I have sold to John **Pinson** over the Creek and what Mr. **Turk's** tract and James **Pucket** interferes and in lieu of what I have sold to Mr. **Pinson**, I sell unto sd. **Johnston** 3 or 4 acres which is John **Pinsons** interference running over Cane Creek in the field. Witness Richd. **Duty**, John (P) **Pinson**, Elizbeth (E)

Pinson. Signed John **Cole**. Witness oath by John (P) **Pinson** 27 May 1797 to Angus **Campbell** J.P. Laurens Co. [No record date.]

Page 223-225 Lease & Release, 24 & 25 Nov 1769, William **Wright** (Berkley Co.) hunter to Benjamin **Heaton** (same) Carpenter, for £110 sell one certain Tract of Land containing by Estimation 200 acres more or less, in Craven Co. on a branch of Little River, bounded on all sides by vacant Land. Granted to sd. **Wright** by Letter Patent at Charlestown, 7 May 1767, signed by Ld. Chas. Grenville **Montague** Gov. Paying one pepper corn upon the feast of Saint Michael the arch Angel, if lawfully demanded. Witness Jos. **Wright**, James **Batty** [**Patty** in one ref.], Charity (C) **Wright**. Signed William **Wright**. Witness oath by Joseph **Wright** 25 Nov 1760 [sic] to James **Lindley** J.P. Granvil Co. [No record date.]

Page 225 20 Jan 1797, Thomas **Fakes** (Laurens Co.) for £75 Sterling paid by Nathan **Todd** [Nathen in one ref.] (same), sold all that Tract of Land containing 150 acres, agreeable to the Grant thereof, in sd. Co. on Smiths Creek. Joining land of Widow **Proctor**, John **Meek**, William **Watson** & Vacant land at time of Survey. Granted to me 1 Aug 1785. Witness J. R. **Brown**, Christian **Brown**. Signed Thomas **Fakes**. Witness oath by J. R. **Brown** 24 June 1797 to Angus **Campbell** J.P. Ninety Six Dist. Dower relinquished by Margret (x) **Fakes**, wife of Thomas **Fakes**, 20 Jan 1797 before Jacob R. **Brown** Judge Newberry Co. Rec. 18 July 1797.

Page 225-226 4 July 1797, Thomas **Burton** (Laurens Co.) sell unto Benjamin **Byrd** (same), a Negro Boy Sam in consideration of $220. Witness Ezel. **Roland**, Benjn. **Burton**. Signed Thomas **Burton**. Witness oath by Eze. S. **Roland** 4 July 1797 to John **Davis** J.P. L. Co. Rec. 18 July 1797.

Page 226 10 Feb 1796, John **Weeks** & Benjamin **Weeks** (Newberry Co.) for £86 10sh Sterling paid by John **Hughes** (Laurens Co.), sold all that tract of Land containing 200 acres more or less, in Laurens Co. on both sides of beaverdam branch of Little River. Adjoining E on Patrick **Cuningham**, N on Thomas **Babb**, W on David **Baley**, S on Abel **Boland**. Originally granted to William **Wright**, letter patent at Charlestown 7 May 1767 & conveyed by him to Benjamin **Heaton** by Lease & release 24 & 25 Nov 1769, and left by Will unto John **Weeks** & Benjamin **Weeks**, which Will is recorded in the Clerk's office of Newberry Co. Witness Robert **Paslay**, Jacob **Miller**. Signed John **Weeks**, Benjamin (x) **Weeks**. Witness oath by Robt. **Paslay** 8 July 1797 to Zech. **Bailey** J.P. Laurens Co. Rec. 18 July 1797.

Page 226-227 19 Sept 1794, John **Rodgers** (Laurens Co.) to James **McMahan** Jun. (same), for £90 Sterling sell a certain tract of Land in sd. Co. on Beaverdam Creek, waters of Little River, containing 250 acres more or less, being part of a tract originally granted to Christopher **Hammel** and conveyed from him to William **Drew** dec., and conveyed by Langston **Drew** to John **Rodgers**. Border: branch, **Glenn**, **Chesnut**, Ready branch, **Gibbs**, John **Hughes**. Witness John **Hughes**, John **McMahan**, James **McMahan** Sen.

Signed John **Rodgers**. Witness oath by John **Hughes** 5 July 1797 to Zech. **Bailey** J.P. Laurens Co. Rec. 18 July 1797.

Page 227   17 Nov 1796, John **Wilson** (Laurens Co.) to Joseph **McNeeley** (same), for £60 Sterling sold one Certain tract of Land in sd. Co. on S fork of Rabours Creek. Bounded on **Maczeck, McMahan, Kellet,** branch. Including the house & plantation where Joseph **McNeeley** now lives, containing by Estimation 112 acres more or less. Witness Drewry **Sims** [Drury in one ref.], Samson (x) **Babb** [sic]. Signed John **Wilson**. Witness oath by Sampson (x) **Babb** 15 Apr 1797 to Jno. **Coker** J.P. Laurens Co. Rec. 18 July 1797.

Page 227-228   21 Jan 1797, Elisha **Mitchell** (Laurens Co.) to Isaac **Moseley** (same), for £20 Sterling sold a certain tract of Land in sd. Co. on waters of Cane Creek, containing by Estimation 20 acres more or less, being part of 164 acres conveyed by Patrick **Gibson** to Clabourn **Sims** and originally granted to James **Harley** by Charles Greville **Montague** Gov. Border: sd. **Mitchell,** branch, **Carter,** Joseph **Babb**. Witness Drury **Moseley**, James **Babb**, Isaac **Mitchell**. Signed Elisha **Mitchell**. Witness oath by James **Babb** 18 July 1797 to Zech. **Bailey** J.P. Laurens Co. Dower relinquished by Sarah (x) **Mitchell,** wife of Elisha **Mitchell,** 21 Jan 1797. Witnessed by Drury **Moseley**, James **Babb**. [No record date.]

Page 228-229   24 Apr 1797, John **Hunter** Esq. (Laurens Co.), Attorney for Hercules D. **Bize,** for £23 9sh Sterling paid by John **Stevens** Jun. [**Stephens** in one ref.] and Sarah his Wife, sold all that tract of Land containing 134 acres more or less, on Reedy River, joining William **Holliday,** John **Rodgers,** Reedy River. Being part of 500 acres granted 5 May 1772, to Pierce **Butler,** and by him sold to sd. **Bize**. Witness William **Dunlap,** Oliver **Lowden**. Signed John **Hunter** Atty. for Hercules Dal. **Bize**. Witness oath by Wm. **Dunlap** 18 July 1797 to Reuben **Pyles** J.P. Laurens Co. Plat certified 10 Sept 1793 by John **Hunter** D.S. Rec. 18 July 1797. [Includes plat.]

Page 229   3 June 1797, Robert **Coker** (Laurens Co.) to Philip **Coker** (same), for £40 sold all that tract of Land suppose to contain 100 acres more or less, being part of a Tract granted to John **Abercrombie** 1 Dec 1769, by Wm. **Bull** Esq., in sd. Co. on N side of Rabourn Creek. Border: James **Abercrombie,** sd. Creek. Witness Robert **Coker** Jr., William **Hellums**. Signed Robert (R) **Coker**. Witness oath by Robert **Coker** 18 July 1797 to Jno. **Coker** J.P. Laurens Co. Rec. 18 July 1797.

Page 229-230   3 Feb 1797, James **Smith** (Newberry Co.) to William **Smith** (Laurens Co.), [No consideration noted.] sold all that Tract of Land containing 115 acres more or less, being part of a Tract granted to Fredrick **Ward** 5 Dec 1785, and recorded in Secretary's Office in Book BBBB, page 337, containing 200 acres in Laurens Co. on Smiths Creek, a branch of Saluda River, and conveyed by sd. **Ward** to James **Smith**. Bounding S.W. on Wm. **Smith** and William **Anderson,** N.E. on Thomas **Fakes** and **Proctor,** S.E. on Robert **Gillam** [**Gillmon** on plat.], S.W. on William **Solmon,** at time of original survey. Witness John **Dendey**, Elijah **Stone**, James **Watts**. Signed James (x) **Smith**. Witness oath by Elijah **Stone** 2 July 1797 to Angus **Campbell** J.P. Laurens Co. Dower relinquished by Martha **Smith**, wife of James **Smith**, 30 May 1797 before Jacob R. **Brown** Judge Newberry Court. Plat certified 4 Dec 1793 by William **Caldwell** D.S. Rec. 18 July 1797. [Includes plat.]

Page 230-231   23 Feb 1797, John **Sample** & Peter **Smith** (Laurens Co.) to John **Watts** (same), for £16 Sterling sold a certain parcel of Land in sd. Co. on waters of Cane Creek, containing 82 acres more or less, being part of 249 acres granted to Hugh **Crumbless** in 1791. Border: Jonathan **Puckett**, dry branch, Joseph **Hollingsworth**, William **Wheler** [sic], **Parson**. Witness Simpson **Warrin**, Wm. **Wheeler**, Phillip **Housworth**. Signed John **Sample**, Sarah (x) **Sample**, Peter **Smith**, Dolley (x) **Smith**. Witness oath by William **Wheeler** 15 July 1797 to Angus **Campbell** J.P. Laurens Co. Rec. 18 July 1797.

Page 231   4 Oct 1796, Mary **Johnston** (Edgefield Co.) for 200 Spanish Dollars paid by Richard **Griffin** [Richarg in one ref.] (Laurens Co.) Planter, sold all that tract of Land containing 150 acres more or less, in Laurens Co. on Saluda River. Originally granted to William **Edwards** and by him conveyed to my Father John **Savage**, bounded N.E. by Patrick **Huggens**, N.W. by James **Chapple**. Witness Matthew **Sullivan** [sic], Eliza Ann **Anderson**, Rebecca **Anderson**. Signed Mary **Johnston**. Witness oath by Mathew **Sullivan** 4 Oct 1796 to Wm. **Anderson** Judge Edgefield Co. Rec. 18 July 1797.

Page 231-232   Lease & Release, 27 May 1793, Martin **Martin** (Laurens Co.) to Joseph **Young** (same), for £7 Sterling sold all that tract of Land containing 16 acres more or less, in sd. Co. on waters of Little River. Border: James **Cook**, Joseph **Young**, John **Young**. Being granted to sd. **Martin** on Bounty by Thomas **Pinckney** Esq. then Gov., surveyed 9 Jan 1787. Witness Saml. C. **Stidman**, John **Hutchinson**. Signed Martin (8) **Martin**. Witness oath by Saml. C. **Stidman** 17 July 1797 to Chas. **Smith** J.P. Laurens Co. [No record date.]

Page 232-233   20 Jan 1767, William **Reily**, living in Charles town, is bound unto John **Smith** (S.C.) for £460. Condition that if William **Reily** makes over a tract of Land containing 100 acres on a branch of Dunkins Creek, which was granted to sd. **Reily**, then this obligation to be void. Witness James **Johnson**, Robert **Mitchacel** [sic], Signed William **Reily**. Witness oath by John **Smith** 22 Aug 1797 to Roger **Brown** J.P. Laurens Co. [No record date.]

Page 233   [No date.], John **Hunter** Esq. (Laurens Co.) as Attorney for John **Rutledge** Jun. (Charleston) for £21 paid by Isaac **Thomas** (Laurens Co.), sold all that tract of Land of 100 acres [133 in plat.] more or less, in Laurens Co. on waters of Redy River, being part of 1,300 acres granted to Thos. **Shubuck** and conveyed to John **Rutledge** Esq. Jun. Border: P. **Cuningham**, Widow **Baugh**, sd. Survey. Witness Abel **Thomas**, William **Elleman**. Signed John **Hunter** Atty. for Jno. **Rutledge** Jun. Witness oath by Abel **Thomas** 17 July 1797 to

Joseph **Downs** J.P. Laurens Co. Plat certified 16 May 1791 by John **Hunter** D.S., Rec. 18 July 1797. [Includes plat.]

Page 233-234 10 Mar 1797, John **Cane** (Laurens Co.) for £30 Sterling paid by William **Bush** (same), sold all that tract of Land containing 60 acres more or less, on W side of my Spring branch. Border: Spring branch, S fork of Dunkins Creek. Being part of 200 acres granted to John **Gray** 15 May 1772 by Ld. **Montague** and Recorded in Secretary's Office in Book LLL, page 92. Witness John **Martindill**, Joseph **Huddleston**. Signed John **Cain** [sic]. Witness oath by John **Martindill** 10 Mar 1797 to Geo. **Whitmore** J.P. Laurens Co. Rec. 18 July 1797.

Page 234 10 Mar 1797, George **Bush** (Laurens Co.) for £22 10sh Sterling paid by John **Cain** (same), sold all that tract of Land containing 70 acres more or less, on waters of Dunkins Creek, being part of 100 acres granted to sd. **Bush**, 5 June 1786 by Wm. **Moultrie** Esq. Gov. & recorded in Secretary's Office in Book LLLL, page 41. Witness Joseph **Huddleston**, John **Martindill**. Signed George **Bush**. Witness oath by Joseph **Huddleston** 27 May 1797 to George **Whitmore** J.P. Laurens Co. Rec. 18 July 1797.

Page 234-235 11 Jan 1796, James **Downen** (Laurens Co.) to Sampson **Babb** (same), for £60 Sterling sold one certain Tract of Land in sd. Co. on Raborns Creek, waters of Reedy River, containing 222 acres, part of a Tract granted to James **Downen** by Chas. **Pinckney** Esq. Gov. 10 Nov 1791. Witness Edward **Scar Brough** [sic], Andrew **McKnight**. Signed James **Downen**, Jane **Downen**. Oath by Andw. **McKnight** 15 July 1797, that he saw James **Downen** & Jane his Wife sign the deed. Given before Jno. **Coker** J.P. Laurens Co. Rec. 18 July 1797.

Page 235-236 28 Nov 1794, Sandford **Berry** (Laurens Co.) & Elizabeth his Wife to Spencer **Bobo** (Sparten Co.), for £60 Sterling sold all that tract of Land containing 100 acres, being part of 400 acres formerly granted to James **Allison** & conveyed by him to Wm. **Cox** by Lease & release 4 & 5 Aug 1774, since conveyed by John **Cox**, son of William dec., to sd. Sandford **Berry** by Lease & release 28 & 29 June 1788. Being on S.E. part of above tract. Border: Enoree Bank, old line. Witness Thomas **Berry**, Peter **Brooks**. Signed Sandford (6) **Berry**, Elizabeth (x) **Berry**. Witness oath by Thomas **Berry** 16 July 1796 to James **Saxon** J.P. Ninety Six Dist. Rec. 18 July 1797.

Page 236-237 20 Nov 1795, Angus **Campbell** (Laurens Co.) & Milley his Wife to Spencer **Bobo** (same), for £80 Sterling sold all that tract of Land containing by Estimation 50 acres more or less, being part of 400 acres formerly granted to Jas. **Allison** in sd. Co. on S side of Enoree. Border: Source of Warrior Creek, **McCrery**, Sandford **Berry**, Enoree River, Warrior Creek where it unites with the Enoree. Witness Wm. (a) **Berry**, Howard (x) **Smith**. Signed Angus **Campbell**, Milley (x) **Campbell**. Witness oath by Howard (x) **Smith** 16 July 1796 to James **Saxon** J.P. Laurens Co. Rec. 18 July 1797.

Page 237 7 Jan 1795, James **Durrah** (Laurens Co.) to John **Durrah** (same), for 10sh Sterling sold one certain tract of Land joining James **Durrah**, Kiah **Deak**, Wm. **Norris** & Saml. **Putt**. Containing 102 acres in sd. Co. on waters of Ready River, being part of a tract originally granted to Hugh **Isamell** & from him conveyed to James **Durrah**. Witness Thomas **Cuningham**, David **Dunlap**. Signed James (O) **Durrah**. Witness oath by David **Dunlap** 18 July 1796 to Joseph **Downs** J.P. Laurens Co. Rec. 18 July 1797. [Includes plat.]

Page 237-238 10 Jan 1795, John **Coker** (Laurens Co.) to William **Bowen** (same), for £8 sold a certain Tract of Land in sd. Co. on S fork of Durbens Creek, containing 73 acres more or less. Plat dated 1792, and recorded in Grant Book D, No.5, page 627. Witness Thos. **Goodwin**, William **Pugh**. Signed Jno. **Coker**. Witness oath by Thos. **Goodwin** 23 May 1797 to Daniel **Wright** J.P. Laurens Co. Rec. 18 July 1797.

Page 238-239 Lease & Release, 9 & 10 June 1797, Laird B. **Boyd** (Davidson Co., Tenn.) by his Attorney John **Boyd** to Matthew **McDaniel** (Laurens Co.), for £100 Sterling sell all that tract of Land containing 150 acres on Raiborns Creek, a Creek of Saluda River, bounded on all sides by vacant Land at time of Surveying. Being granted 4 Nov 1762, by Thomas **Boone** Esq. Gov., unto Robert **Box**. Recorded in Secretary's Office in Book WW, page 186. Conveyed by sd. Robert **Box** unto James **Ryan** & by him unto James **Boyd**. Power of Atty. given to John **Boyd**, dated 22 Nov 1796. Witness Joseph **Downs**, William **Hunter**. Signed John **Boyd** Atty. for Laird **Boyd**. Witness oath by William **Hunter** 18 July 1797 to Jas. **Dillard** J.P. Laurens Co. [No record date.]

Page 240 17 Oct 1796, Benjamin **Kevil** (Greenville Co.) to John **House** (Laurens Co.), for £45 sold all that tract of Land containing 300 acres in Laurens Co. on S side of Enoree River on some branches of Durbins Creek, waters of Enoree River, being granted to Nethaniel **Newman** by Patent 6 June 1785 & recorded in grant Book DDDD, page 347. Witness Joab **League**, James **Halks**, Thomas **Kevil**. Signed Ben. **Kevil**. Witness oath by Thomas **Kevil** 17 Oct 1796 to James **Kilgore** J.P. Greenville Co. Rec. 18 July 1797.

Page 240-241 17 Oct 1796, Benjamin **Kevil** (Greenville Co.) to John **House** (Laurens Co.), for £10 sold all that tract of Land supposed to contain 60 acres more or less, in Laurens Co. on S side of Enoree River, being part of 900 acres originally granted to sd. Benjamin **Kevil** by patent 6 Jan 1794. Recorded in Grant Book M, No.5, page 19. Border: Enoree River, **Hooker's** old line. Witness Joab **League**, Jas. **Halks**, Thomas **Kevil**. Signed Benjn. **Kevil**. Witness oath by Thomas **Kevil** 17 Oct 1796 to James **Kilgore** J.P. Greenville Co. Rec. 18 July 1797.

Page 241 1797, William **Hughes** (S.C.) for £25 15sh paid by Robert **Young** (same), sold all that tract of Land of 175 acres in Abbeville Co., being part of 14,832 acres purchased of R. A. **Rapley** Esq. by Nicholas **Eveleigh** Esq. and of him by me, William **Hughes**. Sd. land was conveyed to Robert **Smith**, John

Bee **Holmes** & Edward **Rutledge** by Nicholas **Eveleigh** Esq. and Mary his Wife, by Lease & release 26 & 27 Oct 1789, for the purpose of applying the proceeds toward Satisfaction of his Debts. Witness Robert **Freeman**, Abraham **Hollingsworth**. Signed Wm. (WH) **Hughes**. Witness oath by Robert **Freeman** 17 July 1797 to Zech. **Bailey** J.P. Laurens Co. [No record date.]

Page 241-242 (North Carolina) 1 Oct 1792, William Henry **Crouch** (Fayette Ville, N.C.), late of Charleston, appoint Lewis **Trezevant** Esq. (Charleston) my Lawful Attorney to sell all that tract of Land granted for 100 acres 8 May 1758 to Abraham **Crouch**, now dec., then bounded on all sides by vacant Land. Situate on Indian Creek in the fork between Broad and Saluda Rivers, in Laurens Co., but which by a late Resurvey by John **Hunter** Esq. 3 May 1787, is found to contain 138 acres, bounding N.W. on Isham **East**, N.E. on unknown, S.E. on Josiah **East**. And also for me in my Name to Lease sd. premises as may be necessary. Witness Lemuel **Moyes**, Starling **Wheaton**. Signed Wm. Henry **Crouch**. Recorded in Book of Miscellaneous record lettered CCC, page 476, 14 Nov 1793 & Examd. by Stephen **Ravenel** Dep.Sec. Witness oath by George **Greenland** (Charleston Facten), 14 Nov 1793, that he is well acquainted with the manner & form of the hand writing of William Henry **Crouch**, and that the foregoing is his signature. Given before Stephen **Ravenel** J.P. Charleston. [No record date.]

Page 242-244 28 Oct 1795, John **Edward** & Catherine his Wife (Laurens Co.) planter to David **Mayson** (same), for £200 Sterling sell all that tract of Land containing 628 acres more or less, in sd. Co. on Indian Creek, whereon sd. John **Edwards** [sic] now lives, being composed of Different tracts, granted to Different persons & conveyed to sd. John **Edwards**. One tract of 150 acres granted to John **Mayson** 5 Feb 1769 by Charles G. **Montague**, then Gov. and conveyed by sd. John **Mayson** & Ellenor his Wife by Lease & release to Allen **Wilson** 10 & 11 July 1770, and by sd. **Wilson** conveyed by Lease & release to sd. John **Edwards** 1 & 2 Feb 1773. Also one other tract of 100 acres granted to Abraham **Crouch** 8 May 1758 by William Henry **Littelton**, then Gov. and conveyed by Lease & release to sd. John **Edwards** 13 & 14 Nov 1793 by Lewis **Trezevant** Esq. Atty. for William Henry **Crouch**, Heir to Abraham **Crouch** dec. Also one other tract of 52 acres, being part of 250 acres granted to John **Entrican** 4 Dec 1770 by Charles Gr. **Montague**, then Gov. & by sd. **Entrican** conveyed to Susanna **Deen** 6 Feb 1785, and by her conveyed to sd. John **Edwards** 16 Mar 1787. And also such part of 383 acres granted to John **Edwards** 5 June 1786 by William **Moultrie**, then Gov. as is included within the lines of the plat hereunto annexed & not mentioned in sd. Conveyance as included in older grants. Also such part of 174 acres granted to John **Edward** 5 Mar 1787, as is included within the lines of sd. plat. Border: Thomas **East**, David **Mayson**, Large Survey, **Greenland**, Isham **East**. Witness James **Lindsey**, Stephen (S) **Sparks**. Signed John **Edwards**, Catherine **Edwards**. Witness oath by Stephen **Sparks** [No signature.] 20 Feb 1797 to P. **Williams** P. Plat certified 26 Oct 1795 by John **Hunter** D.S. [No record date.] [Includes plat.]

Page 244 30 Oct 1795, John **Edwards** & Catherin [sic] his Wife (Laurens Co.) planter to David **Mayson**, for £700 Sterling sold all that tract of Land containing 97 acres more or less, being part of 383 acres granted to John **Edwards** 5 June 1786 by William **Moultrie** Esq., then Gov., situate in sd. Co. on Indian Creek. Border: John **Edwards**. Land granted. Witness James **Lindsey**, Stephen (S) **Sparks**. Signed John **Edwards**, Catherine **Edwards**. Witness oath by Stephen [sic] 13 Feb 1797 to P. **Williams** P. Plat certified 27 Oct 1795 by John **Hunter** D.S. [No record date.] [Includes plat.]

Page 245 28 Oct 1795, Dower relinquished by Catherine **Edwards**, Wife of John **Edwards**, to 628 acres more or less, in Laurens Co. on waters of Indian Creek, whereon sd. John **Edwards** then resided. Certified by John **Hunter** J.L.C. [No record date.]

Page 245-246 16 May 1797, William **Dendey** Sen. (Laurens Co.) for $10 paid by William **Dendey**, son of Thomas, (same), sold one Tract of Land on Norths Creek in sd. Co. containing 33 acres, part of a certain Tract granted to William **Dendey** Sen. Border: Cornelius **Dendey**, Thomas **Dendey**, William **Hall**. Witness Thos. **Dendey**, Jas. **Parker**, Thos. C. **Dendy**. Signed William **Dendey**, Clary (C) **Dendey**. Witness oath by Thos. **Dendy** [sic] 16 May 1797 to Wm. **Mitchell** P. Laurens Co. Dower relinquished by Clary (C) **Dendy** [sic], wife of William **Dendy** [sic], 16 May 1797 before Wm. **Mitchell** J.L.C. [No record date.]

Page 246 15 Nov 1796, John **Wilson** (Laurens Co.) to Sampson **Babb** (same), for £40 Sterling sold one certain Tract of Land in sd. Co. on S fork of Raiborns Creek. Border: near mouth of a branch, E fork of branch, Abner **Babb**, Samson **Babb** [sic], Joseph **McNeeley**. Including where John **Wilson** now lives, containing by Estimation 80 acres more or less. Witness Drury **Sims**, Joseph **McNeely** [sic]. Signed John **Wilson**. Witness oath by Joseph **McNeely** 15 July 1797 to Jno. **Coker** J.P. Laurens Co. [No record date.]

Page 247 10 Sept 1795, William **Burris** (Laurens Co.) & Rachel his Wife to John **Blackwell** (same), for £100 Sterling sold one certain Tract of Land containing 200 acres in sd. Co. on a branch of Raiborns Creek, bounding S.W. Joseph **Babb**, all other sides on vacant land. Witness James **Abercrombie**, John **Pinson**. Signed William (W) **Burrows** [sic], Rachel (R) **Burrows** [sic]. Witness oath by John **Pinson** 18 July 1797 to Joseph **Downs** J.P. Rec. 18 July 1797.

Page 247 27 Jan 1797, Hutchins **Burton** (Laurens Co.) to Stephen **Plant** (same), for £50 Sterling sold all that tract of Land containing 100 acres in sd. Co. on waters of Beaverdam of Little River. Joining on W on Fredrick **Sullivant**, S on Stepen **Plant** [sic], Jesse **Meeks**, Isaac **Rodgers**, E & N by John **Godfrey**, F. **Sullivan**. Being part of a tract originally granted to John **Martin** containing 740 acres & conveyed by him to sd. **Burton**. Witness John **Moseley**, Howel **Moseley**. Signed Hutchins (J) **Burton**. Witness oath by John **Moseley** 18 July 1797 to Charles **Saxon** J.P. Laurens Co. [No record date.]

Page 248   22 Mar 1793, Joseph **Gallegly** (Laurens Co.) to David **Speers** (same), for £40 Sterling sold all that tract of Land in sd. Co. on a certain branch of Dunkins Creek, waters of Enoree, containing by Estimation 159 acres more or less, granted by Charles **Pinckney** Esq. 3 Jan 1791. Recorded in Grant Book C, No.5, page 142. Bounding E on Wm. **Williamson**, N.W. on not known, S.E. on Andw. **Endsley**, other sides on vacant land at time when Surveyed. Being originally granted to James **Cummings** and by him conveyed to sd. Joseph **Gallegly**. Witness Jean **Hunter**, Wm. **Dunlap**. Signed Joseph **Gallegly**. Witness oath by Wm. **Dunlap** 18 July 1797 to James **Abercrombie** [No title.]. [No record date.]

Page 248-249   28 Dec 1796, John **Hunter** Esq. (Laurens Co.) Attorney for John **Rutledge** Esq. Jun. (S.C.), for £47 5sh Sterling paid by John **Elleman** (Newberry Co.) sold all that tract of Land containing 189 acres in sd. Co. on waters of Ready River, being part of 1,300 acres granted to Thomas **Shubrick**, conveyed by him to William **Williamson** and by him to John **Rutledge** Esq. Jun. Border: James **Abercrombie**, Edwd. **Thomas**, part of Survey, Wagon Road to fish Dam ford. Witness Wm. **Dunlap**, William **Elleman**. Signed John **Hunter** Atty. for Jno. **Rutledge** Jun. Witness oath by William **Elleman** 28 Dec 1796 to Angus **Campbell** J.P. Laurens Co. Plat certified 14 Nov 1792 by John **Hunter** D.S. [No record date.] [Includes plat.]

Page 249   15 Sept 1797, John **Garman** (Laurens Co.) for £30 Sterling sold unto Hastings **Dial**, one Bay Mare 3 years old, about 13 hands high; one red Cow marked in left ear with a Crop, in right 2 Nicks; one white Cow, both ears red unmarked; 1 Heifer red & white unmarked; 1 Bull red & white unmarked; 10 head of hogs, the left ear cropped, right ear slited; 2 Beds and furniture, 1 small pott, 6 pewter plates, 1 Dish, 8 acres of Corn, 10 pounds of Tobacco and Quantity of fodder. Witness Robert **Allison**, Hastings **Dial**. Signed John (I) **Garman**. Witness oath by Hastings **Dial** 16 Aug 1797 to Chas. **Smith** J.P. Laurens Co. Rec. 16 Aug 1797.

Page 249   24 Apr 1797, Thos. William **Fakes** (Laurens Co.) sold unto Robert **McCurley** (same), one small Black Horse about 14 years old, one Sorrel mare about 9 years old, one bay horse Colt 2 years old, 2 feather beds & furniture, 1 Larke Iron pott, one Dutch Oven, all my household furniture & stock of Hoggs, Cows & Sheep. Witness John **McCurley**. Signed Thos. Wm. **Fakes**. Condition if Thos. Wm. **Fakes** shall pay unto Jno. **Ritchey** on or before 25 Sept 1798, £15 Sterling with Interest, then this property shall return to him. Witness oath by John **McCurley** 18 July 1797 to James **Abercrombie** J.P. [No record date.]

Page 250   17 Aug 1797, John **Dunlap** (Cambridge) for £50 paid by James **Johnston** (Laurens Co.), sold all that part of 1,000 acres granted to Moses **Kirkland** & sold by the Commissioners of Confiscated Estates to Robert **Cooper** (that is not included within the boundaries of Lands Granted of a prior date), containing 500 acres. Sd. tract originally containing 605 acres, in sd. Co.

in fork of Raburns Creek, a branch of Reedy River, the whole of which is conveyed to sd. **Johnston** except 100 acres laid out to Joseph **Holmes** by Jonathan **Downs** Esq. Bounding on Jonathan **Downs** Esq., John **Camock**, Moses **Kirkland**, James **Irwin**, land laid out to John **Calhoon**, **Cuningham**, David **McCaa**, Hannan **Nuffen**, S fork of Raburns Creek, N fork of Raburns Creek. Original boundaries containing by a resurvey 1,224 acres, 605 acres only is not included within the boundaries of Lands Granted as above mentioned. Witness Taliaferro **Livingston**, David **Smith**. Signed J. **Dunlap**. Witness oath by David **Smith** 16 Aug 1797 to Julius **Nichols** J.P. Abbeville Co. Plat certified 12 Apr 1792 by Jonthn. **Downs** D.Sur. [No record date.] [Includes plat.]

Page 251 1 Aug 1797, Edmond **Learwood** (Laurens Co.) to John **Workmon** (Newberry Co.), for £100 Sterling sold one certain Tract in afsd. Co. containing 200 acres more or less, on waters of Little River of Saluda. Border: **Ragsdales** Spring branch on the Beaverdam, **Osborn**, below Meeting house Spring, **Shackelford**, **Cox**, **Comes**, **Moore**, **Learwood**. Witness Mark **Moore**, William **Moore**. Signed Edmond (E) **Learwood**. Witness oath by William **Moore** 16 Aug 1797 to Chas. **Smith** J.P. Laurens Co. Rec. 16 Aug 1797.

Page 251 18 Feb 1796, John Archer **Elmore**, Samuel **Saxon** and James **Saxon** (Laurens Co.) are bound unto Simion **Theus** and John G. **Guignard**, Treasurers of S.C., for £1,000 Sterling. Condition that if John Archer **Elmore** shall faithfully behave himself in the Office of Tax Collector of sd. Co., then this Obligation to be void. Witness John **Cockran** D.C. Signed John A. **Elmore**, Samuel **Saxon**, James **Saxon**. [No witness oath.] [No record date.]

Page 251-252 19 Sept 1797, James **McDavid** (Laurens Co.) for £12 Sterling paid by William **Byrd** (same), sell a parcel of Land divided off from a Tract of 150 acres granted to John **McDavid** dec., containing 58 acres more or less. Bounding by sd. **Byrd** on S & W, N by William **Murphey**, E by sd. James **McDavid**. Witness Benjn. **Byrd**, Jas. **Davis**. Signed James **McDavid**. Witness oath by Benjn. **Byrd** 19 Sept 1797 to John **Davis** J.P. Laurens Co. Rec. 29 Sep 1797.

Page 252 1793, Martin **Martin** (Laurens Co.) to William **Rodgers** (same), for £6 Sterling sell one certain tract of Land containing 12 acres more or less, on head of Norths Creek in sd. Co. Joining S on Wm. **Harris**, N.E. on Abros **Hudgens**, S.E. on Jno. **Menary**, N.W. on lands laid out. Granted 4 June 1787, and made over sd. 12 acres. Recorded in Book BBBB, page 451. Witness Joshua **Downs**, Daniel **Williams**. Signed Big: Martin (8) **Martin** [sic]. Witness oath by Joshua **Downs** 29 Sept 1797 to Joseph **Downs** J.P. Laurens Co. Rec. 29 Sept 1797.

Page 252-253 16 Sept 1796, Claborn **Sims** hatter (Laurens Co.) to John **Powell** Planter (same), for £100 sold all that tract of land containing by Estimation 150 acres more or less, in sd. Co. Being part of 281 acres granted by Arnoldus **Vanderhorst** Gov. Witness Geo. **Wright**, John **Hazlet**, Wm.

Sims. Signed Claborn **Sims**. Witness oath by James **Hazlet** 30 Sept 1797 to James **Saxon** [No title.]. Rec. 30 Sept 1797.

Page 253   2 Oct 1797, William **Conner** (Aberville Co.) for £45 paid by William **Washington** (Laurens Co.), sold all that 250 acres on N.E. side of Saluda River and bounding S.W. by Saluda River, all other sides by vacant Land. Witness Ste. C. **Wood**, Nimrod **Chiles**. Signed Wm. **Conner**. Witness oath by Nimrod **Chiles** 2 Oct 1797 to Julius **Nichols** J.P. Aberville Co. Dower relinquished by Mary **Conner**, wife of Wm. **Conner**, 2 Oct 1797 before Andrew **Hamilton** J.A.C. Rec. 9 Oct 1797.

Page 254   21 Sept 1797, Vincent **Sprouse** (Laurens Co.) for £100 Sterling sold unto Ebenezar **Murphey** & Ezekiel S. **Roland** (same), the following personal property, seven head of Cattle: three Cows and Calves and one Steer, Twenty head of Hoggs, six marked with a Crop in one Ear and a swallow fork in the other, the rest in my possession and all my house hold and kitchen furniture & crop of Corn. Witness Wm. **Burnside**, Chas. **Smith**. Signed Vincent (^) **Sprouse**. Witness oath by W. **Burnside** 21 Sept 1797 to Chas. **Smith** J.P. Laurens Co. [No record date.]

Page 254-255   10 Mar 1797, Robert **Hunter** & Ebbey **Hunter** (Laurens Co.) for $100 paid by John **Brown** (same), sold all that Tract of Land containing 100 acres more or less, on N side of Dunkins Creek in sd. Co. Originally granted to John **Hunter** dec. 1 Aug 1785 and recorded in Secretary's Office in Grant Book EEEE, page 263. Border: sd. John **Brown**. Witness Bennett **Langston**, James **Morehead**. Signed Robert **Hunter**, Ebbey (II) **Hunter**. Witness oath by Bennett **Langston** 24 Mar 1797 to Roger **Brown** J.P. Laurens Co. Dower relinquished by Ebbey (x) **Hunter**, wife of Robert **Hunter**, 9 Oct 1797 before Chas. **Allen** J.L.C. [No record date.]

Page 255-256   7 July 1775, James **Lawfin** (Ninety Six Dist.) to James **Bryson** Farmer (same), for £230 Current money sold all that tract of Land containing 150 acres on Carsons Creek, a branch of Little River. Bounding on all sides by vacant Land at time of original Survey. Original grant to sd. James **Lawfin** 6 Apr 1768, by Chas. Grevil **Montague**, then Gov. Witness John **Ritchey**, John **Hunter**, William **Ritchey**. Signed James **Lawfin**. Witness oath by John **Hunter** 5 Oct 1775 to John **Caldwell** J.P. Ninety six Dist. [No record date.]

Page 256   10 Oct 1797, By virtue of a writ issued by the Laurens Co. Court at the suit of **Wadsworth** & **Turpin** against John and James **Powell**, the Sheriff of sd. Co., William **Hunter**, seized a certain Tract of Land and did on 7 Oct 1797, publicly sell same to William **Simms** for $35. Tract situate in sd. Co. on waters of Cain Creek, containing 150 acres more or less, being part of 281 acres granted to Claiborn **Sims**, adjoining William **Simms**, Andrew **Burnside**, Samuel **Wharton**, John **Osborn**, Hutchins **Burton**. Witness William **Mitchell**, Robert **Creswell**, Signed William **Hunter** S. Witness oath by R. **Creswell** 10 Oct 1797 to Wm. **Mitchell** J.P. L.Co. [No record date.]

Page 256-257 6 Feb 1796, By virtue of a writ issued from the Clerks Office of Laurens Co. at the suit of Joseph **Gallegly**, Joshua **Downs** & John F. **Wolff** against the property of William **Thomason** Sen., the Sheriff of sd. Co., William **Dunlap**, did seize a certain Tract of Land and on the above date sold at public sale unto sd. John F. **Wolff** for £25 5sh 11p f [sic] Sterling, but sold subject to a Mortgage of £29 13sh Sterling dated 11 Feb 1793 with Interest. Tract contains 200 acres more or less, being part of 400 acres originally granted to Solomon **Niblet** and from him conveyed to Joseph **Kellett**. The remaining 123 acres being part of sd. 400 acres. From sd. Joseph **Kellett** the sd. 200 acres conveyed to sd. William **Thomason** Sen. Granted by Charles Grevil. **Montague** Gov. 22 Mar 1769. Being in sd. Co. on N fork of Raiborn Creek. Conveyed sd. 200 acres together with sd. 123 acres. Border: John **Williams**, John **Thomason**, Raburns Cr., Thomas **Garner**, John F. **Wolff**. Witness John **Cargill** va., James **McCaa**. Signed William **Dunlap**. Witness oath by James **McCaa** 14 Oct 1797 to Chas. **Smith** J.P. Laurens Co. Surveyed 6 Sept 1796 by John **Rodgers** D.Sur. Rec. 14 Oct 1797. [Includes plat.]

Page 257-258 9 May 1792, William **Compton** and Elizabeth **Compton** (Greenville Co.) to John **McDowel** (Laurens Co.), for £20 Sterling sell all that tract of Land containing 100 acres in Laurens Co., S.W. Side of Durbins Creek on a small branch. Bounding N on James **McClurkin**, S.E. on Thomas **Wier**. Granted to David **Wier** 30 Sept 1774 & recorded in Secretary's Office in Book XXX, page 456. Witness Solomon **Goodwin**, Theophilus **Goodwin**, John **Power**. Signed William **Compton**, Elizabeth (x) **Compton**. Witness oath by Solomon **Goodwin** 21 Dec 1795 to Daniel **Wright** J.P. Laurens Co. Rec. 18 Oct 1797.

Page 258 25 Oct 1797, William **Gilmore** (Laurens Co.) for £8 2sh 8p paid by Elihu **Creswell** & Co. (same), sell one feather Bed & furniture, with all my last Crop now on the plantation of William **Tweedy**, containing Tobacco, Corn, Fodder & Shucks. Provided that if the sum is paid on or before 25 Dec next, for the Redemption of the above property, then the present sale shall be void. Witness Nehemiah **Franks** Jr., John **Martin**. Signed Wm. (x) **Gilmore**. Witness oath by Nehemiah **Franks** 26 Oct 1797 to Charles **Saxon** J.P. Laurens Co. Rec. 26 Oct 1797.

Page 259 20 May 1797, David **Madden** (Laurens Co.) to Thomas **Burton** (same), for £7 Sterling sold all that tract of Land containing 8 acres & 30 Rod [32 on plat.], in sd. Co. on little Beaver Dam. Adjoining land whereon sd. **Burton** now lives, Chas. **Simmons**, Isaac **Rodgers**, Alexr. **Hamilton**. Originally granted to Jesse **Meeks** and conveyed by him to John **Martin** & by him to David **Madden**. Witness Ezel. S. **Roland**, Benjamin **Burton**. Signed David **Madden**. Witness oath by Ezekiel Stephens **Roland** 6 Nov 1797 to Chas. **Smith** J.P. Laurens Co. Plat certified 27 June 1792 by John **Rodgers** Dep.Sur. Rec. 6 Nov 1797. [Includes plat.]

Page 259-260 15 Nov 1782, Mary **Edwards** Widow (Ninety Six Dist.) to William **Neiley** planter (same), for £14 14sh Current money sold 20 acres of

Land laid out for a Mill Seat, being part of 150 acres Surveyed for Mary **Edwards** 12 Dec 1770. Situate in Craven Co. on a Branch of Cain Creek. Bounding S.W. on Willm. **Purse**, John **Evans**, N.E. on Benjn. **Moore**, all other sides Vacant at time of original Grant. Granted by Lord Charles Grenville **Montague** 8 Feb 1773 unto sd. Mary **Edwards**. Witness Tho. Willm. **Fakes**, John **Puckett**, John **Neiley**. Signed Mary (x) **Edwards**. Witness oath by John **Neiley** 23 Nov 1797 to Angus **Campbell** J.P. Laurens Co. We jointly bind ourselves to William **Neiley** for £100 Sterling, 15 Nov 1782. Condition that if sd. **Neiley** remains in possession of a certain tract containing 20 acres and sold to him by Mrs. Mary **Edwards**, then this obligation shall be void. Witness Thos. Wm. **Fakes**, John **Puckett**, John **Neiley**. Signed Mary (x) **Edwards**. Rec. 25 Nov 1797.

Page 260-261 2 June 1797, John & William **Cuningham** (Laurens Co.) Exors. of Patrick **Cuningham** dec., for £43 6sh 8p Sterling paid by David **Whiteford** (same), sell all that tract containing 40 acres more or less. Situate in sd. Co. on waters of Cain Creek, being part of 820 acres granted to Patrick **Cuningham** dec. Witness John **Strain**, William (x) **McMurtrey**. Signed John **Cuningham**, William **Cuningham**. N.B. There being a small piece of the 40 acre tract taken away by an older title then Patrick **Cuningham** dec. possessed, I acknowledge receipt of 5sh 8d Sterling as full compensation for the loss. Witness John **Strain**. Signed David **Whiteford**. Witness oath by William (x) **McMurtrey** 29 June 1797 to Angus **Campbell** J.P. Laurens Co. Rec. 25 Nov 1797.

Page 261 13 Sept 1797, Ann **Tinsley** (Laurens Co.) for £100 Sterling paid by Marthy **Tinsley** (same), sold all that tract of Land containing 200 acres more or less, in sd. Co. on waters of Bush River, adjoining lands with Wm. **Cason**, including the plantation where Philip **Tinsley** formerly lived, being a tract originally granted to Thomas **Farr** Sen. Witness Thos. **Cason**, Abraham **Tinsley**. Signed Ann (x) **Tinsley**. Witness oath by Abraham **Tinsley** 10 Oct 1797 to William **Neill** J.P. Laurens Co. Rec. 6 Dec 1797.

Page 262 7 Oct 1797, Clabourn **Sims** (Laurens Co.) to John **Fowler** (same), for £26 sell all the tract of Land containing 150 acres more or less, being part of 535 acres originally granted unto Thomas **Fare** 8 July 1774, on waters of Warrier Creek, W by John **Hall**, N by William **Berry** & Angus **Campbell**, E by Robert **McCrery**. Warrant against claim of sd. Clabourn **Sims** as Son and Heir of William **Sims** dec. Witness William **Young**, Samuel **Young**. Signed Claborn **Sims** [sic]. Witness oath by William **Young** 13 Dec 1797 to James **Saxon** J.P. Rec. 20 Dec 1797.

Page 262-263 26 Feb 1772, Mary **Caldwell** (Barkley Co.) to John **Millwee** (same), for £100 Current Money sold all that Tract of Land containing 100 acres on waters of Little River, bounded S.E. on lands laid out to Edward **Seaburn**, other sides on Vact. Land. Original Grant to Mary **Callwell** [sic] & in Secretary's Office Recorded in Book EEE, page 34. Granted by William **Bull** Lieut. Gov. 12 Sept 1768. Witness William **Millwee**, Robt. **Johnston**,

Richard **Griffin**. Signed Mary (O) **Callwell**. Witness oath by Richard **Griffin** 25 Dec 1797 to Angus **Campbell** J.P. L.Co. Witness oath by William **Millwee** 3 July 1773 to John **Caldwell** J.P. Ninety six Dist. Rec. 27 Dec 1797.

Page 264-265 4 Jan 1774, Silvanus **Walker** (forks of Broad and Saluda Rivers, Berkley Co.) planter to Ambrose **Hudgens** (Berkley Co.), for £250 Current Money sold 200 acres, granted 10 Nov 1768 by Lord Charles Gr. **Montague** Capt. Gen. Gov. unto Silvanus **Walker**. Situate in sd. Co. on waters of Little River, bounded S on Michael **Wilson** and Vacant land, N.E. on land laid out to Moses **Gregory**, N on land laid out to Moses **Caldwell**, all other sides on Vacant land. Witness Samuel **Jordan**, John (J) **Dacus**, Thomas **Cargill**. Signed Silvanus **Walker**, Sarah (F) **Walker**. Oath by Thomas **Cargill** 27 Jan 1774, that he saw Silvanus **Walker** and Sarah his Wife sign the Release and Lease. Given before James **Lindley** J.P. Ninety Six Dist. Rec. 27 Dec 1797.

Page 265-266 9 Feb 1774, John **Millwee** and his Wife Mary (Ninety Six Dist.) to Ambrose **Hudgens** (same), for £159 7sh Current Money sell all that tract of Land containing 100 acres in S.C. on waters of Little River. Bounded S.E. on lands laid out to Edward **Seaburn**, all other sides on Vacant land at time of original Survey. Originally granted to Mary **Caldwell** 12 Jan 1786 by Lord Chas. Greville **Montague** Gov., and by sd. Mary **Caldwell** conveyed to sd. John **Millwee** by Lease & release 25 & 26 Feb 1772, a Memorial of which was entered in Auditor's Office in Book I, No.9, page 221, 27 Feb 1769. Witness Isaac **Williams**, John **Dunlap**, John **Entrekin**. Signed John **Millwee**, Mary (x) **Millwee**. Witness oath by Isaac **Williams** 23 Feb 1774 to Jonathan **Downs** J.P. Ninety Six Dist. [No record date.]

Page 266-267 5 May 1778, Ambrose **Hudgens** and his Wife Joanna (Ninety Six Dist.) to James **Henderson** (same), for £850 Current Money sold all that Tract of Land containing 100 acres in S.C. on waters of Little River, bounding S.E. on land laid out to Edward **Seaburn**, all other sides on Vacant land at time of original Survey. Originally granted to Mary **Caldwell** 12 Jan 1768 by then King **George III**, under Lord Chas. Greville **Montague** Gov. Conveyed by sd. Mary **Caldwell** to John **Millwee** by Lease & release 25 & 26 Feb 1772. A Memorial was entered in the Auditor's Office in Book I, No.9, page 221, 27 Feb 1769, and by sd. John **Millwee** conveyed to sd. Ambrose **Hudgens** by Lease & release 8 & 9 Feb 1774. Witness Isaac **Williams**, Elisabeth (x) **Henderson**, John **Entrekin**. Signed Ambrose **Hudgens**, Joanna (J) **Hudgens**. Witness oath by John **Entrekin** 23 Dec 1797 to William **Neill** J.P. Rec. 27 Dec 1797.

Page 267-268 16 Feb 1774, Ambrose **Hudgens** (St. Marks Parish) and Margret his Wife to James **Henderson** (same), for £475 Current Money sold all that Tract of Land containing 200 acres in Barkley Co. on Simmonds branch of Little River. Bounding S on Michael **Wilson** & Vacant land, N.E. on land laid out to Moses **Gregory**, N on land laid out to Moses **Caldwell**, all other sides on Vacant land at time of original Survey. Granted to Silvanus

Walker 10 Nov 1768 by Lord Chas. G. **Montague** Capt. Gen. Gov. By sd. Silvanus **Walker** conveyed to sd. Ambrose **Hudgens** by Lease & release 3 & 4 Feb 1774, a Memorial of which was entered in Auditor's Office in Book L, No.11, page 478, 21 Oct 1772. Witness Isaac **Williams**, Wm. **Hudgens**, Sml. **Henderson**. Signed Ambrose **Hudgens**, Margret (x) **Hudgens**. Witness oath by Samuel **Henderson** 22 Feb 1774 to John **Caldwell** J.P. Ninety Six Dist. [No record date.]

Page 268-269 27 Dec 1797, John **Williams** (Laurens Co.) to Robert **Franks** (same), for £50 sell one certain tract of Land containing 183 acres, granted to sd. John **Williams** by Thomas **Pinckney** Esq. Gov. 4 June 1787. Situate in sd. Co. on Little River, waters of Saluda. Border: Richd. **Win**. Witness Benjamin **Nabers**, Randolph **Cook**. Signed John **Williams**. Witness oath by Ben. **Nabers** 30 Dec 1797 to Chas. **Smith** J.P. Laurens Co. Rec. 30 Dec 1797.

Page 269 13 Jan 1797, Benjamin **Jones** (Laurens Co.) to Thomas **Jones** (same), for £50 Sterling sold a certain Tract of Land on N.W. Fork of Bush River, containing 200 acres, being granted to Henry **Neely**, 20 Sept 1766. Conveyed to James **Young**, from him to Charles **Saxon**, from him to sd. **Jones**. Witness Robt. **Young**, Nancy (x) **Jones**, Benj. (x) **Jones**. Signed Benjn. **Jones**, Molly (x) **Jones**. Oath by Robt. **Young** 28 Feb 1797, that he saw Benjamin **Jones** and Molly his Wife sign the deed. Given before Wm. **Neill** J.P. Laurens Co. [No record date.]

Page 270 9 Aug 1797, James **Puckett** (Laurens Co.) for £10 paid by John **Smith** Sen. (same), sold all that Tract of Land in sd. Co. containing 12-1/2 acres, lying on waters of Saluda River on Edwards Creek. Adjoining Mr. **Purse**, John **Edwards**. Lying on both sides of the above Creek for Compliment. Witness Peter **Smith**, Michael **Finney**. Signed James **Puckett**. Witness oath by Peter **Smith** 2 Jan 1798 to Angus **Campbell** J.P. Laurens Co. Rec. 18 Jan 1798.

Page 270 19 July 1797, William **McMurtrey** Sen. (Laurens Co.) to Richard **Puckett** Jun. (same), for £5 Sterling sold a certain parcel of Land in sd. Co. on waters of Cane Creek, containing 100 acres more or less, being part of a Tract granted to Cristopher **Parsons**. Witness William **McMurtrey** Jun., Peter **Smith**, Doley (x) **Smith**. Signed William (x) **McMurtrey**, Mary (x) **McMurtrey**. Witness oath by Peter **Smith** 13 Jan 1798 to Angus **Campbell** J.P. Laurens Co. Rec. 18 Jan 1798.

Page 271 1 July 1797, John **Martin** (Laurens Co.) to Thomas **Burton** (same), for £15 Sterling sold all that Tract of Land containing by Estimation 104 acres, on waters of Little River of Saluda. Being part of two tracts of 640 acres each, one tract granted to John **Martin** aforesd. & the other to William **Hix**. Sd. **Hix's** part first conveyed to sd. John **Martin**. Witness Ezekl. S. Roland, Benjamin **Burton**. Signed John **Martin**. Witness oath by E. S. **Roland** 6 Feb 1798 to Chas. **Smith** J.P. Laurens Co. Rec. 7 Feb 1798. [Includes plat.]

Page 271-272 24 Jan 1798, John **Godfrey** (Laurens Co.) for £21 7sh sold unto Thomas **Burton** (same), six head of Cattle, being all I now possess, two Feather Beds and Furniture, my Working Tools, all my household & Kitchen furniture. Witness Ezekl. S. **Roland**, Thos. (x) **Ford**. Signed John **Godfrey**. Thos. **Burton** recd. one pen knife in lieu of a full Delivery of the within Property. Witness oath by E. S. **Roland** 6 Feb 1798 to Chas. **Smith** J.P. Laurens Co. Rec. 7 Feb 1798.

Page 272-273 1797, Thomas **Wadsworth** Merchant (S.C.) for the same value in Land conveyed to me by William **Turpin**, conveyed unto sd. William **Turpin** all my right to the following tracts of Land, they having fallen to him on a division of certain tracts, which were held jointly by Thomas **Wadsworth** and William **Turpin**. Situate in Laurens Co., one tract containing 252 acres on Abners Creek, S side Enoree River. Surveyed by A. **Thompson** 11 Apr 1785 for William **Willson** and granted by Gov. **Moultrie** 5 Feb 1787. One other tract containing 225 acres on Duncans Creek. Surveyed by Robert **Hannah** 25 Oct 1790 and granted to Alexr. **McNary** by Gov. Charles **Pinckney** 6 Dec 1790. One other tract containing 313 acres on waters of Dunkins Creek. Surveyed by John **Hunter** for John **Rodgers** 3 Apr 1791 and granted to him by Gov. Charles **Pinckney** 4 July after & conveyed by sd. **Rodgers** to **Wadsworth** & **Turpin** 18 Feb 1795, recorded in Laurens Co. Book E, page 345. One other tract containing 640 acres on Beaver Dam of Little River. Granted to John **Martin** Jun. by Gov. **Moultrie** 6 Mar 1786, lying on Ready Lick, a branch of William Creek. Bounded at time of original Survey by Edmond **Learwood** & Vacant land. John **Martin's** deed to **Wadsworth** & **Turpin** dated 17 July 1793 & recorded in Laurens Co. Book D, page 163. Witness James **Boyce**, Wm. **Turpin** Jun. Dower relinquished by Jane **Wadsworth**, wife of Thomas **Wadsworth**, 6 June 1797 before Wm. **Mitchell** Judge Laurens Co. Witness oath by William **Turpin** Jun. 25 Jan 1798 to P. **Bonnetheau** J.Q. Charleston. Rec. 17 Feb 1798.

Page 273 3 Aug 1797, William **Conner** and Mary **Conner** (Abberville Co.) for £20 paid by Robert **Carter** (Laurens Co.), sold all that Tract of Land containing 100 acres on Cain Creek. Bounded by sd. **Carter**. Originally granted to John **Foster** 22 Aug 1771. Witness Jonan. **Johnston**, Ste. C. **Wood**. Signed William **Conner**, Mary **Conner**. Dower relinquished by Mary **Conner** 5 Aug 1797 before Charles Jones **Colcock** J.P.Qu. Ninety Six Dist. Witness oath by Jonan. **Johnston** 4 Nov 1797 to Angus **Campbell** J.P. Laurens Co. Rec. 17 Feb 1798.

Page 273-274 3 Nov 1797, Robert **Carter** & Elizabeth **Carter** (Laurens Co.) for $35 paid by John **Pinson** Sen. (same), sold all that Tract of Land on Cane Creek, containing 35 acres more or less, being part of a Tract originally granted to John **Foster** and by him conveyed to John **Savage**, and by William and Mary **Conner**, heirs of sd. **Savage**, conveyed to sd. Robert **Carter**. Border: middle of Cane Creek, a little below fish trap Shoal, Jonan. **Johnston**. Bounded S.W. side over the Creek by Jonan. **Johnston**, N.W. by sd. **Pinson**, N.E. by sd. **Pinson**, S.E. by Robert **Carter**. Witness Jonan. **Johnston**, Richd.

Book F

Duty, Howard **Pinson**. Signed Robert **Carter**, Elizth. (O) **Carter**. Witness oath by Jonan. **Johnston** 14 Nov 1797 to Angus **Campbell** J.P. Laurens Co. [No record date.]

Page 274-275 28 Dec 1797, Abraham **Eddens** (S.C.) for $200 paid by Josiah **Chandler** (Laurens Co.), sold all that tract of Land containing 100 acres more or less, in aforesd. Co. on a branch Simmons Creek, waters of Little River. Bounding at time of original survey, N.W. on **Williamson**, N.E. on Wm. **Millwee**, S on David **Burns**. Granted 16 Feb 1786. Witness Joseph **Young**, Isaac **Chandler**, Robt. (R) **Young**. Signed Abraham (A) **Eddens**. Dower relinquished by Sarah (x) **Eddens**, wife of Abraham **Eddens**, 3 Jan 1798 before Wm. **Mitchell** J.L.C. Witness oath by Isaac **Chandler** 13 Jan 1798 to Wm. **Mitchell** [No title.] L.Co. Rec. 17 Feb 1798.

Page 275 19 Sept 1796, Thomas **Wadsworth** & William **Turpin** Merchants (S.C.) for £50 Sterling paid by John **Maulden** (Laurens Co.) planter, sold all that Tract of Land containing 51 acres, on a small branch of Casons Creek, waters of Little River. Granted to **Wadsworth** & **Turpin** 7 Dec 1795. Together with all that part of a tract which sd. **Wadsworth** & **Turpin** bought of Thomas **Norris**. Originally granted to Thomas **Edghill**, supposed to contain 160 acres, bounding by Laugley **Hunter**, John **Cason**, William **Teague** & above 51 acres, held by heirs of Robert **Simpson** and part of original Survey. Witness James **Boyce**, Joel **Walker**. Signed Thomas **Wadsworth**, William **Turpin**. Dower relinquished by Jane **Wadsworth**, wife of Thomas **Wadsworth** 19 Sept 1796 before William **Turpin** J.Q. Dower relinquished by Mary **Turpin**, wife of William **Turpin**, 19 Sept 1796 before Thomas **Wadsworth** J.L.C. Mrs. **Turpin** resides in Charleston. Witness oath by James **Boyce** [No signature.] 28 Oct 1797 to John **Johnson** J.P. [No record date.]

Page 276 3 Aug 1797, Drury **Smith** planter (Laurens Co.) to Henry **Vaughn** planter (same), for £20 Sterling sold one certain tract of Land in sd. Co. on S side of a branch of Warriors Creek, containing 50 acres more or less, granted to Drury **Smith** in 1786 by William **Moultrie** Esq. Gov. Witness William **Vaughn**, James **Smith**. Signed Drury (x) **Smith**. Witness oath by James **Smith** 19 Sept 1797 to Joseph **Downs** J.P. Laurens Co. Rec. 17 Feb 1798.

Page 276-277 21 Dec 1797, Randolph **Cook** and Mary my Wife planter (Laurens Co. for £40 paid by James **Bumpass** (same), sold a Tract of Land containing 212 acres more or less, on Branches of Reedy fork, waters of Little River. Bounded by **Bazie**, spring branch, N by Estate of Stephen **Potter** dec., E by John **Brown**, S by William **Brown**, W by Abner **Harden**. Witness John **Potter**, William **Potter**. Signed Randolph **Cook**, Polley **Cook**. Dower relinquished by Polley **Cook** 1 Jan 1798 before Chas. **Allen** J.L.C. Witness oath by John **Potter** 1 Jan 1798 to Chas. **Allen** J.P. Laurens Co. [No record date.] [Includes plat.]

Page 277 10 Apr 1797, John **Ritchey** planter (Laurens Co.) and Margaret my Wife for £30 paid by Margaret **Fakes** (same), sold a certain tract of Land containing 100 acres more or less, on waters of Cain Creek, joining lands granted to William **Dudgeon**, land of James **McGill** on S, Stephen **Wood** on W. Being part of 252 acres originally granted to Saml. **Harris** by William **Moultrie** Esq. 3 Mar 1796, and released by sd. **Harris** unto William **Caldwell** Esq., and from him unto sd. John **Ritchey**. Witness Joseph **Groves**, Jean (x) **Harris**, Rebecca (M) **Groves**. Signed John **Ritchey**, Margaret (M) **Ritchey**. Witness oath by Joseph **Groves** 12 Feb 1798 to Zech. **Bailey** J.P. Laurens Co. Rec. 14 Feb 1798.

Page 277-278 14 Dec 1796, James **Gidden** Sen. and his son James (Tlbord? Co., Ga.) to Alexander **Mills** (Laurens Co.), for £35 Sterling sold all that tract of Land of 100 acres more or less, being part of 200 acres granted to Stephen **Hudson** by William **Bull** Esq. Gov. Recorded in Aud. Office in Book K, No.10, page [blank], 16 Oct 1770. Witness John **McClintock**, James **Mills**. Signed James **Giddens** Sen. [sic], James **Giddens** [sic]. Witness oath by John **McClintock** 16 Feb 1798 to Starling **Tucker** J.P. Laurens Co. Rec. 17 Feb 1798.

Page 278-279   7 Sept 1793, John **Hunter** Esq. (Laurens Co.) to John **Cammeck** [**Cammack** in one ref.] (same), for £22 16sh Sterling sold all that Tract of Land containing 176 acres [276 on plat], being part of 500 acres granted to Pierce **Butler** and by him conveyed to Hercules D. **Bize**. Border: Saml. **Elliot, Jenen?**, John **Camack**, James **Cuningham**, part of survey land sold to L. B. **Harvey**. Also one other tract of 144 acres more or less. Border: Benjn. **Eliot**, John **Manley**, part of survey. Being part of different Tracts originally granted to Pierce **Butler**, and by him conveyed to Hercules Daniel **Bize** 9 July 1792, and now conveyed by sd. John **Hunter**, by power of Attorney from Hercules Danl. **Bize**, dated 1 June 1793. Witness Jonthn. **Downs**, David **Gary**. Signed John **Hunter** Atty. for Hercules Danl. **Bize**. Both tracts on waters of Raburns Creek in sd. Co. Witness oath by David **Gary** 20 Feb 1798 to Reuben **Pyles** J.P. L.C. Plat of 176 acres certified 3 Sept 1793 by John **Hunter** D.S. Plat of 144 acres certified 5 Sept 1793 by John **Hunter** D.S. Rec. 19 Feb 1798. [Includes two plats.]

Page 279-280 15 Dec 1797, Andrew **Endsley** (Laurens Co.) for £30 Sterling paid by Joshua **Southerlin** (same), sold all that certain Tract of Land whereon sd. Joshua **Southerlin** now lives, containing 125 acres, being part of 250 acres granted to John **Cuningham**, and by him conveyed to Thomas **McClurkin**, and by him conveyed unto sd. **Endsley**. Situate in sd. Co. on Beards fork, a branch of Duncans Creek. Bounded at time of original Survey on all sides by Vacant Land. Now bounded by William **Glidewell**, Adam **Gordon**, John **Rodgers** & James **Endsley**, on other part of sd. 250 acres, the Creek being the dividing line. Plat signed by William **Bull** Esq. Lieut. Gov. and recorded in Book GGG, page 273. Witness Wm. **Prather**, Robt. (R) **Spence**. Signed Andrew **Endsley**, Jean (a) **Endsley**. Dower relinquished by Jean (J) **Endsley**, wife of Andrew **Endsley**, 26 Dec 1797 before Wm. **Mitchell** J.L.C. Witness oath by Robert (R) **Spence** 20 Feb 1798 to Zech. **Bailey** J.P. [No record date.]

Page 280 13 Aug 1797, James Robert **Mayson** (Edgefield Co.) planter for £60 paid by William **Dendy** (Laurens Co.) planter, sold all that Tract of Land containing 100 acres more or less, agreeable to a dividing line drawn through 200 acres originally granted to Fredrick **Ward**. Situate in Laurens Co. on Smith Creek, a branch of Saluda River. Witness Richd. **Pollard**, James **Watt**, John **Dendy**. Signed Jas. Robert **Mayson**. Dower relinquished by Nancy **Mayson**, wife of James Robert **Mayson**, 13 Aug 1797 before James **Mayson** Judge Newberry Co. Witness oath by [blank] 6 Sept 1797 to Jas. **Mayson** J.N.C. Rec. 20 Feb 1798.

Page 280-281 18 Aug 1797, George **Hearn** (Laurens Co.) to John **McGee** (same), for £15 Sterling sold a tract of Land containing 157 acres more or less, being part of a tract granted to Thomas **Hughes**, conveyed from him to Lewis **Saxon**, and from him to George **Hearn**. Being on waters of Reedy River in sd. Co. Border: **Bowman**, Henry **Hazel**. Witness Drury **Moseley**, John (x) **Moseley**. Signed George (x) **Hearn**, Lucey (x) **Hearn**. Witness oath by John (x) **Moseley** 20 Feb 1798 to James **Abercrombie** J.P. Laurens Co. [No record date.]

Page 281-282 18 Nov 1794, Elizabeth Jane **Ravenel** Exrx. of her late Husband Daniel **Ravenel** to Samuel **Wier**, for £18 8sh sold all that tract of Land on waters of Bush River in Ninety Six Dist. containing 230 acres more or less, part of 3,000 acres originally granted to sd. Daniel **Ravenel** and known in the General plan of the same as 12, and was by him in his last Will and Testament directed to be sold by his Exrx. and Exors. Witness Daniel **Ravenel**, Rene **Ravenel**, Peter **Porcher** Jun. Signed Elizabeth Jane **Ravenel**. Witness oath by Peter **Porcher** Jun. 11 Dec 1797 to Stephen **Ravenel** J.Q. Rec. 20 Feb 1798.

Page 282-283 1 Apr 1797, Mansfield **Walker** (Laurens Co.) planter for £75 Sterling paid by James **Bailey** (same) planter, sold all that tract of Land containing 130 acres more or less, one whole original Survey and part of another. Border: Samuel **Powell**, William **Hall**, James **Young**, head of a branch, Little River, Robert **Roland**, Patrick **Cuningham**, James **Bailey**. Witness Silv. **Walker** Sen., Wm. **Bailey**. Signed Mansfield **Walker**. Dower relinquished by Janey (x) **Walker**, wife of Mansfield **Walker**, 1 Apr 1797 before Wm. **Mitchell** J.L.C. Witness oath by Silv. **Walker** and Wm. **Bailey** 1 Apr 1797 to Wm. **Mitchell** J.P. Laurens Co. Rec. 20 Feb 1798.

Page 283 15 Nov 1797, John **ONeal** (Laurens Co.) in consideration of the Love, good will and Affection I have towards my Loving Daughter Margret **Scott** (same), wife of Thomas **Scott**, give unto her a Negro Girl Lucy. Witness James **Golding**, Charles (x) **Murphey**. Signed John (x) **ONeal**. Witness oath by Charles **Murphey** [No signature.] 27 Jan 1798 to Angus **Campbell** J.P. Laurens Co. [No record date.]

Page 283-284 13 Jan 1796, David **Smith** and Ann his Wife (Union Co.) to Thomas **Lee** (same), sold all that Right of Dower belonging to sd. Ann **Smith** arising from Edward **Musgrove's** land on Enoree, known by name of Musgroves Mill Tract of 150 acres. Dower of Ann **Smith**, formerly Ann **Musgrove**, Widow to Edward **Musgrove** dec. In consideration of £50 Sterling. Witness Absalom **Bobo**, Leah **Musgrove**. Signed David **Smith**, Ann **Smith**. Witness oath by Absalom **Bobo** 15 Feb 1798 to Roger **Brown** J.P. Laurens Co. Rec. 21 Feb 1798.

Page 284 4 Dec 1797, Whereas Ebenezer **Murphey** (Laurens Co.) became indebted to George **Brock** (same) for £10 9sh 6p to be paid on or before 20 Dec 1797. For the better securing the sum, Mortgage unto sd. George **Brock**, 1,600 pounds of Tobacco, 100 bushels of Corn, 4 head of Cattle, 15 head of Hoggs, one Bay Mare, branded R.M. on near Shoulder and Buttock & all my household furniture and plantation tools &c. Providing that if the sum is paid, then this Instrument of Writing shall be void. Witness John **Wilson**, John **Coats**. Signed Ebenezer **Murphey**. Witness oath by John **Coats** 3 Apr 1798 to James **Abercrombie** J.P. Laurens Co. Rec. 5 Apr 1798.

Page 284-285 6 Sept 1797, Joseph **Young** (Laurens Co.) for £185 Sterling paid by James **Cook** (S.C.), sold all that tract of Land containing 293 acres more or less, being part of one tract granted to James **Young** and another Tract granted to Martin **Martin** by William **Bull**, 1769, the other by Thomas **Pinckney** in 1787. Border: Little River, James **Cook**. Witness Andw. **Rodgers** Jun., Daniel **Mitchell**, John **Young**. Signed Joseph **Young**. Witness oath by A. **Rodgers** Jun. 6 Sept 1797 to Wm. **Mitchell** J.P. Laurens Co. [No record date.]

Page 285-286 1 Nov 1796, John **Rutledge** (Charleston) for £125 paid by William **Nichels** (Laurens Co.), sold all that tract of Land containing by Resurvey 509 acres more or less, being originally Surveyed for Abram **Hollingsworth** and granted to John **McQuin** for 300 acres. Situate in Laurens Co. on Mudlick Creek. Bounding on James **Nichels**, Matthew **Hunter**, Nethaniel **Nichels**, Widow **Hollingsworth**, **Hood**. Subdivided agreeable to the plat & sold to which purchasers sd. William **Nichels** is authorised to convey. [Plat shows 100 acres sold to Matthew **Hunter**, 100 acres to James **Nicholds** [sic], 124 acres to Nathl. **Nicholds** [sic], 195 acres to William **Nicholds** [sic].] Witness Eliza **Laurens**, Fredrick **Rutledge**. Signed J. **Rutledge**. Witness oath by Fredrick **Rutledge** [No signature.] 1 Dec 1796 to John **Hunter** [No title.]. Plat certified 10 Apr 1791 by John **Hunter** D.S. [No record date.] [Includes plat.]

Page 286 26 Jan 1798, Whereas William **Farrow** (Laurens Co.) standeth Indebted unto John **Simpson** Mert. (same) for $167 to be paid upon a Bond with Condition of payment on 25 Dec next. For the better securing of payment, sold unto sd. John **Simpson**, one Sorrel Mare about 4 years old big with Colt & one Sorrell Mare likewise big with Colt about 11 years old with their Colts, three Feather Beds, five head of Cattle, about twenty Hoggs. Condition that if the sum be paid, then this present Writing shall be void.

Witness John **Gallegly**, Richd. (x) **Johnston**. Signed William **Farrow**. Witness oath by John **Gallegly** 20 Feb 1798 to William **Neill** J.P. Rec. 22 Feb 1798.

Page 286-287 16 Feb 1798, William **Nichels** (Laurens Co.) for £25 paid by James **Nichels** (same), sold all that Tract of Land containing 100 acres more or less, being part of Land originally surveyed for Abraham **Hollingsworth** and granted John **McQuin** for 300 acres. Situate in sd. Co. on Mudlick Creek and conveyed by John **Rutledge** to sd. Wm. **Nichels**. Border: James **Nichels**, sd. Survey, unknown. Witness John **Hunter**, Mathew **Hunter**. Signed William **Nichels**. Dower relinquished by Elizabeth (x) **Nickels**, wife of Wm. **Nickels** [sic], 16 Feb 1798 before Wm. **Mitchell** J.L.C. Witness oath by Mathew **Hunter** 22 Feb 1798 to Wm. **Mitchell** J.P. L.Co. Laid off 10 Apr 1791 by John **Hunter** D.S. Rec. 22 Feb 1798. [Includes plat.]

Page 287 20 Jan 1798, Thomas **Lee** (Union Co.) sold unto George **Gordon** (Laurens Co.) all that Right of Dower belonging to Ann **Smith** arising from Edward **Musgrove's** land on Enoree River known as Musgroves Mill Tract of 150 acres. Deed from David & Ann **Smith** to sd. Thomas **Lee**, dated 13 Jan 1796. Sold the one third part of sd. Land, for £20 Sterling, during the Natural Life of sd. Ann **Smith**, formerly Ann **Musgrove**, Widow of Edward **Musgrove** dec. Witness Andw. **Torrance**, Joseph **Lee**. Signed Thomas (t) **Lee**. Witness oath by Joseph **Lee** 20 Feb 1798 to John **Davis** J.P. Laurens Co. [No record date.]

Page 287-288 13 Mar [No year.], Clabourn **Sims** (Laurens Co.) and Pattey his Wife to William **Bailey** (same), for £10 sold all that tract of Land containing 19 acres on waters of Little River. Bounded N.E. by Samuel **Powel**, S.E. by Tyre **Glen**, S.W. by **Rayford**, N.W. by William **Bailey**. Originally granted unto sd. Clabourn **Sims** by Arnoldus **Vanderhorst** Gov. 2 Feb 1795. Witness Wm. **Mitchell**, Lewis **Banton**, Saml. (x) **Powel**. Signed Claborn **Sims** [sic]. Dower relinquished by Pattey (x) **Sims** 13 Mar 1797 before Wm. **Mitchell** J.L.C. Witness oath by Lewis **Banton** 13 Mar 1797 to Wm. **Mitchell** J.P. Laurens Co. [No record date.]

Page 288-289 12 Aug 1797, Fredrick **Ward** (Edgefield Co.) Blacksmith for £60 Sterling paid by James Robt. **Mayson** (same) planter, sold all that Tract of Land containing 100 acres more or less, agreeable to a Dividing Line drawn through 200 acres. Originally granted unto Fredrick **Ward**. Situate in Laurens Co. on Smith Creek, a branch of Saluda River. Witness John **Dendy**, Danl. **Ferguson**, Peter (x) **Ferguson**. Signed Fredrick **Ward**. Dower relinquished by Mary (x) **Ward**, wife of Fredrick **Ward**, 12 Aug 1797 before James **Mayson** Judge Newberry Co. Witness oath by John **Dendy** [No signature.] 6 Sept 1797 to James **Mayson** J.N.C. [No record date.]

Page 289 13 Jan 1798, John **Arnold** (Laurens Co.) to Perry **Perritt** (same), for £33 Sterling sold all that Tract of land containing 70 acres in sd. Co. on Horse Creek. Being part of 200 acres originally granted unto William **Turner** dec. and conveyed by Elizabeth **Turner**, wife and sole Exor. of sd. William **Turner** dec., to Moses **Tomerlin** by a certain Lease and release 1 & 2 Sept 1791, recorded in Clerks Office, sd. Co. on 26 Jan 1792, in Book D, page 90-93, and conveyed from sd. Moses **Tomlin** [sic] to John **Arnold** by Deed 26 May 1792, and recorded in same Co. 27 Aug 1792 in page 260. Witness David **Ridgeway**, Andrew (A) **Arnold**. Signed John **Arnold**. Witness oath by David **Ridgway** [sic] 22 Feb 1798 to Zech. **Bailey** J.P. Laurens Co. [No record date.]

Page 289-290 17 Feb 1798, John **Monro** in consideration of £14 14sh paid by Thomas **Wier** Gentleman, sold all that Tract of Land on waters of Bush River in Ninety Six Dist., containing 147 acres more or less & is part of 3,000 acres originally granted to Daniel **Ravenel** and by him in his Last Will and Testament directed to be sold by his Exrs. or Exors. & is known in the General plan of same by No. 10. Sold, providing my Right is good from Elizabeth Jane **Ravenel** Exrx. of her Husband Daniel **Ravenel** dec., if not, neither me nor my heirs are under any obligation to pay any Damage. Witness Samuel **Wier**. Signed John **Monro**, Serrey **Monro**. Witness oath by Samuel **Wier** 21 Feb 1798 to John **Coker** J.P. Laurens Co. [No record date.]

Page 290 7 Apr 1798, Alexander **Manary** (Laurens Co.) for £15 Sterling paid by Richard **Styles** (same), sold a certain Tract of Land containing 100 acres, being part of 325 acres in sd. Co. on a branch of Duncans Creek. Border: Thos. **McClurkin**, Alexander **McNary** [sic], Land laid out to Rawley **McCarley**. Witness Robt. **Rodgers**, Wm. (x) **Glidewell**. Signed Alexander **Menary** [sic]. Witness oath by William (x) **Glidewell** 8 Apr 1798 to Jno. **Davis** J.P. L.Co. [No record date.] [Includes plat.]

Page 290-291 27 Jan 1798, David **Speers** (Laurens Co.) for £20 Current Money paid by Daniel **Johnston** (same), sold all that Tract of Land where sd. Daniel **Johnston** now lives, being part in Newberry Co. and part in Laurens Co. on W side of Carsons Creek, containing 85 acres more or less, being part of 350 acres granted originally to Wm. **Griffin** Sen. 5 June 1772, and since conveyed by sd. Wm. Griffin **Sen.** to Wm. **Griffin** Jun. his son by Will, then conveyed by sd. Wm. **Griffin** Jun. to James **Griffin** his Brother by Deed, and since conveyed by sd. James **Griffin** to sd. David **Speers**. Bounding on lands now held by Hugh **ONeal**, land laid out to John **Simpson** Merct. & land held by Jas. **Lefan**, and part on Original Survey, Carsons Creek being the Dividing line between the 85 acres and the original Survey. Witness Thomas **Gary**, James **Griffin**. Signed David **Speers**. Witness oath by Thomas **Gary** 20 Feb 1798 to Joseph **Downs** J.P. Laurens Co. [No record date.]

Page 291 15 Aug 1797, William **Shandley** [sic] in consideration of the natural affection &c give unto my Son Thomas & Daughter Anna **Shanley**, one Negro Girl Milley. Witness Jno. **Cook**, Jonan. **Johnson**. Signed William **Shanley**. Witness oath by John **Cook** and Jonan. **Johnson** 17 Feb 1798 to Angus **Campbell** J.P. Laurens Co. [No record date.]

Book F

Page 291-292   17 Dec 1792, Charles **Parks** (Laurens Co.) to Peter **Roberts** (same), for £65 sell one Certain Tract of Land in sd. Co. on waters of Mudlick Creek, containing 100 acres, being part of a Tract granted to John **Dunneho** Sen. and conveyed by him to Cornelius **Donohoe**, and conveyed by him to sd. Charles **Parks**. Witness Jno. **Standfield**, Richd. **Shackelford**, George **Shackelford**. Signed Charles **Parks**. Witness oath by Richard **Shackelford** 20 Feb 1798 to Cha. **Smith** J.P. Laurens Co. [No record date.]

Page 292   13 Dec 1797, John **Simpson** & Mary his wife (Laurens Co.) for £30 Sterling paid by Robert **Blake** (same), sold all that Tract of Land containing 86 acres, being part of 350 acres originally granted on or about 18 May 1771 to Charles **Harvey** by William **Bull** Esq. Gov., being in sd. Co. on Casons Creek, a branch of Little River. Border: Alexr. **Simpson**, John **Blake**, John **Simpson**, near Old Waggon Road. The original was transferred by sd. Charles **Harvey** by Lease and Release 22 June 1772 unto Jacob **Jones**, and by him transferred unto Henry and Roland **Rugeley**, 22 Feb 1773, and by sd. **Rugeley's** Attorney James **Mayson** transferred unto John **Simpson**, 13 July 1789. Witness Jno. **Gallegly**, James **McCary**. Signed John **Simpson**, Mary **Simpson**. Witness oath by John **Gallegly** 24 Feb 1798 to James **Saxon** J.P. [No record date.]

Page 292-293   17 Oct 1797, William **Savall** [sic] and Lucey **Savell** (Laurens Co.) for £32 10sh paid by James **Powell** (same), sold all that Tract of Land granted unto John **Hall** on both sides of Walnut Creek. Border: land formerly William **Moore**. Including 200 acres more or less, but in case sd. Land should take any part of a Tract that belongs to John **Piece** dec., sd. **Piece** shall have his bounds according to Law and by these presents is made known. Witness William **South**, Edward **Leavell**, Robert **Gaines**. Signed William **Savell**, Lucey (x) **Savell**. Witness oath by Robert **Gaines** 26 Feb 1798 to Reuben **Pyles** J.P. Laurens Co. [No record date.]

Page 293   23 Oct 1797, John F. **Wolff** (Laurens Co.) for $300 paid by William **Thomason** 2d. Jun. (same), sold part of a Tract of Land containing 200 acres more or less, being part of a Tract originally granted to Solomon **Niblet**, containing 400 acres, and by him conveyed to Joseph **Kellet**, and by him conveyed to William **Thomason** Sen., and granted by Charles Graville **Montague** Gov. 22 Mar 1769. The above parcel was taken and sold by Executions Subject to a Mortgage and bought by John Frances **Wolff**. Being in sd. Co. on N fork of Raborns Creek on W side of sd. Creek. Border: Thomas **Garner**, branch, Raiburns Creek, John **Williams**, John **Thomason**. Witness Anderson **Arnold**, John **Guttery**. Signed John F. **Wolff**. Witness oath by Anderson **Arnold** 24 Feb 1798 to Joseph **Downs** J.P. Laurens Co. [No record date.] [Includes plat.]

Page 294   2 Aug 1769, John **Copeland** (Berkley Co.) Weaver to Isaac **Abercrombie** (same) planter, for £150 sold all that Tract of Land containing 100 acres in sd. Co. on Raiborns Creek, a branch of Saluda. Bounding on all sides Vacant. Original grant was to John **Copeland**. Witness John **Abercrombie**, James **Abercrombie**. Signed John (J) **Copland** [sic]. Witness oath by John **Abercrombie** 27 Feb 1798 to James **Abercrombie** J.P. Laurens Co. [No record date.]

Page 295 8 Nov 1797, Isaac **Abercrombie** (Ansan Co., N.C.) free holder to James **Abercrombie** (Laurens Co.) for $250 sell one certain Tract of Land on a branch of Rabourns Creek in sd. Co. Granted to John **Copland** by Graville **Montague** by patent 6 Apr 1768. Tract contains 100 acres more or less, and conveyed from sd. John **Copland** to sd. Isaac **Abercrombie** 2 Aug 1769. Witness Hastings **Dial** [Hastings **Diel** Sen. in one ref.], William **Johnson**. Signed Isaac **Abercrombie**. Witness oath by William **Johnson** 8 Nov 1797, that he saw the Deed delivered to James **Abercrombie** Jun. Given before James **Abercrombie** J.P. Laurens Co. [No record date.]

Page 295-296 22 Feb 1798, James **Abercrombie** (Laurens Co.) planter for $365 paid by Anderson **Arnold** (same), sold all that tract of Land containing 100 acres more or less, in sd. Co. on N fork of Rabourns Creek of Redy River. Border: Anderson **Arnold**, John **Thomason**, Samuel **Evans**, John Frances **Wolff**. Originally granted to John **Copeland** 6 Apr 1768, and conveyed from him to Isaac **Abercrombie** by Lease & Release, and from him to James **Abercrombie** 8 Nov 1797. Witness William **Thomason**, Joseph **Camp**. Signed James **Abercrombie**. Dower relinquished by Ann (I) **Abercrombie**, wife of James **Abercrombie**, 22 Feb 1798 before Jonthn. **Downs** J.L.C. Witness oath by William **Thomason** 28 Feb 1798 to Joseph **Downs** J.P. Laurens Co. [No record date.]

Page 296 18 Oct 1785, Benjamin **Wofford** planter (Spartenburg Co.) to James **Allison** (Laurens Co.), for £10 Sterling sold all that Tract of Land containing 5 acres more or less, on both sides Durbens Creek. Bounding W on John **Brockman**, all other sides by sd. James **Allison**. Being part of 600 acres on both sides of Enoree River and granted to Bartley **Brown** by Arther **Dobs** Gov. of No. Carolina, being within the Bounds of a Tract afterwards granted to Benjamin **Vines** by the Gov. of So. Carolina. Sd. 5 acres is to include part of the Mill and Mill Shoals, where sd. James **Allison** now has a Mill on Durbins Creek. Also sd. Tract is to Include the house or Cabbin where Marah **Campbel** formerly lived. Witness Benjamin **Wofford** Jun., Thomas **York**. Signed Benj. **Wofford**. Witness oath by Thomas **York** 14 Mar 1798 to Charles **Saxon** J.P. Laurens Co. [No record date.]

Page 296-297 20 Feb 1798, William **Nickels** (Laurens Co.) for £25 paid by Mathew **Hunter** (same), sold all that Tract of Land containing 100 acres more or less, being part of a Tract originally surveyed for Abram **Hollingsworth** and granted to John **McQuin** for 300 acres, in sd. Co. on Mudlick Creek, waters of Little River and conveyed by John **Rutledge** Esq. to sd. William **Nickels**. Border: Part of sd. Survey, Matthew **Hunter** [sic], **Hood**. Witness Samuel **Goodman**, Mathew **Hunter**. Signed William **Nickels**. Dower relinquished by Elizabeth (x) **Nickels**, wife of Wm. **Nickels**, 24 Feb 1798 before Wm. **Mitchell** J.L.C. Witness oath by Mathew **Hunter** Jun. 24 Feb

1798 to Wm. **Mitchell** J.P. Plat certified 10 Apr 1791 by John **Hunter** D.S. [No record date.] [Includes plat.]

Page 297 1 Feb 1797, William **Nickels** (Laurens Co.) for £25 paid by Nethaniel **Nickels** (same), sold all that Tract of Land containing 124 acres more or less, being part of Land originally granted to John **McQuin** for 300 acres, in sd. Co. on Mudlick Creek, waters of Little River and conveyed by John **Rutledge** Esq. to sd. William **Nickels**. Witness James **Nickels**, John **Hunter**. Signed William **Nickels**. Dower relinquished by Elizabeth (x) **Nickels**, wife of Wm. **Nickels**, 16 Feb 1798 before Wm. **Mitchell** J.L.C. Witness oath by James **Nickels** 24 Feb 1798 to Wm. **Mitchell** J.P. [No record date.]

Page 298 30 Sept 1797, Jeremiah **Page** (Newberry Co.) Eldest Son and Heir of Robert **Page** dec., for £25 Sterling paid by William **Ball** Sen. (Laurens Co.), sold all that tract of Land containing 50 acres more or less, in Laurens Co. on Cain Creek. Originally granted to Barbara **Moles** 14 Oct 1774, and conveyed to David **Cuningham**, and by him conveyed to Robert **Page**. Witness Abia **Griffin**, Elijah **Watson**. Signed Jeremiah (x) **Page**. Witness oath by Abia **Griffin** 30 Sept 1797 to Angus **Campbell** J.P. Laurens Co. [No record date.]

Page 298 12 Jan 1798, John **Godfrey** (S.C.) for £160 paid by James **Sullivant** (same), sold all that Tract of Land in aforesd. Co. on a branch of Ryans Creek, including the plantation Tract on which I now live: 83 acres & a tract joining the same bought of John **Martin** containing 157 acres. Making in the whole 200-1/2 [sic]. Witness Ezel. S. **Roland**, James **Sullivant**. Signed John **Godfrey**. Witness oath by Ezel. S. **Roland** 26 Mar 1798 to Cha. **Smith** J.P. Laurens Co. [No record date.]

Page 298-299 21 Dec 1796, James **Tindsley** [sic] (Columbia Co., Ga.) for £30 Sterling paid by William **Tinsley** (Laurens Co.), sold all that Tract of Land containing 70 acres more or less, in sd. Co. on N side of N fork of Bush River. Adjoining land of John **Hunter** Esq. and William **Cason**. Being part of 200 acres originally granted to George **Dalrymple**, whereon Ann **Tinsley** now lives and including all that to the N side of N fork of sd. Bush River, the N fork to be the line between sd. William **Tinsley** & his Brother Abraham. Witness William **Dunlap**, Abraham **Tinsley**. Signed James **Tinsley**. Witness oath by Abraham **Tinsley** 10 Oct 1797 to William **Neill** J.P. Laurens Co. [No record date.]

Page 299-300 20 May 1796, William **Brodey** (Laurens Co.) to John **Brodey** (same), for £10 Sterling sold all that parcel of Land containing 120 acres more or less, in sd. Co. on waters of Raiborns Creek. Being part of Sundry tracts granted to Charles **Brodey** dec. Border: **Watkins**, Alexr. **Brodey**, Raborns Creek, Old Survey, Spring branch, not known. Witness John **Cochran**, Henry **Box**. Signed William **Brodey**. Witness oath by John **Cochran** 21 Apr 1798 to Cha. **Smith** J.P. Laurens Co. [No record date.] [Includes plat.]

Page 300 15 Sept 1797, John **Martin** (Laurens Co.) to Thomas **Burton** late of same place, for $150 sold all that tract of Land containing 210 acres, in sd. Co. on waters of Raburns Creek. Border: Oliver **Matthews, Elliot,** Jno. **Rodgers** Esq., Charles **Lowry,** not known. Witness Ezel. S. **Roland,** John **Rodgers.** Signed John **Martin.** Witness oath by Ezel. S. **Roland** 23 Apr 1798 to Cha. **Smith** J.P. Laurens Co. [No record date.] [Includes plat.]

Page 300-301 17 Mar 1798, John **Camack** (Laurens Co.) planter for £75 paid by John **Harris** (same) Blacksmith, sold all that Tract supposed to contain 100 acres more or less. Originally granted to sd. John **Camack** for 125 acres, bounded N on Jonathan **Downs,** E on Wm. **Williamson,** S on James **Cuningham,** W on Wm. **Milwee.** Also one other tract of 176 acres, joining the above tract. Originally granted to Pierce **Butler** & by him conveyed to Harculas D. **Bizee,** and by John **Hunter** as Attorney for sd. H. D. **Bizee,** to John **Camack.** Witness Lewis **Saxon,** John **Williams.** Signed John **Camack.** Dower relinquished by Margaret (O) **Camack,** wife of John **Camack,** 17 Mar 1798 before Cha. **Allen** J.L.C. Witness oath by John **Williams** 17 Mar 1798 to Charles **Allen** J.P. Laurens Co. [No record date.]

Page 301-302 5 May 1798, William **Atteway** (Laurens Co.) for £20 paid by Ansel **Dollar** (S.C.), sold 150 acres of Land more or less, being part of 623 acres granted to David **Smith** by William **Moultrie** Esq., 3 Apr 1786, and conveyed by sd. **Smith** to Stephen **Potter** dec. and afterwards the above 150 acres conveyed by John **Potter,** Admr. of sd. Stephen **Potter** dec., to William **Atteway.** Situate in Ninety Six Dist. on Ready Fork, a branch of Little River. Border: sd. **Dollar,** head of Wolf branch, Creek, N & E by Elizabeth **Goolsbey** and Larrance **Barker,** S & W by John **Potter** and Isham **Histelow.** Witness Joseph **Atteway,** Thomas **Waldrop.** Signed William (x) **Atteway.** Dower relinquished by Elizabeth (x) **Atteway,** wife of William **Atteway,** 5 May 1798 before Cha. **Allen** J.L.C. Witness oath by Thomas **Waldrop** 5 May 1798 to Cha. **Allen** J.P. Laurens Co. [No record date.]

Page 302 3 Mar 1795, Isaac **Fowler** (Laurens Co.) to Elias **Stone** (same), for £30 sold part of a tract of Land to contain 100 acres more or less, lying between Enoree and Jacks branch. Joining Thomas **Moor,** Nathen **Bramlett.** Original grant to Richard **Fowler** 1 June 1789 by Charles **Pinckney,** then Gov. and recorded in Secretary's Office in Book ZZZZ, page 372. Witness Nathen **Bramlett,** Reuben **Bramlett.** Signed Isaac (x) **Fowler.** Witness oath by Nathen **Bramlett** 7 Aug 1793 [sic] to Daniel **Wright** J.P. Laurens Co. [No record date.]

Page 302-303 11 Nov 1797, Nicholas **Garrett** (Laurens Co.) to Nathen **Bramlett** (same), for £7 sold part of a Tract of Land on E side of Beaverdam, waters of Enoree River. Border: John **Stone,** Nicholas **Garrett.** Containing 20 acres. Witness John **Stone** Sen., John **Stone** Jun. Signed Nicholas **Garrett.** Witness oath by John **Stone** 4 Apr 1798 to Daniel **Wright** J.P. Laurens Co. [No record date.]

Page 303   24 July 1797, Robert **Coker** Sen. (Laurens Co.) to James **Coker** [**Coke** in one ref.] (same), for 20sh sold a certain tract of land containing 100 acres more or less, on S side of Raiborn Creek, waters of Saluda River. Bounded S by James **Abercrombie**, other sides by Big Surveys and Richard **Owens** when first laid out. Granted 21 Dec 1769 by William **Bull** Esq. Gov., a memorial entered Auditor Genl's. Office in Book K, No.10, page 634, 24 Jan 1770 and recorded in Secretary's Office in Book EEE, page 11. Witness Robert **Coker**, Thomas **Coker**. Signed Robert (R) **Coker**. Witness oath by Robert **Coker** 14 May 1798 to John **Coker** J.P. Laurens Co. [No record date.]

Page 304-306   Lease & Release, 17 & 18 Nov 1794, Elizabeth Jane **Ravenel** Exrx. of her late husband Daniel **Ravenel**, to William **Johnson**, for £35 4sh Current money sold a certain Tract of Land on waters of Bush River, containing 320 acres more or less, part of 3,000 acres originally granted to sd. Daniel **Ravenel**, and by him in his last Will and Testament directed to be sold by his Exrx. and Exors., and known in the General plan by No.2. Witness D. **Ravenel**, Rene **Ravenel**, Peter **Porcher** Jun. Signed Elizabeth Jane **Ravenel**. Witness oath by Peter **Porcher** Jun. 16 Dec 1797 to Stephen **Ravenel** J.Q. [No record date.]

Page 306   1 Jan 1796, Elizabeth Jane **Ravenel** Exrx. of Daniel **Ravenel** dec. for £23 10sh paid by Larkin **Shepherd**, sold all that Tract of Land on waters of Bush River, containing 235 acres more or less, part of 3,000 acres originally granted to sd. Daniel **Ravenel** and by him in his last Will and Testament directed to be sold by his Exrx. or Exors. and is known in the General plan by No.3. Witness George **Porcher**, Isaac **Porcher**, Peter **Porcher** Jun. Signed Elizabeth Jane **Ravenel**. Witness oath by Peter **Porcher** Jun. 16 Dec 1797 to Stephen **Ravenel** J.Q. [No record date.]

Page 306-307   4 Aug 1796, William **Harris** (Laurens Co.) for £45 Sterling paid by Peter **Kelley** (same), sold all that certain Tract of Land whereon sd. William **Harris** now lives, containing 200 acres more or less, being part of 300 acres granted to William **Harris** Sen. & by him conveyed to sd. William **Harris** Jun., Son & Heir to aforesd. William **Harris** Sen. The other 100 acres of sd. Tract is sold and laid off and conveyed to William **Rodgers**. Sd. tract is situate in sd. Co. on waters of Little River. Bounded at time of original survey on all sides by Vacant Land, but sd. 200 acres is now bounded by Robert **Cooper**, Thomas **Blakely**, Gilbert **Mcnary**, William **Rodgers** and Large Survey. Witness Robert **McClintock**, Jno. **Simpson**. Signed William **Harris**. Dower relinquished by Frankey (C) **Harris**, wife of William **Harris**, 21 Aug 1796 before John **Hunter** J.L.C. Witness oath by Robert **McClintock** 9 May 1798 to Joseph **Downs** J.P. Laurens Co. [No record date.]

Page 307-308   19 Apr 1797, Charles **Hutchings** and Elizabeth his Wife (Washington Co., Tenn.) to Jesse **Dodd** (Union Co.), for £100 Sterling sold all that Tract of 150 acres of Land more or less, in Laurens Co. on N side of Duncans Creek. Originally granted to William **Coller** [sic] and recorded in Secretary's Office in Book LLL, page 169. Bounding S by **Kilgore**, all other sides by Vacant lands. Sd. William **Colter** did make to John **Colter** by Lease and release 16 Mar 1773, and sd. John **Colter** did make unto John **McCrary** by Lease & release 14 July 1774, and sd. John **McCrary** did make unto sd. Charles **Hutchings** by Lease and release 15 Feb 1786. Witness Amos **Richardson**, Thomas **Dillard**, Thomas (x) **Hutchings**. Signed Charles **Hutchings**, Elizabeth **Hutchings**. Witness oath by Amos **Richardson** 2 Aug 1797 to James **Dillard** J.P. Laurens Co. [No record date.]

Page 308   24 Sept 1796, Claborn **Sims** (Laurens Co.) to James **Culbertson** (same), for £5 Sterling sold all that Tract of Land containing 100 acres more or less, on long lick Creek in sd. Co., being part of 281 acres granted to Claborn **Sims** by Arnuldus **Vanderhorst** Esq. Lieut. Gov. 20 Jan 1795. Border: **Barmore**, John **Sims**, John **Hazlet**. Witness Geo. **Wright**, Wm. **Sims**, David **Burris**. Signed Claborn **Sims**. Witness oath by William **Sims** 30 Dec 1797 to Zechr. **Bailey** J.P. [No record date.]

Page 308-309 22 May 1797, Joseph **Babb** (Laurens Co.) for £20 Sterling paid by James **Culbertson** (same), sold all that Tract of Land on Beaver Dam, waters of Little River in sd. Co. Containing 60 acres more or less, being part of a Tract originally granted to Joseph **Babb** dec. Border: land granted to John **Philpot**, **Pasley**, Creek, Eldrige **Fuller's** new line. Witness Eldrige (x) **Fuller**, James **Babb**, Elizabeth (x) **Babb**. Signed Joseph **Babb**, Mary (x) **Babb**. Oath by Eldrige (x) **Fuller** 5 May 1798, that he saw Joseph **Babb** & Mary **Babb** his Wife, sign the deed. Given before Zech. **Bailey** J.P. Laurens Co. [No record date.]

Page 309   2 Feb 1797, John **Boyd** (Laurens Co.) for $20 paid by Henry **Atkinson** (same), sell all the tract of Land on Southmost side of Little River, being bounded on N by Henry **Atkinson**, W by Silv. **Walker**, S by main run of branch that leads from John **Davis'** spring into Little river on E side from mouth of sd. branch up main run of Little River to Henry **Atkinson's** line. Being part of Land originally granted to James **Ryan**. Witness John **Davis**, Silv. **Walker** Sen., William **Hunter**. Signed John **Boyd** Atty. for Ephrim **McClain**. Witness oath by Silv. **Walker** 17 Mar 1797 to John **Davis** J.P. [No record date.]

Page 309-310 24 Jan 1797, John **Philpot** (Laurens Co.) for £30 Sterling paid by Eldridge **Fuller** (same), sold all that Tract of Land whereon Daniel **Fuller** formerly lived. Border: Joseph **Babb**, Zechariah **Bailey**, Spring on a branch that I live on, big Branch, Glaid branch. To include 100 acres of Land and to strike John **Rodgers'** line. Witness James **Culbertson**, Martin **Milley** [**Miller** in one ref.]. Signed John (O) **Philpot**, Susanah (x) **Philpot**. Witness oath by James **Culbertson** 5 May 1798 to Zech. **Bailey** J.P. Laurens Co. [No record date.]

Page 310 22 May 1797, Joseph **Babb** (Laurens Co.) for £20 Sterling paid by Eldrige **Fuller** (same), sold all that Tract of Land on Bever Dam, waters of Little River in sd. Co. Containing 60 acres more or less. Border: land granted to John **Philpot**, sd. **Fuller's** spring, near old house stead, **Pasley**, Creek, **Glen**. Witness James **Culbertson**, James **Babb**, Elizabeth (x) **Babb**. Signed Joseph **Babb**, Mary (x) **Babb**. Witness oath by James **Culbertson** 5 May 1798 to Zech. **Bailey** J.P. Laurens Co. [No record date.]

Page 310-311 26 Feb 1798, John **Howard** Sen. (Greenville Co.) for £40 Sterling paid by William **Collins** (Laurens Co.), sold 75 acres of Land, being part of 150 acres in Co. aforesd. on a branch of Durbins Creek, waters of Enoree River, granted unto Mayo **Nevill** 20 Sept 1774, and from sd. **Nevill** to John **Nevill** by heirship, and from him conveyed to sd. John **Howard** Sen. Border: **Boyds** old waggon Road. Witness Wm. **Gilbert** Jr., Samuel **Howard**. Signed John (I) **Howard**. Witness oath by William **Gilbert** 27 Feb 1798 to Daniel **Wright** J.P. Laurens Co. [No record date.]

Page 311 6 Dec 1797, William **Bowen** (Laurens Co.) for £40 Sterling paid by William **Gilbert** Jun. (same), sold 193 acres of Land, being part of 3,000 acres, in sd. Co. on Durbins Creek, waters of Enoree River, granted unto Alexander **Frasher** about 20 July 1772 & conveyed unto James **Frasher** & from him conveyed to sd. William **Bowen**. Border: branch, William **Gilbert** Sen., tract laid off for John **Deen**. Witness John **Pugh**, Nathen **Pugh**. Signed William **Bowen**. Witness oath by John **Pugh** 27 Feb 1798 to Daniel **Wright** J.P. Laurens Co. [No record date.]

Page 311-312 19 July 1797, James **Gilbert** (Laurens Co.) for £25 Sterling paid by William **Collins** (same), sold 120 acres of Land more or less, being part of 250 acres in sd. Co. on Durbins Creek, waters of Enoree, granted unto James **Gilbert** 5 June 1786. Sd. 120 acres border: **Boyds** old road. Witness Wm. **Gilbert** Jun., John **Gilbert**. Signed James **Gilbert**. Witness oath by William **Gilbert** Jr. 27 Feb 1798 to Daniel **Wright** J.P. Laurens Co. [No record date.]

Page 312 18 Dec 1793, Joseph **Burchfield** (Laurens Co.) planter to William **Collins** (same) planter, for £60 Sterling sold a Tract of Land containing 100 acres more or less, being part of 204 acres granted 21 Jan 1785 by Benjamin **Grenard** Gov. unto Joseph **Burchfield**, in sd. Co. on branches of Durbins Creek, waters of Enoree River. Recorded in Grant Book AAAA, page 256. Border: branch, creek, Isaac **Barton**, branch whereon Stephen **Marchbanks** now lives, **Nevill** old line. Witness Wm. **Gilbert**, Joel (x) **Holcomb**. Signed Joseph (J) **Burchfield**. Witness oath by William **Gilbert** Jun. 5 July 1794 to Hudson **Berry** J.P. Laurens Co. [No record date.]

Page 312-313 13 Feb 1798, Thomas **Butler** (Edgefield Co.) for £13 paid by William **Collins** (Laurens Co.), sold part of a Tract of Land granted unto Thomas **Farr** Sen. 8 July 1774 and recorded in Grant Book RRR, page 143. Joining sd. William **Collins'** land. To include 92 acres, being the E part of sd. Thomas **Farr** Tract containing 865 [acres] and from sd. **Farr** to Charles Jones **Colcock**, and from him to Thomas **Butler**. Witness William **Jones**, Nethaniel

(x) **Austin**. Signed Thos. **Butler**. Witness oath by William **Jones** 13 Feb 1798 to Daniel **Wright** J.P. Laurens Co. [No record date.]

Page 313 13 Feb 1798, Thomas **Butler** (Edgefield Co.) planter for £15 paid by Nethaniel **Austin** Jun. (Laurens Co.), sold all that Tract of Land in Greenville [sic] Laurens Co. containing 105 acres, being part of a Tract granted to Thomas **Farr** Sen. containing 865 acres 8 July 1774. Recorded in Grant Book RRR, page 143. Witness James **Halks**, William **Collins**. Signed Thos. **Butler**. Witness oath by James **Halks** 13 Feb 1798 to Daniel **Wright** J.P. Laurens Co. [No record date.]

Page 313-314 13 Jan 1794, James **King** Sen. planter (Laurens Co.) to James **King** Jun. (same) planter, give 100 acres of land more or less, upon N side of Saluda River. Border: Saluda River, mouth of a creek, Edward **Conneway**, branch. The sd. land and premises where sd. James **King** now lives. Witness Daniel (x) **Brown**, James (x) **Waldrop**, Hugh (x) **Thompson** [**Tompson** in one ref.]. Signed James **King**. Witness oath by James (x) **Waldrop** 11 Apr 1798 to Reuben **Pyles** J.P. Laurens Co. [No record date.]

Page 314-315 2 May 1797, William **Turpin** Merchant (S.C.) for the same value in Land conveyed to me by Thomas **Wadsworth**, conveyed all my Right to the following tracts, having fallen to him on a Division of Certain Tracts which were held jointly by Thomas **Wadsworth** & William **Turpin**. One tract containing 200 acres in Laurens Co., N side Reedy River, surveyed by Jonathan **Downs** 12 Jan 1787 for John **Hall** & granted to Thomas **Wadsworth** by William **Moultrie** esq. 5 Feb 1787. One other tract in Pendleton Co. on a branch of Twenty three Mile Creek, containing 315 acres, surveyed by Joshua **Saxon** 5 June 1785 and granted to Thomas **Wadsworth** by William **Moultrie** esq. 7 Nov 1785. Also one other tract containing 295 acres on a branch of Twelve Mile River, waters of Savannah River, surveyed by John **Hunter** for Nancey **Wadsworth** 2 Sept 1785 and granted by William **Moultrie** 7 Nov 1785. Also one other tract containing 405 acres in Pendleton Co. on a branch of Twelve Mile River, surveyed for Nancey **Wadsworth** 3 Sept 1785 and granted by William **Moultrie** Esq. 7 Nov 1785. Witness James **Boyce**, Wm. **Turpin** Jun. Signed William **Turpin**. Dower relinquished by Mary **Turpin**, wife of William **Turpin**, 8 May 1797 before Peter **Bounetheau** J.Q. Witness oath by James **Boyce** 21 Aug 1797 to William **Neill** J.P. Laurens Co. [No record date.]

Page 315-316 8 May 1797, William **Turpin** (S.C.) Merchant for £150 Sterling paid by Thomas **Wadsworth** Merchant (same), sell the following Tracts of Land in Laurens Co. on Simmons Creek and Little River and waters thereof, being all that belonged to **Wadsworth** & **Turpin** at that place. A Tract containing 11 acres bought of Hugh **ONeall**, called **Milton**, the titles dated 27 & 28 Aug 1787. One other Tract containing about 9 acres bought of Jane **Thompson**, the titles dated 24 & 25 Sept 1788. One other Tract containing about 18 acres granted to **Wadsworth** & **Turpin** 21 Sept 1787. One tract bought of Samuel **Eallin** containing about 150 acres, titles dated 15

Aug 1792. One tract bought of Joseph **Blackerby** containing about 100 acres, titles dated 30 & 31 Oct 1793. One other tract bought of Joseph **Young** containing about 17-1/2 acres, titles dated 6 & 7 Aug 1793. One other tract containing about 6-1/2 acres bought of William **Osborn**, titles dated 15 & 16 Nov 1793. One other tract containing about 6 acres granted to **Wadsworth & Turpin**. One other tract containing by original grant to John **Young**, 200 acres, bought at two separate purchases of Galvanus **Winn** by titles dated 11 & 12 Feb 1793. One other tract bought of Thomas **Norris** containing about 71 acres, granted to Thomas **Edgehill** Jun. for 100 acres, titles from **Norris** to **Wadsworth & Turpin** dated 20 Dec 1792. One other tract granted to **Wadsworth & Turpin** 5 Oct 1795, containing about 70 acres. One other tract containing about 100 acres bought of Thomas **Norris**, titles dated 20 Dec 1792. All sd. tracts lay adjoining together with the Mill, Mill house, Still house, Tan Yard &c. One other tract bought of John **Simpson** containing about 80 acres on S side of Little River containing a small Mountain, titles dated 4 Mar 1793. Also one other tract containing about 150 acres, being the balance of a tract bought of Thomas **Norris**, the other part having been sold to John **Maulden**, titles dated 20 Dec 1792. Witness James **Boyce**, William **Turpin** Jun. Signed William **Turpin**. Dower relinquished by Mary **Turpin**, wife of William **Turpin**, 8 May 1797 before Peter **Bounetheau** J.Q. Witness oath by James **Boyce** 21 Aug 1797 to William **Neill** J.P. Laurens Co. [No record date.]

Page 316   2 May 1797, William **Turpin** (S.C.) Merchant for £175 Sterling paid by Thomas **Wadsworth** Merchant (Laurens Co.), sold all my half of Two following Tracts of Land. One Tract bought by **Wadsworth & Turpin** of Hugh **ONeall**, containing by original Survey 150 acres on both sides of Little River, waters of Saluda in sd. Co., granted to his Father Hugh **ONeall** 26 July 1774, and at time of Original Survey bounded by land laid out to John **Chesnut**, Hugh **ONeall**, Henry **ONeall**, Thomas **Carter**, Vacant Land, and Land granted to John **Purcel**. Also one other Tract containing 200 acres on both sides of Little River, bounded on two whole squares by above Tract, granted to Hugh **ONeall**, sd. 200 acres originally granted to John **Purcel** 21 June 1764 by William **Bull** Esq. Also one other tract bought of John **Maulden** supposed to contain 105 acres more or less, containing part of two original Surveys, one granted to John **McClintock**, the other to James **Young**, sd. Tract lays on S.W. side of Little River, adjoining the above described Tract bought of Hugh **ONeall**. If any part thereof should ever be lost, the part lost to be valued without regard to buildings or improvements at an average value with the whole, which whole is never to be estimated higher than the conditions here expressed, say £175. Witness James **Boyce**, William **Turpin** Jr. Signed William **Turpin**. Dower relinquished by Mary **Turpin**, wife of William **Turpin**, 8 May 1797 before Peter **Bounetheau** J.Q. Witness oath by James **Boyce** 21 Aug 1797 to William **Neill** J.P. Laurens Co. [No record date.]

Page 316-317   2 May 1797, William **Turpin** Merchant (S.C.) for the same value in Land conveyed to me by Thomas **Wadsworth**, convey all my Right to the following Tracts of Land, fallen to him on a division of Certain Tracts of

Land which were held jointly by Thomas **Wadsworth** & William **Turpin**. The following tracts situate in Laurens Co. One Tract containing 241 acres on Raborns Creek, granted to John **Ritchey** by William **Moultrie** Esq. 6 Feb 1786, by him to William **Arnold** Sen. and by him sold to **Wadsworth** & **Turpin**. One other tract containing 100 acres bought of Hutchin **Burton** by **Wadsworth** & **Turpin** on Ryans Creek, waters of Little River, originally granted to John **Martin** by William **Moultrie** Esq. 2 Oct 1786. One other Tract containing 242 acres, surveyed by John **Hunter** Esq. 13 Dec 1785, and granted 3 Apr 1786 to Thomas **Wadsworth** on branches of Indian Creek, waters of Broad River. One other tract containing 130 acres conveyed 18 Feb 1786 for Landron **Farrow** and granted to Thomas **Wadsworth** 5 Feb 1787, on S side of Enoree River. One other tract containing 365 acres, surveyed by Robert **Hanna**, 27 Jan 1786, on a small branch of Little River, joining land of John **Rodgers** and Robert **Cooper** at time of original Survey. Also a Lot at Laurens Court house purchased by **Wadsworth** & **Turpin** of the Judges of sd. Co. Witness James **Boyce**, William **Turpin** Jun. Signed William **Turpin**. Dower relinquished by Mary **Turpin**, wife of William **Turpin**, 8 May 1797 before Peter **Bounetheau** J.Q. Witness oath by James **Boyce** 21 Aug 1797 to William **Neill** J.P. Laurens Co. [No record date.]

Page 317-318 4 Oct 1796, John **Maulden** and Nancey my Wife (Laurens Co.) planter for £50 Sterling paid by Thomas **Wadsworth** Merchant (S.C.), sold part of Two tracts of Land on Little River, part of one Tract sold by Joseph **Young**, originally granted to James **Young**, to John **Maulden** supposed to be 50 acres more or less. Also part of a Tract sold by Robert **Young**, originally granted to John **McClintock**, to sd. **Maulden** supposed 50 acres more or less. Border: Little River, tract granted to John **Caldwell**, land granted to Hugh **ONeall**. Witness Jno. **Babb**, Absalom **Rhodes**. Signed John **Maulden**, Nancey (x) **Maulden**. Dower relinquished by Nancy (x) **Maulden** [sic] 18 Oct 1798 [sic] before John **Hunter** J.L.C. Witness oath by John **Babb** 18 Oct 1796 to John **Hunter** [No title.]. [No record date.]

Page 318 29 Nov 1793, David **McGladry** (Laurens Co.) Yeoman am bound to William **Lloyd** (same) yeoman, in £50 Sterling. Witness Robert **Todd**, William **Suter**. Signed David (D) **McGladry**. Condition of the obligation that if David **McGladry** shall keep covenants and agreements mentioned in a certain Deed which he is to make to sd. William **Lloyd**, of 100 acres of Land on waters of Reedy River in sd. Co., bounded by David **Green** on one side, land of David **McGladry** on two sides, land up the River owned by sd. **McGladry**, being part of same Tract sold sd. **Lloyd**, the above bond to be void. Witness Robert **Todd**, William **Sooter** [sic]. Signed David (D) **McGladry**. Witness oath by Robert (R) **Todd** 14 May 1798 to Chas. **Smith** J.P. Laurens Co. [No record date.]

Page 318-319 17 Jan 1798, Horatio **Walker** (Laurens Co.) sold unto Thomas & William **Burnside** (same), a Negro man Ned for £100 Sterling. Witness Andrew **Rodgers** Jun., Wm. A. **Rodgers**. Signed Hor. **Walker**. Witness oath by Wm. A. **Rodgers** 14 May 1798 to John **Davis** J.P. Laurens Co. [No record date.]

Page 319 29 Mar 1792, James **Puckett** (Laurens Co.) am bound unto John **Fincher** (Sparting Co.) in the sum of £12 Sterling to be paid by 1 Aug next for value recd. Condition if James **Puckett** shall sign and deliver a good title to 6 acres of Land joining the river against sd. **Finchers**, more or less, joining lands of Ann **Musgrove** & John **Billups**, then the above to be void. Witness Thomas **Bishop**. Signed James **Puckett**. 17 May 1797, I assign over all my title to the within Bond to George **Gordon**. Witness Charles (x) **Puckett**. Signed John (J) **Fincher**. Witness oath by Thomas **Bishop** 18 Jan 1798 to Jno. **Martindale** J.P. Union Co. Witness oath by Charles (x) **Puckett** 15 Feb 1798 to Roger **Brown** J.P. Laurens Co. [No record date.]

Page 319-320 James **McDavid** (Laurens Co.) planter for $400 paid by Archibald **Smith** (same) planter, sold all that Tract of Land bordering Dunkins Creek, mouth of small branch. Containing 282 acres more or less, in sd. Co. on waters of Dunkuns Creek. Bounded N by Wm. **Byrd**, W by Mathw. **Cuningham** & Benjamin **Byrd**, S by Aaron **Harlen**, E by Thos. **Murphey**. Being part of two tracts originally granted unto John **McDavid**, the first of 250 acres granted 17 Feb 1767, recorded in Book H, No.8, page 182, Auditors Office 3 Apr 1767 & the second tract of 150 acres granted 3 Apr 1786, recorded in Secretary's Office grant Book JJJJ, page 378. Witness Alexr. **Morison**, Wm. **Byrd**. Signed James **McDavid**. Witness oath by William **Byrd** 15 May 1798 to Chas. **Smith** J.P. Laurens Co. [No record date.] [Includes plat.]

Page 320 19 Oct 1797, James **Oliphant** (Laurens Co.) for 5sh Sterling paid by Joseph **Cox** (same), sold all that Tract of Land in sd. Co. on N side of Little River containing by estimation 100 acres more or less, being part of Land originally granted unto James **Ryan**, and afterward conveyed to James **Boyd**, and sd. **Boyd** at his Death left it to his Daughter Polley, now the wife of Ephraim **McClain**, and conveyed by John **Boyd**, Attorney of sd. Polley & Ephraim to James **Oliphant**. Witness John **Davis**, Thomas **Cox**. Signed James (O) **Oliphant**. Witness oath by Thomas **Cox** 19 Oct 1797 to John **Davis** J.P. L.Co. [No record date.]

Page 321-322 Lease & Release, 28 & 29 Nov 1788 [1780 in lease.], Benjamin **Rainey** (Laurens Co.) to Isreal **Eastwood** (same), for £40 Sterling sold all that Tract of Land containing 100 acres more or less, on N fork of Rayborns Creek, waters of Saluda River, in sd. Co. Bounded on all sides by Vacant land at time of Surveying. Originally granted unto Joseph **Livingston** by Charles G. **Montague**, then Gov. 6 Apr 1768. Conveyed by lease and release unto sd. Benjamin **Rainey** by David **Livingston**, Brother and heir unto sd. Joseph **Livingston** dec., 6 Aug 1783. Witness William **Head**, Thomas **Head**. Signed Benjamin **Rainey**. Witness oath by William **Head** 10 Sept 1796 to Saml. **Woods** J.P. Elbert Co., Ga. [No record date.]

Page 322   20 Nov 1796, Isreal **Eastwood** (Laurens Co.) and Elizabeth his Wife to Jesse **Childers** (same), for £60 Sterling sold a certain Tract of Land on waters of Rayborns Creek in sd. Co. Granted to Joseph **Livingston** by Lord Charles **Montague**, Apr 1768, for 100 acres. Witness Richard **Childers**, John **Childers**. Signed Israel (J) **Eastwood**. Elizabeth (E) **Eastwood**. Witness oath by Richard **Childers** 11 Apr 1797 to John **Coker** J.P. Laurens Co. [No record date.]

Page 322-323   13 Dec 1797, John **Craddock** (Winton Co.) planter for $50 paid by Bartholemew **Craddock** [Bartholamew in one ref.] (Laurens Co.), sell all that tract of Land in Laurens Co. on Little River, waters of Saluda, containing 50 acres more or less, being part of 300 acres originally granted to David **Craddock**. Border: mouth of sd. Bartholamew **Craddock's** Spring Branch, Little River, land laid out to James **Ryan**, land laid out to John **McNees**. Witness John **Dendy**, Daniel **Craddock**. Signed John **Craddock**. Witness oath by Daniel **Craddock** 8 June 1798 to Wm. **Mitchell** J.L.C. [No record date.]

Page 323   13 Jan 1798, William **Spurgin** for $367-1/2 paid by James **McClintock**, sold one Negro Wench Bet with future Issue. Witness Sterling **Tucker**, Samuel **Fleming**. Signed William **Spurgin**. Witness oath by Samuel **Fleming** 16 May 1798 to James **Saxon** J.P. Laurens Co. [No record date.]

Page 323-324   12 Mar 1798, Elizabeth **Goodwin** Admx. of Mark **Goodwin** dec. (Laurens Co.) for 4,000 Weight of Tobacco paid by Robert **Bumpass** (same), sold a parcel of Land containing 250 acres more or less. Being part of 1,000 acres originally granted to James **Smith** dec. Situate in sd. Co. on waters of Little River, waters of Saluda River. Border: **Goodwin**, John **Powers**, Robert **Bumpass**, **Williams**, **Smith**. Witness Marshall **Franks**, Chas. **Smith**, Jacob **Neighbours**. Signed Elizabeth (x) **Goodwin**. Witness oath by Marshall **Franks** 14 June 1798 to Chas. **Smith** J.P. Laurens Co. [No record date.] [Includes plat.]

Page 324   30 Sept 1796, William **Bowen** (Laurens Co.) for £40 paid by Reuben **Bramlet** (same), sell a parcel of Land supposed to be 200 acres more or less, being part of 3,000 acres granted about 20 July 1772 unto Alexander **Fraser**, conveyed to sd. William **Bowen**. Situate in sd. Co. on S fork of Durbins Creek, waters of Enoree River. Border: John **Childers**, William **Gilbert**, Waggon Road, Caleb **Hugh**, William **Allison**, South fork of Durbins Creek, mouth of second branch. Witness Benjamin **Brown**, Samuel (A) **Allison**. Signed William **Bowen**. Witness oath by Benjamin **Brown** 27 Feb 1798 to Daniel **Wright** J.P. Laurens Co. [No record date.]

Page 324-325   8 Jan 1798, Ansel **Magee** (Laurens Co.) to Thomas **Williamson** (same), for $55 sold a tract of Land in sd. Co. on Beaver Dam branch of Reedy River, bounding on land laid out to **Goodwin**, William **Arther**. Originally granted to sd. Ansel **Magee** 20 Aug 1793 for 84 acres more or less. Witness Thomas **Meares**, James **Kinman**, Cornelius **Cook**. Signed

Ansil (x) **Magee** [sic], Mary (x) **Magee**. Oath by Thomas **Meares** 19 June 1798, that he saw Ansil **Magee** & Mary his Wife, sign the Deed. Given before Reuben **Pyles** J.P. Laurens Co. [No record date.]

Page 325   22 Feb 1798, William **Bowen** (Laurens Co.) for £30 Sterling paid by James **Gilbert** (same), sold 160 acres of Land, being part of 3,000 acres in sd. Co. on Durbins Creek, waters of Enoree River. Granted unto Alexander **Freasher** about 20 July 1772, and conveyed unto James **Frasher**, and from him conveyed to sd. William **Bowen**. Sd. 160 acres border: William **Gilbert** Sen., Wm. **Gilbert** Jun. Witness John **Pugh**, Elisha **Holcomb**. Signed William **Bowen**. Witness oath by John **Pugh** 2 Feb 1798 to Daniel **Wright** J.P. Laurens Co. [No record date.]

Page 325-326   4 Jan 1798, William **Lowery** (Jefferson Co., Ga.) for £40 paid by Daniel **Drummond** (Laurens Co.), sold all that tract of Land containing 100 acres more or less, in Laurens Co. on waters of Mudlick Creek, whereon sd. Daniel **Drummond** now lives. Originally granted to sd. William **Lowry** [sic] 12 Apr 1771. Bounded on one side by lands laid out to William **Nash**, all other sides by Vacant land at time of original Survey. Witness Nethl. **Drummond**, Charles **Porterfield**. Signed William **Lowrey** [sic]. Dower relinquished by Rhoda **Lowery** [Rhody **Lowrey** in signature.], wife of William **Lowery**, 4 Jan 1798 before Jacob Robert **Brown**, J.N.C. Witness oath by N. **Drummond** 28 Mar 1798 to Zech. **Bailey** J.P. Laurens Co. [No record date.]

Page 326   4 Oct 1797, William **Bowen** (Laurens Co.) for £40 paid by Reuben **Higgins** (same), sold all that tract of Land containing 100 acres more or less, being part of Land granted to Alexander **Frasher** about 20 July 1772, containing 3,000 [acres], conveyed to James **Frasher** and from him to sd. William **Bowen**. Lying on Durbins Creek, waters of Enoree River. Border: Creek, Frances **Allison**. Witness Joseph **Lyon**, Nancy **Pugh**. Signed William **Bowen**. Witness oath by Joseph **Lyon** 7 June 1798 to Daniel **Wright** J.P. Laurens Co. [No record date.]

Page 327   22 Feb 1798, Joseph **Holcomb** (Laurens Co.) for £10 paid by Stephen **Caudle** (same), sold a parcel of Land containing 130 acres more or less, being part of 500 acres granted to Joseph **Holcomb** by Charles **Pinckney** Esq. 1 May 1797. Situate on Durbins Creek, waters of Enoree River. Bounded by Henry **Wood**, John **Freeman**, vacant land, Frances **Allison**. Recorded in Grant Book 2, No.5, page 329. Witness Joseph **Lyon**, Elisha **Halcomb**. Signed Joseph (L) **Halcomb** [sic]. Witness oath by Elisha **Halcomb** 27 Feb 1798 to Daniel **Wright** J.P. Laurens Co. [No record date.]

Page 327-328   22 Feb 1798, Elisha **Halcomb** (Laurens Co.) for £40 paid by Abraham **Deyson** (same), sold a parcel of Land containing 70 acres more or less, being part of Two certain Grants, both for 640 acres, granted by Benjn. **Garrard** Esq., one to John **Williams**, the other to Martin **Williams**, both on 21 Jan 1785, and both recorded in grant Book DDDD, page 38, and 200 acres conveyed from John **Williams** to Frances **Allison** & 100 acres conveyed from Frances **Allison** to Elisha **Halcomb**, also 10 acres conveyed from Martin **Williams** to sd. Elisha **Halcomb**, both on Durbins Creek, waters of Enoree River. Border: Creek, Frances **Allison**, Reuben **Bramlet**, Wm. **Bowen**. To include all that part on N side of the Creek conveyed from sd. **Allison** & Martin **Williams** to Elisha **Halcomb**. Witness Joseph **Lyon**, Solomon **Halcomb**. Signed Elisha **Halcomb**. Witness oath by Joseph **Lyon** 27 Feb 1798 to Daniel **Wright** J.P. Laurens Co. [No record date.]

Page 328   22 Feb 1798, Elisha **Halcomb** (Laurens Co.) for £30 paid by Stephen **Caudle** (same), sold a parcel of Land containing 30 [acres] more or less, being part of 640 acres granted to John **Williams** by Benjamin **Guarrard** Esq. 21 Jan 1785, and recorded in Grant Book DDDD, page 38, and 200 acres conveyed to Frances **Allison** and 100 acres conveyed from sd. **Allison** to Elisha **Halcomb**, also 20 acres of sd. Tract conveyed from John **Williams** to Elisha **Halcomb**. Situate on S fork of Durbins Creek, waters of Enoree River. Border: **Allison**, Creek. Including the whole of that piece which John **Williams** conveyed to Elisha **Halcomb** and also part of that which Frances **Allison** conveyed to sd. **Halcomb**. Witness Joseph **Lyon**, Solomon **Halcomb**. Signed Elisha **Halcomb**. Witness oath by Joseph **Lyon** 27 Feb 1798 to Daniel **Wright** J.P. Laurens Co. [No record date.]

Page 328-329   27 Feb 1798, Reuben **Bramlet** (Laurens Co.) for £30 paid by Benjamin **Brown** (same), sold a parcel of Land containing 100 acres more or less, being part of 3,000 [acres] granted about 20 July 1772 unto Alexander **Fraser** & conveyed to James **Fraser**, from him to William **Bowen** & from sd. **Bowen** about 200 acres conveyed unto Reuben **Bramlet**. Situate in sd. Co. on Durbins Creek, waters of Enoree River. Border: Frances **Allison**, Creek, second branch, John **Deen**, William **Gilbert** Jun., sd. **Bramlet**. Witness Joseph **Lyon**, William **Gilbert** Jun. Signed Reuben **Bramlet**. Witness oath by Joseph **Lyon** 27 Feb 1798 to Daniel **Wright** J.P. Laurens Co. [No record date.]

Page 329   19 Aug 1797, Frances **Allison** (Laurens Co.) for £60 paid by Elisha **Halcomb** Blacksmith (same), sold a Tract of Land containing 100 acres more or less, being part of 640 acres on Durbins Creek, waters of Enoree River in sd. Co. Granted unto John **Williams** and conveyed unto Frances **Allison**, the grant dated 21 Jan 1785, by Benjn. **Guerard** Esq. Recorded in Grant Book DDDD, page 38. Sd. 100 acres bounded by William **Brown**, sd. Frances **Allison**, Reuben **Bramlet**. Witness Joseph **Lyon**, John **Carr**. Signed Frances (J) **Allison**. Witness oath by Joseph **Lyon** 27 Feb 1798 to Daniel **Wright** J.P. Laurens Co. [No record date.]

Page 329-330   20 Dec 1797, Joseph **Halcomb** (Laurens Co.) for £20 paid by Elisha **Halcomb** (same), sold a parcel of Land containing 40 acres more or less, being part of 3,000 acres granted about 20 July 1772 unto Alexander **Fraser** & conveyed to James **Fraser**, from him to William **Bowen** & from sd. **Bowen** about 83 acres conveyed unto sd. Joseph **Halcomb**. Situate in sd. Co. on Durbins Creek, waters of Enoree River. Sd. 40 acres border: Joseph **Lyon**, old road leading from Martin **Williams'** old place to sd. Elisha **Halcomb's**, branch. Witness Joshua **Halcomb**, Joseph **Lyon**. Signed Joseph (L) **Halcomb**. Witness oath by Joseph **Lyon** 3 Jan 1798 to Daniel **Wright** J.P. Laurens Co. [No record date.]

Page 330 31 July 1797, John **Williams** (Pendleton Co.) for £10 paid by Elisha **Halcomb** Black Smith (Laurens Co.), sold a Tract of Land containing 20 acres more or less, being part of 640 acres on So. Durbins Creek, waters of Enoree River in Laurens Co. Granted unto sd. John **Williams** 21 Jan 1785 by Benjamin **Guerard**. Recd. in Grant Book DDDD, page 38. Sd. 20 acres border: **Allison**. Witness Frances (F) **Allison**, William (8) **Heartgrave**. Signed John (W) **Williams**. Witness oath by Frances (x) **Allison** 27 Feb 1798 to Daniel **Wright** J.P. Laurens Co. [No record date.]

Page 330-331 14 Nov 1797, Martin **Williams** (Pendleton Co.) for £5 paid by Elisha **Halcomb** Black Smith (sd. Co.), sold 12 acres of Land more or less, being part of 640 acres granted unto Martin **Williams** by Benjamin **Guerard** Esq. 21 Jan 1785 & recorded in Grant Book DDDD, page 38. Situate on So. Durbins Creek, waters of Enoree in sd. Co. Sd. 12 acres border: William **Brown**, sd. Elisha **Halcomb**. Witness John (M) **Williams**, Lewis **Shelton**. Signed Martin **Williams**. Witness oath by John (M) **Williams** 2 Feb 1798 to Daniel **Wright** J.P. Laurens Co. [No record date.]

Page 331 6 Mar 1798, William **Bowen** (Laurens Co.) for £40 paid by Levy **Young** (same), sold a parcel of Land containing 180 acres, being part of 3,000 acres granted unto Alexander **Fraser** about 20 July 1772. Situate on Durbins Creek, waters of Enoree River and conveyed from sd. **Fraser** to James **Fraser** and from him conveyed to sd. William **Bowen**. Sd. 180 acres border: branch, Waggon Road, Joseph **Lyon**, Reuben **Bramlet**, Caleb **Hughes**, Elisha **Halcomb**. Witness Joseph **Lyon**, James **Bowen**. Signed William **Bowen**. Witness oath by Joseph **Lyon** 28 Apr 1798 to Jonthn. **Downs** J.P. Laurens Co. [No record date.]

Page 331-332 22 Feb 1798, Joseph **Halcomb** (Laurens Co.) for £5 paid by Frances **Allison** (same), sold a parcel of Land containing 50 acres more or less, being part of 500 acres granted to Joseph **Halcomb** by Charles **Pinckney** Esq. 1 May 1797. Recorded in Grant Book 2, No.5, page 329. Situate on Durbins Creek, waters of Enoree River. Border: Frances **Allison**, Stephen **Caudle**, John **Freenan** [sic], near a Road. Witness Joseph **Lyon**, Elisha **Halcomb**. Signed Joseph (x) **Halcomb**. Witness oath by Elisha **Halcomb** 27 Feb 1798 to Daniel **Wright** J.P. Laurens Co. [No record date.]

Page 332 Last day July 1797, Samuel **Neighbours** (Laurens Co.) for £32 paid by Elisha **Eastis** (same), sold all that Tract of Land in sd. Co. adjoining the Old Indian boundary, being the W line of sd. Co. Lying on line Creek. Witness Joel **Webb**, Fleet **Neighbours**. Signed Samuel **Neighbours**. Witness oath by Fleet **Neighbours** last day July 1797 to Reuben **Pyles** J.P. Laurens Co. [No record date.]

Page 332-333 18 Nov 1797, Cornelius **Dendy** (Laurens Co.) for $400 paid by Wm. **Mitchell** (same), sold one certain Tract of land containing 285 acres more or less, being part of Two tracts, 180 acres being part of a Tract granted unto Benjn. **Powell** by Wm. **Bull** Esq. Gov. 25 June 1771, containing 250 acres and conveyed by sd. **Powell** unto Thomas **Dendy** by Lease & release 20 Dec 1773, and conveyed by sd. Thomas **Dendy** Sen. unto Cornelius **Dendy** 30 May 1792. The other 5 acres being a parcel reserved by sd. Thomas **Dendy** out of a Tract conveyed to Wm. **Mitchell** 6 Nov 1794, and conveyed by sd. Thomas **Dendy** to Cornelius **Dendy** 17 Nov 1797. Border: lower line of sd. 250 acres, N side of Norths Creek, small branch, Wm. **Leek**. Witness Tho. **Dendy**, Isaac **Mitchell**, Mary (x) **Dendy**. Signed Cornelius **Dendy**. Witness oath by Thos. **Dendy** 17 July 1798 to Jonthn. **Downs**. J.P. Laurens Co. [No record date.]

Page 333-334 23 Jan 1798, Elisha **Atteway** (Laurens Co.) for £182 10sh Sterling paid by George **Mosely** (same), sold all that parcel of Land containing 250 acres more or less, being part of three tracts, the original grantee was Joseph **Atteway**, William **Booling** & Thos. **Deen**. Border: John **Atteway**, sd. **Moseley** [sic], Joseph **Atteway**, Warriers Creek, James **Saxon** Esq., **Patterson**, Vincent **Brown**. Being in sd. Co. Witness Samuel **Fleming**, James **Saxon**, John **Moore**. Signed Elisha (x) **Atteway**. Witness oath by John **Moore** 23 Jan 1798 to Starling **Tucker** J.P. Laurens Co. Dower relinquished by Lettice (nn) **Atteway**, wife of Elisha **Atteway**, 18 July 1798 before Chas. **Allen** J.L.C. [No record date.]

Page 334 25 Apr 1798, Matthew **Hunter** (Ninety Six Dist.) for £20 Sterling paid by Charles **Little** (same), sold all that tract of Land containing 100 acres, being part of 476 acres originally granted to Wm. **Hudelston** by William **Bull** Lieut. Gov. 11 Aug 1774. Conveyed by sd. **Hudelston** to Matthew **Hunter**. Being on waters of Dunkins Creek on Browns Creek. Bounded S.W. on lands formerly John **Jones**, S.E. by John **Adair**, S.W. on Joseph **Adair**, N.W. on part of sd. tract, S.W. on unknown, according to plat drawn by John **Hunter** Dep. Sur. Witness Andrew **Middleton**, Answorth **Middleton**. Signed Matthew **Hunter**, Margret (x) **Hunter**. Oath by Answorth **Middleton** 18 July 1798 that he saw Matthew **Hunter** and Margret his Wife sign the deed. Given before William **Neill** J.P. [No record date.]

Page 334-335 30 Apr 1798, James **Greer** (Laurens Co.) planter for $300 paid by Josias Prayter **John** of Basil (same) blacksmith, sold all that Tract of Land containing 150 acres more or less, on Dunkins Creek. Joining E on Colo. Robert **McCrery**, N on Basil **Prayter**, W on John **Rammage**, S on Dunkins Creek. Witness John **Prater**, William **Bell**. Signed James (J) **Greer**. Witness oath by William **Bell** 5 May 1798 to Geo. **Whitmore** J.P. Laurens Co. Dower relinquished by Elisabeth **Greer** [Elizabeth in one ref.], wife of James **Greer**, 3 May 1798 before Wm. **Mitchell** J.L.C. [No record date.]

Page 335 18 Oct 1797, John **Adair** and Jane **Adair** (Laurens Co.) for $109 paid by David **Little** (same), sold 109 acres of Land in sd. Co., being part of Two Surveys, one originally granted to William **Huddleston**, the other to sd John **Adair** and joining each other. Bounded by Patrick **Bryan**, Thomas **Holland**, Matthew **Hunter**, John **Adair**, lands granted to Joseph **Glenn**. Witness Robt. **Adair**, Elisha **Adair**. Signed John **Adair**, Jane (x) **Adair**. Oath by Robt. **Adair** 17 July 1798, that he saw John **Adair** and Jane his wife sign the deed. Given before Jonthn. **Downs** J.P. Laurens Co. [No record date.]

Page 335 16 July 1798, Thomas **Camp** (Laurens Co.) to Joseph **Camp** (same), for £100 Sterling sold a certain Tract of Land containing 150 acres more or less, in sd. Co. on N side of South fork of Rayborns Creek, being part of a Tract granted to Owen **Reed** by the Gov. 22 Sept 1769. Border: Widow **Reeds** branch, Creek. Witness Robert **Atkins**, Benjn. (x) **Camp**. Signed Thomas (C) **Camp**. Witness oath by Robert **Atkins** 17 July 1798 to Joseph **Downs** J.P. Laurens Co. [No record date.]

Page 336 3 Aug 1797, Drewry **Sims** (Laurens Co.) to Thomas **Matthews**, for £70 Sterling sold one certain Tract of Land in sd. Co. on both sides of Raiborns Creek. Bounded by Tulley **Choice**, Thomas **McDonald**, Raiborns Creek, Mr. **Anderson's** land where Sarah **McHaffee** now lives, James **Nesbet**, **Sims'** fence, Edward **Nash**. Includes the house where Drury **Sims** [sic] now lives and contains by estimation 160 acres more or less. Granted to Samuel **Bolling** & Drury **Sims** by William **Moultrie** Gov. Witness Solomon **Hopkins**, Henry **Morgan**. Signed Drury **Sims**, Ruth **Sims**. Witness oath by Henry **Morgin** [sic] 18 July 1798 to John **Coker** J.P. Laurens Co. [No record date.]

Page 336 2 Jan 1796, William **Dudgeon** (Virginia) planter for $50 paid by William **Nickels** (Laurens Co.), sold all that tract of Land containing 300 acres in Laurens Co. on Cain Creek, waters of Saluda. Border: **Fendley**, **Carter**. Witness A. **Rodgers** Jun., John **Rodgers**, Jacob **Levy**. Signed William **Dudgeon**. Witness oath by Andrew **Rodgers** Jun. 18 July 1798 to Zech. **Bailey** J.P. Laurens Co. [No record date.]

Page 337 13 Jan 1798, William **Edings** (Laurens Co.) for £50 Sterling paid by Joseph **Young** (same), sold all that tract of Land containing 100 acres in sd. Co. on waters of North Creek, being part of 150 acres originally granted to Thomas **Dendy**. Witness James **Henderson**, Isaac **Chandler**, Josiah **Chandler**. Signed William (x) **Eddens** [sic]. Witness oath by Isaac **Chandler** [Josiah **Chandler** signature.] 13 Jan 1798 to Wm. **Mitchell** J.P. L.Co. Dower relinquished by Rebecca (x) **Eddens**, wife of Wm. **Eddens**, 13 Jan 1798 before Wm. **Mitchell** J.L.C. [No record date.]

Page 337-338 10 Oct 1797, Elizabeth **Bryson** Widow of James **Bryson** dec., William **Bryson** Brother of sd. James **Bryson**, Joseph **Young** who married sd. James **Bryson's** Sister Mary (Laurens Co.) for £70 Sterling paid by John **Bryson** (same), sold all that Tract of Land containing 150 acres in sd. Co. on Carsons Creek, a branch of Little River, bounded on all sides at time of

Original Survey by Vacant Land. Granted to James **Lefan** by Charles Graville **Montague** 6 Apr 1768, and by sd. **Lawfin** [sic] sold to James **Bryson** by lease & release 7 July 1775. Witness Chas. **Smith**, Robt. **Hutcheson**. Signed Elizabeth (&) **Bryson**, William **Bryson**, Joseph **Young**. Witness oath by Robert **Hutcheson** 10 Oct 1797 to Chas. **Allen** J.P. Laurens Co. Dower relinquished by Jane **Bryson** & Mary **Young**, Wives of William **Bryson** & Joseph **Young**, 10 Nov 1797 before Wm. **Mitchell** J.L.C. [No record date.]

Page 338 20 Feb 1796, Richard **Giddeons** (Laurens Co.) for £20 Sterling paid by William **Jones** (same), sold a certain Tract of Land containing 178 acres on Beards fork, a branch of Dunkins Creek. Granted to Edward **Giddeons** 2 Dec 1793 and recorded in Secretary's Office in Book J, No.5, page 421. I am the owner of the premises in my own right as an Estate of Inheritance. Witness Robert (x) **Glidewell**, James **Leek**. Signed Edward **Giddens** [sic], Elizabeth (x) **Giddens**. Oath by James **Leak** [sic] 25 Apr 1798 that he saw Edward **Giddens** and his Wife sign the deed. Given before Roger **Brown** J.P. Laurens Co. [No record date.]

Page 338-339 14 Nov 1796, James **Leek** (Laurens Co.) for $50 paid by William **Leek** (same), sold a Tract of 200 acres on branches of Beards fork of Dunkins Creek in sd. Co. Bounded E by Joseph **Glenn**, N by Hannah **Jones**, S.W. by Wm. **Jones** and Andw. **Endsley**, S.E. & S by sd. James **Leek** & Robert **Glidewell**. Witness Wm. **Rodgers**, William **Jones**. Signed James **Leek**, Franky (x) **Leek**. Witness oath by Wm. **Jones** 25 Apr 1798 to Roger **Brown** J.P. Laurens Co. Dower relinquished by Frankey (x) **Leek** [sic], wife of James **Leek**, 21 May 1798 before Wm. **Mitchell** J.L.C. [No record date.]

Page 339 15 Oct 1794, Matthew **Bowen** (Laurens Co.) planter to Rolly **Bowen** [Rolley in one ref.] (same) planter, for £40 Sterling sold a Tract of Land containing 100 acres more or less, in sd. Co. on South fork of Durbins Creek, waters of Enoree River. Granted 16 June 1795 by William **Moultrie** Esq. Gov. unto William **Bowen** and recorded in Grant Book DDDD, page 425. Conveyed by sd. William **Bowen** to Matthew **Bowen** by lease and release. Border: Benjn. **Vines**. Witness William **Gilbert**, John **Gilbert**. Signed Matthew **Bowen**. Witness oath by John **Gilbert** 21 July 1798 to Daniel **Wright** J.P. Laurens Co. [No record date.]

Page 340 25 Apr 1798, William **Jones** (Laurens Co.) for $125 paid by James **Leek** (same), sold a Tract of 118 acres of Land, being part of 178 acres on branches of beards fork of Dunkins Creek in sd. Co. Bounded on lands held at this time by William **Leek**, James **Brown**, William **Taylor**, Bazil **Holland**, Alexander **Fairbarn**, William **Glidewell** and rest of tract held by James **Jones**. Witness William **Leek**, Enoch **Gilndn**? Signed William **Jones**. Witness oath by William **Leek** 25 Apr 1798 to Roger **Brown** J.P. Laurens Co. Dower relinquished by Mary (O) **Jones**, wife of William **Jones**, 21 May 1798 before Wm. **Mitchell** J.L.C. [No record date.]

Page 340-341 25 Nov 1795, Watson **Allison** (Laurens Co.) planter to Joseph **Hammon** (same) planter, for £35 Sterling a Tract of Land in sd. Co. on waters of Rayborns Creek, supposed to be 100 acres more or less, being part of land granted to Hasting **Dial** by Thos. **Pinckney**, recorded in Grant Book XXXX, page 73, dated 2 June 1788. Sold by sd. **Dial** to Watson **Allison**, part of sd. Tract. Border: old line supposed to be run for Jane **McClurkin**. To include that plantation whereon Mordecia **Moore** now lives. Witness John **Childers**, Jacob **Manord**. Signed Watson **Allison**. Witness oath by Jacob (x) **Mayner** [sic] 18 July 1798 to Chas. **Smith** J.P. Laurens Co. [No record date.]

Page 341 13 Oct 1795, Watson **Allison** (Laurens Co.) planter to Jacob **Mayner** (same) planter, for £40 Sterling sold a Tract of Land containing 152 acres in sd. Co. Including the plantation whereof Samuel **Allison** now lives, being the N & W part of 288 acres on waters of Rayborns Creek, waters of Reedy River, granted 3 Dec 1792 by Chas. **Pinckney** Gov. unto Watson **Allison**. The Old Grant is recorded in Grant Book F, No.5, page 276. Witness Isreal (x) **Eastwood**, Joel (x) **Johnston**, Elizabeth (x) **Eastwood**. Signed Watson (A) **Allison**. Witness oath by Isreal (J) **Eastwood** 13 Oct 1795 to Hudson **Berry** J.P. Laurens Co. [No record date.]

Page 342 10 May 1798, John & William **Cuningham** (Laurens Co.) Exors. of Patrick **Cuningham** dec. for £100 Sterling paid by Silvanus **Adams** (same), sold all that Tract of Land containing 200 acres more or less, in sd. Co. on waters of Reedy River granted to Peter **Mehl** in June 1774 & conveyed by him & his Wife Mary by lease & release 2 & 3 Nov 1774 to Patrick **Cuningham**. Witness James **Forrest**, Elijah **Burgess**. Signed John **Cuningham** for himself & Brother William **Cuningham**. Witness oath by Elijah **Burgess** 14 July 1798 to Zech. **Bailey** J.P. Laurens Co. [No record date.]

Page 342-343 28 Jan 1791, John **Stephenson** Weaver (Fairfield Co.) to John **Robertson** (Laurens Co.), for £20 Sterling sold a certain Tract of Land containing 150 acres in Berkley Co. but now Laurens in the fork between Broad & Saluda Rivers, the S.W. side of Enoree River. Bounded N.E. by sd. River, N.W. by land laid out to Thos. **Gordon**, S.W. by land laid out to John **Odall**, S.E. by Vacant land. Granted unto sd. John **Stevenson** [sic] 4 May 1775 & recorded in Secretary's Office in Book AAA, page 415. Witness John **Johnston**, Alexr. **Rosbrough**. Signed John **Stevenson**. Witness oath by John **Johnston** 30 Apr 1796 to Geo. **Whitmore** J.P. Laurens Co. [No record date.]

Page 343 16 Sept 1797, John **Roberson** (Laurens Co.) for £60 paid by James Odall **Robertson** [**Roberson** in one ref.] (same), sold all that tract of Land containing 150 acres in Berkley Co. now Laurens in the fork between Broad & Saluda Rivers, the S.W. Side of Enoree River. Bounded N.E. by sd. River, N.W. by land laid out to **Gordon** Thos. [sic], S.W. by land laid out to John **Odall**, S.E. by Vacant Land. Granted unto John **Stevenson** 4 May 1775 & Recorded in Secretary's Office in Book AAA, page 415. Conveyed by sd. **Stevenson** to sd. John **Roberson** 28 Jan 1791. Witness Moses **Whitten**, John R. **Hendley**. Signed John (J) **Roberson**. Witness oath by John Roberson

Hendly [sic] 20 Apr 1798 to Geo. **Whitmore** J.P. Laurens Co. [No record date.]

Page 343-344 2 Nov 1797, William **Partridge** (Laurens Co.) for $200 paid by Odell **Garrett** (same), sold 62 acres of Land of a certain Tract upon two small drafts of Dunkins Creek, waters of Enoree river in sd. Co. Bounded by Henry **Davis**, land surveyed for Andw. **McCrery**, sd. **McCrery**, land laid out to Geo. **Whitmore**. Being one half of 124 acres originally granted to Geo. **Whitmore** 6 Aug 1792 by Charles **Pinckney** Esq. Gov. and recorded in Secretary's Office in grant book E, No.5, page 113. Witness Henry **Davis**, Elizabeth **Davis**. Signed William **Partridge**. Witness oath by Henry **Davis** 16 July 1798 to Geo. **Whitmore** J.P. Laurens Co. [No record date.]

Page 344-345 4 Nov 1797, Sarah, Lydda, Margret, Anney and Mary **Whitmore**, Joint heirs of the Estate of John **Whitmore** dec. (Laurens Co.) for £110 paid by George **Young** (same), sold all that Tract of Land containing 250 acres upon the Drafts of Dunkins Creek in Berkley Co. when surveyed but now Laurens, whereon sd. George **Young** now lives. Granted unto sd. John **Whitmore** dec. 31 Aug 1774 by William **Bull** Esq. late Lieut. Gov. and recorded in grant Book SSS, page 525, in Secretary's Office. Bounded S.W. by lands part laid out Andrew **McCrery** & part Vacant, N.W. by part laid out to Joseph **Whitmore** & part Vacant, N.E. by lands part laid out to Lifus **Rayley** & part Vacant, S.E. by lands part laid out to Thomas **McCrery** & part Vacant. Witness John **Watson**, Andrew **McCrery**. Signed Sarah (x) **Duckett**, Lydda (x) **Duckett**, Margret (x) **Prude**, Anney (x) **Whitmore**, Mary (x) **Duckett**. Witness oath by John **Watson** 4 Nov 1797 to Geo. **Whitmore** J.P. Laurens Co. Dower relinquished by Alsey (A) **Whitmore** [Alis in one ref.], Widow & Relict of John **Whitmore** dec., 17 July 1798 before Jonthn. **Downs** J.L.C. [No record date.]

Page 345 2 Jan 1796, Fredrick **Freasure** Esq. (Charleston) by his Attorney John **Hunter** Esq. to Isaac **Chandler** (Laurens Co.), for £24 Sterling sold all that Tract of Land containing 174 acres more or less, in Laurens Co. on waters of Simmons Creek, being part of 2,000 acres originally granted to William **Bull** Jun. 21 Feb 1772, and by sd. **Bull** conveyed to William **Williamson** by lease & release 7 June 1772, and recorded in Registers Office mean [sic] Conveyance in Book Z, No.3, page 203, 30 Oct 1772, and conveyed by sd. **Williamson** to sd. Fredrick **Frasure** [sic] 24 Nov 1779 & now conveyed by virtue of a power of Attorney from sd. **Freasure** 20 Mar 1795. Witness Joseph **Gallegly**, James **Henderson**, William (x) **Eddins**. Signed John **Hunter** Atty. for Fredrick **Freasure**. Recd. of Robert **Cannin** & William **Young** a Bond payable to Joseph **Winthrop** for £24. Witness oath by James **Henderson**, William (x) **Eddins** 2 Jan 1796 to William **Neill** J.P. Laurens Co. [No record date.]

Page 345-346 29 Oct 1796, Benjamin **Camp** (Laurens Co.) to George **Thomason** (same), for £30 Sterling sold all that tract of Land that sd. George **Thomason** lives on at this time of 100 acres more or less, in sd. Co. on middle fork of Mountain Creek, waters of Rabourns Creek. Granted 15 July 1793 for 500 acres and conveyed from John **Hunter** to Benjamin **Camp**. Witness Robt. **Atkins**, Wm. **Arnold**. Signed Benjamin (XX) **Camp**. Witness oath by Robert **Atkins** 22 Mar 1797 to Joseph **Downs** J.P. Laurens Co. [No record date.]

Page 346 14 Apr 1798, George **Brock** (Laurens Co.) Mercht. for $34.11 paid by Roger **Murphey** planter (same), sold one Cow & Calf, one Cow & one 2 year old Heifer, five head of hogs, seven pewter Basons, two pewter Dishes, six pewter plates, six knives and forks, one pail, one pr. Cotton Cards, three Cups & Saucers, one Skillet, one Dutch Oven, one Bed & furniture and bed stead, one drawing knife, one Screw Auger, one Ax, one set Swingle trees, two Clevices, four Chains, one plough, all sd. property now in hands of Ebenezer **Murphey**. Witness Jas. **Hollingsworth**, John **Wilson**. Signed George **Brock**. Witness oath by John **Wilson** 9 July 1798 to James **Abercrombie** J.P. Laurens Co. [No record date.]

Page 347 12 July 1790, Martha **Lazenby** Widow (Laurens Co.) give unto my Daughter Sarah **Duckett**, wife of Jacob **Duckett** (same), a certain Negro Girl about 4 years old, Jane. Witness Joseph **Jeanes**, John Prather (x) **Odell**, Elizabeth **Davis**. Signed Martha **Lazenby**. Witness oath by Jno. Prather (x) **Odell** 5 May 1791 to James **Montgomery** J.P. Laurens Co. [No record date.]

Page 347 25 Oct 1797, Daniel **Brown** (Laurens Co.) for £50 paid by Kitt **Smith** (same), sold all that Tract of Land on N side of Saluda River in sd. Co., being part of three Tracts and there are three Deeds made for same, one Deed made to sd. Daniel **Brown** by James **King** Sen. for 100 acres, bordering sd. James **King's** Spring, branch, James **Waldrop**. The second Deed for the other part was made to Daniel **Brown** by Joseph **Waldrop** for 50 acres, bordering Saluda River, branch. All the above mentioned is sold to Kitt **Smith**, only a few acres excepted sold joining Maxwells Bridge, not exceeding 12 [acres] and a Deed made for same. Witness Lidda (x) **Wilson**, Margret (x) **Stevens** [**Stephens** in one ref.], Samuel **Mares**. Signed Daniel (B) **Brown**, Elizabeth (A) **Brown**. Oath by Samuel **Meares** [sic] 8 June 1798, that he saw Daniel **Brown** with Elizabeth **Brown** his Wife (he thinks sign seal) deliver the Deed. Given before Reuben **Pyles** J.P. L.C. [No record date.]

Page 348 13 Jan 1794, James **King** Senr. (Laurens Co.) planter to Daniel **Brown** (same) planter, give 100 acres of Land more or less, upon N side of Saluda River. Border: sd. James **King** Senr. Spring, branch, river, James **Waldrop**. Witness James (x) **Waldrop**, Hugh (x) **Thompson**, James (x) **King** Junr. Signed James **King**. Witness oath by James (x) **Waldrop** 17 Nov 1796 to Reuben **Pyles** J.P. L.Co. [No record date.]

Page 348-349 7 Apr 1796, Joseph **Waldrop** (Laurens Co.) to Daniel **Brown** (same), for £20 Sterling sold 50 acres of Land more or less. Border: Saluda River, branch. Being part of 174 acres granted to sd. Joseph **Waldrop** by Charles **Pinckney**. Situate in sd. Co. on a branch that empties into Saluda River. Witness Jas. (x) **Waldrop**, William (D) **Dunlap**, George **Swindle**.

Signed Joseph **Waldrop**, Hanner **Waldrop**. Witness oath by William (D) **Dunlap** 19 Nov 1796 to Reuben **Pyles** J.P. L.C. [No record date.]

Page 349   23 Jan 1797, John **Young** (S.C.) for £40 Sterling paid by Reuben **Higgins** (Laurens Co.), sold all that Tract of Land containing 100 acres more or less, on a branch of Warriors Creek, being originally granted to Solomon **Niblet**. Border: near Spring where sd. **Niblet** formerly lived, Samuel **Dunlap**, main branch. Including the Houses & plantation where John **Coker** formerly lived. Witness John **Creecy**, Enoch **Jones**. Signed John (J) **Young**. Witness oath by Enoch **Jones** 28 Jan 1797 to Daniel **Wright** J.P. Laurens Co. [No record date.]

Page 349   16 Oct 1797, George **Clarke** (Newberry Co.) to Almon **Gaunt** (same), for £31 Sterling sold all that Tract of Land containing 100 acres more or less, in Laurens Co. on waters of Warrior Creek. Bounded N.E. & N.W. on Vacant Land, S.E. & S.W. on old Survey at time of Surveying. Being granted to James **Simpson** by Wm. **Bull** Esq. Gov. 4 May 1773 & recorded in Book XXX, page 393. Witness James **McClintock**, John **Patterson**. Signed George **Clarke**. Witness oath by John **Patterson** 20 June 1798 to Starling **Tucker** J.P. Laurens Co. [No record date.]

Page 349-350   12 Jan 1798, Reuben **Higgins** (Laurens Co.) for £35 paid by Peter **Hammonds** (same), sold all that Tract of Land containing 100 acres more or less, on a branch of Warriors Creek in sd. Co., being originally granted to Solomon **Niblet**. Border: Spring where sd. **Niblet** formerly lived, Samuel **Dunlap**, main branch. Including the houses & plantation where John **Coker** formerly lived. Witness William **Robertson**, William **Hammonds**. Signed Reuben (3) **Higgins**. Witness oath by William **Hammonds** 24 [No month.] 1798 to Daniel **Wright** J.P. Laurens Co. [No record date.]

Page 350   10 Nov 1790, Abner **Babb** (Laurens Co.) to John **Blackwell** (same), for £200 Sterling sold one certain plantation of Land containing by estimation 200 acres more or less. Being in sd. Co. on Raiborns Creek, a branch of Saluda. Bounded on all sides by Vacant Land when Surveyed. Granted to Oliver **Matthews** and by him conveyed to Joseph **Babb** and including the plantation whereon sd. John **Blackwell** now lives. Witness Richard **Jowell**, Thos. **Babb**. Signed Abner **Babb**, Martha (x) **Babb**. Oath by Thomas **Babb** 18 July 1798, that he saw Abner **Babb** & Martha **Babb** his Wife sign the deed. Given before Zech. **Bailey** J.P. Laurens Co. [No record date.]

Page 351   13 May 1798, David **Ridgeway** (Laurens Co.) to Andrew **Arnold** (same), for £50 Sterling sold a Tract of Land containing 80 acres more or less, in sd. Co. on Reedy River. Border: John **Arnold**, Peter **Acker**, Reedy River. Being originally granted to James **Tate** 4 Feb 1793, recorded in Secretary's office in Grant Book F, No.5, page 517, and conveyed from sd. **Tate** to David **Ridgway** [sic] by Deed recorded in Clerk's office in sd. Co. in Book E, page 259. Witness Wm. **Arnold**, Perry **Perritt**. Signed David **Ridgway**. Witness oath by Perry **Perritt** last day of June 1798 to Reuben **Pyles** J.P. L.Co. [No record date.]

Page 351-352   13 July 1798, Andrew **Rodgers** Sen. (Laurens Co.) for £30 Sterling paid by Andrew **Rodgers** Jun. (same), sold all that certain Tract of Land whereon sd. Andrew **Rodgers** now lives containing 84 acres more or less, being part of Two different Tracts, one containing 100 acres granted to Philimon **Harvey** & recorded in Book TTT, page 132 & by him conveyed to sd. Andrew **Rodgers** Sen. The other containing 182 acres granted to Andrew **Rodgers** Sen. & recorded in Book KKKK, page 510. Sd. tract situate in sd. Co. on beards fork of Duncans Creek, bounded by John **Rodgers**, Andw. **Rodgers** Sen., Andrew **Endsley**, James **Endsley**. Witness Ezel. S. **Roland**, Wm. **Boyd**. Signed Andrew **Rodgers**. Witness oath by Ezel. S. **Roland** 18 July 1798 to Wm. **Mitchell** J.L.C. Dower relinquished by Ann (A) **Rodgers**, wife of Andrew **Rodgers** Sen., 18 July 1798 before Wm. **Mitchell** J.L.C. [No record date.] [Includes plat.]

Page 352-353   Lease & Release, 28 June 1788, John **Sills** & Wife Caty (Ninety Six Dist.) to Richard **Hatter** (same), for £5 sold all that Tract of Land containing 53 acres in Laurens Co. on a small branch of Saluda River, being a tract laid out to sd. John **Sills**, bounding W on **Gordon**, S.E. on Vacant, S.W. on land laid out to Wm. **Luthgow**. Witness George **Peterson**, Benjamin **Hatter**, Amos **Day**. Signed John **Sills** Jun., Caty (x) **Sills**. Witness oath by Benjamin **Hatter**, Amous **Day** [sic] 11 Dec 1789 to Angus **Campbell** J.P. Laurens Co. [No record date.]

Page 353-354   13 May 1798, Margret **Holt** (Laurens Co.) hath put her Son George Washington **Holt** voluntarily as an apprentice to John **Watts** planter (same) to learn his art, trade or mystery during the Term of 9 years next ensuing. He shall serve and gladly obey his sd. Master, not see damage done by others without giving notice thereof. He shall not waste his master's goods nor lend them to others. He shall not commit Fornication nor contract Matrimony within sd. Term. He shall not play Cards, Dice or any unlawful Game. He shall not absent himself form his service nor Haunt Ale houses, Taverns or play houses. Sd. Master shall teach and instruct sd. apprentice in the Trade he occupieth & provide him sufficient meat, drink, apparel, lodging & washing. Witness Benjn. **Hatter**, Jno. **Owen**. Signed Margret (x) **Holt**, John **Watts**. Witness oath by Benjn. **Hatter** 16 July 1798 to Angus **Campbell** J.P. Laurens Co. [No record date.]

Page 354   12 May 1798, Margret **Holt** (Laurens Co.) hath put her Son William **Holt** voluntarily as an apprentice to Benjamin **Hatter** planter (Aberville Co.) to learn his art, trade or mystery during the Term of 7 years next ensuing, He shall obey, do no damage to his sd. Master nor see it done by others without giving notice thereof. He shall not waste his goods nor lend them to others. He shall not commit Fornication nor Contract Matrimony within sd. Term. He shall not play at Cards, dice or any unlawful Game. Sd. Master shall teach & instruct him in the Trade he now occupieth and provide sufficient Meat, Drink,

Apparel, Lodging & Washing. Witness John **Watts**, John **Owen**. Signed Margret (x) **Holt**, Benj. **Hatter**. Witness oath by John **Watts** 16 July 1798 to Angus **Campbell** J.P. Laurens Co. [No record date.]

Page 354-355 28 May 1798, James **Underwood** (Laurens Co.) for $200 paid by John **Copeland** (same), sold all that certain Tract of Land whereon sd. Jno. **Copeland** now lives, containing 288 acres more or less, being part of a Tract originally granted to Wm. **Gibbs** containing 1,090 acres, recorded in Book LLL, page 76 & by him conveyed to sd. James **Underwood** the above 288 acres, being laid of the N end or Square of the original granted land. Bounding on **Stuart**, Philimon **Harvey**, Patrick **Briant**, Andw. **Endsley**. Being in sd. Co. on waters of Dunkins Creek. Witness Thos. **Dendey**, Andrew **Endsley** Jun., John **McElvy**. Signed James (J) **Underwood**. Witness oath by Thos. **Dendy** [sic] 28 May 1798 to Wm. **Mitchell** J.L.C. Dower relinquished by Mary (m) **Underwood**, wife of James **Underwood**, 28 May 1798 before Wm. **Mitchell** J.L.C. [No record date.]

Page 355 30 Apr 1798, James **Underwood** (Laurens Co.) for $300 paid by John **McElvey** (same), sold all that certain Tract of Land whereon sd. John **McCalvey** [sic] now lives containing 300 acres more or less, being part of 1,090 acres originally granted to William **Gibbs**, recorded in Book LLL, page 76, and by him conveyed unto sd. James **Underwood**. Situate in sd. Co. on branches of Dunkins Creek & Bush River. Bounded at time sd. Tract laid out by Obediah **Earrige**, Peter **Kelly**, Philimon **Harvey**, Patrick **Bryant**. Witness John **Studdard**, Mary **Mitchell**. Signed James (J) **Underwood**. Witness oath by John **Studdard** 30 Apr 1798 to Wm. **Mitchell** J.L.C. Dower relinquished by Mary (m) **Underwood**, wife of James **Underwood**, 30 Apr 1798 to Wm. **Mitchell** J.L.C. [No record date.]

Page 356 23 Oct 1797, William **Gilliland** (Laurens Co.) to Henry **Morgan** (same), for £30 Sterling sold one certain Tract of Land in sd. Co. on S fork of Raiborns Creek. Border: sd. Creek, some stones near the Sholes. Containing 100 acres granted to George **Thomason** by William **Bull** Gov. in 1779. Witness Thomas (TM) **Matthews**, Robert **Gilliland**. Signed William **Gilliland**. Witness oath by Thomas (TM) **Matthews** 18 July 1798 to Jno. **Coker** J.P. Laurens Co. [No record date.]

Page 356-357 30 Dec 1794, William **Kellet** (Laurens Co.) to John **Kellet** (same), for £50 Sterling sold all that part of a Tract of Land containing 423 acres in sd. Co. on Raborns Creek, waters of Saluda River. Including in sd. tract 140 acres. Border: Creek, Cornelius **McMahan**, James **Downen**. Leaving out 3 acres at the Still. Witness Edwd. **Scarbrough**, Martin **Kellet**, James **Ryley**. Signed William **Kellet**. Witness oath by James **Ryley** 18 July 1798 to Jno. **Coker** J.P. Laurens Co. [No record date.]

Page 357 27 Feb 1798, Charles **Henderson** (Laurens Co.) to Edward **Harris** (same), for £110 Sterling sell all that Tract of Land containing 150 acres more or less, in sd. Co. on Warriors Creek, bounded N.E. on land laid out to Wm.

Vaughan, all other sides by Vacant land at time of original Survey. Being part of a Tract granted to John **Cox** by Charles G. **Montague** by plat 4 Dec 1771. Witness Charles **Gillam**, David (x) **Gibson**. Signed Charles **Henderson**, Edy (x) **Henderson**. Oath by Charles **Gillam** 18 July 1798 that he saw Charles **Henderson** & Edy his Wife sign the deed. Given before Jno. **Coker** J.P. Laurens Co. [No record date.]

Page 358-359 Lease & Release, 8 & 9 May 1784, Robert **Hanna** Esq. (Ninety Six Dist.) to Ludowick **Laird** (same), for £70 Sterling sell all that tract of 150 acres of Land on Duncans Creek, bounded N.E. & S by Robert **Hanna**, N.E. by James **McClure**, W on Benjn. **Negain** [**Nugen** in one ref.]. Surveyed for himself 24 Dec 1778. Recorded in Secretary Genl. Office in Charleston in Book CCCC, page 227. Witness Jos. **McClure**, Thomas **Searls**, George **Ross**. Signed Robert **Hanna**. Witness oath by Thomas **Searls** 12 May [No year.] to James **Montgomery** J.P. Laurens Co. [No record date.]

Page 359-360 Lease & Release, 21 & 22 Mar 1787, Ludowick **Laird** (Ninety Six Dist.) to Basil **Holland** (same), for £71 8sh 6p Sterling sold all that Tract of 225 acres of Land in Two Surveys adjoining each other, situate on both sides of Duncans Creek in sd. Dist. The first of 100 acres originally granted to James **Barton** 25 Apr 1765 and recorded in Secretary's Office in Book YY, page 456 and conveyed by sd. James **Barton** & Rebecca his Wife to James **McNees** & by him to sd. **Laird** 9 May 1777. The other survey of 150 acres was originally granted to Robert **Hanna** 25 Jan 1785 and conveyed by him to sd. **Laird** 9 May year last above. Sd. two surveys as aforesd. except 25 acres formerly conveyed to Robert **Lard**. Witness Robert **Hanna**, John **George**, Robt. **Lard**. Signed **Ludowich** (LL) **Laird**, Eliz. (C) **Laird**. Oath by Robert **Hanna** 12 Mar 1791, that he saw Ludowich **Laird** and Elizabeth **Laird** his Wife sign the deed. Given before John **Hunter** J.P. [No record date.]

Page 360 30 Apr 1798, Ambrose **Downs** sold unto William **Gary**, one lot of Blacksmiths Tools consisting of one Anvill, Vice, Bellows, Hammers, Tongs &c., in consideration of £7 10sh 2p Sterling. Provided that if sd. **Downs** shall pay the sum on the last day of June next, for redemption of the bargained premises, then this Bill of Sale to be void. Witness Joseph **Downs**, John **Kelly**. Signed Ambrose **Downs**. Witness oath by Joseph **Downs** 30 July 1798 to Jonthn. **Downs** J.P. Laurens Co. [No record date.]

Page 361 22 Oct 1797, John & William **Cuningham** (Laurens Co.) Exors. of Patrick **Cuningham** dec. for £21 14sh Sterling paid by John **McGowen** (same), sold all that Tract of Land containing 93 acres more or less, being part of 820 acres originally granted unto sd. Patrick **Cuningham**. Should sd. John **McGowen** lose any part of the aforementioned Tract by any Superior Claim, we oblige ourselves to refund $1 per acre for every acre he shall lose. Witness Margt. (m) **Cuningham**, Robert A. **Cuningham**. Signed John **Cuningham**, Wm. **Cuningham**. Witness oath by Robert A. **Cuningham** 2 June 1798 to Angus **Campbell** J.P. Laurens Co. [No record date.]

Page 361 11 Aug 1797, John **Sample** (Laurens Co.) to John **Riley** (same), for £45 Sterling sold one certain Tract of Land on waters of Cane Creek in sd. Co. containing 80 acres more or less. Granted to Christopher **Parsons** in 1775 by Charles Graville **Montague** Gov. Witness Aquila **Rusing**, Wm. **Wheeler**. Signed John **Sample**, Sarah (O) **Sample**. Oath by Aquila **Rusing** 14 July 1798, that he saw John **Sample** and Sarah his Wife sign the deed. Given before Angus **Campbell** J.P. Laurens Co. [No record date.]

Page 362 10 Feb 1792, George **Hollingsworth** and Susanna his Wife (Laurens Co.) to Robert **Hollingsworth** (same), for 10sh Sterling sold all that Tract of Land containing 140 acres, being part of 300 acres granted to Thomas **North**. Situate in sd. Co. on waters of Mudlick and Cane Creeks, commonly called and known as the Liberty Spring Tract. By sd. Thomas **North** conveyed to John **Williams** by lease & release 22 & 23 Nov 1773, and by sd. **Williams** conveyed to Abraham **Hollingsworth** by lease & release 10 & 11 Jan 1778, and devolving to sd. George **Hollingsworth** by heirship. Witness Wm. **Wheeler**, Joseph **Hollingsworth**, Lucy **Hollingsworth**. Signed George **Hollingsworth**, Susannah (x) **Hollingsworth**, Susannah (x) **Hollingsworth** [sic]. Witness oath by William **Wheeler** [No signature.] 25 [No month.] 1792 to Angus **Campbell** J.P. Laurens Co. [No record date.]

Page 362-363 12 Apr 1798, Andrew **Rodgers** (Laurens Co.) sold unto John Frances **Wolff**, one Negro Boy Paul, for $400. Witness Reuben **Pyles**, Mansil **Crisp**. Signed A. **Rodgers**. Witness oath by Reuben **Pyles** 12 Apr 1798 to Joseph **Downs** J.P. Laurens Co. [No record date.]

Page 363 30 Mar 1798, Received of John F. **Wolff** $400 for a Negro Jacob, about 26 years old. Witness Elihu **Creswell**, Frances **Ross**. Signed John **Thompson**. Witness oath by Frances **Ross** 19 July 1798 to Joseph **Downs** J.P. Laurens Co. [No record date.]

Page 363-364 (Newberry Co.) 6 July 1793, Mary **Kelly** Widow (Charles Ton Dist.) to John **Loner** (Newberry Co.) planter, for £50 sell all that Tract of Land containing 100 acres originally granted unto Lucia **Schichem** by Wm. **Bull** Esq. 19 Feb 1770 and recorded in Secretary's office in Book EEE, page 333, being in Craven Co. on the big branch of south fork, bounded N.W. by Johannes Andrew **Mitchell**, S.W. by John Jacob **Webber**, all other sides at time of original survey on Vacant Land. Whereas sd. Lucia **Schichem** died Intestate, the 100 acres devolved to sd. Mary **Kelly**, she being the heir at Law. Witness John **Subben** [Sebben in one ref.], John Adam **Sume**. Signed Mary **Kelly**. Witness oath by Major John Adam **Sumer** [sic] 23 Dec 1793 to John **Hampton** J.Q. Orangeburgh Dist. [No record date.]

Page 364 10 Jan 1794, John **Loner** (Orangburgh Dist.) planter to John **Greer** (Ninety Six Dist.), for £50 Sterling sold all that Tract of Land containing 100 acres more or less. Originally granted unto Lucia **Schichem** by Wm. **Bull** Esq. 19 Feb 1770 and recorded in Secretary's office in Book EEE, page 333, being in Laurens Co. on the big branch of the South fork. Bounded N.W. Johanna

Andrew **Mitchell**, S.W. by John Jacob **Webber**, all sides at time on Vacant land. Whereas sd. Lucia **Schichem** died Intestate, the 100 acres devolved to Mary **Kelly**, she being the heir at Law, then transferred unto sd. John **Loner**. Witness Benedict **Mayer**, Josiah **Greer**, L. A. **Hauseal**. Signed John (HL) **Loner**, Mary (x) **Loner**. Oath by Josiah **Greer** 5 June 1798 that he saw John **Loner** & Mary **Loner** his Wife sign the deed. Given before Geo. **Whitmore** J.P. Laurens Co. [No record date.]

Page 364-365 29 Dec 1797, Robert **Spence** (Laurens Co.) for £17 10sh Sterling paid by Frances **Gill** (same), sell all that certain Tract of Land containing 62-1/2 acres, being part of 250 acres granted to John **Williams** and by him conveyed unto Alexander **Manary** and by him unto sd. Robert **Spence**. Situate in sd. Co. on a branch of Duncans Creek. Border: Luke **Weeks**, land laid out to John **Williams**, land laid out to Alexr. **Manary**. Witness Robt. **Rodgers**, Richard (R) **Styles**. Signed Robert (R) **Spence**. Witness oath by Richard (R) **Styles** 9 Oct 1798 to Wm. **Mitchell** J.L.C. Dower relinquished by Agness (A) **Spence**, wife of Robert **Spence**, 9 Oct 1798 to Wm. **Mitchell** J.L.C. [No record date.] [Includes plat.]

Page 365 21 Apr 1798, William **Hughes** (Laurens Co.) for £10 15sh sold unto Robert **Paslay**, one Bay Mare about 4 ft 6 in high, named Lilley. Witness Zechariah **Bailey**, John **Adams**. Signed William (WH) **Hughes**. Witness oath by Zech. **Bailey** J.P. Laurens Co. 24 Sept 1798, certified by me. [No record date.]

Page 365-366 21 Apr 1798, Thomas **Hughes** (Laurens Co.) for £10 15sh Sterling sold unto Robert **Paslay** (same), one Black Mare about 4 ft 5 in, named Pyor, and Saddle & Rifle Gun. Witness Zechariah **Bailey**, John **Adams**. Signed Thos. **Hughes**. Witness oath by Zech. **Bailey** J.P. Laurens Co. 24 Sept 1798, certified by me. [No record date.]

Page 366 29 June 1798, Samuel **Ridgway** (Laurens Co.) for £50 Sterling paid by John **Ridgway** (same), sold all that Tract of Land containing 140 acres more or less, on E side of Reedy River. Bounded Genl. **Hugear**, S fork of Peachlands Creek including all the land that lies in the bounds of Samuel **Ridgway's** Survey from the back line to the head of John **Ridgway's** Spring branch, **Hugar** [sic]. Including the plantation whereon sd. John **Ridgway** now lives, being part of a tract originally granted to Samuel **Ridgway** by Wm. **Moultrie**, then Gov., 5 June 1786. Witness Benjn. **Nabers**, Sarah **Downs**. Signed Samuel (S) **Ridgway**. Dower relinquished by Catherine (x) **Ridgway**, wife of Saml. **Ridgway**, 29 June 1798 before Jonthn. **Downs** J.L.C. Witness oath by Benj. **Nabers** 30 June 1798 to Jonthn. **Downs** J.P. Laurens Co. [No record date.]

Page 366-367 8 Oct 1798, John **Hunter** Esq. (Laurens Co.) for £5 paid by Roger **Brown**, Thomas **Ewing** & John **Ewing** Trustees for the Use of the Baptist Church & Meetinghouse (same), sold all that tract of Land containing 2 acres on waters of Dunkins Creek in sd. Co. Being part of a tract granted to

John **Hunter** Esq. for 363 acres. Border: Ninety Six Rd. Plat certified 3 Nov 1797 by Wm. **Dunlap** D.S. Witness Jerh. **Burdine**, Wm. (x) **Cason**. Signed John **Hunter**. Witness oath by Wm. (x) **Cason** 8 Oct 1798 to James **Dillard** J.P. L.Co. [No record date.] [Includes plat.]

Page 367 3 Mar 1796, Alexander **Adair** (Laurens Co.) and Mary his Wife for £20 Sterling sold unto Benjamin **Wilson** all that Described premises and Tract of Land containing 100 acres, being part of a larger granted to sd. **Adair** by William **Moultrie**, then Gov., for 234 acres 23 Dec 1784, in the fork of Duncans Creek on lands laid out to sd. Benjn. **Wilson**, John **Walker** and sd. Benjamin **Wilson** formerly laid out by a Bounty Warrant and a large Survey formerly made by Moses **Kirkland**. Sd. 100 acres to be laid off S.E. end of aforesd. Tract. Grant recorded in Secretary's Office in Book HHH, page 197. Witness James **Lindsey**, John **Entrekin**. Signed Alexander **Adair**, Mary (x) **Adair**. Witness oath by John **Entrekin** 9 Apr 1796 to William **Hunter** J.P. Laurens Co. [No record date.]

Page 368-369 Lease & Release, 10 & 11 Feb 1771, Isaac **Grey** (Berkley Co.) Shoe Maker to Jane **Curry** (same) Sole Trader, for £500 Current money sell all that tract of Land containing 500 acres in Bartley Co. [sic] on Enoree River at a place Called Durbens Sholes. Bounding S.E. on Enoree River, all other sides by Vacant Land. Witness William **Martin**, Hannah **Rutledge**. Signed Isaac **Gray** [sic]. Witness oath by Wm. **Martin** [No signature.] 26 Feb 1772 to Wm. **Arther** J.P. Berkley Co. [No record date.]

Page 369-370 Lease & Release, 11 & 12 Jan 1785, Jane & Stepn. **Curry** Widow & planter (Camden Dist.) to John **Brockman** (Ninety Six Dist.) planter, for £150 Sterling sold all that tract of Land containing 500 acres on S side of Enoree River, known by name of Derbin Shouls. Bounded on all sides on Vacant Land at time of Survey (Except a certain Mill Seat on Durbins Creek which is reserved to sd. Jane & Stepn. **Curry**). [Release states that Mill Seat is now in dispute between sd. Jane & Stepn. **Curry** and James **Allison** who now has a Mill on sd. Seat.] Witness Nicholas **Grubb**, Judith (x) **Gambell**. Signed Jane **Curry**, Stepn. **Curry**. Witness oath by Nicholas **Grubbs** [sic] [No signature.] 12 Jan 1785 to Timo. **Rives** J.P. [No record date.]

Page 371 17 Aug 1798, George **Livingston** & Martha my Wife (Ninety Six Dist.) for £1 8sh paid by Thomas **Horner** (same), sold all that tract of Land containing 7 acres more or less, being part of a Tract formerly granted to Isaac **Livingston** by Wm. **Bull** Esq. Lieut. Gov. 23 Aug 1774, and now conveyed by George **Livingston** Son & heir of sd. Isaac **Livingston**. Situate in Laurens Co. on a small branch of Indian Creek. Border: Thomas **Horner**, land formerly Andw. & Ainsworth **Middleton** [Ainnworth in one ref.]. Witness Jacob **Horner**, Daniel (x) **Davis**. Signed George **Livingston**, Martha (x) **Livingston**. Witness oath by Daniel (x) **Davis** 8 Oct 1798 to Wm. **Neill** J.P. Plat surveyed 16 Aug 1798 by William **Hunter** D.S. [No record date.] [Includes plat.]

Page 371 26 Mar 1798, George **McCrery** & Margaret **Adair** (Laurens Co.) for £16 paid by Alexander **George** (same), sold 2/3 of all that tract of Land in sd. Co. on Dunkins Creek, a branch of Enoree, on a branch thereof called Allisons branch. Bounded when surveyed on all sides by Vacant Land. Originally granted to William **Hanna** by William **Bull** Lieut. Gov. 21 Dec 1769 and recorded in Grant Book EEE, and containing 100 acres. Witness William **Bolan** Jr., Moses **Lindsey**, Bordy **Roberts**. Signed George **McCrery**, Mararet (x) **Adair** [sic]. Witness oath by William **Bolan** [No signature.] [No date.] to George **Whitmore** J.P. [No record date.]

Page 372 Oct 1798, Thomas **Davis** (Newberry Co.) for £20 paid by David **Mayson** (Laurens Co.), sold all that tract of Land containing 90 acres more or less, in Laurens Co. on waters of Indian Creek, waters of Enoree River, bounded N.E. by John **Edwards**, N.E. by Clement **Davis**, S.E. by land supposed to be Wm. **Turpin's**, S.E. on John **Ryan**, S.E. on Ellener **Lewis** dec. Recorded in Secretary's Office in Book XXXX, page 56, granted by Thos. **Pinckney** 28 May 1788. Witness Isaac **Taylor**, John **Williams**, Elizabeth **Williams**. Signed Thomas **Davis**. Witness oath by Isaac **Taylor** [No signature.] 6 Oct 1798 to Provedence **Williams** J.P. Newberry Co. [No record date.]

Page 372-373 26 Mar 1798, Robert **Scott** (Laurens Co.) Capt. for £8 paid by Alexander **George** (same) Yeoman, sold all that tract of Land containing 90 acres in sd. Co. on Allisons branch of Dunkins Creek. Bounded by land laid out to Thomas **Allison**, land originally laid to William **Hanna**, Allisons branch. Being part of 130 acres granted to me by Wm. **Moultrie** Gov. 3 Apr 1786. Recorded in Grant Book KKKK, page 238. Witness William **Bolan**, Moses **Lindsey**, Bordy **Roberts**. Signed Robert **Scott**. Witness oath by William **Bolan** [No date.] to George **Whitmore** J.P. Dower relinquished by Isabella (x) **Scott** [Isbell in one ref.], wife of Robert **Scott**, 9 Oct 1798 before Jonthn. **Downs** J.L.C. [No record date.]

Page 373-374 25 Sept 1798, Richard **Bell** (Laurens Co.) to Benjamin **Wilson** (same), for £70 Sterling sold all that Tract of Land containing 150 acres, being granted to Elizabeth **Bowles** Widow, in sd. Co. on a small branch of Enoree River, known as South of Dunkins Creek, all sides by Vacant Land. Conveyed by sd. **Bowles** to Robert **Bell** by Lease and release in Mar 1783, then fell to Richard **Bell** by dec. of Robert **Bell**, his Father. Being the plantation where Richard **Bell** now lives. Witness Morgan **Layson** [**Lason** in one ref.], Elizabeth (x) **Wilson**, Moses **Lindsey**. Signed Richard **Bell**. Witness oath by Moses **Lindsey** 8 Oct 1798 to Geo. **Whitmore** J.P. Laurens Co. Dower relinquished by Elizabeth (E) **Bell**, wife of Richard **Bell**, 8 Oct 1798 before Jonthn. **Downs** J.L.C. [No record date.]

Page 374 2 Feb 1796, Darling Duke **Fuller** (Laurens Co.) sold unto Nancy **Simson**, one Sorrell Mare, four head of Cattle, also seven head of hogs, being for consideration of £2 cash paid by sd. Nancy, wife of William **Simson**.

Witness Peter **Roberts**. Signed Darling Duke **Fuller**. Witness oath by Peter **Roberts** 4 Aug 1798 to Zech. **Bailey** J.P. Laurens Co. [No record date.]

Page 374-375 29 Sept 1796, William **Bowen** (Laurens Co.) for £45 paid by William **Brown** (same), sold a parcel of Land containing 160 acres, being part of 3,000 acres granted about 20 July 1772 unto Alexr. **Fraser** and conveyed to James **Fraser**, from him conveyed to sd. William **Bowen**. Situate in sd. Co. on South fork of Durbins Creek, waters of Enoree River. Border: big survey, Moses **Allison**, Waggon Road, branch. Witness Joseph **Brown**, Benjamin **Brown**. Signed William **Bowen**. Witness oath by Benjamin **Brown** 8 Oct 1798 to John **Coker** J.P. Laurens Co. [No record date.]

Page 375 4 Sept 1798, James **Gambal** and Rachel my Wife (Ninety Six Dist.) for £20 paid by John **Taney** [**Tanney** in one ref.] (same), sold all that Tract of Land containing 70 acres more or less, being part of a tract originally granted to William **Paxton** dec. 27 Nov 1770. Situate in Laurens Co. on a small branch of Indian Creek. Bounded by Thos. **Horner**, George **Livingston**. Plat dated 24 Dec 1772, drawn by P. **Cuningham**. Witness Thomas **Horner**, Ambrose **Johnston**, John **Gamble**. Signed James (x) **Gambal**, Rachel (x) **Gambal**. Witness oath by John **Gambel** [sic] 8 Oct 1798 to William **Neill** J.P. [No record date.]

Page 375 15 Dec 1797, John **Coker** (Laurens Co.) to Bradock **Harris** (same), for £10 sold a certain Tract of Land containing 112 acres in sd. Co. on Bever Dam Creek, waters of Enoree River. Witness Richard **Owings**, William **Owings**. Signed John **Coker**. Witness oath by William **Owings** 16 June 1798 to Starling **Tucker** J.P. Laurens Co. [No record date.]

Page 376 17 Aug 1795, James **Garrett** (Laurens Co.) planter to George **Hughes** (same) planter, for £40 sold a certain part of a tract of Land containing 150 acres more or less, in sd. Co. on S.E. side of Warriors Creek, waters of Enoree River, which is part of 313 acres granted to sd. James **Garrett** 5 Mar 1792. Bounded E on Edward **Garrett**, part on land not known, S.W. on **Bass**, W on William **Vaughan**, N on Warrior Creek. Witness Stephen **Mullings**, Stephen **Garrett**. Signed James **Garrett**. Witness oath by Stephen **Muillings** 15 Sept 1798 to Roger **Brown** J.P. Laurens Co. [No record date.]

Page 376-377 15 Sept 1798, Stephen **Mullings** (Warriors Creek, Laurens Co.) for £30 Sterling paid by George **Hughes** (sd. Co.), sold all that tract of Land containing 30 acres more or less, being part of Land granted to William **Vaughan** containing 200 acres, 26 July 1774, and recorded in Secretary's Office in Book RRR, page wore out [sic]. Premises lie on S side of Warriors Creek. Border: Original Corner, John **Garrett**, Creek. Witness Nicholas **Garrett**, John (G) **Garrett**. Signed Stephen **Mullings**. Witness oath by Nicholas **Garrett** 15 Sept 1798 to Roger **Brown** J.P. Laurens Co. [No record date.]

Page 377 14 July 1798, John **Garrett** (Warriors Creek, Laurens Co.) for $200 paid by George **Hughes** (Warrior Cr.), sold all that Tract of Land containing 120 acres more or less, on S side of sd. Creek in sd. Co., being part of 300 acres originally granted to Thomas **Farr** 8 June 1774. Witness John (a) **Ashley**, Darkis (x) **Mullings**. Signed John **Garrett**. Witness oath by John (a) **Ashley** 14 July 1798 to Roger **Brown** J.P. Laurens Co. [No record date.]

Page 377-378   7 Mar 1798, Alexander **Fairbern** (Laurens Co.) in consideration of good Maintenance till my Death and then a Decent Christian Burial by my only Son James **Fairbern** (same), sold all that tract of Land containing 113 acres, 100 acres was granted to me by William **Bull** 11 Aug 1774, and recorded in Secretary's Office in Book RRR, page 583. The other 13 acres joins the first tract on E side and was originally granted to Joseph **Barton** & lies between sd. first tract and another tract which I still reserve for myself. Sd. premises lie on waters of Dunkins Creek in sd. Co. Witness Mathew **Brown**, David **Brown**. Signed Alexr. **Fairbern**. Witness oath by Mathew **Brown** 7 Mar 1798 to Roger **Brown** J.P. Laurens Co. [No record date.]

Page 378 17 July 1797, James **McDavid** (Laurens Co.) for £30 Sterling paid by Mathew **Cuningham** (same), sold all that tract of Land containing by Estimation 75 acres on S side of Duncans Creek in sd. Co., bounded W by Wm. **Byrd** and James **McLaughlin**, S by Benjamin **Byrd**, E by sd. **McDavid**. Witness John **McLaughlin**, James **Carwile**. Signed James **McDavid**. Witness oath by John **McLaughlin** 9 Oct 1798 to Joseph **Downs** J.P. Laurens Co. [No record date.]

Page 378-379 20 Nov 1797, Charles **Goodwin** (S.C.) Attorney at Law for $100 paid by John **Dendy** (Laurens Co.), sold all that tract of Land containing 150 acres more or less, being granted to John **McNees** 12 Oct 1771. Situate in sd. Co. on a branch of Little River, waters of Saluda River. Border: James **Martin**, David **Craddock**. The date having been first altered from 28 Apr 1798 to the 20 Nov 1797 [sic]. Witness Silv. **Walker** Jun., R. **Gantt**. Signed Chas. **Goodwin**. Witness oath by Silvs. **Walker** Jun. 9 Oct 1798 to Wm. **Mitchell** J.L.C. [No record date.]

Page 379 9 Aug 1798, Robert **Young** Sen. (Laurens Co.) for £125 paid by Charles **Goodman** (same), sold all that Tract of Land containing 200 acres more or less, in sd. Co. on waters of Little River, being part of two tracts originally granted, the one to George **Anderson**, the other to Robert **Young**. Border: Little River, James **Burnside**, Mrs. **Goodman**, Norths Creek. Witness Andrew **Rodgers** Jun., James (M) **White**. Signed Robert **Young**. Witness oath by A. **Rodgers** Jun. 20 Oct 1798 to Wm. **Mitchell** J.L.C. Dower relinquished by Rebeccah (x) **Young**, wife of Robert **Young**, 20 Oct 1798 before Wm. **Mitchell** J.L.C. [No record date.]

Page 379-380 9 Aug 1798, Received of David **Caldwell** $265 for one Negro Girl Beck. Witness R. **Creswell**. Signed Jas. **Irwin**. Witness oath by Robert **Creswell** 15 Oct 1798 to Joseph **Downs** J.P. Laurens Co. [No record date.]

Page 380 24 Jan 1796, Burgess **Guldsby** [**Gooldsby** in one ref.] (Laurens Co.) to John **Lowry**, for £30 Sterling sold all that tract of Land containing 50 acres in sd. Co. on a branch of Raburns Creek. Bounded W by Jas. **Boyd**, N.E. by land laid out for David **Smith**, S by Pierce **Butler**. Being part of a Tract originally granted to John **Williams** 7 Feb 1791 by Charles **Pinckney** Gov., recorded in Secretary's Office in Book C, No.5. Conveyed from sd. John **Williams** to Stephen **Potter**. Witness Thos. **Burton**, Charles (C) **Lowry**. Signed Birdgis **Goolsbe** [sic], Elizabeth (x) **Goolsbe**. Witness oath by Charles (C) **Lowry** Sen. 22 Oct 1798 to James **Abercrombie** J.P. Laurens Co. Received of John **Lowry** £30. Witness Jesse **Adams**. Signed Birdgess **Goolsbe** [sic]. [No record date.]

Page 380-381 24 Oct 1798, Thomas **Cox** (Laurens Co.) give unto my well beloved Son Thornton **Cox** (same), one Negro Woman Rachel, one Negro Boy Joe about 7 years of age, one Negro Girl Silvy about 3 years old, one Negro Woman Milley and her child, one Negro Man Landy about 27 years old, one Negro Girl Fanny about 12 years old, also one Negro Boy Charles about 14 years old, and also all my Household furniture and Stock, and all other substance. Witness John **Martin**, Ezel. S. **Roland**. Signed Thomas **Cox**. Witness oath by Ezel. S. **Roland** 24 Oct 1798 to Chas. **Smith** J.P. Laurens Co. [No record date.]

Page 381-382 Lease & Release, 10 & 11 July 1770, Frances **Phillips** (Charles Town) Gun Smith to Isaac **Grey** (Berkley Co. [Craven Co. in release.]) Shoe Maker, for £40 sold a certain Tract of Land containing 200 acres in Berkley Co. on Beaverdam branch. Bounded on all sides by Vacant land. Witness Richd. **Burkloe**, Philand. **Burkloe**. Signed Frances **Phillips**. Witness oath by Richard **Burkloe** [No date.] before [blank]. [No record date.]

Page 382-383 28 Feb 1772, Isaac **Grey** (Berkley Co.) to Abraham **Grey** (same), for 5sh Curt. Money sold a certain tract of Land containing 200 acres in Craven Co. on Beaverdam branch, bounded on all sides by vacant land at time of Surveying. Witness Andrew **McCrery**, Robt. **McCrery**, Isaac **Gray** Jun. Signed Isaac **Gray** Sen. [sic]. Witness oath by Robt. **MacCrery** [sic] 21 Mar 1772 to James **Ford** J.P. Berkley Co. [No record date.]

Page 383 30 Oct 1797, John **Bradshaw** & James **Bradshaw** (Christa Co., Canetuckee) for £100 paid by Elisha **Attaway** (Laurens Co.), sold all that parcel of Land in Laurens Co. granted to Francis **Phillips** by **George III**, on both sides of Beaverdam Creek, then bounded on all sides by Vacant Land. Conveyed from sd. **Phillips** to Isaac **Gray**, and from him to Abraham **Gray**, and from him to John & James **Bradshaw**. Witness Saml. **Persons**, John **Patterson**, John **Barton**. Signed John **Bradshaw**, James **Bradshaw**. Witness oath by Saml. **Persons** 6 Nov 1798 to Starling **Tucker** J.P. Laurens Co. [No record date.]

Page 383-385   Lease & Release, 20 & 21 June 1793, Robert **Gillam** Sen. (Newberry Co.) to Robert **Stuart** (Laurens Co.), for £26 14sh Sterling sold a certain tract of Land containing 89 acres in Laurens Co., being part of 348 acres granted to Robert **Gillam** Sen. about 22 May 1786, on a branch of Saluda River. Bounding Jas. **Mayson**, S.E. & N.E. on John **Cole**, N.W. on Daniel **Wood**, N.E. on Robert **Gillam**. [Plat also shows 100 acre plat of John **Cole** bordered by sd. 89 acres, Robt. **Gillam**, George **Taylor**.] Witness Wm. **Swift**, Uriah **Stone**, Jas. (x) **Taylor**. Signed Robert **Gillam** Sen. Witness oath by James (x) **Taylor** 11 May 1795 to Angus **Campbell** J.P. Laurens Co. [No record date.] [Includes plat.]

Page 385   17 Aug 1798, James **Jones** (Laurens Co.) in consideration of the Love, Good will and affection I bear towards my Son Miles **Jones** (same), give a certain Negro Boy Tom about one year old. Witness Jesse **Jones**, Joseph **Jones**. Signed James **Jones**. Witness oath by Jesse **Jones** 17 Aug 1798 to George **Whitmore** J.P. Laurens Co. [No record date.]

Page 385   17 Aug 1798, James **Jones** (Laurens Co.) in consideration of the Love, Good will & affection I bear towards my Son Benjamin **Jones** (same), give a certain Negro Boy about 3 years old, called Squire. Witness Jesse **Jones**, Joseph **Jones**. Signed James **Jones**. Witness oath by Jesse **Jones** 17 Aug 1798 to George **Whitmore** J.P. Laurens Co. [No record date.]

Page 385-386   29 Oct 1798, John **Workman** (Laurens Co.) for $200 paid by Edmond **Lear Wood** (same), sold all that Tract of Land containing 100 acres more or less, being part of 600 acres originally granted to sd. Edmond **Lear Wood** 3 Oct 1785 by William **Moultrie** Esq. Gov. Border: Daniel **Osbourn**, Mark **Moore**. Situate in sd. Co. on Beaver Dam Creek. Witness Samuel **Franks**, William **Moore**. Signed John **Workman**. Witness oath by Samuel **Franks** 29 Oct 1798 to Chas. **Smith** J.P. L.Co. [No record date.]

Page 386   12 Sept 1798, David **Ridgeway** (Laurens Co.) for $300 paid by James **Poole** (S.C.), sold all that Tract of Land containing 141 [acres] more or less, on W side of Reedy River, 100 acres granted to Jonathan **Downs** & 25 granted to Elijah **Majors** and 16 to James **Tate**, bounded S & S.E. on Jas. **Poole**, S & S.W. John **Arnold**, N & N.W. on Andrew **Arnold**, E by sd. River. Conveyed from sd. Jonathan **Downs** & James **Tate** to sd. David **Ridgeway**. Witness Andrew (x) **Arnold**, William **Downs** Jun. Signed David **Ridgway** [sic]. Witness oath by Andrew (x) **Arnold** 12 Sept 1798 to Jonthn. **Downs** J.P. Laurens Co. Dower relinquished by Elizabeth (x) **Ridgway**, wife to David **Ridgway**, 12 Sept 1798 before Jonthn. **Downs** J.L.C. [No record date.]

Page 387   12 Sept 1798, Andrew **Arnold** (Laurens Co.) for 130 [No currency.] paid by James **Poole** (S.C.), sold all that Tract of Land containing 78 acres more or less, on W side of Ready River. Granted to James **Tate** and from him conveyed to David **Ridgway** and from him conveyed to sd. Andrew **Arnold**. Witness David **Ridgway**, William **Downs** Jun. Signed Andrew (x) **Arnold**. Witness oath by David **Ridgway** 12 Sept 1798 to Jonthn. **Downs** J.P. Laurens Co. Dower relinquished by Polley (x) **Arnold**, wife of Andrew **Arnold**, 12 Sept 1798 to Jonthn. **Downs** J.L.C. [No record date.]

Page 387-388 29 Dec 1797, Lewis **Saxon** (Laurens Co.) to Drury **Goolsby** (same) planter, for £60 sold all that Tract of Land containing 200 acres more or less, in sd. Co., on Buck Head branch of Enoree. Bounded when surveyed S on Joseph **Parsons**, all other sides on Vacant land. Originally granted to Thos. **Hughes** by William **Moultrie** Esq. Gov. and by sd. **Hughes** conveyed to Lewis **Saxon**. Witness Mansil **Crisp**, Joseph (J) **Parsons**. Signed Lewis **Saxon**. Witness oath by Joseph (J) **Parsons** 26 Nov 1798 to Starling **Tucker** J.P. Laurens Co. [No record date.]

Page 388-389 Lease & Release, 1 Mar 1781, Robert **McNees** (Craven Co.) planter to William **Taylor** (same) planter, for £700 Current Money sold all that Tract of Land containing 150 acres on waters of Little River, bounded N.W. on land laid out on bounty proprietors name not known, all other sides on Vacant land when Surveyed. Granted 27 Nov 1770 by William **Bull** Esq. Lieut. Gov. unto Robert **Tweedy**. Recorded in Secretary's office in Book K, No.10, page 319. Robert **Tweedy** did on 1 Oct 1777, give a lease and release unto sd. Robert **McNees**. Witness Robt. **Ross**, Robt. **Speer**, Augness (x) **Taylor** [sic]. Signed Robert **McNees**. Witness oath by Agness (x) **Taylor** 26 July 1798 to Roger **Brown** J.P. Laurens Co. [No record date.]

Page 390 26 Mar 1791, William **Price** am bound unto William **Taylor** for £90 Sterling to be paid on or before 2 Dec next. Condition is such that if William **Price** makes a good right to 50 acres of Land more or less, adjoining sd. **Taylor**, unto above Wm. **Taylor** on or before 25 Dec next, then the obligation is void. [No witnesses named.] Signed Wm. **Price**. Oath by William **Taylor** 20 July 1798, that William **Price**, now deceased, signed the within Bond. Given before Roger **Brown** J.P. Laurens Co. [No record date.]

Page 390 21 Nov 1794, Clabourn **Sims** (Laurens Co.) to William **Taylor** Jun. (same), for £21 Sterling sold a certain Tract of Land containing 200 acres more or less, being part of 450 acres granted unto William **Williamson** 2 Apr 1773 by William **Bull**, on Buck head creek, waters of Enoree River. Border: **Marada**, Luke **Waldrop**, branch. Witness David **Speers**, Andw. **Speers**, Richard **Taylor**. Signed Claborn **Sims** [sic]. Witness oath by Richard **Taylor** 26 July 1798 to Roger **Brown** J.P. Laurens Co. [No record date.]

Page 390-391 26 Nov 1798, Drury **Goolsbey** (Laurens Co.) for $200 paid by Samuel **Parsons** (same) planter, sell three feather Beds and furniture; two Saddles; twelve head of Hogs; one Cow; three Cow hides; one Brown Bay Gilden, 14-1/2 hands high, 4 years old; one Bay Gilden, 13-1/2 hands high, 5 years old; one Roan Mare, 7 years old, 13 hands high; one Black Colt; one pair of Saddle Bags; one Hackele; one chest; one linning wheel; two arm chairs;

three augers; two Chizzel; one pair of Stillards; one sledge & three Hand hammers; one Rifle Gun; one Shot Gun; one pair of Chain Traees; one bedstead and nine pewter Basons; twelve pewter plates; three Dishes; one dozen knives & forks; one Coffee pot; two Iron Pots; one Dutch Oven & Skillet; one Plough; one Hoe; one Mattock; one Ax; two flat Irons; one padlock. Witness Sterling **Tucker** [sic], James (x) **Hughes**. Signed Drury **Gollsbey**. Witness oath 24 Dec 1798, by Starling **Tucker** J.P. Laurens Co. for himself. [No record date.]

Page 391 26 Nov 1798, Drury **Goolsbey** (Laurens Co.) to Samuel **Persons** (same) planter, for £60 sold all that Tract of Land containing 200 acres more or less, in sd. Co. on Buck head branch of Enoree. Bounding when Surveyed S on Joseph **Persons**, all other sides on Vacant land. Originally granted to Thomas **Hughes** by William **Moultrie** Esq. Gov. and by sd. **Hughes** conveyed to Lewis **Saxon**. Witness Starling **Tucker**, James (x) **Hughes**. Signed Drury **Goolsbey**. Witness oath 24 Dec 1798, by Starling **Tucker** J.P. Laurens Co. for himself. [No record date.]

Page 391-392 9 Oct 1791, Thomas **Wadsworth** & William **Turpin** (S.C.) to John **Milam** (same), for £45 Sterling sold all that Tract of Land containing 150 acres more or less, on E side of Little River, being part of a Tract originally granted to John **Cargill**, and by him Transmitted to his Son Cornelius, and by him sold to David **Bailey**, which sd. tract was purchased by sd. **Wadsworth** & **Turpin** at Sheriff's Sale. Witness Silv. **Walker**, Joseph (J) **Groves**. Signed Thomas **Wadsworth** for **Wadsworth** & **Turpin**. Witness oath by Silv. **Walker** 1 Dec 1798 to Jno. **Davis** J.P. Laurens Co. [No record date.]

Page 392-393 10 June 1794, George **Ross** and Isabala [sic] his Wife (Laurens Co.) to John **Craig** (same), for £25 Sterling sold all that tract of Land containing 100 acres in Ninety Six Dist. on Duncans Creek, being a Survey made by Robert **Hanna** Dep. Surv., certified for 12 June 1784. Originally granted unto sd. George **Ross** 3 Apr 1786, recorded in Secretary's Office in Grant Book JJJJ, page 104. Witness Joseph **Mitchell**, William **Craig**. Signed George **Ross**, Isabell **Ross**. Witness oath by William **Craig** 20 Dec 1798 to James **Dillard** J.P. Laurens Co. [No record date.]

Page 393 17 Sept 1798, John **Craig** (Laurens Co.) for $255 paid by Alexander **Filson** [**Fillson** in one ref.] (same), sold all that Tract of Land containing 150 acres more or less, on both sides of Duncans Creek, 100 of which was originally granted to George **Ross** 3 Apr 1786, as represented by a plat 12 June 1784 and recorded in Grant Book JJJJ, page 104.The other 50 acres being part of 200 acres granted to James **Adair** Sen. 11 Aug 1774 & sd. James **Adair** and Elener his Wife did in Feb 1784 convey unto John **Jones** 50 acres, border: John **McCrery's** spring branch, John **Adair**, Vacant land, James **Montgomery**, John **McCrery**. Hannah **Jones** and William **Jones** her Son and Mary his Wife did convey 50 acres of aforesd. Tract unto sd. John **Craig**, laying on N side of sd. tract, bordering on Montgomerys branch, **Montgomery**, John **Craig**. Witness William **Craig**, James **Craig**. Signed John

(C) **Craig**. Witness oath by William **Craig** 20 Dec 1798 to James **Dillard** J.P. Laurens Co. Dower relinquished by Issaballa (x) **Craig**, wife of John **Craig**, 19 Sept 1798 before Wm. **Mitchell** J.L.C. [No record date.]

Page 394 15 Nov 1796, Lewis **Devall** (Laurens Co.) for £40 paid by Elizabeth **Duke** (same), sold all that Tract of 500 acres more or less, being part of 903 acres in sd. Co. on a branch of Warriors Creek. Surveyed 19 Jan 1792 by John **Rodgers** D.S., entered in Secretary's Office Book F, No.5, page 352, signed by Gov. **Moultrie** 4 Mar 1793. Border: branch, Reubin **Kelly**, John **Word**. Witness Abel **Parker**, Earbin (x) **Cornet**. Signed Lewis **Duvall** [sic]. Witness oath by Abel **Parker** 16 Jan 1799 to Joseph **Downs** J.P. Laurens Co. [No record date.]

Page 394-395 12 Dec 1798, Thomas **Roberts** (Laurens Co.) for £30 Current Money paid by John **Copeland** black smith (same), sold all that Tract of Land containing 79 acres more or less in sd. Co. on Bush River or Creek. Being part of 250 acres originally granted to James **Anderson** dec. and since conveyed by John **Hunter** & George **Anderson** Esq. to Thomas **Roberts**. Witness Wm. **Saxon**, Jas. (J) **Underwood**. Signed Thomas **Roberts**. Witness oath by Wm. **Saxon** 12 Dec 1798 to Wm. **Mitchell** J.L.C. Dower relinquished by Mary (x) **Roberts**, wife of Thomas **Roberts**, 12 Dec 1798 before Wm. **Mitchell** J.L.C. [No record date.]

Page 395 12 Dec 1798, Thomas **Roberts** (Laurens Co.) for £14 Current Money paid by John **Copeland** black smith (same), sold all that Tract of Land containing 37-3/4 acres in sd. Co. on Bush River or Creek. Being part of 250 acres granted to Michael **Dickson** and by him sold to Rev. Robert **McClintock** and above 37-3/4 acres conveyed to sd. Thomas **Roberts**. Witness Wm. **Saxon**, James (J) **Underwood**. Signed Thomas **Roberts**. Witness oath by Wm. **Saxon** 12 Dec 1798 to Wm. **Mitchell** J.L.C. Dower relinquished by Mary (O) **Roberts**, wife of Thomas **Roberts**, 12 Dec 1798 before Wm. **Mitchell** J.L.C. [No record date.]

Page 396 12 Dec 1798, Thomas **Roberts** (Laurens Co.) for £50 Current Money paid by John **Copeland** Black Smith (same), sold all that Tract of Land containing 112 acres more or less, in sd. Co. on waters of Bush River, being part of 140 acres originally granted to James **Doherty**, conveyed from him to James **Young**, from sd. **Young** to Samuel **Saxon**, from sd. **Saxon** to sd. Thomas **Roberts**. Witness Wm. **Saxon**, Jas. (J) **Underwood**. Signed Thomas **Roberts**. Witness oath by Wm. **Saxon** 12 Dec 1798 to Wm. **Mitchell** J.L.C. Dower relinquished by Mary (x) **Roberts**, wife of Thomas **Roberts**, 12 Dec 1798 to Wm. **Mitchell** J.L.C. [No record date.]

Page 396 14 July 1797, Marah **Barker** on her oath sayeth that a certain Rosannah **Wooten**, which passed for a Widow, was Married to Laurens **Barker**. Some years after they were married, it was reported that her Husband John **Wooten** was yet alive and sd. Rosannah for some time denied her Husband John **Wooten** was alive, but after some time she confessed that he was yet alive and that she would leave sd. Laurens **Barker** and would not live any longer with him for if she lived and died so she should go to heal and accordingly she left sd. **Barker**, acknowledging she was no Lawful wife to sd. Laurens **Barker**. Witness Daniel **Wright** J.P. Signed Marah (x) **Barker**. [No record date.]

Page 397   17 Oct 1793, Harculas Daniel **Bize** by his Attorney John **Hunter** (Laurens Co.) to Lewis **Saxon** (same), for £15 Sterling sold all that tract of 225 acres of Land in sd. Co. on waters of Reaburns Creek. Bounding on John **Manley**, James **Cuningham**, James **Irwin**, Lewis **Saxon**, Benjamin **Williams**, Berry **Harvey**. Being part of 500 acres originally granted to Pierce **Butler** Esq. and by him conveyed to Harculas Daniel **Bize** 9 July 1792, and now by John **Hunter** by virtue of a power of Attorney from sd. **Bize** 1 June 1793. Witness Lyall **Allen** [sic], Thomas **Holmes**. Signed John **Hunter** Atty. for Harculas Danl. **Bize**. Witness oath by Lydall **Allen** 2 Feb 1797 to Chas. **Allen** J.P. L.Co. Plat certified 17 Oct 1793 by John **Hunter** D.Sur. [No record date.] [Includes plat.]

Page 397-398   8 Jan 1799, William **Rodgers** (Laurens Co.) to Peter **Kelly** (same), for £16 6sh 8p Sterling sold one certain Tract of Land in sd. Co. on Norths Creek, a branch of Little River, bounding N.E. by Michael **Waldrop**, S.E. by Wm. **Rodgers**, S.W. by Wm. **Harris**, containing 50 acres more or less. Witness John **Strain**, James **Hendricks**. Signed Wm. **Rodgers**. Witness oath by John **Strain** 10 Jan 1799 to Wm. **Mitchell** J.L.C. Dower relinquished by Nancy (x) **Rodgers**, wife of William **Rodgers**, 10 Jan 1799 before Wm. **Mitchell** J.L.C. [No record date.] [Includes plat.]

Page 398   20 May 1798, Elijah **Barker** (Laurens Co.) for £35 Sterling sold unto James **Mills** (same), a Dun Mare and a Cow and Yearling, ten head of hogs, 7 acres of Corn and all my Household furniture. Witness Francis **Glenn**. Signed Elijah **Barker**. Condition is such that if sd. Elijah **Barker** pays the sum above before 25 Dec 1799, then the obligation is void. Witness oath by Francis **Glen** [sic] 5 Nov 1798 to Chas. **Smith** J.P. Laurens Co. [No record date.]

Page 398-399   20 Nov 1798, Charles **Miller** (Laurens Co.) for £20 Sterling paid by Bennet **Langston** (same), sold all that tract of Land containing 67 acres more or less, being on N side of Duncans Creek, on waters of sd. Creek in sd. Co. Originally granted to Anthony **Miller** 15 Mar 1775 by William **Bull** and recorded in Secretary's Office in Book WWW, page 35. Witness David **Dunlap**, William **Miller**. Signed Charles **Miller**. Witness oath by David **Dunlap** 20 Nov 1798 to Joseph **Downs** J.P. Laurens Co. [No record date.]

Page 399   1 Jan 1796, Randolph **Cook** (Laurens Co.) to John **Lowery** (same), for £20 Sterling paid by Burgess **Goolsby** in behalf of John **Lowery**, for a certain Tract of Land in sd. Co. on Reedy fork, a branch of Little River, containing 88 acres more or less. Border: **Butler**. Being part of a Tract conveyed from John **Hunter** to Randolph **Cook**, and from him to Burges **Goolsby** [sic], and now conveyed from sd. **Goolsby** to John **Lowery**. Witness

Charles **Lowry** Jun. [**Lowery** in one ref.], Charles (C) **Lowry** Sr. Signed Randolph (O) **Cook**, Polly **Cook**. Witness oath by Charles (C) **Lowery** Sen. [sic] 22 Oct 1798 to James **Abercrombie** J.P. Laurens Co. [No record date.]

Page 400 5 June 1798, Whereas by virtue of a writ issued from the Court of Common pleas at suit of Elizabeth **Swift** against the Admrs. of William **Swift** dec., directed William **Tennent** (Sheriff of Ninety Six Dist.) to seize a certain Tract of Land. The tract was exposed to public sale at Cambridge in sd. Dist. and struck off to sd. Elizabeth **Swift** for $160. Sd. tract being in sd. Dist. on waters of Mudlick, containing 150 acres more or less, being part of 300 acres surveyed for William **Caldwell** 25 Mar 1768. One other tract containing 200 acres more or less, on waters of Mudlick, surveyed for John **Robertson** 28 Jan 1771. Also one other Tract containing 150 acres more or less, on waters of Little River, surveyed for Oliver **Telles** 18 Nov 1768. Witness Jas. **Scott**, Stan More **Butler**. Signed Wm. **Tennent**, Shiff. 96 Dist. Witness oath by Stan More **Butler** Gentleman 9 Apr 1799 to Wm. **Nibbs** J.Q. Ninety Six Dist. [No record date.]

Page 400-401 17 Nov 1798, Elizabeth **Wright** (Pittsylvania Co., Va.) appoint my Husband **Wright** my Attorney to recover and receive of Lewis **Graves** Exor. of Margaret **Hendrick** dec. (Laurens Co.) Admr. of Hance **Hendricks** dec., who was my Father, every sum of Money due me from the Estate of sd. Hance **Hendricks**, and which may be due me by the last Will and Testament of sd. Margaret **Hendricks** [sic]. [No witness.] Signed Eliza. (\\) **Wright**. Acknowledged 19 Nov 1798 at Court for Pittsylvania Co. by Elizabeth **Wright** and ordered the Letter of Attorney be recorded. Signed Will. **Tunstall** C.P.C. Certification on 23 Nov 1798, that the Letter of Attorney was recorded by William **Tunstall** Clerk of Pittsylvania Co., Va. Court. [No record date.]

Page 401 10 Oct 1797, William **Spurgin** and John **Spurgin** (Laurens Co.) for 135 Silver Dollars paid by James **McClintock** planter (same), sold one certain Negro Girl Silvy, about 12 years old. Provided that if sd. William and John **Spurgin** shall pay the sum on or before 2 Jan 1799, then this Bill of Sale shall be void. Witness Starling **Tucker**, John **McClintock**. Signed William **Spurgin**, John **Spurgin**. Witness oath 12 Jan 1799, by Starling **Tucker** J.P. Laurens Co., for himself. [No record date.]

Page 401-402 22 Oct 1798, Joseph **Babb** (Laurens Co.) to Abner **Pyles** (same), in consideration of a Negro Boy [No name.] for which he has my Bill of Sale, sold a certain tract of Land in sd. Co. on waters of Kain Creek, containing 100 acres more or less, being part of 150 acres granted to Cornelius **Cargill** dec. Border: head of bee branch, **White**, John **Carter**, Paul **Finley**, **Dudgen**. Witness Richard **Shackelford**, George **Shackelford**. Signed Joseph **Babb**. Witness oath by Richard **Shackelford** 9 Feb 1799 to Chas. **Smith** J.P. Laurens Co. [No record date.]

Page 402 11 Feb 1799, John **Davenport** (Laurens Co.) sold unto Ezekiel Stephen **Roland**, one certain Negro Boy Joe, for £25. Witness George

Madden, Chas. **Smith**. Signed John (x) **Davenport**. Witness oath by George **Madden** 11 Feb 1799 to Charles **Saxon** J.P. Laurens Co. [No record date.]

Page 402-404 Lease & Release, 6 & 7 Sept 1774, Joseph **Babb** (Ninety Six Dist.) to John **Ferguson** (same), for £100 Current money sold all that Tract of Land containing 100 acres in Craven Co., on waters of Mudlick Creek, being part of 350 acres originally granted to John **Filpot** 25 Aug 1769 by William **Bull** Esq. Lieut. Gov. Conveyed by sd. **Filpot** unto sd. Joseph **Babb** by lease and release 12 & 13 July 1772. Border: Joseph **Babb**, Allen **Brown**. Witness Hugh **McMurry**, Hugh **Abernathey**, Ellener (x) **Tweed**. Signed Joseph **Babb**, Mary **Babb**. Witness oath by Hugh **Abernathey** 3 Apr 1790 to George **Anderson** J.P. Laurens Co. Plat certified 6 Sept 1774 by John **Caldwell** D.Sur. [No record date.] [Includes plat.]

Page 404 [No date.], Pursuant to an order of Council dated this day, I certify for Richard **Ballard** a Tract of 150 acres in Berkley Co. on Reedy River, surveyed for him 21 Mar 1771. Bounding N.E. on Robert **Box**, N.W. on Jacob **Wright**, all other sides on Vacant Lands. [No signature.] [No record date.]

Page 404 10 Aug 1789, I promise to pay unto Mary **Ferguson** £100 Sterling to which I bind myself. Condition that if James **Ferguson** shall make a Good Right to a certain Tract of Land containing 100 acres, whereon John **Ferguson** formerly lived on Mudlick waters, then the note to be void. Signed George **Anderson**, Benjamin **Carter**. Signed James **Ferguson**. Witness oath by George **Anderson** 20 Feb 1799 to Ruben **Pyles** J.P. Laurens Co. [No record date.]

Page 404-405 15 Jan 1799, John **Elleman** (Newberry Co.) planter for £70 Sterling paid by Abel **Thomas** (Laurens Co.), sold all that Tract of Land containing 189 acres in Laurens Co. on waters of Reedy River, being part of 1,300 acres granted to Thomas **Shubrick** and conveyed by him to William **Williamson**, and by him to John **Rutledge** Esq. Jun., and from him to John **Hunter** Esq., Attorney to sd. John **Rutledge**, to sd. John **Elleman**. Recorded by Clerk of Laurens Co. in Book F, page 248. Witness Even **Thomas**, Joanna **Pearson**, Richard **Clegg**. Signed John **Elleman**. Witness oath by Even **Thomas** 18 Feb 1799 to James **Abercrombie** J.P. Laurens Co. [No record date.]

Page 405 7 May 1795, David **Speers** (Laurens Co.) to John **Steward** Stiller (same), for £10 Sterling sold a certain Tract of Land containing 37 acres in sd. Co. on Beards fork, waters of Dunkins Creek. Bounded N.E. by land laid out to David **Studdart**, S.W. by large Survey & Vacant land. Witness John **Copeland**, Robert (R) **Spence**. Signed David **Speers**. Witness oath by Robert (R) **Spence** 18 Feb 1799 to Zech. **Bailey** J.P. Laurens Co. [No record date.]

Page 405-406 24 July 1798, John **Rutledge** (Charleston) by my Attorney John **Hunter** Esq. (Laurens Co.) for £42 Sterling paid by Richard **Gains** (sd. Co.), sold all that Tract of Land containing by Imputation 160 acres more or less.

Situate in Laurens Co. in the fork of Saluda & Reedy Rivers on Walnut Creek. Joining land laid out to John **Robertson**, **Williamson**, **Robertson**, Waggon Road. Being part of 3,000 acres granted to Thomas **Shubrick** and by him conveyed to William **Williamson** & by him to sd. John **Rutledge**. Witness James **Powell**, Thomas **Gaines**. Signed John **Rutledge** by his Atty. John **Hunter**. Witness oath by James **Powell** 18 Feb 1799 to Joseph **Downs** J.P. Laurens Co. [No record date.]

Page 406 4 Jan 1799, Charles **Tennent** (Charleston) for $100 paid by Robert **Gains** (Laurens Co.), sold all that Tract of Land containing 100 acres in sd. Co. on waters of Reedy River, bounded E on Robert **Box**, N on unknown. Witness Wm. **Tennent**, Jas. **Scott**. Signed Chas. **Tennent**. Witness oath by Jas. **Scott** 4 Feb 1799 to Wm. **Nibbs** J.Q. Ninety Six Dist. [No record date.]

Page 406-407 29 Jan 1799, Wm. G. **Foster** (Laurens Co.) planter for £60 Sterling paid by John **Stils** (same), sold all that Tract of Land containing 110 acres more or less, being part of 500 acres, dated 31 July and granted to James **Smith**, lying on Coxes Creek, waters of Enoree in sd. Co. Border: Aaron **Lynch**, John **Lynches** Spring branch, Jesse **Holder**, Samuel **Stils**. Witness John **Lynch**, Samuel **Stile** [sic]. Signed Wm. G. **Foster**, Judah (x) **Foster**. Witness oath by John **Lynch** 29 Jan 1799 to Roger **Brown** J.P. Laurens Co. [No record date.]

Page 407 28 Dec 1799, Silvanus **Adams** (Laurens Co.) to Henry Main **Stromer** (Charleston Dist.), for £200 Sterling sold all that Tract of Land containing 200 acres more or less, according to a plat to the Original Grant, but by a Resurvey containing 325 acres. Situate in sd. Co. on waters of Reedy River. Granted to Peter **Meal** in June 1774, and conveyed by him by Lease & Release to Patrick **Cuningham** & from thence by Deed 10 May 1798 to sd. Silvanus **Adams**. Witness William **Jones**. Signed S. **Adams**. Witness oath by William **Jones** 20 Dec 1798 to Wm. **Dunington** J.P. Charleston Dist. [No record date.]

Page 407 15 Jan 1799, Samuel **Powell** (Laurens Co.) sold unto Daniel **Osborn** Sen., one Negro Girl Silvey, for $300. Witness Silv. **Walker** Jun., Wm. **Glenn**, Sarah **Walker**. Signed Samuel (x) **Powell**. Witness oath by Silv. **Walker** Jun. 18 Feb 1799 to Chas. **Smith** J.P. Laurens Co. [No record date.]

Page 408 10 Oct 1798, John **Gent** (Abberville Co.) for £100 Current Money paid by David **Mayson** (Laurens Co.), sold all that Tract of Land containing 100 acres more or less, in sd. Co. on waters of Bush River. Originally granted unto Jacob **Jones** 19 Nov 1772, and fell unto his Son Charles **Jones** as heir at Law, and by him conveyed by Lease and Release 31 Mar 1796 unto Benjamin **Lewis**, and from him conveyed unto John **Gent** by Lease and Release. Bounded at time of original survey on land laid out unto Thomas **Dalrymple**. Witness Jonthn. **Downs**, John **Mitchell**. Signed John **Gent**. Witness oath by Jonthn. **Downs** 15 Nov 1798 to John **Coker** J.P. Laurens Co. Dower relinquished by Susannah **Gent** [Sukey in signature.], wife of John **Gent**, 10 Oct 1798 before Jonthn. **Downs** J.L.C. [No record date.]

Page 408-409   14 Jan 1799, John **Comer** (Union Co.) for $50 paid by John **Cox** (Laurens Co.), sold all that Tract of Land conveyed by Richard **Rowland** to John **Comer** and is a part of land conveyed by Aquilla **Hall** by Lease and Release to Isaac **Neighbours** and from him to Charles **Parret**. Bounded on N by Mark **More**, E by sd. John **Cox**, S by a small Creek which divides it from part of sd. original tract now sold to Joseph **Cox** and a Bond given sd. Joseph for the conveyance thereof. Containing by estimation 34-1/2 acres more or less. Witness John **Davis**, Mansfield **Walker**. Signed John (x) **Comer**. Witness oath by Mansfield **Walker** 14 Jan 1799 to John **Davis** J.P. Laurens Co. [No record date.]

Page 409   18 Oct 1798, Silvanus and Horatio **Walker** (Laurens Co.) for $428.57 paid by Samuel **Powell** (same), sold one Negro Man Ceasar, 25 years old. Witness G. **Watts**, Memn. **Walker** [Mansfield in one ref.], John **Davis**. Signed Silv. **Walker**, Hor. **Walker**. Witness oath by George **Watts** 18 Feb 1799 to Zech. **Bailey** J.P. Laurens Co. [No record date.]

Page 409-410   23 Nov 1798, Moses **Saunders** and Mary his Wife (Franklin Co., Ga.) to James **Holly** (Laurens Co.), for £100 sold one certain Tract of Land in Co. aforesd. on Beaverdam Creek, containing 250 acres more or less. Bounded S.E. on lands laid out to Henry **Oneal**, N.W. on land laid to Henry Stone **Parris**, all other sides Vacant. Granted 22 Dec 1772. Witness Jonthn. **Downs**, Moses **Saunders** Jun. Signed Moses **Saunders**, Mary **Saunders**. Witness oath by Jonthn. **Downs** 19 Feb 1799 to William **Neill** J.P. Laurens Co. Dower relinquished by Mary (x) **Saunders**, wife of Moses **Saunders**, 24 Nov 1798 before Jonthn. **Downs** J.L.C. [No record date.]

Page 410-411   3 Sept 1796, Fredrick **Frasure** Esq. (Charleston) by his Attorney John **Hunter** Esq. (Laurens Co.), for £83 paid by Lydall **Allen** (Co. aforesd.), sold a certain Tract of Land containing 420 acres more or less, 200 of which was granted to Thomas **Lantriss** by Wm. **Bull** Lieut. Gov. 10 July 1770. Pursuant to a precept by John **Troup** Esq. Dep. Surv. Genl. 3 Feb 1767, surveyed and laid out unto Thomas **Lantriss**, 200 acres on N side of Saluda River on Raiborns Creek. Bound S.E. by land surveyed for Thomas **Owens**, other sides by vacant. The other 220 acres being part of 950 acres originally granted to Wm. **Williamson** and conveyed by him to sd. Fredrick **Frasure** by Lease and Release 23 & 24 Nov 1779. Border: Zack. **Matthews**, land laid out to Thos. **Lantriss**, Widow **Martin**, part of sd. survey. Both tracts adjoining each other on Rabourns Creek, waters of Reedy River in Laurens Co. Witness Wm. **Dunlap**, Margret **Dunlap**. Signed John **Hunter** Atty. for Fredrick **Frasure**. Witness oath by Wm. **Dunlap** 19 Feb 1799 to Joseph **Downs** J.P. Laurens Co. Plat certified 20 May 1767 by Richd. **Winn** D.S. Plat certified 10 Oct 1793 by John **Hunter** D.S. True copy taken from the original and examined 24 Jan 1792 by Peter **Bremar** Pro. Surv. Genl., Columbia. [No record date.] [Includes plats.]

Page 411-412 (Greenville Co.) 18 Oct 1798, Philip **Sherril** (sd. Co.) to Isaac **Dial** (Laurens Co.), for £100 Sterling sold all that tract of Land containing 250 acres more or less, in Laurens Co. on waters of Rabourns Creek on a branch formerly known as Hellums branch. Bounded N.E. by John **Williams** and Vacant land, N.W. by John **Williams**, S.E. & N by Vacant land at time of surveying. Original grant recorded in Secretary's Office in Book OOO, page 634. Witness Benjamin **Holley**, Briton (N) **Neal**. Signed Philip (x) **Sherril**. Witness oath by Benjamin **Holley** [No signature.] 18 Oct 1798 to George **Salmon** J. Greenville Co. Dower relinquished by [blank] **Sherril**, wife of Philip **Sheril**, 18 Oct 1798 before George **Salmon** J.G.C. [No record date.]

Page 412 27 Dec 1798, Oath by Thomas **Cargill** that about 25 or 30 years ago, he was present when David **Craddock** and John **Caldwell** the Surv. was running the dividing line between sd. **Craddock** and John **McNees**, and all concerned admitted to be the right Divisional line. The same line has on 15 Dec 1778, been run again by sd. Thos. **Cargill**. Given before John **Davis** J.P. Laurens Co. Border: Jno. **Dendy**, **Craddock**, Little River, branch. Plat of 74-1/2 acres certified 15 Dec 1798 by Thos. **Cargill** D.S. I certify that the above plat contains 9 acres and 36 Perches, 15 Dec 1798, by Thos. **Cargill** D.S. [No record date.] [Includes plat.]

Page 412-413 31 Mar 1798, Richard **Puckett** (Laurens Co.) for $334-1/4 paid by James **Mauldin** (same), sold all that Tract of Land containing 100 acres more or less, in sd. Co. on waters of Cane Creek. Bounding on John **McGown**, Robert **Cuningham**, John **Robertson**, Capt. Jno. **Watts**, Joseph **Hollingsworth**, Jno. **Riley**, Levey **Hollingsworth** [Levy in one ref.], spring branch. Originally granted to Christopher **Parsons**, and by the heirs of sd. **Parsons** conveyed to Mary **Puckett**, and by William **McMurtrey**, husband of sd. Mary, conveyed to Richard **Puckett**. Witness Clemment **Wells**, Jonan. **Johnson**. Signed Richard **Puckett**. Witness oath by Clemment **Wells** 29 Sept 1798 to Zech. **Bailey** J.P. Laurens Co. [No record date.]

Page 413 31 Dec 1792, Langston **Drew**, Joshua **Roberts** & Sarah **Roberts** his wife (Laurens Co.) sold unto John **Simpson** (same) for £60 Sterling the following Negroes: Beck & her Son Solomon with their future increase. Witness Andrew **Smyth**, David **Speers**. Signed Langston **Drew**, Joshua (x) **Roberts**. Witness oath by David **Speers** 18 May 1793 to Wm. **Hunter** J.P. Laurens Co. [No record date.]

Page 413-414 30 Jan 1799, Andrew **Endsley** (Laurens Co.) for $130 paid by William **Prather** (same), sold all that tract of Land containing 129 acres by accurate admeasurement. Situate in sd. Co. on branches of Beards fork of Duncans Creek. Border: John **McKelvey**, Andrew **Endsley**, pond. Witness John **McCelvey** [sic], Mary **Mitchell**. Signed Andrew **Endsley**. Witness oath by John **McCelvey** 30 Jan 1799 to Wm. **Mitchell** J.L.Co. Dower relinquished by Jane (O) **Endsley**, wife of Andrew **Endsley**, 30 Jan 1799 before Wm. **Mitchell** J.L.C. [No record date.] [Includes plat.]

Page 414-415 17 Oct 1797, Joel **Hart** (Laurens Co.) to Henry **Box** (same), for £37 sold all that piece of Land containing 117 acres more or less, in sd. Co. on waters Rabourns Creek. Originally granted to Hastings **Dial** by Thomas **Pinckney** Esq. 2 June 1786 and recorded in Secretary's Office book KKK, page [blank]. Bounded at time of Surveying on S by John **Henderson**, E by James **Williams**, N by Charles **Bradey**, W by William **Watkins**. Witness John **Moore**, Benjamin **Sooter**. Signed Joel **Hart**, Beththiah (x) **Hart**. Oath by John **Moor** [sic] 17 Oct 1797, that he saw Joel **Hart** and his Wife sign the deed. Given before James **Abercrombie** J.P. Laurens Co. [No record date.]

Page 415 10 Nov 1791, Henry **Byram** (Laurens Co.) planter to Joel **Hart** (same) planter, for £50 Sterling sold a Tract of Land containing 117 acres, being part of 485 acres in sd. Co., granted 2 June 1788 by Thomas **Pinckney** Esq. unto Hastings **Dial**, and by him sold to Henry **Byram** 13 Oct 1799. Bounded N on Charles **Bradey**, N.W. on **Watkins**, S on John **Henderson**, E on James **Williams**. Witness John **Henderson**, John **Byram**. Signed Henry (B) **Byram**, Bethier (x) **Byram**. Oath by John **Byram** 17 Dec 1791, that he saw Henry **Byram** and his Wife Bethier sign the deed. Given before Geo. **Anderson**. Plat certified 15 Aug 1791 by John **Rodgers** Dep.Sur. [No record date.] [Includes plat.]

Page 415-416 4 Aug 1798, Hastings **Dial** (Laurens Co.) planter for £50 Sterling paid by John **Woody** (same) planter, sold all that Tract of Land containing 140 acres more or less. Border: William **Hellums**, land laid out to James **Abercrombie**, Vacant land, Old Survey, Joseph **Hammond**, Jacob **Hammond**. Situate in sd. Co. on Raybourns Creek and in N part of a Tract granted 2 June 1788 to sd. Hastings **Dial** for 240 acres, recorded in Book XXXX, page 73. Witness Richard **Owings**, William **Fowler**. Signed Hastings **Dial**. Witness oath by Richard **Owings** 19 Feb 1799 to Joseph **Downs** J.P. [No record date.]

Page 416 22 Oct 1798, John **Rutledge** Esq. Jun. by my Attorney John **Hunter** Esq. for £17 2sh Sterling paid by Humphrey **Gains** (Laurens Co.), sold all that Tract of Land containing 114 acres more or less, as it is now laid off. Situate in sd. Co. on waters of Walnut Creek and Reedy River. Bounding on land called **Williamson's** Land, Land sold to Widow **Swain** & John **Robertson** and is the same that was bargained to John **Daniel**, being part of 3,000 acres granted to Thomas **Shubrick** & by him conveyed to John **Rutledge**. Witness Thomas **Gains**, Joseph **Waldrop**. Signed John **Rutledge** by his Atty. John **Hunter**. Witness oath by Thomas **Gains** 18 Feb 1799 to Joseph **Downs** J.P. Laurens Co. [No record date.]

Page 417 [No date.], John **Rammage** (Laurens Co.) made over unto Benjamin **Rammage** (same), all that Tract of Land containing 100 acres more or less, in sd. Co. on Duncans Creek, waters of Enoree River. Border: Nathan **Davis**, John **Buoys**, Josiah **Rammage**, branch. Duncans Creek. Being part of 500 acres originally granted to John **Rammage** by [remainder blank.].

Page 417 16 Feb 1799, John **Rammage** (Laurens Co.) for 10sh Sterling paid
by Benjamin **Rammage** (same), sold all that Tract of Land containing 100
acres more or less, in sd. Co., Duncans Creek, waters of Enoree River. Border:
Nathen **Davis**, John **Buoys**, Josiah **Rammage**, branch, Creek. Being part of
500 acres originally granted to sd. John **Rammage** by Charles Greenville
Montague 20 Jan 1773. Witness Alexander **Fillson**, Josiah **Rammage**. Signed
John (JR) **Rammage**. Witness oath by Josiah **Rammage** 18 Feb 1799 to Chas.
Allen J.P. Laurens Co. Dower relinquished by Jane **Rammage**, wife of John
Rammage, 18 Feb 1799 before Chas. **Allen** J.L.C. [No record date.]

Page 418 16 Feb 1799, John **Rammage** (Laurens Co.) for 10sh Sterling paid
by Josiah **Rammage** (same), sold all that Tract of Land containing 110 acres
more or less. Situate in sd. Co. on Duncans Creek, waters of Enoree River.
Being part of 500 acres originally granted to sd. John **Rammage** by Charles
Greenville **Montague** 20 Jan 1773. Witness Alexander **Fillson**, Benjamin
Rammage. Signed John (JR) **Rammage**. Witness oath by Benjamin
Rammage 18 Feb 1799 to Chas. **Allen** J.P. Laurens Co. Dower relinquished
by Jane **Rammage**, wife of John **Rammage**, 18 Feb 1799 before Chas. **Allen**
J.L.C. [No record date.]

Page 418-419 1 Dec 1791, William Hasell **Gibbes** (Charleston) for £109 paid
by James **Underwood** (Laurens Co.) planter, sold all that body of Land in
Laurens, formerly Craven Co., on branches of Duncans Creek, containing
about 1,090 acres more or less. Bounding S.E. on Edmund **Reily**, land
unknown, Patrick **Bryant**, Michael **Dixon**, S.W. on James **Barton**, William
Sanders, N.W. on Benjamin **Barton**, near William **Bull** Jun., N.E. on William
Taylor, Andrew **Rodgers**. Witness James **Cleaton**, William **Underwood**,
David **Burns**. Signed Wm. Hasell **Gibbes**. Witness oath by David **Burn** [sic]
and William **Underwood** 19 Feb 1799 to Robert **Hutcheson** J.P. Dower
relinquished by Eliza **Gibbes**, wife of William Hasell **Gibbes**, 10 Feb 1797
before Wm. **Blamyer** J.Q. Charleston Dist. [No record date.]

Page 419-420 18 Feb 1799, Zechariah **Bailey** (Laurens Co.) for $75 paid by
Edmond **Ragsdale** (Greenville Co.), sold all that tract of Land containing 50
acres more or less, in Laurens Co. on Reedy River. Border: Peter **Acker**, Peter
Ragsdale, Reedy River. Being part of 197 acres originally granted to sd.
Zechariah **Bailey** 7 Jan 1793, recorded in Secretary's Office in Grant Book F,
No.5, page 411. Witness Hewlet **Sullivant**, John (x) **Blunt**, Ambrose **Hall**.
Signed Zech. **Bailey**. Witness oath by Hewlet **Sullivant** 18 Feb 1799 to
Jonthn. **Downs** J.P. Laurens Co. Dower relinquished by Winneford **Bailey**
[Wine **Bailey** in signature.], Wife of Zechariah **Bailey**, 18 Feb 1799 before
Jonthn. **Downs** J.L.C. [No record date.]

Page 420 22 Aug 1798, William **Johnson** Jun. Blacksmith (Laurens Co.) for
£20 Sterling paid by Joseph **Mitchell** (Laurens Co.) Planter, sold all that tract
of Land on the Dividing ridge between Enoree River and Duncans Creek
containing 100 acres [150 in plat.] more or less, being part of a Tract originally

granted to Eleaner **Craig** which at her decease falling into possession of John **Craig** her Son, was conveyed by him and Isabella his Wife unto William **Johnson** Sen. Black Smith, then by him conveyed by a Deed of Gift unto above William **Johnson** Jun. Border: Vacant land, Waggon Road, Spring. Witness Goerge **Ross**, James **Davis**, Isabella **Ross**. Signed William **Johnston** [sic]. Witness oath by George **Ross** 15 Jan 1799 to Roger **Brown** J.P. Laurens Co. Dower relinquished by Martha **Johnston**, wife of William **Johnston** Jun., 7 Sept 1798 before Wm. **Mitchell** J.L.C. [No record date.] [Includes plat.]

Page 421 4 Oct 1798, Josiah **Greer** (Laurens Co.) for £18 Sterling paid by William **Hugins** [**Hudgins** in one ref.] (same), sold all that tract of Land containing 112 acres more or less, being part of 280 acres granted to sd. **Greer** in sd. Co. on South fork of Duncans Creek. Bounding on Anne **McClure**, Daniel **Ravenel**, Samuel **McConnethy**. Witness Jno. **Hunter**, Wm. **Dendy** S. of T. Signed Josiah **Greer**. Witness oath by Wm. **Dendy** 2 Feb 1799 to Wm. **Mitchell** J.L.C. [No record date.]

Page 421 14 Nov 1798, Nancy **Baugh** Widow of William **Baugh** Sen. dec. and Mother of William **Baugh** Jun. dec. and David **Baugh** (Laurens Co.) for £30 paid by David **Culbertson** (same), sold a Tract of Land supposed to contain 100 acres more or less, on E side of Reedy River, being part of 150 acres originally granted to William **Baugh** dec. Border: Reedy fork Creek, Reedy River. Containing part of the original Survey of 150 acres that lies below the Reedy fork Creek, which part was by William **Baugh** Sen. dec. in his last Will and Testament willed & given unto William **Baugh** Jun. dec. and above David **Baugh**. Witness Thomas **Hood**, Abel **Thomas**, John **Hill**. Signed Nancey (x) **Baugh** [sic], David **Baugh**. Witness oath by Thomas **Hood** 19 Feb 1799 to James **Abercrombie** J.P. Laurens Co. [No record date.]

Page 422 2 Feb 1799, William **Camp** (Laurens Co.) for $100 paid by Elisha **Casey** (same), sold all that tract of Land containing 155 acres more or less, in sd. Co. on waters of Raburns Creek, waters of Reedy River. Border: Henry **Morgin**, Raburns Creek, Thomas **Camp**, Eli **Cashaw**. Being part of 225 acres originally granted to sd. William **Camp**. Witness Thomas (C) **Camp**, Starling **Camp**. Signed Wm. **Camp**. Witness oath by Thos. **Camp** 18 Feb 1799 to Reuben **Pyles** J.P. L.C. [No record date.]

Page 422-423 1 Feb 1799, James **Abercrombie** (Laurens Co.) to Elisha **Casey** (same), for £6 Sterling sold 12 acres of Land, being part of 200 acres, granted 5 Nov 1792 to Lewis **Saxon** and made from him to sd. **Abercrombie**. Situate on S side of Rabourns Creek in sd. Co. and South fork of sd. Creek. Border: **Reid**, Creek, Owing **Reid**. Witness Wm. **Camp**, Thomas **May**. Signed James **Abercrombie**. Witness oath by Wm. **Camp** 18 Feb 1799 to Reuben **Pyles** J.P. L.Co. [No record date.]

Page 423 1 Feb 1798, Thomas **Camp** (Laurens Co.) to Elisha **Casey** (same), for £60 sold all that Tract of Land supposed to contain 100 acres more or less, in sd. Co. on South fork of Raburns Creek and on S side of sd. Creek. Being part of a Tract granted to Owin **Reid**, 22 Sept 1769. Conveyed by George **Vaughan** Attorney for William **Reid**, lawful heir of Owin **Reid**, to Thomas **Camp**. Witness Wm. **Camp**, Elizabeth (x) **Camp**. Signed Thomas (C) **Camp**. Witness oath by Wm. **Camp** 18 Feb 1799 to Reuben **Pyles** J.P. L.C. [No record date.]

Page 423-424 1 Jan 1799, John **Rammage** (Laurens Co.) for £30 Sterling paid by Nathen **Davis** (same), sold all that tract of Land containing 94 acres more or less, in sd. Co. on Duncans Creek, waters of Enoree River. Being part of 500 acres originally granted to sd. John **Rammage** by Charles Greenville **Montague** 20 Jan 1773. Witness Thomas **East**, Benjamin **Rammage**. Signed John **Rammage**. Witness oath by Benjamin **Rammage** 18 Feb 1799 to Chas. **Allen** J.P. Laurens Co. Dower relinquished by Jane **Rammage**, wife of John **Rammage**, 18 Feb 1799 before Chas. **Allen** J.L.C. [No record date.]

Page 424 1 Mar 1798, John **Potter** (Laurens Co.) to Lawrence **Barker** (same), for £20 Sterling sold one certain Tract of Land in sd. Co. on branches of Reedy fork of Little River, containing 70 acres more or less. Border: Stephen **Potter**, John **Arnold**, Samuel **Birk**. Being part of a Tract surveyed for John **Arnold**. Witness William **Potter**, Huriel **Nickson**. Signed John **Potter**. Witness oath by William **Potter** 1 Feb 1799 to Chas. **Allen** J.P. Laurens Co. [No record date.]

Page 425-426 10 Dec 1787, John **Lewis** (Randolph Co., N.C.) appoint Jacob **Lewis** (Wilks Co., Ga.) my Attorney irrevocable to sell all my real Estate in Ninety Six Dist., one tract of Land containing 200 acres, one containing 150 acres, also one other containing 100 acres. Also to recover and receive all Debts and demands which now are due and owing unto me. Witness Zebedee **Wood**. Signed John **Lewis**. Acknowledged 10 Dec 1787, that John **Lewis** received full satisfaction for the premises and this memorandum shall be sufficient Receipt. Acknowledged by Zebedee **Wood**, Dec Sept 1787 [sic], the power of Attorney from John **Lewis** Sen. Given before J. **Harper** Clk., Randolph Co. N.C. [No record date.]

Page 426 6 Feb 1799, Martin **Kellett** (Laurens Co.) to Andrew **McKnight** Sen. (same), for £29 3sh 4p Sterling sold one certain tract of Land in sd. Co. on Rabourns Creek, waters of Reedy River, containing 100 acres more or less. Border: Robert **Sims**, Creek, branch, James **McCaa**, Waggon Road, Drury **Boyce**. Being granted by William **Moultrie** Esq. Gov. 7 Mar 1775. Witness James **McCaa**, William Mart. **Dixon**. Signed Martin **Kellet** [sic]. Witness oath by James **McCaa** 19 Feb 1799 to James **Abercrombie** J.P. Laurens Co. [No record date.]

Page 427 18 Dec 1797, Thomas **Camp** Jun. (Laurens Co.) for $225 sold unto Martin **Mehaffey** (same), all that Tract of Land on N.E. side of South fork of Raybourns Creek in sd. Co., containing 100 acres more or less, being part of a tract originally granted to Owen **Reid**, and by the heirs of sd. **Reid** sold unto sd. Thomas **Camp** Jun. Border: Widow **Reid's** spring branch, Raybourns

Creek, land sold to M. **Mehaffee**. Witness Benjn. H. **Saxon**, Solomon **Hopkins**. Signed Thomas (C) **Camp** Jun. Witness oath by Solomon **Hopkins** 13 Aug 1798 to Jonthn. **Downs** J.P. Laurens Co. Dower relinquished by Susannah (x) **Camp**, wife of Thomas **Camp** Jun., 13 Aug 1798 before Jonthn. **Downs** J.L.C. [No record date.] [Includes plat.]

Page 427-428 24 July 1798, John **Rutledge** (Charleston) by my Attorney John **Hunter** Esq. (Laurens Co.) for £7 Sterling paid by John **Box** (same), sold all that Tract of Land containing by computation 50 acres more or less, in sd. Co. on waters of Reedy River. Being part of 3,000 acres granted to Thomas **Shubrick** and by him conveyed to William **Williamson** & by him to sd. John **Rutledge**. Border: part of big survey, John **Box**, **Mahon**. Witness James **Powell**, Thomas **Gaines**. Signed John **Rutledge** by his Atty. John **Hunter**. Witness oath by Thomas **Gains** [sic] 8 Dec 1798 to Reuben **Pyles** J.P. Laurens Co. Plat certified 10 Jan 1792, by John **Hunter** D.Sur. [No record date.] [Includes plat.]

Page 428 20 Apr 1791, Abraham **Box** made oath that about 6 years ago that he heard his Uncle Henry **Box** tell sd. Depnt's Father John **Box** that he gave to him the title of a certain tract of Land on Reedy River in Laurens Co., being then occupied by David **Alexander**. Given before Joseph **Downs** J.P. Laurens Co. [No record date.]

Page 428 11 June 1796, William **Davis** (Newberry Co.) for Love and Affection I bear unto my Step Sister Prisila **Davis** and unto my Youngest Step Brother Van **Davis**, being Infants under age, both now under the care of their Mother Jean **Davis** Widow, give the Tract of Land containing 100 acres, being part of a larger Tract granted to William **Davis** dec. by William **Bull**, then Gov., in Sept 1769, recorded in Secretary's Office in Book DDD, page 595, for 200 acres. Sd. William **Davis** being the heir unto the Deceased. The Mother of sd. Pricilla **Davis** [sic] and Van **Davis**, to have the use and privilege of sd. Land, houses and plantation during her natural live or Widow hood. Witness John **Davis**, James **Lindsey**. Signed William (W) **Davis**. Witness oath by James **Lindsey** 11 June 1796 to James **Dillard** J.P. Laurens Co. [No record date.]

Page 428-429 21 Oct 1798, William **Owens** formerly of Laurens Co. to James **Cammock** (same), for $500 sold all that tract of Land containing 150 acres, on waters of Rabourns Creek in sd. Co. on a branch formerly called Hellom's branch. Being originally granted to John **Williams** 10 Sept 1765 and recorded in Secretary's Office in Book ZZ, page 445, and by sd. **Williams** conveyed to John **Owens** by Lease and Release 9 & 10 Aug 1772. Bounded at time of surveying on all sides by Vacant Land. Now conveyed by sd. Wm. **Owens**, lawful heir to sd. John **Owens**, unto sd. James **Cammock**. Witness John **Hughes**, John **Harris**. Signed William **Owins** [sic]. Witness oath by John **Harris** 19 Feb 1799 to Charles **Saxon** J.P. Laurens Co. [No record date.]

Page 429-430 6 Dec 1798, John **Bowman** (Mercer Co., Caintuckey) to Zechariah **Arnold** (Laurens Co.), for £50 Sterling sold all that tract of Land containing 100 acres more or less, being all the land on the S side of Reedy River belonging to a tract containing 150 acres granted to Richard **Ballard** by Wm. **Bull** Esq. Gov. 2 Apr 1773. Witness Lewis **Graves**, John (x) **Willard**, George (-) **Morgan**. Signed John **Bowman**. Witness oath by Lewis **Graves** 18 Feb 1799 to James **Abercrombie** J.P. Laurens Co. [No record date.]

Page 430 4 Aug 1798, Hastings **Dial** (Laurens Co.) planter for £50 Sterling paid by Richard **Owens** (same) planter, sold all that Tract of Land containing 217 acres. Border: James **Abercrombie**, not known, Joseph **Downs**, sd. Hastings **Dial**. Situate in sd. Co. on Peachland branch, waters of Rabourns Creek and is the south part of a Tract granted 2 Mar 1795 to sd. Hastings **Dial** for 206 acres [sic] recorded in Book P, No.5, page 132. Witness John **Woody**, William **Fowler**. Signed Hastings **Dial**. Witness oath by John **Woody** 19 Feb 1799 to Joseph **Downs** J.P. Laurens Co. [No record date.]

Page 430 18 Feb 1799, John **Hazlet** (Laurens Co.) sold unto Paul **Fendley** (same), twelve head of Cattle, twenty head of Hoggs, three Bee gums, twenty Geese, two feather Beds & furniture and all my working Tools and one Set of Waggon Wheels & Boxes, in consideration of £65 Sterling. Witness Ezekl. S. **Roland**, Larkin **Sullivan**. Signed John **Hazlet**. Recd. 21 Feb 1799 of Paul **Fendley** 50sh as well as £62 which he paid before to John **Hazlet**. Signed Mary **Hazlet**. Witness oath by Ezekl. S. **Roland** 21 Feb 1799 to Jno. **Davis** J.P. [No record date.]

Page 431 1 Sept 1798, Thomas **Gary** (Laurens Co.) for $400 paid by James **Adair** (same), sold two Negroes, one Negro Woman Cynthia, a Negro Girl Jemina. Witness P. **Williams**, David **Mason**. Signed Thomas **Gary**. Witness oath by David **Mason** 19 Feb 1799 to Roger **Brown** J.P. Laurens Co. [No record date.]

Page 431 18 Feb 1799, Sandford **Berry** (Laurens Co.) planter for $50 Sterling [sic] paid by James **Lynch** (same), sold all that Tract of Land containing 40 acres in sd. Co. on Lynches Creek a branch of Enoree River, part of a Survey of 550 acres originally granted to Thomas **Fare** 8 July 1774. Border: Aron **Lynch**, Mirey branch, Creek. Witness John **Lynch**, Jessee **Lynch**. Signed Sanford (96) **Berry** [sic]. Witness oath by John **Lynch** 21 Feb 1799 to Reuben **Pyles** J.P. L.C. [No record date.]

Page 431-432 21 Feb 1799, William **Bryson** (Laurens Co.) for $350 paid by William **Mitchell** (same), sold a certain Negro Woman Beck, about 35 years of age. Witness Thomas **Dendy**, Robert **Bryson**. Signed William **Bryson**. Witness oath by Thos. **Dendy** Jr. 23 Feb 1799 to Jonthn. **Downs** J.P. Laurens Co. [No record date.]

Page 432-433 18 June 1797, John **Middleton** (Laurens Co.) Exor. of Ainsworth **Middleton** dec. to James **Anderson** (same), for £5 sold all that

Tract of Land containing 150 acres in sd. Co. on W wide of Reedy River. Granted to sd. Ainsworth **Middleton** by William **Bull** Esq. Gov. in 1774, and sd. **Middleton** by his last Will and Testament directed his Exors. to make a right of above Land to sd. James **Anderson**. Witness Thomas **Davenport**, Jno. **Davenport**, Jas. **Clements**. Signed John **Middleton**. Witness oath by Thos. **Davenport** 18 July 1798 to Zech. **Bailey** J.P. Laurens Co. [No record date.]

Page 433 17 Aug 1798, James **Jones** (Laurens Co.) for the Love, goodwill and Affection I bear towards my Son Dred **Jones** (same), give a certain Negro Boy Toney, about 5 years old. Witness Jessee **Jones** [sic], Joseph **Jones**. Signed James **Jones**. Witness oath by Jesse **Jones** 17 Aug 1798 to George **Whitmore** J.P. Laurens Co. [No record date.]

Page 433 17 Aug 1798, James **Jones** (Laurens Co.) for the love, good will and affection I bear towards my Son Joseph **Jones** (Newberry Co.), give a certain Negro Girl Bett, about 7 years old. Witness Jessee **Jones**, Dred (x) **Jones**. Signed James **Jones**. Witness oath by Jessee **Jones** 17 Aug 1798 to George **Whitmore** J.P. Laurens Co. [No record date.]

Page 433 6 Oct 1798, Recd. of Matthew **McDoniel**, Cattle, Potts, Loom, Saddle, wearing Cloaths with the Crosebard Sivut, according to the Contents of the Will of my Sister's Will Rachel **Turk** dec. Signed Margaret (x) **McDonald**. 6 Oct 1798. Recd. of Matthew **McDonial** [sic] Exor. of Estate of Rachel **Turk** dec., the third of the Cattle and third of the Potts, according to the Testator's Will. Signed Archibald (x) **McDonald**. [No record date.]

Page 433-434 16 Dec 1784, Thomas **Boyce** and Ellenor **Boyce** his Wife (Ninety Six Dist.) to Zachariah **Green**, for £15 Sterling sold all that Tract of Land containing 100 acres in sd. Dist. on bullet branch of Rabourns Creek. Bounding N on land laid out unknown, S on land claimed by Thomas **Hooker**, all other sides by Vacant land at time this was laid out. Surveyed 5 Mar MDCCLXXIII and granted to Eleaner **Tweed** that is now the wife of sd. Thomas **Boyce**, by William **Bull**, then Lieut. Gov. 4 May M:CCLXXV [sic]. Witness David **Green**, James (x) **Green**, John (x) **Dunhue** [**Dunhow** in one ref.]. Signed Thomas **Boyce**, Alanor (x) **Boyce** [sic]. Witness oath by David **Green** 17 [No month.] 1784 to Geo. **Anderson** J.P. 96 Dist. [No record date.]

Page 434-435 14 July 1798, Ann **Garrett**, John **Garrett** & William **Garrett** Admrs. of the late Edward **Garrett** dec. (Warriors Creek, Laurens Co.) in consideration of Edward **Garrett** having given with his Daughter Elizabeth to John **Ashley** 100 acres of Land and never made sd. **Ashley** any legal Right or Title and it appearing that sd. Land is his Full Share of sd. Estate, sell unto sd. John **Ashley** all that tract of Land containing 100 acres more or less, being part of 500 acres originally granted to sd. Deceased in Nov 1770 and recorded in Secretary's Office in Book JJJ, page 383. Border: branch, Bishops branch. Witness Nicholas **Garrett**, Jesse **Garrett**. Signed Anne (x) **Garrett** [sic], John (G) **Garrett**, William **Garrett**. Witness oath by Nicholas **Garrett** [No signature.] 14 July 1798 to Roger **Brown** J.P. Laurens Co. [No record date.]

Page 435   21 Feb 1799, Wm. **Bryson** (Laurens Co.) for $2 paid by Wm. **Mitchell** (same), sold all that tract of Land containing by Estimation one acre more or less, in sd. Co. on a branch of Norths Creek, waters of Little River. Border: near head of sd. **Mitchell's** Mill pond, Creek, sd. **Mitchell**. Witness Thos. **Dendy**, Zacee (x) **Tinsley**. Signed Wm. (x) **Bryson**. Witness oath by Thos. **Dendy** Jr. 23 Feb 1799 to Jonthn. **Downs** J.P. Laurens Co. [No record date.]

Page 435-436   22 Oct 1796, John **Neely** (Laurens Co.) for £20 Sterling paid by David **Whiteford** (same) planter, sold all that Mill Seat and Tract of Land containing 20 acres, part of 150 acres more or less in sd. Co. on waters of Cane Creek, originally granted to Mary **Edwards** and by her conveyed to John **Neely**. Bounding S.W. on Wm. **Pierce** and John **Evans**, N.E. on Benjamin **Moore**, all other sides Vacant Land at time of original grant. Granted by Lord Charles Greenville **Montague** 8 Feb 1773 to sd. Mary **Edwards**. Witness William (x) **McMurtrey**, Sary (x) **Campbell**, Robt. **Campbell**. Signed John **Neely**, Joseph **Neely**, Wm. **Neely**. Witness oath by William **McMurtrey** [No signature.] 7 Jan 1797 to Angus **Campbell** J.P. Laurens Co. [No record date.]

Page 436   1 Oct 1797, James **King** (Laurens Co.) to John **Maxwell** (Abberville Co.), for £3 Sterling sold 10 acres of Land more or less, now in John **Maxwell's** possession, being part of a Tract belonging to sd. James **King** in sd. Co. joining sd. John **Maxwell's** Bridge. Border: mouth of a branch of May laye River. Witness James **Hodges**, Edmund **Ware**. Signed James **King**. Witness oath by James **Hodges** 1 Nov 1797 to Adam Crain **Jones** J. A.C. [No record date.]

Page 436-437   26 Mar 1790, Denney **Anderson** (Spartinburg Co.) to William **Roundtree** (Union Co.), for £60 Sterling sold a Tract of Land containing 200 acres in Laurens Co. on Dirbans Creek, a branch of Enoree River. Bounding S.E John **Willis**, S.E. Isaac **Gray**, N.E. on old lines, N.W. on David **Welch**, N.E. and W on Vacant land. Witness Benjn. **Kilgore**, Edwd. **Mitchusson**, Jon. **Penington**. Signed Denney **Anderson**. Witness oath by Benja. **Kilgore** 26 Mar 1790 to Wm. **Mitchusson** J.P. [No record date.]

Page 437   29 Sept 1798, Stephen **Plant** (Laurens Co.) for £40 Sterling paid by Leonard **Brown** (same), sold all that Tract of Land containing 40 acres more or less, in sd. Co. on branches of rean Creek, being part of a Tract originally granted to Richard **Winn** and conveyed to sd. **Plant**. Bounded dry branch, S by James **Sullivan**, E by sd. **Winn**, W by Moses **Madden**. Witness Robt. (x) **Brown**, Nathan (x) **Henderson**. Signed Stephen (x) **Plant**, Leae Bes (x) **Plant** [sic]. Witness oath by Robt. (x) **Brown** 19 Feb 1799 to Jno. **Davis** J.P. L.Co. Dower relinquished by Elizabeth (x) **Plant**, wife to Stephen **Plant**, 30 Mar 1799 before Chas. **Allen** J.L.C. [No record date.]

Page 437-438   29 Sept 1798, Moses **Madden** (Laurens Co.) for £200 Sterling paid by Leonard **Brown** (same), sold all that Tract of Land containing 153 acres more or less, in sd. Co. on branches of Rean Creek. Bounded S by James **Sullivan**, W by Wm. **Hicks**, N by John **Martin**, E by Richard **Winn**. Witness Robt. (x) **Brown**, Nathan (x) **Henderson**. Signed Moses **Madden**, Caty **Madden**. Witness oath by Robt. (x) **Brown** 19 Feb 1799 to John **Davis** J.P. L.Co. Dower relinquished by Catharine (x) **Madden**, wife of Moses **Madden**, 30 Mar 1799 to Chas. **Allen** J.L.C. [No record date.]

Page 438   3 Jan 1799, Mary **Turk** (Laurens Co.) for $500 paid by Joseph **Motes** (same), sold all that Tract of Land containing 163 acres more or less, being on N side of Little River, 100 acres being part of a Tract originally granted to Gilbert **Turner** 3 May 1764 by Thomas **Boone** Esq. The other 63 acres originally granted to John **Caldwell** 8 July 1774 by William **Bull** Esq., being part of 1,250 acres, joining the above 100 acres. Border: sd. Gilbert **Turner**. Being the plantation where I now live. Witness John **Gallegly**, James **Sproll**. Signed Mary (x) **Turk**. Witness oath by John **Gallegly** 11 Mar 1799 to Charles **Griffin** J.P. Newberry Co. [No record date.]

Page 438-439   6 Nov 1797, Lewis **Duvall** (Laurens Co.) to John **McClintock** (same), for £70 Sterling sold a Tract of Land containing 600 acres more or less, in sd. Co. on branches of Warriors Creek and Beaverdam, being part of 903 acres granted to sd. Lewis **Duvall** 4 Mar 1793 by Wm. **Moultrie** Esq. Gov., recorded in Secretary's Office in Book F, No.5, page 552. Border: John **Vaughan**, branch, old line. Witness James **McClintock**, James **Hunter**. Signed Lewis **Duvall**. Witness oath by James **McClintock** 12 Jan 1799 to Starling **Tucker** J.P. Laurens Co. [No record date.]

Page 439   2 Jan 1799, John **Coker** (Laurens Co.) sold unto John **Simpson** (same), one Negro Girl Venas [sic] for $200. Condition that if John **Coker** shall pay the sum at or before the last day of May next, then John **Simpson** shall give up sd. Negro Wench Venus. Witness Peter **Hammons**, Thomas (T) **Simpson**. Signed Jno. **Coker**. Witness oath by Peter **Hammons** 18 Mar 1799 to Robert **Hutcheson** J.P. [No record date.]

Page 439-440   21 Jan 1799, William Hasell **Gibbes** (Charleston) for £28 paid by John **Allison** [**Ellison** in one ref.] (Little River), sold all that Tract of Land in Laurens Co. on branches of Little River of Saluda. Originally granted in 1772 to William **Gibbes**, bounding N.W. and S.E. on Estate of Charles **Simmons**, N.W. and W by Majr. Pierce **Butler** and Robert **Hooper**. Being within about a Mile of Laurens Court House. Witness Edward **Thomas**, Matthew **Hall**. Signed Wm. Hassell **Gibbes** [sic]. Witness oath by Matthew **Hall** 14 May 1799 to James **Abercrombie** J.P. Laurens Co. Dower relinquished by Eliza **Gibbes**, wife of William Hassell **Gibbes**, 21 Jan 1799 before Jacob **Crayton** J.Q. [No record date.]

Page 440   29 Jan 1799, James **Abercrombie** [James A. **Crombie** in one ref.] (Ninety Six Dist.) to Sarah **Jeffres** (same), for £15 Sterling sold a certain Tract of Land on W side of Raibourns Creek, containing by Estimation 50 acres more or less, being granted by Charles **Pinckney** Esq. Gov. to Lewis **Saxon** and recorded in Secretary's Office in Grant Book 5 Nov 1792. Being part of 200 acres granted to sd. **Saxon**. Border: Mouth of Rock house branch, original line, William **Camp**, Creek. Witness Joseph **Dunklin**, Sarah (x) **Dunklin**. Signed James **Abercrombie**. Witness oath by Joseph **Dunklin** 16 Mar 1799 to John **McElroy** J.P. Greenville Co. [No record date.]

Page 440   13 May 1799, William **Watson** (Laurens Co.) doth bind to Moses **Butler** (same), his Son John **Watson** for the 4 years & 11 months, from date. He shall not absent himself from his Master's business without leave, and all that shall be instrusted to him. Moses **Butler** shall find sufficient meat, drink, lodging and Wearing Apparel & shall give him 12 months Schooling and at the Expiration thereof give him a Horse, Saddle & Bridle & a suit of Clothes to be valued $100. Witness Wm. **Burnside**, George (x) **Gryson**, Thos. **Burnside**. Signed William (x) **Watson**, Moses (x) **Butler**. Witness oath by Wm. **Burnside** J.P. Laurens Co. [No date.], for himself. [No record date.]

Page 441   24 Apr 1799, Nehemiah **Franks** Sen. (Laurens Co.) give unto Nehemiah **Franks** Jun. (same), all the Tract of Land whereon I now live. Witness Chas. **Smith**, John **Garner**. Signed Nehemiah **Franks**. Witness oath by Chas. **Smith** 25 June 1799, for himself. [No record date.]

Page 441   6 Apr 1799, John **Brockman** and James **Allison** (both of Laurens Co.) have agreed and run the dividing line between our Tract of Land on Enoree River & Durbens Creek. Border: Enoree River, sd. **Brockman**, Durbens Creek, fork, **Arguar**?, old line, sd. **Allison**. Witness Daniel **Wright**, Emanuel **York**, Thomas **Parks**. Signed John **Brockman**, Jas. **Allison**. Witness oath by Emanuel **York** 6 Apr 1799 to Daniel **Wright** J.P. Laurens Co. [No record date.]

Page 441-442   31 Jan 1798, William **Harriss** (Laurens Co.) for $85 (Spanish Milled) paid by John **Cuningham** (same), sold all that tract of Land containing 200 acres, being all my part of a 500 acre tract on Dunkins Creek and Rittle River [sic]. Surveyed 18 July 1796 for Patrick **Cuningham** and William **Harriss**, and granted 6 Feb 1797 to John **William** & Robert **Cuningham** & William **Harriss**. Should sd. John **Cuningham** lose sd. tract of any part by a Superior Claim made known, then I oblige myself to refund at the rate of $85 for 200 acres that he shall lose. Witness Elijah **Burgess**, Thomas (x) **Redden**. Signed William **Harriss**. Witness oath by Eijah **Burgess** 9 Mar 1798 to Zech. **Bailey** J.P. Ninety Six Dist. Dower relinquished by Frances (H) **Harris**, Widow of within William **Harriss**, 13 May 1799 before Jonthn. **Downs** J.L.C. [No record date.]

Page 442   3 Dec 1798, Cornelius **Cargill** (Washington Dist., Greenville Co.) on 7 Jan 1790 did sell unto Patrick **Cuningham** (Laurens Co.), one Negro Wench Hannah and her Child Lewis for £70 Sterling. Now, for $50 in Specie paid by John & William **Cuningham**, Exors. of sd. Patrick **Cuningham** dec., sold the sd. Negro Wench's other four Children having been born since she became the property of sd. Patrick **Cuningham**, consisting of two boys & two girls, Jeofry & Sam, Margaret & Ritter, with the future increase of the females, with the future issue of sd. Negro Wench unto sd. John & William **Cuningham**. Witness Anne **Cuningham**, Elijah **Burgess**. Signed Cornelius **Cargill**, Sarah (C) **Clary**. Witness oath by Elijah **Burgess** [No signature.] 2 May 1799 to Lewis **Graves** J.P. Laurens Co. [No record date.]

Page 442-443 (Aberville Co.) 16 Feb 1799, Robert Andrew **Cuningham** (same) for $120 paid by John **McGowen** (Laurens Co.), sold a certain Tract of Land containing 40 acres more or less, in Laurens Co. Adjoining lands of David **Whiteford** on W, Clement **Wells** on N.W., John **McGowen** on N, Jas. **Maulden** on E, on waters of Cane Creek, waters of Saluda River. Witness John **Chiles**, Elisha (x) **Riley**. Signed Robert A. **Cuningham**. Witness oath by Elisha **Riley** [No signature.] 25 Mar 1799 to Angus **Campbell** J.P. Laurens Co. [No record date.]

Page 443 1 Nov 1797, Richard **Puckett** and Mary **Macmurty** [sic] (Co. aforesd.) for £20 Sterling paid by Robert A. **Cuningham** (same), sold all that tract of Land containing 40 acres more or less. Witness Moses **Wells**, Margret (m) **Cuningham**. Signed Richard **Puckett**, Mary (x) **McMurtrey** [**McMurtray** in one ref.]. Witness oath by Moses **Wells** [No signature.] 23 Mar 1798 to Angus **Campbell** J.P. Laurens Co. [No record date.]

Page 443 22 Oct 1797, Moses **Wells** (Laurens Co.) for £20 Sterling paid by Margret **Cuningham** (same), sold all that tract of Land containing 50 acres more or less, on waters of Cain Creek, being part of 100 acres granted to John **Wells** by Peter **Casety** 2 Apr 1789, and conveyed away by sd. **Wells** to sd. Margret **Cuningham** 17 Oct 1797. Witness Robert A. **Cuningham**, Fielder **Wells**, Martha **Cuningham**. Signed John **Wells**, Moses **Wells**. Witness oath by Robert A. **Cuningham** 29 Jan 1798 to Angus **Campbell** J.P. Laurens Co. [No record date.]

Page 443-444 31 Dec 1798, Cornelius **Dunnahoo** (Laurens Co.) planter for $150 paid by James **Burnside** (same), sold all that tract of Land containing 100 acres in sd. Co. on waters of Mudlick Creek, being part of a tract originally granted to John **Dunnahoo** by Charles Greenville **Montague** Esq. 21 May 1772 containing 300 acres, and by sd. **Dunnahoo** conveyed to sd. Cornelius **Dunnahoo** by lease and release 1 & 2 Feb 1789. Border: John **Dunnahoo**, Jno. **Clement**, Jas. **Burnside**. Witness Wm. **Coleman**, Joseph **Babb**. Signed Cornelius (S) **Donahoo** [sic]. Witness oath by Joseph **Babb** 1 June 1799 to Wm. **Burnside** J.P. Laurens Co. Dower relinquished by Elizabeth (x) **Dunnahoo**, wife of Cornelius **Dunnahoo**, 31 Jan 1799 before Wm. **Mitchell** J.L.C. [No record date.] [Includes plat.]

Page 444 3 Feb 1797, John **Philpot** (Laurens Co.) planter for £60 paid by James **Burnside** (S.C.), sold 200 acres [219 acres on plat.] of Land, being part of two tracts granted to sd. **Philpot**, the first granted by William **Moultrie** 4 Feb 1793. The second [blank]. Border: Cornelius **Dunnahoo**, Chesnut, Eldridge **Fuller**, Zachariah **Bailey**, branch. Witness James **McMahen**, Wm.

A. **Rodgers**. Signed John (O) **Philpot**. Witness oath by James **McMahen** 1 June 1799 to Wm. **Burnside** J.P. Laurens Co. [No record date.] [Includes plat.]

Page 444-445 16 July 1798, Jesse **Holder** (Laurens Co.) for $50 paid by Solomon **Holder**, sold all that tract of Land containing 50 acres more or less, being part of 100 acres originally granted to Margaret **McCulle** in Sept 1760 and recorded in the Secretary's Office in Book EEE, page 1. Premises lie on N.W. side of Coxes Creek, a branch of Enoree. Bounded S.E. by sd. Creek, W by Henry **Langston** Branch. Witness Henry **Langston**, Sarah (x) **Langston**. Signed Jesse **Holder**. Witness oath by Henry **Langston** 16 July 1798 to Roger **Brown** J.P. Laurens Co. [No record date.]

Page 445 8 Jan 1799, James **Russell** (Laurens Co.) for £50 paid by Joseph **Barton** Sen. (same), sold a parcel of Land containing 100 acres more or less, being in two grants, the one being part of a Tract granted unto Alexander **Harper** and conveyed to James **Russell**, supposed to contain 44 acres more or less. Border: N side of Durbins Creek at mouth of School House branch, **Harper**, **Hughes**, Waggon Road, part of **Harper's** Tract, James **Gilbert**, being 56 acres of a Resurvey granted to James **Russell** 3 Dec 1798, recorded in Grant Book L, No.5, page 335. Witness William **Gilbert** Jun., David **Barton** (x). Signed James **Russell**. Witness oath by David (x) **Bartin** [sic] 23 Feb 1799 to Danl. **Wright** J.P. Laurens Co. [No record date.]

Page 445-446 23 Feb 1796, Whereas Henry **Lindauer** late of Charleston dec. was in his lifetime and at the time of his death among other real Estate possessed of a Tract, in his last Will and testament 28 Sept 1787, did order his Exors. to sell the tract. Daniel **Strobel**, Jacob **Williman** and Abraham **Markley** surviving Exors. did sell the tract unto John Christopher **Faber** (sd. City) for £17 8sh Sterling. Tract lies in Laurens Co. on Warriors Creek, branch of Enoree River, containing 850 acres. Border: Vacant Land, **Vaughan**, Thos. **Simlin**, Jno. **Cox**, Joshua **Simpson**, Drury **Smith**, Warriors Creek, Warren Creek, Coxes Branch. Witness Jacob **Martin**, Casimir **Patrick**. Signed Daniel **Strobel**, Jacob **Williman**, Abrm. **Markley**. Witness oath by Jacob **Martin** [No signature.] 22 Aug 1796 to Danl. **Smith** J.P. Survey for Henry **Lindauer** 6 Dec 1772 by Jon. **Downs**. Resurveyed 6 Apr 1791 by Jonthn. **Downs** D.Sur. [No record date.] [Includes plat.]

Page 446-447 24 Dec 1798, John Christopher **Faber** (Charleston) Clergyman for $700 Spicie paid by Daniel **Abbot** Planter (Laurens Co.), sold all that tract of Land in Laurens Co. on Warriors Creek, branch of Enoree River which had been on 6 Dec 1772 laid out for Henry **Lindauer** (S.C.) and which on 6 Apr 1791 was resurveyed by Jonathan **Downs** Esq. Dep.Sur. (S.C), containing 850 acres more or less. Witness Thomas **Matthis** Jun., Ezekiel (x) **Matthis**, William **Moer**. Signed John Christopher **Faber**. Witness oath by Ezekiel (x) **Mathews** [sic] 24 June 1799 to Jonthn. **Downs** J.P. Laurens Co. Dower relinquished by Mary Margaret **Faber**, wife of within named, 24 Dec 1798 before James **Nicholson** J.Q. [No record date.]

Page 447 6 Jan 1706 [sic] and the 20th of Independence, Ezekiel **Matthews** (Laurens Co.) to John Frances **Wolff** (same) Merchant, for £20 Sterling sold all that tract of Land containing 45 acres more or less. Situate on Rabourns Creek in sd. Co. Being part of 56 acres granted to sd. **Matthews** 5 Oct 1789 by Charles **Pinckney** Esq. Gov. Ezekiel **Matthis** [sic] until execution of these presents shall stand seized in his right of an Estate of inheritance in sd. tract. Witness Jesse **Garrett**, Isham **Hestelo**. Signed Ezekiel (x) **Matthews**, Rebecka (x) **Matthews**. [No witness oath.] [No record date.]

Page 447-448 11 May 1796, John **Dunklin** (Mercer Co., Canetuckey) to John F. **Wolff** (Laurens Co.), for £66 Current Money sold one certain Tract of Land on W side of Raibourns Creek, containing 133 acres more or less, being granted by William **Moultrie** Esq. Gov. to John **Ritchey** & recorded in Secretary's office in Grant Book 6 Feb 1786. Bounding N.W. on John Ewen **Calhoon**, S.W. on John **Goucher**. Witness John **Rodgers**, Hewlet **Sullivant**. Signed John **Dunklin**. Witness oath by John **Rodgers** 11 May 1796 to Joseph **Downs** J.P. Laurens Co. Plat certified 16 Aug 1792 by P. **Cuningham** D.S. [No record date.] [Includes plat.]

Page 448 31 Dec 1792, Ezekiel **Matthews** (Laurens Co.) planter to John F. **Wolff** Merchant (same), for £5 Sterling sold one piece of Land containing 9-1/2 acres in sd. Co. Bounded by sd. John F. **Wolff**, Widow **Morgan**, sd. Ezekiel **Mathews** [sic]. To include one half the Spring of Water which sd. John F. **Wolff** now makes use of and is to have free egress & regress. Being part of 56 acres originally granted to sd. Ezekiel **Matthis** [sic] 5 Oct 1789 by Charles **Pinckney** Esq. Gov. Lying on Rayborns Creek. Witness James **McCaa**, Samuel **Evens**. Signed Ezekiel (x) **Matthews**, Rebeckah (x) **Matthews**. Witness oath by James **McCaa** 7 Mar 1793 to Joseph **Downs** J.P. Laurens Co. [No record date.]

Page 449 11 May 1796, John **Dunklin** (Mercer Co., Cantuckey) to John F. **Wolff** (Laurens Co.), for £4 Current Money sold one certain Tract of Land on W side of Rabourns Creek containing 36 acres more or less, being granted by William **Moultrie** Esq. Gov. to John **Gocher**. Bounding E on John F. **Wolff**, S.E. on Patk. **Cuningham**. [Plat shows 38 acres, bordering William **McFerson**, J. E. **Calhon**.] Witness John **Rodgers**, Hewlet **Sullivant**. Signed John **Dunklin**. Witness oath by John **Rodgers** 11 May 1796 to Joseph **Downs** J.P. Laurens Co. [No record date.] [Includes plat.]

Page 449 24 Jan 1799, Recd. from John F. **Wolff** $300 for a Negro Boy Billy, about 12 years old. Witness John **Jones**, Isham (x) **Histerlo**. Signed R. **Owens** [Richard **Owens** in one ref.]. Witness oath by Isham (x) **Histerlo** 27 May 1799 to Joseph **Downs** J.P. Laurens Co. [No record date.]

Page 449-450 29 Sept 1798, Samuel **Saxon**, Attorney for Robert Goodloe **Harper** (Abberville Co.), to Joseph **Bolton** (Laurens Co.), for £130 Sterling sold all that tract of Land containing 390 acres more or less, in Laurens Co. on

Walnut Creek, waters of Reedy River, formerly belonging to James **Braden** dec. and purchased by sd. Robert G. **Harper** under an Execution against the Estate of sd. **Braden**. Bounded at time of original Survey by Thomas **Elliott**, Joseph **Box**, James **Braden**, Vacant land. Witness Mathew (x) **Bolton**, John **Saxon**. Signed Saml. **Saxon** for R. G. **Harper**. Witness oath by Mathew (D) **Bolton** 6 July 1799 to James **Abercrombie** J.P. Laurens Co. Plat certified 3 Mar 1798 by John **Rodgers** D.S. [No record date.] [Includes plat.]

Page 450 23 Aug 1798, John **Ritchey** & Margaret my Wife (Laurens Co.) to John Caldwell **Burns** (same), for £20 Sterling sold a certain Tract of Land containing 100 acres more or less, on waters of Cain Creek, adjoining Wm. **Nickels**, John **Ritchey**, **Fachs**. Being part of 262 acres originally granted by Wm. **Moultrie** Esq. 3 Mar 1786 to Samuel **Harriss** and released by him to Wm. **Caldwell** Esq., and released by him to John **Ritchey**. Witness William **Nickels**, Charter (O) **Nickels**, Joseph **Hooges**. Signed John **Ritchey**, Margaret (x) **Ritchey**. Witness oath by William **Nickels** 19 July 1799 to Joseph **Downs** J.P. Laurens Co. [No record date.]

Page 451 13 July 1799, Charles **North** (Edgefield Co.) for $100 paid by Thomas **Rodgers** (Laurens Co.), sold all that tract of Land formerly belonging to Robert **Hood** in Laurens Co. on waters of Mudlick, bounding N.W. on land laid out the property of Thos. **North** & land not known, S.E. on Wm. **Williamson**, N.W. on Richard **North**. Witness Thos. **Scott**, Patrick **Rodgers**. Signed Charles (x) **North**. Witness oath by Patrick **Rodgers** 13 July 1799 to Wm. **Burnside** J.P. Laurens Co. [No record date.]

Page 451 Jan 1799, Joseph **Martindale** and Mary his Wife (Union Co.) to Moses **Martindale** (Laurens Co.), for $300 sold a Tract of Land in co. aforesd. on waters of Enoree River. Bounded by William **Gilbert**, Thos. **McCrery**, Vacant land. Granted unto sd. Joseph **Martindale** the tract of 139 acres more or less. Sd. Jos. **Martindale** is until Execution of these presents possessed of an Estate of inheritance in sd. tract. Witness Jesse **Martindale**, William (x) **Potts**. Signed Joseph (x) **Martindale**, Mary (x) **Martindale**. Witness oath by Jesse **Martindale** 20 Mar 1799 to John **Martindale** J.P. Union Co. [No record date.]

Page 452 16 Mar 1799, Mary **Mayzek** [sic] exrx of J. **Mazyck** (Charleston) for £50 Sterling paid by William **Washington** (Laurens Co.), sold all that Tract of Land containing 400 acres more or less. Situate in Craven Co. between and upon waters of Reedy River and Saluda, bounding S.E. on John **Savage** (Ninety Six), Mark **Freeman**, all other sides on Vacant land. Witness John **Findley**, J. H. **Mitchell**. Signed Mary **Mazyck**. Witness oath by John **Findley** 18 Mar 1799 to [No name.]. [No record date.]

Page 452 24 Dec 1798, George **Wright** (Laurens Co.) for £30 paid by William **Washington** (same), sold 100 acres of Land, on N.E. side of Saluda River. Border: **McDoles** ford on River. Part of a Tract granted to Thomas **Foster** by Charles **Pinckney** Esq. 7 Sept 1789 and recorded in Grant Book

ZZZZ, page 475. Examined by Peter **Freneiu** Sec. Witness Daniel **Cox**, Jobe **Deen** [Joab in one ref.], Saml. **Freeman**. Signed George **Wright**. Witness oath by Samuel **Freeman** 19 Feb 1799 to James **Abercrombie** J.P. Laurens Co. [No record date.]

Page 453   24 Dec 1798, George **Wright** (Laurens Co.) for £10 Sterling paid by William **Washington** (same), sold all that Tract of Land containing 80 acres more or less, being part of 640 acres granted to Thomas **Foster** by Charles **Pinckney** 17 Sept 1789 & recorded in Grant Book ZZZZ, page 475. Examined by Peter **Freneiu**. Border: James **Wood** formerly conveyed by **Foster** to Wm. **Arthur**, George **Gorthard**, line to leave room for 100 acres between it and 100 conveyed to above **Washington** before of sd. Tract. Witness Daniel **Cox**, Job **Deen**, Saml. **Freeman**. Signed George **Wright**. Witness oath by Saml. **Freeman** [No date.] to James **Abercrombie** J.P. Laurens Co. [No record date.]

Page 453   20 July 1799, William **Rennolds** (Laurens Co.) for £30 Sterling paid by Robert **Neeley** (same), sold all that Tract of Land containing 54 acres in sd. Co. on Beverdam Creek, waters of Little River, being part of 74 [acres] granted to Stephen **Mullins**. Witness Thos. **Babb**, John **Hughes**. Signed William (W) **Runnels** [sic]. Witness oath by John **Hughes** 20 July 1799 to Chas. **Allen** J.P. Laurens Co. Dower relinquished by Alsey (x) **Rennels**, wife of William **Runnels**, 20 July 1799 before Chas. **Allen** J.L.C. [No record date.]

Page 454   23 Feb 1799, Constant **Hellums** to Archey **Owings**, for £10 or her maintenance during her natural life, sold all that tract of Land containing 100 acres more or less, on Rabourns Creek where William **Hellums** dec. formerly lived, being part of 200 acres granted to sd. William **Hellums** dec., bounded E by Joseph **Hammons**, N by John **Woody**, W by John **Childers** and Richard **Owings** Sen., S by big Survey. Witness Thomas **Childres**, Samuel **Nisbit**. Signed Constant (J) **Hellums**. Witness oath by Thomas **Childress** [sic] 23 Feb 1799 to Jno. **Coker** J.P. Laurens Co. [No record date.]

Page 454   21 Feb 1799, John **Coker** (Laurens Co.) to Archabel **Owings** (same), for £70 Sterling sold all that Tract of Land containing 100 acres more or less, on Rabourns Creek where William **Hellums** dec. formerly used to live, which was Willed to Jonathan **Hellums** by his Grand Father William **Helums** Sen. dec., being part of a Tract granted to sd. William **Helums** Sen. dec., containing 200 acres, bounded E by Joseph **Hammon**, N by John **Woody**, W by John **Childress** and Richard **Owings** Sen., S by Big Survey. Witness Thomas (x) **Childress**, Samuel **Nesbitt**. Signed Jno. **Coker**. Witness oath by Samuel **Nesbitt** 18 July 1799 to Joseph **Downs** J.P. Laurens Co. [No record date.]

Page 454-455   17 July 1799, John **Milam** (Laurens Co.) for $300 paid by Reubin **Carter** (same), sold all that tract of Land containing by Estimation 100 acres more or less, in sd. Co., being part of 300 acres originally granted to John **Cargill** 31 Oct 1769, and by him conveyed by Will to Cornelius **Cargill** his Son, and by him conveyed to David **Bailey**, and by him conveyed to Thos. **Wadsworth**, and by him conveyed to sd. John **Milam**. Sd. tract taken off the lower End of above 300 acres. Border: Little River, **Hall's** spring branch, other branches, S.E. on James **Young** and Thomas **Dendy**, N.E. on Ambrose **Hall**. Witness Abram **Hall**, Henry **Hall**. Signed John **Milam**. Witness oath by Abram **Hall** 17 July 1799 to Wm. **Mitchell** J.L.C. Dower relinquished by Nancy (x) **Milam**, wife of John **Milam**, 17 July 1799 before Wm. **Mitchell** J.L.C. [No record date.]

Page 455 7 Feb 1790 and until 4 July the 23rd year of Independence, James **White** (Orange burgh Dist.) for $125 paid by James **Gibson** (Laurens Co.), sold 100 acres of Land upon the S side of Enoree River, being part of 300 acres originally granted to Andrew **Owings** by William **Bull** Esq., then Lieut. Gov., in Sept 1768 and recorded in Auditor's Office in Book J, No.9, page 250. Witness Geo. **Whitmore**, Martha (x) **Whitmore**. Signed James **White**. Witness oath by Geo. **Whitmore** 17 July 1799 to Starling **Tucker** J.P. Laurens Co. [No record date.]

Page 456 5 Apr 1797, Lod **Dulin** (Spartenburgh Co.) for £50 Sterling paid by John **Thomson** (Laurens Co.), sold 300 acres of Land more or less. Border: Long branch, old conditional line. Being part of a Tract granted to sd. Lod **Dulin** by Arnoldus **Vanderhost** 3 Aug 1795, recorded in Secretary's Office in Book J, No.5, page 340. I defend sd. premises unto sd. **Thomson**, against myself and my heirs, but not from any other persons. Witness John **Bollan**, James (2) **Thomson**. Signed Lod **Dulin**. Witness oath by John **Bollan** 5 Apr 1797 to Geo. **Whitmore** J.P. Laurens Co. [No record date.]

Page 456-457 6 Feb 1796, By virtue of a Writ issued from the Clerk's Office of County Court at Suit of James **Park** and George **Gordon** against Michael **Waldrop**, William **Dunlap** Sheriff of Laurens Co. did seize a certain Tract of Land and on the above date exposed the tract to sale at the Court House and struck off to John **Waldrop** for £20. Tract lies in sd. Co. on waters of Norths Creek, bounding Andrew **Rodgers** Sen., William **Harris** Jun., all other sides Vacant at time of Survey. Originally granted to William **Harris** Sen. 26 Feb 1768. Witness Wm. **Rodgers**, Mary Ann **Waldrop**. Signed William **Dunlap** Sheriff. Witness oath by Wm. **Rodgers** 17 July 1799 to Chas. **Allen** J.P. Laurens Co. Pursuant to an Order of Council dated this day, I certify for William **Harris** a Tract of 150 acres of Land surveyed for him 26 Feb 1768. Situate in Berkley Co. on Norths Creek, a branch of Little River, bounding N.E. on land laid out to Andrew **Rodgers**, S.E. on land laid out to William **Harris** Sen., all other sides on Vacant Land, this 6 Nov 1771 by John **Caldwell** Dep.Sur., John **Bremar** Surv.Gen. [No record date.] [Includes plat.]

Page 457 8 Oct 1796, James **Green** (Laurens Co.) to William **McDavid** (same), for £66/4/8 Sterling sold all that Tract of Land containing 93 acres more or less, in sd. Co. on Reedy River, bounded by David **Dunlap**, John **Rodgers**, **Berd**, Reedy River. Being part of 500 acres originally granted to Rives? **Butler** and by him conveyed to Herculas Daniel **Bize** 9 July 1792 &

conveyed by John **Hunter** by power of Attorney from sd. **Bize** dated 1 June 1793 & from sd. **Hunter** to James **Green**. Witness John **Dorrah**, David **Dunlap**. Signed James **Green**, Nancy (x) **Green**. Dower relinquished by Nancy **Green**, wife of James **Green**, 29 Nov 1796 [No official.]. Recd of Wm. **McDavid** £42 4sh 8p and also a Bond for £24 payable 25 Dec 1797, this 8 Oct 1796. Witness oath by John **Dorrah** 19 July 1799 to Joseph **Downs** J.P. Laurens Co. [No record date.]

Page 457-458   10 Apr 1799, Sherod **Camp** [sic] (Laurens Co.) for £40 Sterling paid by James **Camp**, sold all that Tract of Land containing 305 acres in sd. Co., Reedy River. Border: Reedy River, Nathen **Camp**. Being a tract originally granted to Sherod **Camp** 19 Sept 1798 and recorded in Secretary's Office in Grant Book S, No.5, page 221. Witness Jesse **Allen**, Wm. **Camp**. Signed Shearwood **Camp**. Witness oath by Jesse **Allen** 11 Apr 1799 to Jno. **Coker** J.P. Laurens Co. [No record date.]

Page 458-459   30 Apr 1799, Edmond **Penman** (Charleston) Merchant for $250 paid by Thomas **Chapman** & Stephen **Vitteto** (Laurens Co.), sold all that Tract of Land containing 250 acres, being the one half of 500 acres granted to William **Savage** and James **Simpson** 9 Nov 1774, bounded N.W. by John **Long**, S.E. by Patrick **Welsh** and Robert **Cuningham**, N.E. by Vacant land, S.E. by other half of sd. Tract. Witness Alexr. **McNeill**, Wm. **Anderson**. Signed Edmd. **Penman** by his Atty. James **Gairdner** Witness oath by W. **Anderson** 3 June 1709 [sic] to Charles **Davenport** J.P. Abbeville Co. Plat on waters of Saluda River certified 30 Apr 1799 by Wm. **Anderson** D.S. [No record date.] [Includes plat.]

Page 459-460   12 Apr 1799, Frances **Luster** [sic] (Laurens Co.) for $100 paid by Thomas **Wilks** (same), sold all the several tracts of Land. One tract of Land containing 110 acres more or less, in sd. Co. on both sides of Norths Creek, being part of two tracts, one granted to George **Anderson**, the other to Arthur **Spence** and bounded by John **Milam**, **Hardie** [**Hardey** in one ref.], **Gafford**, James **Burnside**, John **Pamfillin**, Norths Creek, branch. Conveyed by sd. **Anderson** to Silvs. **Walker**. One other tract containing 135 acres more or less, being part of two tracts granted to Margret **Wiseman** for 100 acres and conveyed by her to George **Norwood** dec. & by Nathaniel Son & heir to sd. Dec. to Thomas **Gafford** the 35 acres a part of a Tract granted to sd. George **Norwood** & bounded Jas. **Burnside**, S side of Norths Creek, **Wilkes**, **Luster**, **Hardy**, Wm. **Hollin**, **Hall**, **Owins**. The two described tracts on both sides of Norths Creek, reserving the Mill pond as now marked off with the land below the Mill. Witness Edmond **Roberts**, William **Hall**. Signed Frances **Lester**. Witness oath by William **Hall** 2 May 1799 to Wm. **Mitchell** J.L.C. Dower relinquished by Elizabeth **Lester**, wife of Frances **Lester**, 2 May 1799 before Wm. **Mitchell** J.L.C. Plat certified 4 Apr 1799 by John **Hunter** D.S. [No record date.] [Includes plat.]

Page 460   12 Mar 1799, Henry **Woodward** (Fairfield Co.) to Thomas **Jones** (Laurens Co.), for $17 sold a certain Tract of Land joining sd. **Jones**, being part of sd. **Woodward's** Survey containing 14 acres. Border: Henry **Woodward**, David **Vance**, Thomas **Jones**. Witness E. **Young**, Abner **Young**. Signed Hen. **Woodward**. Witness oath by Abner **Young** 18 July 1799 to Roger **Brown** J.P. Laurens Co. [No record date.] [Includes plat.]

Page 460 30 Mar 1799, John and Rebeckah **Wells** (Laurens Co.) for $70 paid by David **Tweed** (same), sold all that tract of Land containing 60 acres more or less, on waters of Mudlick and Cain Creek, being part of a 250 acre Survey originally granted to John **Owens** and by him conveyed to William **ONeal** and by him conveyed to sd. John **Wells**. Border: Thomas **Crosson**, Meeting house tract, **Hamelon**, **Hamelton**. Witness William **McMurtrey**, Thomas **Crosson**, Robert (x) **Hambilton**. Signed John **Wells**, Rebeckah (x) **Wells**. Witness oath by Robert (x) **Hambleton** [sic] 10 June 1799 to Angus **Campbell** J.P. Laurens Co. [No record date.]

Page 461 8 Feb 1797, John and Moses & Clement **Wells** (Laurens Co.) for £30 Sterling paid by Margret **Cuningham** (same), sold all that tract of Land containing 50 acres in sd. Co. on waters of Cain Creek, being part of 100 acres originally granted from Peter **Casuty** to John **Wells** and being part of Land where sd. **Wells** now lives. Witness Robert Andw. **Cuningham**, John **McGowen**, Caleb (x) **Maulden**. Signed John **Wells**, Moses **Wells**, Clement **Wells**. Witness oath by John **McGowen** 2 June 1798 to Angus **Campbell** J.P. Laurens Co. [No record date.]

Page 461 26 Oct 1796, Alexander **Fearbearn** (Laurens Co.) for £80 sold unto Reazin **Holland** all that Tract of Land containing 300 acres more or less, in sd. Co. on branches of Duncans Creek. Bounded E by Wm. **Price**, S by James **Underwood**, N.W. by sd. **Price** and others. Witness Robert **Hannah** [**Hanna** in one ref.], Abraham (Ax) **Holland**. Signed Alexr. **Fearbearn**. Witness oath by Abraham (Ax) **Holland** 9 Mar 1799 to James **Dillard** J.P. Laurens Co. Dower relinquished by Christian **Fearbearn**, wife of Alexander **Fearbearn**, 1 Mar 1799 before Wm. **Mitchell** J.L.C. [No record date.]

Page 461-462 18 July 1799, Robert **McCurley** (Laurens Co.) for £20 Sterling paid by Richard **Styles** (same), sold all that certain tract of Land containing 250 acres more or less. Originally granted to Rowley **McCarley** and by him conveyed to sd. Robert **McCarley** [sic], Son & heir of aforesd. Rowley **McCarley**. Situate in sd. Co. on waters of Duncans Creek, bounded at time of original survey N.W. & N.E. by Andrew **Rodgers**, all other sides by Vacant Land, but sd. Tract is now bounded by Luke **Weeks**, Joshua **Palmore**, Robert **Taylor**, Adam **Gordon**, sd. Richard **Styles**, **Wadsworth** & **Turpin**. Witness Andrew **Burnside**, Lewis **Graves**, Wm. **Cuningham**. Signed Robert (x) **McCurely**. Witness oath by A. **Burnside** 18 July 1799 to Jno. **Davis** J.P. Laurens Co. [No record date.]

Page 462-463 11 Jan 1798, Holleway **Power** [sic] (Laurens Co.) & Tabitha his Wife to John **Pugh** (same), for $350 sold a certain Tract of Land containing 100 acres more or less, on S side of Enoree River in sd. Co., being part of a Tract granted to James **McClurken** & by him conveyed to sd. Halloway **Power**. There is an older survey that takes part of sd. Tract. Whatever number of acres should be taken out of the 100 acres, sd. **Power** grants unto sd. John **Pugh** as much land adjoining sd. Tract sold out of 200 acres which was conveyed to sd. **Power** by Mordecia **Moore**. Sd. **Power** until Execution of these presents shall stand seized of an Estate of Inheritance in the premises. Witness Joseph **Lyons**, William **Pugh**. Signed Halloway **Power**, Tabitha (x) **Power**. Witness oath by Joseph **Lyon** [sic] 27 Feb 1799 to Daniel **Wright** J.P. Laurens Co. Dower relinquished by Tabitha (x) **Power** 11 Jan 1798 before Jonathn. **Downs** J.L.C. [No record date.]

Page 463 1 Nov 1796, Zachr. **Turner** (Laurens Co.) for £50 paid by William **Parker** (same), sold all that tract of Land containing 100 acres more or less, on a branch of Beaverdam Creek, waters of Enoree River. Bounded S by Robert **Allison** Sr., N by old lines, all other sides by Vacant land at time of being granted. Granted unto Thomas **Allison** by William **Bull** then Gov. 2 Feb 1773. Witness Joseph (a) **Allison**, Elizabeth (A) **Allison**. Signed Zachr. **Turner**. Witness oath by Joseph (a) **Allison** 21 Feb 1797 to Daniel **Wright** J.P. Laurens Co. [No record date.]

Page 463-464   28 Mar 1799, Jesse **Arther** (Lexington) Carpenter for £62 Sterling paid by Martin **Pugh** (Laurens Co.), sold all that tract of Land containing 350 acres in formerly Craven Co., now Laurens Co., between Broad and Saluda Rivers. Granted unto William **Arther** on Walnut Creek, a branch of Reedy River, bounding S.E. on land claimed by Daniel **Williams**, S by **Braganaw**, other sides by Vacant Land. Witness Danl. **Friday**, Robert **Huskinson**. Signed Jesse **Arther**. Witness oath by Robert **Huskinson** 23 July 1799 to James **Abercrombie** J.P. [No record date.]

Page 464 8 Dec 1798, Thomas **Burton** (Laurens Co.) for £25 6sh 8p Sterling paid by David **Smith** (S.C.), sold all that Tract of Land containing 133 acres in sd. Co. on branches of Dirty Creek. Border: Oliver **Matthis**, unknown, Charles **Lowery**, John **Rodgers**, **Elliot**. Witness McNees **Rodgers**, Walter **Matthews**. Signed Thomas **Burton**, Witness oath by Walter **Matthews** 25 July 1799 to Chas. **Smith** J.P. Laurens Co. [No record date.] [Includes plat.]

Page 464-465   27 May 1799, Lewis **Saxon** (Laurens Co.) for $150 sold unto Walter **Matthews** (same), sold all that Tract of Land containing 175 acres more or less, on waters of Rabourns Creek in sd. Co. Bounded N on James **Cuningham**, S on John **Cochran**, W on Thomas **Johnston**, S.W. on Lewis **Saxon** & James H. **Lowrey**. Being part of a tract originally granted to Pierce **Butler** Esq. & by him sold to Hercules Daniel **Bize** and by John **Hunter** Esq. Attorney for sd. **Bize**, sold to sd. Lewis **Saxon** 17 Oct 1792. Witness Robert **Matthews**, William (x) **Neighbours**. Signed Lewis **Saxon**. Witness oath by Robert **Mathews** [sic] 25 July 1799 to Chas. **Smith** J.P. Laurens Co. [No record date.] [Includes plat.]

Page 465 7 Mar 1795, William **Anderson** and Molley his Wife (Laurens Co.) to John **Middleton** (same), for £50 Sterling sold part of a certain Tract of Land containing 100 acres more or less, in sd. Co. on E side of Long lick Creek, waters of Reedy River. Border: long lick creek, John **Foster**, Lewis **Banton**, **Cason's** Road, David **Anderson**. Granted to sd. William **Anderson** by William **Bull** Esq. Gov. in 1774. Witness James (J) **Rains**, Wm. **McCall**, Luke **Demcey**. Signed Wm. **Anderson**, Molley (x) **Anderson**. Witness oath by Luke **Demcey** 3 Aug 1799 to Lewis **Graves** J.P. Laurens Co. [No record date.]

Page 465-466 5 Aug 1797, William **Conner** and Mary **Conner** (Abberville Co.) for £50 Sterling paid by John **Middleton** (Laurens Co.), sold all that Tract of Land containing 150 acres on Long lick Creek, a branch of Reedy River. Originally granted to John **Foster** 15 July 1768 and by him conveyed to John **Savage**. Witness Jonan. **Johnson**, Ste. C. **Wood**. Signed William **Conner**, Mary **Conner**. Witness oath by Ste. C. **Wood** 13 Jan 1798 to Zech. **Bailey** J.P. Laurens Co. Dower relinquished by Mary **Conner**, wife of William **Conner**, 5 Aug 1797 before Charles Jones **Colcock** J.Q. Ninety Six Dist. [No record date.]

Page 466 21 Dec 1798, John **Rily** (Laurens Co.) to Lazrus **Hitt** (same), for £45 Sterling sold one certain Tract of Land on waters of Cain Creek in sd. Co. containing 80 acres more or less. Granted to Christopher **Parsons** in 1775 by Charles Graville **Montague** Gov. Witness Henry **Hitt**, Curtis **Curnal**, Wm. **Wheeler**. Signed John (x) **Rily**, Sarah (x) **Rily**. Witness oath by Henry **Hitt** 8 Aug 1799 to Zech. **Bailey** J.P. Laurens Co. [No record date.]

Page 467 17 Apr 1795, William **Ball** (S.C.) Gentleman to Henry **Hitt** (Ninety Six Dist.) planter, for £50 Current money sold a certain Tract of Land, bounding N & N.E. on **Purse**, S.E. **Geddis**, S.W. on Wm. **Senior**, N.W. **Smith** Jun. Granted 10 Aug 1768 by Lord Charles Graville **Montague** Gov. and recorded in Secretary's Office in Book CCC, page 100. Witness Lazarus **Hitt**, Reuben **Martin**. Signed William **Ball**. Witness oath by Lazarus **Hitt** 8 Aug 1799 to Zech. **Bailey** J.P. Laurens Co. [No record date.]

Page 467 10 Apr 1799, Robert **Gillam** (Ninety Six Dist.) for $10 paid by John **Sadlar** (same), sold all that Tract of Land in Laurens Co. on waters of Mudlick Creek containing 144-1/2 acres more or less, agreeable to a plat made 23 June 1792, being part of a Tract granted to John Lewis **Bourquit** for 300 acres and sold by an Execution at the suit of **Hurt** & **Wailey** as appears by Sheffs. Titles 7 Jan 1799. Witness Robert **Stewart**, William **Sadlar**, Enoch (x) **Hensley**. Signed Robert **Gillam**. Witness oath by William **Sadler** 11 Apr 1799 to Anguish **Campbell** J.P. Laurens Co. Dower relinquished by Elizabeth **Gillam**, wife of Robert **Gillam**, 10 Apr 1799 before Ro. **Brown** J.N.C. [No record date.]

Page 468 21 Feb 1799, Robert **Gillam** (Newberry Co.) for £10 Sterling paid by Mary **Hensley** Widow (Laurens Co.), sold all that tract of Land containing 38 acres in Laurens Co. Bounded N.E. on Robert **Stewart**, S.W. on John **Cole**,

S.E. on George **Taylor**. Being part of a Tract originally granted to Robert **Gillam** 4 Sept 1786, containing 348 acres. Witness John **Sadler**, Joshua **Gillam**, Sarah **Martin**. Signed Robert **Gillam**. Witness oath by John **Sadler** 11 Mar 1799 to Angus **Campbell** J.P. Laurens Co. [No record date.]

Page 468 2 Mar 1799, John **Frost** (Newberry Co.) to Gracey **Kernell** (Laurens Co.), for £140 Sterling sold a certain Tract of Land in Laurens Co. on Banks Creek, waters of Saluda River containing 100 acres more or less, granted to Jonathan **Frost** in 1774. Bounding S.W. on **Purse** and Peter **Hitt**. Witness Peter **Hitt**, Curtis **Kearnal** [**Curnal** in one ref.], Wilson (x) **Sanders**. Signed John **Frost**. Witness oath by Peter **Hitt** 11 May 1799 to Angus **Campbell** J.P. Laurens Co. [No record date.]

Page 468-469 29 July 1799, David **McClure** and Ellender my Wife (Laurens Co.) for $150 paid by Robert **Ritchey** (same), sold all that tract of Land containing by Estimation 125 acres more or less, being part of 250 acres originally granted to John **Williamson** 31 Aug 1774 and by him conveyed to Hugh **Young** and by him conveyed to Alexander **McNary** and by him conveyed to Margret **Ritchey** and by her conveyed to Ellender **Ritchey**, the above Ellender **McClure**. Sd. 125 acres to be taken off the E side of sd. Tract. Being in sd. Co. on Lam reeds fork of Dunkins Creek. Joining Joshua **Palmore**, Jas. **Blakely**, Wm. **Cuningham**, Alexander **Tanney**, Adam **Gordon**, rest of original Survey, Frank **Gill**. Witness Adam (x) **Gordon**, Mary **Mitchell**. Signed David (d) **McClure**, Ellender (o) **McClure**. Witness oath by Adam (O) **Gordon** 27 July 1799 to Wm. **Mitchell** J.L.C. Dower and Estate and Inheritance relinquished by Ellender (o) **McClure**, wife of David **McClure**, 6 Aug 1799 before Wm. **Mitchell** J.L.C. [No record date.]

Page 469-470 13 Aug 1799, James **Blakely** (Laurens Co.) for £40 Sterling paid by Benjamin **Smith** (same), sold all that Tract of Land originally granted unto Robert **Tweedy** in sd. Co. on waters of Little River and containing 200 acres more or less. Bounded at this time by John **Blakely**, Benjamin **Atkins** [**Adkins** on plat.], **Butler**, John **Allison**. Witness Robert **Creswell**, Chas. **Allen**. Signed James **Blakely**. Witness oath by Chas. **Allen** 30 Aug 1799 to Chas. **Smith** J.P. Laurens Co. Dower relinquished by Agness (x) **Blakely**, wife of James **Blakely**, 30 Aug 1799 before Chas. **Allen** J.L.C. Surveyed 7 Mar [No year.] by John **Caldwell**, granted 17 Dec 1772. [No record date.] [Includes plat.]

Page 470 26 Aug 1799, Roger **Murphey** (Laurens Co.) for £20 Sterling paid by William **Sprouse** (same), sold all that Tract of Land containing 87 acres, being part of 300 acres originally granted to William **Golden** by William **Bull** Esq. Gov. Border: S side of original tract, branch, Thomas **Wadsworth**, Ace **Turner**, **Starns**. Witness John **Newman**, Michael **Burtey** Jun., Silvanus **Adams**. Signed Roger **Murphey**. Witness oath by S. **Adams** 26 Aug 1799 to Lewis **Graves** J.P. Laurens Co. [No record date.]

Page 470-471   3 Sept 1791, Barnabas **McGill** and Elizabeth his Wife, Daughter and Exrs. of James **McCain** dec. (S.C.) to Joseph **Holmes** (Laurens Co.), for £50 Sterling sold all that Tract of Land containing 50 acres more or less, on W side of Rayborns Creek. Bounding S.E. by Jane **Hollingsworth**, W by John **Hollingsworth**, N.E. by sd. Creek. Being part of a Tract originally granted to Daniel **Allen** and from him conveyed to James **McCain** by Lease & Release 1 May 1768 and recorded in Book S, No.3, page 304 in the Register's Office 8 Apr 1771, a memorial entered in Auditor's Office in Book L, No.11, page 242, 2 Jun 1772, and by sd. James **McCain** bequeathed and devised sd. 50 acres to sd. Elizabeth. Witness Jas. **Floyd**, Thomas **Parker**. Signed Barnabas (x) **McGill**, Elizabeth (x) **McGill**. Witness oath by James **Floyd** 2 Mar 1792 to Joseph **Downs** J.P. Laurens Co. [No record date.]

Page 471   17 Aug 1799, James **Adair** (Laurens Co.) planter by virtue of a Power from Ruth **Adair** (Georgia), for $300 paid by Bazil **Prather** [Basil **Prater** in one ref.] (Laurens Co.) Black Smith, sold all that Tract of Land containing 150 acres more or less, being the half of 300 acres on Northmost Side of Dunkins Creek, bounding S.E. on sd. Creek, all other sides on Vacant Land. Granted by William **DeBrahm** Esq. 17 Mar 1756 to John **Greer**. Witness John Daniel **Kern**, Obediah **Roberts**, Samuel **Bishop** Jun. Signed Ruth **Adair**. Oath by Samuel **Bishop** 17 Aug 1799, that he saw James **Adair** assign the name of Ruth **Adair** to the deed. Given before James **Dillard** J.P. Laurens Co. [No record date.]

Page 471-472   20 Sept 1799, John **Abercrombie** (Laurens Co.) for $500 paid by Jonathan **Abercrombie** (same), sold all that Tract of Land containing 150 acres more or less, in sd. Co. on waters of Raybourns Creek, bounded W and N.W. by Lewis **Saxon**, N & N.E. by Thomas **Johnston**, S by William **Johnston**. Conveyed by Job **Smith** unto sd. John **Abercrombie** 1 Dec 1788. Witness John **Cochran**, Margaret (x) **Cochran**. Signed John **Abercrombie**. Witness oath by John **Cochran** 21 Sept 1799 to Chas. **Smith** J.P. Laurens Co. [No record date.]

Page 472   29 Sept 1799, Received of James **Adear** [sic] $5 for my undivided part of a certain Tract of Land containing in the whole 300 acres in Laurens Co. on waters of Enoree River, late property of Thomas **Pearson** and left to me by James **Mountgomery** Esq. dec. in his last Will and Testament. Witness George **Ross** Jun., Samuel **Farrow**. Signed George **Ross**. Witness oath by S. **Farrow** 28 Oct 1799 to A. **Casey** J.P. [No record date.]

Page 472   [No date.], Grand Jurors for Laurens Co. consider it a great Grievance that no method is adopted to Establish a sufficient number of Poore Schools throughout this State to facilitate the education of Poore Children which with that advantage might not only become ornamental but useful numbers of Society. We view with concern a letter written by Judge **Grimkie**. Signed Richd. **Shackelford** foreman, George **Whitmore**, Wm. **Roundtree**, Jno. **Blakely**, Jno. **Simpson**, Chas. **Smith**, Saml. **Williams**, John **Williams**, Jno. **Wilson**, Thos. **Wilks**, Wm. **Berry**, Wm. **Hutcheson**. [No record date.]

Page 473   28 Dec 1798, Jacob **Buller** (Newberry Co.) for $375 paid by Thomas **Lindley** (Laurens Co.), sold all that Tract of Land containing 500 acres more or less, in Laurens Co. Granted to Herman **Nuffer** dec. by patent at Charleston 23 Nov 1772. Conveyed to sd. Jacob **Buller** by his intermarriage with Mary the Daughter of sd. dec. Herman **Nuffer**. Witness James **Copeland**, Wm. **Abercrombie**, Thomas **ONeall**. Signed Jacob **Buller**. Witness oath by Wm. **Abercrombie** 13 Aug 1799 to Jonthn. **Downs** J.P. Laurens Co. Dower relinquished by Mary **Buller**, wife of Jacob **Buller**, 20 May 1799 before Jacob R. **Brown** J.N.C. [No record date.]

Page 473-474   1 Oct 1799, Lewis **Banton** (Laurens Co.) for $759 paid by James **Crocker** (same), sold all that Tract of Land containing 253 acres in sd. Co. on waters of Reedy River, being part of a tract whereon sd. **Banton** now lives. Granted to James **Lang**. Border: branch. Witness Silvs. **Walker** Jun., John **Middelton** [**Middleton** in one ref.], Robt. **Paslay**. Signed Lewis **Banton**. Witness oath by Silvs. **Walker** Jun. 1 Oct 1799 to Wm. **Mitchell** J.L.C. Dower relinquished by Jededah (J) **Banton**, wife of Lewis **Banton**, 1 Oct 1799 before Wm. **Mitchell** J.L.C. [No record date.]

Page 474   10 Jan 1799, William **Owens** (Newberry Co.) for $400 paid by Frances **Lester** (Laurens Co.), sold all the tract of Land containing 421 acres more or less, in Laurens Co. on Norths Creek, being part of two tracts, the one granted to Patrick **Hinds**, the other granted to Robert **Sims**. Conveyed by sd. **Hinds** & **Sims** to John **Owens**, which part is now conveyed to sd. **Lester** by sd. William **Owens**, Son of sd. John **Owens**. Border: Galanus **Winn**, part of a survey held by G. **Smith**, **Mitchell**, **Couter**, Abner **Rage**, **Roberts**, **Wilks** & **Lester**, Norths Creek. Witness John **Hunter**, Wm. **Dunlap**. Signed William **Owens**. Witness oath by John **Hunter** 13 Oct 1799 to Wm. **Mitchell** J.P. Laurens Co. Plat certified 10 Jan 1799 by John **Hunter** D.S. [No record date.] [Includes plat.]

Page 475   20 Nov 1798, Absalom **Coleman** (Laurens Co.) for $100 paid by John **Stokes** (same), sold all that part of Land bordering, branch, John **Moseley**, Joseph **Babb**, Absalom **Coleman**. Being 100 acres of Land. Witness Absalom **Bailey**, Clement **Wharton**, John **Moseley**. Signed Absalom **Coleman**. Witness oath by Clement **Wharton** 25 Nov 1799 to Wm. **Mitchell** J.L.C. Surveyed 7 Feb 1798 by Thos. **Cargill** D.S. [No record date.] [Includes plat.]

Page 475   16 Sept 1799, Silvanus **Walker** (Laurens Co.) for $350 paid by Saml. **Fleman** (same), sold one Negro boy Gideon. Witness Robert **Hunter**, John **Hunter**. Signed Silvs. **Walker**. Witness oath by Robt. **Hunter** 15 Oct 1799 to Joseph **Downs** J.P. Laurens Co. [No record date.]

Page 476   29 Dec 1797, Charles **Smith** (Laurens Co.) for £15 paid by John **Williams** (same), sold all that tract of land in sd. Co. on waters of Little River. Being part of 1,000 acres originally granted to James **Smith** dec. & conveyed to Mark **Goodwin** dec. & by him conveyed to Charles **Smith**. Containing 100 acres. Border: Chas. **Smith**, branch, Robt. **Bumpass**, John **Williams**. Witness Chas. **Allen**, Ann **Neighbours**. Signed Chas. **Smith**. Witness oath by Ann **Neighbours** 29 Dec 1797 before Chas. **Allen** J.P. Laurens Co. Dower relinquished by Lucy **Smith**, wife of Charles **Smith**, 29 Dec 1799 before Chas. **Allen** J.L.C. [No record date.] [Includes plat.]

Page 477 19 July 1799, John **Arnold** (Laurens Co.) for £27 15sh 9p Sterling sold unto James **Mills** (same) a tract of Land containing 146 acres more or less, on waters of Little River. Bounded on Jamima **Potter**, Chas. **Smith**. Likewise 3 Beds and furniture, 3 Dishes and 3 plates of Putter, two Fields of Corn, two Cows & Calves, three Heifers. Witness William **Hopper**, Francis **Glen**. Signed John (J) **Arnold**. Condition that if sd. John **Arnold** pays the sum above on or before 1 Nov next, then the obligations to be void. Witness oath by William **Hopper** 29 Oct 1799 to Chas. **Smith** J.P. L.Co. [No record date.]

Page 477 22 Nov 1799, E. S. **Roland** (L. Co.) to J. F. **Wolff** (same), [No consideration mentioned.] a certain Negro Girl 12 or 13 years old named Lacey, being a Girl which James **Sullivan** Senr. raised. Witness Thos. **Lewers**, A. **Morrison** [R. D. **Morrison** in one ref.]. Signed Ezel. S. **Roland**. Witness oath by Thos. **Lewers** 22 Nov 1799 to Chas. **Smith** J.P. Laurence Co. [No record date.]

Page 478 22 July 1799, Joseph **Gallegy** [sic] (Laurens Co.) planter for £200 paid by John **Simpson** Mert. (same), sold 1 negro Fellow Sampson, one Negro woman Darkis, one negro boy Mose, one Negro boy David & two horses, fifteen head of Cattle, two Feather Beds and Furniture, one wagon. Dated at Belpoth. One pen knife delivered in behalf of the Hole. Witness John **Gallegly**. Signed Jo. **Gallegly**. Witness oath by John **Gallegly** 3 Oct 1799 to Chas. **Griffen** J.P. [No record date.]

Page 478-479 5 Aug 1799, By virtue of a Writ issued from the Court of Common Pleas at suit of Joseph **Downs** against James **Irwin**, William **Butler** (Sheriff of Ninety Six Dist.) did seize a certain Tract of Land and did on the day above expose the same at Cambridge, and was struck off to sd. Joseph **Downs** Esq. for $30. Tract being in sd. Dist. containing 150 acres more or less, being part of a Tract originally granted to **Lindley**, bound S & E on sd. Joseph **Downs**, W on Jonathen **Downs** Esq. Witness Jno. **Dunlap**, Thos. **May**. Signed Wm. **Butler**. Witness oath by Thos. **May** 10 Oct 1799 to Chas. **Smith** J.P. Laurens Co. [No record date.]

Page 479 11 June 1799, Henry **Geddes** (Charleston) for £35 paid by Clabourn **Brown** (S.C.), sold all that Tract of Land in Laurens Co. on waters of Little River containing 280 acres more or less, being part of 350 acres surveyed and granted to George **Saxby** and sold by the Commissioners of Confiscated Estates to Henry **Geddes**. Border: Silvanus **Walker** Jun. Donil **Osburn**, Silvs. **Walker** formerly Tandy **Walker**, Waggon Road. Witness Robt. **Creswell**, Robt. **Flemming**. Signed Henry **Geddes**. Witness oath by Robt. **Creswell** 16

Oct 1799 to Jno. **Davis** J.P. Laurens Co. Plat certified 6 May 1799 by John **Hunter** D.S. [No record date.] [Includes plat.]

Page 480 19 May 1797, Elizabeth **Goodwin** Admx. of Mark **Goodwin** dec. (Laurens Co.) for 4,000 weight of Tobacco paid by Charles **Smith** (same), sold a Tract of Land containing 250 acres more or less, being part of 1,000 acres originally granted to James **Smith** dec., in sd. Co. on waters of Little River, waters of Saluda River. Border: John **Williams**, Marshall **Franks**, Robt. **Bumpass**, Widow **Goodwin**, branch L. River. Witness John **Williams**, Thomas **Goodwin**, McNees **Rodgers**. Signed Elizabeth (O) **Goodwin** Admx. Witness oath by John **Williams** 20 Oct 1799 to Charles **Saxon** J.P. Laurens Co. [No record date.] [Includes plat.]

Page 480-481 2 Nov 1799, John **Penington** (Spartenburgh Co.) for £25 Sterling paid by Elisha **Atteway** Sen. (Laurens Co.), sold all that parcel of Land containing 50 acres more or less, in Laurens Co. on S side of Enoree River. Originally granted to Robert **Hanna** dec., bounded N.E. by sd. River, W on land laid out to sd. **Hanna**, all other sides Vacant when laid out. Being granted by Charles Graville **Montague** 10 May 1766 and recorded in Secretary's Office 30.CC, page 194. The lines extending to Abraham **Gray** & **Oliphant**. Witness Isaac **Lindsey**, Ellis (x) **Cheek**, John (x) **Power**. Signed Jno. **Penington**. Witness oath by Isaac **Lindsey** 2 Nov 1799 to Starling **Tucker** J.P. Laurens Co. [No record date.]

Page 481-482 2 Dec 1786, Whereas Joseph **Mahon** and Dixon **Mahon** (same Dist., S.C.) were seized of a certain Tract of Land in Berkley Co. on Reedy Creek, a branch of Saluda River, but now in Laurens Co. Surveyed on the Bounty for John **Reedy** 8 Feb 1768 and granted to him 13 May next ensuing by Lord Charles Graville **Montague** Esq. Gov. and recorded in Secretary's Office in Book DDD, page 144. The other Survey for Elizabeth **Burke** on the Bounty the tract of 100 acres granted to her by the same Gov. Joining lines with the Tract granted to sd. **Ready** [sic], below his land. Bounded S & S.W. on John **Ready**. Both tracts containing in the whole 200 acres, whereon Joseph **Mahon** now lives. John **Bowie** Esq. (same) in April Term 1786, impleaded sd. Joseph and Dixon **Mahon** in the Court of Common pleas held for Ninety Six Dist. in an Action for Recovery of £43 5sh 8p Current Money and sd. **Bowie** Esq. did obtain a Judgment for £20 14sh 4p Current Money for his Damage and Cost of Suit. By virtue of a writ issued by Henry **Pendleton** Esq. one of the Justices of sd. Court at Ninety Six 21 Mar 1786, Edmond **Martin** Esq. now Sheriff of sd. Dist. Did seize the tract before mentioned and exposed to public out cry 2 Dec 1786. Sd. 200 acres more or less, in two separate tracts sold unto Robert **Maxwell** Esq. for £26 10sh. Situate in Laurens Co. formerly Berkley Co. on Reedy Creek now Reedy River. Witness Richd. **Tutt** Jun., George **Vaughan**. Signed Edmond **Martin**. Witness oath by Richd. **Tutt** Jun. 3 Sept 1799 to Wm. **Nibbs** J.Q. Ninety Six Dist. [No record date.]

Page 482 29 Oct 1798, James **Russell** Sen. (Laurens Co.) am bound unto John **Willson** (Greenville Co.) for $600. Condition is such that if James **Russell**

makes unto sd. John **Wilson** [sic] a Good Right to a certain Tract of 130 acres of Land more or less, by 25 Dec next, then the above obligation is void. Situate on S side of Durbins Creek, waters of Enoree River, bounding on John **Deen**, Calib **Hughes**, George **Watson**, sd. James **Russell**, Creek, branch, old ford, supposing to extend to **Gilbert's** line. Being granted to Alexander **Harper**. Witness Wm. **Bowen**, Micajah **Hughes**. Signed James **Russell**. Witness oath by Wm. **Bowen** 9 Oct 1799 to Wm. **Rountree** J.P. Laurens Co. [No record date.]

Page 483 31 Oct 1799, John **Workman** (Laurens Co.) for 5sh paid by George **Montgomery** (York Co.), sold all that Tract of Land lately granted to sd. John **Workman** by Edmond **Wood** and includes the plantation whereon William **Ragsdale** lately lived (Except what of sd. Tract was sold previous to Nov 1798 to Edmond **Wood** and William **Moore**.), more or less. Possession, however, not to be given to sd. **Montgomery** until the Death of sd. John **Workman** and his Wife Elizabeth **Workman**, unless sd. John should leave his Wife and live Separate from her or treat her so cruelly in the Judgment of two or three honest neighbours as to force her to leave him, then sd. **Montgomery** to have possession, yet so that his Sister Elizabeth **Workman** have possession during her natural life. Witness Jno. **Davis**, David **Glen**, James **Glen**. Signed John **Workman**. Witness oath by David **Glen** 31 Oct 1799 to John **Davis** J.P. Laurens Co. [No record date.]

Page 483-485 29 Feb 1772, Isaac **Gray** (Barkley Co.) Cordwainer to Abraham **Gray** (same), for £175 Curt. Money sold all that Tract of Land containing 200 acres in Croven Co. [sic] on beaver dam branch, bounded on all sides by Vacant Land at time of Surveying. Granted 1 Dec 1769 by William **Bull** Esq. Lieut. Gov. unto Francis **Philips** (Charles town) B.Smith. Witness Andrew **McCrery**, Robt. **McCrary**, Isaac **Gray** Jun. Signed Isaac **Gray** Sen. Witness oath by Robert **McCrery** [sic] 21 Mar 1772 to James **Ford** J.P. Berkly Co. [No record date.]

Page 485-486 21 Feb 1784, Abraham **Gray** (96 Dist.) Sadler to James & John **Bradshaw** (same), for £100 Sterling sold 200 acres in sd. Dist. on a branch of Beaverdam, bounded on all sides by Vacant land at time when laid out. Granted 1 Dec 1769 by Wm. **Bull** Esq. then lieut. Gov. unto Francis **Philips**, recorded in secretary's office in Book KK, page 49, 1 Dec 1769. Conveyed unto sd. Abrm. **Gray** from sd. **Philips** in the year 47 [sic]. Witness John **Hall**, Matthew **McCrery**, James **Lard**. Signed Abram **Gray** [sic]. Witness oath by John **Hall** 21 Feb 1784 to James **Montgomery** J.P. [No record date.]

Page 486 16 Nov 1799, Robt. **Morgan** (Laurens Co.) sold unto David **Speers** (same), one Rifle Gun, double Triggered & mounted with Brass with a Stare on her breach, for $35. Witness Saml. C. **Stidman**, John **Simmons**. Signed Robert **Morgan**. Witness oath by Saml. C. **Stidman** 16 Nov 1799 to Robt. **Hutcheson** J.P. Laurens Co. [No record date.]

[Two pages not numbered.] [No date.], Multiple plats and adjacent owners with names: Susannah **Long** (2), Jacob **Jones**, William **Ewing**, Thomas **Ewing**, Benjn. **Gregory**, Jonah **Greyer**, **Hannah**, Thos. **Allison**, Wm. **Hannah**, Bounty Land (7), James **Pogue**, Robt. **Proctor**, Ann **Crossing**, Widow **Bowl**? [Page torn.], John **Gray**, Andw. **McCrary**, Thomas **McCrary**, James **Greer**, James **Proctor**, William **Boland**. Four branches shown. Total of included plats: 2,000 acres. [Includes plats.]

Page 487 5 June 1799, Daniel **Ravenel** (Saint Johns Parish) for £150 Sterling paid by John Archer **Elmore**, Benjamin Harper **Saxon** and James **Dillard** (Laurens Co.), sold all that Tract of Land containing 2,000 acres more or less, in Laurens Co. in the fork between Broad and Saluda Rivers on branches of Dunkins Creek. Original grant to Daniel **Ravenell** by Charles Greenville **Montague** 13 Oct 1772. Witness Philip Gender **Prioleau**, George **Gordon**. Signed Daniel **Ravenel**. Witness oath by George **Gordon** 12 Nov 1799 to Roger **Brown** J.P. Laurens Co. Dower relinquished by Catherine **Ravenel**, wife of Daniel **Ravenel**, 6 June 1799 before George **Reid** J.Q. Charleston Dist. [No record date.]

Page 488 22 Nov 1799, Jesse **Allen** (Laurens Co.) sold unto Lyddall **Allen** (same) a certain Negro Boy Slave Boston for $270. Witness John F. **Wolff**, Saml. **Cooper**. Signed Jesse **Allen**. Witness oath by J. F. **Wolff** 22 Nov 1799 to Joseph **Downs** J.P. Laurens Co. [No record date.]

Page 488 21 Aug 1798, Joseph **Martin** (Laurens Co.) for $320 sold unto Cornelius **Donohoe** a Negro Woman Slave Ryna. Witness Henry **Williamson**, Hugh **Abernathey**. Signed Joseph **Martin**. Witness oath by Hugh **Abernathey** 28 Sept 1799 to Zech. **Bailey** J.P. Laurens Co. [No record date.]

Page 488-489 16 July 1799, George **Hearn** (Laurens Co.) to Zechariah **Arnold** (same), for £3 sold all that Tract of Land containing 8 acres in sd. Co. on waters of Reedy River. Border: Wm. **Arnold**, near sd. Wm. **Arnold's** gate, John **Watson**, Zechariah **Arnold**. Witness Drury **Mosely**, Levi **Hill**, Reuben **Arnold**. Signed George (x) **Hearn**, Lucy (x) **Hearn**. Oath by Drury **Mosely** 27 July 1799, that he saw George **Hearn** and Lucy **Hearn** his Wife sign the deed. Given before Lewis **Graves** J.P. Laurens Co. [No record date.]

Page 489 30 Dec 1798, William **Thomason** Jun. (Laurens Co.) for $220 sold unto Hugh **Mehaffey** (same), all that tract of Land on N.E. side of South fork of Rabourns Creek in sd. Co., containing 100 acres more or less, being part of a Tract granted to Lewis **Saxon** and conveyed to James **Abercrombie**, and from him to William **Thomason** Jun. Border: sd. Creek, Thomas **Camp**, Sarah **Jeffery**. Witness Robert **Coker** Junr., Alexander **Mehaffey**. Signed William (x) **Thomason**. Witness oath by Alexr. **Mehaffey** 20 Nov 1799 to Joseph **Downs** J.P. Laurens Co. Dower relinquished by Sarah (x) **Thomason**, wife of William **Thomason**, 20 Sept 1799 before Jonthn. **Downs** J.L.C. [No record date.]

Page 490 11 Oct 1797, Robert **Carter** and Elizabeth **Carter** (Laurens Co.) for $30 paid by Jonathan **Johnston** (same), sold all that Tract of Land containing 30 acres more or less. Situate on Cane Creek, bounding on sd. Carter S.E. and S.W. on Jonathan **Johnson** [sic], N.W. on sd. **Johnson** and **Pinson**. Being part of a Tract originally granted to John **Foster** 22 Aug 1771, and by him conveyed to John **Savage**, and by William **Conner** and Mary **Conner** (Heirs of sd. **Savage**) conveyed to Robert **Carter**. Witness Dabney **Pucket**, Martha (x) **Carter**, Sarah (x) **Carter**. Signed Robert **Carter**, Elizabeth (x) **Carter**. Witness oath by Dabney **Puckett** 14 Nov 1799 to Angus **Campbell** J.P. Laurens Co. [No record date.]

Page 490-491 13 Dec 1799, By virtue of a writ issued from the County Court of Fairfield at the Suit of John **Smith** against Kemp T. **Strother** and Henry **Hunter**, William **Hunter** Esq. (Sheriff of Laurens Co.) did seize under Execution a certain Tract of Land and on 1 June in year above publicly sell the same at the Court House as the Property of Colo. Henry **Hunter**, and was struck off to Robert **Frank** (Laurens Co.) for £80. Tract lies on branches of Raburns Creek, bounding when surveyed on Kitt **Shote**, all other sides Vacant Land, containing 600 acres more or less. Originally granted to Samuel **Elliott** & by him said to be conveyed to Col. Henry **Hunter**. Witness Jno. **Davis**, Lewis **Saxon**, Saml. C. **Stidman**. Signed William **Hunter** S.L.C. Witness oath by Saml. C. **Stidman** 13 Dec 1799 to Chas. **Smith** J.P. Laurens Co. Warrant to me directed by John **Bremar** Esq. D.S.Genl. 5 Nov 1771, I have admeasured and laid out unto Saml. **Elliott** a Tract of 600 acres in Berkley Co. on waters of Raburns Creek, bounded on part of S.W. side by Kitt **Shote**, all other Vacant. Plat certified 24 Jan 1792 by Pat. **Cuningham** D.S. True copy examined by Peter **Bremar** pro.Sur.Genl. Columbia, 26 Mar 1796. [No record date.] [Includes plat.]

Page 491 6 Dec 1797, Frances **Scurlock** (Laurens Co.) to James **Pinson** (same), for $57 sold one certain Tract of Land in sd. Co. on waters of Reedy River, being part of a Tract originally granted to James **Goodman** containing 58 acres more or less, and conveyed by him to Ann **Scurlock**. Plat certified by Pat. **Cuningham** dec. Witness Thomas **Davenport**, J. W. **Swancy**, Thomas **Wathers**. Signed Frances (x) **Scurlock**. Recd. $57 by me. Signed Sten. C. **Wood**. Witness oath by Thos. **Davenport** 17 Mar 1798 to Zech. **Bailey** J.P. Laurens Co. [No record date.]

Page 492 6 Dec 1797, Stephen Chilton **Wood** & Sarah **Wood** (Laurens Co.) for $350 paid by James **Pinson** (same), sold all that Tract of Land on waters of Reedy River containing 93 acres more or less, as by a plat certified by Pat. **Cuningham** dec. Granted to George & William **Anderson** and conveyed to Ste. C. **Wood**. Witness Thos. **Davenport**, J. W. **Swancey**, Thos. **Weathers**. Signed Ste. C. **Wood**, Sarah **Wood**. Witness oath by Thos. **Davenport** 11 Mar 1798 to Zech. **Bailey** J.P. Laurens Co. Dower relinquished by Sarah **Wood**, wife of Ste. C. **Wood**, [No date.] before Wm. **Mitchell** J.L.C. [No record date.]

Page 492-493 5 July 1799, Charles **Madden** (Laurens Co.) for $100 Sterling [sic] sold unto Robert **Todd** (same), all that Tract of 220 acres in sd. Co. on Todds branch of Rabourns Creek. Being first conveyed to sd. **Madden** 5 Jan 1795. Border: Pat. **Cuningham**, John **Todd**, Benjn. **Suter**, not known, Jacob **Williams**, **Abercrombie** Road. Witness John (x) **Todd**, David **McCaa**. Signed Charles **Madden**. Witness oath by John (x) **Todd** 27 Dec 1799 to Joseph **Downs** J.P. Laurens Co. [No record date.] [Includes plat.]

Page 493 16 Jan 1798, Charles **Madden** (Laurens Co.) am bound unto Robert **Todd** (same) for £60 Sterling. Whereas Charles **Madden** sold unto sd. Robert **Todd** a certain Tract of Land containing 220 acres more or less, bounded N.E. on sd. Robert **Todd**, N.W. on Mabre **Madden** & John **Blackwell**, S on land laid out for David **Burriss** & Adam **Garman**. Condition that if Charles **Madden** shall keep sd. Robert **Todd** free from Suits or damages, then the obligation to be void. Witness John **Todd** (x), Abraham **Madden**. Signed Charles **Madden**. Witness oath by John (x) **Todd** 27 Dec 1799 to Joseph **Downs** J.P. Laurens Co. [No record date.]

Page 493-494 20 Mar 1793, William **Johnson** (Laurens Co.) planter to Matthew **Johnson** (same), for £40 Sterling sold a certain tract of Land on waters of Rabourns Creek containing 100 acres, bounding S by Thomas **Lindley**, S.E. by Merma Duke **Pinson**, N.E. by Philip **Sherrel**, N by John **Abercrombie**, W by Thomas **Elliot** and James **McClanehan**. Witness James **Johnson**, Thomas **Johnson**. Signed William **Johnson**. Witness oath by James **Johnson** 25 Mar 1793 to Joseph **Downs** J.P. Laurens Co. [No record date.] [Includes plat.]

Page 494-495 6 Sept 1799, Absalom **Coleman** & Elizabeth his Wife (Laurens Co.) for $335 paid by James **White** (same), sold all that Tract of Land containing 259-1/2 acres & 28 perches in sd. Co., being part of a Tract originally granted to James **White** Sen. on waters of Cane Creek. Border: Absalom **Coleman**, John **Stokes**, John **Mosley**, John **Cureton**. Witness George **Crosslay**, John **Carter**. Signed Absalom **Coleman**, Elizabeth (C) **Coleman**. Witness oath by George **Crosslay** 23 Nov 1799 to Zechariah **Bailey** J.P. Laurens Co. Plat surveyed 14 Feb 1799 by Thos. **Cargill** D.S. [No record date.] [Includes plat.]

Page 495-496 6 Jan 1796, Ezekiel **Matthews** (Laurens Co.) to John Frances **Wolff** (same) Merchant, for £20 Sterling sold all that Tract of Land containing 45 acres more or less, on Rabourns Creek in sd. Co. Being part of 56 [acres] granted to sd. **Matthews** 5 Oct 1789 by Charles **Pinckney** esq. Gov. Sd. Ezekiel **Matthews** is until the Execution of these presents possessed of an Estate of inheritance. Border: John F. **Wolff**, William **Gary**, Ezekle **Matthews** [sic], Reaburns Creek, spring. Witness Jesse **Garrett**, Isham (x) **Histelo**. Signed Ezekiel (x) **Mathews** [sic], Rebecka (x) **Matthews**. Witness oath by Isham (x) **Histielo** [sic] 18 Jan 1800 to Joseph **Downs** J.P. Laurens Co. [No record date.] [Includes plat.]

Page 496 5 Nov 1799, Dower relinquished by Elizabeth (x) **Coleman**, wife of Absalom **Coleman**, unto James **White**. Given before Wm. **Mitchell** J.L.C. [No record date.]

Page 496-498 10 Feb 1792, George **Hollingsworth** and Susannah his wife (Laurens Co.) to Levi **Hollingsworth** (same), for £150 sold all that tract of Land containing 150 acres in sd. Co. on a branch of Cane Creek, adjoining Robert **Hollingsworth**, Robert **Hambleton**, Widow **Cunningham**, Patrick **Cunningham**, Richard **Hollingsworth**. Being part of a tract originally granted to Thomas **North** for 300 acres, commonly known as the Liberty Springs, and by sd. Thomas **North** conveyed to John **Williams** by Lease and release 22 & 23 Nov 1773, and by sd. **Williams** conveyed to Abraham **Hollingsworth** by Lease and release 10 & 11 Jan 1778, and devolving to sd. George by heirship. Witness William **Wheeler**, Joseph **Hollingsworth**, Robert **Hollingsworth**. Signed George **Hollingsworth**, Susannah (x) **Hollingsworth**, Susannah (x) **Hollingsworth** [sic]. Witness oath by William **Wheeler**, Joseph **Hollingsworth** and Robert **Hollingsworth**, [No signatures.] 25 Apr 1792 to Angus **Campbell** J.P. Laurens Co. [No record date.]

Page 498-499 18 Oct 1798, James **Cook** (Laurens Co.) planter for $9-1/2 paid by Thomas **Wadsworth** (same) Merchant, sold all that tract of Land containing 9-1/2 acres in sd. Co. on both sides Norths Creek and on E side of Little River, bounded W by sd. River, E by sd. **Cook**, Norths Creek, sd. **Wadsworth**. Being part of Land originally granted to James **Young** and sold by Joseph **Young** to James **Cook**. Witness James **Young**, James **Atwood**. Signed James **Cook**. Witness oath by James **Young** 27 Feb 1800 to Robert **Creswell** C.C.C.Ps. [No record date.] [Includes plat.]

Page 499-500 1 Jan 1797, Elizabeth Jane **Ravenel** Exrs. of Daniel **Ravenal** [sic] dec. for £13 paid by John **Charles** Gentleman, sold all that tract of Land on waters of Bush River, containing 130 acres more or less, a part of 3,000 acres originally granted to Daniel **Ravenal**, and by him in his last Will and Testament directed to be sold. Known in the general plan by number 111. Witness Peter **Porcher** Jun., Elizth. D. **Braughton**. Signed Elizabeth J. **Ravenall** [sic]. Witness oath by Peter **Porcher** Jun. 24 Oct 1797 to Wm. **Turpin** J.Q. [No record date.]

Page 500 30 Dec 1796, Boland **Bishop** (Laurens Co.) for £50 Sterling paid by William **Brown** (same), sold all that tract of Land containing 200 acres more or less, in sd. Co. on Reedy Fork of Little River, being part of 400 acres originally granted to Garner **Williams**, recorded in Grant Book AAA, page 359. Joining: John **Brown**, Robert **McNees**. Witness Isaac **Edwards**, Matthew **Brown**. Signed Boland (x) **Bishop**. Witness oath by Matthew **Brown** 30 Dec 1796 to Roger **Brown** J.P. Laurens Co. [No record date.]

Page 501-502 25 Dec 1799, Wm. **Arnold** Sen. (Laurens Co.) to Zacheriah **Arnold** his son (same), for £10 sold all that tract of Land containing 78 acres in sd. Co. on Beaverdam, a branch of Reedy River. Granted to Jacob **Wright** by Wm. **Moultrie** Esq. 12 Nov 1784, and from him descended to his widow and son George, and by them conveyed to Wm. **Arnold** Sen. 6 Nov 1795. Witness George **Harn** [**Hearn** in one ref.], Saml. (x) **Arnold**, Lewis **Watson**. Signed Wm. **Arnold**, Mary (x) **Arnold**. Witness oath by Saml. (x) **Arnold** 26 Dec 1799 to Lewis **Graves** J.P. Laurens Co. [No record date.]

Page 502-503 4 Apr 1794, James **Crooks** (Laurens Co.) to Joseph **Dean** (same), for £20 Sterling sold one certain tract of Land containing 100 acres more or less, in sd. Co. on N side of Bratchers creek, 3 acres included on S side of sd. Creek, whereon the spring is, being the E end of two tracts originally granted to James and William **Crooks** 10 Feb 1781. Witness William **Crooks**, Thomas **Dean**, Joseph **Hall**. Signed James (x) **Crooks**, Magaret (x) **Crooks** [sic]. Oath by Thomas **Dean** 23 Jan 1800, that he saw James **Crooks** and Margaret his wife sign the deed. Given before James **Saxon** J.Q. Laurens Dist. [No record date.]

Page 503-504 14 June 1799, Thomas **May** (Laurens Co.) for $500 paid by Henry **Burrow** [**Borow** in one ref.] (same), sold all that tract of Land containing 296 acres on the branches of Reedy River and Rabourns Creek in sd. Co. Originally granted to Elizabeth **Shote** and conveyed by her to **Camp**, and from **Camp** to Thomas **May**. Bounding N on Isaac **Hugus**, S on William **Tait**, S.E. on Joseph **Dorset**, N.W. on Robert **Cooper**, formerly known as Hickory Tavern, now New Markett. Witness Hezekiah **Dyer** [**Dial** in one ref.], Wm. (x) **Atkins**. Signed T. **May**. Witness oath by Hezekiah **Dyer** 17 Feb 1800 to Reuben **Pyles** J.P. Laurens Co. [No record date.]

Page 504-505 27 July 1799, James **Delong** and Agness my wife for $100 paid by John **Patterson** (Laurens Co.), sold a tract of Land containing 62 acres in sd. Co. on a small branch of Beaverdam Creek, waters of Enoree River, joining to Nathen **Higgins**, being in W side of a tract originally granted to Benjamin **Kilgore** 22 Jan 1785 and recorded in Book GGGG, page 579. Border: Isaac **Gray**. Witness Newton (x) **Bramblett**, Wm. (x) **Ball**. Signed James **Delong**, Nancy (x) **Delong**. Oath by Newton (x) **Bramlett** [sic] 15 Feb 1800, that he saw James **Delong** and Nancy his wife sign the deed. Given before Starling **Tucker** J.P. Laurens Dist. [No record date.]

Page 505-506 12 Sept 1796, John **Martin** and William **Martin** (Laurens Co.) to William **Hobb** (same) planter, for £30 Sterling sold all that piece of Land containing 97 acres more or less, in sd. Co. on Red Lick Branch, waters of Little River. Bounded S by Horatio **Walker**, W by John **Todd**, N by Peter **Faysour**, E by Mrs. **Barby**. Being part of 640 acres originally granted to sd. William **Martin** 3 Apr 1786. Witness Mancel **Crisp**, Margit **Crisp** [sic]. Signed John **Martin**, William **Martin**. Dower relinquished by Elizabeth **Martin**, wife of John **Martin**, and Sally **Martin**, wife of William **Martin** [No signatures.], 21 Feb 1796 [sic] before Jonathan **Downs** J.Q. Laurens Co. Oath by Mancel **Crisp** 11 Oct 1796, that he with his wife Margaret saw the deed signed. Given before Reuben **Pyles** J.P. Laurens Co. Surveyed 10 Sept 1796 by John **Rodgers** D.S. [No record date.] [Includes plat.]

Page 507 12 Nov 1799, William **Barrett** (Laurens Co.) for $62 paid by James **Hutcheson** (same), sold a Sorrel Horse, about 8 years old, 13-1/2 hands high with a star in his face; a yellow Cow and yearling calf, both unmarked; a white heifer with a red Head; two beds and clothing. Witness Thomas **Dean**, Samuel **Young**. Signed William **Barrett**. Witness oath by Saml. **Young** 21 Feb 1800 to Robert **Hutcherson** J.P. Laurens Dist. Delivered to Jas. **Hutcheson** 18 Oct 1803. [No record date.]

Page 507-508 25 Feb 1779, Received of Samuel **Bell** two Bonds for £4,100 due him by John **Black** and Moses **Casey** Planters, the one of £1,600 payable 1 May, the other of £2,500 value 25 Dec, both this current year. I acknowledge to be in part of the price a plantation sold by me to sd. Samuel **Bell**. Signed James **Oliphant**. Recorded at the same time £400 on the aforesd. acct. Oath by Moses **Casey** Sen. that he was very well acquainted with the hand writing of James **Oliphant** Esq. dec. and he believes the within Receipt with the Signatures to be the hand writing of sd. **Oliphant**. Sworn 12 Feb 1800 before A. **Casey** J.P. Spartanburg Co. [No record date.]

Page 508-509 1 Aug 1799, Samuel **Anderson** (Laurens Co.) planter to John **Creasy** (same) Doct., for $250 sold sd. John **Creacy** [sic] a certain tract of Land containing 100 acres more or less, in place aforesd. on Reedy River, being part of a tract laid out for William **Anderson** and part of a tract granted to **Foster** by Wm. **Bull** Esq. Gov. in 1774. Border: Geo. **Wright**, David **Anderson**, **Cunning**, **Anderson**, sd. River. Witness Ezekiel S. **Roland**, David **Anderson**. Signed Samuel (x) **Anderson**. Witness oath by David **Anderson** 21 Jan 1800 to Zach. **Bailey** J.P. Laurens Co. [No record date.]

Page 509-510 29 Dec 1798, James **Clardy** (Laurens Co.) for $400 paid by William **Hencock** (S.C.), sold a tract of Land containing 150 acres more or less, in sd. Co., being part of a tract granted to George **Anderson**. Border: Mariah **Goodman**, James **Cook**, Thomas **Woodard**, Stephen **Harris**. Witness Thomas **Dendy**, John **Milam**. Signed James **Clardy**. Dower relinquished by Mary Wilkuson **Clardy**, wife of James **Clardy**, 29 Dec 1798 before Wm. **Mitchell** J.L.C. Witness oath by Thomas **Dendy** 29 Dec 1798 to Wm. **Mitchell** J.L.C. [No record date.]

Page 510 24 Oct 1797, John & Elizabeth **Huston**, Robert and Mary **Hannah**, Hanna **Davies** (Laurens and Spartanburg Cos.) for £50 to us by Jno. B. **Kennedy** V.D.M. (Co. aforesd.), sold all that tract of 150 acres of Land in Co. aforesd. on McCauls fork of Duncans creek. Bounded N.E. by land formerly Bounty Land now in possession of Heirs of sd. **Davies**, N.W. by land laid out for Joseph **Adair** Sen., S.E. by land laid out for Daniel **Long** dec. Memorial entered in Auditor's Office Book L, No.11, page 109, 14 Jan 1772. Witness Robert **Long**, Thos. **McCrery**, Cassey (x) **McCrery**. Signed John **Huston**, Elizbeth (x) **Huston** [sic], Robert C. **Hanna** [sic], Mary (x) **Hanna** [sic], Hanna (x) **Davies**. Oath by Thos. **McCrary** [sic] 16 July 1799, that he saw John **Huston** & Elizabeth his wife, Robert C. **Hanna** and Mary his Wife, and

Hanna **Davies** sign the deed. Given before James **Dillard** J.P. Laurens Co. [No record date.]

Page 511 13 Sept 1799, Thomas **Dendy** Sen. (Laurens Co.) for £150 Sterling paid by my Son William **Dandy** [sic] (same), sold all that tract of Land whereon I now live containing 300 acres more or less, being part of three different tracts, one part supposed to contain 278 [acres] granted to William **Dandy** Sen. for that amount, the other supposed to contain 20 acres granted to John **Cragill** [sic], being part of the same, the other part supposed to contain nearly about 10 acres granted to Benjn. **Powell**. Situate in sd. Co. on Norths Creek, joining Wm. **Mitchell**, Jas. **Roberts**, John **Milam**, Jas. **Young**, Henry **Hall**, Abram **Hall**, sd. William **Dandy**. Witness William **Dandy** Sen., Samuel (x) **Leak**, John **Hunter**. Signed Thomas **Dandy** [sic]. Witness oath by Samuel (x) **Leak** 30 Dec 1799 to Wm. **Mitchell** J.L.C. [No record date.]

Page 512 5 Feb 1798, By virtue of a writ issued from the Court of Common Pleas at suit of Alexander **Chollath** against the Estate of James **Oliphant**, William **Tennant** (Sheriff of Ninety Six Dist.) did seize a certain Tract of Land and did on the day above mentioned expose the land to public sale at Cambridge in sd. Dist. Sd. land was struck off to Sturling **Tucker** [Sterling in one ref.] for £100. Tract lies in Laurens Co. on Beverdam Creek, waters of Enoree River, joining sd. Sturling **Tucker**, Elisha **Attaway**, James **Higgins**. Containing in the whole 300 acres more or less. Witness James **Saxon**, John **Wright**. Signed Wm. **Tennant** Sheff. 96 Dt. Witness oath by James **Saxon** 13 Mar 1800 to Robt. **Creswell** C.C. [No record date.]

Page 513 5 Sept 1797, John **Wallis** Sen. (Laurens Co.) for £32 10sh paid by John **Wallis** Jun. (same), sold all that tract of land containing 120 acres more or less. Border: Robert **Hana**, William **Rountree**, Henry **Feagin**. Granted 1 Jan 1787 by William **Moultrie** Esq. Gov., recorded in Grant Book OOOO, page 517. Witness William **Sparks**, William **Roundtree** [sic]. Signed John **Wallis** Sn. Witness oath by William **Sparks** [Parks in one ref.] 13 Feb 1798 to Daniel **Wright** J.P. Laurens Co. [No record date.]

Page 514 15 Aug 1796, John **Word** (Laurens Co.) planter for £20 paid by Thomas **Word** (same) planter, sold all that Tract of Land containing 136 acres, being part of 903 acres laid out to Lewis **Duvall** and conveyed to John **Word**, on waters of Warriors Creek, a branch of Enoree, and joining William **Turner**. Witness Robert **Word**, Samuel **Word**. Signed John **Word**. Witness oath by Robert **Word** 19 Mar 1800 to Sterling **Tucker** J.P. Laurens Dist. [No record date.]

Page 514-515 1 Oct 1797, John **Maxwell** (Abberville Co.) to James **King** (Laurens Co.), for £3 Sterling sold 20 acres of Land more or less, now in James **King's** possession, being part of Land granted to John **Maxwell** in Laurens Co., joining sd. James **King**, branch. Witness James **Hodges**, Edmund **Ware** [Edmond in one ref.]. Signed John **Maxwell**. Witness oath by James **Hodges** 3 Sept 1798 to Reuben **Pyles** J.P. [No record date.]

Page 515-516   7 Jan 1799, John **Childers** (Laurens Co.) to James **King** (same), for $25 sold 50 acres of Land more or less, now in John **Childers'** possession, being part of a tract granted to Joseph **Waldrop** 3 Sept 1792 by Charles **Pinckney** Esq. Gov. Border: branch, road. Witness Kitt **Smith**, Ambrose Joshua **Smith**. Signed John **Childress** [sic]. Witness oath by Kitt **Smith** 13 Feb 1800 to Reuben **Pyles** J.P. Laurens Co. [No record date.]

Page 516-517   27 Feb 1800, William **Fulton** (Laurens Co.) planter for $80.75 paid by John **Simpson** (same) Storekeeper, sold one Bay mare, about 13-1/2 hands high, star & snip, no brand nor Docks; one Rid cow; one yearling; one Rid & White Hafer, all marked two swoller Fork, one in each year; Two father beds & furniture; one large Trunk; two pots; one dutch oven; a quantity pewter; ten barrels of corn; one pen of corn Blade? Witness John **Gallegly**. Signed William **Fulton**. Witness oath by John **Gallegly** 21 Mar 1800 to William **Mitchell** J.Q. [No record date.]

Page 517-518   10 Oct 1798, John **Gent** (Abbeville Co.) to David **Mason** (Indian Creek settlement, Laurence Co.), for £100 Current money sold all that Tract of Land containing 100 acres more or less, being part of 200 acres granted to George **Dylerimple** 19 Nov 1754, and conveyed by sd. **Dylrymple** [sic] unto Thomas **Dylrimple** and from him conveyed 100 acres unto John **Gent** for £50 current money, being one half the sd. 200 acres. Bounding W and N on remaining part of sd. 200 acres, all other sides vacant when laid out. Witness Jonathn. **Downs**, John **Mitchell**. Signed John **Gent**. Dower relinquished by Susannah **Gent** [Sukey in signature.], wife of John **Gent**, 10 Oct 1798 before Jonathan **Downs** J.L.C. Witness oath by Jonathan **Downs** 22 Mar 1800 to John **Davis** J.P. Laurens Dist. [No record date.]

Page 518-519   19 Dec 1793, Lewis **Duvall** & Teressa **Duvall** his wife (Laurens Co.) to John **Word** (same), for £14 sold one certain tract of Land on waters of Warriors Creek, a branch of Enoree in sd. Co. Containing 136 acres more or less, joining William **Turner**. Being part of 903 acres laid out to sd. **Duvall**, in a plat 12 Feb 1793. Witness Thomas **Word**, Robert **Word**. Signed Lewis **Duvall**. Witness oath by R. **Word** 19 Mar 1800 to Sterling **Tucker** J.P. Laurens Dist. [No record date.]

Page 519-520   13 Dec 1798, Thomas **Word** Jun. (Penalton Co.) planter for $120 paid by George **Hughs** (Laurens Co.), sold a part of land containing 100 acres more or less, being part of 903 acres granted to Lewis **Duvall** & conveyed to John **Word** & from him to Thomas **Word**. Lying on waters of Warriors Creek, a branch of Enoree River. Joining land which did belong to William **Turner**, excepting what **Abbit's** line takes of sd. Land. Witness Stephen **Mullings**, Austen **Moore**. Signed Thomas **Word**. Witness oath by Stephen **Mullings** 15 Feb 1800 to Roger **Brown** J.P. Laurens Co. [No record date.]

Page 520-521   24 Dec 1798, William **Ball** (Laurens Co.) for £40 paid by Richard **Griffin** (same), sold all that tract of Land containing 50 acres more or less, which was granted to Barbara **Male** 2 Mar 1773, now lying in sd. Co. & adjoins Peter **Ball**, sd. Richard **Griffin**, Cane Creek. Plat made by David **Cunningham**. Witness James **Watson**, Anthony **Watson**. Signed William **Ball**. Witness oath by James **Watson** 5 Jan 1800 to Joseph **Downs** J.P. Laurens Co. Dower relinquished by Mary **Ball**, wife of Wm. **Ball**, 19 Apr 1799 before Wm. **Mitchell** J.L.C. [No record date.]

Page 521-522   24 Dec 1798, Peter **Ball** (Laurens Co.) for $428-1/2 paid by Richard **Griffin** (same), sold all that tract of Land whereon I now live containing 169 acres in sd. Co. on cain creek, waters of Saluda river, being part of a tract originally granted to Wm. **Anocum**, Aron **Lacock** & Josep **Kirshaw**. Witness James **Watson**, Anthony **Watson**. Signed Peter **Ball**. Witness oath by Anthony **Watson** 19 Nov 1799 to William **Nibbs** J.Q. Ninety Six Dist. Dower relinquished by Lelah (x) **Ball**, wife of Peter **Ball**, 19 Nov 1799 before Wm. **Nibbs** J.Q. Ninety Six Dist. [No record date.]

Page 522-523   13 Feb 1800, Micajah **Hendrix** (Laurens Co.) to Wm. Win **Hendrix** (same), for £50 sold all that tract of Land containing 300 acres in sd. Co. Border: Reedy River, original Grant. Granted to Hans **Hendrick** by Wm. **Bull** Esq. 23 June 1774 and descended to sd. Micajah **Hendrick** [sic], being his heir. Witness John **Wait**, Elijah **Burgess**, Jacob **Niswanger**. Signed Micajah (x) **Hendrix**. Witness oath by Elijah **Burgess** 13 Feb 1800 to Lewis **Graves** J.P. Laurens Dist. [No record date.]

Page 523-525   22 Sept 1797, Stephen C. **Wood** and Sarah his wife (Laurens Co.) to John **Davenport** (same), for $300 sold all the remaining part of a Tract of Land in sd. Co. on waters of Ready River on long lick creek supposed to contain 150 acres more or less, which was granted unto Nathan **Hampton** by Ld. Chas. Greenville **Mountage** Capt. Gov., containing 200 acres and conveyed by lease and release to Joseph **Pinson** and conveyed by him to sd. **Wood**. Sd. 150 acres is estimated as above. Border: David **Anderson**, sd. **Wood**, George **Wright's** old Road, Lewis **Banton**, William **Mitchell**. Witness Thomas **Davenport**, Thomas **Davenport** Jun., Lewis **Banton**. Signed Ste. C. **Wood**, Sarah **Wood**. Witness oath by Lewis **Banton** 16 Dec 1797 to Zach. **Bailey** J.P. Laurens Co. Dower relinquished by Sarah **Wood**, wife of Stephen Chilton **Wood**, 16 Mar 1798 before Wm. **Mitchell** J.L.C. [No record date.]

Page 525-526   21 Oct 1799, Bradford **Camp** (Laurens Co.) for $48 paid by John H. **Hughes** (same), sold all that tract of Land supposed to contain 100 acres more or less. Border: branch, creek, Ralph **Humphrey's** old line, Reaburns Creek. Sd. tract is part of 500 acres originally granted to sd. Bradford **Camp** by Charles **Pinckney** Esq. Gov. 26 Sept 1798. Witness Lewis **Saxon**, Larkin **Camp**. Signed Bradf. **Camp**. Witness oath by Lewis **Saxon** 21 Mar 1800 to Joseph **Downs** J.P. Laurens Dist. [No record date.]

Page 526-527 15 Mar 1800, William **Hancock** (Laurens Co.) for $400 paid by Abner **Pyles** (same), sold all that tract of land containing 150 acres more or less, in sd. Co., being part of land formerly granted unto George **Anderson**. Border: Mariah **Goodman**, James **Cook**, Thomas **Woodard**, **Harris**. Witness William **Pyles**, Wm. **Hudgins**. Signed William **Hancock**. Witness oath by Wm. **Hudgins** 18 Mar 1800 to Reubin **Pyles** J.P. Laurens Dist. [No record date.]

Page 527 16 Nov 1799, Authur **Taylor** (Laurens Co.) for $300 paid by John **Harper** (same), sold all that piece of Land in sd. Co. on waters of Reedy River containing 132 acres more or less. Bounding N & N.E. on lands lately owned by Richd. **Pugh** dec., S on Samuel **Cooper**, W on David **Dunlap**. Being part of 232 acres granted unto sd. Authur **Taylor** by John **Hunter** Esq. Attorney for Harculus Daniel **Bize** by lease & release 9 & 10 Sept 1793. Witness John **Cockran**, James **McClannehan**. Signed Authur **Taylor**. Witness oath by Jno. **Cockran** 18 Mar 1800 to Reuben **Pyles** J.P. Laurens Co. [No record date.]

Page 528 24 Jan 1800 at Belfast, William **Farrow** (Laurens Co.) planter for $566 paid by John **Simpson** Mercht. (same), sold one Knife; twelve head of cattle marked a crop, 2 holes, one underkiel; two 2 year old calves; one brown horse; one Bay mare; one Iron Gray horse about 14-1/2 hands high; eighteen Head of hogs marked 2 crops, 2 hole, underkiel; two Feather Beds and furniture; plantation Tools; Kitchen furniture; likewise one negro Fellow Harry. Witness John **Gallegly**. Signed William **Farrow**. Witness oath by Jno. **Gallegly** 25 Feb 1800 to Charles **Griffin** J.P. [No record date.]

Page 528-529 15 Mar 1800, Joseph **Gallegly** (Laurens Dist.) for $600 paid by John **Simpson** Mercht. (same), sold a certain Tract of Land containing 50 acres more or less, laid out for Augustinns **Warnar** on Bush River, waters of Salluda, now Laurens Dist., 2 Mar 1756. Border: Samuel **Jones**, all other sides on vacant Land. Conveyed by Saml. **Jones** to Joseph **Gallegly** and likewise 50 acres granted 22 Aug 1771 to Kitt **Smith** and conveyed by him to Joseph **Gallegly**. Lying on Bush River now Laurens Dist. Bounding N.E. and N.W. on William **Neely**, S.E. on James **Anderson**, S.W. & N.W. on James **Dickinson** &c. And likewise 50 acres, part of 200 acres granted to James **Dickinson** and conveyed to Joseph **Gallegly**. Border: Kitt **Smyth** [sic], waters of Bush River, sd. Dist. Witness James **Hunter**, John **Gallegly**. Signed J. **Gallegly**. Witness oath by John **Gallegly** 15 Mar 1800 to Robert **Hutcheson** J.P. [No record date.]

Page 529 15 Mar 1800, Benjamin Johnston **Raney** (Laurens Dist.) in consideration of being security for payment of $100 to Wm. **Colemun** [**Coleman** in one ref.] for purchase of 90 acres of Land, has unto Stephen **Jones**, all sd. Land, one mare, one cow and calf, my stock of hogs and house hold furniture. Being the tract of Land whereon I now live. Subject to be void on payment of sd. $100 to Wm. **Calmun** [sic]. Witness William **Mathews**, David **Anderson**. Signed Benjamin Johnson **Rany** [sic]. Witness oath by

William **Mathews** 15 Mar 1800 to David **Anderson** J.Q. Laurens Dist. [No record date.]

Page 530 22 Aug 1799, Joseph **Holmes** (Laurens Co.) for $165 paid by Mr. Jonathan **Cox** (same), sold all that tract of land containing 50 acres more or less, on Raiburn Creek. Bounding S.E. on Jane **Holingsworth** [sic] dec., now Nathan **Hollingsworth**, W by John **Hollingsworth**, N.E. by sd. Creek. Being part of a Tract originally granted to Daniel **Allen** & by him conveyed to James **McCain** by Lease & release 1 May 1768, and by him bequeathed by his last will & Testament, the sd. 50 acres unto his Daughter Elisabeth **McCain**, alias Elisabeth **McGill**, and by her & her Husband Barnabas **McGill** sold to sd. Joseph **Holmes** by lease & release 3 Sept 1791. Witness Jonthn. **Downs**, Henry **Buckner**. Signed Joseph **Holms** [sic]. Dower relinquished by Ann **Holmes**, wife of Joseph **Holmes**, 22 Aug 1799 before Jonthn. **Downs** J.L.C. Witness oath by Jonthn. **Downs** 28 Jan 1800 to Joseph **Downs** J.P. Laurens Co. [No record date.]

Page 531 6 Apr 1799, James **McClanahan**, Son & heir of the late John **McClanahan** dec. (Laurens Co.) and Mary **Pugh** (formerly Mary **McClanahan** and widow of John **McClanahan** dec.) for £125 Sterling sold unto Marmaduke **Pinson** (same), all that tract of Land in sd. Co. on waters of Reaburns Creek on Dirty creek (formerly Hallums Branch). Bounded by vacant land on all sides at time of surveying. Sd. Tract of 150 acres was granted to John **Williams** 7 May 1767 & by him conveyed to James **Lindly** esq. 19 Jan 1773, & by him sold unto sd. John **McClanahan** 28 Aug 1778. Witness John **Cochran**, John **McClannahan** [sic]. Signed James **McClanahan**, Mary (x) **Pugh**. Witness oath by Jno. **Cochran** 22 June 1799 to James **Abercrombie** [No title.] Laurens Co. [No record date.] [Includes plat.]

Page 532-533 31 Aug 1799, Thomas **Baird** [**Beard** in one ref.] (Laurens Co.) for $350 paid by William **Dorough** (same), sold all that tract of land containing 100 acres more or less, in sd. Co. on N.E. side of Reedy River. Bounded Widow **Bard**, Wm. **Nary**, S.E. on sd. River, N on William **Norris**. Being one half of 200 acres originally granted to Hugh **Baird** & by him sold to William **Baird** dec. and by his last will & Testament did give sd. Tract unto sd. Thomas **Baird** & Wm. **Baird** to be equally divided between them, Wm. **Baird** to have the S side or half. The land intended to be conveyed is the N side or one half of sd. 200 acres. Witness Salley **Saxon**, Lewis **Saxon**. Signed Thomas **Baird**. Witness oath by Lewis **Saxon** 16 Dec 1799 to Joseph **Downs** J.P. Laurens Co. Pursuant to direction of Court of Common Pleas of Cambridge, I have laid out unto Thomas **Baird** 104-1/4 acres, 9 Dec 1799 by Jonthn. **Downs** D.Sur. [No record date.] [Includes plat.]

Page 533-534 19 Mar 1800, Exors. of Henry **Adkison** dec. (Laurens Co.) for $300 and 9 Sterling [sic] paid by Joseph **Cox** Sen. (same) planter, sold a certain Tract of Land containing 103 acres more or less, being part of a tract originally granted to David **Craddock** dec. and conveyed by him to James **McDowel**, and by him to sd. Henry **Adkison** dec. Border: Bridget **McLaney**,

John **Davidson**, Joseph **Cox**, Mr. **Glass**, Little River. Witness Joseph **Cox**, Thomas **Cox**, Jessee **Cox**. Signed Mary (x) **Adkinson**, Drury (x) **Dupree** [**Deupree** in one ref.], John **Dacus**. Dower relinquished by Mary (x) **Adkinson**, widow of Henry **Adkinson**, 19 Mar 1800 before Wm. **Mitchell** J.Q. Laurens Dist. Witness oath by Thomas **Cox** 19 Mar 1800 to Wm. **Mitchell** J.Q. Laurens Dist. Surveyed 13 Aug 1799 by John **Rodgers** Dep.Sur. [No record date.] [Includes plat.]

Page 534-535 8 Mar 1799, William **Runnolds** (Laurens Co.) for £80 Sterling paid by Henry **Fuller** (same), sold all that Tact of Land containing 171 acres, being part of a Tract originally granted to John **Fields** containing 196 acres in sd. Co. on waters of Rabourns Creek, or Starnes branch. Witness Benj. **Carter**, Silvanus **Adams**. Signed William (W) **Reynolds** [sic]. Dower relinquished by Alsey (x) **Runolds**, wife of Wm. **Runnolds**, 17 Mar 1800 before Chas. **Allen** J.Q. Laurens Dist. Witness oath by S. **Adams** 17 Mar 1800 to Chas. **Allen** J.Q. Laurens Dist. [No record date.]

271

Teague: Elia., 109;
William, 159
Telles: Oliver, 202
Templeton:
Archabald, 44;
David, 27, 44;
James, 44; John,
68, 74, 79, 84;
Robert, 54, 84
Tenison: Zachariah,
19
Tennant: William,
239
Tennent: Charles,
204; William,
106, 202, 204
Thedford: Simeon,
34
Thelford: Simon,
106
Thetford: Simon, 98
Theus: Simion, 152
Thomas, 215; Abel,
146, 203, 209;
Ann, 67; Edwd.,
151; Even, 203;
Isaac, 146; John,
53, 67, 112
Thomason: George,
184, 188; John,
79, 154, 165,
166; Sarah, 233;
William, 166;
William 2d. Jun.,
165; William
Jun., 233;
William Sen., 79,
154, 165
Thompson: A., 158;
Agnes, 38;
Burrel, 115;
Daniel, 38;
Flanders, 141;
Henery, 125;
Hugh, 23, 123,
172, 185;
Isabella, 38;
James, 23, 123;

Jane, 172; John,
86, 190; Joseph,
95; Mary, 95;
W., 21; William,
38, 54, 132
Thomson: Andrew,
54; Cynthia H.,
105; James, 222;
John, 222;
Robert, 105
Thornton: John, 71,
72
Thurston: James,
20, 34
Tillotson: Francis,
110
Tindsley: James,
167
Tinsley: Abraham,
155, 167; Ann,
155, 167; James,
167; Marthy,
155; Philip, 155;
William, 167;
Zacee, 214
Tinsly: Elisebeth, 5
Todd: Jane, 135;
John, 119, 235,
237; Nathan,
144; Nathen,
144; Robert, 88,
105, 135, 174,
235; Thomas, 12
Tomerlin: Moses,
164
Tomlin: Moses, 45,
64, 164; Pamelia,
117; Rachel, 117
Tompson: Hugh,
172
Tomson: John, 97,
98
Torrance: Andw.,
163
Torrence: Andw.,
106
Townsend, 14

Trezevant: Lewis,
149
Trimble: Hugh, 111
Trotti: Gasper, 87,
137
Troup: John, 86,
101, 205
Truman: William,
20
Tucker: Elijah, 124;
Elisha, 138;
Starling, 82, 90,
160, 180, 186,
194, 197, 198,
199, 202, 215,
222, 231, 237;
Sterling, 42, 126,
176, 199, 239,
240; Sturling,
239
Tumblin: Rachel,
127
Tunstall: William,
202
Turk, 143; Mary,
215; Rachel, 213;
Theodocias, 3;
William, 67
Turner: Ace, 227;
Deborah, 126;
Elizabeth, 164;
Gilbert, 215;
Joseph, 21, 62;
Richard, 126;
William, 38, 91,
121, 126, 164,
239, 240; Zachr.,
91, 225;
Zechariah, 90
Turpin, 41, 46, 47,
53, 105, 106,
153, 224; Mary,
159, 172, 173,
174; William, 4,
7, 9, 10, 15, 16,
31, 32, 41, 48,
49, 64, 70, 71,
74, 75, 79, 87,